Contents

WITHDRAWN

Corporate Finance

A Model-building Approach

SECOND EDITION

MICHEL SCHLOSSER
IFL

PRENTICE HALL

New York   London   Toronto   Sydney   Tokyo   Singapore

First published 1989
This second edition published 1992 by
Prentice Hall International (UK) Ltd
Campus 400, Maylands Avenue
Hemel Hempstead
Hertfordshire, HP2 7EZ
A division of
Simon & Schuster International Group

© Prentice Hall International (UK) Ltd, 1989, 1992

All rights reserved. No part of this publication may be
reproduced, stored in a retrieval system, or transmitted,
in any form, or by any means, electronic, mechanical,
photocopying, recording or otherwise, without prior
permission, in writing, from the publisher.
For permission within the United States of America
contact Prentice Hall Inc., Englewood Cliffs, NJ 07632

Typeset in 11/13 pt Bembo
by Columns Design & Production Services Ltd.

Printed and bound in Great Britain
at the University Press, Cambridge

Library of Congress Cataloging-in-Publication Data

Schlosser, Michel.
Corporate finance : a model-building approach / Michel
Schlosser.
– 2nd ed.
p. cm.
Includes bibliographical references and index.
ISBN 0–13–176322–9 (PBK)
1. Corporations–Finance. 2. Corporations–Finance–Data
processing.   I. Title.
HG4026.S3 1992   92–5340
658.15′0285′5369–dc20   CIP

British Library Cataloguing in Publication Data

A catalogue record for this book is available from
the British Library
ISBN 0–13–176322–9 (pbk)

---

4   5   96   95   94

PART VI   WHICH DISCOUNT RATE TO USE?   287
     The Cost of Capital Issue

Preface

This book, because of its original approach, renders modern corporate finance easily accessible to management students and non-financial practising executives.

If you are one of the above, this book will help you learn how to build and use financial models and, more generally, how to use modern corporate finance approaches and concepts in order to perform effective business analyses and plans.

This book uses extensively the potential of personal computer technology and its user-friendly software (particularly spreadsheet packages). Most importantly, it will provide you with the theoretical framework you need to use this technology effectively and to avoid the many mistakes which result from its misuse.

The full benefit of this book is obtained when the reader has access to a personal computer and a spreadsheet – whatever make. You can, however, make valuable use of this book even if this equipment is not available.

For whom was this book written?

We wrote this book for two particular groups of people:

- management students
- non-financial practising executives

but we believe that it will also be valuable for financial executives and management teachers and trainers.

If you are a management student, you will find in this book a comprehensive introduction to modern corporate finance for under- and post-graduate management courses. It will enable you to learn about modern corporate finance and how to use it. It is one of the first textbooks in the field which uses the full potential of the personal computer as a learning tool.

If you are a non-financial practising executive, you will find this book a valuable self-learning tool. It is also a textbook in corporate finance for courses in general management and in finance for non-financial executives. It will help you learn about corporate finance and will enable you to introduce relevant financial concepts and theories in the analyses and models you make for your business investigations, decisions and plans.

If you are a financial executive, this book will help you develop more effective spreadsheet models – a new activity which differs quite significantly from traditional modelling. This book will also help you teach other managers how to develop skills for using financial models for preparing their decisions, plans and budgets.

Finally, if you are a management teacher or trainer, you are probably aware of the dramatic potential impact of information technology on management and management education. This book will provide you with a comprehensive example of how to use information technology in your professional activities. We believe that information technology cannot be considered as a mere addition to management courses: it rather invites teachers and trainers completely to rethink what they teach and how they teach it. The material in this book has already been used with success in a variety of courses aimed at students and practising managers. If you decide to adopt it in your own professional activities we are at your disposal to provide you with suggestions drawn from our own experience.

What will you learn from working with this book?

This book is about using modern corporate finance effectively for management decisions in the age of personal computers and spreadsheets.

Modern corporate finance

We strongly disagree with the view that corporate finance is a matter for specialists only; on the contrary, corporate finance is part of the toolkit that any manager can – and probably should – use for decision-making. Corporate finance is a very powerful tool which helps managers quantify, model, understand and decide – and the good news is that corporate finance is much easier to use now, with the widespread diffusion of the personal computer and spreadsheets.

This book covers all the topics of modern corporate finance except those which are only of interest to specialists.[1] Among the topics covered are:

- The language of financial accounting.[2]
- Financial budgeting and planning: how to build cash flow and, more generally, financial statements for various purposes, in various conditions and for various time horizons.
- Working capital management: the impact of growth and inflation.
- The impact of operational strategies on cash generation (forecast driven v. demand pulled operations).
- The concepts of return and of value.
- Risk analysis: how to build models to understand risk.
- Interest and foreign currency exposures.
- Capital budgeting: how to evaluate new projects and, more generally, any strategic alternative.
- How to value acquisitions and joint ventures.
- Market efficiency, risk–return relationship; models for evaluating stocks; cost of the different sources of financing.
- Cost of capital and capital structure.
- Introduction to option valuation: its potential for financial modelling.
- Financial modelling as a framework which enables you to integrate a variety of other management approaches (marketing, strategy, etc) and to understand more clearly complex competitive situations.

Spreadsheets[3]

Starting with VisiCalc and reaching a wide diffusion with Lotus 1-2-3, spreadsheets have made computer power available to all managers. The two unique advantages of spreadsheets are those of being:

- General purpose languages which impose few constraints on the thinking of the user – with a spreadsheet, you work very much as you do with a piece of paper and a pencil.
- Extremely easy to learn: mastering the fundamentals of any spreadsheet is a matter of hours; continuing to learn about spreadsheets comes very naturally through use.

The bad news, however, is that, like many other powerful technologies, spreadsheets can be used very effectively, or very badly, depending on the methodological skills of the user. With this book, you will learn:

- How to use spreadsheets effectively – a new management skill.
- How to master the basic technique of any spreadsheet. Although this book is biased towards the most widely diffused spreadsheet (Lotus 1-2-3),[4] it will enable you to work with any other spreadsheet (Excel, Quattro, VP Planner, SuperCalc, Lucid 3-D, Multi-plan, Framework, Symphony, etc.).

Management issues

This book will help you develop skills for using modern corporate finance and spreadsheet models to address such issues as:

- How to build a financial plan or budget. How to build a cash budget.
- How to assess the value of a marketing plan or, more generally, of a business plan. How to assess alternative strategies.
- Which is it more important to look at, cash or profit?
- Is growth always desirable? What is healthy growth?
- What is the impact of stocks and accounts receivable?
- What is the cost of working capital needs?
- What is the impact of inflation on the performance of a business?
- How to assess the profitability and risk of a new contract or project. How to build its financial statements.
- How to conduct a risk analysis.
- How do accounting measures of performance (ROA, ROCE, etc) relate to criteria like NPV and internal rate of return?
- How can you value a lease proposal?
- What is the cost of the different sources of financing?
- Is it a good idea to borrow?
- How to build a strategy for launching a new product.
- How to prepare for an acquisition negotiation.
- How to design and implement co-operative strategies.
- How to model the impact of experience.

How will you learn from this book?

This book consists of text and case studies drawn from real business situations. In order to benefit fully, we recommend that you:

Try to solve these cases by yourself.
Then compare your solutions with ours.
Ultimately, try to solve these cases again by yourself.

The text and the cases will invite you to build a series of PC-based financial models which will help you to learn about modern corporate finance and how to use it.

The unique benefits of the modelling approach

- The modelling approach has enabled us to adopt an original structure for the material that will help you develop a progressive step-by-step understanding of the essentials of modern corporate finance: cash flows, value, risk, risk return relationship, corporate finance as an integrative approach, the potential of the option valuation framework.
- The modelling approach will enable you to acquire a full understanding of finance and to develop skills in using finance to prepare effective business analyses, decisions and plans. The case studies and their analyses performed through building models will help you develop skills at specifying problems, searching for and analyzing relevant information, selecting adequate financial approaches, defining relevant variables and relationships, building them into effective models, understanding the outcome of these models, testing them against concepts and theories. The case studies presented describe business situations which are rich enough to help you develop skills you can easily transfer to real business situations. When used with the support of a PC, these cases allow for much more experimentation and learning than the material of traditional textbooks.
- The modelling approach will enable you to develop and understand the different topics of corporate finance and of corporate finance as a whole. In order to work with corporate finance effectively, one should acquire a global understanding of the discipline. The material presented and analyzed in the book enables you to construct models which will help you to develop this global perspective on finance and financial modelling.
- The modelling approach will enable you to develop the new skills required to use personal computers and spreadsheets effectively. It will help you to learn with a personal computer and to develop skills for further learning with this technology.

What kind of equipment do you need?

Although you can benefit from this book without having access to a personal computer, its full benefit is obtained with a personal computer and spreadsheet software, any personal computer and any spreadsheet!

How familiar should you be with PCs and spreadsheets before you start working with this book?

This book does not assume any prior knowledge of PCs and spreadsheets.

The Second Edition

Among the many changes that have taken place in management since 1989, the date of the first edition, we would like to single out two series of innovations which have guided us when preparing this new edition:

- Many organizations have introduced streamlined, decentralized operations with reduced staff functions and have undertaken dramatic change programmes called 'Total Quality', 'Customer Focus', 'Fast Flow Operations', etc. Experience shows that these new approaches require that managers become 'bilingual' and be fully conversant in the language of operations and the language of finance. Managers should master the language of operations and use it to map, simplify, speed-up, measure, and reorient. They should also master the language of finance and use it by themselves to create more value. In this second edition we have kept all the material that will help you relate operations and finance and we have introduced a number of further valuable ideas: speculative vs non speculative operations, just-in-time operations, quality and cost of low quality, cost of working capital, etc. In order to reflect the growing internationalization of business, we have also introduced more material on foreign currency and interest exposure.
- Another far reaching innovation is the emergence of new ways to compete through cooperation and strategic alliances. In order to answer this new dimension we have introduced a totally new Part VIII devoted to acquisitions, mergers, joint ventures and strategic alliances. This part is based on a case drawn from a real business negotiation. It will provide you with opportunities to develop and use models in a variety of new situations: how to assess the value of a business? How to design and value a joint venture? How to create and implement cooperative, win-win strategies? How to create value out of differences? How to reduce risk through imaginative uses of time?

Finally, when preparing this new edition, we have considered that spreadsheets are now much better known than they were in 1989. As a consequence, we have suppressed the final appendix introducing spreadsheets but we have kept all the references that will enable non-users to work with the book without any difficulty.

NOTES

1 In this book, priority is given to the development of a cohesive presentation of the essential topics of modern corporate finance within a manageable volume of material. As a result, some topics found in traditional textbooks have been omitted. This is not a problem since these topics do not present any special difficulty, and can easily be dealt with when you have fully understood the fundamental principles of corporate finance which are presented here.

2 This book will help you to develop skills in relating economic facts to accounting figures. Even though financial modelling should go far beyond the production of financial statements, it is almost impossible in practice to build financial models without a good mastery of the language of financial accounting.

3 We decided in this book not to introduce any specialized financial modelling language. Although these languages are of great value, their common characteristic is to adopt the language of the finance specialists – which makes them very effective for the specialists but creates obstacles for the generalist. (In some cases these obstacles are very small but experience shows that even very small obstacles may create enormous difficulties.)

4 All the instructions in the text are valid with the different versions and releases of Lotus 1-2-3.

Acknowledgments

When writing this book based on the experience of designing and running learning situations, it is a great pleasure for me to think about all the people I had the chance to work with and to learn from. Among those I would like to pay a special tribute to:

- The executives who participated in the Ti0, the international program organized by IFL for ABB, AGA, Alfa-Laval, Atlas Copco, Fläkt, Axel Johnson Group, Nokia, Saab Scania, Sandvik, Skandia International and Stora.
- The teachers of management who participated in the 1974–1979 and in the 1985–1992 editions of the ITP.
- The executives who participated in the EMP of Ericsson, in the CFD of Isvor Fiat, in the AMP IMP and MBF of Philips, in the management program of Rolls-Royce and in the Profitability in Marketing programs of Atlas Copco.
- Teachers and executives who attended courses I have been involved in at the AACSB, the BBTC, De Baak, the London Business School and LPPM.
- Academics who, in their position as heads of institutions or programs, provided me with exceptional opportunities and support: James Baughman, André Blondeau and Per-Jonas Eliæson.
- Executives who helped me learn about management and management development. Among those, I would like to thank Colin Buckingham, JA Darlin, Bertil Ericksson, Gordon Fithen, Ron Giffin, Hans Holmquist, Bo Johansson, Fadil Kamar, Claude Levy, Lars Otterbeck, Antti Räikkönen, Åke Stavling, Giovanni Testa and JMB van Straaten.
- Colleagues with whom I enjoyed working and learning about helping others to learn. Among those, I would like to thank Alexander Bergmann, Anthony Berry, Damir Borsic, Derek Bunn, Richard Flavell, Xavier Gilbert, Anders Lindström, Foster Rogers, Severino Salvemini, Bonifacius Suwartojo and Stuart Timperley.
- Among those colleagues, two deserve a very special tribute as this book draws on many exciting joint teaching experiences with them: Bernard Dubois and Sherwood Frey.
- Finally, among colleagues, I want to thank two course administrators I had the chance to work with: Karen Myring and Vanja Ekberg.

Also, I should like to pay a tribute to educational institutions I had the chance to be associated with:

- The Centre Hec-Isa where I started my career as a teacher of management.
- The Harvard Business School which helped me understand what is excellence in teaching.

- IFL where I discovered the unique value of an effective cooperation between industry and an academic institution as well as the challenge of management development in a truly international environment.

Finally, and without mentioning names as they would be too many, I would like to thank the information technology industry: I always found hardware and software firms very supportive and without their help I would not have been able to experiment and write this book.

Introduction

CHAPTER 1

Corporate Finance using a Modelling Approach

R.T.C. LIBRARY, LETTERKENNY

1.1 THE VALUE OF QUANTIFICATION

Managers base their decisions on their intuition or business sense. Management is a practice and good management is an art. Most managers feel more at ease, however, in exercising their judgement when decisions have been prepared by some kind of formal analysis, particularly quantitative analysis. The value of quantification, ie the specification of some relationships and numbers, even very simple, comes from the fact that quantification significantly improves:

- Understanding of business situations. When you structure problems, formalize alternative actions and evaluate them, you do not get definite answers but you do learn about the real nature of the problem and the opportunities for action.
- Comparison of different business situations and the transfer of experience and insight from one to another.
- Design and selection of plans for moving more effectively towards a desirable future.
- Communication with other managers about situations, problems, alternative actions, yardsticks for control and areas of responsibility.
- Monitoring of the results of courses of action that have been chosen.
- Development of intuition. Complex situations and systems may not behave as immediate intuition suggests; quantification often helps you get a better feel of the overall behaviour of complex systems and as a result helps you educate your intuition.

The need to improve our judgement is evidenced by the growing literature in the field of cognitive psychology.[1] As shown by many authors, and in particular by R Hogart,[2] the human mind has strong limitations when acquiring and processing information – which is a serious problem when you consider the growing complexity of management situations. Quantification is an aid we can use in order to educate our intuition and better deal with management issues.

1.2 THE NATURE AND VALUE OF MODELS

Modelling is a very fundamental and common human activity as, if we believe Patrick Rivett: 'the whole history of man, even in his most non-scientific activities, shows that he is essentially a model-building animal'.[3] Models are not very popular with managers, however, as they often consider that models can only be complex and built by specialists.

In this book:

- We define as a model any kind of quantitative description of a business situation: a five-line income statement is a model according to this definition.
- We only consider the models that any generalist is able to build by him/herself.

This book is very much about what we can call *personal modelling*. By personal, we mean an activity which can be undertaken by any manager for his or her own benefit. This activity is not necessarily individual as it may equally involve a manager or a group of managers, but it is private to those members and often unique to that group. In many instances, personal modelling simply helps a manager or a group of managers to understand and master a unique situation.[4] (In these cases the model is often scrapped as soon as the situation is mastered; learning and experience accumulate but learning aids lose their value as soon as they have served their purpose.)

In some instances, personal modelling also helps managers to develop models which will become of standard use (corporate planning models, budgetary models, etc). This generality of use will require a complete change in the nature of the original model which will have to lose its personal character and become a heavy duty operational tool to be used by a wide range of people in the organization. This transformation will generally be done by specialists in charge of corporate modelling and procedures. We do not deal with heavy duty corporate models in this book.

In order to understand more clearly what a model is and how a model can be used to prepare a business decision, let us consider the example shown in Figure 1.1.

Figure 1.1 can help us clarify a number of important concepts.

- The decision to be made is the fixing of the price of the new product: should it be 150 000FFR, 200 000FFR or 250 000FFR?
- The objective pursued by Mr Leblanc when making his decision is to maximize profit from the new product. Mr Leblanc has also defined how this profit should be measured.
- What kind of model could help Mr Leblanc reach a decision?
  - · A model which has the same objective as Mr Leblanc, ie maximization of profit.

Mr Leblanc, General Manager of Alfa SA, a subsidiary of the Alfa group, a machine tools producer, is thinking about how he should price the new product the company is about to introduce on to the market.

Mr Leblanc wants to fix this price so that Alfa SA would enjoy maximum profitability on this new product in 1993.

Mr Leblanc defines the profitability derived from this new product as the difference between the sales generated and the resulting costs when buying the product from the parent company.

A study prepared by the marketing department of Alfa SA indicates that:

1. The total market for the new product can be estimated at 2500 units in 1993.
2. The market share of the new product will depend on its price:
   With a price of 200 000FFR, a market share of 10% can be envisaged.
   With a price of 250 000FFR, the market share would fall to 8%.
   With a price of 150 000FFR, the market share would reach 12%.

Mr Leblanc also knows that the parent company will charge Alfa SA 100 000FFR per unit.

Figure 1.1 A decision.

· A model which defines profit in the same way as he does, ie sales – transfer costs.
· A model which relates profit to the variables that explain it, ie total market, market share and price.

		(in 000FFR)
Total market	2 500	2 500	2 500
Unit market price	150	200	250
Market share	0.12	0.1	0.08
Units sold	300	250	200
Sales	45 000	50 000	50 000
Unit transfer cost	100	100	100
Total transfer cost	30 000	25 000	20 000
Profit	15 000	25 000	30 000

Maximum profit is achieved with a price of 250 000FFR.

Figure 1.2 A model.

Let us use the example of the model in Figure 1.2 for some basic definitions. Like any model, the model in Figure 1.2 is characterized by:

1. Its objectives. The model shown in Figure 1.2 aims to maximize profit. However, this maximization is not done by the model itself but by its user, who has to compare the profits achieved by the different pricing levels. This type of model, which shows the impact of alternative decisions and leaves the user to decide which decision is best, is called a *simulation model*. On the other hand, a model which itself determines the best decision is called an *optimization model*. In this book, we will primarily deal with simulation models, since we believe they are the most useful as far as personal modelling is concerned.
2. Its variables: total market, unit market price, market share, number of units sold, sales, unit transfer cost, total transfer cost and profit. These variables do not have the same nature and can be classified into four distinct categories:

· Outcome variables allow you to evaluate the decision. In this case, there is only one outcome variable, profit. Other names for outcome variables are: measure of performance, attribute, yardstick for success, output variable, etc.

· Decision variables correspond to a decision you can make. Here there is only one decision variable, the unit selling price. Another name for decision variables is controllable variables.

· Uncontrolled variables are those which you consider to be external to the decision you model and consequently as imposed by the environment. Here the uncontrolled variables are total market, market share and unit transfer cost. One thing you should realize is that uncontrolled variables are often uncontrolled because of your decision. Even though there are very few truly uncontrollable variables, it is often a good idea to simplify a problem and consider that a number of variables are uncontrolled, ie beyond the scope of the analysis. Another name for uncontrolled variables is exogenous variables.

· Intermediate variables enabling you to relate the decision and uncontrolled variables to each other and to the outcome variables. Here the intermediate variables are number of units sold, sales and total transfer cost.

3. The relationships between the variables. In Figure 1.2, these relationships can be described as:

$$\text{Total market} \times \text{Market share} = \text{Units sold}$$
$$\text{Units sold} \times \text{Unit market price} = \text{Sales} \qquad (1)$$
$$\text{Unit transfer cost} \times \text{Units sold} = \text{Total transfer cost} \qquad (2)$$
$$(1) - (2) = \text{Profit}$$

4. The constraints imposed on the value of the variables. In the example, the following constraints are imposed:

· Only one possible value for total market and transfer price.

· Only three possible values for the two variables, unit selling price and market share. In real life, there are very few absolute constraints but, for the sake of the analysis, you will often decide to impose constraints on the value of a number of variables.

1.3 CORPORATE FINANCE AS A MODELLING FRAMEWORK

Finance and accounting make available to managers the most powerful approach for quantifying – or, more exactly, modelling – the preparation of a large number of business decisions. Why is this?

▪ Finance and accounting are the only universally accepted quantitative approaches for describing business organizations but they can also describe the various units of these organizations and the various decisions to be made in the organizations and their units. The unique value of finance and accounting is to carry *consistency* across business analysis.[5]

- Finance encourages you to look at the impact of your decisions on organizations as a whole. One danger when looking at a business situation is to define it too narrowly in order to keep the analysis tractable. Managers tend to define their problems as marketing, production or people problems and to forget about the broader view of the organization as a whole.

- Finance and accounting provide managers with a powerful methodology for integrating various decisions and uncontrolled variables and relating them to outcome variables. One great advantage of the framework provided by finance is that it invites you to make sure that you have all relevant information before you attempt to evaluate a situation.[6]

- Finance also provides managers with invaluable help for identifying appropriate outcome variables and helps them avoid one major pitfall in quantitative analysis and model-building, the selection of inadequate outcome variables.

- Finance invites you always to integrate risk into your analyses and provides you with a framework for doing so.

- Finally, finance tells managers which objective should be pursued: the creation of maximum additional value for the whole organization is a clear, future-orientated, and motivating objective. This objective enables managers to evaluate alternatives easily and, as a result, to develop their creativity.[7]

As with any powerful approach, finance also presents dangers. The two major ones are:

Finance tends to encourage you to oversimplify business situations.
Finance invites you to use standard approaches which may become mechanical.

These dangers are real but they should not prevent you from using the powerful structuring tool that finance is – you should simply use this tool with a few precautions.

R.T.C. LIBRARY
LETTERKENNY

A paradox

If finance and financial models are so useful for decision-making why are there still managers who do not use them every day?

The first reason for this is that finance and accounting use a special language which needs frequent practice for the user to remain conversant with it; relationships between accounting and financial variables are not easy to remember and are somewhat cumbersome to manipulate 'by hand'.

The second reason is that managers traditionally believe that models and financial models belong to specialists, because financial models often require the use of a computer – traditionally another specialist skill.

Leaving the building of models to specialists involves serious drawbacks, however:

- The learning one can achieve from models is not limited to the analysis of the results. *In general, the most useful learning you can achieve with models takes place when you build them.*
- Building financial models is usually more fun than using them. As stated by Russell Ackoff: 'one can enjoy a game played by others but one can only have fun by playing it oneself'.[8]

The emergence of the personal computer and its user-friendly software should dissolve this paradox.

NOTES

1 Cognitive psychology is concerned with internal mental processes, mental limitations and the way in which the processes are shaped by limitations. For an introduction to cognitive psychology, refer to: L Bourne *et al.* (1986), *Cognitive Processes*, Prentice Hall.

2 R Hogart (1980), *Judgement and Choice: The psychology of decision*, John Wiley. Refer particularly to Chapter 9, pp 155–81.

3 P Rivett (1980), *Model Building for Decision Analysis*, John Wiley.

4 As their purpose is to be thinking aids, personal models should remain manageable and therefore relatively small, given human mental constraints.

5 The literature of cognitive psychology has shown that one of the main limitations of human information processing is the lack of consistency. Refer, for example, to: E Bowman (1963), 'Consistency and optimality in management decision making', *Management Science*, **10**: 310–21.

6 One common bias in human information acquisition is the excessive reliance on information which is readily available. Refer for example to: D Kahneman, P Slovic and A Tversky (eds) (1986), *Judgement under Uncertainty: Heuristics and biases*, Part IV, pp 163–208, Cambridge University Press.

7 As shown by D Campbell ('Blind variation and selective retention in creative thought as in other knowledge processes', *Psychological Review* (1960) **67**: 380–400), creativity implies the production of alternatives (variations), a consistent evaluation and selection process and a mechanism for preserving and reproducing the creative alternatives. The two unique advantages of computer-based financial models lie in their ability to help you evaluate alternatives quickly and to help you understand how these alternatives create value, a very powerful aid for reproducing valuable alternatives.

8 R Ackoff (1978), *The Art of Problem Solving – Accompanied by Ackoff's Fables*, John Wiley.

Part I   Bibliography

Ackoff R (1978), *The Art of Problem Solving – Accompanied by Ackoff's Fables*, John Wiley.

Bourne L, Dominowski R, Loftus E and Heavy A (1986), *Cognitive Processes*, Prentice Hall.

Bowman E (1963), 'Consistency and optimality in management decision making', *Management Science*, **10**: 310–21.

Brealey R and Myers S (1991), *Principles of Corporate Finance*, McGraw-Hill.

Campbell D (1960), 'Blind variation and selective retention in creative thought and in other knowledge processes', *Psychological Review*, **67**: 380–400.

Gilder G (1988), 'The revitalization of everything: the law of the microcosm', *Harvard Business Review*, March–April, pp 49–61.

Hogart R (1980), *Judgement and Choice: The Psychology of Decision*, John Wiley.

Kahneman D, Slovic P and Tversky A (eds) (1986), *Judgement under Uncertainty: Heuristics and Biases*, Cambridge University Press.

Rivett P (1980), *Model Building for Decision Analysis*, John Wiley.

Financial Accounting as the Foundation for Financial Models

In Part II, we invite you to develop the basic skills needed for financial modelling: how to describe business activity, conditions and strategies with accounting and financial figures and how to use these figures to assess business success.

We will start from the situation of International Textiles and explore a very straightforward issue: how much cash is going to be generated by the operations of the company? You should make the effort to solve the case by yourself before reading our analysis.

We will then address a somewhat more complex question: how much profit are these same operations going to generate? This will lead us to define key accounting principles, state the difference between cash and profit, and show how income statements, balance sheets and cash flow statements are built. We will end by proposing a cash flow statement format which is very useful for building PC-based financial models.

Part II has been written for people who do not know anything about accounting and finance, using an original[1] approach practised by the author in a variety of educational programmes. Unless you are an expert in finance and accounting, please forget everything you know about this subject for the moment and approach the material in Part II with a fresh mind. If you are an expert, just skim through Chapters 2, 3 and 4 in order to understand the logic of the presentation (which may be useful when you have to introduce people to accounting and finance concepts), and to understand the cash flow model we are going to use in subsequent chapters.

KEY LEARNING POINTS

MODELS

- A model of cash generation in a business firm – *Figure 2.2, page 19*
- Three cash flow statement models – *Figures 4.6, 4.7 and 4.8, pages 40 and 41*

FINANCIAL ACCOUNTING

- The concept of operations – *Chapter 2, page 15*
  Cash from operations, CFO – *Figures 3.6 and 3.8, pages 30 and 32*
- Six accounting principles for assessing profit:
  · Revenue recognition – *Chapter 3, page 20*
  · Expenditure recognition – *Chapter 3, page 22*
  · CGS and matching – *Chapter 3, page 23*
  · Depreciation – *Chapter 3, page 25*
  · Business entity – *Chapter 4, page 34*
  · Historical value – *Chapter 4, page 35*
- The differences between profit and operational profit – *Figures 3.3, 3.5 and 3.7, pages 26, 30 and 31*
- Profit, CFE, changes in working capital needs and CFO – *Figure 3.6, page 30*
- Four financial statements:
  · Income statement – *Figure 3.4, page 27*
  · Balance sheet – *Figure 4.1, page 35*
  · Uses and sources of funds – *Figures 4.4 and 4.5, pages 38 and 39*
  · Cash flow statement – *Figure 4.8, page 41*

NOTE

1 This approach, initially tested in the International Teachers Programme by the author and Xavier Gilbert, Professor at IMD (Switzerland), is original in the sense that it differs from most introductions to accounting and finance. The main differences are the order of presentation (cash then profit v profit then cash) and the focus on planning. As accounting and finance have been taught by a considerable number of people for many years, it would be very adventurous to claim that this approach is new. In fact, we know of at least one predecessor, P Hunt, who used a similar approach in the MBA programme at the Harvard Business School in the sixties.

For more about financial accounting, refer to: C Horngren and G Sunden (1983), *Introduction to Financial Accounting*, Prentice Hall; and R Anthony and J Reece (1989), *Accounting: Text and cases*, R D Irwin.

INTERNATIONAL TEXTILES

The International Textiles Company is a textile trading company. At the beginning of 1993, Mr Rolland, the General Manager, wants to estimate how much cash the company will be left with at the end of the year and how successful its trading activities will be in terms of their cash generation in 1993.

In order to carry out this analysis, Mr Rolland collected a list of all the cash receipts and disbursements that were expected to take place in 1993. This list is reproduced in Figure A.1.

		$000
1	Receipts from sales to department stores	2 000
2	Receipts from sales to supermarkets	1 000
3	Receipts from sales to individual customers	4 000
4	Receipts from sales to foreign customers	900
5	Receipts from disposal of treasury bonds	1 000
6	Payments to suppliers of wool cloth	600
7	Payments to suppliers of synthetics	1 800
8	Payments to suppliers of cotton	1 400
9	Payment of salaries	1 600
10	Payment of overtime and bonuses	400
11	Payment of advertising expenditures	300
12	Payment of promotion expenditures	100
13	Payment of various administrative expenditures	600
14	Payment of corporation tax	612
15	Payment of interest to Industrial Bank	100
16	Repayment of part of the loan made by Industrial Bank	200
17	Payment of dividend	100
18	Payments related to the opening of new shops	700
19	Payments related to the purchase of new vehicles	200

Figure A.1 Expected cash receipts and disbursements.

At the beginning of 1993 International Textiles has $200 000 cash in hand.

CHAPTER 2

Assessing the Cash Generated by Operations

The International Textiles case raises two questions:

1. What will the cash position of the company be at the end of the year?
2. How successful will the activities of the company be during the year?

The answer to the first question is straightforward. It merely requires the calculation of the total expected receipts, the total expected disbursements, the calculation of the difference between these receipts and disbursements and its addition to the opening cash balance of the company:

	$000
Total receipts	8 900
− Total disbursements	(8 712)
= Net	188
+ Opening cash balance	200
= Ending cash balance	388

If things happen as Mr Rolland expects, International Textiles will be left with a cash balance of $388 000 at the end of the year.

The answer to the second question is less obvious.

- International Textiles will certainly generate a lot of cash in 1993 but when we look at the expected receipts it is clear that the disposal of treasury bonds is not really related to the usual activity of a trading company. If your aim is to assess the results of the usual activity of the company, you should exclude such exceptional items.
- Among the disbursements expected in 1993, some concern relationships with a bank and with shareholders (items 15, 16 and 17). These disbursements do not relate strictly to the business of trading but rather to the financing decisions made by Mr Rolland in 1993 and before. Had these financing decisions been different, the financial disbursements such as items 15, 16 and 17 would also have been different – and would have been different whatever the cash outcome of the trading activity itself.

- Finally, and again returning to the expected disbursements, some relate to the trading activity in 1993 (payments to suppliers, payments to labour, payments of selling and administrative expenditures, payment of taxes) but some relate to that activity both in 1993 and in future years. New shops and new vehicles are acquired in order to sustain the activity over several years to come.

In order to assess the success of a firm's activity we need a concept that helps us define this activity and the related cash flows more precisely. This concept is the concept of operations.

2.1 THE CONCEPT OF OPERATIONS

The only actions undertaken by a firm which are considered as belonging to operations are those which:

- Take place during a specific period of time (the period of study).
- Are directly related to the economic purpose of the firm.
- Are not of a financial nature.
- Have a short-term scope (ie a scope limited to the period of study).

Assessing the success of a firm means assessing whether or not its operations (or the actions that belong to the operations) generate enough cash.

When applied to International Textiles the concept of operations enables us to measure how much cash the trading activity of the company should generate during the year (see Figure 2.1).

In order to assess the success of International Textiles' operations in 1993, only the receipts and disbursements related to its usual trading activity should be taken into account. This excludes exceptional items (the disposal of treasury bonds, item 5), all financial items (interest, reimbursement of loans and dividend, items 15, 16 and 17), and all items with a scope extending beyond 1993 (new shops and vehicles, items 18 and 19, these generally being known as capital expenditures).

The concept of operations calls for some comments.

- Operations always relate to a specific period of time. The activity of a firm is certainly an on-going process that extends over a long span of time, but it would be inconvenient to have to wait until the economic activities of a firm have come to an end before assessing its success. Accounting and finance have therefore designed periodic evaluations of a business firm's degree of success. The periods used vary, although the most popular time period used is probably the year. The rationale for the widespread use of the year as a

time period may be summarized as follows:
· The year is a sufficiently long period of time for smoothing out the impact of seasonal factors.
· The year has traditionally been used as the main time period in the financial community (banks, stock markets, etc). In addition, banks and financial institutions in most countries calculate the price of money they provide to firms on a yearly basis.

■ In practice it can be difficult to distinguish between those flows which are of a short-term scope and those which are not. In the International Textiles case it is obvious that disbursements related to new shops and new vehicles are long-term in scope, longer than the one year time period chosen to assess the success of the operations. However, we may wonder about the scope of some other disbursements, for example, those related to advertising expenditures. Most of their impact will surely take place in 1993, but one could argue that it could also extend beyond 1993 and contribute to building up the image of the company in the long term. In practice, the distinction between short- and long-term actions is not clear cut, and is often a matter purely of judgement. We will see later, however, that this distinction is not really crucial for assessing the success of operations.[1]

		$000
OPERATIONAL RECEIPTS		
1 Receipts from sales to department stores	2 000	
2 Receipts from sales to supermarkets	1 000	
3 Receipts from sales to individual customers	4 000	
4 Receipts from sales to foreign customers	900	7 900
OPERATIONAL DISBURSEMENTS		
6 Payments to suppliers of wool cloth	600	
7 Payments to suppliers of synthetics	1 800	
8 Payments to suppliers of cotton	1 400	
9 Payment of salaries	1 600	
10 Payment of overtime and bonuses	400	
11 Payment of advertising expenditures	300	
12 Payment of promotion expenditures	100	
13 Payment of various administrative expenditures	600	
14 Payment of corporation tax*	612	7 412
CASH FROM OPERATIONS (CFO)		488

* Let us assume that corporation tax is strictly related to operations, an assumption which we will check at a later stage.

Figure 2.1 Cash generated from the operations.

2.2 HOW MUCH CASH SHOULD OPERATIONS GENERATE?

In 1993 the operations of International Textiles should generate $488 000. Is this good or bad?

When asked such a question we are often tempted to look for a basis for comparison: is cash generation expected in 1993 better than the one achieved the year before at International Textiles? Is the expected cash generation better than those of similar companies, if such companies exist? Making comparisons will, however, never provide us with really satisfactory answers because these comparisons do not indicate whether the cash generation of International Textiles in 1993 is good or bad but only whether it is better or worse than that with which we have compared it.

So what are the criteria we can use in order to assess whether or not International Textiles' cash generation is satisfactory or not?

- First of all, the operations of a company should generate a cash excess. A company that does not generate a positive cash flow from its operations is potentially in trouble since operations are the only engine that generates cash. Should this engine stop generating cash excesses and generate cash deficits instead, how could these be covered?
  - · By recourse to bank credit? Banks may agree to help a company whose operations generate cash deficits. One should, however, realize that using bank credit will oblige the firm both to pay interest and to reimburse the amount borrowed. In order to face such cash outflows the firm will have to generate cash from its operations in the future. (If not, it will only be able to cope with its interest and repayments by raising new debts – which is not very healthy.
  - · By recourse to shareholders? Shareholders may agree to provide new capital but in the long run the firm will have to deal with extra dividend payments. These will also require extra cash to be generated from operations.
- In general, though, *cash from operations should be more than just positive.* Returning to the International Textiles case, merely generating positive cash flow from operations in 1993 would not be sufficient since the company has to cope with the cash outflows related to its debt contracts. Since these cash flows result from contractual commitments made in the past, they are compulsory and should be taken care of, regardless of the situation. Cash generated from operations should be at least enough to cover these compulsory cash flows.

  Another important point to remember is that in order to generate cash from its operations, a business has to invest. The cash from operations which International Textiles generates in 1993 is most probably the result of capital expenditures made in 1993 and earlier. As a consequence, cash from operations should not be just positive but superior to the capital expenditures that were necessary to its generation.[2] Comparing cash from operations with capital expenditures is complex, however, since:

· It is difficult to identify exactly which capital expenditures and which cash from operations correspond to each other. This is, generally, possible for current capital expenditures and future cash from operations but impossible for current cash from operations and past capital expenditures.

· A problem related to timing immediately arises. Cash from operations related to specific capital expenditures is generally spread over several years: should we account for this delay, and, if so, how? How should we account for the fact that in some cases the delay is long whereas in others it is much shorter? These very important issues are dealt with in Chapter 14.

Cash generation in a business, and at International Textiles in particular, can be summarized by the model reproduced in Figure 2.2. The model shows that:

■ The change in cash balance is the result of a series of many different actions and does not mean anything in itself. The most important points to look at when attempting to assess the financial situation of a business are:
· Cash generated from operations
· Cash available for strategic uses
· Strategic outflows
· Need for external financing
· New external financing

■ The financial success of a business can be assessed by evaluating in turn:
· The amount of cash the business generates from its operations. Is this amount large enough compared with the capital expenditures that were made in order to generate it?
· The amount the business is left with after it has met its compulsory outflows. Depending on the magnitude of these compulsory outflows, which in turn depends on previous decisions, more or less cash from operations will be needed.
· The nature of the strategic outflows: are the capital expenditures adequate? Are the dividends sufficient?
· The nature of its external financing: if new debts are raised, they will create compulsory future outflows which will earmark future cash from operations and therefore decrease management's room for manoeuvre. So, raising too much debt may be potentially dangerous. Raising new equity, however, will create dividend commitments which are much less binding.

■ The overall financial planning of a business corresponds to a process which can be summarized as follows:
· First, estimate the cash operations will generate. Is it positive? How can it be increased?

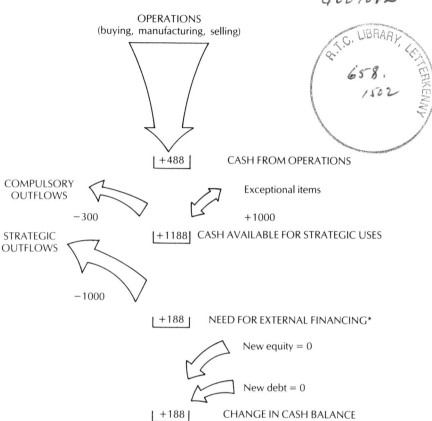

R.T.C. LIBRARY, LETTERKENNY
658,
1502

OPERATIONS
(buying, manufacturing, selling)

| +488 | CASH FROM OPERATIONS

COMPULSORY
OUTFLOWS   Exceptional items

−300   +1000

STRATEGIC
OUTFLOWS | +1188 | CASH AVAILABLE FOR STRATEGIC USES

−1000

| +188 | NEED FOR EXTERNAL FINANCING*

New equity = 0

New debt = 0

| +188 | CHANGE IN CASH BALANCE

* No need for external financing here since strategic outflows are less than the cash available for strategic uses.

Figure 2.2 A model of cash generation in a business firm

· Then compare this cash with the compulsory cash outflows. Is it enough to cover these? If not, how can these be covered?
· Next, evaluate the potential capital expenditures and identify those worth undertaking, ie those that will generate enough additional cash from the operations. The way to do this is discussed in Parts IV, V and VII. Finally, when external financing is needed, choose the most adequate sources. This is discussed in Part VI.

NOTES

1 Please refer to Chapter 11.

2 A number of companies actually define cash from operations as the difference between CFO and capital expenditures. The logic behind this is explained in Chapter 14.

R.T.C. LIBRARY
LETTERKENNY

CHAPTER 3

Assessing the Profit Generated by Operations

3.1 BASIC ACCOUNTING PRINCIPLES

As indicated above, financial analysis and planning require primarily an assessment of cash flows and especially of the cash generated from operations. However, people also refer to the profit or the income generated by the operations. How can this be calculated? Calculating how much cash is generated by operations is fairly straightforward since it is merely a matter of computing the difference between the receipts and disbursements related to these operations. However, calculating how much profit, or income, operations generate is far more complex since the concept of profit is rather sophisticated:

- When trying to measure how much profit is generated by the operations we are in fact trying to measure by how much the value of the company, or rather the value of the company for its owners, has increased due to these operations. Value is a much broader concept than cash since it includes a wide spectrum of things of value such as claims on customers, holdings of inventories, etc, and, obviously, cash.[1]
- In order to calculate how much profit is generated by operations, one has to follow a number of rules or accounting principles.

Let us try to calculate how much profit the operations of International Textiles will generate in 1993.

The recognition principle for revenues

At International Textiles, selling cloth to customers in 1993 will result in total cash receipts of $7 900 000. Does this mean that the company will in fact become richer by this amount? In 1993 International Textiles will deliver products to its customers and, as is usual in most trades, some customers will pay cash for these products whereas some will get them on credit (ie on the basis of their promise to pay at a later date). Let us assume that, at the beginning of 1993, total customer promises to pay were equal to $1 000 000.

They related to deliveries made in 1992 which were to be paid in 1993. At the end of 1993 they are expected to amount to $2 000 000. These customers' promises to pay are recorded in accounts called accounts receivable.

As far as accounting is concerned the company creates value as soon as it delivers products or services. Both deliveries paid for in cash, and deliveries made on credit, should therefore be considered as revenues or sales. This first accounting principle enables us to calculate the sales of International Textiles in 1993. These will equal:

- The cash receipts in 1993
- To which should be added the customers' promises to pay resulting from deliveries to be made in 1993 (or accounts receivable end, ie $2 000 000)
- And from which should be deducted the cash receipts related to deliveries made in 1992 (or accounts receivable open, ie $1 000 000)

	$000
Cash receipts from customers in 1993	7 900
+ Accounts receivable end	2 000
− Accounts receivable open	(1 000)
= Sales in 1993	8 900

Because of the way in which accounting defines sales, one realizes that, as soon as customers are allowed credit, the cash received from selling lags behind the sales by a period equal to the duration of the credit granted to customers. This credit duration is also called the *collection period*. As indicated above, sales not yet collected are recorded in accounts called accounts receivable or debtors. In some economic activities, such as banking, one would not use the term accounts receivable but instead the term *accrued revenues* which has basically the same meaning.[2]

Cash receipts, however, do not always necessarily lag behind revenues; they may also precede or lead them. Publishing companies, for example, sell subscriptions for magazines that customers pay for in advance. If subscription money is received in 1993 for magazines to be delivered in 1994, the amount is not considered as a revenue in 1993 but rather as a debt or liability of the company towards its subscribers. All revenues paid for in advance are recorded in accounts called *deferred income* (deferred revenue would be a better term).

Let us go back to the International Textiles case. As shown above the company will create revenues amounting $8 900 000. But in order to do so, the company will also incur expenses, and the profit generated will equal the difference between revenues and expenses.

The assessment of expenses results from three basic accounting principles:

- Expenditure recognition
- Matching
- Allowance for depreciation.

The recognition principle for expenditures

The expenditure recognition principle is very similar to the revenue recognition principle: expenditures are recognized during a specific accounting period only if they correspond to goods actually received from suppliers during that period (or to services performed by suppliers, employees and various agents). Because goods and services are generally not paid for in cash when they are delivered, the expenditures of a specific accounting period usually do not equal the disbursements in this same period: generally, like receipts, disbursements lag behind expenditures.

In 1993 International Textiles expects that among the operational items listed in Figure A.1, all will be paid for in cash except those related to suppliers. Let us assume that, at the end of 1993, International Textiles' promises to pay its suppliers amount to $600 000. At the beginning of 1993, they were equal to $400 000. Promises to pay suppliers are recorded in accounts called *accounts payable* or *creditors*.[3]

Purchases in 1993 at International Textiles will be calculated as follows:

	$000
Cash payments to suppliers in 1993	3 800
+ Accounts payable end	600
− Accounts payable open	(400)
= Purchases in 1993	4 000

Since all the other expenditure items will be paid for in cash in 1993, the other expenditures will equal the corresponding cash disbursements and the total of expenditures including purchases will amount to:

	$000
Purchases	4 000
Labour expenditures	2 000
Other expenditures	1 000
Corporation tax	612
Total expenditures	7 612

Because of the accounting principle used for recognizing expenditures, expenditures will therefore, in general, not equal cash disbursements. In most cases, like the purchases above, they will precede or lead the cash disbursements. Amounts due to suppliers are recorded as indicated above in accounts payable. The time lag between purchases and cash payments to suppliers is called the *payment period*. Amounts due to persons who, unlike suppliers, have not submitted an invoice for the amount owed (for example, employees whose wages are not yet fully paid) are recorded in an account called *accrued expenses*. Amounts due to tax authorities when there is a lag in tax payments are recorded in an account called *tax payable*. It is obvious, however, that payments do not always lag behind, since, in some cases, these will be made in advance, for example, insurance policies. Such expenditures are recorded in an account called *prepaid expenses* or *deferred charges*.[4]

The matching principle for expenses

According to the 'matching expenses with revenues' principle, accounting considers that, in order to calculate the profit in a given accounting period, one should deduct from the revenues of this period only those expenditures which helped generate the recognized revenues or sales. These are called *expenses*.

This rule is very important because it is unusual that goods bought or manufactured in a given period are delivered to the customers during that same period. In most cases, the purchase and manufacturing of goods lead deliveries, which explains the existence of inventories of goods at any moment in time. The matching principle has very important implications in terms of the profit calculation: in the extreme case where no revenues are recognized, there should be no expenses either, an almost perfect built-in insurance against losses (provided that selling price is higher than purchasing or manufacturing price).

Two methods exist of applying the matching principle. The first one is popular in the UK, the USA and in a number of other countries, while the second one is popular in continental Europe and elsewhere. In order to show how these methods are used, let us go back to the International Textiles case. We know that in 1993, revenues or sales will amount to $8 900 000 and expenditures will amount to $7 612 000.

In addition to this information, the company knows that part of the purchases do not relate to sales to be made in 1993 but rather to sales to be made in subsequent years. These purchases relating to future sales amount to $1 500 000 and will be recorded at the end of the year in accounts called *inventories*. At the beginning of 1993, inventories were equal to $1 000 000 corresponding to goods to be sold in 1993.

The matching principle as used in the UK and the US

In order to calculate the profit generated in 1993 at International Textiles, we should deduct from the sales:

- not, all the expenditures incurred during the year,
- but only, those expenditures related to sales made during the year.

Among the expenditures incurred in 1993, purchases correspond to both sales of 1993 and sales to be made after 1993. We also know that some of the sales in 1993 will be made from the goods stored in inventory at the beginning of the year. So the purchases that match the sales made in 1993 are equal to:

	$000
Purchases	4 000
+ Opening inventory	1 000
− Ending inventory	(1 500)
= Cost of goods sold/Cost of sales	3 500

At International Textiles, the other expenditures (labour, other expenses, etc) are not identified as related to specific sales. Instead, they appear to correspond to the 1993 period and are therefore to be considered as expenses and deducted as they are from sales. This allows for a profit estimation as shown in Figure 3.1.

	$000
Sales	8 900
Cost of goods sold (CGS)	3 500
Other expenses	3 000
Corporation tax	612
Cash flow earnings (CFE)*	1 788

* When calculated in this way, the profit is called Cash flow earnings or Working capital provided by the operations.

Figure 3.1 Estimating profit: UK/US method.

This approach requires that a distinction be made between expenditures[5]:

- Some are considered as being directly related to sales and are called *product expenditures*. These expenditures should match the sales and if the firm incurs more of these expenditures than it sells, the extra expenditures are to be stored in an inventory. The reverse is true also; if sales are more than incurred expenditures, extra expenses have to be charged to sales from a reduction in the inventory. Such expenditures are purchases, labour and other items directly related to the selling or the manufacturing process. The amount of product expenditures that match the sales is called the *cost of goods sold* or cost of sales.
- Other expenditures are considered as being related to the period in which they occur and are called *period expenditures*. These expenditures are charged

to the period in which they occur, whether or not sales are made and they are never stored in inventory. General overhead expenditures are a good example of period expenditures. Their existence means losses are much easier to make than if there were only product expenditures.

The matching principle the continental European way

With this approach one does not calculate the cost of goods sold but merely adjusts the difference between revenues and expenditures incurred by the change in inventories, as shown in Figure 3.2.

	$000
Sales	8 900
Ending inventory	1 500
Opening inventory	1 000
Purchases	4 000
Other expenses	3 000
Corporation tax	612
Cash flow earnings (CFE)	1 788

Figure 3.2 Estimating profit: continental European method.

Both approaches lead to the same estimation of profit or rather cash flow earnings.[6] The continental European approach may, however, be somewhat confusing since the ending inventory appears as revenues and the opening inventory as expenses. Actually, the opening and ending inventories are only introduced so that expenses match sales (ie in order to reduce the expenditures).

One thing to note is that the matching principle is a particular application of a much more general accounting principle, the *accrual principle* according to which the *financial data generated in the accounting system should be allocated to the specific periods to which they are judged to relate.*

The depreciation principle

The notion of cash flow earnings which has been introduced above is generally considered by accounting as an over-optimistic view of what profit will be or has been. The reason for this, according to accounting, is that the concept of cash flow earnings does not account for any expense related to the use of fixed assets. In accounting, fixed assets are defined as all those items which have a long life-span (a life of more than one year). In the International Textiles case, the payments for the acquisition of new shops and vehicles are capital expenditures which are made in order to acquire such fixed assets.

- When assessing the cash generated from the operations we disregarded capital expenditures on the basis that they cannot be traced to a specific year – and particularly to the one in which they are paid.

- Accounting views the problem quite differently and advocates that the amount of any capital expenditures for the acquisition of fixed assets should be charged to those accounting periods or years in which the fixed assets will be used. In order to do so accounting requires, for example, that the amount of capital expenditure be divided by the number of years of supposed use, and that the amount obtained, (which is called allowance for depreciation, or, more simply, depreciation) be charged as an expense to each of the years in which the fixed asset will be used.[7]

Returning to International Textiles, let us assume that its estimate of the allowance for depreciation is $500 000 for 1993. The profit calculation has to be adjusted accordingly.

	$000
Sales	8 900
Cost of goods sold	3 500
Other expenses	3 000
Corporation tax	612
Cash flow earnings (CFE)	1 788
Depreciation	500
Operational profit after tax	1 288

Figure 3.3 Estimating operational profit after tax.

3.2 THE INCOME STATEMENT AND THE CALCULATION OF CORPORATION TAX

The income statement or profit and loss account is a statement produced by accounting, the purpose of which is to report the profit or loss made by a business during a specified period of time. Presentations of income statements depend on the business concerned and on the countries in which these firms operate since accounting follows different traditions or rules in different countries.[8]

According to conventions prevailing in the USA, the income statement of International Textiles would look as shown in Figure 3.4.

The income statement of International Textiles shown in Figure 3.4 is close to the calculation of operational profit after tax shown in Figure 3.3. There are, however, some major differences.

	$000
Sales	8 900
Cost of goods sold	3 500
Labour expenses	2 000
Other expenses	1 000
Depreciation	500
Interest	100
Profit (or income) before taxes	1 800
Corporation tax	612
Profit (or income) after tax	1 188

Figure 3.4 Income statement.

R.T.C. LIBRARY
LETTERKENNY

- When calculating the profit of a company, accounting deducts *interest* and therefore mixes up operational and financial items. In addition, when calculating profit, accounting also considers the *exceptional items* if any. Here the assumption is that the treasury bonds are sold for the price at which they were bought, so no exceptional profit is made upon the disposal of such bonds. The reason why the calculation of profit is not limited to the operational items is that accounting aims at giving a comprehensive view of the revenues and expenses whether they are operational or not. It should be realized that this comprehensive scope is achieved at the expense of the homogeneity of the concept of profit which generally includes operational items and non-operational items. To assess the profit generated by operations, you should adjust the profit reported by accounting and remove the impact of financial and exceptional items.
- The income statement in Figure 3.4 shows an intermediate balance called profit before tax (or taxable profit). Profit before tax in Figure 3.4 is equal to $1 800 000. Since corporation tax is equal to $612 000 this means that the implied corporation tax rate is 34%.

The calculation of corporation tax calls for two comments at this stage.

- When calculating taxable profit, interest expenses are deducted but not dividends. Debt is a source of financing that is favoured by Tax Authorities in most countries around the world.[9]
- When calculating taxable profit, the allowance for depreciation is deducted. The more you depreciate, the less you pay taxes or more exactly, the quicker you depreciate, the slower you pay taxes. This is why in all countries Tax Authorities define very precise guidelines for computing the allowance for depreciation. The allowance for depreciation stated by Tax Authorities is sometimes called *capital allowance*. In some countries, Tax Authorities may grant very generous capital allowances which enable the firms which invest to defer their income tax to a very significant extent.[10] However, the existence of generous capital allowances creates a problem for the reporting

of profit. In order to illustrate this problem, let us consider the following hypothetical example.

· Early in 1993, the Taylor company purchases a 30 000 SEQ[11] asset which is expected to have a three year economic life. The company is entitled to claim a 100% capital allowance in 1993. The company expects its profit before depreciation and tax to be as follows in the period 1993–1995:

1993	1994	1995
60 000	70 000	80 000

How can the company estimate its profit after tax?

Alternative 1: 'tax' profit

	1993	1994	1995	Cumulative
Profit before depreciation and tax	60 000	70 000	80 000	210 000
Depreciation (capital allowance)	30 000			30 000
Profit before tax	30 000	70 000	80 000	180 000
Tax at 40%	12 000	28 000	32 000	72 000
Profit after tax	18 000	42 000	48 000	108 000

Alternative 2: 'fair' profit

	1993	1994	1995	Cumulative
Profit before depreciation and tax	60 000	70 000	80 000	210 000
Depreciation (fair depreciation)	10 000	10 000	10 000	30 000
Profit before tax	50 000	60 000	70 000	180 000
Tax at 40%	20 000	24 000	28 000	72 000
Profit after tax	30 000	36 000	42 000	108 000

The two alternatives lead to the same cumulative tax and profit after tax over the period and the advantage of Alternative 1 is a timing effect only. The problem with Alternative 1 is that it tends to underestimate the profit in 1993 and to overestimate it afterwards (provided you believe that since the equipment will be used over three years, you should allocate its cost evenly over this period). The solution to this problem is the *deferred tax* concept: this concept enables you to reconcile 'tax' and 'fair' profit considerations:

	1993	1994	1995	Cumulative
Profit before depreciation and tax	60 000	70 000	80 000	210 000
Depreciation (fair depreciation)	10 000	10 000	10 000	30 000
Profit before tax	50 000	60 000	70 000	180 000
Tax (from Alternative 1)	12 000	28 000	32 000	72 000
Provision for tax (deferred tax)	8 000	−4 000	−4 000	0
Profit after tax	30 000	36 000	42 000	108 000

Each year, provision for tax is equal to the difference between actual tax (from Alternative 1) and 'fair' tax (from Alternative 2). Provision for tax is accumulated in a balance sheet account called deferred tax. This account cancels itself out at the end of the life of the asset. One thing to note is that the concept of deferred tax is not universally accepted. Although it is common practice in the UK, the USA and countries with similar accounting philosophies it is not used in most continental European countries.[12] In these countries, profit should be reported as it is calculated for tax purposes, as in Alternative 1. The consequence of this is that when capital allowances are generous, annual reported profits are not generally 'fair'. This obviously creates serious difficulties when you want to compare the profitability of companies operating in different countries.

3.3 RECONCILING PROFIT WITH CASH, WORKING CAPITAL NEEDS, CASH AS A SUPERIOR YARDSTICK

In the International Textiles case, we have estimated profit from cash generated from operations. We may now try to do just the opposite and estimate cash from operations from profit. Let us assume that we are given the profit figure shown in Figure 3.4 (profit reported in the income statement) and that we want to estimate the amount of cash generated from operations.

In order to do this, we will have to make a series of adjustments.

- We must remove the impact of the interest charges from the profit shown in the income statement. This is done by adding the amount of interest to the profit.
- We should adjust the profit in order to get an estimate of the cash generated.
  - · First, we should remember that when calculating profit, allowance for depreciation has been deducted. From a cash viewpoint such a deduction is not to be made; in order to cancel the impact of allowance for depreciation we have to add it back to profit.
  - · We should also remember that sales correspond to deliveries of goods and not to cash receipts. In order to get cash receipts we have to deduct the increase in accounts receivable, if any, from profit.
  - · We should also remember that cost of goods sold and not purchases have been considered as expenses in the profit calculation. From a cash viewpoint, purchases and not cost of goods sold matter. We therefore have to deduct from profit the increase in inventory, if any.
  - · Finally, purchases correspond to cash disbursements only if accounts payable have not changed. Since these are to increase, we again have to add that increase to profit in order to replace purchases with cash disburse-

	$000	
PROFIT AFTER TAX	1 188	(from Figure 3.4)
+ Interest	100	
= OPERATIONAL PROFIT AFTER TAX	1 288	(as in Figure 3.3)
+ depreciation	500	
= CASH FLOW EARNINGS (CFE)	1 788	(as in Figures 3.1 and 3.2)
− increase in accounts receivable	1 000	
− increase in inventories	500	
+ increase in accounts payable	200	
= CASH FROM OPERATIONS (CFO)	488	(as in Figure 2.1)

Figure 3.5 Reconciling profit with cash.

ments. These successive adjustments are shown in Figure 3.5.

Ignoring the impact of interest expenses, Figure 3.5 allows us to single out the reasons why profit (or, more specifically, operational profit) may differ quite substantially from the cash generated from operations.

- Profit is calculated after deducting the allowance for depreciation.
- The profit calculation ignores the fact that part of the sales are not yet paid for, that an inventory exists, and that part of the purchases are not yet paid for. When calculating cash, one has therefore to deduct from profit the net balance of the increase in accounts receivable, inventories and accounts payable; this net balance is called the *change in working capital needs*.

The reconciliation of profit with cash from operations may be summarized as in Figure 3.6 which allows us to understand one very important fact of business life: despite making a profit, a firm may not generate any cash from its operations. This can easily happen if the increase in working capital needs is more than cash flow earnings. A firm whose receivables and/or inventories

PROFIT AFTER TAX
+ depreciation*

= CASH FLOW EARNINGS (CFE)†

− increase in working
capital needs

= CASH FROM OPERATIONS (CFO)

* And more generally all non cash expenses.

† This presentation may help you understand why some people call CFE working capital provided by operations: cash is generated provided that more working capital than needed is generated.

Figure 3.6 Reconciling profit with cash: a summary.

increase too much in relation to its profit can find itself fairly quickly in this kind of situation. In this case, profit and cash from operations will give different signals. A positive profit will tend to indicate a favorable situation, but cash from operations will indicate that the situation is not acceptable – and this will be the relevant signal since what a firm actually needs to reimburse its debts and make new investments is cash.[13]

Removing the tax impact of interest

In Figure 3.6 we assume that corporation tax is totally related to operations, but this is not true. When calculating its taxable profit, International Textiles has deducted interest expenses which have enabled it to reduce its corporation tax.

Without any deduction of interest expenses, taxable profit would have been equal to $1 900 000 and corporation tax to $646 000. With the deduction of interest expenses, taxable profit is $1 800 000 and tax only $612 000. We should therefore consider that tax related to operations is $646 000 and that the difference between this amount and the amount paid ($34 000) is the tax shield due to interest. This leads to the estimate of cash from operations shown in Figure 3.7.

	$000
PROFIT AFTER TAX	1 188
+ Interest	66
= OPERATIONAL PROFIT AFTER TAX*	1 254
+ depreciation	500
= CASH FLOW EARNINGS (CFE)	1 754
− increase in accounts receivable	1 000
− increase in inventories	500
+ increase in accounts payable	200
= CASH FROM OPERATIONS (CFO)	454*

* 34 less than in Figure 3.5, since tax related to operations is considered to be 34 more due to the absence of interest related tax shields.

Figure 3.7 Reconciling operational profit with cash.

This in turn leads to an adjustment of Figure 2.1 (p 16) also: it becomes Figure 3.8.

		$000
OPERATIONAL RECEIPTS		
1 Receipts from sales to department stores	2 000	
2 Receipts from sales to supermarkets	1 000	
3 Receipts from sales to individual customers	4 000	
4 Receipts from sales to foreign customers	900	7 900
OPERATIONAL DISBURSEMENTS		
6 Payments to suppliers of wool cloth	600	
7 Payments to suppliers of synthetics	1 800	
8 Payments to suppliers of cotton	1 400	
9 Payment of salaries	1 600	
10 Payment of overtime and bonuses	400	
11 Payment of advertising expenditures	300	
12 Payment of promotion expenditures	100	
13 Payment of various administrative expenditures	600	
14 Payment of corporation tax (operational)	646	7 446
CASH FROM OPERATIONS (CFO)		454

Figure 3.8 Cash generated from the operations.

NOTES

1 In financial literature there are not many definitions of profit. The most famous is probably the one proposed by Hicks: Profit is the measure of how much value can be withdrawn from the firm over an accounting period without leaving it worse off than before. For more about the definition of profit, refer to: J Treynor, 'The trouble with earnings' in *Modern Developments in Investment Management*, J Lorie and R Brealey (eds), Praeger (1972), pp 663–7.

2 When a bank lends money it charges interest and this interest is considered as a revenue for the bank. In some cases the borrower does not pay interest immediately on using the credit. For example, a credit granted in 1993 to be reimbursed in 1995 may commit the borrower to pay interest only in 1995, when the credit is reimbursed. When calculating its revenue in 1993, the bank will consider that it has earned interest, even though it has not yet been paid by the borrower. This interest, or claim on the borrower, will be recorded as accrued interest revenue in the books of the bank.

3 More precisely accounts payable trade or trade creditors, since promises to pay may also be made in relation to non-operational actions like the acquisition of new equipment or machinery (or capital expenditures in general).

4 Deferred charges are like prepaid expenses but have a longer-term scope (ie a scope extending over several periods). Restructuring costs are a typical example of deferred charges. Because of their long scope, deferred charges are often depreciated or *amortized*.

5 In practice, this distinction is not easy to make and is often a matter of judgement. Consequently, be careful when comparing the cost of goods sold in different companies.

6 One thing to note is that, since they do not distinguish between product and period expenditures, continental European accounts do not enable you to estimate cost of goods sold.

7 It should be noted that the annual allowance for depreciation is not necessarily constant over the life of an asset. For some assets one could, for example, charge higher depreciation at the beginning and less at the end of their life. In any case the sum of the annual allowances for depreciation over the life of an asset is necessarily equal to its acquisition value.

8 In some countries the presentation of income statements must be made according to a very detailed format specified by law. In others there are certain traditions which are supported by some legally specified rules. For an analysis of the reporting practices in the UK, refer to *Survey of Published Accounts*, and *Accounting Standards*, two annual publications of the Institute of Chartered Accountants, Moorgate Place, London EC2P 2BJ. For a comprehensive review of US accounting standards, refer to P Delaney, J Adler, B Epstein and M Foran (1992), *GAAP Interpretation and Application*, John Wiley & Sons. For a presentation of the international accounting standards, refer to *International Accounting Standards*, a publication of the International Accounting Standards Committee, 167 Fleet Street, London EC4A 2ES.

9 This seems strange when we consider that debt financing may be dangerous (as shown in Chapter 21). For an argument in favour of recognising interest on equity as a cost of doing business, refer to: R Anthony, 'Equity interest – its time has come', *Journal of Accountancy*, Dec 1982.

10 In a number of countries there have been situations where companies have benefited from capital allowances equal to 100% of the value of the assets in the first year of their acquisition. In some countries, companies are even able to claim capital allowances before they acquire the asset. This was, for example, the case in Sweden where companies were allowed to deduct from their taxable income a provision related to assets they planned to acquire in subsequent periods. This provision was posted to a balance sheet account called reserve for investment.

11 The currency of an hypothetical country.

12 Deferred tax is not an easy concept. For a discussion of some of the problems it poses, refer to: S Zeff and T Keller, *Financial Accounting Theory*, 3rd edn, McGraw-Hill (1985) Section 7, H, pp 423–49.

13 Even though accountants have traditionally put more emphasis on profit than on cash, there is now a considerable interest in cash. Some authors are even recommending that cash flow accounting be adopted for financial reporting. For some of the arguments in favour and against cash flow accounting, refer to: S Zeff and T Keller, op. cit., Section 5, pp 235–82.

CHAPTER 4

Balance Sheets and Cash Flow Statements

The calculation of profit aims at measuring how much an organization has created value over a specified period of time. Accounting does not limit itself, however, to the measurement of the profit which is achieved through the construction of income statements. Accounting also aims at presenting at specific time intervals a description of the value situation of organizations. This periodical description, or snapshot view, at a specified moment in time, is called the balance sheet.

4.1 THE BALANCE SHEET

The balance sheet is a list of:

- On one side, all those things of value the organization owns. These are called *assets*.
- On the other side, all the obligations of the organization to outsiders or the claims against these assets. These are called *liabilities* and *owners' equity*.

By definition, the total value of the liabilities and owners' equity equals the total value of the assets. This definition may seem strange at first; since some assets are financed by debt, claims exist against them, but how can claims exist against all the assets? The answer to this question comes from a further accounting principle, the concept of *business entity*.[1] According to this principle, balance sheets should reflect the situation of the company and not that of its owners. As, in the end, the firm belongs to its owners, these have claims on total assets minus the claims of other external parties (lenders, suppliers, etc). The total of the claims of the owners is called owners' equity, or shareholders' equity, or net worth.

Although the presentation of balance sheets, like those of the income statements, varies from country to country, balance sheets in most countries include the same broad categories. International Textiles' balance sheet as at the end of 1993 is presented according to a US model in Figure 4.1.

	$000		$000	
Cash	388	Accounts payable	600	
Accounts receivable	2 000	Current liabilities		600
Inventories	1 500	Long term debt	800	
Current assets	3 888			
Financial assets	100	Owners' equity:		
Gross fixed assets	10 900	Common stock	4 000	
– accumulated depreciation	5 300	Retained earnings	4 188	
Net fixed assets	5 600			
		Total liabilities and		
Total assets	9 588	owners' equity	9 588	

Figure 4.1 Balance sheet at year end.

Let us examine the items shown on the balance sheet of International Textiles as at December 31, 1993.

Assets

Assets are shown as either *current* or *fixed*.

■ *Current assets* are assets which are currently in the form of cash or which are expected to be converted to cash within one year. The headings in the International Textiles balance sheet are self explanatory: cash, accounts receivable, inventories. Other items which are found among current assets are those such as prepaid expenses, short term financial investments, etc.

■ *Fixed assets* are properties which have a relatively long life-span (more than one year). Fixed assets may be of a financial or a physical nature. Examples of financial assets are outstanding long term loans to a subsidiary, equity holdings, etc. Examples of physical assets are machinery and equipment, buildings, land. For reporting the value of physical assets three accounts are used:

· Gross fixed assets represent the amount of fixed assets at their acquisition value. A further accounting principle is that of *historical value*.[2]

· Accumulated depreciation corresponds to the cumulative amount of allowance for depreciation which has been made over the years regarding the fixed assets presently owned by the company.

· Net fixed assets correspond to the difference between gross fixed assets and accumulated depreciation.

In order to illustrate the working of the fixed assets accounts, let us consider an example. Let us assume that at the beginning of 1993 a company buys a machine worth $6 000 that it plans to use for 3 years. Let us further assume that the company will depreciate this machine over three years for an annual amount of $6 000/3 = $2 000. How will the machine be recorded by accounting during its life time?

- At the beginning of 1993: the machine has just been acquired.

gross fixed assets	6 000
− accumulated depreciation	(0)
= net fixed assets	6 000

- At the end of 1993: The machine was bought almost one year ago and a $2 000 allowance for depreciation is made in 1993.

gross fixed assets	6 000
− accumulated depreciation	(2 000)
= net fixed assets	4 000

- At the end of 1994: The machine was bought two years ago and in 1994 another $2 000 allowance for depreciation is made.

gross fixed assets	6 000
− accumulated depreciation	(4 000)
= net fixed assets	2 000

- At the end of 1995: The machine has reached the end of its planned life and the last allowance for depreciation is made in 1995.

gross fixed assets	6 000
− accumulated depreciation	(6 000)
= net fixed assets	0

What will happen next? If the machine is actually kept for longer than originally planned then nothing else is done as far as accounting is concerned: the machine is fully depreciated, its net value is zero, and no further accounting action will be taken. On the other hand, if the machine is disposed of, some accounting actions will take place. First, the amount of $6 000 will be cancelled from both gross fixed assets and accumulated depreciation in order to clear the books. Second, any profit or loss resulting from the disposal of the machine will be recorded. In the books, the machine is worth nothing; if it is disposed of for any amount of money, a profit will occur. This profit will be reported in the income statement as an exceptional item.

Liabilities and owners' equity

- Liabilities correspond to claims that people other than the owners have on the company.
- Owners' equity corresponds to the claims that the owners have on the company.

Liabilities and owners' equity, like assets, are also shown as either *current* or *long term*.

- Short term (current) liabilities correspond to those obligations which are due within a year. In International Textiles' balance sheet, only one short term liability item is reported. In other cases, under the heading of current liabilities, one would find items such as accrued expenses, taxes payable, deferred income, short term loans, long term debt current portion (the portion of long term debt which is to be paid within the year), dividends to pay, etc.
- Long term liabilities and shareholders' equity correspond to obligations which are due in more than one year. Shareholders' equity, or net worth, shown in Figure 4.1, comprises two components: *capital stock* and *retained earnings*. Capital stock corresponds to the amount of capital that shareholders have brought in over the history of the company. Retained earnings correspond to the cumulative sum of non-distributed profit over the years. Since profit is the property of shareholders, retained earnings (the part of profit they have not yet received as dividends) is obviously theirs.

4.2 THE USES AND SOURCES OF FUNDS STATEMENT

There are many different expressions used to describe this statement: statement of changes in financial position, sources and applications of funds statement, fund flows statement, etc. Here we will keep to the expression uses and sources of funds statement.

This statement is built on the comparison of the opening and ending balance sheets for a specified period of time.

- Uses of funds are defined as any increase in an asset item or any decrease in a liability or owners' equity item. Examples of uses of funds are an increase in inventories or a decrease in short term debt (reimbursement of a debt being unquestionably a use).
- Sources of funds are defined as any increase in a liability or owners' equity item or any decrease in an asset item. Examples of sources of funds are increases in long term debt and decreases in accounts receivable (obviously when customers pay that is a source of money to the company).

Uses and sources of funds are calculated by computing the difference between the items of the opening and ending balance sheets. Even though this may appear fairly straightforward, it is worth taking some precautions.

Let us try to build the uses and sources of funds statement for International Textiles in 1993. The opening and ending balance sheets are given in Figure 4.2.

The following steps are used to build the uses and sources of funds statements:

1. Start from an opening and an ending balance sheet (see Figure 4.2).[3]

	$000				$000	
	Open	End			Open	End
Cash	200	388	Accounts payable		400	600
Accounts receivable	1 000	2 000	Long term debt		1 000	800
Inventories	1 000	1 500				
Financial assets	1 100	100	Owners' equity		7 100	8 188
Net fixed assets	5 200	5 600	Total liabilities			
Total assets	8 500	9 588	and owners' equity		8 500	9 588

Figure 4.2 Balance sheet: opening and ending balances.

2. Calculate the difference between each balance sheet item, record it as a use or a source, and regroup the uses and the sources together. This is shown in Figures 4.3 and 4.4.

	Open	End	Change	Nature		Open	End	Change	Nature
Cash	200	388	188	**Use**	Accounts payable	400	600	200	**Source**
Accounts receivable	1 000	2 000	1 000	**Use**	Long term debt	1 000	800	−200	**Use**
Inventories	1 000	1 500	500	**Use**					
Financial assets	1 100	100	−1 000	**Source**	Owners' equity	7 100	8 188	1 088	**Source**
Net fixed assets	5 200	5 600	400	**Use**	Total liabilities				
Total assets	8 500	9 588			and owners equity	8 500	9 588		

Figure 4.3 Balance sheet: changes.

USES	$000	SOURCES	$000
Increase in cash	188	Decrease in financial assets	1 000
Increase in accounts receivable	1 000	Increase in accounts payable	200
Increase in inventory	500	Increase in net worth	1 088
Increase in net fixed assets	400		
Decrease in long term debt	200		
Total uses	2 288	Total sources	2 288

Figure 4.4 Uses and sources of funds.

Before proceeding any further, a check should be made to confirm that total uses equals total sources. As uses and sources are calculated as the difference between two balanced statements, total uses should equal total sources.

3. Think what these uses and sources mean and, more precisely:

   · What does the change in net fixed assets mean?
   · What does the change in shareholders' equity mean?

At International Textiles, the change in shareholders' equity is equal to 1 088 (a source). This change is the net difference between:

· The profit after tax of 1 188 (a source). See Figure 3.4.
· The dividend of 100 (a use). See Figure A.1, item 17.

On the other hand, the change in net fixed assets is equal to 400 (a use). This change is the net difference between:

· The investment in new fixed assets for a total of 900 (a use). See Figure A.1.
· The allowance for depreciation, 500 (a source). The reason why depreciation is considered as a source is far from being obvious. The truth of the matter is that depreciation should be ignored in uses and sources statements, depreciation is neither a source nor a use but a conventional allocation of costs previously incurred. What you must realize is that considering depreciation as a source is aimed at ignoring it: when we say in Figure 4.5 that profit after tax is the outcome of operations, we should not forget that when calculating profit we have deducted depreciation or in other words we have considered depreciation as a use of funds. Considering it now as a source of an identical amount is a complicated but effective way to eliminate depreciation from the uses and sources statement.

We can now replace the change in shareholders' equity and the change in net fixed assets by the factors that explain their change. This is done in Figure 4.5.

USES	$000	SOURCES	$000
Dividend	100	Profit after tax	1 188
Investment in fixed assets	900	Depreciation	500
Increase in cash	188	Decrease in financial assets	1 000
Increase in accounts receivable	1 000	Increase in accounts payable	200
Increase in inventory	500		
Decrease in long term debt	200		
Total uses	2 888	Total sources	2 888

Figure 4.5 Adjusted uses and sources of funds.

Uses and sources statements are widely used and in most countries it is a requirement that, in addition to publishing at least once a year an income statement and a balance sheet, a uses and sources of funds statement must also be published. No standard presentation for the uses and sources of fund statement exists. The one we find most useful is the one described below, which will be called hereafter the cash flow statement.

4.3 THE CASH FLOW STATEMENT

The statement in Figure 4.5 can be rearranged so as to show clearly in Figure 4.6:

- The cash flow earnings.
- The change in working capital needs.
- The cash from operations.

	$000
PROFIT AFTER TAX	1 188
+ Depreciation	500
= CASH FLOW EARNINGS (CFE)	1 688
− Increase in accounts receivable	1 000
− Increase in inventory	500
+ Increase in accounts payable	200
= CASH FROM OPERATIONS (CFO)	388
+ Exceptional items	1 000
− Debt repayment	200
− Dividend	100
− New investments	900
= Change in cash	188

Figure 4.6 Cash flow statement: a first presentation.

Figure 4.6 is merely a rearrangement of the uses and sources of funds statement. The items shown are exactly the same as in Figure 4.5; only the presentation changes. But it enables us to identify how much cash is generated by the operations. Identifying the true value of cash from operations (CFO) requires, however, one further adjustment, the removal of the impact of interest expenses. This is done in Figure 4.7.

	$000
PROFIT AFTER TAX	1 188
+ Interest after tax	66
= OPERATIONAL PROFIT AFTER TAX	1 254
+ Depreciation	500
= CASH FLOW EARNINGS (CFE)	1 754
− Increase in accounts receivable	1 000
− Increase in inventory	500
+ Increase in accounts payable	200
= CASH FROM OPERATIONS (CFO)	454
+ Exceptional items	1 000
− Debt repayment	200
− Interest after tax	66
− Dividend	100
− New investments	900
= Change in cash	188

Figure 4.7 Cash flow statement: a second presentation.

Since Figure 4.7 starts with net profit after tax, which is the bottom line of the income statement, we may integrate the income statement as shown in Figure 3.4 and the cash flow statement as shown in Figure 4.7. This integration is done in Figure 4.8. This last presentation of the cash flow statement, which starts with sales and ends with the change in cash balance, is the one we will use hereafter (with some adjustments when needed).

	$000
SALES	8 900
− Cost of goods sold	3 500
− Labor expenses	2 000
− Other expenses	1 000
− Depreciation	500
− Interest	100
= Profit before tax	1 800
− Corporation tax	612
= Profit after tax	1 188
+ Interest after tax	66
= OPERATIONAL PROFIT AFTER TAX	1 254
+ Depreciation	500
= CASH FLOW EARNINGS (CFE)	1 754
− Increase in accounts receivable	1 000
− Increase in inventory	500
+ Increase in accounts payable	200
= CASH FROM OPERATIONS (CFO)	454
+ Exceptional items	1 000
− Debt repayment	200
− Interest after tax	66
− Dividend	100
− New investments	900
= Change in cash	188

Figure 4.8 Cash flow statement: our favorite presentation.

NOTES

1 The concept of business entity is a fundamental principle in accounting. However, as mentioned by R Anthony in 'We don't have the accounting concepts we need' (*Harvard Business Review*, Jan/Feb 1987, pp 75–83), this concept is not fully accepted by accounting since its full application would require the recognition in the income statement of a cost attached to the use of the money made available to companies by their shareholders.

2 This general principle is not applied, however, in high inflation countries. Among the large multinational companies, one has been for not using historical accounting, the Dutch-based Philips company.

3 One difficulty when building uses and sources of funds statements from the balance sheets published by companies is that they show a lot of accounts and sub-accounts. For example, fixed assets are generally broken down into sub-accounts such as equipment and machinery, buildings, land, etc. In many cases, the gross and the net values of fixed assets are also reported. So as not to be overwhelmed with too many details from the start of the analysis, a good idea is to aggregate sub-accounts in order to limit the asset accounts to cash, accounts receivable, inventory, other current assets, financial assets and net fixed assets. Similarly, equities accounts can be aggregated into loans, accounts payable, other current liabilities, provisions and net worth. Remember it is always possible to reintroduce more details into the analysis if necessary.

Part II   Bibliography

Anthony R (1982), 'Equity interest – its time has come', *Journal of Accountancy*, December, 76–93.

Anthony R (1987), 'We don't have the accounting concepts we need', *Harvard Business Review*, Jan/Feb, pp 75–83.

Anthony R and Reece J (1989), *Accounting: Text and Cases*, R D Irwin.

Delaney P, Adler J, Epstein B and Foran M (1991), *GAAP Interpretation and Application*, John Wiley & Sons.

Horngren C and Sunden G (1988), *Introduction to Financial Accounting*, Prentice Hall.

The Institute of Chartered Accountants, *Survey of Published Accounts*, Moorgate Place, London EC2P 2BJ.

The Institute of Chartered Accountants, *Accounting Standards*, Moorgate Place, London EC2P 2BJ.

The International Accounting Standards Committee, *International Accounting Standards*, 167 Fleet Street, London EC4A 2ES.

Treynor J (1972), 'The trouble with earnings', in Lorie J and Brealey R (eds) *Modern Development in Investment Management*, Praeger Publishers.

Zeff S and Keller T (1985), *Financial Accounting Theory*, 3rd edn, McGraw-Hill.

Cash Flow Models for Planning

Part III deals with one of the most popular applications of financial modelling: the preparation of the overall financial plan of a company. In this part, we will help Delta Metal, a trading company, prepare their financial plan for the year(s) to come. This case is drawn from a real business situation and we would like to ask you to start by carefully reading and analyzing this case by yourself: we suggest that you devote at least one and a half hours to this.

Part III aims to:

- Help you reinforce the skills acquired in Part II. In particular, we would like you to realize that *profit and cash have no independent existence* – they only reflect how successful a business is – and that high profit and cash generation are only a signal of the strategic strength of a business. In case of difficulties with accounting figures and concepts (particularly if you have problems when preparing the Delta Metal case), do not hesitate to go back to Part II. You can use the table on page 12 as an index to Part II.
- Introduce you to spreadsheet modelling.
- Help you understand some key business phenomena such as the *impact of volume growth and inflation*.
- Finally, and most important, help you understand and master the *modelling process*. As it is very difficult to learn such a process without practising, we invite you to build all the models described in Part III, to keep track of what each model makes you understand about the problem, and finally to revise your learning process with the help of the table on page 46. If you find difficulties in your learning process do not be discouraged, since learning how to do things or procedural learning, even though very rewarding, is not easy.[1] If you need help with Part III, refer to the Key Learning Points on page 47 to find reference points and to determine the stage you have reached in relation to the overall goal.

A final suggestion for practising managers: when you have worked through Part III, why not leave the book for a while and try to build a model aimed at helping you prepare the overall financial plan of your own business? If you do so, make a rule to start with a simple model.

R.T.C. LIBRARY
LETTERKENNY

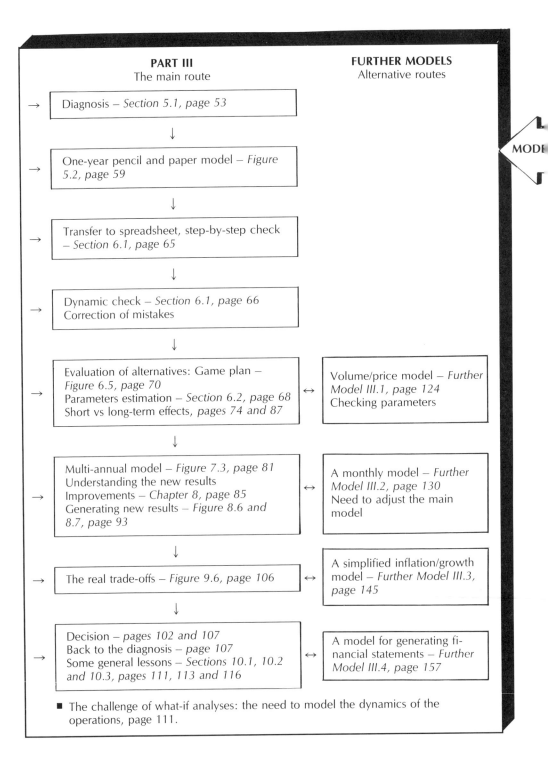

PART III
The main route

FURTHER MODELS
Alternative routes

→ Diagnosis – *Section 5.1, page 53*

↓

→ One-year pencil and paper model – *Figure 5.2, page 59*

↓

→ Transfer to spreadsheet, step-by-step check – *Section 6.1, page 65*

↓

→ Dynamic check – *Section 6.1, page 66*
Correction of mistakes

↓

→ Evaluation of alternatives: Game plan – *Figure 6.5, page 70*
Parameters estimation – *Section 6.2, page 68*
Short vs long-term effects, *pages 74 and 87*

↔ Volume/price model – *Further Model III.1, page 124*
Checking parameters

↓

→ Multi-annual model – *Figure 7.3, page 81*
Understanding the new results
Improvements – *Chapter 8, page 85*
Generating new results – *Figure 8.6 and 8.7, page 93*

↔ A monthly model – *Further Model III.2, page 130*
Need to adjust the main model

↓

→ The real trade-offs – *Figure 9.6, page 106*

↔ A simplified inflation/growth model – *Further Model III.3, page 145*

↓

→ Decision – *pages 102 and 107*
Back to the diagnosis – *page 107*
Some general lessons – *Sections 10.1, 10.2 and 10.3, pages 111, 113 and 116*

↔ A model for generating financial statements – *Further Model III.4, page 157*

■ The challenge of what-if analyses: the need to model the dynamics of the operations, page 111.

KEY LEARNING POINTS

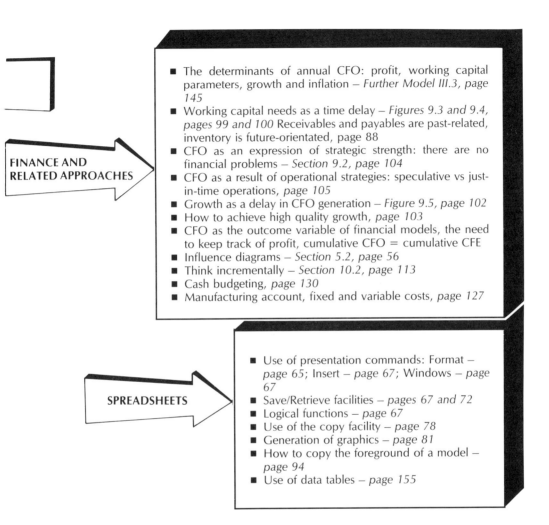

FINANCE AND RELATED APPROACHES

- The determinants of annual CFO: profit, working capital parameters, growth and inflation – *Further Model III.3, page 145*
- Working capital needs as a time delay – *Figures 9.3 and 9.4, pages 99 and 100* Receivables and payables are past-related, inventory is future-orientated, page 88
- CFO as an expression of strategic strength: there are no financial problems – *Section 9.2, page 104*
- CFO as a result of operational strategies: speculative vs just-in-time operations, *page 105*
- Growth as a delay in CFO generation – *Figure 9.5, page 102*
- How to achieve high quality growth, *page 103*
- CFO as the outcome variable of financial models, the need to keep track of profit, cumulative CFO = cumulative CFE
- Influence diagrams – *Section 5.2, page 56*
- Think incrementally – *Section 10.2, page 113*
- Cash budgeting, *page 130*
- Manufacturing account, fixed and variable costs, *page 127*

SPREADSHEETS

- Use of presentation commands: Format – *page 65*; Insert – *page 67*; Windows – *page 67*
- Save/Retrieve facilities – *pages 67 and 72*
- Logical functions – *page 67*
- Use of the copy facility – *page 78*
- Generation of graphics – *page 81*
- How to copy the foreground of a model – *page 94*
- Use of data tables – *page 155*

NOTE

1 As stated by J Anderson (1983) in *The Architecture of Cognition*, Harvard University Press, Ch 6, pp 215–60: The procedural learning mechanisms which are gradual and inductive, contrast sharply with the abrupt and direct learning which is characteristic of the declarative learning.

DELTA METAL SA

In December 1992, Mr Lauru, the Chief Executive Officer of Delta Metal SA, was preparing the company's financial plan for 1993.

Mr Lauru expected that this planning exercise would help him find answers to a number of questions related to the future of the company. Among these questions, two were very important for him:

1. Should Delta Metal SA introduce in 1993 the plan prepared by the finance manager which was aimed at reducing the volume of the accounts receivable?
2. How would the new market regulations which the EC planned to introduce in 1993 affect the operations of Delta Metal SA?

When trying to answer these questions, Mr Lauru wanted to focus on how the cash generation of Delta Metal could change. Delta Metal's cash generation had been generally low in the past and Mr Lauru wanted to improve it.

THE COMPANY

Delta Metal SA was the French subsidiary of the Delta Metal Group, one of the few large independent traders in special steels in Europe. Delta Metal SA, like other subsidiaries of the group in Europe, was in competition with trading companies belonging to the large steel manufacturers as well as with a large number of small independent distributors.

Over the last ten years, the market for special steels in Europe had generally been growing in volume but, due to the harsh competition prevailing in the sector, margins had been gradually eroded at the same time.

Despite being of a different nature, 1991 and 1992 had both been very difficult years for Delta Metal SA.

- In 1991, sales had developed well but the company had faced a severe cash shortage. It also had difficulties in securing new loans with its banks.
- In 1992, the market was sluggish and, in order to remove excess inventory, Delta Metal SA decided to conclude several contracts at what could be considered as sacrificial prices. This resulted in a loss; the company was able, however, to decrease its borrowing as requested by its bankers.

The financial statements of Delta Metal SA for 1990, 1991 and 1992 are reproduced in Figures B.1, B.2 and B.3.

Notes on the calculation of collection period, inventory turnover and payment period

- The *collection period* measures the number of days of sales that are not yet paid at the end of the year. It also corresponds to the number of days it takes for the customers to pay the company.

		(000FFR)
	1991	1992*
Sales	129 524	115 757
Cost of goods sold	103 826	95 752
Operating expenses	16 821	15 919
Depreciation	300	340
Operational profit before tax	8 577	3 746
Tax	0	0
Operational profit after tax	8 577	3 746
Depreciation	300	340
Operational cash flow earnings	8 877	4 086
Receivables open	41 972	63 953
Receivables end	63 953	58 893
Inventory open	20 239	27 068
Inventory end	27 068	16 709
Payables open	30 632	33 234
Payables end	33 234	39 944
Other current assets open	1 994	7 011
Other current assets end	7 011	5 616
Other current liabilities open	4 068	11 679
Other current liabilities end	11 679	3 839
Cash from operations	−14 737	19 770
Interest after tax†	6 206	6 800
Debt reimbursement	11	3 076
New capital expenditures	2 318	2 336
New long term debt	3 000	2 020
New short term debt	18 166	−10 411
Change in cash	−2 106	−833

* Provisional figures.

† As no corporation was paid in 1991 and 1992 (carry forward of losses), interest after tax is equal to the actual amount of interest (see income statement in Figure B.2).

Figure B.1 Delta Metal: cash flow statements.

Collection period as at the end of 1992:

$$\frac{\text{Accounts receivable end}}{\text{Daily sales}} = \frac{58\,893}{\dfrac{115\,757}{365^2}} \approx 186 \text{ days}^1$$

- The *inventory turnover* measures how many times the inventory is renewed during the year.

  Inventory turnover as at the end of 1992:

$$\frac{\text{Cost of goods sold}}{\text{Inventory end}} = \frac{95\,752}{16\,709} \approx 5.73 \text{ times}$$

This inventory turnover of 5.73 corresponds to the time that goods stay on average in inventory:

$$\frac{365}{5.73} \approx 64 \text{ days}$$

The *payment period* measures the number of days of purchases that are not yet paid as at the end of the year. It also corresponds to the number of days it takes for the company to pay its suppliers.

Payment period as at the end of 1992:

$$\frac{\text{Accounts payable end}}{\text{Daily purchases}} = \frac{39\,944}{\dfrac{(95\,752 + 16\,709 - 27\,068)^3}{365}} \approx 171 \text{ days}$$

PROSPECTS FOR 1993

Mr Lauru expected the market to remain extremely competitive in 1993. He was convinced that margins would stay low, but not as low as in 1992 when Delta Metal SA had decided to remove its excess inventory. A cost of goods sold equal to 80% of sales was to be expected in 1993.

The assumptions which Mr Lauru considered reasonable for 1993 were:

> Operating expenses: 14% of sales
> Inventory turnover: four times a year
> Collection period: six months or about 183 days
> Payment period: four months or about 122 days

The sharp reduction in the payment period envisaged for 1993 was motivated by the urgent need to improve relationships with suppliers: in 1992, Delta Metal SA had delayed its payments a great deal and this obviously could not be continued indefinitely.

The collection period reduction plan

During its history, Delta Metal SA had often experienced cash shortages caused by excessive volumes of inventories and of accounts receivable. The success of actions taken in 1992 for reducing inventory reinforced Mr Ladouce's position as finance manager; he had, for many years, been arguing in favour of shortening the collection period.

Mr Ladouce recommended that Delta Metal SA offer discounts to its customers for prompt payments. According to Mr Ladouce, it was possible to reduce the average collection period to 122 days, losing only 4% of the sales price on average.

The new EC regulations

The EC was trying to introduce new regulations aimed at promoting healthier competition within the steel industry. For Delta Metal SA these new regulations (which were not yet fully defined) were likely to mean:

(000 FFR)

	1990	1991	1992*
Sales	96 793	129 524	115 757
Cost of goods sold	75 931	103 826	95 752
Operating expenses	14 519	16 821	15 919
Depreciation	203	300	340
Profit before interest and tax	6 140	8 577	3 746
Interest	3 048	6 206	6 800
Profit before tax	3 092	2 371	−3 054
Tax†	0	0	0
Profit after tax	3 092	2 371	−3 054
Growth rate of sales	0.15	0.34	−0.11
CGS/sales	0.78	0.80	0.83
Operating expenses/sales	0.15	0.13	0.14
Profit before interest and tax/sales	0.06	0.07	0.03
Profit after tax/sales	0.03	0.02	−0.03

* Provisional figures.

† The corporation tax rate is 45%; losses made in 1992 can be carried forward against future profits.

Figure B.2 Delta Metal: income statements.

(000 FFR)

	1990 Dec 31	1991 Dec 31	1992* Dec 31
Cash	3 195	1 089	256
Other current assets	1 994	7 011	5 616
Accounts receivable	41 972	63 953	58 893
Inventory	20 239	27 068	16 709
Net fixed assets	2 464	4 482	6 478
Total assets	69 864	103 603	87 952
Bank short term	19 417	37 583	27 172
Other current liabilities	4 068	11 679	3 839
Accounts payable	30 632	33 234	39 944
Long term debt current	11	3 076	2 245
Long term debt	5 000	4 924	4 699
Net worth	10 736	13 107	10 053
Total equities	69 864	103 603	87 952
Collection period (days)	158	180	186
Inventory turnover	3.75	3.84	5.73
Payment period (days)	136	110	171
Current ratio	1.25	1.16	1.11
Quick ratio	0.87	0.84	0.88
Debt/Net worth	2.28	3.48	3.39

Current ratio is equal to current assets/current liabilities
Quick ratio is equal to (current assets − inventory)/current liabilities
Debt/Net worth is equal to total interest bearing (or financial) debt/net worth

* Provisional figures.

Figure B.3 Delta Metal: balance sheets.

- An increase in the gross margin. Cost of goods sold could well fall to 74% in 1993 (instead of 80%) due to subsidized purchase prices.
- A need to increase the level of stocks. According to Mr Lauru, they could mean an inventory turnover equal to three (instead of four as expected without the new regulations).

Market volume in 1993

Mr Lauru was not very optimistic about 1993: he expected the market to remain sluggish. There would, however, be a very small increase in sales (2%) for Delta Metal SA due to the specificity of its product mix and of the marketing efforts made in 1992. Mr Lauru did not, however, completely disregard the hypothesis of a higher volume increase (about 10%). The steel market would grow in the long run but nobody could tell when growth would start again. Some data about the industry are given in Figure B.4.

Throughout western Europe the demand for special steels had been growing in the 80s and more growth was expected in the future. In spite of this basic trend towards growth, the market was very cyclical.

Production of special steel was concentrated in a very small number of manufacturers (four major ones in Europe) and distribution was ensured by the trading companies of these manufacturers, hundreds of small independent traders, and a few large stockists, among which was Delta Metal.

In the early 90s price competition had been severe on this market and some manufacturers did not hesitate to cut their prices when the volume of their sales did not match their expectations, or their production.

Buyers of special steel had the choice either to purchase direct from the factory or to buy from stocks. In the first case, the price was lower but a long lead time was to be expected (6 months or more). In the second, delivery was almost immediate but the price was higher. In the early 90s, more and more customers seemed to prefer buying from the factory in spite of the long lead time, but the new EC regulations could reverse this trend.

In the market segment Delta Metal operated in, the customers were relatively few (about a hundred spread over Europe). Very often these customers had special technical requirements which obliged their engineering departments and those of the manufacturers to cooperate. Due to the diversity of the problems raised by the customers and the variety of possible technical solutions, even the large traders like Delta Metal could not envisage their own engineering department.

In the early 90s, the manufacturers' own trading companies became very aggressive on the market and there was no sign that this aggressiveness would decline in the near future.

Market conditions were different in each country in Europe but the trend described existed everywhere. In some countries, the situation for stockists like Delta Metal was made even more difficult by the existence of long collection periods: this was the case in France and Italy, for example. On the other hand, business was rendered somewhat easier by the 15 days' collection period prevailing in a country like Norway.

Figure B.4 Delta Metal: evolution of the industry.

NOTES

1 Collection period could also be expressed in months.

2 When dividing annual sales by 365 one gets a figure that corresponds to theoretical daily sales, ie daily sales if sales were made in equal amounts on each of the 365 days of the year. Actual daily sales often differ quite significantly from this theoretical amount because they vary from one day to another and are made on fewer days than 365.

3 Purchases are equal to cost of goods sold + inventory end − inventory open.

CHAPTER 5

The Foundations for Cash Flow Models

5.1 DIAGNOSING THE PROBLEM

Mr Lauru is eager to take actions which could improve the cash generation of Delta Metal. Looking at the balance sheets of the company (Figure B.3), we understand what motivates him to do so. Delta Metal has not been able to pay any dividend to the group (changes in net worth equal annual net profit or loss) and outstanding loans are very high, a direct consequence of inadequate cash generation. Figure B.1 enables us to understand why cash generation is very poor at Delta Metal.

- In 1991, the increase in working capital needs exceeded cash flow earnings. This was due to poor profitability and to major growth in working capital needs:
  - Accounts receivable increased under the combined pressure of extended collection period and growth in sales.
  - Stocks increased due to the higher level of activity.
  - Accounts payable did not increase as much as they should have, due to prompter payments to suppliers.
  - The company experienced an adverse change in its other current assets which was fortunately more than compensated for by a favourable change in its other current liabilities.
- In 1992, the results were very different but not necessarily much healthier:
  - Profits fell, due to the decision to sell inventory at sacrificial prices.
  - Working capital needs decreased due to the sharp decrease in stocks, the decrease in accounts receivable (due to the decrease in sales) and the increase in accounts payable (due to slower payments to suppliers).
  - Other current assets decreased but the development of other current liabilities was adverse.

It is clear that the cash generation in 1992 was much better than in 1991 (34.4mFFR more) but the actions taken could be a matter for concern: how easy will it be to make customers accept normal prices when they benefited from favourable prices in 1992? As inventories are very low at the end of 1992, will it not be necessary to increase them substantially in 1993? Was it reasonable to delay payments to suppliers and for how long can this be continued?

The poor cash generation of Delta Metal is perfectly consistent with the characteristics of its industry.[1] In the special steel sector, large independent stockists are in a difficult position:

- Stockists are expected to carry inventory, which means high working capital needs. In a country like France, working capital needs are even higher due to the tradition of long delays in payment.
- Customers seem to be in a strong bargaining position as far as prices and delays are concerned: their pressure on prices explains the low margins of Delta Metal, their pressure for long payment periods and large inventory availability causes the high working capital needs. As the case suggests, there are many factors that explain this strong bargaining position. Most of the customers seem to be large firms; as most of the products they need are standardized, they can play one supplier off against another. As the actual number of producers is very small, customers may easily get full information from them and, as a result, put middlemen in a difficult position.
- The problem for Delta Metal is that suppliers in their turn also have a strong bargaining position which enables them to exert strong pressure on prices and delays: Delta Metal's profitability is probably reduced by high purchase prices, and its working capital needs cannot be reduced by stretching the payment period (what happened in 1992 seems to be exceptional). As indicated in the case, the strong bargaining position of the suppliers is also explained by several factors. They seem to be large firms; they are the only ones who can offer the special services that some customers may require; as customers are relatively few, they can easily obtain information about them and, as a result, do not need to involve middlemen. In fact, one might think that producers have realized that they no longer need middlemen and their move towards direct distribution is a real threat to Delta Metal as the company seems to have very limited weapons to combat this threat.
- Delta Metal is also under pressure from other distributors. The existence of numerous small distributors is due to the low cost of entry to the market. Because of the slow growth of the industry and the largely standardized products and services, distributors seem to be engaged in fierce competition. The problem here for Delta Metal is that its scope for product/service differentiation seems to be fairly narrow, so rendering the company very vulnerable to competition.
- Delta Metal is probably also under pressure from its banks, who might well start worrying about its ability to repay its debt. This might explain why the company had to take actions aimed at releasing cash in 1992.

When preparing Delta Metal's financial plan for 1993, Mr Lauru is particularly interested in investigating two specific issues which could have a significant impact on the cash generation of the company:

1. Should Delta Metal introduce the new credit plan recommended by the finance manager?
2. What could Delta Metal expect from the new EC regulations?

How can we help Mr Lauru? He has already done something essential: he has specified the problem. Among the many issues related to the future of Delta Metal, he has decided to investigate only two in particular: what would be the impact of a *decision* (to implement the new credit plan), and a *change in the environment* (the new EC regulations)? Mr Lauru has also defined a general approach to the problem: he wants to know how this decision and this environmental change would modify Delta Metal's cash generation. He – and we – must therefore:

- First estimate the cash generation of the company in 1993 if no decision to implement the credit plan is taken and if no change occurs in the environment. This will provide us with a basis for comparison (or *base solution*).
- Then estimate what the cash generation would be if the new credit plan were implemented. If this plan increases the cash generation, then it should be recommended.

However, the problem with evaluating the new credit plan is that we do not know whether or not the EC will implement new regulations in 1993. As a consequence, we have to evaluate the impact of the new credit plan both if the regulations are changed and if they are not. It is quite possible that the best decision regarding the new credit plan is not the same when the environment is different.

A further problem is that we do not know what the growth rate might be: 2% or 10%, according to Mr Lauru. Consequently, we have to envisage all of the above scenarios twice, with 2% growth, and then with 10%. Let us ignore the uncertainty about growth for the moment and consider that it will be 2%.

5.2 APPROACHES FOR BUILDING CASH FLOW MODELS

Before we start making calculations, let us decide on a methodology, or model, which we will use for each individual simulation. Deciding which model we want is a matter of answering two basic questions:

1. What do we want the outcome variable of the model to be?

2. How do we want the model to generate this outcome variable?

In order to answer this second question, we must identify:

- The variables we want to consider: decision, uncontrolled and intermediate variables.
- The relationships we want to have between these variables, including the outcome variable.

The influence diagram approach

One useful way to approach the building of models is to draw first what is called an influence diagram.[2] An influence diagram is a display of:

- All the variables related to a strategic problem.
- All the influence relationships among these variables.

We may adopt the following conventions for building an influence diagram:

- Decision variables are represented by a rectangle.
- Uncontrolled and intermediate variables are represented by a circle.
- Outcome variables are represented by an ellipse.
- The influence exerted by one variable on another is shown by an arrow, the arrow showing the direction of the influence.

An influence diagram describing the model we need to solve Mr Lauru's problem is shown in Figure 5.1.[3] Even for a relatively simple problem like the one Mr Lauru has defined, influence diagrams are not easy to construct since identifying all variables and their influence relationships on a diagram is not obvious.[4]

You must also note that, in order to build a model from Figure 5.1, you must not limit yourself just to recognizing influences but you must also specify the nature of the relationships. We will look at this later.

The decision and uncontrolled variables are those which are not influenced by any others: new credit plan, EC regulations, market conditions, etc. The distinction between decision variables and uncontrolled variables depends very much on the definition of the problem. For example, the payment period is considered here as an uncontrolled variable, which it currently is for Mr Lauru. However, this is not generally the case and this may well change for Mr Lauru at a later stage.

It is not easy to identify *pure quantitative decision and uncontrolled variables*. Adopting the new credit plan is a clear decision variable but it is not quantitative. On the other hand, cgs/sales is a quantitative variable but it is not a pure decision variable since it is affected by more factors than merely the new credit plan.

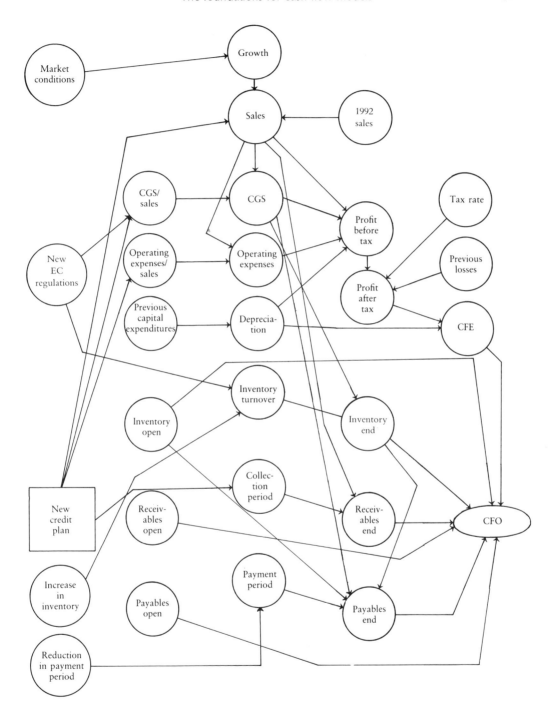

Figure 5.1 An influence diagram.

The uncontrolled variables are not all of the same nature. Some are pure data and their value is certain: 1992 sales, depreciation, etc, but some are basically uncertain, like the growth rate. One thing to realize is that any intermediate variable which is influenced by an uncertain uncontrolled variable is, in its turn, uncertain – as are most of the intermediate variables in Figure 5.1. Let us decide therefore to call all the variables which are certain, *constants*, and all the variables which are uncertain, *parameters*.

The cash flow statement approach

The cash flow statement approach we introduced in Chapter 4 can simplify the model building process since:

- It invites you to select an *outcome variable* that makes sense for the organization as a whole. When evaluating strategic alternatives, you need to assess their overall impact on the organization: evaluating the additional cash from operations (CFO) they may generate is an effective way to do so.[5]
- It helps you to identify quickly the decision variables, parameters, data and intermediate variable you need to evaluate CFOs.
- It provides you with a *general architecture* for relating these various variables to one another and to CFOs.
- It provides you with a set of *standard relationships* which do not need to be reinvented each time you build a model.
- It provides you with a *standard methodology* that has two major advantages:
  - As it is close to the way in which data is recorded by accounting, the cash flow statement approach gives you access to a large volume of quantitative past data (both internal and external).
  - As it is a widely accepted approach, the cash flow statement approach enables you to build models other managers can easily understand.

A cash flow statement approach to Mr Lauru's problem is shown in Figure 5.2. The framed area in Figure 5.2 is a good example of how financial models are generally presented. It also shows which variables are displayed and those which are not.

- *Parameters* are displayed: growth rate, cgs/sales, etc. In Figure 5.2, all headings corresponding to parameters are in lower case (not capital letters). Parameters correspond to:
  - Decision variables (eg collection period).
  - Uncertain uncontrolled variables (eg growth rate).
  - A combination of decision and uncontrolled variables (eg cgs/sales).
  The reason for displaying the parameters is obvious; any manager who looks at the financial model can see the assumptions which lead to the results.
    One thing you should note here is that the decision variable (new credit

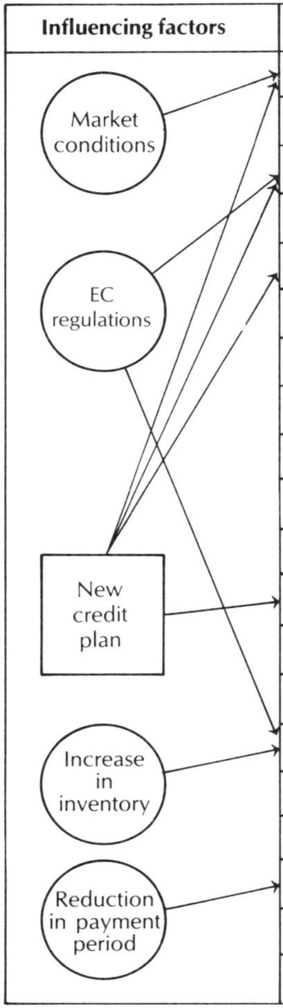

Influencing factors	Parameters	Constants	Quantitative variables	Numbers	Relationships
Market conditions	Growth rate		Growth rate	0.02	
		1992 sales	SALES	118072	115757*(1.02)
	CGS/sales		CGS/sales	0.80	
			CGS	94458	118072*0.80
EC regulations	Operating expenses/sales		Oper. exp/sales	0.14	
			OPERATING EXPENSES	16530	118072*0.14
		Depreciation	Depreciation	400	
		Tax rate	OPERATIONAL PBT	6684	118072-94458-16530-400
		Previous losses	OPERATIONAL PAT	3676	0.55*6684
			OPERATIONAL CFE	4076	3676+400
		Receivables open	Receivables open	58893	58893
New credit plan	Collection period		Collection period	183	365/12*6
			RECEIVABLES END	59036	118072/365*183
		Inventory open	Inventory open	16709	16709
Increase in inventory	Inventory turnover		Inventory turnover	4	
			INVENTORY END	23614	94458/4
		Payables open	Payables open	39944	39944
Reduction in payment period	Payment period		Payment period	122	365/12*4
			PAYABLES END	33788	(94458+23614−16709)/365*122
			CFO	−9128	4076+58893−59036+16709 −23614−39944+33788

Figure 5.2 Using the cash flow approach to build a model.

plan) and the environmental change (new EC regulations) do not correspond to any specific parameter because:

· Two parameters are used to describe the new credit plan, cgs/sales and collection period.

· Two parameters are used to describe the EC regulations, cgs/sales and inventory turnover.

· One parameter is used in the description of the decision and of the environmental change, cgs/sales.

■ *Intermediate variables* are also displayed: CGS, OPERATING EXPENSES, etc. In Figure 5.2, the headings corresponding to intermediate variables are in capitals.

■ *Constants* are not generally shown. This is the case for 1992 sales. Since these variables cannot be changed, one can make the model more compact by not showing them. Note, however, that some constants and uncontrolled variables are shown: depreciation, accounts receivable open, inventory open, etc. Since such variables are part of the usual structure of financial models, they are generally displayed.

Managers who use financial models are generally not as rigorous as management scientists and, as a result, what their models display cannot be analyzed according to clear-cut categories, but as they find their approach is effective, why reject it?

Which approach to use?

When building financial models, both the cash flow statement and influence diagram approaches are useful. As a consequence, we recommend that you always consider using both of them:

■ *Use the cash flow statement approach to structure your problem*. More precisely, use the cash flow statement approach to:
   · Define the broad architecture of your model.
   · Generate a list of key quantitative variables. Having such a list is very useful since it enables you to check that you have enough data in order to start building your model.
   · Define the key relationships between variables and between variables and CFOs.[6]
■ *Use the influence diagram approach to analyze your problem in more depth*. The influence diagram methodology has some special advantages. It invites you to reflect on how each of the cash flow statement variables is generated:
   · Is it a decision variable, an uncontrolled variable or a combination of both? Is it a constant or a variable?
   · Is it rather a purely intermediate variable?

It invites you to reflect on the relationships. Among the many relationships suggested by the cash flow statement approach, some are not a matter of choice, but some are, and these should be investigated. As an example of this, operating expenses at Delta Metal are assumed to be proportional to sales: is this true in all circumstances, and in particular when prices and/or volume change?

It helps you explore in more detail some parts of the model. In the Delta Metal case, sales in 1993 are determined as the result of 1992 sales multiplied by a growth factor. The company thinks this is the appropriate calculation, but it could be worth investigating more variables that could explain the level of sales in 1993: evolution of total market, pricing, market share, etc.[7] An influence diagram could help identify these variables and find out how they relate to each other.

5.3 FOREGROUND AND BACKGROUND OF FINANCIAL MODELS

Financial models, as they are usually prepared by managers, can be analyzed at two very different levels called the foreground and the background.

The foreground of a financial model is what managers write down on the piece of paper (or spreadsheet or worksheet) which they use for building and presenting the model. One possible foreground of the model for simulating the cash generation at Delta Metal is shown in Figure 5.2 (framed area).

- The foreground is not limited to the presentation of the outcome variable; it also shows parameters and intermediate variables, those that the manager finds useful for constructing, presenting and using the model. The display of intermediate variables is called for by the fact that managers, while primarily interested in the outcome variable, also want to check the value taken by such intermediate variables as total cgs, total operating expenses, operational profit, etc. Frequently, managers not only want solutions which achieve a good end result, but they also want these solutions to be globally consistent, to correspond to satisfactory values for a series of intermediate variables.[8]
- The foreground generally does not show the relationships between variables. The basic reason for keeping these relationships implicit is that financial models use accounting relationships which are supposed to be known by all managers, an hypothesis which is not always totally realistic.
- The structure of the foreground varies as it depends very much on the manager who builds the model and the company in which he/she works. Although managers generally use worksheets to show the foreground of their models, they may also use graphs, an alternative foreground for financial models.

- *The background* of a financial model is made up of these generally invisible relationships between variables which constitute the *logic* of the model and make it able to generate the results or, in other words, to propagate[9] the values of parameters.

- As with the foreground, the background may be presented in different ways. A possible description of the background of the model for Delta Metal is given by the equations in Figure 5.2. Another possible description is given by the influence diagram in Figure 5.1.

- As the background drives the foreground, one might think that financial models should systematically be built from their background, as professional modellers do. *Experience shows however that managers generally prefer to work from the foreground.* Experience also shows that managers generally tend to limit the use of tools such as equations and influence diagrams to the exploration of special issues, such as the construction of a sub-model for generating the volume of sales, or a special model for evaluating a replacement decision, etc.

- The background of models, however, when made explicit, is an invaluable communication tool. Understanding models built by others from their foreground is not easy and may even present serious dangers as it is difficult to be sure that you have understood all the relevant implicit assumptions made by the model-builder.[10]

NOTES

1 A methodology for industry analysis is described in: M Porter, *Competitive Strategy – Techniques for Analyzing Industries and Competitors*, The Free Press (1980) Chapter 1, pp 3–33.

2 For more about influence diagrams, refer to: S Bodily, *Modern Decision Making*, McGraw-Hill (1985).

3 In this diagram and later on in the various steps of the analysis, we consider that other current assets and liabilities are not going to change. As the evolution of these accounts is very difficult to predict, assuming they will not change simplifies our task a great deal. However, we should remember that the results we will obtain could be modified by changes in other assets and liabilities; the history of these accounts actually shows that they are not stable. Even though the case does not tell us anything about the nature of these accounts, we can imagine that other current assets may correspond to deposits made by Delta Metal with suppliers when placing special orders. Other current liabilities may correspond to deposits made by customers with Delta Metal and to operating expenses which have not yet been paid.

4 Spreadsheets do not offer influence diagram facilities. However, there is one

commercially available PC software that combines the features of spreadsheets and enables you to use influence diagrams (and other powerful modelling features): Javelin. One interesting feature of Javelin is the possibility to build 'local' influence diagrams.

5 Obviously, financial criteria like CFO are not the only possible yardstick for assessing the performance of organizations. Another thing to note, which we will establish in Chapter 15, is that CFO is not the true outcome variable of financial models. The true outcome of financial models is the difference between the present value of CFOs and the present value of capital expenditures required for generating the CFOs.

6 In many respects, the cash flow statement approach, when fully mastered and assimilated, is what cognitive psychologists call a production system, an automatically pre-registered procedure which, when activated, enables your mind to operate without perceived effort, a very powerful aid which helps you structure problems quickly and so frees your time for further thinking. For more about the concept of production systems, refer to: A Newell and H Simon, *Human Problem Solving*, Prentice Hall (1972). An overview of this book is given in 'Human problem solving: the state of the theory in 1970', *American Psychologist* (1971) **26**: 145–59.

7 For an example of this, please refer to Part VII.

8 In most cases, this global consistency is not defined explicitly. Intermediate variables to be checked and their satisfactory levels are loosely defined, and are always susceptible to being ruled out if the end result is very good.

9 Relationships enable managers to visualize all the implications of a local change: impact on the end result and impact on key intermediate variables. For more about the concept of propagation of numerical values in models, refer to: P H Winston, *Artificial Intelligence*, Addison Wesley (1984) p 72.

10 This danger has become a serious one with the diffusion of spreadsheet models in business organizations and the need to audit them when they are used by people other than their authors.

CHAPTER 6

Building and Using a First One-year Spreadsheet Model

6.1 TRANSFERRING THE MODEL ONTO A SPREADSHEET

Analyzing the results of the pencil and paper analysis: why is CFO negative?

According to the pencil and paper model displayed in Figure 5.2, the operations of Delta Metal are going to generate a cash deficit in 1993. Is this a result we should have expected?

As we realized earlier, the high cash generation achieved in 1992 should be considered as exceptional and nothing as good can be expected in 1993. It is true that profitability should improve due to better selling prices, but working capital needs should increase substantially due to the need to build up inventory and to accelerate payments to suppliers. The result shown in Figure 5.2 is therefore perfectly consistent with our expectations.

Entering the analysis on the electronic spreadsheet and checking the results

The first thing we have to do in order to transfer our pencil and paper model to a spreadsheet is to change the relationships or formulas shown in Figure 5.2 and to express them according to a spreadsheet approach. This is done in Figure 6.1.

In Figure 6.1, formulas are shown according to the approach common to Lotus 1-2-3 and almost all other spreadsheets.[1] In order to simplify the presentation of the text, we have decided to refer to one spreadsheet only in general (Lotus 1-2-3). As most spreadsheets are very close to Lotus 1-2-3, this should not create any difficulties for you and at the beginning we will use footnotes to tell you the basic instructions for working with Excel, Quattro and SuperCalc.

The next step is to enter the headings,[2] numbers and formulas onto the electronic spreadsheet.

One great feature of spreadsheets is that they enable you to check that any

	A	B	Background of column B
1	Growth rate	0.02	0.02
2	SALES	118 072	115 757*(1+B1)*
3	cgs/sales	0.8	0.8
4	CGS	94 458	+B3*B2
5	Operating expenses/sales	0.14	0.14
6	OPERATING EXPENSES	16 530	+B2*B5
7	Depreciation	400	400
8	OPERATIONAL PROFIT BEFORE TAX	6 684	+B2−B4−B6−B7
9	OPERATIONAL PROFIT AFTER TAX	3 676	0.55*B8
10	OPERATIONAL CFE	4 076	+B9+B7
11	Receivables open	58 893	58 893
12	Collection period	183	365/12*6
13	RECEIVABLES END	59 036	+B2/365*B12
14	Inventory open	16 709	16 709
15	Inventory turnover	4	4
16	INVENTORY END	23 614	+B4/B15
17	Payables open	39 944	39 944
18	Payment period	122	365/12*4
19	PAYABLES END	33 788	(B4+B16−B14)/365*B18
20	CFO	−9 128	+B10+B11−B13+B14−B16−B17+B19

R.T.C. LIBRARY LETTERKENNY

* With Excel, all formulas should start with +, − or =; (in B2 enter + 115 757*(1+B1))

Figure 6.1 Preparing a spreadsheet model: the general approach.

relationship you enter returns the result you expect, the same result as your pencil and paper model. We recommend that you use this feature and check systematically the result of each formula you enter before proceeding further. If the spreadsheet returns a result which differs from the one you expected, check the reason for the difference and correct the mistake immediately, in the spreadsheet or in your pencil and paper analysis.

One problem you will face as early as cell B2 is that spreadsheets do not display rounded up figures except when asked to do so. If you want to display integer numbers, you have to use the Format command. With Lotus 1-2-3,[3] you can proceed as follows:

- First select an integer display for the whole worksheet: / W (worksheet) G (global) F (format) F (fixed) 0 [R] ([R] for return).
- Then select for three cells (B1, B3 and B5) a display with two decimals. For B1, position the cursor in B1, then: / R (range) F (format) F (fixed) [R] [R]. Then repeat for B3 and B5.

Obviously, when selecting a format for display, the calculations are not affected. They are still performed using all decimal places required.

After you have checked that the results are the same as those shown in Figure 6.1, the next two steps are:

- Save the model on a diskette. Losing one's work and having to repeat it is

frustrating. With Lotus 1-2-3, you proceed as follows:[4]
place a formatted diskette in drive B; type in / F (file) S (save) delta [R] (delta being the name of the model). You may choose any short name for the model (space between the letters or digits is not allowed).

- Check the model further. At present, you know that your spreadsheet model returns the same CFO as your pencil and paper model when the parameters have the value envisaged in the base model: growth rate = 0.02, cgs/sales = 0.80, operating expenses to sales = 0.14, etc. But how sure are you that your spreadsheet model will return adequate results when you assign different values to the parameters? As you are going to use the model in order to calculate CFOs for different values of the parameters, you had better make sure that your model works in all cases before proceeding any further. It is, however, extremely difficult to be sure of this. You can obviously check again that the background of each cell contains the formulas you specified in the pencil and paper analysis, but how sure are you about them? You can check by changing the value of some parameters and check that CFO changes according to what you expect:

- If you decrease cgs/sales, CFO should increase – does this happen if you change cgs/sales to 0.70 for example?

- If you decrease collection period, CFO should increase – does this occur if you change collection period to 100 for example?[5]

    This *dynamic verification* of financial models is very useful and should always be performed before you start using them. It is not easy to do, however:

    · You may forget to check some parameters; try to be as systematic as possible.

    · This approach can only be used when you know what the model should return when the value of a specific parameter is changed, which is obviously not always the case. For example, what should happen to CFO if you increase the growth rate? Some people would instinctively expect it to increase, but this is wrong, as we will see later. Under the same conditions as those in Delta Metal, finance theory says that CFO should decrease when growth increases and this is how the model behaves.

- It is not enough to be able to predict the direction of change of the outcome variable. In order to check the model properly, you should also be able to predict the magnitude of the change. For example, when you alter the values of the parameters, you realize that CFO seems to be more sensitive to a variation in collection period than to a variation in cgs/sales – is this correct?

From the outset, you should keep one essential characteristic of modelling in mind. It is an activity which requires the exercise of judgement and a lot of care.

Improving the model

Checking that the model works is not only a matter of checking that the outcome variable (CFO) behaves as you expect, but also that intermediate variables do the same.

When changing the value of cgs/sales and operating expenses/sales, you realize that, when a loss is made, corporation tax becomes negative. You may also realize that we have not accounted for the fact that the loss made in 1992 can be carried forward against the 1993 profit.

In order to improve the model, we should change the calculation of profit after tax. The process for doing so is described in Figure 6.2.

---

1 Introduce a blank row above row 9: position the cursor in A9 then type: / W (worksheet) I (insert) R (row) [R]*
2 Type in A9: cumulative profit before tax;
  type in B9: −3 054+B8
3 Enter a new formula for the calculation of profit after tax in B10:
  @IF(B8<0, B8, @IF(B9<B8, @IF(B9>0, B8−(0.45*B9), B8), (1−0.45)*B8))†

---

* With Excel:
  Point A9 press and hold SHIFT and press the space bar / E (edit) I (insert)
  with Quattro:
  Point A9 / R (row) I (insert) [R]
  with SuperCalc4:
  Point A9 / I (insert) R (row) [R]

† In Excel and SuperCalc, functions do not start with @; with Excel: = (or +) IF(B8<0, B8, etc.); with SuperCalc: +IF(B8<0, B8, etc.)

Figure 6.2 Correcting the profit after tax calculation.

When following the instructions in Figure 6.2, you obtain:

- a profit after tax equal to 5 051
- a CFO equal to −7 754

You can then save the new model. You can actually save it under the same name so that the new model replaces the old one; with Lotus 1-2-3: / F (file) S (save) [R][6] R (replace).

The problem with this modified model is that, since it has 21 lines, you can no longer see all of it at once on the screen. To see part of the model and the outcome variable (CFO in line 21), you can open two windows on the screen. To do this with Lotus 1-2-3:

- position the cursor in row 19
- type in: / W (worksheet) W (window) H (horizontal)[7]
- then scroll row 21 in the lower window with the cursor; in order to jump from one window to another with the cursor, just depress the F6 key.

6.2 USING THE SPREADSHEET MODEL TO UNDERSTAND MORE ABOUT THE PROBLEM – THE VALUE OF A GAME PLAN

Evaluating the alternatives – how to estimate the parameters

The most immediate use of the spreadsheet model we have just built is to simulate the outcome of:

- the decision to implement the new credit plan;
- the possible introduction of the new EC regulations.

The results of these simulations are given in Figures 6.3 and 6.4.

	Situation 1	Situation 2	Situation 3	Situation 4
Growth rate	0.02	0.02	−0.02	−0.02
SALES	118 072	118 072	113 349	113 349
cgs/sales	0.80	0.75	0.83	0.78
CGS	94 458	88 627	94 458	88 627
Operating expenses/sales	0.14	0.14	0.15	0.15
OPERATING EXPENSES	16 530	16 530	16 530	16 530
Depreciation	400	400	400	400
OPERATIONAL PROFIT BEFORE TAX	6 684	12 515	1 961	7 793
CUMULATIVE OPERATIONAL PROFIT BEFORE TAX	3 630	9 461	−1 093	4 739
OPERATIONAL PROFIT AFTER TAX	5 051	8 258	1 961	5 660
OPERATIONAL CFE	5 451	8 658	2 361	6 060
Receivables open	58 893	58 893	58 893	58 893
Collection period	183	183	122	122
RECEIVABLES END	59 036	59 036	37 783	37 783
Inventory open	16 709	16 709	16 709	16 709
Inventory turnover	4	3	4	3
INVENTORY END	23 614	29 124	23 614	29 124
Payables open	39 944	39 944	39 944	39 944
Payment period	122	122	122	122
PAYABLES END	33 788	33 681	33 788	33 681
CFO	−7 754	−10 164	10 410	8 491

Key
Situation 1: No new credit plan and no new EC regulations
Situation 2: No new credit plan and new EC regulations
Situation 3: New credit plan and no new EC regulations
Situation 4: New credit plan and new EC regulations

Figure 6.3 Simulation results in full (000 FFR).

Figures 6.3 and 6.4 are good examples of the problem you soon come across when using models. What should you look at?

- Only the outcome variable?
- The outcome variable and all the intermediate variables?
- The outcome variable and some selected intermediate variables?

Decision variable		Environment variable	Intermediate variable	Outcome variable
			1993	1993
The new credit plan is not implemented			PROFIT	CFO
	and EC does not install new regulations (1)		5 051	−7 754
	and EC installs new regulations (2)		8 258	−10 164
The new credit plan is implemented				
	and EC does not install new regulations (3)		1 961	10 410
	and EC installs new regulations (4)		5 660	8 491

Figure 6.4 Simulation results: key results.

The answer to this question is not easy. As looking at everything may be confusing, it is better to focus on some key variables. Obviously, the outcome variable is the most important, but some intermediate variables are also useful since they may help you understand why a particular value of the outcome variable is generated by the model. Figure 6.4 proposes a solution to this problem: it only shows the outcome variable (CFO) and one key intermediate variable (operational profit after tax).

The results shown in Figures 6.3 and 6.4 call for two immediate comments:

1. Why make four different simulations? Whatever Delta Metal decides about the collection period reduction plan, the EC may or may not install the new regulations: in this sense, the decision about the new plan and the change in the environment are independent of each other and, as a consequence, four different situations are to be envisaged if growth is to be taken as 2%, and eight if growth is to be taken as either 2% or 10%. Let us ignore the uncertainty about growth for the moment.

Decision variable	Environment variable	Parameters				
		Growth	cgs/ Sales	Operating expenses/ Sales	Collection period	Inventory turnover
The new credit plan is not implemented	and EC does not install new regulations (1)	0.02	0.8	0.14	182.5	4.0
	and EC installs new regulations (2)	0.02	0.75	0.14	182.5	3.04
The new credit plan is implemented	and EC does not install new regulations (3)	−0.02	0.83	0.15	121.7	4.0
	and EC installs new regulations (4)	−0.02	0.78	0.15	121.7	3.04

Figure 6.5 A game plan for new simulations.

2. How are these four simulations made? Looking at the impact of a change in a parameter is very easy with a spreadsheet software since it is just a matter of typing the new value of the parameter over its previous value. Evaluating alternative situations is a bit more difficult since you have to enter for each a new *consistent set of parameter values*. A table such as Figure 6.5 can be of considerable help for evaluating the other situations we want to consider.

Comments on the value of the parameters in Figure 6.5

As CFO is a very sensitive outcome variable, you have to be careful when estimating the value of the parameters. In order to get the results of Figure 6.3, you should use the following formulas to estimate their values.

▪ Situation 2. Even if we assume that the new EC regulations are implemented on 1 January 1993, only part of the steel sold in 1993 will be purchased at the new price. This is due to the existence of an opening inventory. As a consequence, cgs will be slightly more than 74% of sales in 1993. The formula for calculating cgs/sales in 1993 is:

$$\frac{\text{New cgs}}{\text{Sales}} = \frac{(((118\,072 - 16\,709/0.8) * 0.74) + 16\,709)}{118\,072} \approx 0.75$$

You should also be careful with the consequence of fixing the value of cgs/sales to 0.75 in 1993. Because of the structure of the model, any increase in cgs causes an increase in inventory end (inventory as of December 1993). In the present case, you do not want that to happen because the goods which will be stored at the end of the year will have been bought at the new price. In order to avoid the adjustment in cgs/sales causing any increase in inventory end, you have to adjust the inventory turnover and make it slightly more than 3. The formula for calculating the inventory turnover in 1993 is:

$$(3 * \text{B3})/0.74 \approx 3.04$$

Obviously, in the years subsequent to 1993, cgs/sales and inventory turnover will be equal to 0.74 and 3 respectively.

▪ Situation 3. The impact of a change in selling price is not easy to analyze either. First of all, cutting the price will decrease the amount of sales: you can introduce this effect by changing the growth rate. The formula for the new growth rate is:

$$(1.02 * 0.96) - 1 \approx -0.02$$

A cut in the selling price will also change the cgs/sales parameter. If the selling price is changed from 1 January, the formula for calculating the new cgs/sales is:

$$0.80/0.96 \approx 0.83$$

Even though operating expenses have been proportional to sales in the past, a reasonable assumption is to consider that a cut in selling price will not cause a reduction in operating expenses (this actually assumes that operating expenses are proportional to the volume of sales). The formula for the new operating expenses/sales is:

$$0.14/0.96 \approx 0.146$$

Finally, the formula for calculating collection period is:

$$365/12 * 4$$

- Situation 4. The values of the parameters can be calculated with the following formulas:

Growth rate: $(1.02 * 0.96) - 1$

CGS/sales: $\dfrac{(((118\,072 - 16\,709/0.8) * 0.74) + 16\,709)}{(118\,072 * 0.96)}$

Operating expenses: $0.14/0.96$

Collection period: $365/12 * 4$

Inventory turnover: $(3 * B3 * 0.96)/0.74$

The usefulness of volume – price models

As shown above, it is not easy to estimate the values of the parameters that correspond to environmental changes and/or strategic decisions:

- The example of Delta Metal demonstrates the difficulty of estimating the impact of changes in prices.
- In general, it may be even more difficult since you may have to analyze simultaneously the impact of changes in prices and in volume. This is very hard to do with a model that estimates items like sales, cgs, etc at an aggregate level.

As a consequence, it may often prove much more effective to build an alternative model that *estimates explicitly the volume and the price components* of sales, cgs, purchases, etc. Such a model is shown in Further Models III.1. As you will realize, models that estimate explicitly the volume and price components have their advantages and disadvantages:

- They require more data.
- Their structure is more complicated.

But
- It is easier to estimate the values of the parameters.
- *As a consequence they may help you to avoid making mistakes in estimating these values.*

We recommend that you:

- Always keep in mind the risk of making estimating errors when working at an aggregate level.
- *Are prepared to use a model that estimates explicitly volume and price factors each time you are in doubt.* In case you are planning for manufacturing activities, we would suggest that you always use a model that estimates explicitly volume and price factors. An example of such an approach is shown in Part VII.

Further comments on the evaluation of alternatives

Changing the value of a parameter has an immediate effect with spreadsheets but even in a simple case like the present one, it is not that easy to perform a series of meaningful simulations. This is because:

- Each simulation should correspond to a cohesive set of values for the different parameters.
- Going from one simulation to another means that the value of each parameter must be reviewed since some change and some do not.

This calls for some precautions which avoid loss of time and the generation of strange results:

- Always prepare some kind of game plan before running simulations: the format of Figure 6.5 is a good example of a game plan that helps you structure your analysis. As soon as you have built Figure 6.5, you know that you have four simulations to perform and also which parameters are to be changed from one to another.
- As soon as several parameters have to be changed from one simulation to another, consider using one of the facilities offered by spreadsheets, the save/retrieve facility.[8] When performing a series of simulations you always start from a base model that you save on a diskette. You then have a choice of either:
  · Working on the same model and progressively modifying it for the sake of each simulation, or
  · Running each new simulation from the base model. In this case, before carrying out each new simulation, you retrieve the base model and, when the simulation is completed, you record its result (on paper or on a diskette) *but do not use the modified model for the next simulation.*

  Although the second method looks, and is, more cumbersome than the first, experience shows that it is much more reliable, and in the end leads to quicker results.

- When introducing new values for the parameters, always type in the formula that corresponds to this new value. This will prevent you from having to use a calculator and from making estimation errors due to approximations.
- Always ensure you understand the results you obtain for each simulation before using them for decision-making purposes.

What do the results tell?

When deciding whether or not to implement the new credit plan from a cash point of view, the results shown in Figure 6.4 are very clear. The new credit plan has a very positive impact and this is true whatever the EC is going to do.

Still from a cash point of view, Figure 6.4 shows that, if they are implemented within the conditions specified in the case, the new EC regulations will not be favorable to Delta Metal. Whatever the company decides to do about the credit plan, the regulations will have a negative impact.

A problem with the results in Figure 6.4, however, is that, when profit rather than cash is used as the outcome variable, things look the opposite:

- In profit terms, the new credit plan should not be recommended as it leads to lower profits, which is true whatever the EC does.
- In profit terms, and if implemented within the conditions specified in the case, the regulations will be favorable to Delta Metal.

The contradiction between the signals given by cash and profit can easily be explained:

- CFO is equal to profit minus increase in working capital needs.
- The new credit plan and the new EC regulations have an impact on profit and working capital needs.
- Both actually have a different impact on profit and working capital needs.
- When analyzing the impact of the plan and of the regulations from the point of view of cash, you measure both their positive and negative consequences, and you can see whether the negative outweigh the positive.
- *As a consequence, Delta Metal is right to attach more importance to cash rather than profit when analyzing this decision and change in the environment.*

We may have a problem however: would the results in Figure 6.4 be the same if we were to perform these simulations over more than one year?

When considering, for example, the impact of the regulations in 1993, it is clear that the additional working capital needs outweigh the additional profitability. But is this not because in 1993 Delta Metal would have to make an exceptional effort to bring the inventory to a higher level? When this is done, the additional working capital needs will be much lower and perhaps, in 1994, they will no longer outweigh the additional profitability which will be nearly the same in 1994 as in 1993 (if sales are about equal). In order to explore this issue further, we have to extend the model over a longer period of time.

NOTES

1 Excel, Quattro, Quattro Pro, SuperCalc, VP Planner, Lucid 3-D, Framework, Symphony, VisiCalc, etc.

2 With most spreadsheets, the headings in Figures 6.1, 6.2 and 6.3 are too long to fit the standard sized column. You will therefore have to use abbreviated headings (which we advise you to do if this is your first experience in dealing with spreadsheets) or enlarge the width of column A to 30 characters. To do so, position the cursor in A1, then:

> With Lotus 1-2-3: / W (worksheet) C (column) S (set) 30 [R]
> With Excel: ☐ Alt ☐ or / T (format) C (column width) 34 [R]
> With Quattro Pro: / S (style) C (column) 30 [R]
> With SuperCalc: / F (format) C (column) [R] W (width) 30 [R]
> With SuperCalc5, / G (global) 1 turns on 'Lotus mode': you can then work with Lotus 1-2-3 commands.

3 With Excel:
Global format:
Press and hold CTRL and SHIFT and press the space bar / T (format) N (number) point at 0 [R] press any arrow key.
Format for B1:
Point at B1 / T (format) N (number) point at 0.00 [R]

With Quattro Pro:
Global format:
/ O (options) F (formats) N (numeric format) F (fixed) 0 [R] Esc Esc
Format for B1:
Point B1 / S (style) N (numeric format) F (fixed) 2 B1.B1 [R]

With SuperCalc:
Global format:
/ F (format) G (global) I (integer) [R]
Format for B1:
Point B1 / F (format) E (entry) [R] $ [R]

4 Excel and Quattro: same as Lotus 1-2-3. With SuperCalc: S (save) DELTA [R] A (all)

5 One common mistake made by beginners is to enter in B13: +B2/365*183. This returns a correct result until you change the value of collection period.

6 Excel and Quattro: same as Lotus 1-2-3. With SuperCalc: / S (save) [R] O (overwrite) A (all)

7 With Excel (in which these kinds of windows are called windowpanes): – T (split) move with the down arrow key the gray split bar to row 19 [R]

With Quattro:
Point at A19 / W (windows) O (options) H (horizontal)

With SuperCalc4:
Point at A19 / W (window) H (horizontal)

8 Save, Load in SuperCalc.
Save, Open in Excel.

CHAPTER 7

Extending a One-year Cash Flow Model over Several Years

7.1 COPYING A ONE-YEAR MODEL

The problem

Building a spreadsheet model over several years for Delta Metal is just a matter of extending the model shown in Figures 6.1 and 6.2. Since spreadsheets perform calculations only where data or formulas have been entered, the extension of the model will require new data and formulas to be entered. The ones you need to extend the initial model to four more years are shown in Figure 7.1.

When you analyze the formulas in Figure 7.1, you realize that:

- From year 1994 onwards (from column C), formulas are very similar across the years. More precisely, they are identical in structure and differ only according to the column they are in. As an example, the formula that generates cost of goods sold always gives the product of the content of the cell two rows above, same column, and the content of the cell one row above, same column, and therefore is expressed (in Lotus 1-2-3 notations) as:

$$+B2*B3 \text{ in column B}$$
$$+C2*C3 \text{ in column C}$$
$$+D2*D3 \text{ in column D etc}$$

In spreadsheets these are called *relative formulas*.
- Formulas in year 1 and year 2 may have the same structure (ie be relative), or may be different:
  - Cgs, operating expenses, operational profit before tax, etc are generated by formulas with the same structure (relative formulas)
  - Sales, receivables open, inventory open and payables open are generated by different formulas in year 1 and year 2. This is a feature of most financial models where the first year differs from subsequent ones due to the fact it is the base year.

	A	B	C	D	E	F
1	Growth rate	0.02	0.02	0.02	0.02	0.02
2	SALES	115 757*(1+B1)	+B2*(1+C1)	+C2*(1+D1)	+D2*(1+E1)	+E2*(1+F1)
3	cgs/sales	0.8	0.8	0.8	0.8	0.8
4	CGS	+B2*B3	+C2*C3	+D2*D3	+E2*E3	+F2*F3
5	Operating expenses/sales	0.14	0.14	0.14	0.14	0.14
6	OPERATING EXPENSES	+B2*B5	+C2*C5	+D2*D5	+E2*E5	+F2*F5
7	Depreciation	400	400	400	400	400
8	OPERATIONAL PROFIT BEFORE TAX	+B2−B4−B6−B7	+C2−C4−C6−C7	+D2−D4−D6−D7	+E2−E4−E6−E7	+F2−F4−F6−F7
9	CUMULATIVE OPER. PR. BEF TAX	−3 054+B8	+B9+C8	+C9+D8	+D9+E8	+E9+F8
10	OPERATIONAL PROFIT AFTER TAX	(1)	(2)	(3)	(4)	(5)
11	OPERATIONAL CFE	+B10+B7	+C10+C7	+D10+D7	+E10+E7	+F10+F7
12	Receivables open	58 893	+B14	+C14	+D14	+E14
13	Collection period	365/2	365/2	365/2	365/2	365/2
14	RECEIVABLES END	+B2/365*B13	+C2/365*C13	+D2/365*D13	+E2/365*E13	+F2/365*F13
15	Inventory open	16 709	+B17	+C17	+D17	+E17
16	Inventory turnover	4	4	4	4	4
17	INVENTORY END	+B4/B16	+C4/C16	+D4/D16	+E4/E16	+F4/F16
18	Payables open	39 944	+B20	+C20	+D20	+E20
19	Payment period	365/3	365/3	365/3	365/3	365/3
20	PAYABLES END	(B4+B17−B15)/365*B19	(C4+C17−C15)/365*C19	(D4+D17−D15)/365*D19	(E4+E17−E15)/365*E19	(F4+F17−F15)/365*F19
21	CFO	(6)	(7)	(8)	(9)	(10)

Key
(1) @IF(B8<0, B8, @IF(B9<B8, @IF(B9>0, B8−0.45*B9, B8), 0.55*B8))
(2) @IF(C8<0, C8, @IF(C9>C8, @IF(C9>0, C8−0.45*C9, C8), 0.55*C8))
(3) @IF(D8<0, D8, @IF(D9>D8, @IF(D9>0, D8−0.45*D9, D8), 0.55*D8))
(4) @IF(E8<0, E8, @IF(E9<E8, @IF(E9>0, E8−0.45*E9, E8), 0.55*E8))
(5) @IF(F8<0, F8, @IF(F9<F8, @IF(F9>0, F8−0.45*F9, F8), 0.55*F8))
(6) +B11+B12−B14+B15−B17−B18+B20
(7) +C11+C12−C14+C15−C17−C18+C20
(8) +D11+D12−D14+D15−D17−D18+D20
(9) +E11+E12−E14+E15−E17−E18+E20
(10) +F11+F12−F14+F15−F17−F18+F20

Figure 7.1 Extending the model four more years.

The copy command[1]

All spreadsheets offer a command that enables you to extend models easily over several years. The concept of this command is *to recopy automatically the background* or content of a cell – or a group of cells – into other cells. In order to use this command, you have to define three things, the *source*, the *target* and *how you want the copy to be made*.

- The source is the position of what you want to be copied. You can only copy numbers or formulas that are already on the spreadsheet. In most spreadsheets, the source can be either a single cell, a range of cells down a column, a range of cells along a row or a range of cells across columns and rows.
- The target is where you want the source numbers or formulas to be copied to. The size of the target must be at least as big as that of the source but may also be bigger since spreadsheets enable you to copy the same source several times, ie in several places, at once. The concepts of source and target can be applied to the extension of the model for Delta Metal. This is done in Figure 7.2.
- Finally, you have to define how you want the copy to be made. Most spreadsheets recopy numbers (and words) exactly as they are, and recopy formulas either strictly as they are (*absolute formulas*), or by keeping the same structure and adjusting it in relation to the new position (*relative formulas*).

With Lotus 1-2-3, you are not asked to specify the copy process at the moment of the copy, but rather *to specify beforehand the components of the formulas as either relative or absolute*.[2] Formulas when written as in Figure 7.1 are copied automatically as relative.[3] If you want a formula or part of it to be recopied as absolute, you must write it differently before using the copy command. For example in the case of a constant growth rate in sales, you should enter the formula in C2:

$$+B2*(1+\$B\$1)$$

If you do so, and copy the formula in D2 and E2, you will get:

$$+C2*(1+\$B\$1) \text{ in D2,}$$
$$+D2*(1+\$B\$1) \text{ in C2, etc}$$

Obviously there is a feature that helps you indicate that a formula or part of it is absolute; you do not have to type the $ sign but just press the [F4] key when entering the component of a formula.[4]

Extending the model

In order to extend the model to four more years keeping all the parameters the same, you can proceed as follows with Lotus 1-2-3:[5]

• Copy of growth rate:

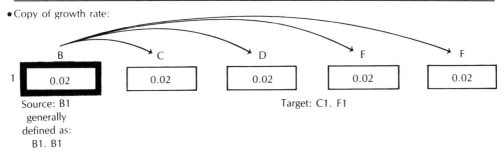

• Copy of sales: first you have to enter a formula in C2: +B2*(1+C1) then, you can copy the content of C2:

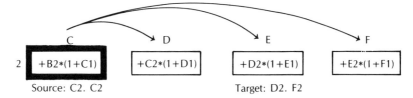

• Copy of cgs/sales, cgs, operating expenses/sales and operating expenses:

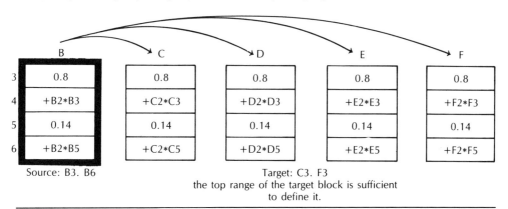

Figure 7.2 Copy command.

- Position the cursor in B1, then: / C (copy) [R] C1.F1 [R]
- Type in a new formula in C2, keep the cursor in C2, then: / C (copy) [R] D2.F2 [R]
- Position the cursor in B3, then: / C [R] C3.F3 [R]
- and repeat as necessary. Be careful to enter new formulas in C9, C12, C15 and C18.

If this is the first time you have made a copy, do it *one row at a time*, and do not be discouraged if you make mistakes. Obviously, if you are more experienced you can copy the model more quickly:

- copy B1 into C1.F1
- enter a new formula in C2 and copy it across
- copy the block B3.B8 at once: position the cursor in B3, then / C B4.B8 [R] C3.F3 [R]
- enter a new formula in C9 and copy it across
- copy the block B10.B11
- enter a new formula in C12, copy it across
- copy the block B13.B14
- etc

In order to show the years on top of the model, you can insert a row above row 1 (position the cursor in A1, then / W (worksheet) I (insert) R (row) [R]). As it is very easy to improve the presentation of a model it is a good idea to delay all embellishments until the end, and to keep your model as compact as possible. If you have enlarged column A and want to see all the years, set the global column width to 7. To do so with Lotus 1-2-3 / W (worksheet) G (global) C (column width) [R].

Useful hints for developing multi-annual models

When building multi-annual models the following method is often very effective:

- First, enter the numbers and formulas for the first year. This should be done after you have prepared an initial model on a piece of paper.
- Then, make sure that this model really works. In order to do so, change some parameters and check that the outcome variable is changed accordingly. Check you understand the magnitude and the direction of change.
- When you are happy with the first year, and only then, start copying the model across. In order to do so you can either:
  - Copy line by line across the years
  - Or alternatively, as the second year is generally slightly different from the first but similar to subsequent ones, you can first build the second year, check it works and then copy it at once across the subsequent years.
- Two further recommendations:
  - Very often it is a good idea initially to copy the parameters across just as they are, and to modify them only if needed in a second stage. Doing this enables you to separate the model-construction phase from the model-use phase and to start working with the model only when you are sure that it is well built.
  - You should be careful with the last year of models. In a number of models the last year presents some specific features.

7.2 A MULTI-ANNUAL MODEL

Analyzing the results with a graph

When the initial model is extended over four more years, you get the results shown in Figure 7.3.

	1993	1994	1995	1996	1997
Growth rate	0.02	0.02	0.02	0.02	0.02
SALES	118 072	120 434	122 842	125 299	127 805
cgs/sales	0.80	0.80	0.80	0.80	0.80
CGS	94 458	96 347	98 274	100 239	102 244
Oper expenses/sales	0.14	0.14	0.14	0.14	0.14
OPERATING EXPENSES	16 530	16 861	17 198	17 542	17 893
Depreciation	400	400	400	400	400
OPERATIONAL PROFIT BEFORE TAX	6 684	6 826	6 971	7 118	7 268
CUMULATIVE OPERATIONAL PROFIT BEFORE TAX	3 630	10 456	17 427	24 545	31 813
OPERATIONAL PROFIT AFTER TAX	5 051	3 754	3 834	3 915	3 998
OPERATIONAL CFE	5 451	4 154	4 234	4 315	4 398
Receivables open	58 893	59 036	60 217	61 421	62 650
Collection period	183	183	183	183	183
RECEIVABLES END	59 036	60 217	61 421	62 650	63 903
Inventory open	16 709	23 614	24 087	24 568	25 060
Inventory turnover	4	4	4	4	4
INVENTORY END	23 614	24 087	24 568	25 060	25 561
Payables open	39 944	33 788	32 273	32 919	33 577
Payment period	122	122	122	122	122
PAYABLES END	33 788	32 273	32 919	33 577	34 248
CFO	−7 754	987	3 193	3 253	3 315
(000FFR)					

Figure 7.3 Multi-annual model.

In order better to visualize the evolution of CFO, you can put it in graph form. To do so with Lotus 1-2-3,[6] provided you have a graphics monitor,

- Position the cursor in B22
- Key in: / G (graph) T (type) B (for drawing a bar graph) A[7] B22.F22 [R] V (view) (in order to view the graph)
- To return to the worksheet, press Esc.

Any graph you define is automatically updated when you change the value of a parameter in the worksheet. When a graph is defined, you do not need to go through the graph command to view it; you need only to press the F10 key. Pressing the F9 key makes you return to the spreadsheet.

Graphs do not need to be saved separately as Lotus 1-2-3 saves them automatically with the corresponding worksheet. In case you want more than one graph attached to a worksheet, you must name these graphs individually (/Graph Name Create). Graphs can also be printed: please refer to the Lotus 1-2-3 manual.

A graph facility such as the one offered by spreadsheets is very useful since graphics are a powerful *communication device* and a very effective *thinking aid*. When analyzing numbers, you can often get a new insight when you display these numbers in one or more graphics forms. Changing the mode of representation of a problem, or expressing it in an alternative thinking language, is often a powerful way to develop your understanding of this problem. As stated by Adams,[8] 'The well-armed problem-finder/solver is fluent in many mental languages and is able to use them interchangeably to record information, communicate with the unconscious and consciously manipulate. Some of these modes are more 'natural' to us than others. They are often more powerful when used in combination with each other than when used alone'.

What do the results tell?

■ From 1994 onwards CFO generation improves a great deal. This may seem strange when you consider that working capital parameters are the same for the whole period 1993–1997. However these parameters are not the same at the end of 1992 and at the end of 1993. The large CFO deficit in 1993 is due to the decrease in inventory turnover and in payment period.

■ The cash excess in 1994 is significantly lower than in subsequent years; why is this so? As it is built, the model assumes that purchases are equally spread over the year. Consequently the inventory build up in 1993 increases the average daily purchases and pushes up the accounts payable end.[9] This might not be a realistic assumption if the inventory build-up is made, for example, at the beginning of the year by one large additional purchase of goods. In such a case the inventory build-up would have no impact on the accounts payable end and as a result CFO would be lower in 1993 and higher in 1994. We will come back to this modelling problem in the next chapter.

NOTES

1 Also called Replicate in some spreadsheets.

2 In Multiplan when the formula is entered as +R2C2 * (1 + R1C3) it is copied automatically as absolute. In order to have it copied as relative it has to be specified as +RC[−1]*(1+R[−1]C).

3 SuperCalc copies formulas automatically as relative. However, SuperCalc gives you the option to do so differently (see below).

4 This works with Excel and Quattro also.

5 With Excel:

To copy B1:

Point at B1 / E(edit) C(copy) point C1 press and hold SHIFT and point at F1 [R]

To copy B3.B8:

Point at B3 press and hold SHIFT and point at B8 / E(edit) C(copy) point at C3 press and hold SHIFT and point at F3 [R]

With Quattro Pro:

To copy B1: E(edit)

Point at B1 / C(copy) [R] C1.F1 [R]

To copy B3.B8:

Point at B3 / E(edit) C(copy) B3.B8 [R] C3.F3 [R]

With SuperCalc:

Position the cursor in B1, then: / C (copy) [R] C1.F1 [R]

Type in a new formula in C2, keep the cursor in C2, then: / C (Copy) D2.F2 [R] When you do so, SuperCalc copies the formulas as relative; if you want part or all of the formula to be absolute, you need to tell it so, after you have defined the target range and before you press [R]. When you do so you then have access to a variety of options:

No-adjust	Each item of the formula is copied absolute
Ask	SuperCalc asks you, for each item of the formula, if you want it to be copied absolute or relative
Values	In this case SuperCalc copies the *foreground* rather than the background of the cell
+, −, *, /	This option is a very useful feature which enables you to modify all the data contained in a range (the target of the copy command). You can add a constant to this data or deduct a constant from this data, or multiply or divide this data by a constant, the constant being the source of the copy command.
Transpose	Transpose rows to columns and vice versa, with adjustment.

- Position the cursor in B3, then / C (Copy) [R] C3.F3 [R]
- Repeat as necessary.

Be careful to enter the new formulas in C9, C12, C15 and C18.

6 With Excel:

Point at B21 press and hold SHIFT and point at F21 press F11. Your graph (a chart in Excel language) is done. If you want to modify this graph, use the / G (gallery) command. This first graph should make you appreciate some very useful features of Excel:

- You can choose among many different types of quality chart.
- The chart can be shown simultaneously with the worksheet.
- The size and position of the window in which the chart is displayed can be modified (Alt or / − command).

With Quattro Pro:

Point at B21 / G (graph) G (graph type) B (bar) S (series) 1 (1st series) B21.F21 [R] Esc V(view)

With SuperCalc:

Point at B21 / V (view) D (data) B1.F21 [R] G (graph type) B (bar) S (show)

7 With Lotus 1-2-3 you can simultaneously graph six ranges of data, these ranges being identified as A, B, C, D, E and F.

8 Adams J (1979), *Conceptual Blockbusting – A guide for better ideas*, W W Norton.

9 You can check this by changing the formula for calculating accounts payable at the end of 1993. When you change this formula to CGS/365 * payment period (+B5/365*B20), you get the following sequence of CFOs:

1993	1994	1995	1996	1997
−10 056	3 131	3 190	3 250	3 312

You can check that the introduction of this new formula only changes the distribution of CFO over the years, particularly 1993 and 1994.

CHAPTER 8

Profit, Working Capital Needs[1] and Cash Generation

Timing Effects

8.1 USING THE MULTI-ANNUAL MODEL TO SIMULATE ALTERNATIVE SITUATIONS

Generating new results

In Figure 6.4, we presented the 1993 results of the four simulations showing their impact on the decision Delta Metal must make regarding the shortening of its collection period and the change in the environment related to the new EC regulations. With the extended model we have just built we can run these four simulations again and analyze the results over a longer period. The new results are shown in Figure 8.1.

In the four simulations shown in Figure 8.1, depreciation and payment period are kept the same as in the base model and constant over the whole period.

- Situation 1. Growth rate = 0.02, cgs/sales = 0.80, operating expenses/sales = 0.14, collection period = 182.5, inventory turnover = 4. All these parameters are kept constant over the whole period.
- Situation 2. Growth rate = 0.02, cgs/sales = 0.75 in 1993 and 0.74 afterwards, operating expenses/sales = 0.14, collection period = 182.5, inventory turnover = 3.04 in 1993 and 3.0 afterwards. Growth rate, operating expenses/sales, collection period and payment period are kept constant over the whole period.
- Situation 3. Growth rate = −0.02 in 1993 and 0.02 afterwards, cgs/sales = 0.83, operating expenses/sales = 0.15, collection period = 121.7, inventory turnover = 4. Except for sales growth, all the parameters are kept the same over the whole period.
- Situation 4. Growth rate = −0.02 in 1993 and 0.02 afterwards, cgs/sales = 0.78 in 1993 and 0.77 afterwards, operating expenses/sales = 0.15, collection period = 121.7, inventory turnover = 3.04 in 1993 and 3.0 afterwards. Operating expenses/sales, collection period and payment period are kept the same over the whole period.

Decision variable	Environment variable	Outcome variable				
		1993 CFO	1994 CFO	1995 CFO	1996 CFO	1997 CFO
The new credit plan is not implemented	and EC does not install new regulations (1)	−7 754	987	3 193	3 253	3 315
	and EC installs new regulations (2)	−10 164	2 586	7 087	7 225	7 366
The new credit plan is implemented	and EC does not install new regulations (3)	10 410	−746	924	939	954
	and EC installs new regulations (4)	8 491	361	4 818	4 911	5 006
(000FFR)						

Figure 8.1 Results over several years.

In order to get the results shown in Figure 8.1, you need to enter the formulas that generate the value of parameters. Please refer to Chapter 6 to see which parameters are generated by formulas. (Be careful with formulas as some should be adjusted.)

When calculating the results of Figure 8.1, you can check *the sensitivity of CFO to the value of the parameters.*

Analyzing the results

When comparing the results of Figure 8.1 with those of Figure 6.4 (which are included in Figure 8.1), you will realize that:

- Whatever the EC does, the new credit plan leads to a higher CFO generation in 1993 and to a lower one afterwards.
- Whatever Delta Metal decides about the credit plan, the new EC regulations lead to a lower CFO generation in 1993 and to a higher one afterwards.

In order to explain why there is such a difference between the immediate and long term impact of the credit plan and the regulations, we have to reflect on how CFO generation is affected by changes in profitability and in working capital parameters.

- We know that the annual cash generation of a company is equal to the difference between its annual profit and the increase in its working capital needs during that year.
- We should also realize that the increase in working capital needs is the result of two sets of factors:
  - The working capital parameters (collection period, inventory turnover and payment period).

· The change in the level of activity.

■ When profitability is increased and kept at the new level in subsequent years, the subsequent profits are all adjusted upwards in a similar proportion, and so are the subsequent CFOs.
■ When working capital parameters are adjusted and then kept at the new level the impact is quite different:
  · In the short run the adjustment of working capital parameters creates a profound change in the working capital needs and, as a consequence, in the CFO as well.
  · In the long run and *because the working capital parameters are kept at their new level*, the working capital needs no longer change, or rather they only change with the level of activity.

As a result, *changes in working capital parameters have a much stronger short-term, rather than long-term, impact*. When applying this framework to Delta Metal, we realize that:

■ The new credit plan has a very favorable short-term impact but a much less favourable long-term one:
  · The short-term advantage is due to the sudden release of funds frozen in accounts receivable caused by the shortening of the collection period. In the short term this advantage outweighs the loss in profitability. As a result CFO is greatly increased in 1993.
  · The long-term disadvantage is due to the loss in profitability. In the long term the loss in profitability is experienced every year but the working capital needs no longer decrease any more. As a result CFOs are lower.
■ The new EC regulations have an unfavorable short-term impact and a favorable long-term one:
  · The short-term disadvantage is due to the need to bring the inventory up to a new level in 1993.
  · In the long run the profit advantage dominates and as a result CFOs are higher.

Consequently, assessing the impact of the credit plan and of the EC regulations is a matter of evaluating trade-offs:

■ Does the initial advantage of the credit plan outweigh its future disadvantages?
■ Do the future advantages of the EC regulations outweigh their initial disadvantage?

One problem, however, at this stage is to assess how sure we can be about our CFO estimates and in particular about the earlier ones: the low values of the 1994 CFOs are not easy to explain.

As it is at the moment, our model estimates ending receivables, inventory and payables on the basis of average sales, cgs and purchases, and assumes that those are *distributed evenly throughout the year*, a simplification which is not necessarily acceptable.

The usefulness of monthly models

A better way to estimate working capital accounts is to analyze the activity of Delta Metal over a shorter period basis, a month, for example, and estimate:

- Accounts receivable end as the sum of July to December sales (and September to December sales when the credit plan is implemented).
- Accounts payable end as the sum of September to December purchases.
- Inventory end as the sum of October to December purchases (and September to December purchases when the new EC regulations are enforced). As inventories are built up in order to prepare for future sales, purchases are made in relation to future rather than current sales, a further improvement to make to our model.

In Further Model III.2 (page 130), you will find monthly models of the CFO generation at Delta Metal in 1993, 1994 and 1995. This monthly modelling shows that our current model has some limitations.

- It ignores the impact of seasonal factors.
- It assumes that the additional purchases needed to bring the inventory to a new level will be made progressively in 1993 and will therefore increase the ending accounts payable, an implicit assumption which results in a transfer of CFO from 1994 to 1993.
- It relates ending inventories to the activity of the years which have elapsed and not, as it should, to the years to come. If *accounts receivable and payable relate to past events*, that is not the case of *inventory which is future oriented*.

The monthly modelling therefore suggests that we:

- Change the formula for calculating inventory end: +C5/B17 in B18; to be copied across.
- Adjust the value of working capital parameters as shown in Figure 8.2. When this is done, you get the new results as displayed in the Figure.

Figure 8.2 shows that when using financial models, you should be very careful about estimating working capital needs:

- When the activity is not equally spread over the year, it is not sufficient to estimate working capital needs based on average sales, cgs and purchases.
- *When working capital needs parameters change, it is necessary to think exactly when*

Decision variable	Environment variable	Parameters		1993 CFO	Outcome variable			
		1993	1994 and after		1994 CFO	1995 CFO	1996 CFO	1997 CFO
The new credit plan is not implemented	and EC does not install new regulations	CP = 183 IT = 4.1 PP = 121	CP = 183 IT = 4.1 PP = 129	−8 024	3 153	3 231	3 292	19 801
	and EC installs new regulations	CP = 183 IT = 3.05 PP = 105	CP = 183 IT = 3.05 PP = 121	−15 008	7 004	7 079	7 217	28 501
The new credit plan is implemented	and EC does not install new regulations	CP = 147 IT = 4.1 PP = 121	CP = 147 IT = 4.1 PP = 129	2 434	1 267	805	817	17 277
	and EC installs new regulations	CP = 147 IT = 3.05 PP = 105	CP = 147 IT = 3.05 PP = 121	−4 058	4 625	4 652	4 742	25 977
(000FFR)								

Figure 8.2 Revised results over several years.

the adjustment is to be made as this will cause a sudden short term change in the CFO generation.

- Finally, estimating the CFOs at the end of the year only is not always enough since different cash positions may exist at some specific dates in the year.

8.2 THE NEED TO ASSESS CASH GENERATION OVER A FINITE PERIOD OF TIME

What should Delta Metal do?

The apparent tradeoffs
Results shown in Figure 8.2 suggest the existence of the following trade-offs associated with the decision to launch the new credit plan:

more cash in 1993
less cash afterwards.

This trade-off is shown in Figure 8.3 as well as the trade-off associated with the new EC regulations.

The true tradeoffs
According to our analysis, the new credit plan would enable Delta Metal to generate more cash in 1993 and less cash afterwards. The key issue is how much less.

	Immediate short term advantage/disadvantage*	Long term annual advantage/disadvantage†
New credit plan: no new EC regulations:	10.5	−2.5
new EC regulations:	10.9	−2.5
New EC regulations: no new credit plan:	−7.0	3.9
new credit plan:	−6.5	3.9

* Difference in 1993 CFOs.

† Difference in 1996 CFOs.

Figure 8.3 Trade-offs.

The best way to answer this question is to abandon our model for a while and come back to the mechanics of the new credit plan: *the introduction of such a plan would not help Delta Metal generate any more cash in the end but would simply help the company generate cash quicker from its sales.* This acceleration would be obtained at the cost of giving away 4% of what would be received without the plan. You can check this by looking at Figure 8.4.

- Cash receipts in July 1993 are 9 900 (ie equal to the sales in January) without the plan, and 9 504 (ie equal to 96% of the sales in March) with it.
- If you compare the receipts corresponding to the sales made in the period January 1993 to June 1994, you realize that:
  · They are received from July 1993 to December 1994 without the new credit plan.
  · They are received from May 1993 to October 1994 with the plan, and are also 4% less.

Figure 8.4 shows that we have to recognize that our modelling of the impact of the new credit plan was not totally correct. A proper comparison of the plan with the base solution over several years (a business cycle for example) will show:

- More cash generated in the year the plan is implemented. This is due to the fact that two months of sales are received more quickly.
- Slightly less cash in each subsequent year, due to the 4% rebate.
- Significantly less cash in the last year of the cycle, due to the fact that, since cash receipts have been accelerated, part of them has already been paid at an earlier date.

This is depicted in the diagram shown in Figure 8.5.

	Cash receipts (base)	Sales	Sales after discount	Cash receipts (new plan)
1993 January		9 900	9 504	
February		9 000	8 640	
March		9 900	9 504	
April		9 900	9 504	
May		10 100	9 696	9 504
June		10 000	9 600	8 640
July	9 900	6 400	6 144	9 504
August	9 000	5 172	4 965	9 504
September	9 900	12 000	11 520	9 696
October	9 900	11 000	10 560	9 600
November	10 100	12 000	11 520	6 144
December	10 000	12 700	12 192	4 965
1994 January	6 400	10 098	9 694	11 520
February	5 172	9 180	8 813	10 560
March	12 000	10 098	9 694	11 520
April	11 000	10 098	9 694	12 192
May	12 000	10 302	9 890	9 694
June	12 700	10 200	9 792	8 813
July	10 098			9 694
August	9 180			9 694
September	10 098			9 890
October	10 098			9 792
November	10 302			
December	10 200			
Total	178 048	178 048	170 926	170 926

Note
Cash receipts in the period January–June 1993 are due to sales made in 1992 and are not changed by the new credit plan. When the new credit plan is implemented, cash receipts in May and June are exceptionally large since the company gets both receipts due to 1992 sales (November and December) and to 1993 sales (January and February).

Figure 8.4 Impact of the new credit plan.

The true impact of the new credit plan

Returning to the mechanics of the new credit plan has enabled us to see more clearly its real impact. Now can we go back to our model and improve it again?

The fundamental idea we have now discovered is that *cash generation can only be assessed over a full business cycle, or more simply over a full and finite period of time.* As we do not have any data about the possible shape of a business cycle at Delta Metal, let us limit ourselves to assessing its cash generation over a five-year period. In order to do this, let us assume the selling activities of Delta Metal stop at the end of December 1997. Delta Metal's cash flows within such an assumption (base solution) are shown in Figure 8.6. The assessment of the various alternatives is shown in Figure 8.7.

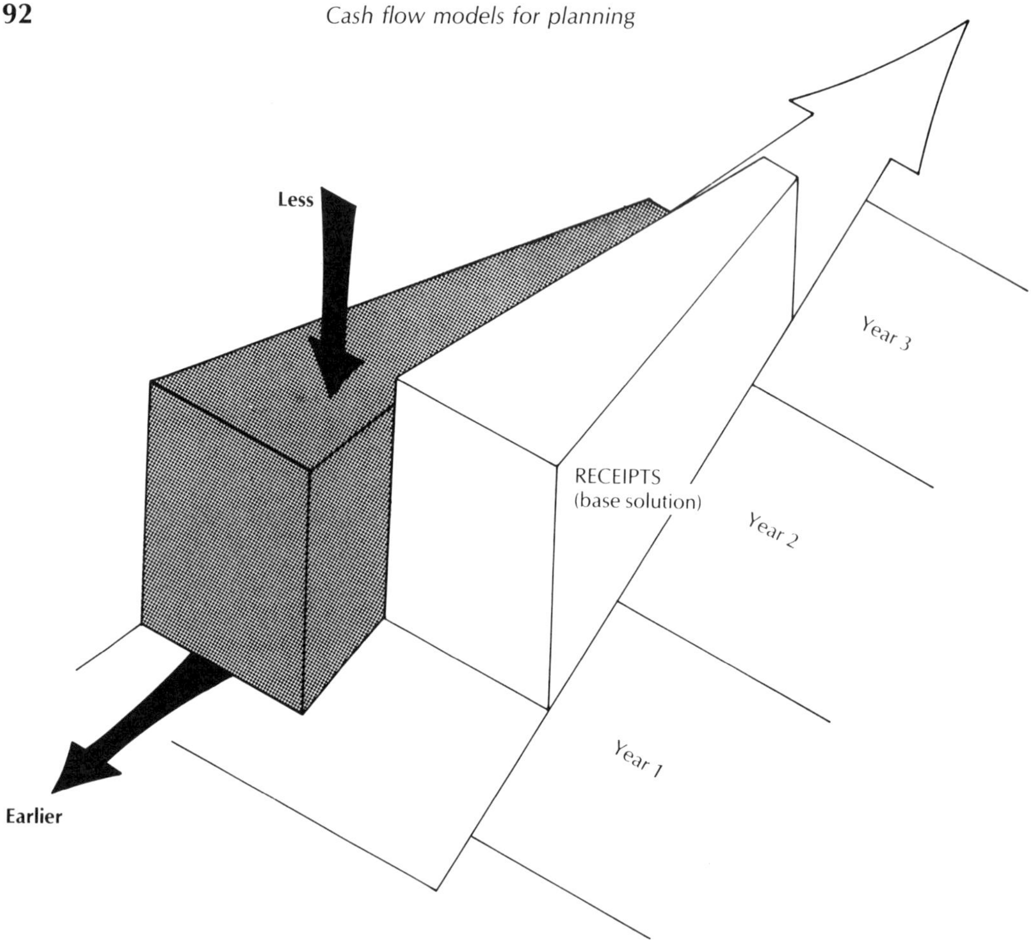

With the new credit plan, Delta Metal receives less, but receives it earlier.
  It receives much more at the beginning,
        slightly less for a time,
        much less at the end.

Figure 8.5 Diagram of the impact of the new credit plan.

The results in Figure 8.6 call for a very important comment:

When you assess profit and cash over a full business cycle their cumulative values are equal:[2] cash and profit only differ when assessed on an annual basis. This is a very important principle which we will clarify in Chapter 11. This will lead us to recommend that you should not be content to look at any single annual CFO but that you should assess CFOs over a longer period. We will also propose, in Chapter 12, a criterion for assessing the value of a series of CFOs, the Net Present Value (NPV). Figure IV.5(a) (see Further Models IV.5) gives a model with an NPV calculation added to it: we recommend that you use this improved model each time you want to assess a strategy.

	A	B	C	D	E	F	G	H
1		1993	1994	1995	1996	1997	1998	cumulated
2	Growth rate (2%)	0.02	0.02	0.02	0.02	0.02		
3	SALES	118 072	120 434	122 842	125 299	127 805		
4	cgs/sales	0.80	0.80	0.80	0.80	0.80		
5	CGS	94 458	96 347	98 274	100 239	102 244		
6	Oper expenses/sales	0.14	0.14	0.14	0.14	0.14		
7	OPERATING EXPENSES	16 530	16 861	17 198	17 542	17 893		
8	Depreciation	400	400	400	400	400		
9	OPERATIONAL PROFIT BEFORE TAX	6 684	6 826	6 971	7 118	7 268		
10	CUMULATIVE OPERATIONAL PROFIT BEFORE TAX	3 630	10 456	17 427	24 545	31 813		
11	OPERATIONAL PROFIT AFTER TAX	5 051	3 754	3 834	3 915	3 998		20 551
12	OPERATIONAL CFE	5 451	4 154	4 234	4 315	4 398		22 551
13	Receivables open	58 893	59 198	60 382	61 589	62 821	64 078	
14	Collection period	183	183	183	183	183		
15	RECEIVABLES END	59 198	60 382	61 589	62 821	64 078		
16	Inventory open	16 709	23 499	23 969	24 449	24 938	0	
17	Inventory turnover	4.1	4.1	4.1	4.1	4.1		
18	INVENTORY END	23 499	23 969	24 449	24 938	0		
19	Payables open	39 944	33 564	34 217	34 902	35 600	27 322	
20	Payment period	121	129	129	129	129		
21	PAYABLES END	33 564	34 217	34 902	35 600	27 322		
22	CFO	−8 024	3 153	3 231	3 292	19 801	36 756	58 209
23	CFO due to 1992 operations	35 658						
24	CFO due to 1993–97 operations	−43 682	3 153	3 281	3 292	19 801	36 756	22 551

Formulas:
H11: @Sum (B11.G11)
H12: @Sum (B12.G12)
G13: +F15
G16: +F18
G19: +F21
G22: +G13+G16−G19

H22: @Sum (B22.G22)

H24: @Sum (B24.G24)
B23: +B13+B16−B19
B24: +B22−B23, to be copied across.

Figure 8.6 Base solution: final analysis.

Decision variable	Environment variable		1993	1994	1995	1996	1997	1998	Cumulated
				Outcome variable: CFOs due to 1993–97 operations					
The new credit plan is not implemented	and EC does not install new regulations	(1)	−43 682	3 153	3 231	3 292	19 801	36 756	22 551
	and EC installs new regulations	(2)	−50 666	7 004	7 079	7 217	28 501	43 005	42 139
The new credit plan is implemented	and EC does not install new regulations	(3)	−33 224	1 267	805	817	17 277	22 091	9 033
	and EC installs new regulations	(4)	−39 716	4 625	4 652	4 742	25 977	28 340	28 621
Impact of the new credit plan									
when there are no new regulations			10 458	−1 887	−2 426	−2 475	−7 524	−14 664	−13 518
when there are new regulations			10 950	−2 379	−2 426	−2 475	−2 524	−14 664	−13 518
Impact of the new regulations									
when there is no new credit plan			−6 984	3 850	3 848	3 924	8 700	6 249	19 588
when there is a new credit plan			−6 492	3 359	3 848	3 924	8 700	6 249	19 588

Figure 8.7 Results over a 5-year period assuming 2% growth.

What should Delta Metal do? Results shown in Figure 8.7 do not portray the new credit plan as a very attractive move. It is true that this plan would accelerate the CFO generation of the company, but this acceleration would cause a cash loss over five years of more than 13 million FFR.

In order to obtain a more accurate assessment of the credit plan we need a criterion that would enable us to evaluate the benefit of the acceleration of the cash generation. Such a criterion is presented in Chapter 12.

The results in Figure 8.7 also show that the new EC regulations might be fairly good for Delta Metal. It is true they would delay the cash generation of the company, but they would increase significantly its cumulative value to about 19 million FFR more over a period of five years.

A methodological comment

One way to generate the results of Figure 8.7 is to:

- Construct the base model (as shown in Figure 8.6) and record and CFOs on paper.
- Save the base model.
- Retrieve it and change the value of selected parameters in order to simulate the second situation (no new credit plan, new EC regulations), record the new CFOs on paper, and save the new model under a new name.
- Retrieve the base model again, change the value of selected parameters in order to simulate the third situation, record the new CFOs on paper, save the model under a third name.
- Continue this process for as many simulations as required.

This is a very effective way to proceed; using information technology does not render paper and pencil obsolete.

However, there is an alternative way which can help you visualize the problem more clearly. As the problem is to assess the impact of the new credit plan as compared to the base solution, it would be useful to show simultaneously on the screen two series of cash flows:[3]

- Those corresponding to the base solution (situation 1).
- Those corresponding to situation 3.

How do you do this? The easiest way is probably to proceed as follows:

- Retrieve the base model.
- Copy the values of the CFOs of the base model into range B26.H26. In order to do so, you can retype them, a cumbersome task, or, better, use Lotus 1-2-3 command:[4]
  · Position the cursor on B24.

· Key in: / R (range) V (value) B24.H24 [R] B26 [R].
- Change the parameters of the base model in order to get the CFOs of situation 3. (see Figures 6.7 and 8.2).

The advantage of this approach is that it enables you to show simultaneously on the screen the CFOs of situations 1 and 3 and to graph them. The disadvantage of this approach, however, is that you must reinitialize the model if you want to display more than two series of cash flows simultaneously.

NOTES

1 The cost of working capital needs is analyzed in Chapter 12, section 5, p 188.

2 More exactly: cumulative CFE = cumulative CFO.

3 You can also decide to display simultaneously the four series of cash flows shown in Figure 8.7. We leave you to work out how this can be done.

4 With Excel:
Point at B24 press and hold SHIFT and point at H24 / E (edit) C (copy)
Point at B26 press and hold SHIFT and point at H26 / E (edit)
S (paste special) V (values) [R] ESC press any arrow key.

With Quattro Pro:
Point at B24 / E (edit) V (values) B24.H24 [R]
Point at B26 [R]

With SuperCalc:
Point at B24 / C (copy) B24.H24 R B26.H26, V (value) [R]

CHAPTER 9

Cash Generation as a Symptom of Strategic Success

9.1 THE CONDITIONS FOR SUCCESSFUL GROWTH

The impact of higher growth at Delta Metal

In our analysis of the situation of Delta Metal, we have not yet considered the fact that the growth of the market could be well above 2%.

Let us run four new simulations changing the growth rate to 10% and compare their results with the ones obtained previously. Running new simulations is, unfortunately, not just a matter of changing the growth rate to 10%: the parameters you need to use are shown in Figure 9.1.

As changes in working capital needs' parameters create a strong disturbance on the short-term cash flows and render their analysis difficult, let us consider the CFOs in 1995. This is done in Figure 9.2.

Figure 9.2 shows some very surprising results:

- In all cases, the higher the growth, the lower the annual cash generation.[1]
- In two cases (corresponding to the situation where the EC does not install new regulations), higher growth even causes negative CFOs.

As the results of the simulations show, higher growth at Delta Metal leads to an increase in annual profit and to a simultaneous and bigger increase in working capital needs. As a result, annual CFO decreases with growth. This phenomenon raises two basic questions:

- Is it a fact of business life that annual CFO decreases when growth increases?
- Can a company accept a negative annual CFO?

Annual CFOs and growth

Businesses are divided into two categories. The first category contains the firms which have positive working capital needs. This is the very large group of firms which normally have higher accounts receivable and inventory

Decision variables	Environment variables	Parameters					
		Growth		cgs/sales*		Working capital:§	
		1993	1994 and after	1993	1994 and after	1993	1994 and after
The new credit plan is not implemented	and EC does not install new regulations (1)	0.1	0.1	0.8	0.8	CP = 183 IT = 4.1 PP = 124	CP = 183 IT = 4.1 PP = 134
	and EC installs new regulations (2)	0.1	0.1	0.75†	0.74	CP = 183 IT = 3.05 PP = 110	CP = 183 IT = 3.05 PP = 127
The new credit plan is implemeted	and EC does not install new regulations (3)	0.06‡	0.1	0.83	0.83	CP = 147 IT = 4.1 PP = 124	CP = 147 IT = 4.1 PP = 134
	and EC installs new regulations (4)	0.06‡	0.1	0.78†	0.77	CP = 147 IT = 3.05 PP = 110	CP = 147 IT = 3.05 PP = 127

* The other parameters are as in the situation with 2% growth.

† New formulas:
  (((127 333−16 709/0.8)*0.74)+16 709)/127 333
  (((122 239/0.96−16 709/0.8)*0.74)+16 709)/122 239
§ From Further Model III.2 Figure III.2(l)).
‡ 1.1*0.96−1

Figure 9.1 Parameters for simulating a 10% growth.

Decision variable	Environment variable	Outcome	
		1995 CFO with 2% growth	1995 CFO with 10% growth
The new credit plan is not implemented	and EC does not install new regulations (1)	3 231	−550
	and EC installs new regulations (2)	7 079	3 313
The new credit plan is implemented	and EC does not install new regulations (3)	805	−2 333
	and EC installs new regulations (4)	4 652	1 530

Figure 9.2 Impact of higher growth.

balances than accounts payable balances. The second category contains those firms which have negative working capital needs. This is the smaller group of firms that normally have lower accounts receivable and inventory balances than accounts payable balances.

The CFO of business firms with positive working capital needs lags behind their profit. The CFOs of firms with negative working capital needs leads on their profit.

The case of firms with positive working capital needs

In firms where this occurs, CFO lags behind profit due to the combined effect of four parameters: collection period, inventory turnover, payment period and growth rate.[2]

Receipts from sales lag behind sales as soon as they are not paid for in cash. If the collection period is six months, the cash receipts in January will be equal to the sales made six months earlier, in July. This would not make any difference if sales were stable but as soon as there is growth this systematically makes receipts from sales lower than sales in each month. The gap between receipts and sales in each month grows with the collection period and the growth rate. This mechanism is shown in Figure 9.3.

Generally, disbursements related to purchases also differ from cost of goods sold. Because of the existence of an inventory, purchases are made in relation to future sales: if the inventory turnover is equal to 4 (a three months' delay), purchases in January are made in relation to sales expected in April. But because of the existence of a payment period, these purchases themselves are not paid for in the month in which they occur. If, for example, the payment period is equal to four months, purchases made in January, and related to April sales, will be paid in May.

As a result, the combined effects of inventory turnover and payment period may make the payments related to purchases either correspond to cost of goods sold (when inventory delay and payment period are equal), lead on cost of goods sold (when inventory delay is more than payment period), or lag behind cost of goods sold (when inventory delay is less than payment period). This latter situation prevails at Delta Metal. As for receipts from sales, the lead or lag does not matter when there is no growth but does when there is. A lead in payments makes them systematically higher than the cost of goods sold. This mechanism is shown in Figure 9.4.

By definition, positive working capital needs correspond to the situation where CFO lags behind profit as the result of the net effect of collection period, inventory turnover and payment period. As shown above, as soon as there is growth – and if all the profitability and working capital parameters are kept constant – the fact that CFO lags behind profit makes CFO systematically lower than profit because cash receipts are lower than sales, and/or disbursements are higher than cgs.

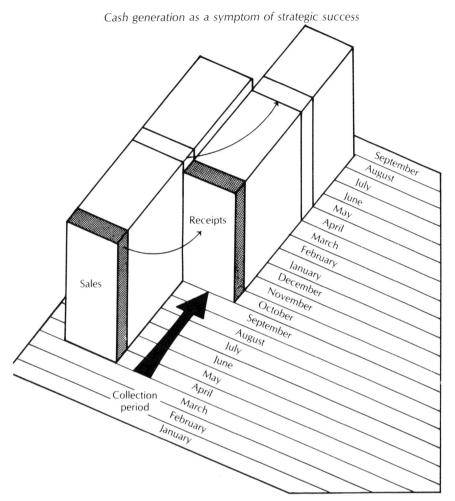

Figure 9.3 Impact of collection period and growth on cash receipts.

The higher the growth, the lower the annual CFO, which ultimately may become negative. CFO will obviously become negative more or less quickly depending on the profitability of the firm. When profitability is high, there is a big difference between sales and cgs and, as a result, receipts should be much lower than sales and/or disbursements much higher than cgs in order to make CFO negative.

The situation where excessive growth causes negative annual CFOs is called *unsustainable growth.*

When there is growth, the only way for a business firm to maintain its annual CFO generation is to increase its profitability and/or reduce its working capital needs. And, obviously, not just maintaining the CFO but increasing it when there is growth, can only be achieved by an even higher increase in profitability and/or reduction in working capital needs.

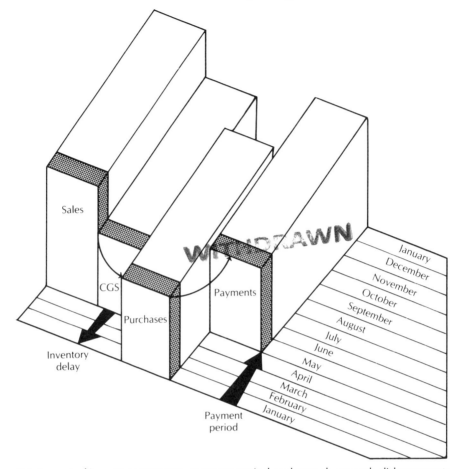

Figure 9.4 Impact of inventory turnover, payment period and growth on cash disbursements.

The case of firms with negative working capital needs

By definition, firms which have negative working capital needs are those in which CFO leads on profit. Let us assume that a supermarket

- Sells on a cash basis to individual customers.
- Carries no inventory.
- Pays its suppliers with a three month delay.

In such a situation cash receipts in each month will equal the sales of the month; cash disbursements in each month will equal the cost of goods sold experienced three months earlier which will be systematically lower than the cost of goods sold of the current month as soon as there is growth.

As a result of growth, annual CFO will therefore be systematically higher than profit. Actually, the higher the growth, the higher the CFO will be.

The value of a simplified model to assess growth

The description of the impact of growth on CFO presented in Figures 9.3 and 9.4 suggests the construction of an alternative model of CFO generation. A much simpler model than the one we have been using so far could estimate CFO as the difference between receipts from sales and disbursements related to purchases.

Such a model is described in Further Model III.3. When referring to it, you will be able to

- Build a simpler model of the annual cash generation of a firm.
- Check that this model gives similar results to the ones we have obtained so far (although it ignores ome complexities like the impact of depreciation and of seasonal factors).
- *Learn more about the impact of growth.* As you will see, the more simple the structure of a model, the better you can organize its utilization, and, consequently, *the more it can help you learn about a problem.*

As you will also realize, a simple model is not that easy to build. The model described in Further Model III.3 requires more understanding of the problem than the one we have built so far. Such a model is therefore not one you will build in the first stages of the analysis but rather when you have already developed a good understanding of the problem. Simple models are the ultimate goal of model building. During the process of building models, it is worth keeping this goal in mind and constantly thinking about alternative *simplified* models rather than more complex ones.

Volume and inflationary growth

Growth may actually be of two different kinds: it can correspond either to volume (real growth) or to price increases.

As shown in Further Model III.3, volume and inflationary growth have basically the same impact as far as accounts receivable and accounts payable are concerned. They differ, however, for inventories. When there is volume growth, holding inventories is costly but as soon as you are able to increase your prices with inflation, holding inventories is neutral.

What are the strategic implications of this? *Even when they do not grow in volume, firms with positive working capital needs may be hurt by inflation.* The net impact of the collection and payment periods may lead to a decrease in annual CFOs as soon as there is inflation. If this is the case, the firms must increase their profitability and/or decrease their working capital needs simply to maintain their CFOs.

Firms with negative working capital needs, on the other hand, are naturally favoured by inflation (provided that the profitability and the working capital parameters do not change); the higher the inflation, the bigger their annual CFOs.

The true impact of growth

Growth decreases the annual cash flows of firms which experience positive working capital needs but it should be realized that the impact of growth is one of pure timing. As the receipt of cash is merely delayed, it should re-appear one day.[3] In order to obtain an adequate perspective on the impact of growth, it should be analyzed over a long enough and *finite period of time*. The principle of such an analysis is shown in Figure 9.5.

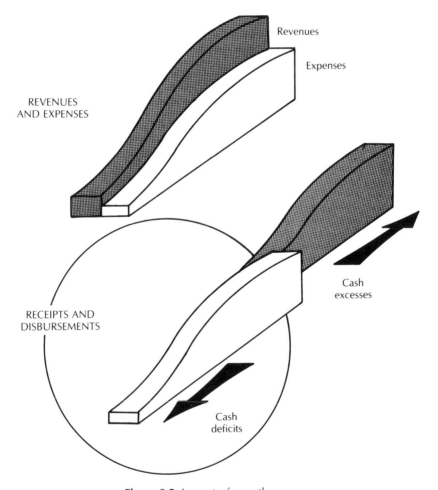

Figure 9.5 Impact of growth.

As Figure 9.5 shows, growth may generate negative annual CFOs, but this is a pure timing effect. Negative annual CFOs caused by growth are bound to be compensated for by positive CFOs in the end, provided that goods are sold at a price which is higher than costs. Negative annual CFOs do raise two problems, however.

- When CFOs are negative, money has to be invested in order to finance operations: the impact of this is analyzed in Chapter 12.
- Negative CFOs due to a systematic anticipation of disbursements over receipts are risky since sales, and therefore receipts, are very rarely certain. In the case where future sales fail to meet expectations, problems may well occur.

The full analysis of the alternatives envisaged at Delta Metal, including higher growth, is shown in Figure 9.6.

High-quality growth

Some companies believe that even though they correspond to a timing effect, the negative cash flows caused by the early stages of growth are not acceptable. These companies tend to be very demanding and to aim at high-quality growth ie, growth that simultaneously creates more volume, more profit and more cash. The model in Figure 9.6 shows that when all operational parameters (margins, operating expenses, ratio, working capital ratios, etc) are kept the same, more growth means less cash. High-quality growth ie, growth that creates more cash now requires that growth is accompanied by operational improvements:

- Higher profit/sales ratio. This can be achieved by a reduction in costs or an increase in prices;
- and/or shorter working capital delays, shorter collection period and/or quicker inventory turnover.

Achieving growth and increase in prices simultaneously is not easy and requires a very strong competitive position. When growth is driven by the customers of the firm who are eager to create more value through the acquisition of more products or services, the firm can probably increase its prices and get a fair share of the additional customers' value.

What should Delta Metal do?

The results in Figure 9.6 do not seem to make the new credit plan any more attractive since, whatever growth is, this plan accelerates the cash generation, but makes Delta Metal incur a large cash loss over a period of five years: 14

million FFR when growth is 2% and 17 million FFR when growth is 10%. Since cash generation is already very low at Delta Metal, reducing it further does not seem to be a good idea.

If we reject the new credit plan, one basic question remains: can Delta Metal continue to do what it has been doing in the recent past? The base solution does not indicate a very promising future and, if you add in the need to cover interest charges, the perspective looks even worse. A model for generating the income statements and balance sheets for Delta Metal in the coming five years is described in Further Model III.4. It shows that the company cannot pursue its present strategy and should implement drastic changes. How can we help them do so?

9.2 CFO AS THE RESULT OF ENVIRONMENTAL FORCES, COMPETITIVE AND OPERATIONAL STRATEGIES

Cash generation is very much dependent on the *competitive forces which prevail in the environment* in which the firm operates: the bargaining power of customers, the bargaining power of suppliers, rivalry among competitors, the threat of new entrants and the threat of substitute products.[4] Due to these forces, some environments are naturally conducive to high cash generation while others are not. What you should realize, however, is that no environment is static, and that appropriate actions aimed at changing the power structure of an environment can make it favorable to cash generation. A fascinating example in this respect is the liquid gas industry in Europe. In the 80s, producers of liquid gas in Europe (Air Liquide in France, Aga in Sweden, etc) had negative working capital needs. When analyzing the history of this industry, you realize, however, how imaginative these firms have been in order to accelerate their cash generation. As prices were very competitive, they tried to improve their cash generation by finding ways to cut down on working capital needs: in contrast to their US counterparts, these firms kept the retail end of the business and encouraged customers to pay cash. Purchasers of gas in cylinders were asked to rent the cylinder (in most cases, this rent was to be paid in advance). When some industrial buyers' needs were large enough to justify their own gas-producing plants, they were asked to contribute to the capital expenditure needed to erect them. On the other hand, when an industrial buyer did not have sufficient needs to justify the erection of a special plant, it was invited to reserve a share of the capacity of a shared plant. In order to do so, it was requested to make an initial payment which was to be recovered through lower prices being charged in the future.

Competitive strategies also influence the CFO generation of a firm. Within the same environment, some firms may generate large CFOs and others not. It is clear that aggressive competitive strategies may deplete cash generation: price cutting, high marketing expenses, lower profitability, granting long payment delays and offering a large range of products, all increase working capital needs. As a result, CFO may decrease, and will decrease even further if the strategy is successful and results in higher growth. Aggressive strategies may succeed if they enable the company to achieve a strong market position within a reasonable time limit. If this is the case, the company can then increase its profitability by charging higher prices and achieve economies of scale and gains from experience. It can also then probably reduce its working capital needs (more pressure put on customers, higher storage efficiency, more pressure put on suppliers). And since, when a company has a high market share, its growth is more or less limited to the growth of the market as a whole, the pressure on CFO due to growth also decreases. The problem, however, is that such aggressive competitive strategies can only succeed if the firm is able to build and maintain a strong competitive advantage. This is possible in some industries but not in others, and at some stages in the development of an industry, but not at others.

Finally, *operational strategies* also shape the CFO generation of a firm. Selling or manufacturing operations can be run according to two extreme strategies:

- Stockists and traditional manufacturers start with preparing a forecast of the future demand. Then, they use this forecast to buy and/or produce which results in the building of an inventory. When customers place an order, they are served from inventory.
- Brokers and 'just-in-time' manufacturers[5] wait until they receive the actual customer orders for triggering purchases and/or production.

These two extreme operational strategies (*'speculative'* vs *'non speculative'*) result in very different CFO profiles:

- Stockists and traditional manufacturers systematically spend much earlier than they get paid which creates large working capital needs.
- Brokers which are paid by a commission incur no working capital needs. Just-in-time manufacturers have very low working capital needs or even negative working capital needs when they request partial payment with the order.

The speculative approach has a number of specific advantages: it enables the firm to offer immediate delivery, it allows for economies of scale (large quantity purchases, manufacturing in large batches) and it enables the firm to organize manufacturing according to its own specific logic. The problem however is that the speculative approach assumes that it is possible to forecast or control demand. As soon as forecasting errors occur, the speculative

Decision variable	Environment variable	Outcome variable: CFOs due to 1993–97 operations						
		1993	1994	1995	1996	1997	1998	Cumulated
The new credit plan is not implemented	and EC does not install new regulations (1)							
	2% growth	−43 682	3 153	3 231	3 292	19 801	36 756	22 551
	10% growth	−47 200	−389	−550	−623	24 620	52 070	27 928
	and EC installs new regulations (2)							
	2% growth	−50 666	7 004	7 079	7 217	28 501	43 005	42 139
	10% growth	−54 574	2 908	3 313	3 626	36 414	61 206	52 892
The new credit plan is implemented	and EC does not install new regulations (3)							
	2% growth	−33 224	1 267	805	817	17 277	22 091	9 033
	10% growth	−35 799	−1 601	−2 333	−2 584	22 463	30 680	10 825
	and EC installs new regulations (4)							
	2% growth	−39 716	4 625	4 652	4 742	25 977	28 340	28 621
	10% growth	−42 766	1 288	1 530	1 665	34 257	39 815	35 790
Impact of the new credit plan when there are no new regulations								
	2% growth	10 458	−1 887	−2 426	−2 475	−2 524	−14 664	−13 518
	10% growth	11 400	−1 212	−1 782	−1 961	−2 157	−21 391	−17 102
when there are new regulations								
	2% growth	10 950	−2 379	−2 426	−2 475	−2 524	−14 664	−13 518
	10% growth	11 809	−1 620	−1 782	−1 961	−2 157	−21 391	−17 102
Impact of the new regulations when there is no new credit plan								
	2% growth	−6 984	3 850	3 848	3 924	8 700	6 249	19 588
	10% growth	−7 375	3 297	3 863	4 249	11 793	9 136	24 964
when there is a new credit plan								
	2% growth	−6 492	3 359	3 848	3 924	8 700	6 249	19 588
	10% growth	−6 966	2 889	3 863	4 249	11 793	9 136	24 964

Figure 9.6 Final results over a 5-year period.

approach has a very poor dynamics. When both the nature and the timing of individual customer orders have not been properly anticipated, keeping the promise of fast delivery generally implies re-work and/or short-notice additional production which might completely disturb the carefully optimized manufacturing schedule and generate substantial additional costs.

Customers' orders pulled, or non-speculative operations exploit the fact that it generally takes less time to purchase and/or manufacture a product than the customer is prepared to wait for it after an order has been placed (for example, a few hours as compared to a few weeks).[6] The advantages of customers' order pulled operations are many:

- Operations can be run in an almost certain environment, which is much easier and cheaper.[7]
- Pressure on operations comes from peaks in customers' demand and not from the 'fire-fighting' climate resulting from not having produced the right thing at the right time. There is little re-work.[8]
- Because of the need for flexibility, operations are generally run in a more decentralized way. They generally rely less on specialists and centralized methods and require less administration. This generally results in an increase in the motivation and the productivity of people.[9]
- More variety can generally be offered to customers.

When adopting the non-speculative approach, companies generally experience very dramatic value improvements.[10]

Reconsidering the problem of Delta Metal

R.T.C. LIBRARY LETTERKENNY

Returning to Delta Metal, it is clear that its low cash generation is due to the fact that it operates in a hostile environment. But the environment does not explain everything and its strategy also has to be questioned. In a fragmented industry like that in which Delta Metal operates, aiming to be big may not be the right strategy since being big does not seem to produce any real advantage. In spite of its size, Delta Metal cannot provide its customers with technical services, cannot increase its prices, cannot achieve greater cost efficiency, cannot shorten delays. In such an industry, a better idea might be to opt for some kind of specialization. Although the environment as a whole is difficult, there are probably certain segments which are easier than others.

- Customers may be less sensitive to prices and delays for some particular types of products. For example a market segment for small orders may exist where product availability is more important than prices or delays in payment. So why not specialize in this kind of segment?
- Some customers may also be less sensitive to prices and payment delays.

Delta Metal should also assess the validity of its business concept. Data in Figure B.4 suggest that it might be better to operate as a broker than as a stockist in this industry. When they are able to forecast, customers buy direct from suppliers who provide them with a better and cheaper service. Consequently, the demand that a stockist has to forecast corresponds to those needs that the customers are not able to anticipate themselves. Forecasting is a very difficult business for Delta Metal and mistakes like the one that was made in 1991 (inadequate purchases) seem inevitable. When considering the future, the situation does not seem likely to improve: the long lead times currently imposed by the manufacturers suggest that these companies have started driving their manufacturing with firm customers' orders. With experience, lead times should decrease thus leaving Delta Metal with an ever smaller – and more volatile segment.

On returning to the solution considered by Mr Lauru to improve the cash generation of Delta Metal (the new credit plan), you realize that it does not sound right. The excessive level of accounts receivable certainly has an impact on the low cash generation but these excessively high accounts receivable are only a symptom of a more serious problem: the weakness of Delta Metal vis-à-vis its customers. Consequently, any serious attempt at improving the cash generation of the company should attack its real cause and attempt to change the relative power position of Delta Metal vis-à-vis its customers (and suppliers). Clearly, the new credit plan does not, and has the major disadvantage of giving something away to customers when the requirement is to get more from them. We observe here a classic effect of attacking the symptoms rather than the real cause of a problem: the only effect of removing symptoms is generally to exacerbate the problem.

The conclusion is very straightforward: Mr Lauru should come back to the problem and imagine new alternative actions which could change the power structure in favor of Delta Metal. The worry you may have at this stage (one you will often have when using models) is that we should have questioned the validity of the new credit plan from the outset: had we made a better diagnosis of the cause of the low cash generation of Delta Metal, we might have been able to reject the new credit plan from the beginning, and focus more quickly on finding more effective alternatives. But we have learned a lot during the modelling process: what seems obvious now was not so when we started. We should, however, draw some important lessons from this first modelling experience:

- The formulation of the problem is a key step in the modelling process, as it largely determines the usefulness of the ensuing modelling work. This formulation should include an *assessment of the real cause* of the problem, not an easy task.
- In order to reach an adequate formulation of a problem, it is essential to spend sufficient time and effort in analyzing the present, and past, situations, and to discover some of the key rules which govern the problem. This thinking backward process as it is called by Einhorn and Hogarth,[11] is a challenging activity which requires the ability to use experience and knowledge, the willingness to consider different formulations and explanations of a problem, the desire to challenge the obvious clues and to seek

better ones, and, in the end, the effort to assess the value of the causal chains you have established.

- When you have done this, and only then, you are ready to look into the future or think forward. The paradox of this appears to be that you should almost know the solution before starting to build a model. In a way this is true; modelling can be seen as the activity which enables you to probe your initial solution and understanding, and most often to discover new and better solutions.

- Finally, you should realize that *there are no financial problems but only strategic problems*. When profit and cash generation are low, they signal to you the existence of a strategic problem which can be changed only by strategic actions.

NOTES

1 These results are consistent with what happened at Delta Metal in 1991 (see Figure B.1).

2 Unless otherwise specified, we will use growth for volume growth.

3 It is probably the reason why rapidly growing firms with negative current CFOs generally can easily raise bank debt in order to finance their growth. Over the years, however, banks have discovered that lending to rapidly growing companies is not without risk. As these companies disburse monies before collecting it and continuously increase their disbursements in the hope of selling more, trouble may result from a collapse in the market which can leave these firms with a large volume of goods they have paid for but which they cannot sell.

4 These are the five competitive forces identified by M Porter in *Competitive Advantage*, New York, Free Press (1985) p 6.

5 'Just-in-time' is one of the many expressions used to describe the new approaches to manufacturing that have developed in the Western world as a reaction to the manufacturing challenge created by Japanese companies. Among the many references on new approaches to manufacturing:
R Harmon and L Peterson (1990), *Reinventing the Factory*, The Free Press.
E Goldratt and J Cox (1989), *The Goal*, Gower.
R Hayes, S Wheelwright and K Clark (1988), *Dynamic Manufacturing*, The Free Press.
R Lubben (1988), *Just-in-Time Manufacturing*, McGraw-Hill.
S Shingo (1988), *Non-Stock Production: The Shingo system for continuous improvement*, Productivity Press.
R Hall (1987), *Attaining Manufacturing Excellence*, Dow Jones-Irwin.
K Suzaki (1987), *The New Manufacturing Challenge*, The Free Press.

6 *Competing Against Time*, G Stalk and T Hout, The Free Press, New York, 1990.

7 Meredith J, *The Management of Operations*, John Wiley & Sons, 1987, p 383. 'With all these potential traps in the implementation process it may come as no surprise that fully 80 percent of all attempts to implement computer-based scheduling systems fail to come near their potential. Yet, this is an improvement – 10 years ago 95 percent of them failed!'

8 Refer to the comparison of factory A and factory B in *Dynamic Manufacturing*, R Hayes, S Wheelwright and K Clark, The Free Press, New York, 1988, p 191.

9 As expressed by several authors, one of the key dimensions of the new manufacturing approaches is to integrate people and technologies in more decentralized, learning organizations. As expressed by R Harmon and L Peterson in *Reinventing the Factory*, The Free Press, New York, 1990: 'For superior results, the reorganization of existing plants into multiple, smaller "factories within a factory" is the single most important feature of productivity improvement.'

10 According to G Stalk and T Hout, 'growth rates of three times the average of their industry with two times the industry profit margins are exciting and achievable targets' for the time-based competitors. In *Competing Against Time*, The Free Press, New York, 1990, p 78.

11 Einhorn H and Hogarth R, 'Decision making: going forward in reverse', *Harvard Business Review* (1987) Jan/Feb.

CHAPTER 10

How to Build Cash Flow Models for Strategic Analysis and Planning

10.1 THE NEED TO MODEL THE DYNAMICS OF THE OPERATIONS

The models that we have built are very useful to understand the outcomes of a variety of strategies and of environmental conditions but they do not enable us to answer a fundamental question: what if we adopt a given strategy and sales are lower than expected? In order to answer such a question, we have to build a model that captures the dynamics of the operations[1] ie, a model that recognizes that, at Delta Metal, several cash outflows are not decided based on actual information. Because of the speculative nature of operations, several cash outflows are decided before actual customers' orders are known and are therefore made on the basis of forecasts:

- Purchases are made in anticipation of future customers' orders.
- Part of the operating expenses correspond to resources which are built in order to deal with the level of future activity that is expected.[2]
- Capital expenditures are made with a view to prepare for future activities.
- Etc.

Figure 10.1 shows the outcomes of the final model (see Figure 8.6) when a segmentation strategy is adopted. Mr Lauru now believes that if Delta Metal focuses on the customers that are less sensitive to prices and delays:

- Margins and collection period will improve substantially.
- Annual growth will amount to 8%.
- The loss of marginal customers will cause a 30% drop in sales in 1993.

What would happen if, in 1995, sales should drop by 15% instead of advancing by the expected 8%? Figure 10.2 shows how the model in Figure 8.6 can be changed in order to answer this question.

Results in Figure 10.2 show the impact of a forecasting error in an extreme situation: sales drop by 15% instead of growing by 8% but purchases and operating expenses remain the same as anticipated (ie, at a level consistent with sales increasing by 8%). As it might be excessively pessimistic, this scenario

	A	B	C	D	E	F	G	H
1		1993	1994	1995	1996	1997	1998	Cumulated
2	Growth rate	−0.3	0.08	0.08	0.08	0.08		
3	SALES	81 030	87 512	94 513	102 074	110 240		
4	cgs/sales	0.78	0.75	0.75	0.75	0.75		
5	cgs	63 203	65 634	70 885	76 556	82 680		
6	Operating expenses/sales	0.22	0.12	0.12	0.12	0.12		
7	OPERATING EXPENSES	18 000	10 501	11 342	12 249	13 229		
8	Depreciation	400	400	400	400	400		
9	OPERATIONAL PROFIT BEFORE TAX	−573	10 977	11 887	12 870	13 931		
10	Cumulative profit	−3 627	7 349	19 236	32 106	46 037		
11	OPERATIONAL PROFIT AFTER TAX	−573	7 669	6 538	7 078	7 662		28 374
12	OPERATIONAL CFE	−173	8 069	6 938	7 478	8 062		30 374
13	Receivables open	58 893	27 010	29 171	31 504	34 025	36 747	
14	Collection period	122	122	122	122	122		
15	RECEIVABLES END	27 010	29 171	31 504	34 025	36 747		
16	Inventory open	16 709	16 008	17 289	18 672	20 166		
17	Inventory turn	4.1	4.1	4.1	4.1	4.1		
18	INVENTORY END	16 008	17 289	18 672	20 166	0		
19	Payables open	39 944	20 720	23 649	25 541	27 585	22 094	
20	Payment period	121	129	129	129	129		
21	PAYABLES END	20 720	23 649	25 541	27 585	22 094		
22	CFO	13 186	7 557	5 113	5 507	20 016	14 653	66 032
23	CFO due to 1992 operations	35 658						
24	CFO due to 1993–98 operations	−22 471	7 557	5 113	5 507	20 016	14 653	30 374

Figure 10.1   A segmentation strategy.

should be considered as a starting point and the model can be used in order to simulate:

- The impact of a quicker adjustment to an unexpected drop of activity. You should however not be overoptimistic and assume a quick response time. Several factors actually render a quick reaction very unlikely: as indicated in Figure B.4, steel should be ordered at least 6 months in advance with the manufacturers, Delta Metal wants to keep a 3 month inventory and finally, in a volatile market, *it is difficult to understand the real meaning of a new information*. What does a sudden drop in customers' orders really mean? Is it the start of a new long term trend of the demand? Is it the start of a new cycle? Is it just a temporary delay that will be quickly compensated by an equal increase in orders?
- The impact of possible reactions aimed at counteracting the unexpected decrease in sales. What will be possible to do when the real meaning of the surprise will be fully recognized? Would it be a good idea to repeat the actions taken in 1992 and to offer discounts? Would other actions be possible also? What would be the most effective reaction[3]?

PROCESS FOR CONSTRUCTING THE MODEL

Starting from the model in Figure 10.1

1 Insert a blank column on the left of column D.
2 In D2: −.15
3 Copy C3.C5 to D3.D5
4 In D7: +E7, in D8: +E8
5 Copy C9.C12 to D9.D12
6 In D13: +E13
7 Copy C14.C15 to E14.E15

8 In D16: +E16, in D18: +E5+E18−D5
9 In D19: +E19, in D21: +E21
10 Copy C22 to D22
11 Check that with a 8% growth, you get the same CFO as expected in 1995: 5113
12 Erase columns G, H and I, as well as ranges A23.I24 and F6.F22

RESULTS:

	A	B	C	D	E	F	G	H
1		1993	1994		1995	1996		
2	Growth rate	−0.3	0.08	−0.15	0.08	0.08		
3	SALES	81 030	87 512	74 385	94 513	102 074		
4	cgs/sales	0.78	0.75	0.75	0.75	0.75		
5	cgs	63 203	65 634	55 789	70 885	76 556		
6	Operating expenses/sales	0.22	0.12		0.12			
7	OPERATING EXPENSES	18 000	10 501	11 342	11 342			
8	Depreciation	400	400	400	400			
9	OPERATIONAL PROFIT BEFORE TAX	−573	10 977	6 855	11 887			
10	Cumulative profit	−3 627	7 349	14 204	19 236			
11	OPTATIONAL PROFIT AFTER TAX	−573	7 669	3 770	6 538			
12	OPERATIONAL CFE	−173	8 069	4 170	6 938			
13	Receivable open	58 893	27 010	29 171	29 171			
14	Collection period	122	122	122	122			
15	RECEIVABLES END	27 010	29 171	24 795	31 504			
16	Inventory open	16 709	16 008	17 289	17 289			
17	Inventory turn	4.1	4.1	1.7	4.1			
18	INVENTORY END	16 008	17 289	33 768	18 672			
19	Payables open	39 944	20 720	23 649	23 649			
20	Payment period	121	129		129			
21	PAYABLES END	20 720	23 649	25 541	25 541			
22	CFO	13 186	7 557	−6 041	5 113			
23								
24								

Figure 10.2 What if sales are 15% less than expected?

10.2 THE VALUE OF INCREMENTAL APPROACHES

In Part III we have pursued two goals, solving Delta Metal's problems and learning how to model cash flows. The approach we adopted has enabled us to attain both goals, in particular the second one, but what if we had only tried to reach the first? Would it have been possible to solve Delta Metal's problem more quickly?

The approach we followed made us simulate each time all the cash flows of the company. Was this really necessary?

■ When you consider the impact of the new credit plan, you realize that it only

affects the sales and the receipts from sales, so why not limit the analysis to these factors and assess how they change the total cash generation?
- When you consider the new EC regulations, you realize that they also have an impact on only a limited number of factors, so, again, why not limit our analysis to these factors?

Let us see how we could have analyzed the impact of the new credit plan[4] using an incremental approach. The only thing we want to assess is the difference between CFOs with the new credit plan and CFOs without it. This difference is equal to the difference between receipts from sales in the two situations:

- Without the new credit plan, cash receipts from sales are equal to sales + receivables open − receivables end (receivables end being estimated from the collection period in Figure 8.2, situation 1).
- With the new credit plan, cash receipts from sales are equal to sales + receivables open − receivables end + tax gain on discount. Sales in this case are to be discounted by 4%; accounts receivables end are to be estimated from the collection period in Figure 8.2, situation 3. The tax gain on discount is due to the need to take into account the fact that the decrease in revenues due to the discount will also cause a decrease in taxable income.
- Cash receipts from sales without and with the new credit plan, as well as the incremental cash flows caused by the new credit plan, are shown in Figure 10.3.

Figure 10.3 shows the format of a spreadsheet model. The formulas to be entered in column B are the following:

$$B6 : 115\ 757*(1+B5)$$
$$B10: +B6/12*B9$$
$$B12: +B6+B8-B10$$
$$B17: +B6*(1-\$B\$16)$$
$$B18: 0.45*B6*\$B\$16$$
$$B22: +B17/12*B21$$
$$B24: +B17+B20-B22+B18$$
$$B26: +B24-B12$$

Except for B6 these formulas can be copied across. Formulas have to be entered in column C for sales and receivables open:

$$C6 : +B6*(1+\$B\$5)$$
$$C8 : +B10$$
$$C9 : +B9$$
$$C20: +B22$$
$$C21: +B21$$

The results in Figure 10.1 are very close to those in Figure 8.7,[5] but they have

	A	B	C	D	E	F	G	H
1		1993	1994	1995	1996	1997	1998	Cumulated
2								
3	CASE WITH NO NEW CREDIT PLAN							
4								
5	Growth	0.02						
6	Sales	118 072	120 434	122 842	125 299	127 805		
7								
8	Receivables open	58 893	59 036	60 217	61 421	62 650	63 903	
9	Collection period	6	6	6	6	6	0	
10	Receivables end	59 036	60 217	61 421	62 650	63 903	0	
11								
12	RECEIPTS FROM SALES	117 929	119 253	121 638	124 071	126 552	63 903	
13								
14	CASE WITH NEW PLAN							
15								
16	Discount	0.04						
17	New sales	113 349	115 616	117 929	120 287	122 693		
18	Tax gain on discount	2 215	2 168	2 211	2 255	2 300		
19								
20	Receivables open	58 893	45 340	46 246	47 171	48 115	49 077	
21	Collection period	4.8	4.8	4.8	4.8	4.8	0.0	
22	Receivables end	45 340	46 246	47 171	48 115	49 077	0	
23								
24	RECEIPTS FROM SALES	129 028	116 877	119 215	121 599	124 031	49 077	
25								
26	DIFFERENCE	11 099	−2 376	−2 423	−2 472	−2 521	−14 825	−13 517

Notes
Global column width: 7. Column A: 22.
In order to get the same results as in Figure 8.7 (solution where the new EC regulations are
implemented, – and Oelta pays taxes), you have to enter the following values for the collection periods:
183/365*12 and 147/365*12.

Figure 10.3 Evaluating the new credit plan: an incremental approach.

been obtained at the price of far less effort. *We hope that this will convince you about the value of incremental approaches, which we recommend you to use as often as possible.*

One further advantage of incremental approaches is that, since they focus on the problem at stake (should we implement the new credit plan?), they can help you to perform some further analysis easily.

- If the new credit plan is not attractive as it stands, which combinations of discount and collection period would be desirable?
- Does our analysis give a fair chance to the new credit plan? When you think about it, the new credit plan is aimed at bringing the collection period down to four months. In our model, we have estimated CFOs on a yearly basis and consequently we have estimated the end collection period at 4.8 months. This gives a fair evaluation of the annual CFOs but may not be a fair estimate of the impact of the new credit plan which is going to pull the monthly

receipts two months forward. A better estimate of the impact of the new credit plan could therefore be obtained by setting the collection period at four (see page 242, for a discussion of this issue).

10.3 MODELLING CASH GENERATION: A DIFFICULT EXERCISE

In Part III, we have developed a general framework for estimating the annual cash generation in a firm. Although this model is generally valid, it should be used with care and the results generated should always be checked against common business sense and theory.

You should always bear in mind that annual CFO *is a very volatile variable*. Minor changes in the level of activity and in working capital needs' parameters may result in brutal short term variations of the annual CFO. The higher the working capital needs are in relation to profit, the more sensitive the CFO. As the volatility of CFO is a fact of life, management has to control it very closely, as is done in all well managed companies. For the modeller, however, CFO is not an easy outcome variable to deal with as it is very easy to make estimation errors.

In order to avoid estimation errors, we recommend that you:

- *Remember that the difference between CFO and profit (or, more exactly CFE) is only a matter of timing.* Consequently, even though you should use CFO as the outcome variable of your models, you should always keep track of two key intermediate variables, profit after tax and CFE. You should always analyze CFO over a long enough and *finite period* of time and check that your model satisfies the basic relationship:

Cumulative CFO = Cumulative CFE

- Be very careful when estimating the value of working capital needs parameters:
  - · Remember that, if accounts receivable and payable end are related to past events, inventory end is primarily future related.
  - · Be careful when estimating working capital needs from average sales, cgs and purchase figures; seasonal factors may introduce significant biases.
  - · Be careful with rounding off approximations.
- *Remember that annual CFO is the cumulative sum of monthly CFOs.* Consequently, it is often a good idea to invest some time in the analysis of the monthly cash generation curve which can tell you about:
  - · The existence of short term cash deficits and excesses.
  - · The significance of the annual CFO. A positive annual CFO can hide large cash deficits during the year.

- *Finally, be critical with the results you get* and always probe them before you use them. Alternative models similar to the ones we built (volume–price model, monthly model, simplified model) enable you to generate CFOs with different approaches and to:
  · Check that your results are correct.
  · Understand the implicit assumptions you have made.

10.4 STEPS FOR BUILDING CASH FLOW MODELS

At the end of this first section, devoted to financial model building for strategic analysis, let us review the successive steps we took. They can be described as follows:[6]

1. Diagnosing the problem

In real business life, there are no problems, there are just problems perceived by managers. Managers are responsible for defining them. In management the word problem defines a situation which satisfies three conditions:[7]

- A manager thinks there are alternative courses of action available.
- That the choice made can have a significant effect.
- That there is some doubt about which alternative should be selected.

This definition has some very important implications.

- As problems are in the eye of the beholder, their definition may well change with his/her understanding of the situation.
- Problems do not necessarily have a negative connotation. Managers have problems when they want to get rid of a difficulty, and also when they want to take advantage of an opportunity.

Diagnosing a problem is not only a matter of identifying the problem (or the opportunity). In order to build an effective model, you need to start from a well documented diagnosis. The diagnosis should define:

- The real nature of the problem.
- The nature of its cause.
- The goal to attain.
- Alternative solutions.

There are many different ways to overcome a problem. Drawing again on Ackoff, a problem may be resolved, solved or dissolved. *Resolving* a problem is selecting a course of action which looks good enough. *Solving* is choosing the best possible course of action. *Dissolving* it is changing the nature of the environment in which the problem is embedded so as to suppress the problem itself. In management, we are primarily interested in resolving problems (finding sufficiently good solutions) but, as the analysis of Delta Metal has shown, considering how the problem can be dissolved instead is often much more productive. The real problem at Delta Metal is not to resolve the accounts receivable problem, it is, rather, to rethink the overall strategy.

2. Constructing an initial paper and pencil model

This model helped us to identify the various parameters and intermediate variables as well as their relationships. It also helped us to generate a first set of numerical outputs which we subsequently used in order to test our spreadsheet model. In order to build this model, we used the cash flow statement format that helped us to structure the problem quickly. We also used the methology of the influence diagram which helped us to formalize some relationships. As soon as this first model was built, we checked that its result was consistent with our understanding of the situation.

3. Transferring the paper and pencil model on to a spreadsheet

A mechanical phase in which you should check the results each time you make a computer entry rather than waiting until the end to discover your mistakes.

4. Checking the initial spreadsheet model, checking for mistakes and making improvements

After making sure that the spreadsheet was returning the same result as the paper and pencil model, we tried to do some dynamic verifications. Does the model return the result we expect when we assign a new value to a specific parameter? During this process, we realized that the tax calculation should be improved, and did so. The good thing about spreadsheet software is that you can easily make such improvements. *It is better to start off simply and progressively refine your approach.*

5. Evaluating new alternatives, discovering new problems, trying alternative routes

As soon as we were *confident enough* in our model, we started using it to test the alternatives identified in the initial diagnosis. Before actually using the model, we prepared a game plan showing:

- The alternatives to be evaluated.
- The values of the different parameters for each of the alternatives.

When evaluating the parameters, we realized that, due to the structure of the initial model, estimating the value of some parameters was not easy. This led us to design a first alternative model describing explicitly the volume and price components of items such as sales, inventories, cgs, etc. (Further Models III.1). This alternative model helped us to:

- Understand the complexity of the impact of changes in prices and volume.
- Check that the values of the parameters used in the initial model were correct.

When analyzing the results for the different alternatives, we realized that a proper analysis of the situation required a longer time horizon. We therefore decided to extend our one-year spreadsheet model to several more years.

6. Extending the initial model to several more years, analyzing the results and checking for mistakes again

When analyzing the results of the multi-annual model we realized that the CFOs of the first two years were fairly different from the subsequent ones. This made us recognize that:

- The decision and the environmental changes under study had different effects in the short and the long term. Modelling a problem helps you learn about it.
- The model we had generated results that were not easy to explain in years one and two.

As a result of the difficulties in interpreting the results of years one and two, we tried a monthly model aimed at helping us to understand the short term effects of the decision and of the environmental change (see Further Model III.2). The construction of this new model made us realize that one implicit assumption of the initial model ie that extra purchases were spread out evenly over the year, was not necessarily realistic and that we had been ignoring the impact of seasonal factors.

7. Making a decision

Having gained confidence in our multi-annual model, we were able to use it for the purpose for which we built it, assessing the desirability of the new credit plan. When assessing the credit plan, we discovered a key dimension of the problem. *The new credit plan does not help us to generate more cash, it only helps us accelerate cash generation.* We decided to verify this concept with a simplified volume-growth model. This model, which is described in Further Model III.3, enabled us:

- To find results similar to the initial model (we used this in order to check the new model).
- To gain a better understanding of the interplay of some fundamental factors governing our problem.

Building models is a process aimed at developing our understanding of strategic problems. When doing so we should always remember Ackoff's aphorism that the greater the understanding we have of a system, the fewer variables we shall need to describe it. Simple models are the ultimate goal of model building.

The great advantage of simple models is that, since they are easy to manipulate, they enable you to explore more alternatives or, in other words, to explore a *wider space* in the environment of your decision.

8. Probing the decision: back to the initial diagnosis

Why does the new credit plan look unattractive?[8] Returning to the diagnosis helped us to realize that the credit plan did not attack the real cause of the low cash generation at Delta Metal. Consequently, new alternatives had to be imagined.

9. Reflecting on the dynamics of the operations

A simple question like 'What if sales were lower than expected?' is not always easy to answer. It requires that your models capture the dynamics of the operations: what are the cash flows which are decided before customers' orders are known? How does the process of adjusting these cash flows work? How are surprises recognized? How long does it take adequately to recognize new information? What can be done when surprises have been recognized?

10. Looking back and realizing there was a much shorter route for getting the results

According to Polya, *looking back* is the fourth and last phase of problem solving.[9] When you have obtained a solution, it is a good idea to look back: can you derive the result differently? Can you see the argument at a glance? Can you use the result or the method for some other problem?

Our approach to the problem was to simulate the total situation of Delta Metal in different conditions. An incremental approach would have been much more effective and we would like to recommend that you always try to define your problems in incremental terms.

This long process requires a lot of patience, thought and the proper mental attitudes.[10] It also suggests some further comments.

1. There is no such thing as a uniquely best model for any specific management decision

On the contrary, you should be aware that, for any specific management decision, the model (or models) used will generally depend on the manager who makes the analysis. The model used will largely depend on the user's understanding of:

- The nature of the problem.
- The nature of the variables and the parameters.
- The nature of their relationships.

This understanding will in turn probably depend on factors such as the business sense of the manager involved, his/her experience, the time he/she is prepared to devote to the analysis, etc.

2. Model building is a very subjective exercise

- *Do not delegate model building to subordinates and/or specialists.*
- *Do try alternative models.* Alternative models help you to check your results, realize your implicit assumptions and understand how the results are generated. Three recommendations at this level:
  · Always check that alternative models give the same result.
  · Do not start building alternative models too early.
  · Do not discard your base model too easily, but be ready to abandon it if need be.

3. The results of models should always be tested against commonsense and experience

It is clear that models are of the most use when they show results indicating that business sense and experience are leading to the wrong conclusion. It is only in such cases that models can lead you to real breakthroughs. You should always keep in mind, however, that such situations are rather exceptional. As a consequence, we recommend that you be very careful each time a model seems to show revolutionary results, and before you accept such results, always try to understand it, and why commonsense or theory could be wrong.

4. Model building is a step-by-step process

Each step makes you learn more about the situation. In order to benefit fully from this learning, *we recommend that you pause after the completion of each step, recognise the learning achieved, and imagine the further progress.* As stated by Ackoff in *The Art of Problem Solving*: 'Art is both creative and recreative. Recreation is the extraction of pleasure here and now; a reward for past efforts. It provides the pause that refreshes and by doing so recreates the creator. Art also produces an unwillingness to settle for what we have.'

Modelling invites you to pay a lot of attention to the process which leads you to decisions: making good decisions is not only a matter of making an adequate, or rational, choice among alternatives but also a matter of generating these alternatives and their consequences through an adequate and sufficiently disciplined process.[11] In many cases it is this process which is the most important.

5. Using alternative representations of the problem can be a great help

Spreadsheets offer you the opportunity to graph variables. Do not forget about this opportunity; use it to gain new perspectives.

6. Model building is a learning process

With models you learn about the problems you have identified, and, it is to be hoped, this learning should make you realize in the end that you could have built much simpler and more powerful models. Never get emotionally attached to your models; be prepared to scrap them and adopt better ones.

7. But effective learning requires feedback

As phrased by J R Anderson:[12] 'Whether the accuracy of the performance improves depends on whether the system can make reliable internal judgements about correctness and so inform the discrimination mechanism. Internal or external feedback is necessary for discrimination but not for strengthening. Both discrimination and strengthening are necessary for improving accuracy; only strengthening is necessary for improving speed.' The good news with spreadsheet models is that it is relatively easy to find a solution to any problem. The bad news is that this solution might be wrong and that spreadsheets can lead you to find the same wrong solution in different situations, and can therefore reinforce decisions based on inadequate skill. This is why it is of paramount importance that you organize your own feedback processes. Does the result make sense? Can it be understood by other people? Is it consistent with theory?[13]

NOTES

1 Operations or 'Industrial' dynamics studies the impact of time delays on the performance of organizations. Pioneering work in this area was made by J Forrester in *Industrial Dynamics*, Productivity Press, 1961.

2 A useful approach is to break costs into variable and fixed costs. Variable costs correspond to those costs which automatically increase or decrease with the level of activity (ie, which are automatically adjusted in case of an unexpected change of activity). Fixed costs correspond to those costs which increase or decrease as a result of a decision.

3 Financial models do not capture the dynamics operations easily. Useful alternative models are the ones proposed by system dynamics like DYNAMO, a PC software of Pugh Roberts Associates, Five Lee Street, Cambridge, MA. See also: *System Enquiry*, E Wolstenholme, 1990, John Wiley & Sons.

4 We leave the analysis of the impact of the new EC regulations to you. It is fair to say that it is more complex than the new credit plan.

5 The difference between the results of Figure 10.1 and Figure 8.7 is due to:
- The value of the collection periods.
- The impact of corporation tax:
  - · The incremental approach ignores the effect of carrying forward the 1992 loss: you can check that the incremental approach gives exactly the same result as the global approach when the new EC regulations are implemented (in this latter case, Delta Metal pays corporation tax in 1993).
  - · When the new EC regulations are not implemented, the global approach shows that the credit plan does not cause any reduction in tax in 1993 (and CFO is consequently lower than that shown by the incremental approach). This reduction is actually postponed to 1994 (which makes CFO higher than that estimated by the incremental approach).

6 You can also refer to the summary of Key Learning Points.

7 This definition is taken from R Ackoff, 'The art and science of mess management', *Interfaces*, **11**(1), 1981.

8 One thing to realize, however, is that we do not yet have the proper criterion for assessing the value of this credit plan. Such a criterion will be developed in Part IV.

9 The three other phases are: understanding the problem; devising the plan; and carrying out the plan. *How to Solve It?* G Polya, Princeton University Press and Penguin Books (1945 and 1990).

10 Among the attitudes which help in the modelling process, we can quote three from J Adams (1979), *Conceptual Blockbusting – A Guide for Better Ideas*, WW Norton:
- The *appetite for chaos* – 'In a sense, problem solving is bringing order to chaos. A desire for order is therefore necessary. However the ability to tolerate chaos is a must.'
- The *ability to incubate* – until a good solution appears.
- The ability to have a questioning attitude or to develop a *constructive discontent*.

11 H Simon, in 'Rationality as process and as product of thought', *Econometrica*, May 1978, stresses the importance of procedural rationality as opposed to substantive rationality. Procedural rationality aims at improving 'the effectiveness, in light of human cognitive powers and limitations, of the procedures used to choose actions'.

12 In *The Architecture of Cognition*, Harvard University Press (1983).

13 Reflection on model building very rapidly raises questions about how our mind works. If you are interested in exploring this issue further, an introduction to cognitive psychology is offered in: L Bourne, R Dominowski, E Loftus and A Heavy, *Cognitive Processes*, Prentice Hall (1986).

Further Models III

FURTHER MODEL III.1
A VOLUME–PRICE MODEL

Items like sales, purchase, cgs, etc, are the result of the product of two factors, volume and unit price.[1] When building financial models you have the choice between estimating, sales purchases, cgs, etc at an aggregate level as is done in Part III, or calculating these same figures from explicit estimates of the corresponding volumes and unit prices.

The problem with working at an aggregate level is that the consequences of changes in volume and price are complex, and this complexity is increased because changes in volume and price have different impacts (see Further Model III.3).

An alternative is to make explicit the volume and unit price factors in your model. This requires:

- Some additional data: the volume and unit price data for Delta Metal are given in Figure III.1(a).

- In 1992, Delta Metal sold 4 148.99 tons at an average price of 27.9 thousand FFR.
- In 1992, the average purchase price of a ton of steel was 22.32 thousand FFR, the price at which the 748.61 tons of the ending inventory were valued.
- In the event that the new EC regulations are not implemented, Delta Metal expects that these average selling and purchase prices will not change in 1993. In order to simplify his simulation exercise, Mr Lauru further assumed that these prices will not change after 1993 if market conditions remain the same.
- When preparing his simulations, Mr Lauru further assumed that, if they take place, changes in EC regulations and collection reduction plan will occur as from 1 January 1993
- Finally, Mr Lauru assumed that operating expenses will grow proportionally with the volume of sales.

Figure III.1(a) Volume and unit price data.

■ An alternative model: the inputs for such a model (using Lotus 1-2-3 notations) are given in Figure III.1(b). The process for extending this model over several more years is described in Figure III.1(c).

	A	B	C	D
1			1993	
2		VOLUME	UNIT PRICE	VALUE
3	Volume growth rate	0.02		
4	Change selling price	0		
5	Change purchasing price	0		
6	SALES	4 148.99*(1+B3)	27.9*(1+B4)	+B6*C6
7	Inventory open	748.61	22.32	16 709
8	Inventory turnover	4		
9	INVENTORY END	+B6/B8	+C10	+B9*C9
10	PURCHASES	+B6+B9−B7	22.32*(1+B5)	+B10*C10
11	CGS			+D10+D7−D9
12	OPERATING EXPENSES			115 757*0.14*(1+B3)
13	Depreciation			400
14	OPERATIONAL PROFIT BEFORE TAX			+D6−D11−D12−D13
15	Cumulative profit bef. tax			+D14−3 054
16	OPERATIONAL PROFIT AFTER TAX			†
17	CFE			+D16+D13
18	Receivables open			58 893
19	Collection period			365/2
20	RECEIVABLES END			+D6/365*D19
21	Inventory open			+D7
22	INVENTORY END			+D9
23	Payables open			39 944
24	Payment period			365/3
25	PAYABLES END			+D10/365*D24
26	CFO			‡

† @IF(D14<0, D14, @IF(D15<D14, @IF(D15>0, D14−0.45*D15, D14), 0.55*D14))

‡ +D17+D18−D20+D21−D22−D23+D25

Note: Use abbreviations for labels when you enter your model on to a spreadsheet.

Fig. III.1(b) Inputs for a volume–price model.

Notes on Figure III.1(b)

The model assumes that inventories are valued according to the FIFO method (first in, first out), and the volume of sales is always superior to the volume of opening inventory.

Analyzing the results

You can check that the results given by this model are the same as those given in Figures 6.3 and 7.3.

You may want to generate the results of the four simulations we ran in

You can display three years simultaneously on the screen provided that you fix the width of column A at 9 characters, the width of columns B, E and H at 8, the width of columns C, F and I at 6 and the width of columns D, G and J at 7. These column widths allow for a two digit format for volume and unit price figures and an integer format for total figures.

The easiest way to extend the model is to:

First copy the range B3.D26 into a range starting in E3 (with Lotus 1-2-3, you just have to specify E3 as the target)

Then correct what has been copied in the range E3.G26 by typing:

$$+B3 \text{ in } E3$$
$$+B6*(1+E3) \text{ in } E6$$
$$+C6*(1+E4) \text{ in } F6$$
$$+B9 \text{ in } E7$$
$$+C9 \text{ in } F7$$
$$+E7*F7 \text{ in } G7$$
$$+B8 \text{ in } E8$$
$$+C10*(1+E5) \text{ in } F10$$
$$+D12*(1+E3) \text{ in } G12$$
$$+G14+D15 \text{ in } G15$$
$$+D20 \text{ in } G18$$
$$+D19 \text{ in } G19$$
$$+D25 \text{ in } G23$$
$$+D24 \text{ in } G24$$

You can then copy the model over one, or several more, years. In order to extend it to 1995, you just have to copy the range E3.G26 into H3.

You can then input the years in F1 and I1 and recopy the labels in the range B2.D2.

In order to see both the top of the model and the CFOs, you can make an horizontal window in row 19.

Finally, you can introduce a calculation of cgs/sales in C11, F11 and I11 and of inventory turnover in C22, F22 and I22. These calculations will show you that the cgs and inventory turnover figures are not exactly the same in 1993 as they are in subsequent years.

Figure III.1(c) Extending the model over several more years.

When volume growth is 2%:

1 No new credit plan, no new EC regulations:
    base model
2 No new credit plan, new EC regulations:
    change in purchasing price: $-0.06/0.8$
    inventory turnover: 3
3 New credit plan, no new EC regulations:
    change in selling price: -0.04
    collection period: $365/12*4$
4 New credit plan, new EC regulations:
    change in selling price: -0.04
    change in purchasing price: $-0.06/0.8$
    inventory turnover: 3
    collection period: $365/12*4$

Figure III.1(d) Parameters for the four simulations.

Chapters 6 to 8, with the model we have just developed. In order to do so, you have to enter the parameters shown in Figure III.1(d) in this model. These simulations will help you check that our estimates of the cgs/sales and operating expenses/sales ratios were correct.

Which of the two models should you use?

Neither the model presented in Chapters 6 and 7 nor the one we have just developed are without disadvantages.

- The model presented in Chapters 6 and 7 has a more simple structure but it requires more care when estimating the value of the parameters. When estimating these values you may make mistakes.
- The model we have just developed has a more complex structure that may be cumbersome when you prepare multi-annual simulations. It also requires more data. You are however, less exposed to mistakes when estimating the value of the parameters.

	Volume	1993 Unit price	Value
SALES	760	65.10	49.48
PRODUCTION LEVEL	960		
OPEN INVENTORY RAW MATERIAL	159	14.78	2.35
END INVENTORY RAW MATERIAL	159	11.00	1.75
PURCHASES RAW MATERIAL	960	11.00	10.56
COST RAW MATERIAL	960	11.63	11.16
PRODUCTION LABOR	960	17.59	16.89
ENERGY, ETC.	960	14.00	13.44
PRODUCTION OVERHEADS	960	3.42	3.28
DEPRECIATION	960	1.55	1.49
COST OF GOODS MANUFACTURED	960	48.19	46.26
OPEN INVENTORY FINISHED GOODS	387	45.47	17.60
END INVENTORY FINISHED GOODS	587	48.19	28.29
CGS	760	46.80	35.57
GROSS MARGIN			13.90
ADMINISTRATIVE COSTS			6.51
INTEREST			8.69
DEPRECIATION			0.35
PROFIT BEFORE TAX			−1.65
TAX			0.0
PROFIT AFTER TAX			−1.65
DEPRECIATION			1.84
CFE			0.19
INVENTORY OPEN			19.95
INVENTORY END			30.04
RECEIVABLES OPEN			28.53
COLLECTION PERIOD			200
RECEIVABLES END			27.11
PAYABLES OPEN			3.52
PAYMENT PERIOD			0.90
PAYABLES END			2.60
TAX PAYABLE OPEN			2.11
TAX PAYABLE END			0.00
CFO			−11.50

Figure III.1(e) Outputs of a model for a manufacturing activity.

Deciding which kind of model to use is a matter of recognizing the complexity of the simulation problem you are confronted with.

- When simulating the cash flows related to a trading activity in which unit prices are relatively stable you will probably prefer the model presented in Chapters 6 and 7.
- When simulating the cash flows related to a business activity in which unit prices are unstable, you will probably prefer a volume–price model. Volume–price models are very useful for analyzing *manufacturing activities*. An example of such a model for a manufacturing activity is given below. The outputs of the model are shown in Figure III.1(e), and the relationships are described in Figure III.1(f).

Notes on Figure III.1(e)
- The production volume commands the volume of all items related to production; the sales volume commands the volume of cgs.
- Production labour, production overheads and depreciation are fixed costs. Their total cost is fixed but their unit cost depends on the level of activity.
- Energy costs are variable; their unit cost is fixed and their total cost depends on the volume of activity.
- Inventories are valued at FIFO and the calculation of the unit costs of ending inventories are valid provided that purchases of raw material and production are not too low.
- The volume of ending inventories is not determined by an inventory turnover but rather by the target level of ending raw materials inventory, the volume of production and the volume of sales.
- Production volume figures are defined in terms of 'equivalent production' that is in terms of equivalent of one completed unit of product. Consistently, finished goods inventories include both finished products and work in process.

NOTE

1 Actually the product of *average volume* by *average unit price*. As the product mix may change over years an effective model may require you to break down accounting items like sales, purchases, cgs, etc into homogeneous product groups.

	A	B	C	D
1			1993	
2		Volume	Unit price	Value
3	SALES	760	65.10	+B3*C3/1 000
4				
5	PRODUCTION LEVEL	960		
6	OPEN INVENTORY RAW MATERIAL	159	14.78	+B6*C6/1 000
7	END INVENTORY RAW MATERIAL	159	+C8	+B7*C7/1 000
8	PURCHASES RAW MATERIAL	+B5+B7−B6	11.00	+B8*C8/1 000
9	COST RAW MATERIAL	+B5	+D9/B9*1 000	+D6+D8−D7
10	PRODUCTION LABOR	+B5	+D10/B10*1 000	16.89
11	ENERGY, ETC	+B5	14.00	+B11*C11/1 000
12	PRODUCTION OVERHEADS	+B5	+D12/B12*1 000	3.28
13	DEPRECIATION	+B5	+D13/B13*1 000	1.49
14	COST OF GOODS MANUFACTURED	+B5	+D14/B14*1 000	+D9+D10+D11+D12+D13
15	OPEN INVENTORY FINISHED GOODS	387	45.47	+B15*C15/1 000
16	END INVENTORY FINISHED GOODS	+B15+B5−B3	+C14	+B16*C16/1 000
17	CGS	+B3	+D17/B17*1 000	+D14+D15−D16
18	GROSS MARGIN			+D3−D17
19	ADMINISTRATIVE COSTS			6.51
20	INTEREST			8.69
21	DEPRECIATION			0.35
22	PROFIT BEFORE TAX			+D18−D19−D20−D21
23	TAX			@IF(D22>0,0.5*D22,0)
24	PROFIT AFTER TAX			+D22−D23
25	DEPRECIATION			+D13+D21
26	CFE			+D24+D25
27	INVENTORY OPEN			+D6+D15
28	INVENTORY END			+D7+D16
29	RECEIVABLES OPEN			28.53
30	COLLECTION PERIOD			200
31	RECEIVABLE END			+D30*D3/365
32	PAYABLES OPEN			3.52
33	PAYMENT PERIOD			90
34	PAYABLES END			+D33*D8/365
35	TAX PAYABLE OPEN			2.11
36	TAX PAYABLE END			+D23
37	CFO			*

* +D26+D27−D28+D29−D31−D32+D34−D35+D36

Figure III.1(f) Relationships in a model for a manufacturing activity.

FURTHER MODEL III.2
A MONTHLY CASH GENERATION MODEL

The purpose of a monthly model

As indicated above, the model developed in Part III may not be completely adequate for estimating the cash generation of the company in the short term (one to two years).

Let us explore how we can build a monthly model for Delta Metal and then compare its results with the ones generated by the model developed in Part III.[1]

Further data about Delta Metal

The monthly sales, purchases and operating expenses for Delta Metal in 1993, 1994, and 1995 are shown in Figure III.2(a).

Complementary data are given in Figure III.2(b).

Building a monthly cash generation model

The general structure of a monthly model with a three-year time horizon is shown in Figure III.2(c). The entries to be made for 1993 are described in Figure III.2(d).

Notes on Figures III.2(c) and (d)
- The process for building the model is first, construct the model for 1993, then extend it to 1994 and 1995, and finally construct the summary in range A21.D40.
- An alternative entry for the monthly purchases is to have a formula estimating them as 80% of the sales three months ahead (from March 93 onwards[2]): in D5: 0.8*G2. This way to calculate purchases is much better as it guarantees the consistency of the model. If you adopt it, note that the estimation of purchases at year end requires figures for sales in the subsequent year.
- Check that cumulative monthly CFO as at the end of December is equal to CFO in the cash flow statement.

In order to extend the model to 1994 and 1995, you can:

- Copy the labels for the months.
- Enter formulas for sales: +B2*1.02 in N2; copy to the range O2.AO2.
- Copy the formula for receipts in M4 in the range N4.AK4.
- Enter a formula for purchases in N5: 0.8*Q2; copy across.
- Copy the formula for payments in the range N7.AK7.

	Jan	Feb	Mar	Apr	May	Jun	Jul	Aug	Sep	Oct	Nov	Dec	Total
1993													
Sales	9 900.1	9 000	9 900	9 900	10 100	10 000	6 400	5 172	12 000	11 000	12 000	12 700	118 072
Purchases	11 400	10 931	8 000	5 120	4 138	9 600	8 800	9 600	10 160	8 078	7 344	8 078	101 249
Operating expenses	1 200	1 220	1 240	1 260	1 290	1 320	1 360	1 380	1 400	1 420	1 800	1 640	16 530
1994													
Sales	10 098	9 180	10 098	10 098	10 302	10 200	6 528	5 275	12 240	11 220	12 240	12 954	120 434
Purchases	8 078	8 242	8 160	5 222	4 220	9 792	8 976	9 792	10 363	8 240	7 491	8 240	96 817
Operating expenses	1 224	1 244	1 265	1 285	1 316	1 346	1 387	1 408	1 428	1 448	1 836	1 673	16 861
1995													
Sales	10 300	9 364	10 300	10 300	10 508	10 404	6 659	5 381	12 485	11 444	12 485	13 213	122 842
Purchases	8 240	8 406	8 323	5 327	4 305	9 988	9 156	9 988	10 570	8 405	7 641	8 405	98 753
Operating expenses	1 248	1 269	1 290	1 311	1 342	1 373	1 415	1 436	1 457	1 477	1 873	1 706	17 198

Notes
Sales in 1994 are calculated as 1.02 * sales in 1993, sales in 1995 as 1.02 * sales 1994.
Purchases are calculated as 80% of the sales three months ahead, starting March 1993.
Purchases in January and February 1993 are higher due to the necessity to build up stocks.
Operating expenses in 1994 are calculated as 1.02 * operating expenses in 1993, etc.

Figure III.2(a) Monthly data.

Payments related to accounts receivable and payable as of
31 December 1992:

Accounts receivable:		58 893
to be received in:		
January 1993	6 293	
February	5 800	
March	12 000	
April	10 900	
May	11 900	
June	12 000	
Accounts payable		39 944
to be paid in:		
January 1993	10 200	
February	10 000	
March	9 800	
April	9 944	

Other payments:
　　Operating expenses are paid for in cash
　　Corporation tax is paid within the year in four equal
　　instalments (March, June, September and December)

Figure III.2(b) Further data.

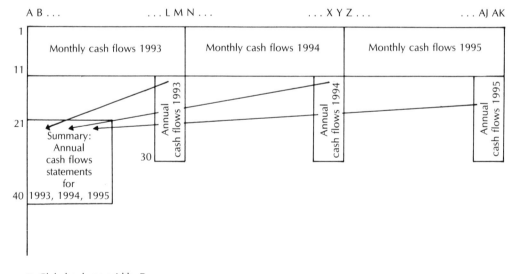

- Global column width: 7
- Global format: fixed, 0 decimal.

Figure III.2(c) General structure of a monthly model.

- Enter a formula for operating expenses: +B8*1.02 in N8; copy across.
- Enter formulas for taxes in March, June, etc. In 1994, the formula is $Y$21/4, in 1995 +$AK$21/4.
- Copy the formula for CFO.
- Enter new formulas for cumulative CFO: +N10 in N11, +N11 + O10 in O11; copy across. This will enable you to cumulate CFO on a yearly basis. Do the same for 1995.
- Copy the annual cash flow statements:
  - Copy range L12.M30 into range X12.Y30.
  - Correct inventory open: +M15 in Y13.
  - Correct cumulative profit: +Y19+M20 in Y20.
  - Correct receivables open: +M25 in Y24.
  - Correct payables open: +M29 in Y28.
  - Copy range X12.Y30 into range AJ12.AK30.
- Finally, if you have not yet done so, a good idea is to enter a formula for purchases in 1993 (starting in March): 0.8*G2 in D5; copy across.

In order to build the summary:

- Copy the labels from range L12.L30 into range A22.A40.
- Enter years in B21, C21 and D21.
- Enter into B22: +M12, into C22: +Y12 and into D22: +AK12.
- Copy the range B22.D22 into range B23.B40.

Comparing the results with those obtained in Chapter 7

The results of the monthly model are shown in Figure III.2(e) and III.2(f). They are compared in Figure III.2(g) with the results generated by the model developed in Chapter 7.

As shown in Figure III.2(f), the two models do not produce the same CFO estimates, in particular in 1993 and 1994. Why is this so?

- The difference in the results of the two models is due to their estimations of ending accounts receivable, inventory and accounts payable; this is shown in Figure III.2(g).[3]
- The model in Chapter 7 estimates ending receivables, inventory and payables on the basis of average daily sales, average cost of goods sold and average daily purchases and therefore ignores the impact of seasonality. Furthermore, this model assumes that the additional purchases made to replenish the inventory are distributed evenly throughout 1993.
- The monthly model:
  - Estimates the accounts receivable at the end of December as the sum of the sales actually made in the last six months (July to December). Due to the seasonal character of the activity at Delta Metal, sales made during the

second semester are slightly more than half of annual sales (0.502 instead of 0.500).

· Estimates the inventories at the end of December as the sum of the purchases made over the last three months (October to December). These purchases are related to the sales Delta Metal expects to make in January, February and March in the subsequent year. Because of the three months' inventory delay, Delta Metal buys in October what it expects to sell in January, in November what it expects to sell in February, and so on. Because of the seasonal character of the business, and in spite of the growth expected, the sum of the purchases over the last quarter of the year is slightly less than a quarter of annual cgs (0.249 v 0.250). The idea that inventory is future-related is a very important one: *inventory is not what you are left with* (even though this may happen if you fail) *but what you have bought/produced to prepare future sales.*

· Further assumes that the additional purchases made in order to build up the inventory with the objective of bringing its turnover from 5.73 in 1992 to 4.0 in 1993 *are made at the beginning of 1993.* As a consequence, these additional purchases increase the total purchases in 1993 but not the accounts payable at the end of the year. Consequently, accounts payable as at the end of 1993 are less than a third of total purchases in 1993.

The model developed in Chapter 7 can be adjusted:

- Either through changes in the formulas that generate receivables end, inventory end and payables end.
- Or through changes in the value of the working capital parameters, collection period, inventory turnover and payment period.

The easiest way is probably to do a bit of both: you can adjust the formulas for calculating inventory end: +C5/B17 in B18; to be copied across; you can then enter the following values for the working capital parameters.

	1993	1994 and afterwards
collection period	183	183
inventory turnover	4.1	4.1
payment period[4]	121	129

When you do so, you get the following values for the annual CFOs:

1993	1994	1995	1996	1997
−8 024	+3 153	+3 231	+3 292	+19 801

(see Fig. 8.2)

	A	B	C	D	E	F	G	H	L	M
1		Jan	Feb	Mar	Apr	May	Jun	Jul	Nov	Dec
2	SALES	9 900.1	9 000	9 900	9 900	10 100	10 000	6 400	12 000	12 700
3	RECEIPTS FROM 1992	6 293	5 800	12 000	10 900	11 900	12 000	10 160		
4	RECEIPTS					+B5		+B2	+F2	+G2
5	PURCHASES	11 400	10 931	8 000	5 120	4 138	9 600		7 344	8 078
6	PAYMENTS FROM 1992	10 200	10 000	9 800	9 944					
7	PAYMENTS									
8	OPERATING EXPENSES	1 200	1 220	1 240	1 260	1 290	1 320	1 360	1 800	1 640
9	TAX			+$M$21/4			+$M$21/4			+$M$21/4
10	CFO	†								
11	CUMULATIVE CFO	+B10	+B11 + C10							

12	SALES	@SUM(B2:M2)
13	INVENTORY OPEN	16 709
14	PURCHASES	@SUM(B5:M5)
15	INVENTORY END	@SUM(K5:M5)
16	CGS	+M13+M14−M15
17	OPERATING EXPENSES	@SUM(B8:M8)
18	DEPRECIATION	400
19	PROFIT BEFORE TAX	‡
20	CUMULATIVE PROFIT	+M19−3 054
21	TAX	‡‡
22	PROFIT AFTER TAX	+M19−M21
23	CFE	+M18+M22
24	RECEIVABLES OPEN	58 893
25	RECEIVABLES END	@SUM(H2:M2)
26	INVENTORY OPEN	+M13
27	INVENTORY END	+M15
28	PAYABLES OPEN	39 944
29	PAYABLES END	@SUM(J5:M5)
30	CFO	§

† +B3+B4−B6−B7−B8−B9

‡ +M12−M16−M17−M18

‡‡ @IF(M19<0, 0, @IF(M20<M19, @IF(M20>0, 0.45*M20, 0), 0.45*M19))

§ +M23+M24−M25+M26−M27−M28+M29

Figure III.2(d) Entries for a monthly model (1993).

	Jan	Feb	Mar	Apr	May	Jun	Jul	Aug	Sep	Oct	Nov	Dec
1993:												
Sales	9 900	9 000	9 900	9 900	10 100	10 000	6 400	5 172	12 000	11 000	12 000	12 700
Receipts from 1992	6 293	5 800										
Receipts from sales			12 000	10 900	11 900	12 000	9 900	9 000	9 900	9 900	10 100	10 000
Purchases	11 400	10 931	8 000	5 120	4 138	9 600	8 800	9 600	10 160	8 078	7 344	8 078
Payments from 1992	10 200	10 000	9 800	9 944								
Payments from purchases					11 400	10 931	8 000	5 120	4 138	9 600	8 800	9 600
Operating expenses	1 200	1 220	1 240	1 260	1 290	1 320	1 360	1 380	1 400	1 420	1 800	1 640
Corporation tax			408			408			408			408
Monthly CFO	−5 107	−5 420	552	−304	−790	−659	540	2 500	3 954	−1 120	−500	−1 648
Cumulative CFO	−5 107	−10 527	−9 975	−10 279	−11 069	−11 729	−11 189	−8 689	−4 735	−5 855	−6 355	−8 003
1994:												
Sales	10 098	9 180	10 098	10 098	10 302	10 200	6 528	5 275	12 240	11 220	12 240	12 954
Receipts from 1993	6 400	5 172										
Receipts from sales			12 000	11 000	12 000	12 700	10 098	9 180	10 098	10 098	10 302	10 200
Purchases	8 078	8 242	8 160	5 222	4 220	9 792	8 976	9 792	10 363	8 240	7 491	8 240
Payments from 1993	10 160	8 078	7 344	8 078								
Payment of purchases	1 224	1 244	1 265	1 285	8 078	8 242	8 160	5 222	4 220	9 792	8 976	9 792
Operating expenses			768		1 316	1 346	1 387	1 408	1 428	1 448	1 836	1 673
Corporation tax						768			768			768
Monthly CFO	−4 984	−4 151	2 623	1 636	2 606	2 344	551	2 550	3 682	−1 142	−510	−2 033
Cumulative CFO	−4 984	−9 135	−6 512	−4 875	−2 269	75	626	3 176	6 857	5 715	5 205	3 172
1995:												
Sales	10 300	9 364	10 300	10 300	10 508	10 404	6 659	5 381	12 485	11 444	12 485	13 213
Receipts from 1994	6 528	5 275										
Receipts from sales			12 240	11 220	12 240	12 954	10 300	9 364	10 300	10 300	10 508	10 404
Purchases	8 240	8 406	8 323	5 327	4 305	9 988	9 156	9 988	10 570	8 405	7 641	8 405
Payments from 1994	10 363	8 240	7 491	8 240								
Payment of purchases	1 248	1 269	1 290	1 311	8 240	8 406	8 323	5 327	4 305	9 988	9 156	9 988
Operating expenses			784		1 342	1 373	1 415	1 436	1 457	1 477	1 873	1 706
Corporation tax						784			784			784
Monthly CFO	−5 084	−4 234	2 675	1 669	2 658	2 390	562	2 601	3 754	−1 165	−520	−2 074
Cumulative CFO	−5 084	−9 317	−6 643	−4 974	−2 316	74	636	3 237	6 992	5 826	5 306	3 232

Figure III.2(e) Results of the monthly model.

	1993	1994	1995
Sales	118 072	120 434	122 842
Inventory open	16 709	23 501	23 971
Purchases	101 249	96 817	98 753
Inventory end	23 501	23 971	24 450
CGS	94 458	96 347	98 274
Operating expenses	16 530	16 861	17 198
Depreciation	400	400	400
Profit before tax	6 685	6 826	6 971
Profit after tax	5 051	3 754	3 834
Receivables open	58 893	59 272	60 457
Receivables end	59 272	60 457	61 667
Inventory open	16 709	23 501	23 971
Inventory end	23 501	23 971	24 450
Payables open	39 944	33 661	34 334
Payables end	33 661	34 334	35 021
CFO	−8 003	3 172	3 232
CFO (as estimated in Figure 7.3)	−7 754	987	3 193

Figure III.2(f) Cash flow statements estimated by the monthly model.

	1992	1993	1994	1995
ACCOUNTS RECEIVABLES END				
Figure 7.3	58 893	59 036	60 217	61 421
Implied collection period		182.50	182.50	182.50
Annual increase		143	1 181	1 204
Monthly model	58 893	59 272	60 457	61 667
Implied collection period		183.23	183.23	183.23
Annual increase		379	1 185	1 209
Difference in the estimates of increase:		236	5	5
INVENTORY END				
Figure 7.3	16 709	23 614	24 087	24 568
Implied inventory turn		4	4	4
Annual increase		6 905	472	482
Monthly model	16 709	23 501	23 971	24 450
Implied inventory turn*		4.1	4.1	4.1
Annual increase		6 792	470	479
Difference in the estimates of increase:		−114	−2	−2
ACCOUNTS PAYABLE END				
Figure 7.3	39 944	33 788	32 273	32 919
Implied payment period		121.67	121.67	121.67
Annual increase		−6 156	−1 515	645
Monthly model	39 944	33 661	34 334	35 021
Implied payment period		121.35	129.44	129.44
Annual increase		−6 283	673	687
Difference in the estimates of increase:		−127	2 188	41
TOTAL DIFFERENCE IN ESTIMATES OF INCREASE		249	−2 185	−39
DIFFERENCE IN CFOs AS ESTIMATED BY THE TWO MODELS		249	−2 185	−39

* Calculated in relation to CGS in subsequent year (4.02 when calculated in relation to current CGS).

Figure III.2(g) Comparison of the estimates.

These new results call for some comment.

- They are not exactly equal to those of the monthly model. In order to get exactly the same results you must enter more precise values for the parameters. This is not really useful.
- The 1997 CFO is very large. This is due to the fact we calculate inventory in relation to future sales. As sales in 1998 are assumed to be zero, the inventory at the end of 1997 is automatically brought down to zero.
- The new values of the parameters are only valid for the base solution. If we want to adjust the model in Chapter 7 for the other situation (new credit plan, new EC regulations), we have to go back to the monthly model and understand the impact of the seasonality in each situation. But before doing so, let us analyze the monthly results.

Analyzing the monthly results

The monthly CFOs as estimated by the model in 1993 and 1994 as well as the evolution of the cumulative CFOs over the year can be shown graphically. This is done in Figure III.2(h) which shows that:

- Normally (in 1994 for example), the annual CFO generation of Delta Metal corresponds to
  - Monthly cash deficits in January, February, October, November and December.
  - Monthly cash excesses in the other months (the cash excess in July being very small).
- In a normal year (1994 again), and if it starts with a zero cash balance, Delta Metal has to borrow until mid-June.
- In 1993 the build-up of inventory makes Delta Metal incur more disbursements at the beginning of the year. If it started with a zero cash balance at the beginning of 1993, it would have to borrow throughout the whole year.

The monthly analysis of the cash generation at Delta Metal suggests some general conclusions.

- In most firms, annual CFOs are not generated at a steady rate over the year.
- Annual CFOs are actually the net results of monthly deficits and excesses.
- Very often these monthly excesses and deficits follow a seasonal pattern.
- When there is such a seasonal pattern, and because this does not change the total cash generation over the year but only its timing:
  - Cash generation in excess of what would be a steady cash generation causes deficits later in the year.
  - Deficits as compared to a steady cash generation cause cash excesses later

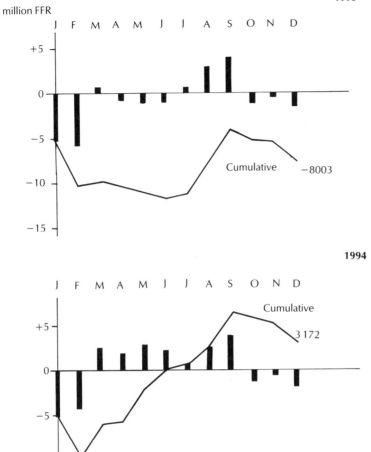

Figure III.2(h) Monthly and cumulative cash generation at Delta Metal.[5]

in the year.

- As the total annual CFO is not affected by these temporary cash excesses or deficits one might thtnk that firms do not care that much about them.
  - In fact, they do. Because deficits should be covered either through debt or through the holding of cash balances, they have a cost which is generally not compensated for by the investment of excess cash balances.
  - As a consequence, when preparing financial plans you should always estimate the annual CFOs and explore the impact of seasonal factors that can cause additional financing costs.

Using the monthly model to simulate alternative situations

New EC regulations

Let us assume that if installed, the new EC regulations will apply from the beginning of January 1993. Let us further assume, as suggested in the case, that these regulations will correspond to subsidized purchase prices.[6] As a result the sales figures will not change, only the purchases figures will. The new purchases figures for 1993, 1994 and 1995 are given in Figure III.2(i).

In order to assess the impact of the new EC regulations, you must enter the values of the purchases shown in Figure III.2(i), or enter new formulas for deriving purchases from expected sales

- In B5 and C5: 11 400/0.8*0.74 and 10 931/0.8*0.74.
- In D5: +G2*0.74 + H2*0.74; in E5: +I2*0.74, copy across.
- Correct the calculation of inventory end in M15, Y15 and AK15.

When you have done so, you get the results shown in Figure III.2(j).

For the model in Chapter 8 to generate similar results, you should run it using the following parameters.

	1993	1994 and afterwards
Collection period	183	183
Inventory turnover[7]	3.05	3.05
Payment period	105	121

New credit plan

In order to assess the impact of the new credit plan (without new EC regulations) you must modify the base monthly model as follows.

	1993	1994	1995
January	10 545†	7 623	7 776
February	10 111‡	7 548	7 699
March	12 136‡‡	4 831	4 927
April	3 827	3 904	3 982
May	8 880	9 058	9 239
June	8 140	8 303	8 469
July	8 880	9 058	9 239
August	9 398	9 586	9 778
September	7 473	7 622	7 774
October	6 793	6 929	7 068
November	7 473	7 622	7 774
December	7 473	7 622	7 774

† 10 545 = 11 400/0.8*0.74
‡ 10 111 = 10 931/0.8*0.74
‡‡ 12 136 = 10 000*0.74+6 400*0.74

Figure III.2(i) Monthly purchases when the new EC regulations are implemented.

	1993	1994	1995
SITUATION (2)			
Sales	118 072	120 434	122 842
Inventory open	16 709	29 211	29 795
Purchases	101 128	89 705	91 499
Inventory end	29 211	29 795	30 391
CGS	88 627	89 121	90 903
Operating expenses	16 530	16 861	17 198
Depreciation	400	400	400
Profit before tax	12 516	14 052	14 341
Profit after tax	8 258	7 729	7 888
Receivables open	58 893	59 272	60 457
Receivables end	59 272	60 457	61 667
Implied collection period	183.23	183.23	183.23
Inventory open	16 709	29 211	29 795
Inventory end	29 211	29 795	30 391
Implied inventory turn*	3.05	3.05	
Payables open	39 944	29 211	29 795
Payables end	29 211	29 795	30 391
Implied payment period	105.43	121.23	121.23
CFO	−14 956	6 943	7 078

* based on CGS in subsequent year.

Figure III.2(j) Cash flow statements: situation 2.

- Introduce a blank row above row 2 and introduce a price discount factor in B2 (this factor will be 1.0 without the new credit plan and 0.96 when the plan is adopted).
- Edit each monthly sales figure in 1993 and multiply it by B2. (A fairly cumbersome task.)
- Then correct the calculation of purchases: +G3*0.8/$B$2 in D6, copy across.
- Then modify the calculation of accounts receivables end in M26, Y26 and AK26.

In order to assess the impact of the credit plan with new EC regulations, start from the model above and introduce the changes caused by the new regulations.

- Enter new values and formulas for monthly purchases: 11 400/0.8*0.74 in B6; 10 931/0.8*0.74 in C6; (G3+H3)*0.74/$B$2 in D6, +13*0.74/$B$2 in E6, copy across.
- Adjust the formulas generating inventory end.

The results associated with the new credit plan are shown in Figure III.2(k).

In order to adjust the model in Chapter 8, you have to use the following working capital parameters.

New credit plan; no new EC regulations

	1993	1994 and afterwards
Collection period	147	147
Inventory turnover[7]	4.1	4.1
Payment period	121	129

New credit plan; new EC regulations

	1993	1994 and afterwards
Collection period	147	147
Inventory turnover[7]	3.05	3.05
Payment period	105	121

What you should note is that, since sales in the last four months of the year are equal to about 40% of yearly sales, accounts receivable end, when the new credit plan is implemented, correspond to more than $365/4 = 122$ average days of annual sales.

Testing the impact of higher growth

We have been able to use the monthly model to estimate the parameters needed for the model in Chapter 8. The problem, however, is that, although these parameters are valid when growth is 2%, they might not be valid for other growth rates. Let us therefore run the monthly model with 10% growth. In order to do so, you can start from the model you built for situation 3 and:

- Insert a row above row 2 and enter a growth factor in B2: 1.02.
- Correct sales:
  · Edit each 1993 sales figure, divide it by 1.02 and multiply it by B2.
  · Enter +B4*$B$2 in N4 and copy across.
- Modify the purchases in January and February 1993; you need only change the February purchases: in C7, enter: @sum(F4.D4)*0.8/B3−(M15+B7−(B4+C4)*0.8/B3)
- Correct operating expenses:
  · In 1993, edit each entry, divide by 1.02 and multiply by B2.
  · In N10, enter: +B10*$B$2; copy across.

When B2 is set to 1.1, you get situation 3 with 10% growth. To obtain situation 1, you have to set the price discount factor to 1 and change the calculation of accounts receivable end. Then, to generate situation 2, you can:

- Change the calculation of purchases:
  · In C7: @sum(F4.D4)*0.74/B3−(M15/0.8*0.74+B7−(B4+C4)*0.74/B3).

	1993	1994	1995
SITUATION (3)			
Sales	113 349	115 616	117 929
Inventory open	16 709	23 501	23 971
Purchases	101 250	96 817	98 753
Inventory end	23 501	23 971	24 450
CGS	94 458	96 347	98 274
Operating expenses	16 530	16 861	17 198
Depreciation	400	400	400
Profit before tax	1 962	2 009	2 057
Profit after tax	1 962	1 596	1 131
Receivables open	58 893	45 792	46 708
Receivables end	45 792	46 708	47 642
Implied collection period	147.46	147.46	147.46
Inventory open	16 709	23 501	23 971
Inventory end	23 501	23 971	24 450
Implied inventory turn	4.10	4.10	
Payables open	39 944	33 661	34 334
Payables end	33 661	34 334	35 021
Implied payment period	121.35	129.44	129.44
CFO	2 388	1 284	804
SITUATION (4)	1993	1994	1995
Sales	113 349	115 616	117 929
Inventory open	16 709	29 211	29 795
Purchases	101 128	89 705	91 499
Inventory end	29 211	29 795	30 391
CGS	88 627	89 121	90 903
Operating expenses	16 530	16 861	17 198
Depreciation	400	400	400
Profit before tax	7 793	9 235	9 428
Profit after tax	5 660	5 079	5 185
Receivables open	58 893	45 792	46 708
Receivables end	45 792	46 708	47 642
Implied collection period	147.46	147.46	147.46
Inventory open	16 709	29 211	29 795
Inventory end	29 211	29 795	30 391
Implied inventory turn	3.05	3.05	
Payables open	39 944	29 211	29 795
Payables end	29 211	29 795	30 391
Implied payment period	105.43	121.23	121.23
CFO	−4 074	4 563	4 651

Figure III.2(k) Cash flow statements: situations 3 and 4.

- In D7: (G4+H4)*0.74/$B$3.
- In E7: +I4*0.74/$B$3; copy across.
- Change the calculation of inventory end.

Finally, to generate situation 4, you can:

- Set the discount factor to 0.96.
- Change the calculation of accounts receivable end.

The results of these models are given in Figure III.2(l).

		1993	1994	1995
The new credit plan is not implemented				
and EC does not install new regulations (1)	SALES	127 333	140 066	154 073
	CGS	101 866	112 053	123 258
	PROFIT AFTER TAX	5 356	4 402	4 864
	CFO	−11 550	−494	−562
	Implied collection period	183.23	183.23	183.23
	Implied inventory turn	4.10	4.10	
	Implied payment period	124.24	133.93	133.93
and EC installs new regulations (2)	SALES	127 333	140 066	154 073
	CGS	95 479	103 649	114 014
	PROFIT AFTER TAX	8 869	9 024	9 949
	CFO	−18 994	3 032	3 318
	Implied collection period	183.23	183.23	183.23
	Implied inventory turn	3.05	3.05	
	Implied payment period	109.98	127.42	127.42
The new credit plan is implemented				
and EC does not install new regulations (3)	SALES	122 239	134 463	147 910
	CGS	101 866	112 053	123 258
	PROFIT AFTER TAX	2 147	1 729	1 475
	CFO	−222	−1 714	−2 352
	Implied collection period	147.46	147.46	147.46
	Implied inventory turn	4.10	4.10	
	Implied payment period	124.24	133.93	133.93
and EC installs new regulations (4)	SALES	122 239	134 463	147 910
	CGS	95 479	103 649	114 014
	PROFIT AFTER TAX	6 068	5 943	6 559
	CFO	−7 258	1 405	1 527
	Implied collection period	147.46	147.46	147.46
	Implied inventory turn	3.05	3.05	
	Implied payment period	109.98	127.42	127.42

Figure III.2(l) Results of the monthly model when growth is 10%.

NOTES

1 Actually, when preparing short term forecasts, financial managers tend to use monthly models.

2 In Figure III.2(a), it is assumed that the additional purchases needed to replenish the inventory are made in January and February 1993.

3 You can also check it by putting into the model of Chapter 7 the end values of receivables, inventory and payables, since these are estimated by the monthly model. When you do so, the model in Chapter 7 generates the same CFOs as the monthly model.

4 Alternatively, you can keep the same value for the payment period over the whole period (129) and change the formula which generates the 1993 ending payables. You can calculate these as 129 days of cgs which is a way of ignoring the purchases corresponding to the replenishment of the inventory.

5 You can generate these graphs with your spreadsheet.

6 Things will probably be a bit more complex as the EC could implement a system enabling stockists to claim a subsidy upon presentation of suppliers' invoices. Within such a system, stockists would probably have to pay suppliers before they get the subsidy.

7 In relation to cgs in the following year.

R.T.C. LIBRARY
LETTERKENNY

FURTHER MODEL III.3
A SIMPLIFIED MODEL TO ASSESS THE IMPACT OF GROWTH[1] AND INFLATION – USING THE DATABASE FACILITIES OF LOTUS 1-2-3

The analysis[2]

During each period (a year, a month, etc) the operations generate an amount of cash which is equal to the difference between the cash receipts related to the operations and the disbursements related to these same operations.

Operational cash receipts: credit to customers, growth and inflation

As soon as credit is extended to customers, cash receipts lag behind sales. When sales are constant over months this lag is immaterial, but when sales are growing, the fact that receipts lag behind sales makes *each month's cash receipts lower than sales.*

When sales are growing at a constant rate, the cash receipts in a designated month are equal to:

$$CR = \frac{S}{(1 + gr)^{cp}}$$

where:

CR = cash receipts in a designated month
S = sales made during the same month
gr = monthly growth rate of sales
cp = collection period (in months)
(all parameters assumed constant)

This formula shows that, as soon as sales grow:

- For the same growth, the longer the collection period, the lower the receipts in relation to sales.
- For the same collection period, the higher the growth, the lower the receipts in relation to sales.

When there is *growth and inflation* the cash receipts become even lower as inflation has the same effect as growth. When there is constant inflation and growth, cash receipts in a designated month are equal to:

$$CR = \frac{V}{(1 + gr)^{cp}} * \frac{usp}{(1 + ir)^{cp}} = \frac{S}{(1 + gr)^{cp}(1 + ir)^{cp}}$$

where:

CR = cash receipts in a designated month
V = volume sold in this month
usp = unit selling price in the same month
gr = monthly growth rate
ir = monthly inflation rate
cp = collection period (in months)

This formula can also be expressed as follows:

CR = Sales * Adjustment for growth * Adjustment for inflation

where:

CR = cash receipts in a designated month
Sales = sales in the same month
$\dfrac{\text{Adj. for}}{\text{growth}} = \dfrac{1}{(1 + gr)^{cp}}$ (This factor is less than 1 as soon as there is growth and a positive collection period.)
$\dfrac{\text{Adj. for}}{\text{inflation}} = \dfrac{1}{(1 + ir)^{cp}}$ (This factor is less than 1 as soon as there is inflation and a positive collection period.)

This formula highlights the impact of growth and inflation. They both reduce the cash receipts as compared with sales; the longer the collection period, the bigger the reduction.

Operational cash disbursements: inventories, growth and inflation

Without inventories and delays in paying suppliers (payment period), the operational cash disbursements are equal to the sum of:

- The purchases that are necessary to make the sales.
- The other expenses.

The existence of an inventory in a trading company reflects the fact that it has to purchase not in relation to current sales but in relation to future sales. *The existence of an inventory therefore causes the disbursements related to purchases to lead on sales.* When sales are constant, this lead has no impact, but, when there is growth, the lead makes the disbursements higher than they would have been if they had been due to the current sales. When sales grow at a constant rate, purchases in a designated month are equal to:

$$\text{PUR} = V * (1 + gr)^{id} * \text{upp} = V * \text{usp} * \frac{\text{upp}}{\text{usp}} * (1 + gr)^{id}$$

$$= S * \frac{\text{upp}}{\text{usp}} * (1 + gr)^{id}$$

where:

PUR = purchases made in a designated month
V = volume sold during the same month
gr = monthly growth rate
id = inventory delay (in months)
upp = unit purchasing price
usp = unit selling price
S = sales made during the same month

What happens when there is growth and inflation? The existence of inflation has no impact provided that the company is able to increase its prices freely. If a company anticipates, in a given month, a growth in volume and an increase in prices over the following months, it will buy more than the level of its current sales *but these purchases will be made at the current price.* So, with growth and inflation, purchases in a designated month are equal to:

$$\text{PUR} = S * \frac{\text{upp}}{\text{usp}} * (1 + gr)^{id}$$

where:

PUR = purchases made in a designated month
gr = monthly growth rate
id = inventory delay (in months)
upp = unit purchasing price
usp = unit selling price
S = sales made during the same month

Operational cash disbursements: credits from suppliers, growth and inflation

The existence of a payment period makes the cash disbursements lag behind the purchases. *Inventories and payment period result in a combined lead and lag.* This combined effect may result in a net lead, a perfect match or a net lag. Again, without growth and inflation, this net lead or lag is immaterial but, when sales grow at a constant rate, the operational cash disbursements in a designated month are equal to:

$$CD = V * \frac{(1 + gr)^{id}}{(1 + gr)^{pp}} * upp = V * usp * \frac{upp}{usp} \quad \frac{(1 + gr)^{id}}{(1 + gr)^{pp}}$$

$$= S * \frac{upp}{usp} * \frac{(1 + gr)^{id}}{(1 + gr)^{pp}}$$

where:

   CD = cash disbursements in a designated month
    V = volume sold during the same month
   gr = monthly growth rate
   id = inventory delay (in months)
   pp = payment period (in months)
  upp = unit purchasing price
  usp = unit selling price
    S = sales made during the same month

When there is growth and inflation, the net lead or lag shown above is changed again and the operational cash disbursements in a designated month are equal to:

$$CD = V * \frac{(1 + gr)^{id}}{(1 + gr)^{pp}} * \frac{upp}{(1 + ir)^{pp}} = V * usp * \frac{upp}{usp} \quad \frac{(1 + gr)^{id}}{(1 + gr)^{pp}(1 + ir)^{pp}}$$

$$= S * \frac{upp}{usp} * \frac{(1 + gr)^{id}}{(1 + gr)^{pp}} * \frac{1}{(1 + ir)^{pp}}$$

where:

   CD = cash disbursements in a designated month
    V = volume sold during the same month
   gr = monthly growth rate
   ir = monthly inflation rate
   id = inventory delay (in months)
   pp = payment period (in months)
  upp = unit purchasing price
  usp = unit selling price
    S = sales made during the same month

The formula can also be expressed as

   CD = Sales * Adjustment for margin * Adjustment for growth * Adjustment for inflation where:

CD = cash disbursements in a designated month

Sales = sales in the same month

$$\text{Adjustment for margin} = \frac{upp}{usp}$$ (As goods are purchased at a lower price than that at which they are sold, disbursements are systematically lower than receipts.)

$$\text{Adjustment for growth} = \frac{(1 + gr)^{id}}{(1 + gr)^{pp}}$$ (This factor can be lower or higher than 1, depending on the relationship between the inventory delay and the payment period.)

$$\text{Adjustment for inflation} = \frac{1}{(1 + ir)^{pp}}$$ (This factor is less than 1 as soon as there is inflation and a positive payment period: *note that the inventory delay has no effect at this level.*)

The formula shows that

- Normally, the cash disbursements are lower than the receipts (because of the margin adjustment).
- A long inventory delay counteracts this difference and may even offset it.
- The payment period in turn counteracts the impact of inventory delay.

Cash generated from the operations when there is growth and inflation

Since, in a designated month, cash generated from the operations is equal to the difference between receipts and disbursements, the general formula with growth and inflation is shown in Figure III.3(a).

$$\text{CFO} = \overbrace{\frac{V * usp}{(1 + gr)^{cp} * (1 + ir)^{cp}}}^{\text{Cash receipts}} - \underbrace{V * usp * \frac{upp}{usp} * \frac{(1 + gr)^{id}}{(1 + gr)^{pp} * (1 + ir)^{pp}} - V * usp * \frac{Oe}{S}}_{\text{Cash disbursements}}$$

where: CFO = cash from operations in a designated month
 V = volume sold in the same month
 usp = unit selling price in the same month
 gr = monthly growth rate in sales
 cp = collection period (in months)
 ir = monthly inflation rate
 upp = unit purchasing price in the same month
 id = inventory delay (in months)
 pp = payment period (in months)
 Oe = other operating expenses divided by sales.
 (assumed to be paid for in cash)
(all parameters assumed constant)

Figure III.3(a) Formula for calculating CFO.

The formulas in Figure III.3(a) can also be expressed as in Figure III.3(b).

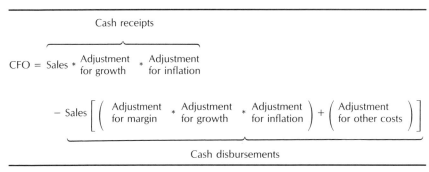

Figure III.3(b) Formula for calculating CFO, alternative expression.

When collection period, inventory delay and payment period exist:

- Growth and inflation reduce cash receipts (adjustments for inflation and growth being less than 1).
- Growth and inflation also increase cash disbursements (adjustment for inflation and growth being more than 1).

The net result of growth and inflation may therefore lead to a situation where cash disbursements are higher than receipts and cash from operations negative. Obviously, as shown by Figure III.3(b), the smaller the margin, the greater the risk that cash from operations becomes negative.

A spreadsheet model

The model

The format of a spreadsheet model is described in Figure III.3(c). The data which reflect the situation at Delta Metal in January 1995 are shown in Figure III.3(d) and the formulas in Figure III.3(e).

Corporation tax

If paid without delay, corporation tax is equal to:

$$(\text{Sales} - \text{purchases} - \text{other expenses}) \times \text{tax rate}$$

This way of accounting for corporation tax is not valid, however, when there is inflation. We considered above that, when there is inflation, inventory holdings are neutral. This corresponds to the fact that inventory increases are cancelled out by equivalent decreases in cgs. This is true when there is no corporation tax but not when there is, as the decrease in cgs due to inflation causes an increase in the corporation tax. *As a result, inventory holdings are generally no longer neutral when there is inflation and corporation tax.*

In Figure III.3(e), corporation tax is adjusted for the decrease in cgs due to inflation, this decrease in cgs being equal to the increase in inventory. When

	A	B	C	D
1	MONTHLY SALES	10 144.2		
2	PURCHASING/SELLING PRICE	0.8		
3	OTHER EXPENSES/SALES	0.14		
4	growth rate (monthly)	0.0017	YEARLY GROWTH RATE	0.02
5	inflation rate (monthly)	0.0000	YEARLY INFLATION RATE	0.00
6	COLLECTION PERIOD (MONTHS)	6		
7	INVENTORY DELAY (MONTHS)	3		
8	PAYMENT PERIOD (MONTHS)	4		
9	=============================		=============================	
10	SALES OF THE MONTH	10 144.20		
11	GROWTH ADJUSTMENT	0.99	profit/sales	0.03
12	INFLATION ADJUSTMENT	1.00	=============================	
13	RECEIPTS OF THE MONTH	10 044.25	adjustment of receipts	0.99
14	CGS ADJUSTMENT	0.80		
15	GROWTH ADJUSTMENT	1.00		
16	INFLATION ADJUSTMENT	1.00	adj for cgs, grth & inf	0.80
17	OTHER EXPENSES ADJUSTMENT	0.14	adj for other exp.	0.14
18	ADJUSTMENT FOR TAX	0.03	adj for tax	0.03
19	DISBURSEMENTS OF THE MONTH	9 796.06	adjustment of disburst	0.97
20	CFO	248.19	cfo/sales	0.02

Width of columns: global: 9, A:30, C:22.

Figure III.3(c) Format of a spreadsheet model.

- As the model assumes that sales are evenly spread out over the year, we have to use a *theoretical amount of sales in January 1995*. Let us make this amount equal to 10 144.2.* We can check that if sales are 10 144.2 in January and then increase by 0.1651% per month (or 2% per year), sales for the whole of 1995 are equal to 122 842 – the same figure as in Figure 8.6
- Other data are: purchasing/selling price   0.80

              other expenses/sales   0.14

              annual growth rate   0.02

              annual inflation rate   0.00

              collection period   6.00

              inventory delay   3.00

              payment period   4.00

  ie the data that correspond to situation 1 (no new EC regulations and no new credit plan).

* As shown in Further Model IV.1 (p 222), the formula for calculating January 1995 sales is:

$$115\ 757 * (1.02)^3 * \frac{(1.02)^{1/12} - 1}{(1.02) - 1}$$

Figure III.3(d) Initial data.

there is inflation, tax is also increased, due to the fact that depreciation, as it relates to equipment bought in the past, decreases in proportion to profit before tax. This effect is not taken into account in Figure III.3(e).

A1:	[W30] "MONTHLY SALES		C12:	[W22] ' =========================
B1:	10 144.2		A13:	[W30] "RECEIPTS OF THE MONTH
A2:	[W30] "PURCHASING/SELLING PRICE		B13:	(F2) +B10*B11*B12
B2:	0.8		C13:	[W22] 'adjustment of receipts
A3:	[W30] "OTHER EXPENSES/SALES		D13:	(F2) +B11*B12
B3:	0.14		A14:	[W30] "CGS ADJUSTMENT
A4:	[W30] "growth rate (monthly)		B14:	(F2) +B2
B4:	(F4) (1+D4) ∧ (1/12)−1		A15:	[W30] "GROWTH ADJUSTMENT
C4:	[W22] 'YEARLY GROWTH RATE		B15:	(F2) ((1+B4) ∧ B7)/((1+B4) ∧ B8)
D4:	(F2) 0.02		A16:	[W30] "INFLATION ADJUSTMENT
A5:	[W30] "inflation rate (monthly)		B16:	(F2) 1/((1+B5) ∧ B8)
B5:	(F4) (1+D5) ∧ (1/12)−1		C16:	[W22] 'adj for cgs, grth & inf
C5:	[W22] 'YEARLY INFLATION RATE		D16:	(F2) +B14*B15*B16
D5:	(F2) 0		A17:	[W30] "OTHER EXPENSES ADJUSTMENT
A6:	[W30] "COLLECTION PERIOD (MONTHS)		B17:	(F2) +B3
B6:	6		C17:	[W22] "adj for other exp.
A7:	[W30] "INVENTORY DELAY (MONTHS)		D17:	(F2) +B17
B7:	3		A18:	[W30] "ADJUSTMENT FOR TAX
A8:	[W30] "PAYMENT PERIOD (MONTHS)		B18:	(F2) 0.45*(1−B2/((1+B5) ∧ B7)−B3)
B8:	4		C18:	[W22] "adj for tax
A9:	[W30] "=============		D18:	(F2) +B18
A10:	[W30] "SALES OF THE MONTH		A19:	[W30] "DISBURSEMENTS OF THE MONTH
B10:	(F2) +B1		B19:	(F2) (B10*((B14*B15*B16)+B17))+B10*B18
A11:	[W30] "GROWTH ADJUSTMENT		C19:	[W22] 'adjustment of disburst.
B11:	(F2) 1/((1 + B4) ∧ B6)		D19:	(F2) +D16+D17+D18
C11:	[W22] 'profit/sales		A20:	[W30] "CFO
D11:	(F2) (1−B2/((1+B5) ∧ B7)−B3)*(1−0.45)		B20:	(F2) +B13−B19
A12:	[W30] "INFLATION ADJUSTMENT		C20:	[W22] "cfo/sales
B12:	(F2) 1/((1+B5) ∧ B6)		D20:	(F2) +D13−D19

Figure III.3(e) Formulas of a spreadsheet model.

Testing the validity of the spreadsheet model

The model generates a figure of 248.19 for the January 1995 CFO. This corresponds to 2.45% of sales. When this percentage is applied to the 1995 sales, it leads to an annual CFO equal to 3 006 in 1995. As shown in Figure 8.6, the model developed in Part III estimates the 1995 CFO at 3 231. The difference of 225 between the two estimates is due to

- The fact that our new model ignores the impact of depreciation. This corresponds to a difference of 180, depreciation*tax rate.
- The fact that working capital parameters of the model developed in Figure 8.6 do not adequately reflect the impact of growth. For example, when there is growth, accounts receivable end with a six month collection period are slightly more than half of the annual sales.

As a consequence, and if we want the model developed in Figure 8.6 to generate the same results as the new model, we have to adjust the value of the working capital parameters.[3] The new values of the working capital parameters to be entered in the model in Figure 8.6 are:[4]

Collection period	183.40
Inventory turnover	4.03
Payment period	122.47

When this is done and when depreciation is set to zero, both models give similar results, and *we can now consider that our new model is valid and use it in order to gain a better understanding of the impact of growth and inflation. As this model is easier to manipulate than the one developed in Chapters 7 and 8, we can expect it to accelerate our learning.*

Using the new spreadsheet model to learn more about the impact of inflation and growth

You can first check that, when there is no growth or inflation, the collection period, inventory delay and payment period do not matter. In order to check this, all that needs to be done is to make yearly growth equal to zero. Whatever are the values of the collection period, inventory delay and payment period, monthly CFO is equal to 335.

You can then initialize the model and check the impact of a higher volume growth rate. The impact of different growth rates on the CFO are given in Figure III.3(f).[5]

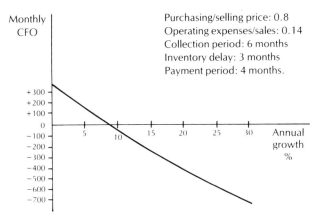

Figure III.3(f) Impact of volume growth on CFO.

As shown in Figure III.3(f), Delta Metal cannot sustain a growth higher than 8% in the conditions of 1995. With a 10% annual growth, monthly CFO is equal to about −73. Since the growth may be equal to 10% in 1995, it is

In order to keep the January 1995 CFO equal to about 250 with a 10% growth, you need to have one of the following:

> Purchasing/selling price ≈ 0.741
> Operating expenses/sales ≈ 0.082
> Collection period ≈ 1.85 months
> Payment period ≈ 9.2 months

By making inventory delay equal to 0, you can only bring CFO up to 116.

Figure III.3(g) Conditions needed to maintain the same annual CFO with higher growth.

possible to discover the values of:

Purchasing/selling price
Operating expenses/sales
Collection period
Inventory delay
Payment period

that would be needed in order to keep CFO at the same level as with a 2% annual growth, ie about 250. The results are shown in Figure III.3(g) and confirm the difficulties facing Delta Metal.

- In order to sustain a 10% growth, the conditions in which the company operates must be dramatically changed. It must seek either higher profitability (six percentage points more) or a much shorter collection period (two months instead of six), or a combination of both.
- As the environment in France probably does not enable Delta Metal to shorten its collection period to two months, the priority is to increase the profitability which probably means that Delta Metal must drastically change its strategy (see Chapter 9).

You can also check that in the conditions in which it currently operates, Delta Metal is highly exposed to the unfavorable impact of inflationary growth. In order to check this, you can initialize the model, make volume growth nil and annual inflation equal to 10%. In these conditions, monthly CFO becomes equal to 30 instead of 335 with no volume gowth and no inflation, or −73 with 10% per year volume growth and no inflation. As the model assumes that inflation has no impact related to inventory holding, inflationary growth decreases CFO generation less than volume growth. However, if prices suddenly increase, Delta Metal will suffer and this will be true even if it is able to increase its selling prices at the same rate as that of its purchase prices increase. In order not to be affected by inflation, Delta Metal should either increase its selling prices more quickly than its purchase prices, or it should improve its working capital parameters, or it should succeed in doing both.

You can also use the model to test the impact of the working capital

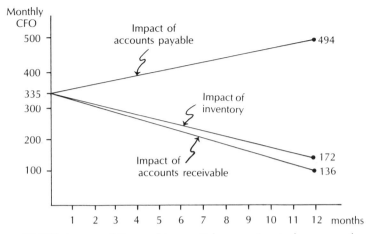

Figure III.3(h) Impact of the working capital parameters (volume growth only).

parameters on the cash generation. Figure III.3(h) demonstrates the impact of different values of working capital parameters within the conditions of January 1995 (sales = 10 144.2, purchasing/selling price = 0.8, operating expenses/ sales = 0.14, annual growth rate = 0.02 and annual inflation = zero). This shows that the parameter with the most unfavorable impact is the collection period. This is generally true, but not always. You can also use the model to check that, when equal to inventory delay, the payment period exactly offsets the inventory delay. Finally, you can use the model to check the impact of the working capital parameters when there is growth and inflation.

Using the data and graph facilities of Lotus 1-2-3[6]

The graph shown in Figure III.3(f) may be generated very quickly with Lotus 1-2-3. In order to do so, proceed as follows:

- Retrieve the new model.
- Set growth rate and inflation rate to zero.
- Construct a table showing the CFOs corresponding to different growth rates. Let us assume that you want to show in the range A21 to A27 annual growth rates ranging from zero to 0.3 and, in the range B21 to B27, the corresponding CFOs.
- In order to do so, first fill up the A21 to A27 range with the values of the growth rate. You can use the Data Fill command:
  · Position the cursor in A21.
  · Type: / D (data) F (fill).

· Enter the fill range: A21.A27 [R].
· As you want to start at zero, press [R] again.
· As you want increments or steps to be equal to 0.05, type: 0.05 [R].
· As you want to stop before 8 191, press [R] again.

■ You now have to make Lotus 1-2-3 calculate the CFOs which correspond to each of these growth rates.
· In B21 type: +B20 (the outcome variable) [R].
· position the cursor in A21 and type: / D (data) T (table) 1 (1 input)
· Enter the table range: A21.B27 [R].
· Enter the input cell (the parameter): D4 [R].

You now have the CFOs that correspond to the growth rates displayed in the range A21 to A27.

■ If you want to display the graph shown in Figure III.3(d)
· Position the cursor in B21.
· Type: / G (graph) T (type) L (line) in order to have a line graph.
· Type A B21.B27 [R].
· Type: V (view) to view the graph.

■ A precaution: fix the value of the CFO which corresponds to a zero growth rate. In order to do so, type 334.76 in B21.

NOTES

1 In Further Model III.3, growth means *volume growth*.

2 This model is derived from the analysis presented in Chapter 9 (refer in particular to Figures 9.3 and 9.4). It applies to *trading activities* but could be extended to manufacturing activities.

3 The idea is the same as in Further Model III.2. The rationale for the adjustment is different however.
· In Further Model III.2, the adjustments aim at reflecting seasonal effects, the timing of a decision and of a change in the environment.
· Here, the adjustment aims at making the model generate the same results as a theoretical model ignoring seasonal effects but enabling us to understand better the long-term or structural impact of growth and inflation on annual CFOs.

4 As shown in Further Model IV.1 (page 222), you can derive the value of the working capital parameters as follows:
· *collection period*:

$$\text{collection period} = \frac{\text{July to December 1995 sales}}{1995 \text{ sales}} * 365$$

$$\frac{\text{July to December 1995 sales}}{1995 \text{ sales}} = \frac{\dfrac{(1 + gr)^{12} - 1}{gr} - \dfrac{(1 + gr)^{6} - 1}{gr}}{\dfrac{(1 + gr)^{12} - 1}{gr}} = \frac{(1 + gr)^{6}}{(1 + gr)^{6} + 1}$$

where gr = monthly growth rate = $1.02^{\frac{1}{12}} - 1$

collection period = $\dfrac{(1 + gr)^6}{(1 + gr)^6 + 1} * 365 \simeq 183.40$

· *Inventory turnover*:

inventory turnover = $\dfrac{1995 \text{ cgs}}{\text{October to November 1995 purchases}}$

$$= \dfrac{\dfrac{(1 + gr)^{24} - 1}{gr} - \dfrac{(1 + gr)^{12} - 1}{gr}}{\dfrac{(1 + gr)^{15} - 1}{gr} - \dfrac{(1 + gr)^{12} - 1}{gr}} = \dfrac{(1 + gr)^{12} - 1}{(1 + gr)^3 - 1} \simeq 4.03$$

· *Payment period*:

payment period = $\dfrac{\text{September to December 1995 purchases}}{1995 \text{ purchases}} * 365$

$$\dfrac{\begin{array}{c}\text{September to December}\\ 1995 \text{ purchases}\\ \hline 1995 \text{ purchases}\end{array}} = \dfrac{\dfrac{(1 + gr)^{12} - 1}{gr} - \dfrac{(1 + gr)^8 - 1}{gr}}{\dfrac{(1 + gr)^{12} - 1}{gr}} = \dfrac{(1 + gr)^{12} - (1 + gr)^8}{(1 + gr)^{12} - 1}$$

payment period = $\dfrac{(1 + gr)^{12} - (1 + gr)^8}{(1 + gr)^{12} - 1} \simeq 122.47$

5 The graph shown in Figure III.3(f) can be generated quickly by using the Data and Graph facilities of Lotus 1-2-3. Please refer to the end of this Further Model.

6 Data table facilities exist in Excel (one-input tables) and in Quattro (what-if tables). Refer to respective manuals.

FURTHER MODEL III.4
A MODEL FOR GENERATING THE FINANCIAL STATEMENTS OF
DELTA METAL

The model described in Chapters 7 and 8 can be extended to generate the financial statements of Delta Metal. In order to do so, you must:

■ Complete the cash flow statement by introducing the non–operating cash inflows and outflows (cash flows related to debt, capital expenditures, dividends and new external financing).

■ Use the variables in the cash flow statement for generating
  · the income statements
  · and the balance sheets.

■ Introduce an iterative feature for the calculation of interest.

The background of a model for generating the financial statements of Delta Metal is shown in Figure III.4(a). The foreground of the model is shown in Figure III.4(b). An alternative approach to the same problem is presented in Figure III.4(d).

Introducing the financing required

Introduce an iterative feature for interest:

> In B23: 0.15*((B53+B56)+(27 172+2 245+4 699))/2
> In C23: 0.15*((C53+C56)+(B53 + B56))/2. Copy across.

When this is done, the model shows the following cash figures in the balance sheet:

	1993	1994	1995	1996	1997	1998
Cash	−14 328	−16 363	−18 729	−18 896	−2 337	30 343

These figures are not acceptable, and new external financing is required in order to make the cash balances positive. In order to keep the cash balance at a level close to its end-1992 level (256), and if you assume that all new external financing will be new short-term loans, you have to enter the following values:

	1993	1994	1995	1996	1997	1998
New short term debt	15 800	4 350	4 550	2 750	−15 000	−33 700

One interesting thing to note when you enter the short-term debt required is that, because of interest, you have to input more new debt than the cash deficit to be financed. When you have entered the amounts of new short-term debt shown above, you get the results displayed in Figure III.4(c).

Analyzing the results

Results in 1997 and 1998 should be analyzed separately as they show an hypothetical situation: what would happen if Delta Metal stopped its activity in 1998? Over the period 1993 to 1996, the results are very poor.

- Profits are very low and, except for 1993, operational profits are lower than interest charges.
- Net worth decreases each year and, as additional debt is required each year, the debt to net worth ratio increases steadily. . . . It might well happen that the banks would refuse to continue lending to Delta Metal.

The hypothetical balance sheet as at the end of 1998 is worth analysis. If Delta Metal were to stop its activity at the end of 1998, and assuming that fixed assets could be sold at their book value and other current assets and other current liabilities could be liquidated for amounts equal to their book value, then shareholders would be left with about 5 million, about half of the net worth at the end of 1992. So why not stop the activity immediately?

An alternative approach

One difficulty with the approach in Figure III.4(a) is the calculation of corporation tax. As the first stage, a theoretical sum for tax is calculated in relation to the result of operations. Then, when interest is known, the tax impact of interest is calculated. In order to avoid this difficulty, you can introduce interest in the calculation of profit. This approach is shown in Figure III.4(d). Although this approach removes the difficulty related to the tax calculation, we do not recommend that you use it as it mixes operational and financial items.

Notes on Figure III.4(a)
1. From the model in Figure 7.1.
2. Interest is assumed to remain the same as it was in 1992. This is an initial assumption.
3. In B26: @IF(B24<0, 0, @IF(B25<B24, @IF(B25>0, 0.45*B25, 0), 0.45*B24)). To be copied across.
4. It is assumed that long term debt will be totally reimbursed over the next four years: 2 245 in 1993, 1994 and 1995 and the remaining balance, 209 in 1996.
5. Capital expenditures in 1991 and 1992 were higher; let us assume that 1 000 is sufficient to sustain the operations.
6. As an initial assumption let us consider that dividend, new equity and new debts are equal to zero.
7. As previously assumed, other current assets and liabilities will not change.

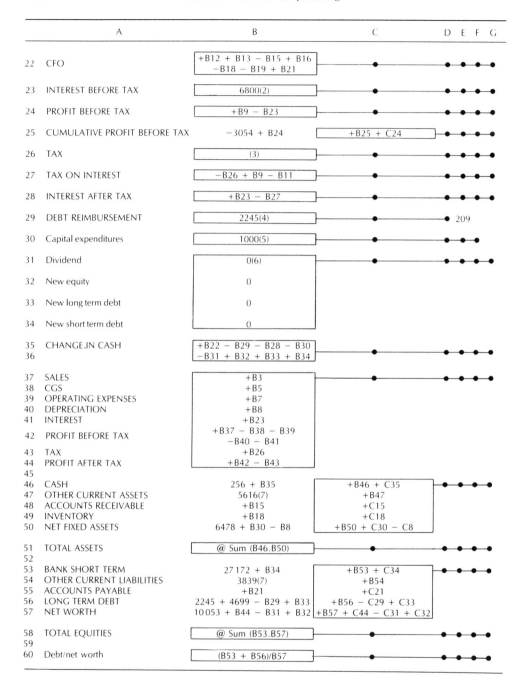

	A	B	C	D E F G
22	CFO	+B12 + B13 − B15 + B16 −B18 − B19 + B21		
23	INTEREST BEFORE TAX	6800(2)		
24	PROFIT BEFORE TAX	+B9 − B23		
25	CUMULATIVE PROFIT BEFORE TAX	−3054 + B24	+B25 + C24	
26	TAX	(3)		
27	TAX ON INTEREST	−B26 + B9 − B11		
28	INTEREST AFTER TAX	+B23 − B27		
29	DEBT REIMBURSEMENT	2245(4)		209
30	Capital expenditures	1000(5)		
31	Dividend	0(6)		
32	New equity	0		
33	New long term debt	0		
34	New short term debt	0		
35	CHANGE IN CASH	+B22 − B29 − B28 − B30		
36		−B31 + B32 + B33 + B34		
37	SALES	+B3		
38	CGS	+B5		
39	OPERATING EXPENSES	+B7		
40	DEPRECIATION	+B8		
41	INTEREST	+B23		
42	PROFIT BEFORE TAX	+B37 − B38 − B39 −B40 − B41		
43	TAX	+B26		
44	PROFIT AFTER TAX	+B42 − B43		
45				
46	CASH	256 + B35	+B46 + C35	
47	OTHER CURRENT ASSETS	5616(7)	+B47	
48	ACCOUNTS RECEIVABLE	+B15	+C15	
49	INVENTORY	+B18	+C18	
50	NET FIXED ASSETS	6478 + B30 − B8	+B50 + C30 − C8	
51	TOTAL ASSETS	@ Sum (B46.B50)		
52				
53	BANK SHORT TERM	27 172 + B34	+B53 + C34	
54	OTHER CURRENT LIABILITIES	3839(7)	+B54	
55	ACCOUNTS PAYABLE	+B21	+C21	
56	LONG TERM DEBT	2245 + 4699 − B29 + B33	+B56 − C29 + C33	
57	NET WORTH	10 053 + B44 − B31 + B32	+B57 + C44 − C31 + C32	
58	TOTAL EQUITIES	@ Sum (B53.B57)		
59				
60	Debt/net worth	(B53 + B56)/B57		

Figure III.4(a) Construction of the financial statements: background of model.[1]

	1993	1994	1995	1996	1997	1998	Cumulated
Growth	0.02	0.02	0.02	0.02	0.02		
SALES	118 072	120 434	122 842	125 299	127 805		
cgs/sales	0.80	0.80	0.80	0.80	0.80		
CGS	94 458	96 347	98 274	100 239	102 244		
Operating expenses/sales	0.14	0.14	0.14	0.14	0.14		
OPERATING EXPENSES	16 530	16 861	17 198	17 542	17 893		
Depreciation	400	400	400	400	400		
OPERATIONAL PROFIT BEFORE TAX	6 684	6 826	6 971	7 118	7 268		
CUMULATIVE PROFIT BEFORE TAX	3 630	10 456	17 427	24 545	31 813		
OPERATIONAL PROFIT AFTER TAX	5 051	3 754	3 834	3 915	3 998		20 551
OPERATIONAL CFE	5 451	4 154	4 234	4 315	4 398		22 551
Receivables open	58 893	59 198	60 382	61 589	62 821	64 078	
Collection period	183	183	183	183	183		
RECEIVABLES END	59 198	60 382	61 589	62 821	64 078		
Inventory open	16 709	23 499	23 969	24 449	24 938		
Inventory turnover	4.1	4.1	4.1	4.1	4.1		
INVENTORY END	23 499	23 969	24 449	24 938	0		
Payables open	39 944	33 564	34 217	34 902	35 600	27 322	
Payment period	121	129	129	129	129		
PAYABLES END	33 564	34 217	34 902	35 600	27 322		
CFO	−8 024	3 153	3 231	3 292	19 801	36 756	58 209
INTEREST BEFORE TAX	6 800	6 800	6 800	6 800	6 800	6 800	40 800
PROFIT BEFORE TAX	−116	26	171	318	468	−6 800	−5 933
CUMULATIVE PROFIT BEFORE TAX	−3 170	−3 144	−2 973	−2 655	−2 187	−8 987	
TAX	0	0	0	0	0	0	
TAX ON INTEREST	1 634	3 072	3 137	3 203	3 271	0	
INTEREST AFTER TAX	5 166	3 728	3 663	3 597	3 529	6 800	
DEBT REIMBURSEMENT	2 245	2 245	2 245	209			
Capital expenditures	1 000	1 000	1 000	1 000	1 000	0	
Dividend	0	0	0	0	0	0	
New equity	0	0	0	0	0	0	
New long term debt	0	0	0	0	0	0	
New short term debt	0	0	0	0	0	0	
CHANGE IN CASH	−16 435	−3 820	−3 677	−1 514	15 272	29 956	
SALES	118 072	120 434	122 842	125 299	127 805	0	
CGS	94 458	96 347	98 274	100 239	102 244	0	
OPERATING EXPENSES	16 530	16 861	17 198	17 542	17 893	0	
DEPRECIATION	400	400	400	400	400	0	
INTEREST	6 800	6 800	6 800	6 800	6 800	6 800	
PROFIT BEFORE TAX	−116	26	171	318	468	−6 800	
TAX	0	0	0	0	0	0	
PROFIT AFTER TAX	−116	26	171	318	468	−6 800	
CASH	−16 179	−19 999	−23 676	−25 190	−9 918	20 037	
OTHER CURRENT ASSETS	5 616	5 616	5 616	5 616	5 616	5 616	
ACCOUNTS RECEIVABLE	59 198	60 382	61 589	62 821	64 078	0	
INVENTORY	23 499	23 969	24 449	24 938	0	0	
NET FIXED ASSETS	7 078	7 678	8 278	8 878	9 478	9 478	
TOTAL ASSETS	79 212	77 646	76 256	77 063	69 253	35 131	
BANK SHORT TERM	27 172	27 172	27 172	27 172	27 172	27 172	
OTHER CURRENT LIABILITIES	3 839	3 839	3 839	3 839	3 839	3 839	
ACCOUNTS PAYABLE	33 564	34 217	34 902	35 600	27 322	0	
LONG TERM DEBT	4 699	2 454	209	0	0	0	
NET WORTH	9 937	9 963	10 134	10 452	10 920	4 120	
TOTAL EQUITIES	79 212	77 646	76 256	77 063	69 253	35 131	
Debt/net worth	3.21	2.97	2.70	2.60	2.49	6.59	

Figure III.4(b) Construction of the financial statements: foreground of the model.

	1993	1994	1995	1996	1997	1998	Cumulated
Growth	0.02	0.02	0.02	0.02	0.02		
SALES	118 072	120 434	122 842	125 299	127 805		
cgs/sales	0.80	0.80	0.80	0.80	0.80		
CGS	94 458	96 347	98 274	100 239	102 244		
Operating expenses/sales	0.14	0.14	0.14	0.14	0.14		
OPERATING EXPENSES	16 530	16 861	17 198	17 542	17 893		
Depreciation	400	400	400	400	400		
OPERATIONAL PROFIT BEFORE TAX	6 684	6 826	6 971	7 118	7 268		
CUMULATIVE PROFIT BEFORE TAX	3 630	10 456	17 427	24 545	31 813		
OPERATIONAL PROFIT AFTER TAX	5 051	3 754	3 834	3 915	3 998		20 551
OPERATIONAL CFE	5 451	4 154	4 234	4 315	4 398		22 551
Receivables open	58 893	59 198	60 382	61 589	62 821	64 078	
Collection period	183	183	183	183	183		
RECEIVABLES END	59 198	60 382	61 589	62 821	64 078		
Inventory open	16 709	23 499	23 969	24 449	24 938		
Inventory turnover	4.1	4.1	4.1	4.1	4.1		
INVENTORY END	23 499	23 969	24 449	24 938	0		
Payables open	39 944	33 564	34 217	34 902	35 600	27 322	
Payment period	121	129	129	129	129		
PAYABLES END	33 564	34 217	34 902	35 600	27 322		
CFO	−8 024	3 153	3 231	3 292	19 801	36 756	58 209
INTEREST BEFORE TAX	6 134	7 309	7 639	8 003	7 068	3 416	39 569
PROFIT BEFORE TAX	550	−483	−669	−885	200	−3 416	−4 702
CUMULATIVE PROFIT BEFORE TAX	−2 504	−2 986	−3 655	−4 540	−4 340	−7 756	
TAX	0	0	0	0	0	0	
TAX ON INTEREST	1 634	3 072	3 137	3 203	3 271	0	
INTEREST AFTER TAX	4 500	4 237	4 503	4 800	3 798	3 416	
DEBT REIMBURSEMENT	2 245	2 245	2 245	209			
Capital expenditures	1 000	1 000	1 000	1 000	1 000	0	
Dividend	0	0	0	0	0	0	
New equity	0	0	0	0	0	0	
New long term debt	0	0	0	0	0	0	
New short term debt	15 800	4 350	4 550	2 750	−15 000	−33 700	
CHANGE IN CASH	31	22	34	33	3	−360	
SALES	118 072	120 434	122 842	125 299	127 805	0	
CGS	94 458	96 347	98 274	100 239	102 244	0	
OPERATING EXPENSES	16 530	16 861	17 198	17 542	17 893	0	
DEPRECIATON	400	400	400	400	400	0	
INTEREST	6 134	7 309	7 639	8 003	7 068	3 416	
PROFIT BEFORE TAX	550	−483	−669	−885	200	−3 416	
TAX	0	0	0	0	0	0	
PROFIT AFTER TAX	550	−483	−669	−885	200	−3 416	−4 702
CASH	287	308	342	375	379	18	
OTHER CURRENT ASSETS	5 616	5 616	5 616	5 616	5 616	5 616	
ACCOUNTS RECEIVABLE	59 198	60 382	61 589	62 821	64 078	0	
INVENTORY	23 499	23 969	24 449	24 938	0	0	
NET FIXED ASSETS	7 078	7 678	8 278	8 878	9 478	9 478	
TOTAL ASSETS	95 678	97 953	100 274	102 628	79 550	15 112	
BANK SHORT TERM	42 972	47 322	51 872	54 622	39 622	5 922	
OTHER CURRENT LIABILITIES	3 839	3 839	3 839	3 839	3 839	3 839	
ACCOUNTS PAYABLE	33 564	34 217	34 902	35 600	27 322	0	
LONG TERM DEBT	4 699	2 454	209	0	0	0	
NET WORTH	10 603	10 121	9 452	8 567	8 767	5 351	
TOTAL EQUITIES	95 678	97 953	100 274	102 628	79 550	15 112	
Debt/net worth	4.50	4.92	5.51	6.38	4.52	1.11	

Figure III.4(c) Financial statements when external financing is introduced.

	1993	1994	1995	1996	1997	1998	Cumulated
Growth	0.02	0.02	0.02	0.02	0.02		
SALES	118 072	120 434	122 842	125 299	127 805		
cgs/sales	0.80	0.80	0.80	0.80	0.80		
CGS	94 458	96 347	98 274	100 239	102 244		
Operating expenses/sales	0.14	0.14	0.14	0.14	0.14		
OPERATING EXPENSES	16 530	16 861	17 198	17 542	17 893		
Depreciation	400	400	400	400	400		
OPERATIONAL PROFIT BEFORE TAX	6 684	6 826	6 971	7 118	7 268		
INTEREST	6 134	7 309	7 639	8 003	7 068	3 416	
PROFIT BEFORE TAX	550	−483	−669	−885	200	−3 416	
CUMULATIVE PROFIT BEFORE TAX	−2 504	−2 986	−3 655	−4 540	−4 340	−7 756	
TAX	0	0	0	0	0	0	
PROFIT AFTER TAX	550	−483	−669	−885	200	−3 416	−4 702
CFE	950	−83	−269	−485	600	−3 416	−2 702
Receivables open	58 893	59 198	60 382	61 589	62 821	64 078	
Collection period	183	183	183	183	183		
RECEIVABLES END	59 198	60 382	61 589	62 821	64 078		
Inventory open	16 709	23 499	23 969	24 449	24 938		
Inventory turnover	4	4	4	4	4		
INVENTORY END	23 499	23 969	24 449	24 938	0		
Payables open	39 944	33 564	34 217	34 902	35 600	27 322	
Payment period	121	129	129	129	129		
PAYABLES END	33 564	34 217	34 902	35 600	27 322		
CFO	−12 524	−1 083	−1 271	−1 508	16 003	33 400	32 956
DEBT REIMBURSEMENT	2 245	2 245	2 245	209			
Capital expenditures	1 000	1 000	1 000	1 000	1 000	0	
Dividend	0	0	0	0	0	0	
New equity	0	0	0	0	0	0	
New long term debt	0	0	0	0	0	0	
New short term debt	15 800	4 350	4 550	2 750	−15 000	−33 700	
CHANGE IN CASH	31	22	34	33	3	−360	
SALES	118 072	120 434	122 842	125 299	127 805	0	
CGS	94 458	96 347	98 274	100 239	102 244	0	
OPERATING EXPENSES	16 530	16 861	17 198	17 542	17 893	0	
DEPRECIATION	400	400	400	400	400	0	
INTEREST	6 134	7 309	7 639	8 003	7 068	3 416	
PROFIT BEFORE TAX	550	−483	−669	−885	200	−3 416	
TAX	0	0	0	0	0	0	
PROFIT AFTER TAX	550	−483	−669	−885	200	−3 416	
CASH	287	308	342	375	379	18	
OTHER CURRENT ASSETS	5 616	5 616	5 616	5 616	5 616	5 616	
ACCOUNTS RECEIVABLE	59 198	60 382	61 589	62 821	64 078	0	
INVENTORY	23 499	23 969	24 449	24 938	0	0	
NET FIXED ASSETS	7 078	7 678	8 278	8 878	9 478	9 478	
TOTAL ASSETS	95 678	97 953	100 274	102 628	79 550	15 112	
BANK SHORT TERM	42 972	47 322	51 872	54 622	39 622	5 922	
OTHER CURRENT LIABILITIES	3 839	3 839	3 839	3 839	3 839	3 839	
ACCOUNTS PAYABLE	33 564	34 217	34 902	35 600	27 322	0	
LONG TERM DEBT	4 699	2 454	209	0	0	0	
NET WORTH	10 603	10 121	9 452	8 567	8 767	5 351	
TOTAL EQUITIES	95 678	97 953	100 274	102 628	79 550	15 112	
Debt/net worth	4.50	4.92	5.51	6.38	4.52	1.11	

Figure III.4(d) Financial statements: alternative approach.

Part III   Bibliography

Ackoff R (1981), 'The art and science of mess management', *Interfaces*, **11** (1).

Adams JL (1979), *Conceptual Blockbusting – A guide for better ideas*, WW Norton.

Anderson JR (1983), *The Architecture of Cognition*, Harvard Unversity Press.

Bodily S (1985), *Modern Decision Making*, McGraw-Hill.

Bourne L, Dominowski R, Loftus E and Heavy A (1986), *Cognitive Processes*, Prentice Hall.

Einhorn H and Hogarth R (1987), 'Decision making: going forward in reverse', *Harvard Business Review*, Jan/Feb.

Forrester J (1961), *Industrial Dynamics*, The Productivity Press.

Goldratt E and Cox J (1989), *The Goal*, Gower.

Hall R (1987), *Attaining Manufacturing Excellence*, Dow Jones Irwin.

Harmon R and Peterson L (1990), *Reinventing the Factory*, The Free Press.

Hayes R, Wheelwright S and Clark K (1989), *Dynamic Manufacturing*, The Free Press.

Lubben R (1988), *Just-in-Time Manufacturing*, McGraw-Hill.

Meredith J (1987), *The Management of Operations*, John Wiley & Sons.

Newell A and Simon H (1972), *Human Problem Solving*, Prentice Hall.

Polya G (1945 & 1990), *How to Solve it*, Princeton University Press and Penguin Books.

Porter M (1980), *Competitive Strategy – Techniques for analyzing industries and competitors*, Free Press.

Porter M (1985), *Competitive Advantage*, Free Press.

Shingo S (1988), *Non-Stock Production: the Shingo System for Continuous Improvement*, Productivity Press.

Simon H (1978), 'Rationality as process and as product of thought', *American Economic Review*, May.

Simon H and Newell A (1972), 'Human problem solving: the state of the theory in 1970', *American Psychologist*, **26**:, 145–59.

Stalk G and Hout T (1990), *Competing Against Time*, The Free Press.

Suzaki K (1987), *The New Manufacturing Challenge*, The Free Press.

Winston PH (1984), *Artificial Intelligence*, Addison Wesley.

Wolstenholme E (1990), *System Enquiry*, John Wiley & Sons.

PART IV

Assessing the Value of a Strategic Opportunity

A characteristic common to most strategic decisions is that they require an initial cash disbursement, or investment. Consequently, assessing the value of strategic moves is generally a matter of comparing an initial investment with expected future cash flows, a key problem in corporate finance, often referred to as capital budgeting.

In Part IV, we are going to help SADE, a civil engineering company, to assess whether it is worth undertaking a new project, the Dhahran Roads contract. Although risk is an essential dimension of civil engineering projects, we would like to defer the discussion of this issue until Part V and focus here only on the issue of assessing whether or not it is worth spending money now in order to get money in the future (when the money in the future is assumed to be certain).

As you will realize, the essential concept in Part IV is *net present value*, a key concept in finance which enables you to summarize all the figures of a multi-annual plan with one single number, which is very useful for comparing alternative plans. However, as you will also realize, the net present value concept is not easy to grasp. Spreadsheet modelling should be of great help.

The second important objective of Part IV is to review the notions of cash and profit, and to answer the key question: *how much cash should a business generate in order to be successful?*

The third objective of Part IV is to help you test further your understanding of accounting concepts and apply them in a specific but often encountered business activity, the running of projects.

In order to benefit fully from Part IV, spend sufficient time preparing the case and solve it by yourself before working with our analysis. One final piece of advice if you are a practising manager: as Part IV deals with only one aspect of evaluating strategies and investments, wait until the end of Part V before using what you have learned to analyze the projects you contemplate in your own business activity.

KEY LEARNING POINTS

- NPV as the outcome variable of any financial model – *Section 15.5, page 211*
- A model for evaluating strategic alternatives – *Section 15.5, page 211, Figures 15.3, 15.4 and 15.5*
- A fundamental check of financial models:
  - Cumulative CFE = Cumulative CFO
  - Cumulative Profit = Cumulative Free Cash Flow
  – *Chapters 11 and 14, pages 169 and 202*
- A comprehensive financial model for evaluating projects – *Figures 11.2 and 12.9, pages 171 and 185*
- A process for evaluating strategies: estimate cumulative profit, explode it into a cash curve, derive an NPV – *Sections 15.3 and 15.4, pages 208 and 211*

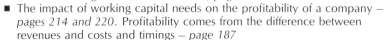

- Creating additional value is a better goal than looking for high returns – *page 205*
- NPV as the additional value created above financing costs and expressed as of today (when the discount rate is the cost of financing) – *pages 181 and 208*
- NPV and profit assess the additional value created, annual CFO does not – *Figure 15.1, page 209*
- In order to create value, a company should generate CFOs, the present value of which is higher than the required capital expenditures – *page 203*
- The value of a cash flow depends on when it is received. A cash flow is defined by its value and date – *page 179*. You cannot compare, add or subtract cash flows generated at different times. Compounding and discounting as the alternatives for reflecting the time value of cash flows – *pages 175 and 179*. Using periods shorter than one year for compounding and discounting – *Further Model IV.1, page 222*

- The impact of working capital needs on the profitability of a company – *pages 214 and 220*. Profitability comes from the difference between revenues and costs and timings – *page 187*
- Working capital needs cost more than the time delays they correspond to. The cost of contractual working capital needs, *page 188*. The cost of speculative working capital needs, *page 189*, the quality costs hidden by working capital needs, *page 189*. What if working capital needs were an 'absolute evil'? *page 190*
- IRR as the discount rate which makes NPV equal to zero – *page 182*
- Beware of the reinvestment assumption in NPV and IRR calculations – *page 190*

- Beware of the real meaning of intermediate accounting or book measures of profitability. ROCE (or RONA) as a better measure than ROA – *page 198*
- There is more than one approach to reporting the annual profits of a project – *Further Model IV.3, page 235*

- NPV and IRR functions – *Section 12.3, page 179*
- EXP and LN functions – *Further Model IV.1, page 213*

DHAHRAN ROADS (A)

On 15 January 1993, Mr Malik, the financial manager of SADE, a Bahraini civil engineering company, was reviewing the contract it had just been awarded by the municipality of Dhahran in Saudi Arabia for the construction of a new road network linking the airport complex and the city. The characteristics of the contract awarded to SADE are described in Figure C.1.

First of all, Mr Malik planned to evaluate the profitability of the contract and to check that it yielded more than the 25% return requested by SADE on projects in Saudi Arabia.[1] Mr Malik also planned to prepare the yearly pro-forma income statements and balance sheets of the contract, which was to be operated as an independent business.

Calculating the annual profit of such a contract was not easy, however, since there were several methods available which led to different results. The two most popular methods for calculating the profit of project activities are described in Figure C.2. Deciding on which profit-reporting method to choose was an important decision to be made, as the yearly dividend SADE obtained from the project would depend directly on the amount of profit reported.

---

1 **Total project value**: 168 million Saudi Rials (SR).

2 **Advance made by the client**: 15% of the total contract value.

3 **Schedule of costs and billings** (in millions SR):

	Costs incurred	Billings
1993	7	11
1994	28	43
1995	31	48
1996	25	39
1997	17	27

In addition to these costs, SADE will have to buy equipment for an amount of 38 million SR (to be paid in 1993).

The equipment will be depreciated over 5 years and SADE does not expect to be able to use it again for other projects. It is also reasonable to assume that SADE will not be able to resell this equipment.

All costs will be paid in the year they occur.

Amounts billed to the customer should be paid in the same year. The customer is expected however to pay only 80% of each invoice. The 20% deduction corresponds to:
- The recovery by the customer of its initial advance (15%)
- A 5% retention for guarantee. Half of this retention is to be reimbursed upon completion (in 1997) and the remaining half in 1998. The

release of the retention funds is however subject to the completed construction being approved by the customer.

4 **Project organization**: the contract is to be executed by a Saudi company created specifically for the purpose. SADE will own 100% of the capital of this company. SADE wishes to invest a minimum and to be able to draw dividends as quickly as possible.

5 **Risks**:* during the past several months, the SADE engineering department has inspected the site, confirmed the surveying and reviewed the drawings that have been provided by the municipality of Dhahran. In the opinion of the Head of the Engineering Department, the project presents no unusual problems. It is very similar to several SADE projects in other countries and these have progressed without any serious difficulties.

The project is to be managed by one of SADE's most experienced project managers, Mr HK Jones. Mr Jones has just completed a major waterworks project in Africa and is noted for strong engineering skills and tight cost control.

As the Bahraini Dinar is pegged to the Saudi Rial, the risk of currency variations is very small.

6 **Taxes**: There are no corporate taxes in Saudi Arabia (and no taxes will have to be paid in Bahrain on the profits of this contract).

---

* The discussion of the risk issue is deferred to Part V. Assume for the moment that everything will happen as expected.

Figure C.1 Dhahran Roads: description of the contract.

1 **Reporting profit (or loss) according to the percentage of completion method**

According to this method, intermediate invoicings are considered as sales and this allows the project to show profit in relation to its progress. The difficulty with this method is that each annual profit to annual sales ratio should be equal to the total profit to total sales ratio. This poses at least two series of problems:
- It may well happen that, in a specific year, invoices are exceptionally high in relation to costs, or that expenses are exceptionally high in relation to invoices. In such cases, adjustments have to be made in order to report a profit which is in the same proportion to sales as total profit to total sales.
- The total profit to sales ratio is not known for certain until the project is terminated; during the life of the project, this ratio is just forecast. Hence the danger of reporting inadequate annual profits during the life of the project and of having to make a substantial adjustment at the end.

2 **Reporting profit (or) loss according to the completed contract method**

According to this approach, intermediate invoicings are not considered as sales. Only the final and total billing at the moment of takeover is considered as sales.

During the execution period, yearly income is equal to the increase in the value of work in progress valued at cost.

Amounts billed to the customer are recorded in an advance account which appears as a liability. This account is offset by the final and total billing at the end.

Figure C.2 Dhahran Roads: two popular approaches for reporting profit in project activities.

NOTE

1 Twenty-five percent was also equal to the cost of financing for SADE for construction projects in Saudi Arabia.

CHAPTER 11

Cash, Profit and Profitability
Some Simple Ideas

11.1 IN THE END, CASH AND PROFIT ARE THE SAME

First of all, let us try to evaluate the Dhahran Roads contract over its entire life.

■ In cash terms, the expected inflows from the contract amount to 168 m SR and the expected disbursements to 146 m SR. The contract will therefore generate a net cash inflow or 'free cash flow'[1] of 22 m SR over its entire life (see Figure 11.1).

■ In profit terms, the conclusion is exactly the same. Total sales (or invoices) will be 168 m SR and total costs 146 m SR leaving a total profit of 22 m SR (see Figure 11.1).

This is an important result and we can generalize as follows.

■ In the end, or in the long run, any contract, project or company generates cash and profit in identical amounts.

■ Cash and profit differ only when contracts, projects and companies are evaluated on a periodic basis. The total of cash and profit is the same, but their timing is generally different.

It is also worth realizing that, when we evaluate the final outcome of the Dhahran Roads contract:

■ The cash receipts and disbursements look the same. The distinction we introduced between operational and strategic flows does not really look necessary. It is only when we split the life of the contract into years that we need to consider that in 1993, the disbursement of 38 m SR needed to acquire the equipment is of a strategic nature and that the disbursement of 7 m SR is of an operational nature.

■ When using a profit approach, costs also look the same. It is only when we analyze the contract on a yearly basis that we need to distinguish between costs which are expenses and costs which give rise to assets. If we analyze the costs incurred in 1993 we have to distinguish between those which are related to the activity of that year (7 m SR) and those which are related to the

Income statement:		Cash flow statement:	
Sales	168	Receipts from sales	168
Operating expenses	108	Payment of operating expenses	108
Depreciation	38	Payment of capital expenditures	38
Profit	22	Free Cash Flow	22

Figure 11.1 Overall income and cash flow statements.

entire life of the contract (38 m SR capital expenditure). On a yearly basis, accounting will consider that the 38 m SR must be stored as an asset and subsequently allocated as an expense against the activity of the different years through an allowance for depreciation.

11.2 PROFITABILITY AND RATE OF RETURN

The concepts of profitability and return enable us to evaluate strategic alternatives and to select from the many possible courses of action the one which is the best.

■ The concept of profitability is based on the comparison of the *cash outflow* required for implementing a strategic alternative with the *cash inflows* that this alternative is expected to generate.

In 1993, SADE is faced with the choice of whether or not to carry out the Dhahran Roads contract. The profitability of this project depends on the relative importance of the cash SADE needs to invest in order to execute the contract and the cash it will receive in return.

If SADE needs to invest a considerable amount in order to obtain the 22 m SR the execution of the contract is expected to generate, the contract will not be profitable. If on the other hand SADE needs to invest only a small amount, then the contract will be profitable. The possibility of using the concept of profitability is actually very wide. One can obviously use this concept in order to decide about the value of executing new contracts, of undertaking new projects, of buying new equipment, etc. But, since most strategic moves require cash to be invested, the concept of profitability is actually useful in a very large number of situations. How can we measure the profitability of strategic alternatives?

■ The *rate of return* is the quantitative measure of the profitability of a strategic alternative. In order to calculate the rate of return, we must compare the cash outcome of the strategic alternative with the cash outcome we would get from depositing with a bank the amount of cash required by this strategic

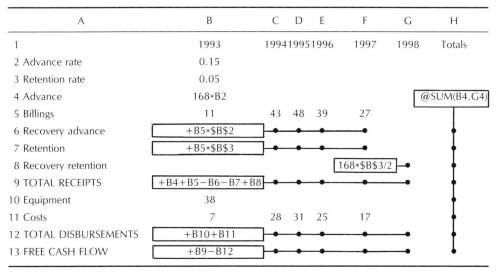

	A	B	C	D	E	F	G	H
1		1993	1994	1995	1996	1997	1998	Totals
2	Advance rate	0.15						
3	Retention rate	0.05						
4	Advance	168*B2						@SUM(B4.G4)
5	Billings	11	43	48	39	27		
6	Recovery advance	+B5*$B$2						
7	Retention	+B5*$B$3						
8	Recovery retention					168*$B$3/2		
9	TOTAL RECEIPTS	+B4+B5−B6−B7+B8						
10	Equipment	38						
11	Costs	7	28	31	25	17		
12	TOTAL DISBURSEMENTS	+B10+B11						
13	FREE CASH FLOW	+B9−B12						

Column width: Global: 7; A:23

Figure 11.2 Spreadsheet model for estimating annual cash flows.

alternative. Since bank deposits generally produce annual interest,[2] this comparison requires that the cash outcome of the strategic alternative be estimated on a yearly basis.

In order to estimate the rate of return of a decision to execute the Dhahran Roads contract, we must first evaluate the yearly cash inflows and outflows of the contract. Figure 11.2 shows a spreadsheet model that enables you to do so. Figure 11.3 shows the results generated by such a model.

Notes on the construction of the model described in Figure 11.2

1. Advance and retention rates are considered as parameters.
2. You can use the copy command to extend the formulas you have entered in B6, B7, B9, B12 and B13.
3. *The rationale for the calculation of totals in column H is to enable you to check that your model is correct.* When the totals are calculated, you can check that:
   · Cumulative recoveries of advance are equal to the initial advance.
   · Cumulative retentions are equal to the recoveries of retentions.
   · Cumulative total receipts are equal to the total value of the contract.
   · Cumulative net cash is equal to 22 m SR.
   When the model is built, you can check its correctness further by changing the advance and the retention rates. As you know that, whatever the advance and retention rates, the net cash should in the end be equal to 22 m SR. You can check that the model agrees with this. *This procedure for testing*

	1993	1994	1995	1996	1997	1998	Cumulated
Initial advance	25.20						25.20
Billings	11.00	43.00	48.00	39.00	27.00		168.00
Recovery of advance	1.65	6.45	7.20	5.85	4.05		25.20
Retention	0.55	2.15	2.40	1.95	1.35		8.40
Recovery of retention					4.20	4.20	8.40
TOTAL RECEIPTS	34.00	34.40	38.40	31.20	25.80	4.20	168.00
Equipment	38.00						38.00
Costs	7.00	28.00	31.00	25.00	17.00		108.00
TOTAL DISBURSEMENTS	45.00	28.00	31.00	25.00	17.00		146.00
FREE CASH FLOW	−11.00*	6.40	7.40	6.20	8.80	4.20	22.00

* A major problem with the 1993 cash flow is its significance: let us assume that SADE will be able to tie up the receipt of the advance with the payment for the equipment (otherwise the 11 m SR deficit could well hide a much bigger deficit). For more about this, refer to Further Model IV.1.

Figure 11.3 Annual cash flows.

the correctness of a model should be used as often as possible. Each time you build a model describing a specific situation, think what the outcome should be in some specific cases, and check that the model agrees with your prediction. (This dynamic verification of models is also explained in Chapter 6.)

As shown in Figure 11.3, the decision to undertake the Dhahran Roads contract would mean that SADE would have to invest 11 m SR in 1993, with a view to obtaining, between 1994 and 1998, a stream of net positive cash flows amounting to a total of 33 m SR (the net amount being 33 − 11 = 22 m SR, the cash excess generated by the project in the end).

A first, and basic, measure of the profitability of the 11 m SR investment required by the contract is that, during its lifetime, the contract will generate a net cash excess of 22 m over the initial investment of 11 m. When expressed as a percentage, this excess represents 200% of the initial investment. Since five years are necessary to achieve this 200%, one can estimate that the annual profitability of the decision to undertake the contract is equal to 200%/5 = 40%. This basic method of measuring profitability is, however, not regarded as fully satisfactory by finance.

NOTES

1 Free Cash Flow is equal to the net cash flow of a project. Cumulated Free Cash Flow is equal to Cumulated Profit. Free Cash Flow is a term coined by M Jensen in 'Agency Costs of Free Cash Flow, Corporate Finance and Takeovers', *American Economic Review*, May 1986, pp 323–9. M Jensen defines the Free Cash Flow of a firm as follows: 'cash flow in excess of that required to fund all projects that have a

positive NPV when discounted at the relevant cost of capital'. The Free Cash Flow of a firm is the surplus or profit it generates after it has exhausted all valuable investment opportunities. *Consequently this free cash flow should be distributed to shareholders*: see M Jensen, 'The Eclipse of the Public Corporation', *Harvard Business Review*, Sept–Oct 1989, pp 61–74. By extension, the free cash flow of a project is the net (ie after investment) cash flow or profit it generates.

2 In some countries interest on bank deposits is calculated on a shorter period than the year. For example, in countries where inflation is very high, interest is calculated on a monthly basis. In this case, you must evaluate the cash outcome of the strategic alternatives on a monthly basis, the same as banks use for their interest calculation (see Further Model IV.1).

R.T.C. LIBRARY
LETTERKENNY

Discounted Cash Flows as the Fundamental Tool for Assessing the Value of Strategic Opportunities

12.1 NET FUTURE VALUE AND INTERNAL RATE OF RETURN

Rate of return

Let us first make the concept of rate of return a bit more operational.

> The rate of return of a strategic alternative is the return you can get from the equivalent deposit with a bank. The equivalent bank deposit is defined as the deposit which:
> - Has the same basic characteristics as the strategic alternative ie the same initial cash outlay and same duration. (By duration of a strategic alternative, we mean the duration of its impact. In practice this duration is often difficult to estimate and may be a matter solely of judgement.)
> - Produces the same final net cash outcome as the project.

Returning to the Dhahran Roads case, let us compare the contract with a bank deposit presenting the same basic characteristics, 11 m SR deposited in 1993 for a duration of five years.

Since our first basic estimation of the rate of return of the contract was 40%, let us see how the contract compares with a 11 m deposit at 40% for five years. These two investment opportunities are shown in Figure 12.1.

In order to compare the contract with the deposit we could simply compare their final outcomes. We see then that the yearly outcomes of the deposit add up to 22 m SR. This seems to show that the deposit is equivalent to the contract and therefore that the contract has a 40% rate of return. In finance, however, we should disregard this method for comparing contracts and deposits since *it ignores the fact that the yearly outcomes of deposits and contracts can be reinvested.*

The concept of future value

When the yearly outcomes of the bank deposit shown in Figure 12.1 are reinvested – or kept with the bank – they themselves generate interest:

	Dhahran Roads contract	Deposit at 40% with same basic characteristics
1993	−11.0	−11.0
1994	6.4	4.4*
1995	7.4	4.4*
1996	6.2	4.4*
1997	8.8	4.4*
1998	4.2	15.4†

* From 1994 to 1998 the deposit produces an interest equal to 11*0.4 = 4.4.
† In 1998 the deposit produces an interest of 4.4 and the initial capital is also reimbursed.

Figure 12.1 Comparison with a 40% deposit.

- The 4.4 m SR generated in 1997 will be reinvested for one year at 40% and will result, in 1998, in an amount of 6.16 m SR. This amount can be calculated in two different ways:

  4.4 m SR plus an interest equal to 40% of the 4.4 m:

  $4.4 + (4.4 \times 0.4) = 6.16$ m SR

  or

  $4.4 \times (1 + 0.4) = 6.16$ m SR

- The 4.4 m SR generated in 1996 will be reinvested for two years and will result, in 1998, in an amount of 8.62 m SR:

  4.4 m SR plus two 40% interests on these 4.4 m (1.76 m SR received in 1997 and 1998) plus one interest on the 1.76 m generated in 1997 and reinvested for one year:

  $$4.4 + 2 \times (4.4 \times 0.4) + (4.4 \times 0.4 \times 0.4)$$
  $$= 4.4 + 2 \times 1.76 + 1.76 \times 0.4$$
  $$= 8.62$$

  or more simply: $4.4 \times (1 + 0.4)^2 = 8.62$

The 6.16 and 8.62 m SR are called the future values or more precisely the 1998 values at 40% of the 1997 and 1996 cash inflows of the deposit. The process of calculating the amount to which a cash flow will grow at a future date when reinvested is known as *compounding*. When the 1998 values of the five cash inflows of the deposit have been calculated, you can add them together: you then get the 1998, or future, value of the deposit. You can then calculate the 1998 value of the contract and compare it with the 1998 value of the deposit. This is done in Figure 12.2.

The concepts of net future value (NFV) and internal rate of return (IRR)

Figure 12.2 shows that the Dhahran Roads contract is better than a 40% deposit as, when intermediate cash flows are reinvested, we get a 73.56 m SR future

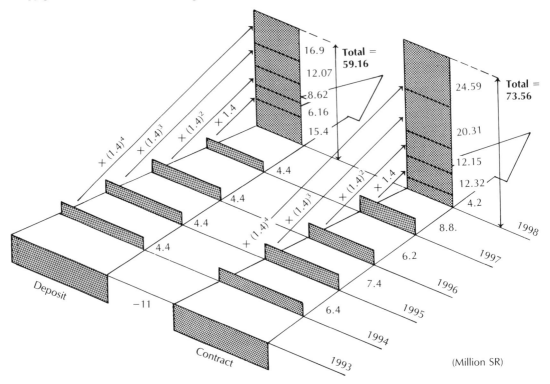

Figure 12.2 Comparison with a 40% deposit when intermediate cash flows are reinvested.

(1998) value for the contract and a 59.16 m SR future value for the deposit. The superiority of the contract over the deposit is a matter of timing only. The deposit and the contract generate as much cash inflow (33 m), but the contract generates this cash flow quicker. We may actually say that the Dhahran Roads contract is equivalent to an 11 m SR deposit for five years at 40%, plus a cash gift in 1998 equal to $73.56 - 59.16 = 14.40$ m SR. Which means that the Dhahran Roads contract obviously has a rate of return higher than 40%. The 14.4 m SR cash gift in 1998 is called the *net future value at 40% of the contract*.

■ The net future value (NFV) of a strategic alternative is equal to the difference between the future value of its expected cash flows and the future value of the expected cash flows attached to a bank deposit having the same characteristics (same initial investment, same duration and same return as the one used for the calculation of the NFV).
■ When the net future value of a strategic alternative is positive, the strategic alternative is superior to the deposit; it is actually equivalent to the deposit plus a cash gift at the end exactly equal to the net future value.
■ When the net future value of a strategic alternative is negative, the strategic

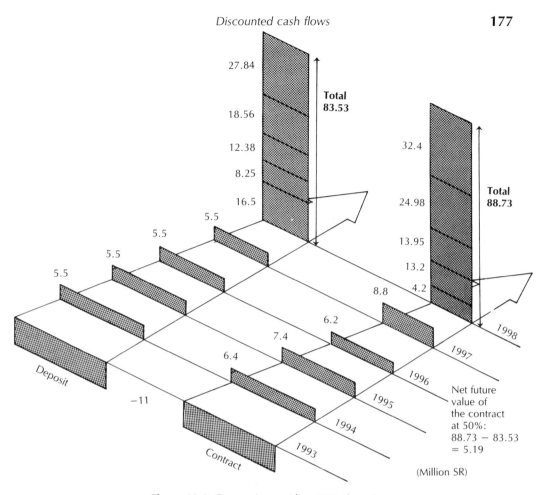

Discounted cash flows

Figure 12.3 Comparison with a 50% deposit.

alternative is inferior to the deposit; it is actually equivalent to the deposit and a further cash outlay at the end exactly equal to the net future value.

- When the net future value of a strategic alternative is nil, the strategic alternative is equivalent to the deposit, ie its rate of return is equal to the rate of the deposit. This rate is called *the internal rate of return* (IRR) of the strategic alternative.

Estimating the IRR of the contract

Internal rates of return can be estimated by trial and error only: How can we estimate the IRR of the Dhahran Roads contract? We know that the contract is equivalent to a 40% deposit plus a cash gift of 14.4 m SR in 1998. Let us compare the contract with a deposit with a higher rate, for example 50%. If the contract is equivalent to such a deposit plus a cash gift in 1998, then its IRR is superior to 50%. If on the other hand the contract is equivalent to such a deposit and a cash outlay in 1998, then its IRR is inferior to 50%. If the contract is superior to a 50% deposit we should then compare it with a deposit at a yet higher rate. If it is inferior we should then compare it with deposit at a rate between 40 and 50%. In Figure 12.3, the Dhahran Roads contract is compared with a 50% deposit.

Since, as shown in Figure 12.3, the Dhahran Roads contract has a return higher than 50%, we should compare it now with a deposit returning more than 50%. Comparisons of the Dhahran Roads contract with deposits returning more than 50% are shown in Figure 12.4.

(million SR)

Deposit rate	Future value of the contract	Future value of the deposit	Net future value of the contract
51%	90.38	86.35	4.02
52%	92.05	89.25	2.80
53%	93.75	92.23	1.53
54%	95.48	95.28	0.20
55%	97.23	98.41	−1.18
56%	99.01	101.63	−2.62
54.15%	**95.74**	**95.74**	**0.00**

Figure 12.4 Comparison with deposits returning more than 50%.

The contract is slightly better than a 54% deposit but not as good as a 55% deposit; in fact, its internal rate of return is close to 54.15%. Since the internal rate of return is found by trial and error, it may take some time to find the rate that makes the net future value exactly equal to zero. In most cases, this is a waste of time since it is enough to say, as for example in this case, that the internal rate of return is about 54%.

12.2 NET PRESENT VALUE

Although net future values are perfectly adequate for assessing the desirability of strategic alternatives, people prefer using net present values. The concept of net present value is actually very close to the net future value concept, and net present values have the same properties as net future values.

The time value of cash flows

Without the opportunity to invest, people should be indifferent to the date at which they receive cash flows; but, as soon as such an opportunity exists,

people prefer to receive cash flows earlier in order to be͏
investment. When the opportunity to invest exists, it is not e͏
cash flow solely by its *amount*; the *date* at which it occurs s͏
also. This has some very important consequences for finan͏

- Two cash flows with identical amounts but occurring at tw͞
  are not equivalent; more generally, you cannot directly compare caʂ.
  occurring at different dates. Before doing such a comparison, you should
  first calculate the value of these cash flows at a common date.
- It does not make much sense to cumulate cash flows occurring at different
  dates. Before working with such cash flows you must re-state them as for
  identical time values.

The present value of a single cash flow

Let us consider one of the cash flows of the Dhahran Roads contract, the 6.2 m
cash flow received in 1996. How can we calculate the value of this cash flow at a
different date? As discussed above, compounding enables you to calculate the
future values of this cash flow:

$$1997 \text{ value} = 6.2 \times 1.4 = 8.68$$
$$1998 \text{ value} = 6.2 \times (1.4)^2 = 12.15$$

In order to calculate the values of this same cash flow at dates earlier than
1996, you have to follow the opposite process, which is known as *discounting*:

$$1995 \text{ value} = \frac{6.2}{1.4} = 4.43$$

$$1994 \text{ value} = \frac{6.2}{(1.4)^2} = 3.16$$

$$1993 \text{ value} = \frac{6.2}{(1.4)^3} = 2.26$$

If today is 1993, the 1993 value of the cash flow is called its *present value*.

The present value of a stream of cash flows

The Dhahran Roads contract is characterized by a series of cash flows occurring
at different dates. If we want to cumulate these cash flows, we must first
express them all on the basis of a common time value. One way to do this is to
express them on the basis of their future, or, more precisely, their 1998, value,
which leads to the calculation of the 1998 value of the stream of cash flows
attached to the contract. As shown in Figure 12.2, the 1998 value of the
contract is equal to 73.56 m SR (at a 40% rate).

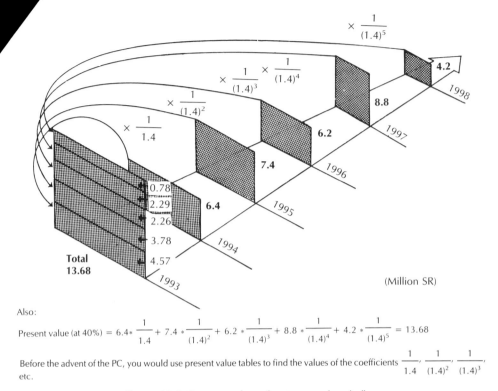

Also:

Present value (at 40%) $= 6.4 * \dfrac{1}{1.4} + 7.4 * \dfrac{1}{(1.4)^2} + 6.2 * \dfrac{1}{(1.4)^3} + 8.8 * \dfrac{1}{(1.4)^4} + 4.2 * \dfrac{1}{(1.4)^5} = 13.68$

Before the advent of the PC, you would use present value tables to find the values of the coefficients $\dfrac{1}{1.4}, \dfrac{1}{(1.4)^2}, \dfrac{1}{(1.4)^3},$ etc.

Figure 12.5 Present value of a stream of cash flows.

Another approach is to express each of the cash flows at their 1993, or present, values and then to cumulate these values: the result is known as the present value of the stream of cash flows. As shown in Figure 12.5, the present value of the stream of cash flows attached to the Dhahran Roads contract is equal to 13.68 m SR (with a 40% rate).

It is important you note the relationship which exists between the present and future values of a stream of cash flows:

$$1993 \text{ value} = 1998 \text{ value} \times \frac{1}{(1.4)^5}$$

and

$$1998 \text{ value} = 1993 \text{ value} \times (1.4)^5$$

What does the present value of a stream of cash flows mean?

The meaning of the present value of a stream of future cash flows at a specified rate is worth emphasising. Saying that the present (1993) value at 40% of the positive cash flows attached to the Dhahran Roads contract is 13.68 m SR

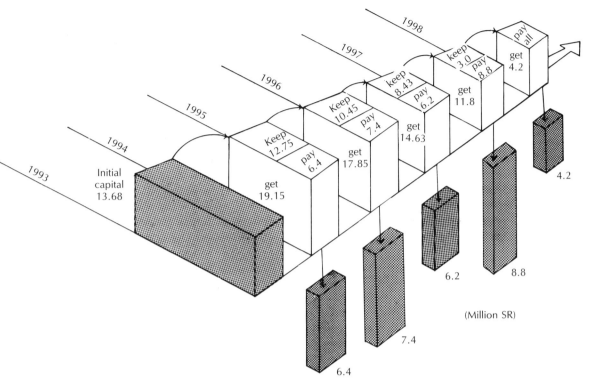

Figure 12.6 Meaning of the present value of a stream of cash flows.

means that you must have 13.68 m SR in 1993 and the opportunity to invest at 40% in order to generate the positive cash flows attached to the Dhahran Roads contract. This is shown in Figure 12.6.

Net present value (NPV)

The net present value concept is very similar to the net future value concept.

- The net present value of a strategic alternative is equal to the difference between the present value of its expected cash flows and the present value of the expected cash flows attached to a bank deposit having the same characteristics (same initial investment, same duration and same return as the one used for the calculation of the NPV).
- When the net present value of a strategic alternative is positive, the strategic alternative is superior to the deposit; it is actually equivalent to the deposit plus a cash gift *today* equal to the net present value.
- When the net present value of a strategic alternative is negative, the strategic alternative is inferior to the deposit; it is actually equivalent to the deposit and a further cash outlay *today* equal to the net present value.

- When the net present value of a strategic alternative is zero, the strategic alternative is equivalent to the deposit, ie its rate of return is equal to the rate of return of the deposit. This rate is called *the internal rate of return* of the strategic alternative.

The net present value can be used exactly in the same way as the net future value. The main reason why people prefer to use net present values is that different strategic alternatives generally have different durations. When this is the case, it is easier to discount their consequences back to one specific date: *today*. Another, and most important, reason is that managers are more interested in knowing the consequences of their decisions today rather than at some date in the future.

Instead of comparing strategic alternatives with deposits, we could compare them with loans or financing sources in general: loans actually work like deposits except for the fact that it is the bank which, in a sense, makes a deposit with you.[1] If we assume that financing in general works as a kind of deposit made with you by suppliers of capital,[2] then you can say that:

- The net present value of a strategic alternative is equal to the difference between the present value of the expected cash flows attached to this alternative and the present value of the expected cash flows attached to the financing or capital required (same amount as the investment required by the alternative and same duration).
- When the net present value of a strategic alternative is positive, then the strategic alternative is worth more than its financing costs; hence this alternative can help the firm create some additional value.
- *The net present value tells you how much value, expressed as of today, is created by the strategic alternative once the financing or capital costs have been taken care of.*

Using NPVs to calculate the IRR of the contract

The concept of net present value enables us to compare the Dhahran Roads contract with bank deposits at different interest rates. In Figure 12.7, the contract is compared with a 40% bank deposit using the net present value approach.

As expected, the net present value of the contract at 40% is positive: it is actually equal to 2.68 m SR. This means that SADE could invest 2.68 m SR more in the project in 1993, or pay a 2.68 m SR commission to an agent in 1993 and still get a 40% return on the execution of the contract.

In order to find out the internal rate of return of the project, one can compare it with deposits with rates higher than 40%. This is done in Figure 12.8.

One obviously finds the same internal rate of return as with net future values.

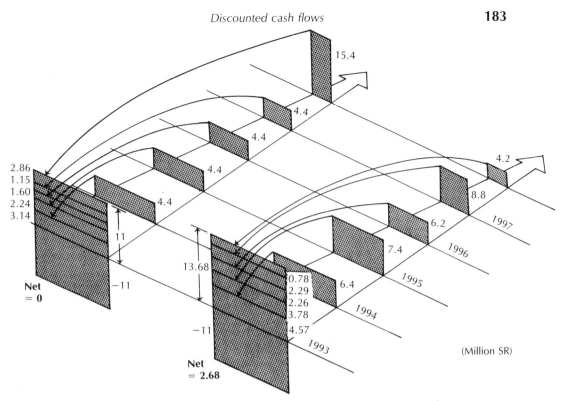

Figure 12.7 Comparison with a 40% deposit using the NPV approach.

			(Million SR)
Deposit rate	Present value of contract	Present* value of deposit	Net present value of contract
0.50	11.68	11.00	0.68
0.51	11.51	11.00	0.51
0.52	11.35	11.00	0.35
0.53	11.18	11.00	0.18
0.54	11.02	11.00	0.02
0.55	10.87	11.00	−0.13
0.5415	**11.00**	**11.00**	**0.00**

* The present value of the deposit is constant and equal to the initial
cash outlay. As indicated in Figure 12.6 the present value of a
stream of cash flows is equivalent to what you need to have now in
order to generate these cash flows in the future through a bank
deposit yielding the discount rate.

Figure 12.8 Comparison with higher rate deposits
using the NPV approach.

The NPV formula

Figure 12.8 shows a remarkable result: whatever the rate is, the present value of the deposit is constant and equal to the initial cash outlay. (You must realize that the net present value definition implies that the net present value at 40% of a deposit having a 40% interest rate is zero.) This result enables us to simplify the net present value calculation considerably:

$$\begin{matrix} \text{NPV} \\ \text{strategic} \\ \text{alternative} \end{matrix} = \begin{matrix} \text{PV} \\ \text{strategic} \\ \text{alternative} \end{matrix} - \begin{matrix} \text{PV} \\ \text{deposit} \end{matrix} \quad \begin{matrix} (\text{NPV} = \text{net present value}) \\ (\text{PV} \quad = \text{present value}) \end{matrix}$$

Since PV deposit = initial cash outlay we have

$$\begin{matrix} \text{NPV} \\ \text{strategic} \\ \text{alternative} \end{matrix} = \begin{matrix} \text{PV} \\ \text{strategic} \\ \text{alternative} \end{matrix} - \text{initial cash outlay}$$

or

$$\begin{matrix} \text{NPV} \\ \text{strategic} \\ \text{alternative} \end{matrix} = \begin{matrix} \text{initial} \\ \text{cash outlay} \\ \text{(a negative figure)} \end{matrix} + \begin{matrix} \text{PV} \\ \text{strategic} \\ \text{alternative} \end{matrix}$$

This is a very popular formula but it is often forgotten, when using it, what is really meant by the initial cash outlay. The initial cash outlay is not only the cash outlay but also the present value of the cash flows of the deposit. Applying this formula to the Dhahran Roads contract, we get

$$\text{NPV} = -11 + \frac{6.4}{(1 + r)} + \frac{7.4}{(1 + r)^2} + \frac{6.2}{(1 + r)^3} + \frac{8.8}{(1 + r)^4} + \frac{4.2}{(1 + r)^5}$$

where r = the deposit or discount rate.

Relationship between NPV and NFV

NPVs and NFVs are obviously related to each other and the relationship is:

$$\text{NPV} = \text{NFV} \times \frac{1}{(1 + r)^d}$$

where: r = discounting/compounding rate
      d = duration in years

In the case of the Dhahran Roads contract we found that at 40% the NFV is 14.40 m SR and the NPV is 2.68 m SR. You can check that $2.68 = 14.40/(1 + 0.4)^5$ and that $14.40 = 2.68 (1 + 0.4)^5$.

  To check your understanding of net future values, net present values and internal rates of return, you should now build the NFV/NPV spreadsheet model which is described in Further Model IV.2.

12.3 CALCULATING NPVs AND IRRs WITH SPREADSHEETS

Calculating NPVs and estimating IRRs without a computer can be frustrating. With spreadsheet software it is almost immediate. Returning to the Dhahran Roads case, we have built a spreadsheet model that calculates the annual cash flows of the project. We can now introduce an NPV calculation into this model.

A first approach

In order to check your understanding of the NPV, proceed as indicated in Figure 12.9. You can then verify that when the discount rate is 0.4, NPV = 2.78 m SR and when the discount rate is 0.5415, NPV = zero.

You can also check that:

- The NPV is equal to 22 m for a zero discount rate. When no reinvestment opportunity exists, the NPV of a stream of cash flows is equal to its simple cumulative sum.
- The NPV at 0.25 is 7.01 m, which means that the contract generates 7.01 m (as of 1993) above the 25% return that SADE requests. Consequently, SADE could well give away a commission of 7.01 m in 1993 and still get a 25% return. In order to check this, add 7.01 m to the costs in 1993 (make them equal to 14.01). The NPV becomes zero.

Foreground of the model A	B	C	D	E	F	G	H
13 Free Cash Flow	−11.0	6.4	7.4	6.2	8.8	4.2	22.00
14 Discount rate	0.4						
15 Time factor	0	1	2	3	4	5	
16 Discount factor	1	0.7142	0.5102	0.3644	0.2603	0.1859	
17 Discounted cash flow	−11.0	4.5714	3.7755	2.2594	2.2907	0.7809	
18 NPV	2.68						

Background of the model
B14, B15, C15, D15, E15, F15, G15, B16: data
C16: 1/(1+$B$14) $\wedge$ C15; to be copied across.
B17: +B13; C17: +C13*C16; to be copied across.
B18: +B17+@SUM(C17.G17) or more simply: @SUM(B17.G17).

Note
In order not to be disturbed by too many decimals, it is a good idea to select a display with two decimals for B18: position the cursor in B18, then / R F F [R] [R].

Figure 12.9 How to introduce an NPV calculation.

Using the built-in NPV function of your spreadsheet

Almost all spreadsheets have a built-in present value function that calculates automatically the present value of the cash flows which follow the initial outlay (in the Dhahran Roads case, the cash flows in years 1994 to 1998).

In most spreadsheets this function only requires you to tell the computer:

- The discount rate you want it to use. The best idea is to make this rate a parameter in order to be able to change it and estimate the IRR.
- The range of the cash flows to be discounted (the position of the first and the last). In Figure 11.2 these are C13 and G13.

In most spreadsheets this function is called net present value, which is a name that does not really correspond to what it does.[3] This is, however, not a major problem if we are aware of this difference in language. Using Lotus 1-2-3 notations, we can introduce a new NPV calculation in the model described in Figure 12.9 by typing:

- in A19: NPV

$$\underbrace{\text{the initial}}_{\text{cash outlay}} + \underbrace{\text{the present value of the cash}}_{\text{flows after the initial cash outlay}}$$

- in B19:
$$+\text{B13} \quad + \quad \underset{\substack{\uparrow \\ \text{the} \\ \text{function} \\ \text{name}^4}}{\text{@NPV}} \quad \underset{\substack{\uparrow \\ \text{the} \\ \text{discount} \\ \text{rate}}}{(\text{B14,}} \quad \underset{\substack{\nwarrow \\ \text{the range of the} \\ \text{cash flows to be} \\ \text{discounted}}}{\text{C13 ... G13)}}$$

To avoid having too many decimals, select a format with two decimals for B19. Check that you get the same NPV as with the first method[5] – and use the built-in NPV function each time you want to calculate a NPV with a spreadsheet.

Using the built-in IRR function of your spreadsheet

Modern spreadsheets also have a built-in facility for estimating IRR. In order to enable you to estimate the IRR of the contract, you must enter:

- in C19: IRR (in order to have this label on the right hand side of the column, position the cursor in C19, then /R(range) L(label) R(right) [R])

- in D19: @IRR(0.4, B13   ...   G13)

$$\underset{\substack{\nearrow \\ \text{a guess} \\ \text{rate}}}{} \quad \underset{\substack{\nwarrow \\ \text{the full range of the cash flows} \\ \text{including the first one}}}{} \quad \underset{\substack{\nearrow}}{}$$

Spreadsheets ask you for a guess rate because their authors made a decision to enable them to return results quickly even for lengthy calculations such as the estimation of an IRR: if your guess rate is too far from a rate which makes NPV equal to zero then Lotus 1-2-3 will abandon the iteration and return an error message (ERR in D19). If this happens, change the guess rate. In order not to get too many decimals, assign a two decimal format to the display of cell D19.

Cleaning up the model

As you no longer need the first calculation of the NPV, why not delete rows 15, 16, 17 and 18? In order to do so, position the cursor in A15; then / W(worksheet) D(delete) R(row) A15.A18 [R]. Now your NPV and IRR as calculated by the built-in functions of Lotus 1-2-3 are in row 15. As the worksheet, or its visible part, is not that big, cleaning up models and removing things which are no longer useful is a very good rule of hygiene, one worth sticking to.

12.4 WHY IS THE IRR OF THE CONTRACT SO HIGH?

A 54% IRR is fairly unusual in business and one may wonder how SADE has obtained such a good deal. Obviously, they were very good at negotiating billing prices which are superior to costs and which result in a net excess of 22 m SR at the end of the contract. But this is only one side of the coin. The high profitability of the contract results from both its 22 m net outcome (and the way in which it is spread over the years) and the initial cash outlay, which is only 11 m SR.

Had the initial cash outlay been different, the profitability of the contract would also have differed, even if the net cash excess of 22 m had been the same. If we look at the economics of the contract, it is obvious that the initial cash outlay depends directly on the amount of the advance made by the customer. Since we have put the advance rate as a parameter, we can simulate the impact of different advance rates (without changing anything else in the contract). This is done in Figure 12.10.

Whatever the advance rate is, the total cash (and profit) generated in the end by the contract is exactly the same, 22 m SR. What the advance rate does is *to modify the timing of these 22 m SR* and, as a consequence, the size of the initial cash outlay. Changes in timing can make the profitability of the contract vary from 22% to 143%. When you set the advance rate to 0.22 and above, there is no longer a cash deficit in 1993 and the concept of return no longer applies.

Advance rate	IRR
0%	22%
5%	27%
10%	36%
15%	54%
20%*	143%

* When you set the advance rate to 0.2, the IRR formula
returns an error message, change the guess rate to 1.

Figure 12.10 Impact of different advance
rates.

12.5 THE COST OF WORKING CAPITAL NEEDS

As we realized in Chapter 8, working capital needs delay cash generation. When you think about it, the initial advance in the Dhahran Roads contract works very much like a negative working capital need. Without this negative working capital need, the profitability of the contract would be 22%; with it, the profitability is 54%. This tells you about one of the consequences of working capital needs on the profitability of firms: high positive working capital needs, such as for Delta Metal, lower the profitability of companies, negative working capital needs increase the profitability of firms which experience them. However, in order to assess the full cost of working capital needs you should go beyond a simple time value of money analysis and examine the real nature of these various working capital needs: even though they all correspond to a time delay, working capital items are of a very different nature as they might either reflect a:

- contractual situation which has not been resolved yet;
- speculative position;
- poor, low quality management.

Depending on their specific nature, working capital needs may have much greater consequences than the simple time value of money.

The cost of contractual working capital needs

Contractual working capital needs may correspond to a variety of situations; retention for guarantee, credit given to customers, raw materials and work in process related to an order received, advances received from customers, credit obtained from suppliers, wages and salaries owed to employees, tax liabilities, etc. Assessing the cost of those contractual working capital needs is a relatively simple matter. It requires the evaluation of:

- The time delay (time value of money).[6]
- The administrative costs. These costs might be significant and are often overlooked. For example, paying suppliers with a delay obliges the company to have an accounts payable department. An alternative approach is to use information technology to generate payments automatically at the reception of goods.[7] Suppressing the accounts payable department may create more value than the interest gain caused by delayed payments.
- The risk involved. Because of the contractual nature of the relationship, the risk is often low and can generally be ignored. However, in the case of amounts to be received or to be paid in a foreign currency, delays create a specific exposure.[8] As the price of these items cannot be changed any longer with a view to offset an eventual variation of the foreign exchange rate, the amount to be received or to be paid is totally dependent on the fluctuations of the exchange rate.

The 'cost' of speculative working capital needs

When a company adopts a speculative strategy for its operations (see Section 9.2), then it incurs expenses before getting actual customers' orders. These expenses, made on the basis of a forecast are stored in inventory until customers' orders materialize. Expenses incurred in the absence of actual customers' orders may correspond to the deliberate and well-motivated decision to build a valuable speculative position: a manufacturer of toys may decide to produce based on an educated guess of the demand, an importer of industrial goods in a high-inflation country may decide to build a speculative stock, a manufacturer of consumer electronics may decide to build a speculative inventory of components which are in short supply, etc.

When inventory is held for building such speculative positions, it is not really relevant to talk about 'inventory costs': you should rather analyze inventory as a speculative investment and assess the value you can derive from it in a variety of scenarios.

The quality costs hidden by working capital needs

Accounts receivable are not always the result of contractual payment delays. They might also correspond to overdue accounts. Non-contractual delays of payment may have a variety of causes related to the customer or to the company itself: customers may delay their payments because they are not satisfied with the quality of the goods they have received (faulty quality, incomplete deliveries, etc), or because of inadequate invoices or because of an absence of monitoring of their payments.

Inventories often hide quality problems also. As depicted by Suzaki,[9] it is common for low-quality companies to hide their problems 'under a sea of inventory'. For these firms, carrying inventory is a way to:

- avoid attacking problems such as absenteeism, poor scheduling, defects, machine breakdowns, line imbalance, long set-up times, etc;
- pretend – and deceive themselves into thinking – that they have a fast response time to customers' needs.[10]

This view on inventory led Shingo to consider *inventory as an absolute evil*[11] that should be totally eradicated.

When working capital needs result from the inability to solve quality problems, they are just a *symptom* of a much broader problem and trying to assess their cost would be a waste of time. The true issue is to refuse the existence of such working capital needs and to go for their suppression. This is the most effective way to reveal all the hidden quality and management problems which have to be solved. When you force down the level of the sea of inventory, then the nasty hidden rocks become visible[12] . . . and can be removed.

12.6 A PARADOX: THE REINVESTMENT ASSUMPTION

The return of the Dhahran Roads contract is 54%: does this mean that, if totally financed by a loan at 54% (obviously a shark loan), the contract would break even? Intuitively it should, since the package of a contract yielding a 54% return and a loan costing 54% should leave the company with a neutral operation. Let us check it and look at the net result of the Dhahran Roads contract and of a loan of 11 m SR at 54%. This is shown in Figure 12.11.

As shown in Figure 12.11, the contract and a loan at 54% do not break even and the loan seems to outperform the contract. This actually highlights the *intermediate cash flows reinvestment assumption*: when the yearly excesses of the contract over the loan are reinvested at 54%, then the contract and the loan break even. This is shown in Figure 12.12.

	1993	1994	1995	1996	1997	1998	Cumulated
Contract	−11	6.4	7.4	6.2	8.8	4.2	22.0
Loan*	+11	−5.96	−5.96	−5.96	−5.96	−16.96	−29.78
Net	0	0.44	1.44	0.24	2.84	−12.76	−7.78

(million SR)

* Loan of 11 million reimbursed in full in 1998

Figure 12.11 Comparison of the contract with a 54.15% loan.

	1993	1994	1995	1996	1997	1998	Cumulated
Contract	−11	6.40	7.40	6.20	8.80	4.20	22.00
Loan	+11	−5.96	−5.96	−5.96	−5.96	−16.96	−29.78
Net	0	0.44	1.44	0.24	2.84	−12.76	−7.78
1998 value of net at 54.15%		2.50	5.29	0.58	4.38	−12.76	0.0

Figure 12.12

When using IRR (and NPV), you should always be aware that:

- IRR and NPV assume that the intermediate cash flows are reinvested at the IRR or at the discount rate (NPV).
- The timing of the cash flows is a factor that contributes to the definition of their IRR and NPV.

The reinvestment assumption poses a crucial problem regarding the validity of using the IRR as a criterion: when we say that the Dhahran Roads contract yields 54%, we are, in fact, saying that it yields 54% provided that the intermediate cash flows (or, more precisely, the intermediate cash flows in excess of the cash flows that would be generated by 11 m SR deposited at 54%) are reinvested at 54%. This in turn means we assume implicitly that SADE will have the opportunity to reinvest these cash flows in projects exactly as profitable as the Dhahran Roads contract.

12.7 SHOULD SADE GO AHEAD WITH THE CONTRACT?

At this stage, it may be worth summarizing what we know about the contract. It is obviously *very profitable* as it would leave SADE with a 7 m SR net present value at 25%. If 25% is the cost of financing incurred by SADE for the project, then the 7 m SR NPV corresponds to the additional value, expressed as at today, which SADE can create in executing this contract. This high profitability, which can also be estimated by the IRR (54%), is due to a satisfactory margin (revenues exceed costs by 22 m) and a favorable timing of cash inflows and outflows. *This contract therefore seems to be a very worthwhile opportunity and SADE should not hesitate to go ahead with it*, after carrying out some risk analysis. This is done in Part V.

The interesting thing to note at this stage is that we have not had to estimate the annual profits of the contract to reach this conclusion. *What matters for evaluating a contract, a project or, more generally, any strategic alternative, is the sequence of its cash flows and not the sequence of its profits.*

If our interest were limited to the assessment of the profitability of the contract, we could well stop here. However, since Mr Malik wishes to construct the annual financial statements of the contract, let us help him to do so.

NOTES

1 For example, an 11 m SR loan at 40% would correspond to the following cash flows:

1993	1994	1995	1996	1997	1998
+11	−4.4	−4.4	−4.4	−4.4	−15.4

2 This is further developed in Part VI.

3 In a net present value calculation, you should generally not discount the first cash flow: for example, we are in 1993 and we want to calculate the net 1993 (present) value of the contract. Therefore the 1993 cash flow should not be discounted. This, however, poses the problem of what we really mean by a 1993 value and it might be worth being a bit more precise and specifying the date in 1993. Here we actually calculate an NPV as of 31 December 1993.

4 In Excel, SuperCalc and Multiplan, the name of the function is simply NPV (without @).

5 An alternative NPV formula with Lotus 1-2-3 is: @NPV(B14,B13.G13)*(1+B14).

6 This may actually be done in different ways: see Figure 15.6 on p 220.

7 In 'Reengineering Work: Don't Automate, Obliterate', *Harvard Business Review*, July–August 1990, 104–12, M Hammer describes the gains captured by Ford when they decided to pay when they got the goods instead of when they got the invoice: head count in accounts payable has been cut by 75%, invoices have been eliminated and accuracy has improved.

8 Refer to Further Models VII.1 and VII.2.

9 *The New Manufacturing Challenge*, The Free Press, 1987. See the diagram on p 17.

10 See G Stalk and T Hout, *Competing Against Time*, The Free Press, 1990, Chapter 2.

11 *Non-Stock Production*, Productivity Press, 1988, p 20.

12 The diagram that naturally follows Suzaki's is in J Meredith, *The Management of Operations*, John Wiley & Sons, 1987, p 394.

CHAPTER 13

Building the Financial Statements of a Project

13.1 PROJECTING THE ANNUAL FINANCIAL STATEMENTS OF THE DHAHRAN ROADS CONTRACT

Before returning to our model, let us make some decisions and assumptions:

- Let us first consider that profit is reported according to percentage of completion (refer to Further Model IV.3 for alternative methods for reporting profits). If so, sales will be equal each year to invoices, and cost of goods sold to the annual costs.
- Let us assume that, since SADE wishes to minimize its equity investment in the company running the contract, it will invest an amount equal to the amount of the cash deficit in 1993 (11 m SR). Let us also assume that the cash inflows and outflows in 1993 are timed in such a way that the maximum cash deficit of the contract at any time will be 11 m SR.
- Let us assume that the equipment is depreciated over the life of the contract according to the following schedule: over six months in 1993 and over a full year in the years 1994 to 1997. This leads to an allowance for depreciation of one ninth of the initial value of the equipment in 1993 and two ninths of the initial value of the equipment in each of the years 1994 to 1997.
- Let us finally assume that SADE aims to draw a dividend equal to the cash generated each year. Such a policy is necessary for SADE to obtain a 54% return on the 11 m it will invest in its subsidiary.

Constructing the income statements and balance sheets of a project is a good exercise for testing your understanding of accounting principles (a comparable exercise was proposed in Further Model III.4). So why not leave the book for a while and try to construct *by yourself, on a piece of paper* the 1993 income statement of the project as well as its balance sheet as at the end of 1993, and the 1994 income statement and the balance sheet as at the end of 1994?

Figure 13.1 shows the results you should get. Figure 13.2 shows how the spreadsheet model described in Figure 11.2 can be extended in order to generate these results (our model has two more rows than in Figure 11.2, one for the discount rate, one for the NPV and the IRR).

	1993	1994	1995	1996	1997	Cumulated
Sales	11.00	43.00	48.00	39.00	27.00	168.00
CGS	7.00	28.00	31.00	25.00	17.00	108.00
Depreciation	4.22	8.44	8.44	8.44	8.44	38.00
Profit	−0.22	6.56	8.56	5.56	1.56	22.00
	31 Dec 1993	31 Dec 1994	31 Dec 1995	31 Dec 1996	31 Dec 1997	31 Dec 1998
Net fixed assets	33.78	25.33	16.89	8.44	0.00	0.00
Retention	0.55	2.70	5.10	7.05	4.20	0.00
Cash	0.00	0.00	0.00	0.00	0.00	0.00
Total assets	34.33	28.03	21.99	15.49	4.20	0.00
Advance	23.55	17.10	9.90	4.05	0.00	0.00
Net worth	10.78	10.93	12.09	11.44	4.20	0.00
Total equities	34.33	28.03	21.99	15.49	4.20	0.00

Figure 13.1 Income statements and balance sheets.

When looking at Figure 13.2 you realize that the quickest way to build the model is probably:

- To enter the labels in column A.
- To enter the formulas in column B.
- To enter the formulas in column C – they are different in general from the formulas in column B.
- To copy all the formulas in column C across columns D to G.

Instead of generating zeros, some formulas may return strange things such as −2E−15 or −9E−16, etc. This is actually equivalent to zero and can be avoided by selecting a two decimal display format.

Accounting issues

You can check that cumulative profit is equal to 22 m SR in Figure 13.1. Calculation of annual profits corresponds to an allocation of the total profit for years 1993 to 1997. You may actually question the allocation shown in Figure 13.1: why report a loss in 1993? This is somewhat inconsistent with the fact that the contract is very profitable and is mainly due to our assumption related to depreciation. Allocating depreciation in relation to time made us charge 11% of the cost of equipment to 1993, whereas only 6% of the total contract is executed in that year. An alternative allocation of total profit, more consistent with the spirit of the percentage completion method is shown in Further Model IV.3.

In the balance sheets, net fixed assets start with a value of 38 m SR (in June 1993) and decrease with the allowance for depreciation. In the end, their value is zero.

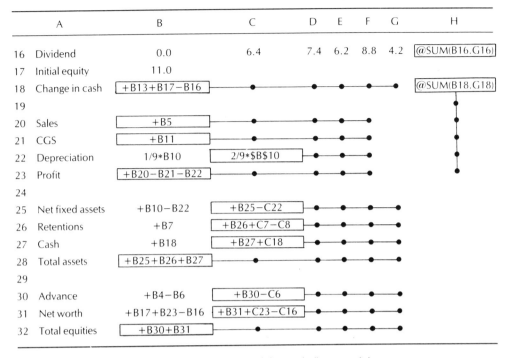

Figure 13.2 Extension of the cash flow model.

Cumulative retentions should be considered as an asset. They correspond to amounts invoiced to the customer and not yet paid (very much like accounts receivable). The amount of the retention account in the balance sheet increases each year by the amount of the annual retention. In 1997 and 1998, it decreases with the recoveries.

Cash in the balance sheet remains equal to zero throughout the period: starting from a zero initial balance, it changes each year by the amount of the change in cash as estimated by the cash flow statement. In 1993, this change in cash is zero due to the fact that initial equity (11 m SR) exactly covers the cash deficit. From 1994 to 1998, the annual change in cash is also zero, since SADE draws a dividend equal to the amount of cash generated.

The advance account on the liability side of the balance sheet corresponds to the initial advance made by the customer. As it is money received in advance of work invoiced, it should be considered as a liability. This account progressively decreases by amounts equal to the annual recoveries of initial advance. At the end, this account is zero.

Net worth starts with a value of 11 m SR (the amount of the initial capital). It then increases by an amount equal to the retained profit (profit minus dividend).

Finally, balance sheets do not show any accounts receivable or payable. This is consistent with the assumption that revenues and expenses are paid for in cash.

Dividends

Results in Figure 13.1 show that our assumption regarding dividends was probably not totally realistic: the general rule about dividends is that they cannot exceed the amount of profit (or, more precisely, the amount of profit and retained earnings). In Figure 13.1, this rule is clearly violated and SADE would have to draw dividend more slowly if this rule were to be respected. This would obviously reduce the return obtained by SADE on the contract. This is a problem often encountered with projects: in order to achieve the return to which they are entitled, shareholders wish to draw cash from the project as soon as it is generated but, since the reference for dividends is profit, not cash, this is, in some cases, difficult to achieve.

It should be mentioned here, however, that means do exist to help shareholders draw the cash as soon as it is generated. Legislation in a number of countries enables shareholders to draw a dividend higher than the amount of profit when it is related to project activities. For the sake of simplification, let us assume here that Sade will be able to draw dividends as shown in Figure 13.1.

Modelling issues

An important point to note is that, when you have built the cash flow statements (down to row 18 in Figure 13.2) *you do not need to enter any new data for estimating income statements and balance sheets*. All the income statement and balance sheet figures are generated by formulas in Figure 13.2. Our model is driven by the cash flow statements, and income statements and balance sheets are just a rearrangement of the data of the cash flow statements.

The independent calculation of total assets and total liability and shareholder's equity provides you with a way of checking the model, a very old checking device used in accounting. In order to benefit from this checking device, you should obviously calculate cash and net worth as in Figure 13.2 and not plug in net worth as is sometimes done. (Plugged in equity would correspond to the following formulas: $+B28-B30$ in B31, $+C28-C30$ in C31, etc: *this is not a correct approach.*)

In order to carry out a dynamic check of the model, you can set the dividends to zero. When you do so, you get the following figures for the balance sheets:

	31 Dec 1993	1994	1995	1996	1997	1998
Net fixed assets	33.78	25.33	16.89	8.44	0.00	0.00
Retentions	0.55	2.70	5.10	7.05	4.20	0.00
Cash	0.00	6.40	13.80	20.00	28.80	33.00
Total assets	34.33	34.43	35.79	35.49	33.00	33.00

Advance	23.55	17.10	9.90	4.05	0.00	0.00
Net worth	10.78	17.33	25.89	31.44	33.00	33.00
Total equities	34.33	34.43	35.79	35.49	33.00	33.00

The balance sheet at the end of 1998 enables you to check once more that cumulative cash equals cumulative profit. The 33 m SR cash balance at the end of 1998 is equal to the net worth, which is itself equal to the sum of the initial capital (11 m SR) and the retained profits (22 m SR).

Keeping the dividends to zero, you can then set the advance rate to zero. If you do so, the balance sheets are still balanced, but cash in the 1993 balance sheet is not acceptable. In order to bring it to zero, you have to increase the amount of initial equity; a minimum initial equity payment of 34.55 m SR (to be entered in B17) is needed to have a positive cash balance at the end of 1993. When you enter a 34.55 m initial equity payment, you get an ending cash balance and net worth amounting to 56.55 m SR. This amount corresponds to the sum of the initial equity of 34.55 m and of the additional value generated by the contract over its life, 22 m SR.

13.2 WHAT DO ACCOUNTING MEASURES OF PROFITABILITY MEAN?

When estimating the internal rate of return of the Dhahran Roads contract, we only considered its annual cash flows and did not refer to its annual profits. This is the correct procedure when evaluating strategic alternatives since their profitability depends primarily on the former, the annual cash flows, rather than the latter, the annual profits. However, managers do also use accounting measures of profitability or book returns. Let us explore what these measures mean.

Return on assets (ROA)

Among the many accounting measures of profitability there is one which is very popular: return on assets (ROA). ROA is defined as annual profit after tax divided by total assets. A number of people prefer to define ROA as profit after tax plus interest after tax over total assets. The rationale behind this adjustment of profit after tax is explained in Part VI. This difference in definition of ROA does not matter, however, in the Dhahran Roads case since there are no interest expenses.

We can easily introduce an ROA calculation in our model.

In A34, type: ROA, in B24 type: +B23/B10
In C34, type: +C23/B28

Copy the content of C34 across the range D34.F34

Enter in G34 a formula for calculating the average ROA over the life of the contract: @SUM(B34.F34)/5

When this is done, you get the results shown in Figure 13.3.

	ROA
1993	−0.01
1994	0.19
1995	0.31
1996	0.25
1997	0.10
Average	**0.17**

Notes
· advance rate: 0.15
· initial equity: 11
· all cash is drawn through dividends (as in Figure 13.2)

Figure 13.3 Returns on assets (ROA).

It is obvious that anyone who is provided only with the figures shown in Figure 13.3 has very little chance of guessing that the return of the project is equal to 54%. Why does ROA give such a poor estimate of the profitability of the contract?

One fundamental defect of ROA is that it compares profit with total assets, a variable which does not really reflect the investment needed for executing the contract. For example, at the end of 1993, total assets amount to 34.33 m SR, but a large part of these assets is actually financed by the customer's advance payment: 23.55 m SR as of December 31 1993. This is why many business organizations prefer using *return on capital employed* (ROCE) *or return on net assets* (RONA) – a different name for the same thing – rather than ROA.

Return on capital employed (ROCE)

Book return on capital employed, or, more simply, return on capital employed, is defined as follows:

$$\text{ROCE} = \frac{\text{operational profit after tax}}{\text{net fixed assets} + \text{working capital needs}}$$

where working capital needs are equal to:

    accounts receivable
+ inventory
+ other operational debtors
− accounts and notes payable trade
− other operational creditors (all other non-interest-bearing liabilities)

When so defined, ROCE reflects more accurately the return on the actual investment needed and is therefore a better measure of profitability than ROA. It remains to be proved, however, that it is a satisfactory measure.

Let us see what it tells us in the Dhahran Roads case. In order to introduce a ROCE calculation in the model you must:

In A35, type: ROCE, in B35 type: + B23/−B13
In C35, type: +C23/(B25+B26−B30) and copy across the range D35.F35
Introduce a formula for calculating the average ROCE in G35.

When this is done, you get the results shown in Figure 13.4.

	ROCE
1993	−0.02
1994	0.61
1995	0.78
1996	0.46
1997	0.14
Average	**0.39**

Note:
· Advance rate: 0.15
· Initial equity: 11
· All cash is drawn through dividends (as in Figure 13.2)
· As the contract is wholly financed by SADE, ROCE is, in this particular case, equal to return on equity (ROE).

Figure 13.4 Returns on capital employed (ROCE).

The results of Figure 13.4 are still not very satisfactory since annual ROCEs vary a great deal from one year to another and their average is different from the return of the project as measured by the IRR, 54%. There are actually three basic reasons why ROCE and IRR give different signals:

- ROCE is calculated in relation to the capital employed as at the beginning of each successive year, whereas IRR is based on the initial investment.
- Annual ROCEs are intermediate and periodic measures of profitability whereas IRR is a global measure.
- Finally, ROCE does not account properly for the timing of the cash flows occurring after the initial investment.

The first discrepancy between ROCE and IRR can easily be eliminated: you merely calculate a return on initial capital employed (ROICE). When you do this, you get the results shown in Figure 13.5.

What do the results in Figure 13.5 tell us?

- The average ROICE is equal to the non-discounted return, the return we calculated at the very beginning of our analysis when we did not account for the reinvestment of intermediate cash flows. On average, ROICE is not that far from IRR except that it ignores a fundamental dimension of the problem: the timing of the positive cash flows. As shown in Further Model IV.4, it is possible to recognize the impact of the timing of the cash flows when using ROICE but this is rather complicated.

	ROICE
1993	−0.02
1994	0.60
1995	0.78
1996	0.51
1997	0.14
Average	**0.4**

Figure 13.5 Returns on initial capital
employed (ROICE).

- Annual ROICEs differ a great deal from one year to another. This is due to the fact that they do not measure the global profitability of the contract but rather the contribution of each year to the building up of this profitability. As the contribution of each year to the global profitability varies due to different levels of sales and different allowances for depreciation,[1] so annual ROICEs differ from one year to another.

What can we conclude about the use of accounting measures of profitability like ROA and ROCE? Potentially, ROA and ROCE can be used for two purposes: decision making and control.

- *As far as decision making is concerned, we do not recommend the use of ROA and ROCE.* The only valid criterion is NPV – please refer to Chapter 15.
- As far as control is concerned, ROA and ROCE should be used with great care. In many industries, ROCE is a better measure than ROA but annual ROCEs are only *intermediate and periodic measures* of profitability.[2] As a result, annual ROCEs mix profitability with the level of activity, which makes their interpretation difficult. Return on initial capital employed (ROICE) would be more satisfactory than ROCE but it is a very difficult measure to use in practice.[3]
- You finally have to bear in mind that ROCE and ROA do not reflect timing effects properly.

As a consequence, when using ROCE and ROA, you must always remember that you are using an indicator of performance which, although it has a strong relationship to profitability, is not really profitability.[4] So why not try to use cash measures for control as well? When the contract is under way, SADE can check each year that the actual cash flows are equal to those expected. If so, the actual return of the contract will also be as expected.

NOTES

1 Further Model IV.3 shows that when you use a pure percentage-of-completion method, annual profits and annual ROICEs are as follows:

	1993	1994	1995	1996	1997
Profit	1.44	5.63	6.29	5.11	3.54
ROICE	0.13	0.51	0.57	0.46	0.32

You can check that in this case each annual ROICE is in the same proportion to total ROICE (200%) as annual profit and sales are to total profit and total sales. In this case, ROICE would be equal to 40% each year, if sales were themselves equal to one-fifth of the total sales each year.

2 In *Relevance Lost*, 1987, Harvard Business School Press, T Johnson and R Kaplan imagine the objectives of the Venetian merchants when accounting was created five hundred years ago: 'To compute overall profitability of the venture and to distribute the net proceeds (the retained earnings) among the initial investors was a worthwhile role for accounting. One has to wonder, however, whether the investors or the Venetian version of the Securities and Exchange Commission or Financial Accounting Standards Board, also asked the accountant to compute the expedition's profit during the third quarter of 1487 when the caravan was traversing the Persian desert *en route* to India.'

3 To assess the profitability of business firms, the French central bank (Banque de France) uses a criterion that is very close to ROICE:

$$\frac{\text{profit before interest and taxes}}{\text{gross fixed assets} + \text{working capital needs}}$$

4 Some people argue that, since the activity of firms consists of a variety of projects at various stages of development, one could assume that there is an averaging-out effect that makes ROCE and ROA good estimators of profitability. Unfortunately, *this is not generally true*. For more about this, refer to: E Solomon and J Laya, 'Measurement of company profitability: some systematic errors in accounting rate of return' in AA Robichek (ed.), *Financial Research and Management Decisions*, John Wiley (1967). Also to: R Shinnar, O Dressler, CA Feng and A Avidan (1989), Estimation of the Economic Rate of Return for Industrial Companies', *Journal of Business*, **62**(3): 417–47 and to: A Steele (1986), A Note on Estimating the Long Run Rate of Return from Published Financial Statements', *Journal of Business Finance and Accounting*, pp 1–13.

R.T.C. LIBRARY
LETTERKENNY

CHAPTER 14

How Much Cash from Operations should a Business Generate?

14.1 CFO SHOULD BE HIGHER THAN CAPITAL EXPENDITURES

To evaluate the profitability of the Dhahran Roads contract, we need to estimate its net annual cash flows but not to make any distinction between CFOs and capital expenditures. Annual CFOs and capital expenditures related to the Dhahran Roads contract are shown in Figure 14.1.

Figure 14.1 can help us set out the terms of the fundamental relationship between cash and profit. These can be stated as follows:

Cumulative CFE = Cumulative CFO
Cumulative PROFIT = Cumulative FREE CASH FLOW

	1993	1994	1995	1996	1997	1998	Cumulated
Profit	−0.22	6.56	8.56	5.56	1.56	0.00	22.00
Depreciation	4.22	8.44	8.44	8.44	8.44	0.00	38.00
CFE*	4.00	15.00	17.00	14.00	10.00	0.00	60.00
− increase in retentions	0.55	2.15	2.40	1.95	−2.85	−4.20	0.00
+ increase in advance	23.55	−6.45	−7.20	−5.85	−4.05	0.00	0.00
CFO	27.00	6.40	7.40	6.20	8.80	4.20	60.00
Capital expenditures	38.00						38.00
FREE CASH FLOW	−11.00	6.40	7.40	6.20	8.80	4.20	22.00

* You can check that the annual values of CFE are independent from the depreciation method you adopt.

Figure 14.1 Annual CFOs and capital expenditures.

Figure 14.1 can also help us understand how much cash a company should generate in order to be successful. As shown above, the Dhahran Roads contract is very profitable because it generates net additional value of 22 m SR. This net additional value is equal to the difference between annual CFOs and capital expenditures:

$$\frac{\text{Net excess value}}{\text{(free cash flow or profit)}} = \text{Cumulative annual CFO} - \text{Capital expenditures}$$
$$22 = 60 - 38$$

When assuming that the discount rate, or cost of financing for SADE, is equal to 25%, we can reformulate the above relationship in terms of present values. The reason why you should use the cost of financing as the discount rate is explained in Part VI.

$$\begin{array}{ccccc} \text{NPV} & & \text{PV} & & \text{PV} \\ \text{(net excess value as of 1993)} & = & \text{of the CFOs} & - & \text{of Capital expenditures} \\ 7 & = & 45 & - & 38 \end{array}$$

Given that the cost of money for SADE is 25%, the contract is profitable because the present value of the CFOs is higher than the present value of the capital expenditures, and it would remain profitable provided that the present value of the CFOs remains higher than 38 m SR. From this example, we can now tell how much CFO a company should generate.

- In order to create excess value, or work at a profit, a company should generate CFOs the present value of which is higher than the present value of the capital expenditures required for generating these CFOs.

As CFOs are usually generated after the capital expenditures, it is not sufficient that non-discounted CFOs be just equal to capital expenditures. In order to break even with financing costs (the discount rate) non-discounted CFOs should generally be significantly higher than capital expenditures. The higher the discount rate, the more the non-discounted CFOs should exceed the capital expenditures in order just to break even. The more spread over time the CFOs are, the more the non-discounted CFOs should exceed the capital expenditures in order just to break even.

Some words of caution

Although it is important to realize that CFOs should exceed capital expenditures, it is even more important to realize that *this is true on a long-term basis but not on an annual one*. During the life of the Dhahran Roads contract CFOs exceed the capital expenditures, but, in 1993, CFO is lower than capital expenditure. There is nothing wrong with this since the 1993 deficit is the condition necessary for creating an excess value. If one insisted that capital expenditures never exceed CFOs on an annual basis, companies would not be able to make many strategic moves. As the essence of most strategic moves is to accept a deficit today in order to create an excess value in the long run, deficits should not be systematically rejected.

When analyzing the past performance of a company it is very difficult to compare its CFOs and its capital expenditures since the latter lead on the CFOs. As an example, let us look at the CFOs and cash generation of the AGA group, a Swedish-based multinational gas company. These are shown in Figure 14.2.

(billion SEK)	1985	1986	1987	1988	1989	1990
CFO*	1.4	1.3	1.6	1.6	1.9	2.2
Capital expenditures†	2.5	0.8	3.1	1.2	1.9	1.4

Source: Annual reports of the company AGA Aktiebolag S-181 81.
Lidingo Sweden and author's estimates.

* CFO before interest (author's estimate).

† net of disposals.

Figure 14.2 Annual CFOs and capital expenditures at AGA.

AGA is in a highly capital-intensive business. During the period 1985–1990, the company went through a heavy capital expenditure programme aimed at reinforcing its competitive edge. Most of the investments made by AGA in the 1985–1990 period will generate CFO for 15 to 20 years. If we compare CFOs and capital expenditures in the period 1985–1990, annual CFOs are generally lower than capital expenditures. On a cumulative basis, CFOs are lower than capital expenditures. *But this is not a valid comparison* because the 1985–1990 CFOs do not correspond to the 1985–1990 capital expenditures. The level of the 1990 CFO may give an indication of how wrong the comparison is.

CHAPTER 15

Net Present Value as the Criterion for Evaluating Strategic Alternatives and as the Outcome Variable of All Financial Models and Plans

To analyze Dhahran Roads, we have used NPV and IRR. NPV, however, is a much better criterion than IRR.

15.1 THE REASONS FOR USING NPV

The first reason for using NPV is that people are in business to create additional value rather than to generate large percentage returns. If, for example, you have $10 million available, a strategy that enables you to invest this $10 million to earn 30% and therefore create an additional value of $3 million is preferable to a move that offers you a 100% return on a $10 000 initial outlay.

The second reason for preferring NPV is its usefulness for strategic decision making. Let us assume that, when evaluating strategic alternatives, you calculate their net present values using the cost of financing as the discount rate. When doing so, the NPV tells you how much value strategic alternatives create beyond their financing costs. What is even more interesting is that the NPV also tells you what this additional value is as of today. You can then not only decide whether or not you want to select different strategic alternatives but also, and most important, you can construct alternative strategies. In the Dhahran Roads case, the contract is presented as it has resulted from the negotiations which took place between Sade and its customer. You should realize, however, that NPV calculations should not be performed when the contract is finalized. *On the contrary, they are most useful when performed during the negotiation phase.*[1] As negotiation is a give and take process, NPV calculations enable you to estimate how much a new demand from the customer would cost you and to imagine ways to avoid this cost or, better still, improve the deal even further. The NPV approach provides managers with a unique opportunity to probe their business ideas: are these ideas going to generate extra value? Would it be possible to find better ideas that would result in even more value? What could destroy this value? Etc. However, a fully effective use of the NPV approach seems to be subject to two basic conditions.

1. NPV calculations should be carried out by the manager who has to make the decision

The NPV approach does not help managers to evaluate situations which already exist; it helps them rather create new alternatives from their unique understanding of a business situation. NPV calculations cannot be delegated for the simple reason that it is only when you carry them out that you discover how to do them and what information you really need. When performed by specialists who do not know enough about the environment of the decision, NPV calculations often look very mechanical and are of little practical use. This may explain why many organizations which have delegated such calculations to specialists have experienced disappointment.[2] The idea of having the decision makers perform NPV calculations by themselves was not realistic before the advent of the new PC/spreadsheet technology; we believe that the situation has changed today.

2. NPV calculations should be carried out early in the decision process

The strategic decision making process is a long and complex organizational process which often progressively reduces the range of possible alternatives. Strategic decisions which imply commitment of funds or capital expenditures might be analyzed according to phases such as identification of ideas, development of ideas, decision and control. NPV calculations should not be confined to the decision phase, as they seem to be in many finance text books, but should also be used in earlier phases when most alternatives are open.[3]

Another and very important reason for preferring NPV to IRR is related to the reinvestment rate assumption. When estimating the IRR at 54%, you assume that the intermediate cash flows are reinvested at 54%, which further assumes that Sade will find a contract exactly as profitable as Dhahran Roads, which is very unlikely. When calculating the NPV at 25%, you assume that the intermediate cash flows are reinvested at 25%. If 25% is the cost of financing to Sade, this reinvestment assumption is very reasonable. The only problem is that, when calculating NPVs, you assume that the discount rate, or financing cost, will remain constant over the period of calculation.

The NPV approach reflects more clearly the way strategic moves are implemented in real business life.

- Managers undertake strategic moves which result in a series of expected cash flows over time. Some of these cash flows are negative and require financing, some others are positive and can be invested.

- In most business organizations, cash management, and funding in general, is done centrally by a treasury department. Consequently, cash deficits are generally financed from a central pool of funds and all cash excesses are transferred to it (in most organizations, managers are not allowed to use the cash they generate).
- When working in an operational unit, you can generally consider that there is a single rate (for a given level of risk, as shown in Part VI) at which you can borrow from the central pool of funds and/or get paid for your cash excesses.
- The NPV translates the series of cash flows over time into one single number, the additional value it creates as of today, after financing costs and investment gains have been accounted for.
- The additional value corresponding to the NPV could not exist without a pool from which funds can be drawn and/or reinvested. As we calculated NPV, these withdrawals and deposits to the pool of funds are assumed to be made on an annual basis.

One last, and equally important, reason for preferring NPV to IRR, is that NPVs are *additive*. When analyzing a complex strategic alternative, you may find it useful to break it down into several components; when using NPV, this poses no problem as the NPV of the total is equal to the sum of the NPVs of the components. When using IRR, it is very difficult since the IRR of the sum is not equal to the sum of the IRRs.

15.2 A POPULAR BUT INCOMPLETE CRITERION: PAYBACK

We should also mention one criterion which is widely used in practice, payback. This measures how long you need to get back the money invested, or how long it takes before the cumulative net cash is positive. The payback of the Dhahran Roads contract is less than two years (1.6 years, if you assume that cash flows are generated evenly over the years). Payback gives you some interesting information about a sequence of cash flows but, since it ignores the magnitude of the total cumulative cash flows, it can only be considered as a secondary criterion. In order to realize the limitations of payback, look at the following sequence of cash flows:

1993	1994	1995	1996	1997	1998
−11	6.4	7.4	0	0	0

This sequence of cash flows has the same payback as the Dhahran Roads contract even though it is definitely less attractive in terms of creation of additional value.[4]

15.3 PROFIT, CASH AND NPV

Both the profit and the cash approach aim to help managers assess how much additional value their activity, or operations, create. But even though they pursue a similar goal, the two approaches differ a great deal.

Profit is an intermediate and periodic measure of how much additional value is created. When a company reports a profit in a given accounting period, this has a very clear meaning: the company has created additional value during that period. Obviously, allocating profit to specific time periods is often a matter of judgement but the eventual allocation mistakes cancel each other out on a cumulative basis. Operational profit estimates the additional value above investment costs. Profit, as calculated in the income statement, estimates the additional value above investment costs and part of the financing costs, those related to debt. If the rule to account for equity costs were adopted by accounting (see Chapter 4), profit would estimate the additional value created above investment and financing costs.

As a periodic and intermediate measure of how much additional value is created, free cash flow is not satisfactory. The cash approach is a total approach which requires the assessment of the initial investment, the estimation of all subsequent CFOs and the calculation of an NPV which summarizes all these cash flows into one single number which corresponds to the additional value created above the financing costs (provided you use the financing cost as the discount rate). Intermediate free cash flows do not correspond to additional value created, only NPV does. Consequently, you can compare NPV and profit but you cannot really compare free cash flows and profit. A comparison of the profit and cash approaches to the Dhahran Roads contract is shown in Figure 15.1.

As it considers the totality of projects and, more generally, of strategic decisions, NPV is especially useful when you want to assess the value of alternatives you are contemplating. On the other hand, profit is especially useful when you want to assess how successful you have been in the period which has just elapsed. NPV is fundamentally future-orientated whereas profit is primarily past-orientated.

NPV takes explicitly into account the effort required by a decision as well as the timing of its outcomes. It does so through the discount rate or cost of financing. NPV corresponds to the additional value created by the decision after the bankers and shareholders have been paid. Profit does not really consider the effort required at the beginning (capital expenditures being spread out through the allowance for depreciation) and ignores a large part of the financing costs (only debt costs are considered). In other words, profit corresponds to the additional value created for the shareholders after banks have been paid. This is a major difference between the profit and the NPV approaches to value.

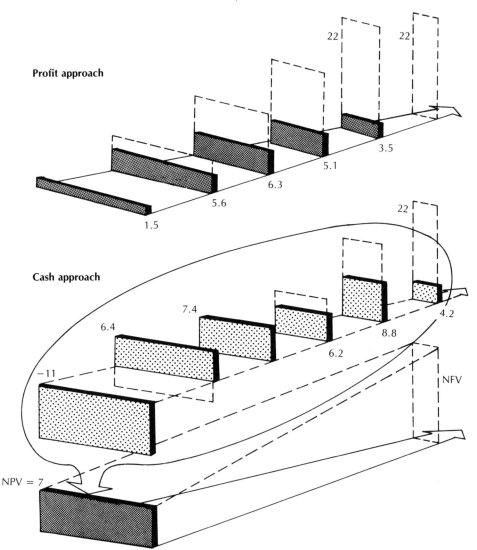

Profits are estimated here according to a pure completion method (see Further Model IV.3).

Figure 15.1 Cash and profit approaches.

NPV expresses the additional value created as at a specific date, today's date. Annual profits are expressed as of the date of the period to which they refer. As different profits correspond to different dates, the cumulative sum of profits is an estimate of additional value which largely ignores the time dimension.

In order to reconcile the profit and NPV approaches, you must do two things. You must account for equity cost in the calculation of profit and express profits in relation to a common date before you cumulate them. When

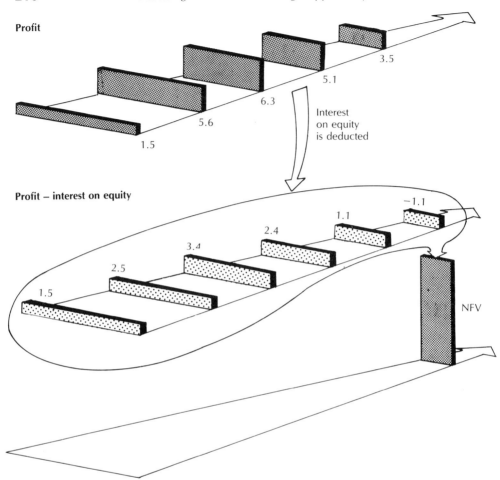

Figure 15.2 Reconciling the profit and NPV approaches.

you express the annual profits after equity costs in 1998 value and add them up, you get a figure equal to the NFV, which demonstrates that the profit and NPV approaches can be reconciled. This is shown in Figure 15.2.

15.4 THE REASON FOR USING BOTH PROFIT AND CASH APPROACHES TO MODEL STRATEGIC ALTERNATIVES

When modelling strategic alternatives, it is useful to use both the profit and the cash approaches in turn.

- Using the profit approach, you can first evaluate the difference between the total revenues and costs associated with a strategic alternative over its entire life. Even though cumulative profit is not an adequate measure of the desirability of a strategic alternative, it is an important item to estimate; a positive cumulative profit is a necessary condition if a strategic alternative is to be valuable, and cumulative profit is relatively easy to estimate.

- You can then explode the cumulative profit into a time-related cash curve, a cash flow analysis. Cash flow analysis is a necessary, but difficult, task. As cash flows are volatile, it is very easy to make estimation errors. This is why it is useful to have, first, an idea of the cumulative value of the cash flows, and then to check that this value is verified in your various analyses. At this stage you should probe your assessment of the cash curve using alternative cash flow models, as we did in Part III.

- The next step is to reconstruct a global value with the help of the NPV. This global value is the only one to be considered when you assess the relative desirability of the various options. Never forget, however, that the quality of your NPV estimate depends very much on the quality of your estimate of the timing of the cash flows. It is clear, for example, that the NPV and IRR of the Dhahran Roads contract depends very much on the assumptions we made in relation to the timing of the cash flows.

In Chapter 5, we highlighted one key contribution of finance to model building for strategic decision making. It provides you with an *outcome variable* that makes sense for the organization as a whole. In Chapter 5, we suggested that this outcome variable was CFO. This is not totally true as *the true outcome variable is NPV*. This means that each time you build a model for evaluating strategic alternatives, you should aim not only to evaluate the CFOs and the capital expenditures, but also to evaluate the NPV. *The NPV is the obvious bottom line of any financial model.* You can refer to Further Model IV.5 to see how NPV and IRR can be used for assessing the new credit plan at Delta Metal. You will also find, in Part VII, an example of using NPV as the outcome variable of a model for evaluating the strategic alternatives related to the launching of a new product.

15.5 NPV AS THE OUTCOME VARIABLE OF ALL FINANCIAL MODELS AND PLANS

Even though they often use NPV for assessing new capital expenditures, many managers do not consider it as the outcome variable of financial plans like those we built for Delta Metal in Part III. By not using NPV for such models, managers deprive themselves of the most powerful criterion which exists for comparing alternative financial plans.

Figure 15.3 shows the foreground of a simple model you can use for

A	B	C	D	E	F	G	H	I	J
1	1989	1990	1991	1992	1993	1994	1995	1996	
2 Growth	26.3%	15.7%	0.2%	0.2%	0.2%	0.2%	0.2%	0.2%	
3 NET SALES	39.5	45.7	45.8	45.9	46.0	46.1	46.2	46.3	
4 Operating income/sales	12%	12%	5%	5%	5%	5%	5%	5%	
5 OPERATING INCOME	4.6	5.7	2.3	2.3	2.3	2.3	2.3	2.3	
6 INTEREST NET	0.4	0.2	0.2	0.4	0.4	0.3	0.3	0.2	
7 PROFIT BEFORE TAX	4.2	5.5	2.1	1.9	1.9	2.0	2.0	2.1	
8 TAX	1.5	2.0	0.9	0.7	0.7	0.7	0.8	0.8	
9 DEPRECIATION	1.3	1.6	1.9	1.8	1.8	1.8	1.8	1.9	
10 CFE	3.9	5.1	3.1	3.0	3.0	3.1	3.1	3.2	
11 Working capital needs/sales	20%	19%	18%	18%	18%	18%	18%	18%	
12 WORKING CAPITAL NEEDS END	7.9	8.5	8.1	8.1	8.1	8.1	8.2	8.2	
13 CFO (after interest)	3.3	4.5	3.5	3.0	3.0	3.1	3.1	3.2	
14 CFO (before interest)	3.6	4.6	3.6	3.3	3.3	3.3	3.3	3.3	
15									8.2
16 PRESENT (92) VALUE 92–96 CFOs (Working capital open 92 deducted)	2.5	3.3	3.9	8.6					
17 INVESTMENTS NET				1.8	1.8	1.8	1.8	1.9	
18 PRESENT VALUE INVESTMENTS				7.1					
19 NET PRESENT VALUE CREATED 92–96				1.5					
20					0% increase over base	0% increase over base			
21	1989	1990	1991	1992	1993	1994	1995	1996	
22									
23 FREE CASH FLOW	0.8	1.2	−0.4	1.1	1.2	1.2	1.3	1.3	
24 DIVIDENDS	0.5	0.7	0.7	0.7	0.7	0.7	0.7	0.7	
25 NEED FOR EXTERNAL CAPITAL	0.3	0.5	−1.1	0.5	0.5	0.5	0.6	0.6	
26 NEW LOANS				0.0	0.0	0.0	0.0	0.0	
27 NEW EQUITY				0.0	0.0	0.0	0.0	0.0	
28 CHANGE IN CASH (Theoretical)				0.5	0.5	0.5	0.6	0.6	
29 LOAN REPAYMENTS (cash excesses)				0.5	0.5	0.5	0.6	0.6	
30 CHANGE IN CASH				0.0	0.0	0.0	0.0	0.0	
31									

32								
33 CASH	5.1	6.8	7.8	7.8	7.8	7.8	7.8	7.8
34 WORKING CAPITAL NEEDS	7.9	8.5	8.1	8.1	8.1	8.1	8.2	8.2
35 NET FIXED ASSETS	11.2	12.7	15.6	15.6	15.6	15.6	15.6	15.6
36 CAPITAL EMPLOYED	24.2	27.9	31.5	31.6	31.6	31.6	31.6	31.6
37								
38 LOANS	8.8	9.4	12.7	12.3	11.8	11.2	10.6	10.0
39 NET WORTH	15.4	18.5	18.8	19.3	19.8	20.4	21.0	21.6
40 CAPITAL EMPLOYED	24.2	27.9	31.5	31.6	31.6	31.6	31.6	31.6
41								
42								
43								
44 ROCE	24%	30%	11%	10%	10%	10%	10%	10%
45 ROCE 2	24%	26%	12%	7%	7%	7%	7%	7%
46 NET DEBT/EQUITY	14%	14%	26%	23%	20%	17%	13%	10%
47 INTEREST COVERAGE	10.7	34.8	12.1	5.2	5.8	6.8	8.3	10.7
48								
49								
50 INTEREST PAID	1.2	1.2	1.5					
51 INTEREST RECEIVED	0.8	1.1	1.3					
52 Interest/loans	14%	13%	12%	10%	10%	10%	10%	10%
53 Net interest/net loans	15%	16%	17%					

* Parameters.

Notes on the model

This model is derived from the situation of a European based international company (data in billion SEK).

  Width of columns: global: 6. To show labels as in the table, you need to set the width of column A to 18 and abbreviate the labels. Format: zero decimals except for percentages.

  Columns B to D are used to recalculate the recent past history of the company (a useful check of the model). Columns E to F portray a base solution ie what would happen if operations were pursued in the conditions of 1991 (the market being expected to allow for a 0.2% growth in sales each year).

  The outcome variable of any scenario for the future (here the base solution) is the NPV in E 19.

  In the period 1992–96, the model assumes that any cash excess is used to repay debts, and that any cash deficit is financed by new loans. In case that outstanding loans become too high, you can enter in the model a new equity issue.

Notes on variables

Net interest is the difference between interest paid on loans and interest received on excess cash balances: because of its international operations, this company cannot totally centralize cash management and as a result the excess balances of some units cannot be used to finance the deficits of others.

  Other net assets are the net sum of: net fixed assets, financial assets, inventories, accounts receivable, other operational assets, accounts payable and other operational or non interest bearing liabilities.

  There are two calculations on Return of Capital Employed (ROCE). The calculation in row 44 excludes financial gains. The second calculation in row 45 includes financial gains (see formulas in Figure 15.4).

Figure 15.3 Foreground of a model for comparing financial plans.

comparing alternative financial plans. Figure 15.4 shows the background of this model and Figure 15.5 shows an alternative presentation of the same model aimed at making its use easier.

The model in Figure 15.3 is extremely simple as it evaluates cash flows from only six parameters:

- Sales growth
- Operating income to sales
- Depreciation to sales
- Tax rate
- Working capital needs to sales
- Capital expenditures.

Three additional parameters are also needed in order to model the financing aspects:

- Dividend as a percentage of profit after tax
- New equity issues
- Interest rate on loans and cash excesses.

These latter parameters, however, have no influence on the value created.

The list of parameters is short, and you may wonder if it is sufficient. Experience shows, however, that these few, particularly the first six, are often enough to enable you successfully to explore alternative strategies. Among them, three are what we can call the three fundamental drivers of value:

- Sales growth
- Margin (operating income/sales)
- Working capital needs.

You can use the model in Figure 15.3 or the one in Figure 15.5 to simulate the relative impact of these drivers on the value created. When doing so, you will check that:

- Working capital needs, as they have only a timing effect, have a strong but limited impact on the value creation process.
- Operating income to sales has the strongest impact on the value creation process.
- Growth contributes to value creation, especially when operating income is high and working capital needs are low.

Even though it focuses mainly on creation of value as assessed by NPV, the model in Figures 15.3 and 15.5 also shows the evolution of return on capital employed (ROCE), a variable which is often used to assess strategies even though its interpretation is often more difficult than NPV (see Chapter 13).

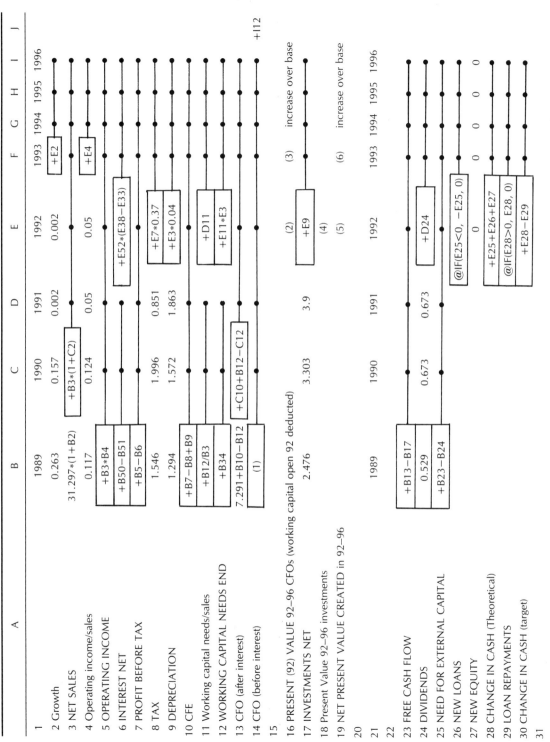

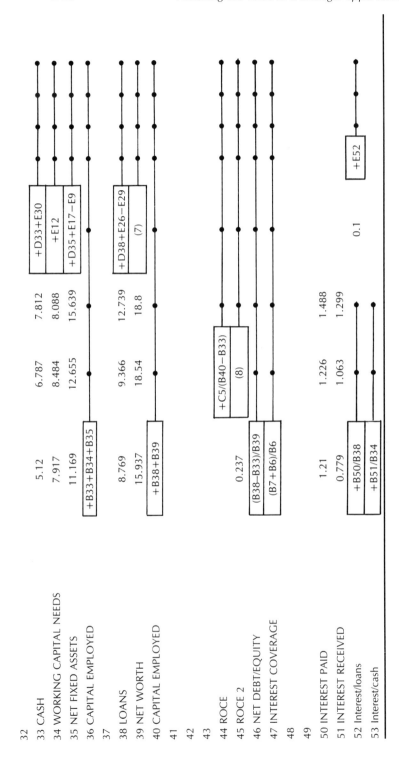

Figure 15.4 Background of the model.

Notes
1 in B14: +B13+B6*(1−B8/B7).
2 +E14+@NPV(0.15, F14. J14)−D12.
3 +E16/8.6−1.
4 +E17+@NPV(0.15, F17. I17).
5 +E16−E18.
6 +E19/1.51−1.
7 +D39+E7−E8−E24+E27.
8 (C5+C51)/((C40+B40)/2)
The model assumes that it is not possible that loans be fully repaid.

The limitations of the model

Although it is very powerful for assessing the value of alternative strategies, this model has a number of limitations of which you should be aware:

1. The model envisages the impact of working capital needs as most financial models do. Here, working capital needs equal to 38% of sales cause a one year delay of an amount equal to 38% of sales. A simple example illustrates that this model of working capital needs is not fully adequate when using NPVs. Let us assume that the working capital needs of a company are limited to a three month collection period. The common financial modelling approach invites you to introduce a one year delay for an amount equal to 25% of the sales which leads you to estimate the cost of the three month collection period as $\frac{(\text{sales} \times \text{collection period}/12)}{(1 + \text{discount rate})}$. A better approach would be to estimate monthly cash flows and to delay them by three months.[5] The model in Figure 15.6 compares these two approaches. Even though the common financial modelling approach is only an approximation, it is generally acceptable and therefore people use it as it is much more manageable.

2. In order to get meaningful results in terms of value, you should make sure that CFOs and capital expenditures correspond to each other. As the model has a very limited time horizon, it is primarily suited to
   - The evaluation of a base plan (continuation of the current activities and strategies). Such a plan should not require many new capital expenditures.
   - The evaluation of *alternative operational strategies*. Such strategies should not require much new capital expenditures either.

   For grand strategic moves involving large new capital expenditures aimed at creating CFOs over a longer time horizon than that of the model, we recommend that you use a different model, based on an incremental approach (refer to Part VII).

3. The model ignores the residual value of the company at the end. Even though you might be satisfied with a model which estimates the value created over the planning horizon, there are situations when this value should include a residual value, as different operational strategies may put the company in different positions at the end of the planning period. Estimating the residual value at the end of the planning period is obviously very difficult, but we can suggest some clues[6]:
   - During the planning period, you are able to formulate superior strategies aimed at creating competitive advantages. This is why you are able, in general, to generate a positive net present value.
   - If your planning period is limited, it is probably because you do not feel that you can imagine superior strategies beyond a certain number of years. Consequently, it is reasonable to assume that, beyond the planning

	A	B	C	D	E	F	G	H	I	J
		←	past	→	←		projection		→	
2		1989	1990	1991	1992	1993	1994	1995	1996	
3	Growth	26.3%	15.7%	0.2%	0.2%	0.2%	0.2%	0.2%	0.2%	
4	Operating income/sales	12%	12%	5%	5%	5%	5%	5%	5%	
5	Working capital needs/sales	20%	19%	18%	18%	18%	18%	18%	18%	
6	Investment net	2.5	3.3	3.9	1.9	1.9	1.9	1.9	1.9	
7	Depreciation/sales	3%	3%	4%	4%	4%	4%	4%	4%	
8	Tax rate	37%	36%	40%	37%	37%	37%	37%	37%	
9	Interest/loans or net loans	14%	13%	12%	10%	10%	10%	10%	10%	
10	Interest/cash	15%	16%	17%						
11	CFO (before interest)	3.6	4.6	3.6	3.3	3.3	3.3	3.3	3.3	
12	PRESENT (92) VALUE 92–96 CFOs (working capital open 92 deducted)				8.6	0% increase over base	0% increase over base			
13	PRESENT VAL INVEST				7.1					
14	NET PRESENT VALUE CREATED 92–96				1.5					
15	ROCE		30%	11%	10%	10%	10%	10%	10%	
16	ROCE 2	24%	26%	12%	7%	7%	7%	7%	7%	
17	PROFIT AFTER TAX	2.6	3.5	1.3	1.2	1.2	1.2	1.3	1.3	
18	DIVIDEND	0.5	0.7	0.7	0.7	0.7	0.7	0.7	0.7	
19	NEED EXTERNAL CAPITAL	0.3	0.5	-1.1	0.5	0.5	0.5	0.6	0.6	
20	NET DEBT/EQUITY	24%	14%	26%	23%	20%	17%	13%	10%	
21		1989	1990	1991	1992	1993	1994	1995	1996	
22	NET SALES	39.5	45.7	45.8	45.9	46.0	46.1	46.2	46.3	
23	OPERATING INCOME	4.6	5.7	2.3	2.3	2.3	2.3	2.3	2.3	
24	INTEREST NET	0.4	0.2	0.2	0.4	0.4	0.3	0.3	0.2	
25	PROFIT BEFORE TAX	4.2	5.5	2.1	1.9	1.9	2.0	2.0	2.1	
26	TAX	1.5	2.0	0.9	0.7	0.7	0.7	0.8	0.8	
27	DEPRECIATION	1.3	1.6	1.9	1.8	1.8	1.8	1.8	1.9	
28	CFE	3.9	5.1	3.1	3.0	3.0	3.1	3.1	3.2	
29	WC NEEDS END	7.9	8.5	8.1	8.1	8.1	8.1	8.2	8.2	
30	CFO (after interest)	3.3	4.5	3.5	3.0	3.0	3.1	3.1	3.2	
31	CFO (before interest)	3.6	4.6	3.6	3.3	3.3	3.3	3.3	3.3	
32	INVESTMENTS NET	2.5	3.3	3.9	1.8	1.8	1.8	1.8	1.9	
33	PRESENT (92) VALUE 92–96 CFOs (working capital open 92 deducted)				8.6	0% increase over base				
34	PRESENT VALUE INVESTMENTS				7.1					
35	NET PRESENT VALUE CREATED 92–96				1.5	0% increase over base				

	1989	1990	1991	1992	1993	1994	1995	1996
36 FINANCING:								
37								
38 FREE CASH FLOW	0.8	1.2	−0.4	1.1	1.2	1.2	1.3	1.3
39 DIVIDENDS	0.5	0.7	0.7	0.7	0.7	0.7	0.7	0.7
40 NEED EXTERNAL CAPITAL	0.3	0.5	−1.1	0.5	0.5	0.5	0.6	0.6
41 NEW LOANS				0.0	0.0	0.0	0.0	0.0
42 NEW EQUITY				0.0	0.0	0.0	0.0	0.0
43 CHANGE IN CASH (Theoretical)				0.5	0.5	0.5	0.6	0.6
44 LOAN REPAYMENTS (cash excesses)				0.5	0.5	0.5	0.6	0.6
45 CHANGE IN CASH				0.0	0.0	0.0	0.0	0.0
46								
47 CASH	5.1	6.8	7.8	7.8	7.8	7.8	7.8	7.8
48 WORKING CAPITAL NEEDS	7.9	8.5	8.1	8.1	8.1	8.1	8.2	8.2
49 NET FIXED ASSETS	11.2	12.7	15.6	15.6	15.6	15.6	15.6	15.6
50 CAPITAL EMPLOYED	24.2	27.9	31.5	31.6	31.6	31.6	31.6	31.6
51								
52 LOANS	8.8	9.4	12.7	12.3	11.8	11.2	10.6	10.0
53 NET WORTH	15.4	18.5	18.8	19.3	19.8	20.4	21.0	21.6
54 CAPITAL EMPLOYED	24.2	27.9	31.5	31.6	31.6	31.6	31.6	31.6
55								
56 ROCE		30%	11%	10%	10%	10%	10%	10%
57 ROCE 2	24%	26%	12%	7%	7%	7%	7%	7%
58 NET DEBT/EQUITY	24%	14%	26%	23%	20%	17%	13%	10%
59 INTEREST COVERAGE	10.7	34.8	12.1	5.2	5.8	6.8	8.3	10.7
60								
61 INTEREST PAID	1.2	1.2	1.5					
62 INTEREST RECEIVED	0.8	1.1	1.3					

Notes
This model is a mere rearrangement of the model in Figure 15.3 which aims at making it easier to use.
In order to get this model, start from the model in Figure 15.3 and:
   Insert a blank page on top of the model.
   Use the Move command to move growth in row 3, operating income/sales in row 4, working capital needs/sales in row 5, interest/loans in row 9 and interest/cash in row 10.
   Introduce investment net, depreciation/sales, tax rate, and dividend in rows 6, 7, 8 and 18; introduce formulas in the model to make use of these parameters.
   Enter formulas in row 12, E13, E14, E15, row 16, row 17, rows 19 and 20 to show the results in the upper part of the model.
   Correct CFO before interest (enter tax as a parameter). Finally, cancel some blank rows.
This process aimed at making a model easier to use is further described in chapter 27.

Figure 15.5 Alternative, simplified model.

horizon, the firm will not earn more than its cost of capital and as a result its new capital expenditures will have net present values equal to zero. This allows you to ignore the impact of any new capital expenditure beyond the planning period.
- The estimate of the residual value then comes down to your assessment of the cash flows that the firm will be able to create beyond the planning horizon due to the competitive advantages built during the planning

	A	B	C	D	E	F	G	H	I	J
			SALES	MONTHLY	ANNUAL					
1				RECEIPTS	RECEIPTS					
2										
3	1993	Jan	100				Discount rate (annual)			0.1
4		Feb	90				Discount rate (monthly)			0.008
5		Mar	120							
6		Apr	100	100						
7		May	80	90						
8		Jun	80	120						
9		Jul	60	100			**Traditional**			**Monthly**
10		Aug	60	80			**Analysis**			**Analysis**
11		Sep	80	80			(end of year			
12		Oct	100	60			cash flows)			
13		Nov	120	60			**NPV:**			**NPV:**
14		Dec	120	80	770		**981**			**1 029**
15	1994	Jan		100			Difference: −4.68%			
16		Feb		120						
17		Mar		120						
18		Apr		0						
19		May		0						
20		Jun		0						
21		Jul		0						
22		Aug		0						
23		Sep		0						
24		Oct		0						
25		Nov		0						
26		Dec		0	340					

Notes
Range C3.C26: data.
Range D3.D26: a formula depending on the collection period; When it is 0: +C3 in D3, copied down; when it is 1 month: +C3 in D4, copied down, etc.
In E/4: @SUM(D3.D14); in E26: @SUM(D15.D26)
In J3: data; in J4: $(1+J3) \wedge (1/12)-1$.
In G14: $+E14/(1+J3)+E26/(1+J3) \wedge 2$.
In J14: @NPV(J4, D3.D26).

· When the collection period is set to zero, the difference between the two approaches is −4.26%.
· When the collection period is set to three months, as in the model the difference between the two approaches is 4.68%.
· When the collection period is set to six months, the difference becomes equal to 4.03%. It is −3.90% with a 9 month collection period.

As a conclusion, the real problem is to decide if you want to discount annually or monthly (see Further Model IV.1). If you go for annual discounting, the commonly accepted method for modelling the impact of working capital needs does not introduce much further bias.
Width of columns: Global: 6; C, D, E and J: 9.

Figure 15.6 Comparing two descriptions of working capital needs.

period. In order to do so, you can look at the cash flow generated at the end of the planning period and try to estimate for how long it could be maintained (and its evolution over this period). You can then estimate the residual value as the present value of these cash flows.[7]

4. The model does not consider that financing (particularly debt financing) can create additional value. This agrees with our own view about the impact of financing (see Part VI) but you should realize that there is still much debate about this issue and that some people consider that the tax deductibility of interest charges can contribute to the creation of value.

NOTES

1 Let us assume a hypothetical situation where SADE is still negotiating the contract. Even though the customer seems to accept the terms of the contract as specified in the case, it is also clear that SADE will not get the contract if it does not act through an agent. Potential agents are very demanding and the problem is to decide on the maximum payment Sade could make and still break even; the answer is given by the NPV, 7 m SR.

Part VIII deals with models as a tool for creating and implementing cooperative strategies.

2 For more about this, refer to: LA Gordon, L Archer and FD Tuggle, 'Informational impediments to the use of capital budgeting models', *Omega*, 7 (1979). You can also refer to a paper showing how Japanese firms prepare capital expenditure decisions with a series of discussions involving a large number of managers: JE Hodder, 'Evaluation of manufacturing investments: a comparison of US and Japanese practices', *Financial Management* (Spring 1986).

3 For more about this, refer to: GE Pinches, 'Myopia, capital budgeting and decision making', *Financial Management* (Autumn 1982). You will also find in this paper a fairly extensive bibliography on capital budgeting.

4 In one very special case, when cash flows are constant and perpetual, the rate of return can be calculated as 1/payback.

5 For discounting with periods shorter than one year see Further Model IV.1.

6 Refer to A Rappaport, *Creating Shareholder Value – The New Standard for Business Performance*, Free Press (1986).

7 Rappaport also suggests (op. cit.) that you estimate this present value as equal to a perpetual stream of the last cash flow. In a number of cases, this might lead to a somewhat optimistic estimate of the residual value.

Further Models IV

FURTHER MODEL IV.1
USING PERIODS SHORTER THAN ONE YEAR FOR COMPOUNDING AND DISCOUNTING – CUMULATIVE VALUES OF COMPOUNDING AND DISCOUNTING FACTORS

In Part IV, we have considered situations where cash flows are generated once a year and where cash flows are compounded on a one-year period basis. This does not correspond to real life since most operating cash flows are generated on a continuous basis and companies have the opportunity to reinvest their cash flows for very short time periods, and also have to finance their cash deficits on a daily basis. Obviously, compounding and discounting can be performed by using periods of less than one year.

Compounding with periods of less than one year

In some very high inflation countries, banks compound interest on a monthly basis, 12% per month for example. If you invest 1 000 at the beginning of the year, at 12% a month compounded monthly, you will have, at the end of the year:

$$1\,000 \times (1.12)^{12} = 1\,000 \times 3.896 = 3\,896 \simeq 3\,900$$

This is the same as if you had invested your money at an annual rate (annually compounded) of 290%:

$$\frac{3\,896}{1\,000} \approx 3.90 = 1 + r \quad \text{hence } r = 2.90 \text{ or } 290\%$$

When interest is compounded on a monthly basis, the annual equivalent interest is much more than twelve times the monthly interest (290% v 144%). The annual equivalent interest (290%) is called the effective rate or the annual percentage rate. The rate you get when you multiply the monthly interest by twelve is generally called the stated interest rate (144%).

The relationship between the stated rate and the effective rate, is as follows:

$$\left(1 + \frac{\text{stated rate}}{12}\right)^{12} - 1 = \text{effective rate}$$

More generally, when you compound m times a year (when you use a compounding period equal to 1 year/m), the relationship between the stated and the effective rates is:

$$\left(1 + \frac{\text{stated rate}}{m}\right)^m - 1 = \text{effective rate}$$

where m = number of compounding periods in a year.

If you compound daily and assume, as many bankers do, that there are 360 days in the year, then:

$$\left(1 + \frac{\text{stated rate}}{360}\right)^{360} - 1 = \text{effective rate}$$

If the stated rate is 144%, as above, then the effective rate becomes:

$$\left(1 + \frac{1.44}{360}\right)^{360} - 1 = 3.21 \text{ or } 321\%$$

The period used for compounding makes a lot of difference but this is true only when interest rates are high; when interest rates are low, the period used has no big influence. For example, with an 8% stated interest rate, the effective rate when compounding monthly is 8.30% and 8.33% when compounding daily.

Continuous compounding

Let us go back to the relationship between the stated and effective rates:

$$\left(1 + \frac{\text{stated rate}}{m}\right)^m - 1 = \text{effective rate}$$

where m = the number of compounding periods within the year.

Denoting m/stated rate as x, we can rewrite the relationship as follows:

$$\left(1 + \frac{1}{x}\right)^{x*\text{stated rate}} - 1 = \text{effective rate}$$

When the compounding period is shortened and the number of periods increases to infinity, the value of $(1 + 1/x)^{xk}$ approaches e^k, where e is a mathematical constant whose value is approximately 2.72 and the value of $(1 + 1/x)^{x*\text{stated rate}}$ approaches $e^{\text{stated rate}}$.

The relationship between stated rate and effective rate becomes:

$$e^{\text{stated rate}} - 1 = \text{effective rate}$$

You can use Lotus 1-2-3 (the built-in function for calculating e^a is @EXP(a)) to calculate the effective rate which corresponds to a stated rate of 144% and continuous compounding: 3.22 or 322%, something very close to daily compounding.

Discounting the quarterly cash flows of the Dhahran Roads contract

In the analysis of the Dhahran Roads contract, we have assumed that cash flows are generated once a year and that they are discounted annually. This is obviously a simplification of what is going to happen and it would be useful to analyze the behaviour of the cash flows over shorter time periods. Let us assume that, when analyzed on a quarterly basis, the cash flows are as follows.

		Quarterly cash flows	Cumulative (annually)
1993	Quarter 1	0	0
	2	−12.80	−12.80
	3	0.20	−12.60
	4	1.60	−11.00
1994	Quarter 1	1.60	1.60
	2	1.60	3.20
	3	1.60	4.80
	4	1.60	6.40
1995	Quarter 1	1.85	1.85
	2	1.85	3.70
	3	1.85	5.55
	4	1.85	7.40
1996	Quarter 1	1.55	1.55
	2	1.55	3.10
	3	1.55	4.65
	4	1.55	6.20
1997	Quarter 1	1.15	1.15
	2	1.15	2.30
	3	1.15	3.45
	4	5.35	8.80
1998	Quarter 1	0.00	0.00
	2	0.00	0.00
	3	0.00	0.00
	4	4.20	4.20

You can enter these cash flows into a spreadsheet and calculate a new NPV. To do so you can input the quarterly cash flows in columns B to Y (let us say B1 to Y1). You can then enter a discount rate in B2 and an NPV formula in B3: +@NPV(B2, B1.Y1).

When the discount rate is zero, you can check that the NPV is equal to 22. But then several problems occur. If calculated as indicated above, the NPV will be as of 31 December 1992, but in Chapter 12, the NPV was calculated as of 31

December 1993. And which discount rate should you use? 0.25 is the annual rate but the quarterly (quarterly compounded) rate which corresponds to a 25% effective annual rate is equal to: $(1.25)^{1/4} - 1 \approx 0.05$ or 5%. When you input a $(1.25)^{1/4} - 1$ rate in the spreadsheet, you get a 5.48 NPV as of 31 December 1992, or $5.48 \times 1.25 = 6.85$ as of 31 December 1993, which is close to the NPV we obtained in Chapter 12 (7.01).

You can use this quarterly model for assessing the impact of different quarterly cash flow patterns. If you change the 1993 cash flows to:

	Quarter 1	Quarter 2	Quarter 3	Quarter 4
Quarterly	0.00	25.20	−37.80	1.60
Cumulative	0.00	25.20	−12.60	−11.00

(all the other cash flows unchanged)

you get a 31 December 1992 NPV of 7.32 and a 31 December 1993 NPV of 9.15. If you change the 1993 cash flows to

	Quarter 1	Quarter 2	Quarter 3	Quarter 4
Quarterly	0.00	−38.00	25.40	1.60
Cumulative	0.00	−38.00	−12.60	−11.00

(all the other cash flows unchanged)

you get a 31 December 1992 NPV of 4.25 and a 31 December 1993 NPV of 5.32.

The assumption according to which SADE will manage to tie up the initial advance and capital expenditure cash flows is very clearly a key assumption; let us assume it is a realistic one.

Discounting continuously generated cash flows

Even though cash flows are usually generated continuously, it is common practice to simplify NPV calculations and to assume that cash flows are generated once a year, at year end. What kind of bias does this simplification introduce in NPV calculations?

Let us assume that in 1993 a project generates a 1 200 cash flow and that this cash flow is generated in equal amounts each month ($1\,200/12 = 100$). If calculated from the year end cash flow, the 31 December 1992 NPV at 20% is:

$$\text{NPV} = \frac{1\,200}{1.2} = 1\,000$$

If calculated from the monthly cash flows, the same 31 December 1992 NPV at 20% is:

$$\text{NPV} = \frac{100}{(1 + r)} + \frac{100}{(1 + r)^2} + \dots + \frac{100}{(1 + r)^{12}} = 1\,089$$

where r $= (1.2)^{1/12} - 1 \approx 0.015$ or 1.5%.

Discounting the year end cash flow leads to an 8% estimation error.

If you repeat this calculation with different discount rates, you find the following results:

Annual discount rate	NPV calculated from monthly cash flows	NPV calculated from year end cash flow	Difference in %
0.08	1 151	1 111	−3%
0.10	1 140	1 091	−4%
0.12	1 129	1 071	−5%
0.15	1 113	1 043	−6%
0.20	1 089	1 000	−8%
0.30	1 044	923	−12%

So, *when you ignore the fact that cash flows are generated continuously, you underestimate the NPV* and this underestimation increases with the discount rate. For low discount rates, the bias is small and can probably be ignored when you consider that NPVs are estimates and not precise figures, but when the discount rate increases, the bias may become unacceptable.

How can you remove this bias? You can discount on the basis of periods of less than one year, as we did above for the Dhahran Roads contract but your model may become unmanageable. Or you can adjust the discount rate you use for discounting year end cash flows. How can this second approach be used?

Coming back to our example of a 1 200 annual cash flow generated evenly each month, you will realize that, in order to get the same result with monthly and year-end discounting, the following equation should be verified:

$$\frac{100}{(1 + r)} + \frac{100}{(1 + r)^2} + \cdots + \frac{100}{(1 + r)^{12}} = \frac{1\,200}{1 + R_a}$$

where r = the monthly rate which corresponds to a 20% effective annual rate and R_a = the adjusted discount rate for discounting the year end cash flow.

Since 100 = 1 200/12, we can simplify:

$$\frac{1\,200}{12} \times \left[\frac{1}{(1 + r)} + \frac{1}{(1 + r)^2} + \cdots + \frac{1}{(1 + r)^{12}} \right] = \frac{1\,200}{1 + R_a}$$

ie

$$\sum_{n=1}^{12} \frac{1}{(1 + r)^n} = \frac{12}{1 + R_a}$$

A useful relationship

To calculate the cumulative value of discount factors over n periods, you can either estimate each factor and their cumulative value or what is better use the following relationship:

$$\sum_{n=1}^{12} \frac{1}{(1 + r)^n} = \frac{1 - (1 + r)^{-12}}{r}$$

This relationship is known as the present value of an annuity formula (see page 231).

Returning to our calculations the equation can be rewritten as:

$$\frac{1 - (1 + r)^{-12}}{r} = \frac{12}{1 + R_a} \text{ or } R_a = \frac{12r}{1 - (1 + r)^{-12}} - 1$$

When $r = (1.2)^{\frac{1}{12}} - 1 \simeq 0.015$, then $R_a \simeq 0.102 \simeq 10.2\%$. Therefore when a cash flow is generated evenly each month, you should either discount the monthly cash flows at 20% (or rather at the monthly rate which is equivalent to 20%, about 1.5%) or discount the year end cash flow at 10.2%. You should check that when you discount the year end cash flow at 10.2% you get the same NPV as with monthly discounting:

$$\text{NPV} = \frac{1\,200}{1.102} = 1\,089^1$$

A spreadsheet model for comparing discounting methods

The model in Figure IV.1(a) will enable you to compare the results given by three different discounting methods when applied to the same series of cash flows.

Method 1: Cash flows are assumed to be generated at year end and are discounted annually.

Method 2: Cash flows are assumed to be generated evenly each month and are discounted monthly.

Method 3: Cash flows are assumed to be generated continuously and are discounted continuously.

The model envisages a period of two years and cash flows which can either remain the same in each period or grow (continuous growth).

The present value PV of a continuously generated cash flow discounted continuously is

$$\text{PV} = \frac{1 - e^{-nk}}{k} * c$$

where n = number of years

k = equivalent continuous discount rate. If R is the annual discount rate,

then $k = \ln(1 + R)$

c = yearly cash flow

	A	B	C	D	E	F	G	H	I	J	K	L	M	N	O	P	Q	R	S	T	U	V	W	X	Y
1	Month	1	2	3	4	5	6	7	8	9	10	11	12	13	14	15	16	17	18	19	20	21	22	23	24
2	Annual amount year 1	1 200																							
3	Annual growth rate		equivalent continuous rate							0															
4	MONTHLY GROWTH RATE	0																							
5	GROWTH COEFFICIENT	1	1	1	1	1	1	1	1	1	1	1	1	1	1	1	1	1	1	1	1	1	1	1	1
6	CUMULATIVE GROWTH COEFFICIENTS	12																							
7	MONTHLY AMOUNT (month 0)	100																							
8	MONTHLY AMOUNT	100	100	100	100	100	100	100	100	100	100	100	100	100	100	100	100	100	100	100	100	100	100	100	100
9	ANNUAL AMOUNT												1 200												1 200
10	Discount rate	0.2								equivalent continuous rate	0.18														
11	PRESENT VALUE (annual cash flow)	1 833																							
12	MONTHLY DISCOUNT RATE	0.02																							
13	PRESENT VALUE (monthly cash flows)	1 996					PRESENT VALUE (continuous)			2 011															
14	ESTIMATION ERROR	−8%								−9%															
15	DISCOUNT COEFFICIENTS	0.98	0.9	0.9	0.9	0.9	0.9	0.8	0.8	0.87	0.8	0.8	0.83	0.8	0.8	0.7	0.7	0.7	0.7	0.7	0.7	0.7	0.7	0.7	0.69

16 DISCOUNTED MONTHLY CASH FLOW	98	97	96	94	93	91	90	89	87	86	85	83	82	81	80	78	77	76	75	74	73	72	71	69

17 ADJUSTED ANNUAL RATE (year 1)   0.10   ADJUSTED ANN. RTE (year 1)   0.09

18 ADJUSTED ANNUAL RATE (year 2)   0.15   ADJUSTED ANN. RTE (year 2)   0.14

19 PRESENT VALUE   1 996   PRESENT VALUE

20 Annual adjusted rate   annual adjusted rate   2 011

Formulas

B4: PR [W5] $(1+B3) \wedge (1/12)-1$
B5: PR [W5] $(1+\$B\$4) \wedge B1$
B6: PR [W5] @SUM(B5..M5)
B7: (F0) PR [W5] +B2/B6
B8: (F0) PR [W5] +B7*(1+B4)
C8: (F0) PR +B8*(1+$B$4)
B11: (F0) PR [W5] $+M9/(1+B10+Y9/(1+B10) \wedge 2$
B12: (F2) PR [W5] $(1+B10) \wedge (1/12)-1$
B13: (F0) PR [W5] @NPV/(B12,B8..Y8)
B14: (P0) PR [W5] +B11/B13−1
B15: PR [W5] $1/(1+\$B\$12) \wedge B1$
B16: (F0) PR [W5] +B8*B15

B17: PR [W5] $1/(@SUM(B16..M16)/B2)-1$
B18: PR [W5] $1/(@SUM(N16..Y16)/Y9) \wedge (1/2)-1$
B20: (F0) PR [W5] $+M9/(1+B17)+Y9/(1+B18) \wedge 2$
M9: (F0) PR [W5] @SUM(B8..M8)
Y9: (F0) PR [W5] @SUM(N8..Y8)
J3: PR [W5] @LN(1+B3)
J10: PR [W5] @LN(1+B10)
J13: (F0) PR [W5] $(M9*(1-@EXP(-2*(J10-J3)))/(J10-J3))$
J14: (P0)+B11/J13−1
J17: PR [W5] $((B2/J13)*(1+(1+B3)/(1+B10))-1$
J18: PR [W5] $(1+J17)*(1+B10) \wedge (1/2)-1$
J20: (F0) PR [W5] $+M9/(1+J17)+Y9/(1+J18) \wedge 2$

Width of columns: global: 4; A: 33, B, J, M and Y: 5.

Figure IV.1(a) Comparing three different discounting methods.

The present value of a continuously generated, continuously growing cash flow discounted continuously is:

$$PV = \frac{1 - e^{-n(k-p)}}{k - p} * c$$

where n = number of years

k = equivalent continuous discount rate. If R is the annual discount rate, then $k = \ln(1 + R)$

p = equivalent continuous growth rate. If G is the annual growth rate, then $p = \ln(1 + G)$

c = yearly cash flow

When you discount over two years, the adjusted rate for the second year is the compounded rate which results from the adjusted rate for the first year and the unadjusted discount rate:

$$\left(1 + \frac{\text{adjusted rate}}{\text{second year}}\right)^2 = \left(1 + \frac{\text{adjusted rate}}{\text{first year}}\right) * \left(1 + \frac{\text{unadjusted}}{\text{discount rate}}\right)$$

Here $(1 + 0.15)^2 = (1 + 0.10)(1 + 0.20)$.

Consequently, when you want to adjust the discount rate to account for continuously generated cash flows, you have to use a different discount rate for each year end cash flow.

When monthly cash flows are growing at a constant rate, the bias introduced by annual discounting is smaller, but not very much.

What should you do in practice?

The first thing to remember is that NPVs are estimates. A 5 to 10% estimation error is very common with NPVs. Estimating cash flows at year end and discounting them on an annual basis is generally acceptable. However, it is a good idea to check that this simplification is valid. In order to do so, you must think about the distribution of cash flows within the yearly periods and work out the pattern of monthly or quarterly cash flows. You can then calculate an NPV based on these quarterly cash flows and compare it with the NPV calculated from the year end cash flows. If the difference is small, keep your annual model; if the difference is large, keep the monthly or quarterly model or, even better, try to adjust the annual model.

A final recommendation: do not adjust the discount rate before carefully analyzing the actual pattern of cash flows within yearly periods.

Cumulative values of discounting and compounding factors

In some circumstances, you need to calculate the cumulative value of discounting or compounding factors. For example, how do you calculate the present value of an annuity of 1 000 to be received in the five years to come? The present value formula is:

$$PV = \frac{1\,000}{1 + r} + \frac{1\,000}{(1 + r)^2} + \cdots \frac{1\,000}{(1 + r)^5}$$

$$= 1\,000 * \left[\frac{1}{(1 + r)} + \frac{1}{(1 + r)^2} + \cdots \frac{1}{(1 + r)^5} \right]$$

Rather than estimate each discount factor and then calculate their cumulative value, you can use the following relationship:

$$\sum_{n=1}^{k} \frac{1}{(1 + r)^n} = \frac{1 - (1 + r)^{-k}}{r}$$

where r = discount rate
     k = number of years (or more generally of periods)

When the sum to be received in each future period grows at a constant rate g, starting from an initial amount in period 1, then the cumulative discount factor to be applied to the initial amount is:

$$\frac{1 - \left(\dfrac{1 + g}{1 + r} \right)^k}{r - g}$$

where g = growth rate
     r = discount rate
     k = number of periods

This can be verified with an example: you expect to receive from 1993 to 1997 the following sums:

20 000 in 1993
22 000 in 1994
24 200 in 1995
26 620 in 1996
29 282 in 1997

The present (1992) value at 15% of these sums growing at 10% is equal to:

$$20\,000 * \frac{1 - \left(\dfrac{1.1}{1.15} \right)^5}{0.05} = 79\,717$$

The relationship for calculating the cumulative value of compounding factors is:

$$\sum_{n=0}^{k} (1 + r)^n = \frac{(1 + r)^{k+1} - 1}{r}$$

This relationship can be used in order to solve problems such as the following:

The sales of a company are growing 20% a year. Sales in 1992 were equal to 12 000. Assuming that there is no seasonality and that monthly sales are growing at a constant rate, what were January 1992 sales equal to? What was the value of sales in the last quarter of 1992?

- Monthly growth rate:

$$g = (1 + G)^{1/12} - 1 = (1.2)^{1/12} - 1 \simeq 0.015$$

where g = monthly growth rate
G = annual growth rate

- Sales in January 1992:

if s = sales in January 1992
S = 1992 sales

$$s[1 + (1 + g) + (1 + g)^2 + \ldots (1 + g)^{11}] = S$$

$$s\left[\frac{(1 + g)^{12} - 1}{g}\right] = S$$

$$s = \frac{S \times g}{(1 + g)^{12} - 1} \simeq 918.57$$

- Sales in the last quarter of 1992:

$$S_{10}^{12} = S_1^{12} - S_1^9$$

$$S_{10}^{12} = 12\,000 - s\left[\frac{(1 + g)^9 - 1}{g}\right]$$

$$\simeq 12\,000 - s \times 9.57 \simeq 3\,208$$

where S_{10}^{12} = sales in the last quarter of 1992
S_1^{12} = 1992 sales
S_1^9 = sales for the period January to September 1992

NOTE

1 When you consider a series of annual cash flows, you should adjust the rate for each cash flow differently, as shown in Figure IV.1(a).

FURTHER MODEL IV.2
THE NPV/NFV MODEL

This is a learning orientated model. It aims to help you understand more clearly the concepts of net future value, net present value and internal rate of return. It uses data from the Dhahran Roads contract but these may be changed.

The screen layout
With Lotus 1-2-3, the screen layout is as shown in Figure IV.2(a).

	A	B	C	D	E	F	G	H
				PROJECT				DEPOSIT	
		Year	Cash	Future	Present		Cash	Future	Present
			flows	value	value		flows	value	value
1	Rate		0.4						
2									
3				PROJECT				DEPOSIT	
4		Year	Cash	Future	Present		Cash	Future	Present
5			flows	value	value		flows	value	value
6			−11				−11		
7		1	6.4	24.59	4.57		4.4	16.9	3.14
8		2	7.4	20.31	3.78		4.4	12.07	2.24
9		3	6.2	12.15	2.26		4.4	8.62	1.6
9		4	8.8	12.32	2.29		4.4	6.16	1.15
10		5	4.2	4.2	0.78		15.4	15.4	2.86
11									
12									
13	Net excess		22				22		
14	Simple return		0.4				0.4		
15	Future/present value			73.56	13.68			59.16	11.0
16									
17	**Net future value (NFV)**			**14.40**					
18	**Net present value (NPV)**			**2.68**					
19	NFV/NPV			5.38					
20	(1+rate)^5			5.38					

Width of columns: Global:8; A:16

Figure IV.2(a) Screen layout.

The model is designed to enable you to compare the Dhahran Roads contract with bank deposits of 11 m SR, lasting 5 years, at various interest rates (in B1).

The cash flows of the contract and of the deposit are in columns B and F respectively. The future values of these cash flows are in columns C and G, and their present values in columns D and H. The future value of the contract is in C15 and the future value of the deposit in G15. The net future value of the contract is in C17. The present value of the contract is in D15, the present value of the deposit in H15 and the net present value of the contract in C18.

With a deposit rate of 40%, the net future and net present values of the contract are positive. Now compare the project with deposits at higher interest rates. When doing so, check that:

Rate	0.4						
			PROJECT			DEPOSIT	
Year	Cash flows		Future value	Present value	Cash flows	Future value	Present value
	−11				+B6		
1	6.4		((1+$B$1)∧(5−$A7))*B7	+B7/((1+$B$1)∧$A7)	−$F$6*$B$1	((1+$B$1)∧(5−$A7))*F7	+F7/((1+$B$1)∧$A7)
2	7.4		((1+$B$1)∧(5−$A8))*B8	+B8/((1+$B$1)∧$A8)	−$F$6*$B$1	((1+$B$1)∧(5−$A8))*F8	+F8/((1+$B$1)∧$A8)
3	6.2		((1+$B$1)∧(5−$A9))*B9	+B9/((1+$B$1)∧$A9)	−$F$6*$B$1	((1+$B$1)∧(5−$A9))*F9	+F9/((1+$B$1)∧$A9)
4	8.8		((1+$B$1)∧(5−$A10))*B10	+B10/((1+$B$1)∧$A10)	−$F$6*$B$1	((1+$B$1)∧(5−$A10))*F10	+F10/((1+$B$1)∧$A10)
5	4.2		((1+$B$1)∧(5−$A11))*B11	+B11/((1+$B$1)∧$A11)	−$F$6*$B$1−F6	((1+$B$1)∧(5−$A11))*F11	+F11/((1+$B$1)∧$A11)
Net excess	@SUM(B6..B11)						
Simple return	+B13/−B6/5				+F13/−F6/5		
Future/present value			@SUM(C7.C11)	@SUM(D7.D11)	@SUM(F6..F11)	@SUM(G7.G11)	@SUM(H7.H11)
Net future value (NFV)	+C15−G15						
Net present value (NPV)	+D15−H15						
NFV/NPV	+C17/C18						
(1+rate)∧5	(1+B1)∧5						

Figure IV.2(b) Inputs for the NPV/NFV model.

- NFV and NPV give the same signal about the profitability of the project.
- NFV and NPV move in relation to one another. The ratio NFV over NPV is always equal to $(1 + \text{interest rate})$,[5] 5 being the duration of both contract and deposit.
- The present value of the deposit is always equal to 11 m SR.

Inputs
You must enter the inputs shown in Figure IV.2(b) in order to build the model.

FURTHER MODEL IV.3
ALTERNATIVE METHODS FOR CALCULATING THE ANNUAL PROFIT OF CONTRACTS AND PROJECTS

In most business activities, the year is a period significantly longer than the operational cycle (purchasing, manufacturing and selling). As a consequence, the yearly profit primarily reflects the result of completed activities. In the case of long-term contracts and projects, however, the year is a period which only permits the reporting of intermediate results since the final results will only be known when the contract or project is completed.

Reporting intermediate results is a very difficult and risky thing to do since the actual profitability of long-term contracts and projects will only be known when the project is completed and intermediate results can therefore give inadequate signals, signals which do not reflect the exact final profit.

When long-term projects and contracts are completed, one should check that cumulated intermediate results correspond exactly to the final outcome. When they do not, since the intermediate results cannot be changed, an adjustment must be made at the end. Accountants do not like such adjustments since they mean that profit reported in previous years has not been true and consequently that the previous years' books are not accurate.

Reporting profit at the end (completed contract method)

One way to avoid reporting intermediate results is to report profit only at the end of contracts and projects. All the intermediate invoices to the customer are to be considered as advances and all costs are to be capitalized in a work-in-progress account (WIP). The results corresponding to this method are shown in Figure IV.3(a). The inputs of the spreadsheet model which generate the results of Figure IV.3(a) are described in Figure IV.3(b).

	1993	1994	1995	1996	1997	1998	Cumulated
Sales	0.00	0.00	0.00	0.00	0.00	168.00	168.00
Costs	7.00	28.00	31.00	25.00	17.00		108.00
Depreciation	4.22	8.44	8.44	8.44	8.44		38.00
Increase WIP	11.22	36.44	39.44	33.44	25.44	−146.00	0.00
Profit	0.00	0.00	0.00	0.00	0.00	22.00	22.00
Net fixed assets	33.78	25.33	16.89	8.44	0.00	0.00	
Retention	0.55	2.70	5.10	7.05	4.20	0.00	
WIP	11.22	47.67	87.11	120.56	146.00	0.00	
Cash	0.00	6.40	13.80	20.00	28.80	33.00	
Total assets	45.55	82.10	122.90	156.05	179.00	33.00	
Initial advance	23.55	17.10	9.90	4.05	0.00	0.00	
Annual advance	11.00	54.00	102.00	141.00	168.00	0.00	
Net worth	11.00	11.00	11.00	11.00	11.00	33.00	
Total equities	45.55	82.10	122.90	156.05	179.00	33.00	

It is assumed that no dividends are paid.

Figure IV.3(a) Completed contract method.

Percentage of completion method

When applying the completion method in Chapter 13, we generated the following annual profits:

1993	1994	1996	1997
−0.22	6.56	5.56	1.56

Such results do not really correspond to the spirit of the percentage of completion method since this method requires contractors to report each year a profit equal to:

$$\text{Sales of the year} * \frac{\text{total expected profits}}{\text{total expected sales}}$$

In other words, when using the percentage of completion method, the relationship between annual profit and annual sales should be the same as the relationship between total expected profit and total expected sales. (When using the percentage of completion method, contractors signal each year to the external analysts the profitability they expect to get when the project is completed.) In order to comply with the percentage of completion method SADE should report each year a profit equal to 22/168 = 13% of its sales. This corresponds to the following annual profits:

1993	1994	1995	1996	1997
1.44	5.63	6.29	5.11	3.54

In order to report such annual profits, the results we calculated in Chapter 13 should be adjusted as follows:

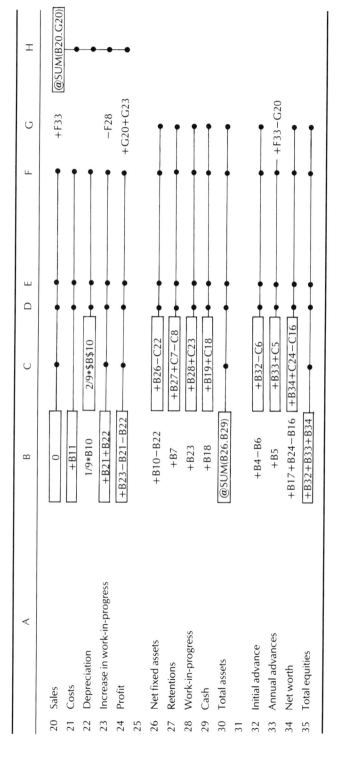

Figure IV.3(b) Inputs for completed contract method.

You need to set the width of column G to 8

	A	B	C	D	E	F	G	H
20	Sales	0					+F33	@SUM(B20.G20)
21	Costs	+B11						
22	Depreciation	1/9*B10	2/9*$B$10					
23	Increase in work-in-progress	+B21+B22					−F28	
24	Profit	+B23−B21−B22					+G20+G23	
25								
26	Net fixed assets	+B10−B22	+B26−C22					
27	Retentions	+B7	+B27+C7−C8					
28	Work-in-progress	+B23	+B28+C23					
29	Cash	+B18	+B19+C18					
30	Total assets	@SUM(B26.B29)						
31								
32	Initial advance	+B4−B6	+B32−C6					
33	Annual advances	+B5	+B33+C5				+F33−G20	
34	Net worth	+B17+B24−B16	+B34+C24−C16					
35	Total equities	+B32+B33+B34						

- As they are lower than the target profits, the profits we initially calculated for 1993 and 1997 should be adjusted upwards. This can be done by deducting from the 1993 and 1997 costs a conventional amount called costs in excess of billings (CIB), 1.66 in 1993 and 1.98 in 1997.
- As they are higher than the target profits, the profits we initially calculated for 1994, 1995, and 1996 should be adjusted downwards. This can be done by deducting from the 1994, 1995 and 1996 revenues a conventional amount called billings in excess of costs (BIC), 0.92 in 1994, 2.27 in 1995 and 0.45 in 1996.
- Costs in excess of billings are considered as an asset and billings in excess of costs as a liability. At the end of the contract, the cumulative values of these two accounts equal each other, and can be offset.

The results of a proper application of the completion method to the Dhahran Roads contract are shown in Figure IV.3(c). The model inputs necessary to generate these results are shown in Figure IV.3(d).

	1993	1994	1995	1996	1997	1998	Cumulated
Sales	11.00	43.00	48.00	39.00	27.00		168.00
Costs	7.00	28.00	31.00	25.00	17.00		108.00
Depreciation	4.22	8.44	8.44	8.44	8.44		38.00
Estimated profit	−0.22	6.56	8.56	5.56	1.56		22.00
Target profit	1.44	5.63	6.29	5.11	3.54		22.00
CIB	1.66	0.00	0.00	0.00	1.98		3.64
BIC	0.00	0.92	2.27	0.45	0.00		3.64
Profit	1.44	5.63	6.29	5.11	3.54		22.00
Net fixed assets	33.78	25.33	16.89	8.44	0.00	0.00	
Retention	0.55	2.70	5.10	7.05	4.20	0.00	
CIB	1.66	1.66	1.66	1.66	3.64	0.00	
Cash	0.00	6.40	13.80	20.00	28.80	33.00	
Total assets	35.99	36.10	37.45	37.16	36.64	33.00	
Advance	23.55	17.10	9.90	4.05	0.00	0.00	
BIC	0.00	0.92	3.19	3.64	3.64	0.00	
Net worth	12.44	18.07	24.36	29.46	33.00	33.00	
Total equities	35.99	36.10	37.45	37.16	36.64	33.00	

It is assumed that no dividends are paid.

Figure IV.3(c) Percentage of completion method.

Profit reserve

One problem with the completion method is that it may lead to reporting intermediate results that can prove to be inadequate in the end. In accordance with a conservative approach, some accountants would recommend splitting the annual profit shown above into an annual allocation to a profit reserve that will be capitalized and considered as profit at the end of the contract only and an annual reported profit.

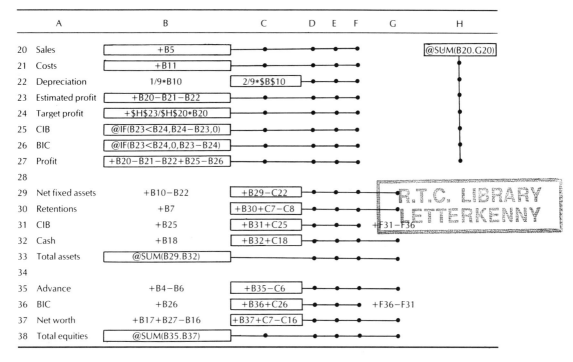

Figure IV.3(d) Inputs for percentage of completion method.

	1993	1994	1995	1996	1997	1998	Cumulated
Sales	11.00	43.00	48.00	39.00	27.00		168.00
Costs	7.00	28.00	31.00	25.00	17.00		108.00
Depreciation	4.22	8.44	8.44	8.44	8.44		38.00
CIB	1.66	0.00	0.00	0.00	1.98		3.64
BIC	0.00	0.92	2.27	0.45	0.00		3.64
Allocation to							
Profit reserve	0.43	1.69	1.89	1.53	−5.54		0.00
Profit	1.01	3.94	4.40	3.57	9.08		22.00
Net fixed assets	33.78	25.33	16.89	8.44	0.00	0.00	
Retentions	0.55	2.70	5.10	7.05	4.20	0.00	
CIB	1.66	1.66	1.66	1.66	3.64	0.00	
Cash	0.00	6.40	13.80	20.00	28.80	33.00	
Total assets	35.99	36.10	37.45	37.16	36.64	33.00	
Advance	23.55	17.10	9.90	4.05	0.00	0.00	
BIC	0.00	0.92	3.19	3.64	3.64	0.00	
Profit reserve	0.43	2.12	4.01	5.54	0.00	0.00	
Capital and							
Retained profit	12.01	15.95	20.35	23.93	33.00	33.00	
Total equities	35.99	36.10	37.45	37.16	36.64	33.00	

It is assumed that no dividends are paid.

Figure IV.3(e) Profit reserve.

The problem when using this approach is obviously to decide on the percentage of profit that should be allocated to the profit reserve. This probably depends on how confident the company is about its estimate of the final profit figure. The less confident it is, the higher proportion of the annual profit it will allocate to the profit reserve.

Figure IV.3(e) shows the results of applying such a method to the Dhahran Roads contract. The results of Figure IV.3(e) have been obtained by allocating 30% of the annual profits to a profit reserve.

The common feature of all profit reporting methods

All the various reporting methods that exist for contracts and projects have one basic common feature. They show the same total cumulative profit. These methods differ in one respect only, the way in which they allocate the total profit to different years.

FURTHER MODEL IV.4
RECONCILING ROICE WITH IRR

Book return on initial capital employed (ROICE) does not capture the impact of the timing of the cash flows which occur after the initial cash outlay. More precisely, the average ROICE is not sensitive to the fact that these cash flows may occur more quickly or slowly than the flows one would receive from investing the initial cash outlay at 54% with a bank. In Figure IV.4(a) the cash flows of the contract are compared with the cash flows of a deposit at 54%.

The cash flows of the contract are generated more quickly than the cash flows from a deposit at 54%. This results in an advantage for the contract, equal to 4.96 m SR if not reinvested, or 12.76 m SR if reinvested at 54%.

It follows that the reinvestment gain on this advantage is equal to

	1994	1995	1996	1997	1998
Contract	6.4	7.4	6.2	8.8	4.2
Deposit (at 54.15%)	5.96	5.96	5.96	5.96	16.96
Advantage of contract over deposit	0.44	1.44	0.24	2.84	−12.76
Cumulative advantage open	0.00	0.68	3.28	5.43	12.75
Advantage of the year	0.44	1.44	0.24	2.84	−12.76
Total advantage invested	0.44	2.12	3.52	8.27	0.0
Interest at 54.15%	0.24	1.15	1.91	4.48	0.0
Cumulative advantage end	0.68	3.28	5.43	12.75	0.0

Figure IV.4(a) Comparing contract and deposit cash flows.

12.76 − 4.96 = 7.78 m SR. These 7.78 m SR correspond to the interest gain (at 54%) on the timing advantage provided by the contract. They also correspond to the annual interest gains of 0.24 in 1994, 1.15 in 1995, 1.91 in 1996 and 4.48 in 1997 (see Figure IV.4(a).

In order to reconcile ROICE and IRR, one can assume that all cash is kept in the project, no dividend is paid, and each year, starting in 1994, an interest gain resulting from the timing advantage is added to the profit. This enables us to calculate a new annual ROICE and its average over five years. This is done in Figure IV.4(b).

	1993	1994	1995	1996	1997	Average
Profit	−0.22	6.56	8.56	5.56	1.56	
Interest gain	0.0	0.24	1.15	1.91	4.48	
Adjusted profit	−0.22	6.80	9.71	7.46	6.04	
ROICE	−0.02	0.62	0.88	0.68	0.55	0.54

Figure IV.4(b) Calculating new annual ROICE.

Figure IV.4(b) shows some important results. It is possible to reconcile ROICE and IRR, provided that we know what IRR is, that we assume that the cash flows in excess of what the cash flows from a deposit at the IRR would be are reinvested at the IRR and that their proceeds are added to the annual profits. This adjustment takes care of the timing characteristics of the project. *As a consequence, ROICE can be reconciled with IRR provided we know what the IRR is.*

What it requires to reconcile annual ROICE with IRR

Accounting measures do not capture the impact of the timing of the cash flows which occur after the initial investment, so ROICE and IRR give, in general, different signals. However, when you know what IRR is, you can adjust profit, through a rather complicated interest calculation, and reconcile average ROICE with IRR. But annual ROICEs are still different from IRR. Is there a way to make them equal to IRR?

Annual ROICEs differ from their average, or rather their total, because annual profits are equal to the yearly contribution of each year to total profit, and capital employed is the total employed capital.

As a result, annual ROICE (which is no longer return on initial capital employed but rather return on annual capital employed) could be reconciled with its average and with IRR if the annual profits were compared with the annual use of capital. This is done in Figure IV.4(c).

From the adjustments made in Figures IV.4(b) and (c), we can see that it is possible, in theory, to reconcile annual ROICE with IRR. Such a reconciliation

	1993	1994	1995	1996	1997	Total
Adjusted profit*	−0.22	6.80	9.71	7.47	6.04	29.80
% of total profit†	−0.01	0.23	0.33	0.25	0.20	1.00
Capital consumed‡	−0.08	2.51	3.58	2.76	2.23	11.00
ROICE§	0.54	0.54	0.54	0.54	0.54	0.54

* Profit plus timing gains (see Figure IV.4(a)).

† Annual adjusted profit/total adjusted profit.

‡ Percentage of total profit * 11. It is assumed that each year the contract consumes total capital in a proportion equal to annual profit. As a consequence, the capital used in 1993 is negative. The economic rationale for this is the following: the total excess value generated by the project over five years is 29.78. At the end of 1993, when the 0.22 loss has been incurred, this value is even greater. As a result, we may say that no capital has been consumed in 1993 but rather that some capital has been generated. This problem does not exist when profits are reported according to a pure percentage of completion method.

§ Adjusted profit/initial capital consumed/5.

Figure IV.4(c) Reconciling annual ROICE with average ROICE and IRR.

needs, however, a long series of successive adjustments.

- IRR should be calculated.
- Timing advantages should be added to profit.
- Annual capital employed should be re-estimated. The consequence of this adjustment is that capital employed becomes different from the figures shown in the balance sheets.

Since it is not really possible to carry out these adjustments in real life, we have to accept that average ROICE differs from IRR, and annual ROICEs differ even more from IRR. The difference between annual ROICE and IRR may be important, as shown above, and this constitutes a serious problem when using ROICE.

Some people argue that the difference between annual ROICE and IRR should not be exaggerated since it is particularly important at the beginning and at the end of the life of projects but is not quite as important in the middle. As the performance of companies results from many projects started at different dates, things should average themselves out. This would be good reasoning if it were in fact true, but it is not, as several studies have shown. So we have to live with this basic fact: *there is no way in practice to reconcile accounting measures of profitability with IRR.*

FURTHER MODEL IV.5
USING NPV TO EVALUATE THE NEW CREDIT PLAN AT DELTA METAL

The NPV/IRR criteria can obviously be used for evaluating the new credit plan at Delta Metal. You can do so with either the incremental model (Figure 10.3 in Chapter 10) or the total model (Figure 8.6 in Chapter 8).

Incremental approach

Using the spreadsheet model in Figure 10.3, you can introduce an IRR calculation in B27. When this is done, you find an IRR equal to:

- 0.23 when the collection period is set to 4.8
- 0.14 when the collection period is set to 4.0 (a more precise way to calculate IRR would be to do it from the difference in monthly cash flows)

0.14 is the correct result. The reason for this is:

- The new credit plan enables the company to cash sales two months earlier.
- The cost of this acceleration is 4% before tax and 2.2% after tax.
- 2.2% for two months is equivalent to about $2.2 \times 6 \approx 13\%$ a year.

When you evaluate the cost of accelerating the receipts from sales at 13% (on an after-tax basis), the plan does not look attractive as any loan with an interest lower than 24% a year is a better solution than the plan.

Global approach

Using the model in Figure 8.6, you can introduce a calculation of the NPV of the 1993–1997 cash flows (see Figure IV.5(a)). If we assume that money costs 20% to Delta Metal, then the NPV of the 1993–1997 cash flows is negative (-10.5 m), which means that it would be better for Delta Metal to close rather than continue in the conditions of 1993. If you change the parameters in order to show the situation with the new credit plan, you will see that the NPV becomes even more negative.

	1993	1994	1995	1996	1997	1998	Cumulated
Growth	0.02	0.02	0.02	0.02	0.02		
SALES	118 072	120 434	122 842	125 299	127 805		
cgs/sales	0.80	0.80	0.80	0.80	0.80		
CGS	94 458	96 347	98 274	100 239	102 244		
Operating expenses/sales	0.14	0.14	0.14	0.14	0.14		
OPERATING EXPENSES	16 530	16 861	17 198	17 542	17 893		
Depreciation	400	400	400	400	400		
OPERATIONAL PROFIT BEFORE TAX	6 684	6 826	6 971	7 118	7 268		
CUMULATIVE PROFIT BEFORE TAX	3 630	10 456	17 427	24 545	31 813		
OPERATIONAL PROFIT AFTER TAX	5 051	3 754	3 834	3 915	3 998		20 551
OPERATIONAL CFE	5 451	4 154	4 234	4 315	4 398		22 551
Receivables open	58 893	59 198	60 382	61 589	62 821		
Collection period	183	183	183	183	183	64 078	
RECEIVABLES END	59 198	60 382	61 589	62 821	64 078		
Inventory open	16 709	23 499	23 969	24 449	24 938		
Inventory turnover	4	4	4	4	4		
INVENTORY END	23 499	23 969	24 449	24 938	0		
Payables open	39 944	33 564	34 217	34 902	35 600		
Payment period	121	129	129	129	129	27 322	
PAYABLES END	33 564	34 217	34 902	35 600	27 322		
CFO	−8 024	3 153	3 231	3 292	19 801	36 756	58 209
CFO due to 1992 operations	35 658						35 658
CFO due to 1993–97 operations	−43 682	3 153	3 231	3 292	19 801	36 756	22 551
Discount rate	0.20						
NET PRESENT VALUE*	−10 487						

* In B26: @NPV(B25,B24.G24).

Figure IV.5(a) Using NPV in the model for Delta Metal.

Part IV   Bibliography

Gordon LA, Archer L and Tuggle FD (1979), 'Informational impediments to the use of capital budgeting models', *Omega*, **7**.

Hammer M (1990), 'Reengineering Work: Don't Automate, Obliterate', *Harvard Business Review* (July/August) pp 104–112.

Hodder JE (1986), 'Evaluation of manufacturing investments: a comparison of US and Japanese practices', *Financial Management*, Spring.

Jensen M (1989), 'The Eclipse of the Public Corporation', *Harvard Business Review* (September/October), pp 61–74.

Jensen M (1986), 'Agency costs of Free Cash Flow, Corporate Finance and Takeovers', *American Economic Review* (May), pp 323–329.

Johnson T and Kaplan R (1987), *Relevance Lost: The Rise and Fall of Management Accounting*, Harvard Business School Press.

Pinches GE (1982), 'Myopia, capital budgeting and decision making', *Financial Management*, Autumn.

Rappaport A (1986), *Creating Shareholder Value – the new standard for business performance*, The Free Press.

Shinnar R, Dressler O, Feng CA and Avidan A (1989), 'Estimation of the Economic Rate of Return for Industrial Companies', *Journal of Business*, **62**(3): 417–47.

Solomon E and Laya J (1967), 'Measurement of company profitability: some systematic errors in accounting rate of return', in Robichek A (ed.), *Financial Research and Management Decisions*, John Wiley.

Steele A (1986), 'A Note on Estimating the Long Run Rate of Return from Published Financial Statements', *Journal of Business Finance and Accounting* (Spring), pp 1–13.

Understanding the Risk Attached to a Strategic Opportunity

Part V deals with one of the most useful applications of PC-based models: trying to understand the risk attached to strategic alternatives. It is not surprising that spreadsheet publishers use the possibility of making what if analyses as a major selling argument, but what if analyses are only an initial step in risk analysis and you should go beyond them.

In this part, we return to the Dhahran Roads case and stop pretending that things are going to happen exactly as expected. Starting from what if simulations we progressively bring more structure to the analysis, and so end up with a full risk analysis.

The concept of risk analysis is not one with which the majority of managers are very comfortable. Although most are ready to accept that any strategic move involves some risk, very few of them actually perform systematic risk analysis. This is often mainly because they consider risk analysis requires the use of sophisticated mathematical approaches.

This ignores the fact that:

- Risk analysis techniques exist which are both effective and accessible to every manager. As we shall see, these techniques often require a fair number of calculations but this is not a problem with a personal computer.
- Most of the recent literature in the various fields of management emphasizes the necessity of recognizing the existence of risk. Perhaps because of the mathematical connotation of the word risk, other expressions are often used instead, turbulence[1] being a popular one, but all the expressions used have basically the same meaning as risk.

The aim of Part V is to help you develop skills in using the power of spreadsheet modelling for more than what if analyses, and for conducting proper risk analyses. As you will rapidly realize, Part V involves very little model building and focuses almost totally on *model using*, a very important dimension of the modelling process.

A fundamental assumption and a basic belief

When trying to understand risk, it is reasonable to start from a fundamental assumption and a basic belief.

The fundamental assumption is that it is impossible to predict the future. The impossibility of predicting the future[2] results from the simple fact that *we never have the information that would enable us to do so.*

In order to predict the future, we would need, first, to have all the available information about the future, to know how all the agents involved in its shaping expect it to look. This is possible in some exceptional cases[3] but not in general. In most businesses today, the environment, the competition, the technology and the organizations themselves have become so complex that no one can claim to have all the available information, or, as the economists phrase it, perfect information.

We also need to have much more. In addition to possessing all the information available today, we need *all the new information that will occur tomorrow.*[4] This is impossible in our present state of knowledge since we are unable to predict how the world will change. If there were not too many changes in the world, this would not be a problem, but reality is quite different. It would appear that, as shown by many researchers:

- Changes are more and more *numerous*. More and more environmental, competitive, technological and organizational characteristics seem to be subject to change.
- Changes seem to be more and more *dramatic*. A number of changes seem to create totally new situations that no experience drawn from the past can help us understand.
- Changes seem to occur at a *quicker rate*.

As a result of the impossibility of predicting the future, risk analysis has necessarily a somewhat modest objective. When analyzing the risk of a strategic alternative we are only aiming at

- Estimating our exposure to future outcomes that could differ for better or worse from the ones we expect.
- Making more conscious decisions and preparing ourselves to react to change.

Realizing that it is impossible to predict the future should also make you tolerant of failure in situations where risk has been carefully analyzed on the basis of all available information, but an adverse outcome has materialized or failure has resulted from totally new information such as an unexpected technological innovation.

The basic belief is that risk analysis helps managers. Whatever its limitations, however, we believe that risk analysis is very helpful. It enables managers to check that strategic alternatives are worth being undertaken in spite of possibly adverse events. Being a successful manager is not a matter of avoiding risk, it is rather a matter of making the decisions that correspond to an *adequate trade-off between risk and results*. Identifying and analyzing risk is not an exercise aimed at scaring managers; it is rather an attempt to make managers recognize which risks are worth being taken and which are not.

It also enables managers to imagine *solutions for reducing their exposure to adverse events*. When managers identify risk they can start thinking about possible reactions, and, most important, can develop attitudes that help them *deal better with change*: sensitivity to change, ability to identify the consequences of change, ability quickly to find new solutions, etc.

Finally, *it helps managers understand their environment*. As expressed by Hogarth,[5] uncertainty does not lie in the environment but in ourselves: 'if you think about it, it is absurd to make a statement of the kind that one situation or venture is more uncertain than another; it is simply you who are more uncertain in one of the situations.' The unique value of risk analysis is to make you progress in your understanding of the environment in which you operate.

KEY LEARNING POINTS

- The two very different functions of what if analyses:
  · The initial step of risk analysis – *Section 16.1, page 252*
  · A learning/creative process – *Section 16.2, page 255*
- When used to understand risk, what if analyses are more useful when structured – *Section 17.1, page 261*. When irrelevant alternatives are ignored and when relevant ones are weighted – *Section 17.2, page 263*
- Risk analysis is a further step which recognizes possible future actions, or options – *Chapter 18, page 272*

MODELS

FINANCE AND RELATED APPROACHES

- Risk diagrams as a description of the mutually exclusive and collectively exhaustive outcomes of a decision – *Section 17.1, page 261*
- Probability assessment – *Section 17.2, page 264*
- Risk profiles – *Figure 17.5, page 268*
- Risk analyses do not aim to scare people away from decisions. Risk is not necessarily negative – *page 259*
- Brief introduction to Expected Utility – *Further Model V, page 282*
- Using influence diagrams to prepare risk analysis – *Figure 16.1, page 253 and Figure 16.2, page 254*

SPREADSHEETS

- The need to adjust models for what if and risk analyses – *Section 17.1, page 261*

NOTES

1 This word has been made popular by I Ansoff.

2 Numerous studies show that forecasts which cover a period of two years or more are generally very inaccurate. If you need to be convinced about this, please refer to: W Ascher, *Forecasting Appraisal for Policy Makers and Planners*, Johns Hopkins University Press (1978).

3 As we will see in Part VI, such a situation seems to exist in well organized capital markets.

4 For more about this, refer to: JA Frenkel, 'Flexible exchange rates, prices and the role of "News": lessons from the 1970s' in DR Lessard (ed.) *International Financial Management: theory and application*, John Wiley (1985) pp 123–50.

5 R H Hogarth, *Judgement and Choice: The psychology of decision*, John Wiley (1980) p 11.

R.T.C. LIBRARY, LETTERKENNY

CHAPTER 16

What If Analysis as a Way to Learn More about a Strategic Decision

16.1 PERFORMING A WHAT IF ANALYSIS

If everything happens as expected in 1993, the Dhahran Roads contract will enable SADE to generate a 7 m SR NPV or will provide SADE with a 54% return on its initial 11 m SR investment.

The problem is that there is very little chance that things will happen exactly as expected and, as a consequence, SADE has to reflect on how the project would look if reality differed from expectations.

The first step in risk analysis is to perform what is called a what if analysis, a systematic exploration of the sensitivity of the final outcome of a strategic alternative to variations of the variables that contribute to this final outcome.

What are the key factors that can jeopardize the profitability of the Dhahran Roads contract? Examination of the economics of the contract would suggest that:

- Equipment costs could be higher.
- Annual costs could be higher.
- Retentions could be lost.
- The customer may delay his payments.

In general, the methodology of the influence diagram we introduced in Chapter 5 can be very helpful for the preparation of what if analyses. When building this influence diagram you can:

- Identify those input variables which are not certain. By convention, any variable which is not certain is marked with a tilde ($\tilde{}$) above the variable. One important thing to realize is that, as soon as a variable is uncertain, all the variables it influences also become uncertain.
- Identify among the influence relationships the ones which are not certain. As an example, one knows that the market share one can achieve depends on the price charged, but the relationship between market share and price is by no means certain. As a convention, uncertain influences are marked by a crooked arrow.

An influence diagram for the Dhahran Roads contract is shown in Figures 16.1 and 16.2.

As shown in Figures 16.1 and 16.2:

- Most of the uncertainty comes from the uncertain level of some parameters, for example, billings, equipment, annual costs, recovery of retentions.
- The rest of the uncertainty comes from the relationships between variables; will billings and costs match each other, as expected?[1]

The spreadsheet model of the Dhahran Roads contract we have built in Part IV can help us simulate the impact of changes in these variables and relationships on the final outcome of the contract. Figure 16.3 shows the results of such simulations.

Generating the results shown in Figure 16.3 can be done very quickly with the spreadsheet model we developed in Part IV.[2] It is, however, worth taking some precautions. The analysis, the results of which are shown in Figure 16.3, corresponds to a *one variable at a time* sensitivity analysis. Such an analysis requires that changes in each parameter be analyzed independently, which means that, before changing a new parameter, you should first re-initialize the model. Re-initializing models is a cumbersome and risky process. In order to avoid going through this process, you can use the save/retrieve facilities offered by spreadsheets. Since the base model (the one corresponding to the initial expectations) is saved, you can retrieve it each time you want to change a

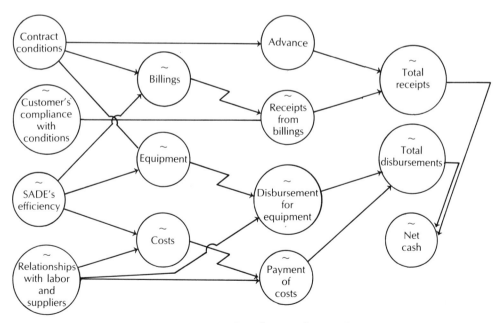

Figure 16.1 Dhahran Roads: influence diagram for year 1.

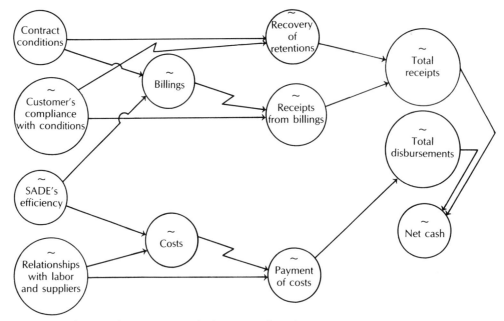

* Years 2, 3 and 4 are similar to year 5 except for the recovery of retentions.
In year 5 recoveries of retention is the only receipt.

Figure 16.2 Dhahran Roads: influence diagram for years 2 to 5.

Risk factors	New total margin	Change in margin	New NPV (@25%)	Change in NPV	New IRR	Change in IRR
Equipment costs are 10% higher	**18.2**	−17%	**3.21**	−54%	0.35	−35%
Annual costs are 10% higher	**11.2**	−49%	**0.11**	−98%	0.25	−53%
Retentions are lost	**13.6**	−38%	**3.91**	−44%	0.45	−17%
Customer delays its payments by one year*	**22.0**	0%	**−10.75**	−253%	0.13	−76%

* All receipts from the customer (except for the initial advance) are delayed by one year. The schedule of receipts becomes:

	1993	1994	1995	1996	1997	1998	1999
Initial advance	25.20						
Receipts from invoices		11.00	43.00	48.00	39.00	27.00	
Recovery of advance		1.65	6.45	7.20	5.85	4.05	
Retentions		0.55	2.15	2.40	1.95	1.35	
Recovery of retentions						4.20	4.20
Total receipts	25.20	8.80	34.40	38.40	31.20	25.80	4.20

Figure 16.3 Impact of changes in key parameters.

parameter, thus avoiding re-initializing the model before changing any parameter.

What do the results in Figure 16.3 tell us about the risk of the Dhahran Roads contract?

It is worth comparing the impact of a variation of each parameter on total margin and on NPV (and IRR).

- A delay in customer's payments causes no losses in terms of total margin but turns the NPV into a negative figure (−10.75 m SR). The contract has, in this case, an IRR of only 13%.
- The loss of retentions causes a higher loss in margin than an increase by 10% in equipment costs. However, the NPV (and the IRR) are much more sensitive to an increase in equipment costs because these take place at the start of the contract.
- Finally, when you compare the respective impacts of a 10% increase in annual costs and of a 10% increase in equipment costs, you realize that, in terms of total margin, a change in annual costs is more than twice as influential as a change in equipment costs. In terms of NPV (and IRR), a change in annual costs is not as influential as that of equipment costs, again due to a timing element.

As a conclusion of the results shown in Figure 16.3, we can say that

- The risk in the Dhahran Roads contract is very much a risk related to changes in the margin *and in the timing of the cash flows.*
- The value of the contract is especially exposed to changes in timings and margins *at the beginning of the contract.*

16.2 THE VALUE AND LIMITS OF WHAT IF ANALYSES

Spreadsheets have made what if analysis popular. What if analyses are indeed very useful but they should not be confused with analyses of risk.

The value of what if analyses

The what if analysis we made of the Dhahran Roads contract can be useful for SADE's management. It helps them understand the economics of the contract, the reasons why it is profitable and the factors which could jeopardize its profitability. As a general rule, when you discover that the final outcome of a decision is sensitive to a variation in a particular parameter, it is worth reflecting how the value of this parameter is generated.

- If it is just a number, where does it come from? How sure are you about the value of this number? How broad is its potential range? Is it worth doing some more research in order to be more certain about its value?
- If the value of this parameter is generated by a relationship, how sure are you about this relationship? What would be the impact of a different relationship? Is it worth doing some more research in order to be more certain about the relationship?

SADE also now has guidelines for actions which could protect the profitability of the contract, such as, to monitor closely the payments from the customer and react quickly to any delay in payment, to allocate adequate human resources to the execution of the contract, and in particular to ensure that it works well from the beginning.

The limits of what if analyses

There are two main reasons why what if analyses are not really analyses of risk:

1. Testing the impact of a variation of 10% in equipment costs tells us about the sensitivity of the NPV to such a variation but not really about the risk attached to a possible variation in equipment costs. In order to analyze such a risk, we should rather reflect on the *possible magnitude of the deviations* of the equipment costs as compared with our initial expectations, and on the *chances* that these deviations will occur.

    In order to identify the possible magnitude of the deviations, we have to reflect on what could go wrong. Changes in supplier's price, variation of the foreign exchange rate, transportation and customs problems, installation difficulties, are all possible. When these adverse events are identified, we then have to evaluate the extra costs they would cause; estimating the magnitude of equipment cost deviations is much more than just playing with a +10% figure.

    Estimating possible deviations is not enough, however. It is also necessary to evaluate the chances that these deviations will occur. In 1979 a storm almost destroyed the installations of a major harbor in Saudi Arabia. All the goods in transit were severely damaged and the contractors who had equipment there lost it. This could obviously happen again but, since it had happened only once in the history of that part of the world, most contractors would disregard this risk completely.

2. Analyzing risk cannot really be done just by looking at one parameter at a time since variations in different parameters can offset each other or, can combine. When serious difficulties are faced in the execution of a contract, these may not only cause cost overruns but also delays in invoicing and collecting payment. There may also be problems when the customer takes

over the contract which may result in the loss of the retentions. In order to analyze risk, one has to think about the possible adverse scenarios and the respective chances of their occurring. Of course, the worst of the worst may always happen but, if this is very unlikely, one should perhaps not attach too much importance to such an unfavorable situation.

The dangers of what if analyses

Experience of running what if analyses with financial models and spreadsheets suggests that these analyses may even be counter-productive, for the following reasons:

- When taken for what they are not, ie analyses of risk, what if analyses can scare managers away from valuable strategic actions.
- When not performed according to a structured plan, they can simply lead to the generation of a lot of numbers and computer printouts which may be of very little help.

The Dhahran Roads (B) case offers an opportunity for going beyond what if analysis and describing risk in a more satisfactory way.

What if analyses as a creative process

A basic characteristic of creative solutions is to appear to be new and unfamiliar. Creative solutions cannot, however, be totally new or totally disconnected from previous experience and knowledge, or at least, not from the previous experience and knowledge of their creators. Innovations are the product of human minds and need to be understood by other human minds in order to be accepted. Investigations into the creative process in fields as diverse as art and science show, as phrased by Rothenberg,[3] that creative persons 'dip into the unknown with firm footing in the known'. Fundamental to this process is the concept of *opposition*. Creative persons are those who are able to consider simultaneously a solution and its opposite and to achieve new understanding through the resolution of their opposition.

What if analysis very much pertains to the general process of using opposition for creating new solutions. You start analyzing a situation with the construction of an initial model which corresponds both to your initial understanding of the situation and to the solution which appears to you to be the most adequate, given your previous experience of comparable situations. If you are driven by the need to innovate, you then try to perform what if analysis, to formulate alternatives, to assess their outcome, to gain a new understanding from their differences, to formulate new alternatives, to gain further understanding until you have created a new solution (or recognized that you are not able to do so).[4]

When seen as a help in the creative process, what if analysis is not to be used as in risk analysis (or, more precisely, as in the initial steps of risk analysis). In order better to understand the nature of a situation, it is often useful to explore its limits. It is often effective to drive what if analyses from a systematic formulation of opposite situations and strategies. If you are considering a conservative pricing strategy, explore what if you were adopting an aggressive pricing strategy instead. Then, if it seems useful, try what if you segmented your markets and simultaneously implemented a conservative *and* aggressive price strategy.[5] Although it is often a highly productive process, formulation of opposites is not easy in practice, as opposites should at the same time be similar in some particular respect, and opposed or specifically resistant to each other in some other respect. One thing to realize also is that the concept of opposites is relative to the specific context in which you work.

NOTES

1 For more about the analysis of uncertain relationships, please refer to the case BA International in Part VII.

2 The analysis of the impact of a delay in customer's payments is slightly more difficult, however. In order to test such a delay, you can
   – Delay all the receipts by one year: zero in 1993, 11 in 1994, 43 in 1995, etc.
   – Change the formulas for recovery of retention, total receipts and net cash.
   – Extend the NPV formula to one more year.

3 A Rothenberg (1979), *The Emerging Goddess: The creative process in art, science, and other fields*, The University of Chicago Press. Refer in particular to Ch 8, pp 207–51.

4 Several authors have shown that reconciling opposites orchestrating tension, designing 'and/also rather than either/or' solutions is an essential ingredient of organizational change and self-renewal. Refer to: R T Pascale (1990), *Managing on The Edge: How the Smartest Companies Use Conflict to Stay Ahead*, Prentice Hall, and to: R Moss Kanter (1989), *When Giants Learn to Dance*, Simon and Schuster.

5 In Part VII, what if analysis is very much used in this way.

DHAHRAN ROADS (B)

While Mr Malik was delighted that the Dhahran Roads contract would generate a substantial value to SADE, he recognized that a favorable result such as this depended on everything proceeding smoothly. Unfortunately, it seemed to him that it would be pure luck if the necessary combination of events were all to occur in his favour. Even though it was unpleasant, his thoughts began to turn to those aspects of the project that could go wrong.

He first wondered which of the various inputs to his evaluation were particularly critical. He decided to make changes to one assumption at a time so that he could see which assumptions had the largest impact on the value of the Dhahran Roads contract.

As he continued to think about the risk in the project, it seemed that there were two key areas in which former projects had run into trouble.

Delayed payments by the client

There had been occasions when SADE had experienced problems in making the contracting payment agency pay in accordance with the agreed billing schedule. SADE was not the only contractor facing these problems. In fact, there had been several informal discussions among contractors in which they had shared their experiences in this area. During these conversations, a pattern of behaviour seemed to emerge. If there were going to be problems in keeping to the billing schedule, the delay seemed to appear in the third year of the longer-term contracts and, recently, one-year postponements of that billing and all subsequent billings had been experienced. It was felt by many of the contractors that the delay occurred at a point in time when the project had gone so far that they could not abandon it, but at a point where delayed payment represented an effective cost reduction to the client. The delays seemed to have occurred recently in about one fourth of the projects and were often justified by the client on the basis of the slightest of deviations from the performance terms of the contract.

Cost overruns

Even though SADE prided itself on its ability to control costs, it occasionally experienced overruns, sometimes rather substantial ones. After reviewing the files of ten completed projects, it seemed that projects could be grouped into four categories:

1. Those projects for which actual costs were very close to the original estimate.

2. Those projects that experienced mild cost overruns in the range of 5 to 10%.

3. Those projects that got into substantial difficulties and had overruns in the vicinity of 15 to 20%.

This case was developed by the author and Sherwood Frey Professor of Business Administration at Colgate Darden Graduate School of Business (USA).

4. Those projects for which actual costs were lower than expected, in the range of 3 to 5% less.

Unfortunately, there had only been one project of this latter variety, while there had been one with serious overruns and two with mild overruns. A closer examination of the files showed that, when cost overruns did occur, they spread fairly equally over the whole life of the contract.

CHAPTER 17

Risk Diagrams and Risk Profiles[1]

The analysis presented in the Dhahran Roads (B) case is a good example of what we can do in order to explore the risk attached to a strategic decision. In his analysis, Mr Malik has successfully identified and specified the various risk factors. Some of the risk factors we thought about in the what if analysis have been ruled out because of their very low likelihood. The relevant risk factors have been described with more precision. Finally, scenarios combining elementary risk factors have been identified. He has also assigned weights to each of the relevant risk factors.

17.1 STRUCTURING THE ANALYSIS: LISTING THE POSSIBLE OUTCOMES

In order to take advantage of the analysis made by Mr Malik, the first thing to do is to identify all possible outcomes that can result from the decision of executing the contract. When making this list of possible outcomes, we should make sure that:

- All the possible outcomes are *mutually exclusive*. Outcomes should be defined in such a way that only one at a time can occur.
- The outcomes are *collectively exhaustive*. Outcomes should be defined in such a way that one or another of them must occur.

The Dhahran Roads (B) case suggests the following list of possible outcomes:

- No postponements of payments occur and there are cost savings.
- No postponements of payments occur and costs are as expected.
- No postponements of payments occur and there are mild cost overruns.
- No postponements of payments occur and there are serious cost overruns.
- Postponements of payments occur and there are cost savings.
- Postponements of payments occur but costs are as expected.

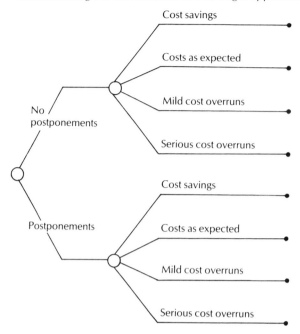

Figure 17.1 Dhahran Roads: risk diagram.

- Postponements of payments occur and there are mild cost overruns.
- Postponements of payments occur and there are serious cost overruns.

These eight possible outcomes are mutually exclusive and collectively exhaustive. They can be represented by a risk diagram as shown in Figure 17.1.

Evaluating the end points and adjusting the model

Each possible outcome corresponds to a path in the risk diagram and can be evaluated by entering in our spreadsheet model of the contract the values of the parameters that correspond to this particular path.

By tradition, we show the value of each outcome at the end (the extreme right) of the path to which it corresponds in the diagram. The values of the outcomes are called end point values.

As it is presently designed, our model is not very convenient for testing the impact of many variations in costs. In order to improve the model, proceed as follows:

- Insert a row above row 5; type in A5: cost adjustment; in B5: 1
- Overtype in B12: 7*B5; in C12: 28*B5; in D12: 31*B5; etc[2]

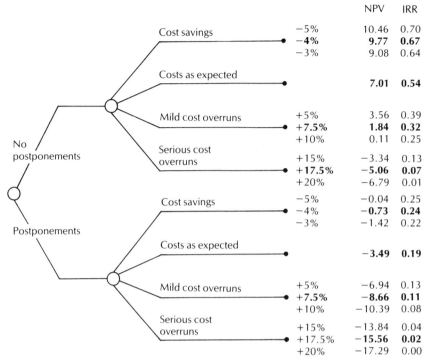

Figure 17.2 Dhahran Roads: risk diagram with end values.

You now have a model that enables you to test the impact of various cost overruns.

In order to test the impact of delays and cost overruns, you can build from this model a second model. In order to do so:

- Insert a new column between column G and H.
- Correct the billings (11, 43, 0, 48, 39 and 27), extend to one more year the calculations of recovery advance, retention, total receipts, total disbursements and net cash.
- Change the formulas for calculating the recovery of retentions.
- Change the calculation of totals in column I. (It is worth checking that delays do not change the cumulative margin.)
- Extend the NPV calculation to one more year. Change the IRR calculation.

This new model should return an NPV equal to −3.49 and an IRR of 0.19 (when costs are as expected).

The end point values corresponding to the eight possible outcomes envisaged by Mr Malik are shown in Figure 17.2.

Figure 17.2 shows twenty end points when there are only eight possible outcomes. This is because cost savings and mild or serious cost overruns are not defined by a value but rather by a range. Figure 17.2 shows the end points corresponding to the extremes of these ranges as well as the end points corresponding to the middle of these ranges. For the sake of simplicity, we will consider below only the end points corresponding to the middle of the ranges.

The results of Figure 17.2 may look very disappointing to Mr Malik, since, when considering the end points corresponding to the middle of the ranges, five possible outcomes out of eight correspond to negative net present values and some of these outcomes are very unfavorable indeed. As a consequence, should Mr Malik consider the Dhahran Roads contract as risky? In order to answer this question, you should not just look at the value of the outcomes but also at the probabilities of these values materializing.

17.2 WEIGHTING THE POSSIBLE OUTCOMES: PROBABILITY ASSESSMENT

In the Dhahran Roads case, all possible events have been defined.

- There can be postponements in the customer's payments. Such postponements happened in the past in one case out of four and did not happen in the remaining three cases.
- There can be cost variations. Cost savings happened in one case out of ten, mild cost overruns happened in two cases out of ten, serious ones in one case out of ten and, obviously, costs were as expected in the remaining six cases.

When describing the chances that one event will materialize, you may do so with words. If SADE's customer behaves as customers normally do, it is more likely that billings will be paid on time rather than be delayed. It is more useful, however, to use a quantitative approach[3] and a scale for describing uncertainty. In practice, there are two possible approaches, probabilities and odds.

With probabilities, the scale goes from zero (absolute impossibility) to 1 (absolute certainty). By definition, the sum of the probabilities of each of the different possible events is equal to 1. In the Dhahran Roads case when considering possible payment delays, delays have a probability of 0.25 and payments on time a probability of 0.75. When considering possible cost overruns, the probability of mild cost overruns is 0.2, the probability of serious cost overruns 0.1 and the probability of no cost overruns 0.6 (and the probability of cost savings is 0.1).

Odds are expressed in the form of 2 to 1, 10 to 1, etc. When considering possible payment delays, the odds are 1 to 3 (and odds against possible payment delays 3 to 1).

Even though both methods are equivalent, the probability approach is easier to use when handling calculations, and we will use it for the rest of this book.

How can we weight the possible outcomes of the Dhahran Roads contract, or assign a probability to each of these outcomes? The first step is to assess probabilities for the possible occurrence of payment delays and cost variations. These probabilities should reflect your degree of certainty regarding such events. The assessment of probabilities is very difficult in practice as it is the complex result of using various techniques and procedures based on past data, assumptions and results taken from models, expert advice, and subjective judgement.[4] In the present case, let us assume that past experience adequately reflects our degree of certainty regarding the possible occurrence of payment delays and cost variations.

The second step is to calculate the probabilities of the eight possible outcomes in the diagram in Figure 17.2. These eight possible outcomes are mutually exhaustive. The sum of their probabilities should therefore be equal to 1.

The eight possible outcomes result from two types of *independent* event, possible payment delays and possible cost variations. The independence of

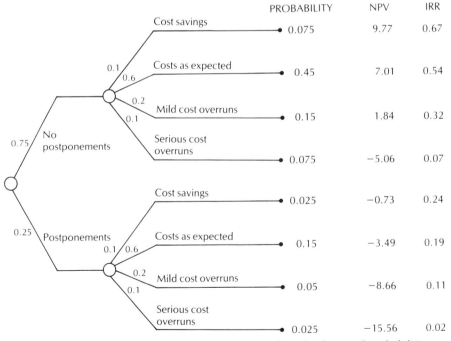

Figure 17.3 Dhahran Roads: risk diagram with end values and probabilities.

payment delays and cost variations is an assumption but it seems a reasonable one. It allows us to calculate the probability of the final outcomes as follows.

- The probabilities of no delay and delay are assigned to each of the two left branches of the diagram in Figure 17.2.
- The probabilities of cost savings, costs as expected, mild overruns and serious overruns are assigned to each of the four top and lower right branches of the same diagram.
- The probabilities of the end points are calculated as the product of the probabilities along the branches leading to this end point. (These probabilities are called conditional probabilities, for example the probability that there is no cost overrun, knowing there is no delay.) The end outcomes together with their probabilities are shown in Figure 17.3. Results such as these enable you to calculate an expected outcome and draw a risk profile.

17.3 ANALYZING RISK

Expected outcome

As shown in Figure 17.3, there are eight possible outcomes for the Dhahran Roads contract. The table also shows that these eight outcomes have a different probability of occurrence, that is, a different weight. The expected outcome of the decision to go ahead with the contract is equal to the weighted average of the eight possible outcomes (the probabilities of the different outcomes being used as weights).

In terms of NPV (the concept of expected IRR does not make much sense):

$$\begin{aligned}
\text{Expected NPV} = {} & (9.77*0.075) + (7.01*0.45) + (1.84*0.15) + (-5.06*0.075) \\
& + (-0.73*0.025) + (-3.49*0.15) + (-8.66*0.05) \\
& + (-15.56*0.025) \\
= {} & 2.42 \text{ m SR.}
\end{aligned}$$

Although outcomes corresponding to very negative NPVs are possible, their probability, or weight, is small enough to make SADE expect an average favorable final outcome. The averaging-out procedure that corresponds to the calculation of an expected NPV aims at picturing the result SADE could expect to get on average if it were running a large number of contracts like the Dhahran Roads one. This should not make you forget, however, that, on the Dhahran Roads contract, SADE *will not get this expected outcome* but rather one of the eight possible outcomes, provided SADE has been good at describing all the possible outcomes.

An alternative way for calculating the expected NPV

The calculation of the expected NPV shown above is not the only possible one since, instead of calculating the probability of each end point, you can fold the diagram back. In order to do so, you start looking at the nodes on the extreme right of the diagram and you replace them and their right hand branches by their expected values. This is done in Figure 17.4(a).

You then obtain a simpler diagram that you can then fold back in order to get the expected NPV. This is done in Figure 17.4(b).

Risk profile

A risk profile is a diagram that shows both the possible outcomes and their probabilities. The risk profile corresponding to the Dhahran Roads contract is shown in Figure 17.5.

The results in Figure 17.5 call for two series of comments:

- Risk profiles do not flatten out the possible outcomes: on the contrary, they keep the possible outcomes visible. In Figure 17.5, you see that the NPV can range between −15 m SR and +10 m SR. You should also realize that, if risk profiles keep the dispersion of the possible outcomes, they also suggest that some weigh less than others. Taken together, the outcomes that

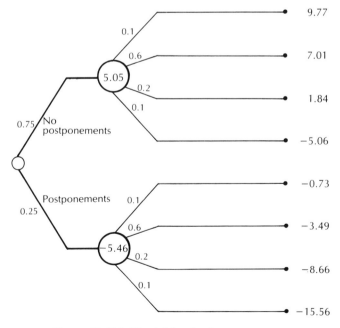

Figure 17.4(a) The folding back process (1).

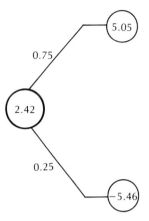

Figure 17.4(b) The folding back process (2).

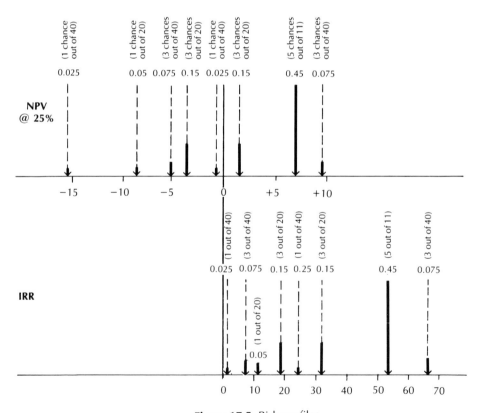

Figure 17.5 Risk profiles.

correspond to positive NPVs have a probability of 67.5%, which may be enough to make you consider the contract as a good one. The superiority of risk profiles over expected values does not really come from a difference in approach but from the fact that *risk profiles stop simplifying data at an earlier stage* than expected value. As a consequence, they leave you, the decision maker, with richer information for exercising your intuition, your business sense.

- Net present value and IRR do not show the same dispersion of outcomes. This is to be expected because of the implicit reinvestment rate assumption. When you discount unfavourable outcomes at 25%, the intermediate cash flows are discounted at 25%, which pushes the NPV down. When using IRR, intermediate cash flows are discounted at the IRR, which is less than 25% with unfavorable outcomes. This obviously limits the fall in the IRR. As a consequence, as soon as you believe that the cost of money for the Dhahran Roads contract is 25%, you should prefer NPV to IRR for your risk analysis since only NPV shows you the real dispersion of outcomes. Another problem with IRRs is that they fail to emphasize that, if the cost of money to SADE is 25%, any IRR below 25% makes SADE lose money. We instinctively consider that any IRR above zero is acceptable, and this is wrong.

Have we missed something?

The analysis above describes the different risk factors as events over which SADE will have no control. SADE will be defenceless if cost overruns occur in addition to the customer delaying payments. As a consequence, the analysis we have made so far is both unrealistic and dangerous. If adverse factors do arise, it is more likely that SADE will have the ability to respond correctively. Since these reactions will aim to counteract adverse events, the final risk for SADE will probably be less than we have envisaged so far. Our present analysis is probably biased in that it over-estimates risk. This is dangerous since it may lead to a wrong decision. The Dhahran Roads (C) case enables us to improve the analysis.

NOTES

1 The process for generating risk profiles with @RISK, a powerful Lotus 1-2-3 add-on is introduced in Further Model VII.2, p 459.

2 If you are using SuperCalc, you can adjust the annual costs with the copy command (see page 83).

3 The basic reason for this is that words describing uncertainty generally have very unclear meanings. For more about this, refer to: PG Moore, 'The manager struggles with uncertainty', *Journal of the Royal Statistics Society*, Series A (General), (1977) **140**: 129–48.

4 Probability is indeed a very difficult concept. As phrased by Schoemaker in 'The expected utility model: its variants, purposes, evidence and limitations', *Journal of Economic Literature*, **20** (June 1982), pp 529–62: 'Historically, probability is a relatively recent construct which lacks primary sensory evidence as to its existence. As such, it might be viewed as an invention rather than a discovery'. Also as shown by LD Phillips and CN Wright in 'Cultural differences in viewing uncertainty and assessing probabilities', in Jungermann and De Zeeuw (eds), *Decision Making and Change in Human Affairs* (Dordrecht, 1977), the concept of probability might be culturally bound. When assessing probabilities you should be very careful. Experience shows that you are exposed to many biases, overconfidence (or wishful thinking), anchoring (the probability of a future outcome is often assessed by anchoring it on a value suggested by past experience), inadequate information (the frequency of well-publicized events is commonly overestimated, many people overreact to new information), overweighting of low probabilities, etc. Refer to *Judgement under Uncertainty: Heuristic and biases*, D Kahneman, P Slovic and A Tversky (eds), Cambridge University Press (1982). For an example of the assessment of probabilities in practice (banking activity), refer to: I Kabus, 'You can bank on uncertainty', *Harvard Business Review* (May/June 1976). For an introduction to the psychological dimensions of probabilities, refer to: LF Bourne *et al.*, *Cognitive Processes*, Prentice Hall (1986), Ch 9. For a weighting system other than probabilities, refer to: D Kahneman and A Tversky, 'Prospect theory: an analysis of decision under risk', *Econometrica* (1979), **47**: 263–91.

DHAHRAN ROADS (C)

Mr Malik was very pleased to have succeeded in building a diagram describing the combined impact of possible cost overruns and payment delays. But he was still not fully convinced that SADE should go ahead with the contract. Certainly the decision to go ahead corresponded to a positive NPV at 25% of 2.42 m SR, but the dispersion of the possible outcomes was wide and some very unfavourable outcomes could occur, especially if SADE were unfortunate enough to experience both payment delays and cost overruns.

When analyzing the problem further, Mr Malik realized that the contract could look much more attractive if SADE had the ability to react against those adverse events that might materialize.

He decided to review previous contracts in which SADE experienced delayed payments. When such problems occurred, SADE always tried to exert some pressure on the customer and, in one case, it even decided to stop the execution of the contract. This firm reaction impressed the customer a great deal and, as a result, he changed his attitude completely. The contract was then restarted and no more payment delays occurred.

Mr Malik thought that such a strategy could be followed if delays in payments occurred in the Dhahran Roads contract. From the discussions he had with commercial and technical managers, he tried to estimate what the receipts and disbursements could be in such a case (see Appendix E.1). In addition, Mr Malik tried to reflect on possible reactions in the case of cost overruns but, unfortunately, none occurred to him.

APPENDIX E.1
IMPACT OF A STRONG REACTION TO PAYMENTS DELAYS

If payment delays occurred in the third year, SADE would try to convince the customer that such delays were a breach of the original contract and it therefore should be brought to a halt. If this approach failed, SADE could well decide to stop the execution of the contract. It was likely that such an action would

- Incur losses for SADE, as it was impossible to stop all the expenses. (There was a 60% chance that costs would be as expected, a 30% chance that there would be mild cost overruns, while serious cost overruns had a 10% probability.)
- Impress the customer sufficiently to enable the contract to be restarted and completed with no further payment delays.

The schedule of receipts and disbursements corresponding to such a situation could be estimated as follows:

This case was developed by the author and Sherwood Frey, Professor of business administration at the Colgate Darden Graduate School of Business USA).

	1993	1994	1995	1996	1997
Receipts	11	43	0*	60*	54*
Disbursements	7	28	5†	39	34

* No receipts at all in 1995, all remaining billings are made and paid in 1996 and 1997. Retentions recovered in 1997 and 1998 as expected initially.

† In spite of the interruption of the execution of the contract, some expenses will have to be met in 1995.

Mr Malik estimated the probability of success of a strong reaction strategy at least 80%. He then tried to estimate what could be the schedule of receipts and expenses if the strategy failed.

	1993	1994	1995	1996	1997	1998
Receipts	11	43	0	15	45	54
Disbursements	7	28	5	39	34	

If this were the case, it would be reasonable to assume that recoveries of retentions would occur in 1998 and 1999.

Decision Diagrams

18.1 BUILDING A DECISION DIAGRAM

The Dhahran Roads (C) case suggests that we should revise our risk analysis in order to take into account not just the risk factors attached to the contract but also the interplay between these risk factors and the possible actions, or decisions, of SADE. The technique for this is to build what is called a decision diagram or tree.

A decision diagram is a map of all

- The *decisions* that can be made in relation to the problem. In the Dhahran Roads case, there are two major decisions: going ahead or not with the contract, reacting or not to payment delays.
- The *risk factors* or *events*. We have already identified the two risk factors of the contract and their eight possible combinations.

A decision diagram is a map of the sequence of decisions and events presented in the order in which the decision maker

- Makes the decision.
- Learns about the events.
- Makes new decisions as a result of this learning.
- Learns about new events.
- And so on.

When building decision diagrams, the usual method is to represent:

- Decision nodes as squares from which originate as many branches as there are alternative actions.
- Event or chance nodes as circles from which originate as many branches as there are possible outcomes.

The decision diagram corresponding to the Dhahran Roads case is shown in Figure 18.1.

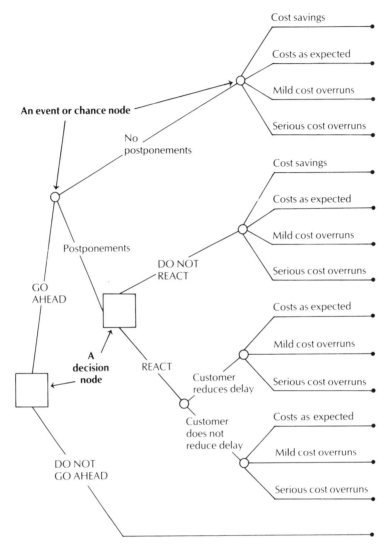

Figure 18.1 Decision diagram.

What is the objective of building a decision diagram such as the one in Figure 18.1? Decision diagrams pursue the same objective as the one we pursued when building risk diagrams: to identify the possible outcomes of a decision and their respective probabilities. Decision diagrams also add one major dimension to the analysis, the existence of possible future reactions to unfavorable events. If you believe that you will have in the future an *option to react* and so avoid part or all of the consequences of unfavorable events, then this risk does not matter for you and you should not take it into account in your analysis. Since SADE has the option to react to payment delays, it will obviously do so if this reaction leads to better results than no action at all. If you believe that a reaction would lead to better results than no reaction, then you should take this into account in the analysis and consider that the consequences of payment delays are adequately described by the scenario of payment delays followed by a reaction from SADE. The more unfavorable situation of payment delays and an absence of reaction from SADE can be disregarded as SADE has the option of avoiding it.

One essential advantage of decision diagrams is that they enable you to prune out alternatives which correspond to irrelevant risk, risk that you have an option to eliminate in the future.[1]

18.2 ANALYZING A DECISION DIAGRAM

How can we analyze the decision diagram shown in Figure 18.1? The first step is to evaluate the end points. The second step is to assign the probabilities. The result of these two steps is shown in Figure 18.2.

From Appendix E1 it can be seen that the cash flows attached to the situations where the customer delays its payments and SADE reacts are as follows:

1. The customer resumes payments according to schedule:

	1993	1994	1995	1996	1997	1998
Initial advance	25.20					
Receipts from billings	11.00	43.00	0.00	60.00	54.00	
Recovery advance	1.65	6.45	0.00	9.00	8.10	
Retentions	0.55	2.15	0.00	3.00	2.70	
Recovery of retentions					4.20	4.20
TOTAL RECEIPTS	34.00	34.40	0.00	48.00	47.40	4.20
Equipment	38.00					
Other costs	7.00	28.00	5.00	39.00	34.00	
TOTAL DISBURSEMENTS	45.00	28.00	5.00	39.00	34.00	
NET CASH	−11.00	6.40	−5.00	9.00	13.40	4.20

2. The customer continues delaying its payments:

	1993	1994	1995	1996	1997	1998	1999
Initial advance	25.20						
Receipts from billings	11.00	43.00	0.00	15.00	45.00	54.00	
Recovery advance	1.65	6.45	0.00	2.25	6.75	8.10	
Retentions	0.55	2.15	0.00	0.75	2.25	2.70	
Recovery of retentions						4.20	4.20
TOTAL RECEIPTS	34.00	34.40	0.00	12.00	36.00	47.40	4.20
Equipment	38.00						
Other costs	7.00	28.00	5.00	39.00	34.00		
TOTAL DISBURSEMENTS	45.00	28.00	5.00	39.00	34.00		
NET CASH	−11.00	6.40	−5.00	−27.00	2.00	47.40	4.20

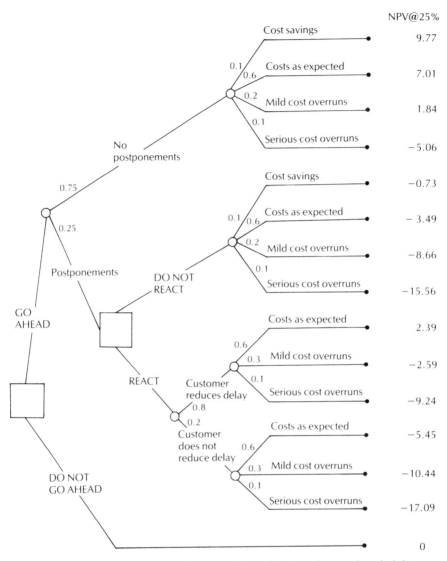

NPV@25%

Cost savings — 9.77

Costs as expected — 7.01

Mild cost overruns — 1.84

Serious cost overruns — −5.06

Cost savings — −0.73

Costs as expected — −3.49

Mild cost overruns — −8.66

Serious cost overruns — −15.56

Costs as expected — 2.39

Mild cost overruns — −2.59

Serious cost overruns — −9.24

Costs as expected — −5.45

Mild cost overruns — −10.44

Serious cost overruns — −17.09

0

Figure 18.2 Decision diagram with end point values and probabilities.

The next step is to prune the decision diagram and eliminate the alternatives for action which are clearly inferior.

- Consider each decision node in turn, starting with the decision node located closest to the end of the diagram (furthest to the right) and then work backwards to the beginning.
- Evaluate each of the alternatives originating from the decision node. This process is known as averaging out. It corresponds to calculating the expected value of the event node.

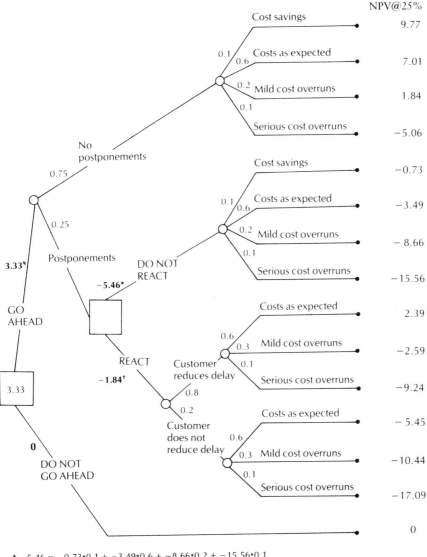

NPV@25%

Cost savings — 9.77

Costs as expected — 7.01

Mild cost overruns — 1.84

Serious cost overruns — −5.06

Cost savings — −0.73

Costs as expected — −3.49

Mild cost overruns — −8.66

Serious cost overruns — −15.56

Costs as expected — 2.39

Mild cost overruns — −2.59

Serious cost overruns — −9.24

Costs as expected — −5.45

Mild cost overruns — −10.44

Serious cost overruns — −17.09

0

* −5.46 = −0.73•0.1 + −3.49•0.6 + −8.66•0.2 + −15.56•0.1
† −1.84 = 0.8•(2.39•0.6 + −2.59•0.3 + −9.24•0.1) + 0.2•(−5.45•0.6 + −10.44•0.3 + −17.09•0.1)
§ 3.33 = −1.84•0.25 + (9.77•0.1 + 7.01•0.6 + 1.84•0.2 + −5.06•0.4)•0.75

Figure 18.3 Folding back.

- Prune the inferior alternatives and replace the decision node by the value of the best alternative. This is another example of folding back.

The process is described in Figure 18.3, and the resulting diagram is shown in Figure 18.4.

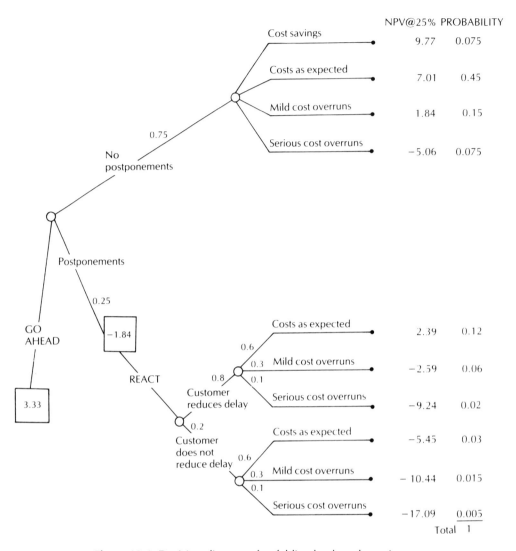

NPV@25% PROBABILITY

Cost savings — 9.77 — 0.075

Costs as expected — 7.01 — 0.45

Mild cost overruns — 1.84 — 0.15

Serious cost overruns — −5.06 — 0.075

0.75

No postponements

Postponements

0.25

GO AHEAD

−1.84

REACT

3.33

0.6 Costs as expected — 2.39 — 0.12

0.3 Mild cost overruns — −2.59 — 0.06

0.8 0.1 Serious cost overruns — −9.24 — 0.02

Customer reduces delay

0.2

Customer does not reduce delay

0.6 Costs as expected — −5.45 — 0.03

0.3 Mild cost overruns — −10.44 — 0.015

0.1 Serious cost overruns — −17.09 — 0.005

Total 1

Figure 18.4 Decision diagram after folding back and pruning.

18.3 DECIDING

The final step is to use our decision diagram to decide what we consider to be the best thing to do. The resolution of the diagram we have just built tells us the expected NPV attached to the decision to go ahead, 3.33 m. But we may not want to limit ourselves to this information but rather keep an idea of the dispersion of the possible outcomes. In order to do so, we can build a risk profile as shown in Figure 18.5.

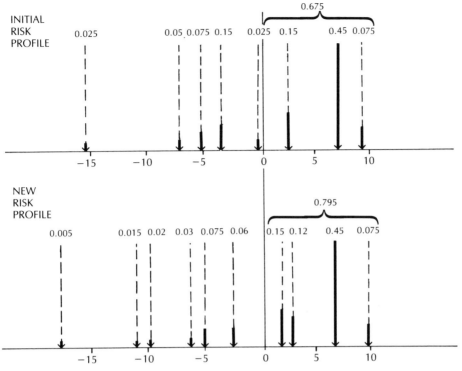

Figure 18.5 Risk profiles.

So, what should SADE do? We are back to the point where the manager must exercise his/her business sense or intuition. Many managers would go ahead on the bases that the expected NPV is positive (3.33 m) and that the dispersion is not too wide. Some managers would not go ahead, however, on the basis that, even taking into account possible reactions against payment delays, several very unfavorable outcomes might materialize.[2]

18.4 SOME REFLECTIONS ON DECISION DIAGRAMS

Decision diagrams do not provide you with definite answers

As stated by PL Keeney and H Raiffa,[3] 'the spirit of decision diagrams is one of *Socratic discovery*, of unfolding what you really believe, of convincing yourself, and of deciding.'

Decision diagrams help you to structure scenarios[4] and strategies for the future. They enable you to identify the decisions which are to be made today, assess the risks involved, identify the choices you can defer (future options), and think how these future choices can be helped by additional information and experimentation. The basic condition for using decision diagrams successfully is to find the right balance between trying to look at all the possibilities (what some call the British Museum Approach) and pruning promising solutions too quickly.

Decision diagrams invite you to adopt a *holistic perspective* and to defer your decision until you visualise all the interactions and evaluate all the consequences. They prevent you from falling into the trap of comparing and selecting alternatives on a one-to-one basis, and of comparing and eliminating alternatives on the basis of one feature at a time.[5]

When considering a risky situation, making the final choice is important, but the phase during which you structure this choice is even more important. The value of decision diagrams is to help you organize the structuring phase. In their book *Taking Risks: The Management of Uncertainty*, KR MacCrimmon and DA Wehrung[6] identify the following three phases in the structuring of risky decisions.

- Recognition of the risky situation.
- Evaluation of the situation. Are the risks acceptable? Is it worth staying in, or entering, this situation? Is it better to opt out, or to stay out?
- Adjusting the risks. Managers who take an active attitude towards risk will try to modify the situation in their favour by gaining time, information and control. They may also attempt to share or shift their responsibility.[7]

Decision diagrams are not built in order to make future decisions today: they deal with present decisions and future options only

One final word about decision diagrams: they are only concerned with decisions to be made today. As decision diagrams envisage future courses of action, some people think that they enable managers to take decisions today for both today and the future. This is not true. Decision diagrams (in spite of the fact that they envisage future decisions) are just a tool for planning, and planning only tells you about the decisions to be made today. As expressed by P Drucker,[8] 'Long range planning does not deal with future decisions. It deals with the futurity of present decisions'.

In the Dhahran Roads case, we envisaged the option to decide to react to payment delays in 1995, but we did not, in fact, take the decision to react. If delays do occur in 1995, SADE will consider the alternatives in 1995 and make the appropriate decision at that time. The reason why we considered the possibility of taking such a decision is because we believe that SADE has, and will keep until 1995, the *option to react*, an option which should enable SADE to escape part of the consequences of delays. We recognized the value of this option by eliminating from the analysis the adverse outcomes that can be avoided by reacting.

Decision diagrams deal with present decisions only but they deal with all the futurity of these decisions, including the options, or the future flexibility, they create. In Part IX, we will see how the theory of option valuation can help you focus on this flexibility and understand the determinants of its value.

NOTES

1 *The only risk which has a negative impact is the risk which corresponds to events from which you have no future flexibility to escape.* As shown in Part IX, the risk attached to situations from which you keep the flexibility to opt out should not be perceived as negative. On the contrary, this risk generally has a positive value. Since risk means that things can result in very bad, or very good, outcomes, then, if you have the flexibility to opt out, you can attach a lot of value to very risky alternatives if they either, at best, give you a great outcome, or, at worst, (if you opt out), nothing.

2 For more about attitudes towards risk, please refer to the introduction to the concept of expected utility in Further Model V.

3 *Decisions with Multiple Objectives: Preferences and Value Tradeoffs*, John Wiley (1976).

4 For scenario planning methodologies, refer to: PB McNamee, *Tools and Techniques for Strategic Management*, Pergamon Press (1985), Chapter 7, pp 212–36 and to: P Wack, 'Scenarios: uncharted waters ahead', *Harvard Business Review* (Sept/Oct 1985), pp 73–89 and 'Scenarios: shooting the rapids', *Harvard Business Review*, (Nov/Dec 1985), pp 139–50.

5 For more about this process of choice, refer to: A Tversky, 'Elimination by aspect: a theory of choice', *Psychological Review* (1972), **79**: 281–99.

6 The Free Press, 1986. Managers' attitudes towards risky situations are described in Chapter 7. Chapter 2 contains an interesting review of the literature dealing with the different phases in managing risk situations (recognition of risks, evaluation of risks, adjustment of risks, choice and tracking of outcomes) and to related issues (risk attitudes and risk measures).

7 Refer, for example, to: I Janis and L Mann, *Decision Making: A Psychological Analysis of Conflict, Choice and Commitment*, The Free Press (1977).

8 In 'Long range planning', *Management Science* (April 1959), p 239.

Further Model V

RECOGNIZING ATTITUDES TOWARDS RISK: THE CONCEPT OF EXPECTED UTILITY

In Chapter 17, we suggested that it is generally not a good idea to rush to calculate the expected outcome (or expected monetary value). A better approach is to keep the dispersion of possible outcomes and use risk profiles as a basis for decision. However, the problem with risk profiles is that they do not provide you with a clear rule for decision making. The alternative to using risk profiles is expected utility. Even though expected utility theory has been one of the major paradigms in the theory of decision making since World War II,[1] its development goes beyond the scope of this book. Let us therefore limit ourselves to a brief introduction to this approach and to selected references for further readings.

In order to introduce expected utility, let us illustrate through an example the limitations of expected monetary value as a criterion for decision making under uncertainty.

Let us examine the case of Mr Lebon who sold, for 300 000 FFR, a property which had a theoretical value of 400 000 FFR.

Mr Lebon owned, as an investor, a block of flats. The flats were rented at abnormally low prices due to local regulations. Consequently, Mr Lebon's property was worth only 200 000 FFR. The election of a new municipal council led Mr Lebon to believe that there was a 50% chance that the local regulations would shortly be changed, that rents could be increased and that the value of his property would jump to 600 000 FFR, its normal market price. The property market was very active and Mr Lebon could expect to sell at a fair price at any time.

Ms Bruno was interested in buying the block of flats and she made a first offer to Mr Lebon who turned it down: 220 000 FFR did not seem acceptable to him. Ms Bruno made a second offer of 260 000 FFR which Mr Lebon again turned down, but, when Ms Bruno came up with an offer of 300 000 FFR, Mr Lebon found it preferable to accept rather than taking his chances with the change in regulations. They concluded the deal at a price which was 100 000 FFR less than the expected monetary value.

People like Mr Lebon who are willing to trade a risky outcome for a sum of money lower than the expected monetary value of the risky outcome are said to be risk averters. If most people seem to be risk averters when making decisions of any importance, there exist also risk lovers (people who regard the certain money equivalent of a bet as being higher than the expected monetary value) and people who are risk neutral (people for whom the certain money equivalent of a bet is simply equal to the expected monetary value).

Attitudes towards risk depend very much on the individual concerned and also on the amounts which are at stake. Expected utility is the approach for incorporating risk attitudes into decisions about risky alternatives.

The following five steps show how to use expected utility in decision making.

- Assess the alternatives and their structure through a decision diagram with decision and chance nodes.
- Evaluate the end points of the diagram and assign probabilities to the branches emanating from chance nodes.

(These two steps are exactly the same as those we went through in chapters 17 and 18.)

- Assess the risk attitude of the decision maker by confronting him/her with a series of lotteries. This step results in the construction of his/her utility function.[2]
- Replace the monetary values of the end points of the diagram by their utility values. In the case of Mr Lebon, an end point showing a value of 300 000 FFR will be replaced by a utility of 0.5.
- Average out and fold back the diagram to calculate the expected utility. (The process for doing so is the same as we used in Chapter 17.)

Selected references

An introduction to expected utility is offered in JS Hammond III (1967), 'Better decisions with preference theory', *Harvard Business Review* (Nov/Dec).

A full treatment of the use of expected utility for strategic decision making is offered in R Schlaifer (1969), *Analysis of Decisions under Uncertainty*, McGraw-Hill; H Raiffa (1970), *Decision Analysis: Introductory Lectures on Choices under Uncertainty*, Addison Wesley; and PL Keeney and H Raiffa (1976), *Decisions with Multiple Objectives: Preferences and tradeoffs*, John Wiley.

A comprehensive review of expected utility theory is offered in PHJ Schoemaker (1982), 'The expected utility model: its variants, purposes, evidence and limitations', *Journal of Economic Literature*, XX, June.

Utilization of expected utility in the theory of finance is offered in TE Copeland and JF Weston (1988), *Financial Theory and Corporate Policy*, Addison Wesley; DE Allen (1983), *Finance: A theoretical introduction*, Martin Robertson and JE Ingersoll Jr (1987), *Theory of Financial Decision Making*, Rowman & Littlefield.

NOTES

1 The pioneering work in this field was the one of J von Neumann and D Morgenstern (1944), *Theory of Games and Economic Behavior*, Princeton University Press.

2 To give an example of the construction of a utility function, let us go back to the example of Mr Lebon. Let us arbitrarily scale the utility of 200 000 FFR (the lowest outcome) at zero and the utility of 600 000 FFR (the highest outcome) at 1. Since Mr Lebon has struck a deal at 300 000 FFR, we can assume that he is indifferent to selling at 300 000 FFR or taking a 50/50 gamble between 600 000 FFR and 200 000 FFR. Consequently, we can say that, for Mr Lebon, 300 000 FFR has a utility which is half way between zero and 1: 0.5. This can be shown as a utility function:

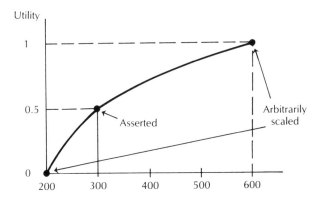

This utility function is drawn from three points only. In order to make a better curve it would be necessary to confront Mr Lebon with a series of bets and to check that his answers are consistent.

Part V Bibliography

Allen DE (1983), *Finance: A theoretical introduction*, Martin Robertson Publishers.

Ascher W (1978), *Forecasting Appraisal for Policy Makers and Planners*, Johns Hopkins University Press.

Bourne LF *et al.* (1986), *Cognitive Processes*, Prentice Hall.

Copeland TE and Weston JF (1988), *Financial Theory and Corporate Policy*, Addison Wesley.

Drucker P (1959), 'Long range planning', *Management Science* (April).

Frenkel JA (1985), 'Flexible exchange rates, prices and the role of "News": lessons from the 1970s', in Lessard DR (ed.), *International Financial Management: Theory and Application*, John Wiley.

Hammond JS III (1967), 'Better decisions with preference theory', *Harvard Business Review* (Nov/Dec).

Hogarth RH (1980), *Judgement and Choice: The Psychology of Decision*, John Wiley.

Ingersoll JE Jr (1987), *Theory of Financial Decision Making*, Rowman & Littlefield.

Janis I and Mann L (1977), *Decision Making: A psychological analysis of conflict, choice and commitment*, The Free Press.

Kahneman D and Tversky A (1979), 'Prospect theory: an analysis of decision under risk', *Econometrica*, **47**: 263–91.

Kahneman D, Slovic P and Tversky A (eds) (1982), *Judgement under Uncertainty: Heuristics and biases*, Cambridge University Press.

Kanter RM (1989), *When Giants Learn to Dance*, Simon and Schuster.

Keeney PL and Raiffa H (1976), *Decisions with Multiple Objectives: Preferences and tradeoffs*, John Wiley.

Kabus I (1976), 'You can bank on uncertainty', *Harvard Business Review* (May/June).

MacCrimmon KR and Wehrung DA (1986), *Taking Risks: The Management of uncertainty*, The Free Press.

McNamee PB (1985), *Tools and Techniques for Strategic Management*, Pergamon Press.

Moore PG (1977), 'The manager struggles with uncertainty', *Journal of the Royal Statistics Society*, Series A (General), **140**: 129–48.

Pascale RT (1990), *Managing on the Edge: How the Smartest Companies Use Conflict to Stay Ahead*, Simon and Schuster.

Phillips LD and Wright CN (1977), 'Cultural differences in viewing uncertainty and assessing probabilities', in Jungermann and De Zeeuw (eds), *Decision Making and Change in Human Affairs*, Dordrecht.

Raiffa H (1970), *Decision Analysis: Introductory lectures on choices under uncertainty*, Addison Wesley.

Rothenberg A (1979), *The Emerging Goddess: The creative process in art, science and other fields*, University of Chicago Press.

Schlaifer R (1969), *Analysis of Decisions under Uncertainty*, McGraw-Hill.

Schoemaker PHJ (1982), 'The expected utility model: its variants, purposes, evidence and limitations', *Journal of Economic Literature*, **XX** (June).

Tversky A (1972), 'Elimination by aspect: a theory of choice', *Psychological Review*, **79**: 281–99.

Von Neumann J and Morgenstern D (1947), *Theory of Games and Economic Behavior*, Princeton University Press.

Wack P (1985a), 'Scenarios: uncharted waters ahead', *Harvard Business Review* (Sept/Oct).

Wack P (1985b), 'Scenarios: shooting the rapids', *Harvard Business Review* (Nov/Dec).

Which Discount Rate to Use?

The Cost of Capital Issue

Part VI deals with a very complex issue which remains unresolved: that of the discount rate or cost of capital.

In Part IV, we introduced the yardstick proposed by finance to help you select possible strategic alternatives.

- The only decisions worth being made are those which are expected to create some additional value for the company.
- *More precisely, the only decisions worth being made are those which correspond to positive net present values ie those which are worth more than they cost.*

Using this yardstick requires one fundamental question to be answered. Which discount rate should be used?

In Part IV we suggested that the discount rate was related to the cost of capital, or the cost of the cash, you need to invest in order to be able to go ahead with the decision you are contemplating. Capital is just like any other resource you may need: *it has a cost which is equal to the price for which its supplier asks.* The price of capital is expressed, however, in a fairly special way since it is normally stated as an interest rate. This interest rate is the return required by the supplier of capital. But there is still some controversy about how the return required by suppliers of capital should be measured. Even more disturbing is the fact that we still do not have clear answers to questions as apparently simple as, why do firms borrow? What is the impact of taxes on alternative financing sources?

The responsibility of the finance department

Calculating the discount rate or cost of capital is complex, and one should accept that most managers in most firms will never be able to estimate it themselves. This is not a major problem, however, since a finance department exists in most firms. The responsibility of this finance department is to:

- Maintain an adequate information system about the cash flows within the whole organization. Which units and projects generate cash excesses? Which

R.T.C. LIBRARY
LETTERKENNY

units and projects need money? How do cash excesses compare with cash needs? How is the situation going to evolve?

- Manage relationships with all the possible suppliers of capital or financial markets. Which are the sources available? What are their costs? How can they be tapped?

Managers in the finance department should be able to tell you about how much the money you need costs. This is obviously not an easy task for them, but there are other areas of business activity which are just as difficult and which require specialized knowledge and skills, for example research and development. So, if you are a generalist it is not a good idea to try to estimate the discount rate or cost of capital by yourself. Call on the finance department. But, even though in practice this is probably the most reasonable answer to give to the discount rate question, we do not like to leave the sole responsibility for any issue to specialists. Consequently we would like to explore this issue further in Part VI and to try to provide you with some clues which can help you start the exploration of this issue and/or understand the answers you may obtain from the finance specialists.

Three final introductory comments about Part VI:

- Because of the material covered, Part VI is not organized around the analysis of a case-study.
- In this part, spreadsheet modelling is not used in order to resolve problems but rather *in order to understand concepts*, a very powerful use of this technology.
- Part VI deals with a number of ideas which require incubation, so do not try to master the contents of this material the first time you read it. Instead, be prepared to sleep on some of the issues developed and to return to them at a later stage. Let us also strongly recommend that you invest time in reading some of the references given in Part VI;[1] some are very exciting to read,[2] some are more difficult, but all are worth reading.

The goods news at the end – you do not need to master the contents of Part VI before you start working with the material of Part VII.

KEY LEARNING POINTS

DISCOUNT RATE
- The discount rate you should use is the cost of the unlevered equity corresponding to the risk class of your decision – *Section 22.3, page 323*
  The APV as a method for taking into account the side effects of financing – *Section 21.2, page 315*
  An alternative approach, WACC – *Section 21.3, page 318*
- Using the unlevered equity rate guarantees value maximization – *Section 22.2, page 321*

COST OF FINANCING SOURCES
- Cost of financing as the price requested by the providers of capital or investors. Explicit and implicit prices – *Section 19.1, page 291*
- Risk as the key determinant of the price requested by investors:
  - This price depends on the type of contract between the firm and the investor – debt or equity – *Section 20.1, page 296*
  - This price depends on what the firm intends to do with the money – *Section 20.5, page 304*
- Two models for evaluating the risk premium requested by the providers of equity:
  - CAPM – *Section 20.3, page 301*
  - APT – *Section 20.4, page 303 and Further Model VI.3, page 335*

FINANCE

CAPITAL STRUCTURE
- Without taxes – *Section 21.1, page 308*
- With taxes and other factors – *page 313*
- Why do companies borrow? – *Further Model VI.5, page 340*

OTHER CONCEPTS
- Efficient markets – *Section 19.2, page 293*
- Diversification – *Section 20.2, page 298*
- Arbitrage – *Further Models VI.3 and VI.5, pages 335 and 340*
- Mean, variance, standard deviation, covariance and correlation coefficient – *Further Model VI.2, page 331*

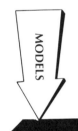

MODELS

MODELS FOR UNDERSTANDING CONCEPTUAL APPROACHES
- How to value a financial lease proposal – *Further Model VI.1, page 327*
- How could you use the APV model for evaluating decisions? A first example using an arbitrage approach – *Further Model VI.3, page 335*
- How can shareholders do or undo leverage by themselves? – *Section 21.1, page 309*
- Debt and corporation and personal taxes. A second example of using an arbitrage approach – *Further Model VI.5, page 340*
- How to reconcile the APV and WACC approaches, the meaning of debt to equity ratio – *Further Model VI.6, page 347*

MODELS FOR DECISION MAKING
- Introducing financing in the Dhahran Roads model – *Further Model VI.4, page 338*

NOTES

1 Several of the sources referred to in Part VI are reprinted in a book of readings: MC Jensen and CA Smith (eds), *The Modern Theory of Corporate Finance*, McGraw-Hill (1986).

2 For example, M Miller, 'Debt and taxes', *Journal of Finance* (1977), **32**: 261–76 and SC Myers, 'The capital structure puzzle', *Journal of Finance*, (1984), **39**: 575–92.

CHAPTER 19

The Cost of Capital Concept

19.1 SOME IMMEDIATE DIFFICULTIES

Estimating the cost of the capital you need for a strategic decision[1] or the return required from this capital, is very difficult in practice since many problems immediately appear.

1. When you need capital to implement a decision there are generally many possible different ways to obtain it. You can get it from within the company itself or from external bodies. When raised externally, capital can be obtained from many different sources and according to many different schemes, debt, equity, convertible debt, leasing, etc. Capital is no exception to the different resources you may want to buy; different types of capital are available at different prices. As a result, there is no such thing as a cost of capital, there is rather a series of different costs for different types of capital.

2. The second difficulty that arises with capital is that its suppliers often do not make explicit the return they require from it. The only exception in this area is capital raised through debt. When you borrow, the lender specifies the interest rate required, and that is your cost of capital. We can even say that, in the case of debt, the lender does not need to specify the return required since you can calculate this return very easily. It is the internal rate of return of the cash flows of the loan. An example of this calculation is given in Figure 19.1.[2]

Cash flows of the loan (from the point of view of the lender)				
	1993	1994	1995	1996	1997
Cash outflow	−1 020				
Cash inflows (interest + reimbursement of capital)		+329	+329	+329	+329
Net cash flows	−1 020	+329	+329	+329	+329
IRR	11%				

Figure 19.1 Calculation of the return required by a lender.

The more general case is illustrated, however, by what happens when capital is raised through equity as then the only thing that is specified is the price of the shares issued. Estimating the return required by investors from this price is not easy as the following example shows.

Deutsche Farbe raises 1 000 000 DM of new equity capital by issuing 10 000 new shares priced at 100 DM each. The only way to estimate the cost of this is to try to put oneself in the position of the investor who buys a share and to try to infer, from the price agreed for payment, the return expected. From a shareholder's point of view, an investment in equity means one cash outflow and a series of expected inflows. If we were able to define this outflow and the expected inflows, we should then be able to calculate, as we did in Figure 19.1, their internal rate of return, which is the return required by the investor.

There is only one possible source of future cash inflows that the investors who bought Deutsche Farbe's new shares could expect, the future dividends.[3] But knowing this does not help us very much since future dividends are never specified by a company when it issues new shares. It is very difficult, therefore, to guess what dividends are expected by an investor when buying a share and consequently to calculate the return demanded. In spite of this extreme difficulty, several authors have proposed models for calculating the return required by shareholders from their dividend expectations. The most famous among these models is the Gordon model:[4]

$$rr = \frac{D}{S} + g$$

where rr = required return
   D = expected dividend next year
   S = current share price
   g = expected dividend growth rate.

From the above evaluations, every source of finance has a cost and the lower the cost the better it is for the company as it enables the company to make investments at a lower cost but will give high returns. It is the case with the following sources of finance ...

19.2 FINANCIAL MARKETS ARE TO BE TRUSTED

The idea of deriving a company's cost of equity capital from an analysis of its share price on the stock market may look very strange to many managers. Stock markets have a fairly poor reputation in many countries: 'prices on these markets behave in an erratic fashion', 'speculation is the rule', 'specialists are at an advantage on these markets', etc.

Recent[5] empirical and theoretical studies of stock markets have proved, however, that they do not deserve their poor reputation. There is now ample theoretical and empirical evidence to show that stock markets are *efficient*, ie they function well and the prices are fair, *and* that prices of shares vary from one day to another in a *random* fashion. [use this to evaluate IPO's as a source of finance.]

Because of the competition that exists between a very large number of investors[6] markets are in equilibrium, and imperfections that could result in special advantages (or arbitrage opportunities or money machines) are almost immediately destroyed. In such competitive markets it is impossible to derive any definite advantage from special knowledge or inside information.[7]

As a result of the competition between investors, share prices reflect all the information that is available on the day when the prices are established. This reflection of all the available information in prices is called *market efficiency*. Market efficiency is generally defined as either weak, semi-strong or strong.

- Weak efficiency corresponds to the situation where prices reflect all the information contained in the record of past prices. As a result you cannot expect to derive a definite advantage from defining investment strategies based on sophisticated statistical studies of past prices.
- Semi-strong efficiency corresponds to the situation where prices do not only reflect past prices but also all the other published information. This rules out the idea of deriving definite advantages from investment strategies based on sophisticated financial and economic analyses, in turn based on published information.
- Strong efficiency corresponds to the situation where prices reflect all the information available. This finally rules out the dream of deriving advantages from brilliant investigations.

Even though statistical studies have shown that some forms of inefficiency exist on the capital markets, (especially as far as semi-strong and strong forms of efficiencies are concerned) the consensus among students of capital markets today is that *one should start from an assumption that markets are efficient*, that markets in general function well, that prices are fair and reflect expectations and that as a consequence consistent extra returns are not to be expected. The best proof of this is probably the fact that most studies of the performance of specialists have shown that it is no better than the one that anybody could achieve.[8]

The fact that share prices vary in a random fashion from one day to another is the direct consequence of the fact that market prices can only change because of new information. This new information that may arrive tomorrow is obviously not known today, because if it were known, it would already be embodied in the prices of today. As they are the result of new information that nobody can predict, changes in prices from one day to another cannot be predicted either. As the world changes from one day to another in a basically unpredictable or random fashion, so do share prices.

What are the implications of these observations on the behaviour of the stock markets for the manager who tries to estimate the cost of capital for his/her company? He/she should:

- Trust market prices and be comfortable with deriving the cost of capital from them.
- Realize that the cost of capital calculated from today's prices will be valid for today, and today only. This limitation is, however, not as serious as one may think. When you are investigating the cost of capital it is because you want to know whether it is worth committing capital today. What the cost of capital will be two months from now is not a problem today, it will affect only the decisions to be made two months from now. So before making decisions in two months' time, you will estimate the cost of capital then.

NOTES

1 In financial literature, the analysis of decisions which require capital to be raised is called capital budgeting. The need for a discount rate is not limited to situations in which you try to evaluate pre-existing strategic alternatives. As we mentioned in Chapter 15, financial calculations are also very useful when constructing a strategy, and, for example, when trying to calculate the price you would like to charge to your customers. In spite of the importance of this use of the discount rate, and for the sake of simplicity, we will limit ourselves to the problem of evaluating pre-existing alternatives in Part VI.

2 There is, however, one special kind of debt, financial leasing, the cost of which is not easy to assess. A spreadsheet model for assessing a financial lease proposal is shown in Further Models VI.1.

3 One may argue that when buying a share an investor does not only consider dividends but also the price at which the share might be resold. The cash flows for the investor could be, for example:

1993	1994	1995	1996	1997
−100	9	10	8	130

The problem then is to estimate both future dividends and the resale value. A solution for estimating the resale value is to say that, if the shareholder will be able to sell the share at 130 in 1997, it is because people will be found on the market who will consider this price fair given their own expectations of future dividends and resale value. As a consequence, we can replace the resale value in 1997 by the future expected dividends from 1997 to infinity. (This, however, assumes that all investors have the same expectations.)

4 This model is derived as follows. Investors buy shares in order to achieve a specific return (or required return). In order to determine the price at which they would be prepared to buy a share, investors estimate its future dividends and discount them at their required return. Consequently, the share price is equal to the present value of the dividends:

$$S = \text{Present value of dividends} = \frac{D_1}{(1 + rr)} + \frac{D_2}{(1 + rr)^2} + \ldots + \frac{D_n}{(1 + rr)^n}$$

Where D_1, D_2, D_n = expected dividend in years 1, 2, ... n
and rr = required return.
When the dividend is constant for eternity ($D_1 = D_2 = \ldots D_n = D$), then:

$$S = \frac{D}{rr}.$$

When the dividend grows at a constant rate g for eternity, then

$$S = \frac{D}{rr - g} \quad \text{or} \quad rr = \frac{D}{S} + g.$$

Some definitions:
· D/S is called the dividend yield. The difference between the required return and the dividend yield is equal to the expected growth.
· Very often investors compare the profit with the share price also. One popular ratio is the price earning (or PE) ratio which is equal to the share price divided by the earnings (or profit) per share. A high price earning ratio means that investors expect high growth in the future.

5 Perhaps not so recent, since the first breakthrough in the understanding of the stock markets dates from 1900: L Bachelier, *Théorie de la Spéculation*, Gauthier Villars. It is fair to say, however, that it is only recently that a cohesive body of theoretical and empirical literature has been developed.

6 Another way to describe speculation.

7 This is true in large western-style stock exchanges, but much more questionable in the many other financial systems which also exist around the world.

8 See for example: M Jensen, 'The performance of mutual funds in the period 1945–64', *Journal of Finance*, (1968) pp 389–416.

CHAPTER 20

The Cost of Equity

20.1 EQUITY IS NECESSARILY MORE EXPENSIVE THAN DEBT

As the cost of capital should be derived from the return requirements of the investors on the capital markets, let us now examine how they view two very popular forms of new capital for business firms, debt and equity.

When investors provide a firm with debt capital, they give money today against the commitment by the firm to pay at precisely defined dates specified amounts corresponding to interest and capital reimbursements. As a result, investors know precisely from the outset the return they will get from their investment and this return will materialize whatever happens to the company, provided, however, that it does not encounter severe financial problems.

When investors provide a firm with equity capital, they are not in a position to determine from the beginning what return will be obtained. When they invest in the equity of a firm, investors acquire the right to future dividends, and also rights attached to the fact that they become partial owners of the company. The future cash flows from the dividends are, however, basically uncertain.[1] As they wish to avoid unnecessary risk, investors would not be prepared to provide equity capital if this did not have a higher expected return than investments in debt capital.

There is a perfect symmetry between the position of the investors and the position of the companies which raise capital.

- Investors can either invest in debt, a lower risk–lower return investment, or in equity, a higher risk–higher return investment.
- Companies can either raise debt, a higher risk–lower cost financing, or equity, a lower risk–higher cost financing.

However logical the arguments given above, are they in fact supported by the reality of financial markets? Testing the fact that equity investments carry a higher return than debt investment (or benefit from a *risk premium* over debt) is difficult in practice since:

- The arguments we developed above apply to *expected returns*. Data you can gather on capital markets is from the past only.

■ The relationship between the expected returns from equity and from debt is obviously a general relationship that holds when markets are in equilibrium. But although, as we stated earlier, markets are in equilibrium in general, they may not be at a precise moment in time, so testing the relationship should be done by analyzing data over a long period of time.

Figure 20.1 shows the average rates of return on common stocks, corporate bonds, government bonds and Treasury bills in the US capital markets over the period 1926–1988.

Over the period 1926–1988: (in per cent per year)		
	Average annual rate of return (nominal)	Risk premium (versus return from Treasury bills)	Average rate of return (inflation deducted)
Common stocks	12.1	8.4	8.8
Corporate bonds	5.3	1.7	2.4
Government bonds	4.7	1.1	1.7
Treasury bills	3.6	0.0	0.5

Source: Ibbotson Associates Inc., *Stocks, Bonds, Bills, and Inflation 1989 Yearbook*, Chicago, 1989.

Figure 20.1 Returns and risk premiums.

The results shown in Figure 20.1 suggest that:

■ A relationship exists between the risk and the return of the different types of security.
■ Debt raised by companies carries a risk premium over safer forms of debt (the risk of the US Government running into financial difficulties is obviously much lower than for companies).
■ Equity capital carries a rather large risk premium (8.4% over the safest form of debt and 6.7% over company debt).

Obviously, the results given in Figure 20.1 provide us with some clues but do not really answer such questions as:

■ What is the risk premium for the equity of an individual company? (This will be explored further in 20.2).
■ How does the risk premium change when interest rates change?
■ Are these historical risk premiums an adequate reflection of the risk premiums investors consider when they compare expected returns?

There is, however, one key result. As we have already stated, there is not one single cost of capital but rather a series of costs associated to each different type. We know now that the *differences in prices of different types of capital depend on their different risks.*

20.2 EQUITY IS NOT AS EXPENSIVE AS ONE MAY IMAGINE: THE IMPACT OF DIVERSIFICATION

Diversification

The higher the risk associated with a specific type of security for the investor, the more return he requires from it. As a result, equity capital is in general more expensive than debt. The problem, however, when you want to estimate the cost of capital of your own company, is that you are not really interested in the cost of equity or of debt in general, but rather in the cost for your individual company. One of the major contributions of financial theory over the last twenty years has been to establish that the general risk-return relationship is also true for individual securities, or companies. As a result, investors will require a higher return when they invest in the equity of companies which carry more risk. But the risk premium required by investors is not a function of the total risk of individual securities, or companies, but a *function of part only of this risk*. As a result the premium required by investors from their investments in individual companies is lower than their risk would first suggest.

In February 1993 Mr Dubois, a French investor, wants to invest 1 million FF on the Paris stock market. For the sake of simplicity let us assume that he is contemplating three possible courses of action only:

1   To invest all his capital in the shares of company Alma.
2   To invest all his capital in the shares of company Opéra.
3   To split his capital equally between Alma and Opéra; (or to *diversify* equally his investment between Alma and Opéra).

Let us further assume that Mr Dubois has made a risk–return analysis on the investments in the equity of Alma and Opéra. Let us finally assume that even though Alma and Opéra are totally different and independent companies, the analysis shows that the risk and return of an investment in either Alma or Opéra are exactly the same – an obviously exceptional case. The risk–return analysis prepared by Mr Dubois is shown below:

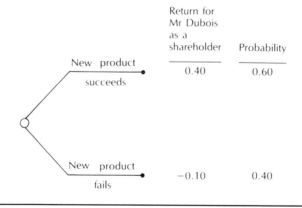

Figure 20.2 Alma and Opéra investment opportunities.

In order to understand why investors cannot require a reward for the whole of the risk of individual companies, we have to put ourselves in their place again and to realize that on any stock market investors can not only buy one single share but also portfolios composed of several different shares. Let us consider the example shown in Figure 20.2.

Let us compare the results for Mr Dubois of investing in either Alma or Opéra or in both Alma and Opéra. These results are shown in the diagram reproduced in Figure 20.3.

Notes on Figure 20.3:

- The results of the new products at Alma and Opéra are independent of one another.
- As Alma and Opéra show similar results of success and failure, and as the investment of Mr Dubois is split into two equal parts:
  - When both Alma and Opéra succeed or fail the return of the investment in both is the same as the return in either of them.

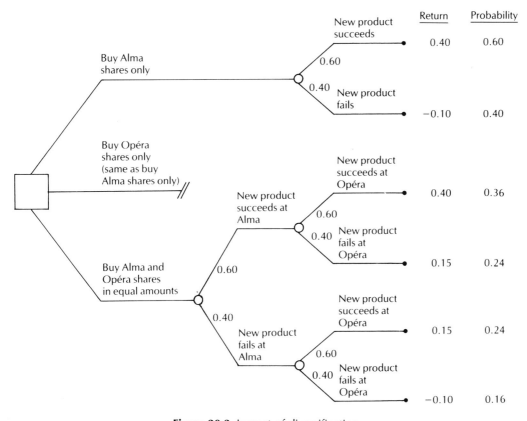

Figure 20.3 Impact of diversification.

· When Alma succeeds and Opéra fails, or vice versa, the return of the investment in both Alma and Opéra is equal to the average of the investment in Alma when it succeeds and in Opéra when it fails, or vice versa.

From the results shown in Figure 20.3, which is the best strategy for Mr Dubois, to invest in either Alma or Opéra, or to divide his investment between Alma and Opéra?

When folding back the diagram in Figure 20.3, you find exactly the same expected value, 20%, for both strategies. So in this case, splitting the investment, or diversification, has no impact on the expected return. However, when looking at their risk profiles, the two alternative strategies show different results. These risk profiles are reproduced in Figure 20.4.

As far as risk is concerned, the diversification of the investment in Alma and Opéra does not eliminate the possibilities of extreme returns very different from the 20% that Mr Dubois expects on average, but it does make these extreme returns less likely to materialize. As diversification enables him to reduce his risk while keeping the same return, Mr Dubois will prefer to invest in both Alma and Opéra rather than in only one of them.

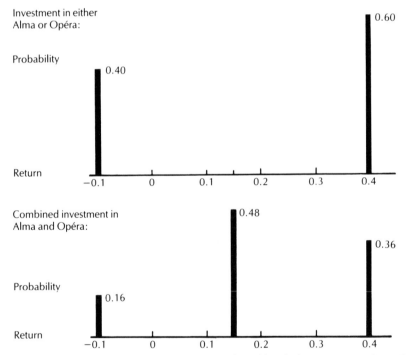

Note: A very popular measure of risk in finance is variance. For an analysis of the risk of an investment in Alma and/or Opéra using variance, please refer to Further Model VI.2.

Figure 20.4 Investment risk profiles.

Diversification, or holding portfolios of shares rather than any individual share, makes a lot of sense for investors on the stock market, since it enables them to reduce their risk for a given level of return or, alternatively, to increase their return for a given level of risk.

Statistical studies have shown that the benefits of diversification are very easily obtained since you only need to hold a few stocks (let us say a dozen of randomly selected stocks).[2] The problem, however, is that diversification does not remove risk totally.

Diversification cannot totally eradicate the risk of investment in the equity of individual companies. This is because all companies are equally exposed to economy-wide hazards. However good your diversification may be, you cannot protect yourself completely against a change in political regime that will affect the results of all companies. This part of the total risk attached to investment in the equity of individual companies that cannot be eliminated through diversification is called the *market risk* or systematic risk.

Diversification can only eliminate that part of the total risk of individual companies which is specific to them. This risk results from the peculiar hazards individual companies face in their specific business environments. As it is highly unlikely that independent companies will all fail in their own business environment, you can reduce your risk with diversification. This part of the total risk that can be eliminated through diversification is called the *specific risk*, or the unique risk or the residual risk.

The good thing about the speculation, or competition as we called it, which prevails on the stock markets, is that investors are unable to demand a premium for the risk they can remove through diversification. As a result the risk premium for individual shares *is a function of their market risk, but is independent of their specific risk and consequently is also not a direct function of their total risk.*

20.3 THE CAPM

The relationship between the return of individual shares and their market risk was formalized in the mid-sixties through a model known as the *capital asset pricing model* (CAPM).[3] According to the CAPM, the relationship between the expected return of an individual share and its market risk can be expressed as follows:

$$r = r_f + \beta(r_m - r_f)^4$$

where r = expected return from an individual share
 r_f = risk free rate (the rate on Treasury bills, see Figure 20.1)

β = beta coefficient which measures the market risk of the individual share

r_m = expected return from an investment in all shares available on the market (market return).

What does the beta coefficient mean?

★■The beta coefficient is a covariance-based measure of the tendency of an individual share to move with the market as a whole.[5] It measures the volatility of an individual share relative to the market as a whole.

■ By definition, the beta coefficient of the market as a whole is equal to 1.

■ Individual shares which have a high beta coefficient are sensitive to movements of the market as a whole. As the latter reflects the expected performance of the economy, companies with high beta coefficients are very much exposed to the performance of the economy as a whole. If the economy is expected to boom, they are expected to generate very good results. On the other hand, if the economy is expected to be depressed, they are in turn expected to generate very poor results. In the USA air transport, real estate, travel and outdoor recreation, electronics and retail department stores are traditional examples of companies with high beta coefficients.[6]

■ Individual shares which have a beta coefficient equal to 1 belong to companies which are basically expected to do exactly as well, or as badly, as the economy.

■ Individual shares which have a low beta coefficient (between zero[7] and 1) are companies whose performance is fairly independent of what may happen to the economy. This may be the case of companies which provide basic products or services which are needed whatever the global economic conditions may be. In the USA utilities, telephone and tobacco are traditional examples of companies with low beta coefficients.[8]

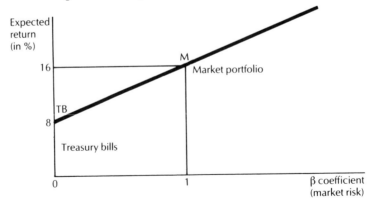

Figure 20.5 Expected return/market risk relationship for the investor.

The relationship between expected return and market risk can be visualized on a graph. This is done in Figure 20.5, in which the line TB–M is called the *security market line*. All individual shares of companies as well as portfolios plot on this line.

How robust is the CAPM and how is it supported by the reality of capital market?

As far as the robustness of the CAPM is concerned, its construction requires many assumptions.[9] A number of theoretical studies have shown that most of these assumptions can be relaxed without changing the basic results of the model.

Answering the second question, whether or not the CAPM is supported by the reality of the capital markets (which is the only valid test), it is fair to say that the problems of measurement are such that no decisive argument has been put forward in favor or against the validity of CAPM.[10]

Finally, it is fair to say that in spite of the doubts people have about the real meaning of the CAPM, beta coefficients are regularly published and are used by the financial community, or, more precisely, by the community of professional investors. This is true in countries with active and sophisticated capital markets.

20.4 AN ALTERNATIVE TO THE CAPM: THE APT

Within the CAPM framework, the return of any individual share is a function of the relationship (or covariance) between its return and the return of one single factor, the market portfolio.

Formulated by Ross in 1976,[11] the arbitrage pricing theory (APT) offers a more general approach to the problem and states that several factors (not just the market portfolio) may explain share returns. The concept then is the same as for the CAPM; for each factor the appropriate measure of risk is the sensitivity of the share return to changes in the factor. *Only systematic risk is rewarded.*[12] An hypothetical example aimed at illustrating how the APT could be used for choosing among alternative strategies is given in Further Model VI.3.

20.5 COST OF CAPITAL DEPENDS MORE ON YOUR DECISION THAN ON YOUR COMPANY

Although the financial community is not really sure about the complete validity of the CAPM itself, the main concepts related to this model are currently widely accepted and they have profound implications for strategic decision making.

The first thing we should remember is that the returns investors expect become returns they require from the point of view of a company that needs to raise capital. The risk return relationship shown in Figure 20.5 becomes the one shown in Figure 20.6.

As all individual securities are plotted on the TB–M security market line, *this security market line describes the cost of capital for all companies in a given economy at a specific date.* As a result, estimating a company's cost of capital is a matter of:

- Estimating the security market line, a general economic relationship that is valid for all companies and that one should therefore be able to obtain from a specialized financial services firm.
- Estimating the company's beta coefficient. As soon as this is established, the cost of capital for the company can be read from the graph in Figure 20.6.
- If beta coefficients are stable over time this obviously simplifies the calculation of the cost of capital a great deal since the only information to be updated is the security market line.

The second thing to specify is what it is that makes the beta coefficient of one company differ from another. We stated earlier that one possible explanation is that the performance of some companies is necessarily more dependent on the performance of the economy as a whole because they are involved in activities which are linked to the performance of the economy. Intuitively, this leads to

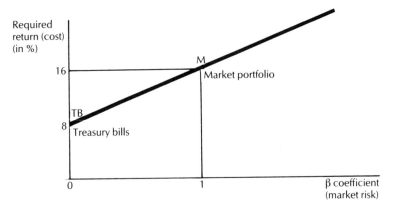

Figure 20.6 Required return/market risk relationship for the company.

the assumption that the beta coefficients of companies are related to the industrial sector in which they operate. This intuition has been confirmed by several statistical studies proving that the beta coefficients of industrial sectors were far more reliable than the beta coefficients of individual companies. The main reason for this is that industry beta coefficients can be estimated from much larger data samples. What are the consequences of this industry return/market risk relationship?

- *The cost of capital depends on the industry with which you are concerned when making a strategic decision that requires funding.* If your strategic decision is related to an industry with a higher beta, you should use a relatively high discount rate. If your strategic decision is related to an industry with a low beta, you should use a relatively low discount rate.[13]
- *The cost of capital does not depend a great deal on the company you are in.* If you take a strategic decision to expand within the industry in which your company operates you should use a cost of capital which is relevant to your company. But if you take the decision to expand into another industry, with a different beta, you should use the cost of capital of the new industry, and not the cost of capital of your own company.
- *So, diversified companies should use different costs of capital* in their different units if these units operate in different industries, each unit using its own industrial sector's cost of capital.
- Stated differently, *when you make a strategic decision in a diversified company, the cost of capital to consider is that of your industry and not that of your company.* The latter is just the result of the portfolio of its different activities in various economic sectors.

This can be illustrated by the hypothetical example given in Figure 20.7.

From the data shown in Figure 20.7, Continental Holdings should use:
- A 21% discount rate for evaluating any new capital expenditures in real estate.
- A 14% discount rate for evaluating any new capital expenditures in tobacco.
- A 20% discount rate for the new capital expenditures it contemplates in the retail sector.

The beta coefficient of the company as a whole will reflect the composition of its different activities. At the moment Continental Holdings has half of its assets in tobacco and half of its assets in real estate, so its beta is

$$0.5 * 0.78 + 0.5 * 1.67 = 1.23$$

NB This overall beta coefficient will change with any shift in the composition of the activities of Continental Holdings. The discount rate corresponding to this beta coefficient is not to be used for evaluating any new single capital expenditure of the company.

Continental Holdings operates in two sectors: tobacco and real estate. It envisages some diversification in the retail sector. The beta coefficients of these sectors are respectively 0.78 (tobacco), 1.67 (real estate) and 1.44 (retail).

Which discount rate(s) should the company use for its new capital expenditures? The security market line is as follows:

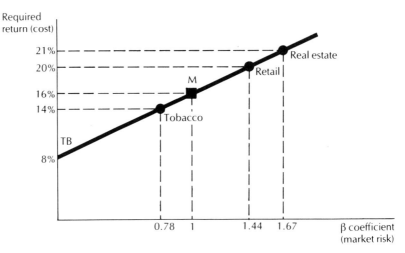

Figure 20.7 A hypothetical example.

NOTES

1 Investors in equity are sometimes guaranteed a minimum dividend. But, since this minimum dividend is extremely low, it is never enough to justify the investment and only constitutes a very limited protection against risk.

2 See, for example, W Wagner and S Lau, 'The effects of diversification on risk', *Financial Analysts Journal*, (Nov/Dec 1971) **26**: 7–13.

3 Developed by W Sharpe, J Treynor, J Lintner and J Mossin. For an intertemporal version of the CAPM, refer to *Continuous-Time Finance*, R Merton, Basil Blackwell, 1990, Chapter 15.

4 Another way to write this relationship is $r - r_f = \beta * (r_m - r_f)$, showing that the risk premium $(r_m - r_f)$ is proportional to the market risk (β).

5 If we call r the expected return from a share and r_m the market return, then:

$$\beta = \frac{\text{cov}(r, r_m)}{\text{var}(r_m)} \qquad \begin{array}{l} \text{cov} = \text{covariance} \\ \text{var} = \text{variance} \end{array}$$

6 See for example: B Rosenberg and J Guy, 'Prediction from investment fundamentals', *Financial Analysts Journal*, (1976) **32**(3): 60–72 and **32**(4): 62–71.

7 A zero beta coefficient is difficult to imagine for an individual company, since it would correspond to a risk-free investment, an investment in Treasury bills.

Because they carry some risk, corporate debt instruments should have a small positive beta; various studies on the US market have evaluated the average beta of the bonds of industrial corporations as from 0.2 to 0.4. For example, I Friend, M Granito and R Westerfield report an average bond beta value of 0.36 (and an average common stock beta of 1.6) in (1978) 'New evidence on the capital asset pricing model', *Journal of Frnance*, June 1978.

8 As stated by WF Sharpe in *Investments* (Prentice Hall, 1978): Stocks of firms whose products are termed necessities tend to respond less than most stocks when expectations about the future health of the economy are revised, while the stocks of firms that manufacture consumer and producer durables and products considered 'luxuries' tend to respond more than most. However, there are significant exceptions.

9 In spite of its apparently simple and intuitive formulation, the CAPM is derived from utility theory (see Further Model V).

10 There are two major problems in testing the CAPM:

- It deals with expected returns, but we can only observe actual returns.
- It envisages a market portfolio including all risk investments but most market indexes contain only a sample of stocks.

For a review of the problems associated with the testing of the CAPM, refer to R Roll, 'A critique of the asset pricing theory's tests', *Journal of Financial Economics*, (May 1977) **4**: 129–76.

11 S Ross, 'The arbitrage theory of capital asset pricing', *Journal of Economic Theory* (Dec 1976), **13**: 341–60.

12 The testing of the APT is not exempt from difficulties either. For more about this, refer to: R Roll and SA Ross, 'An empirical investigation of the arbitrage pricing theory', *Journal of Finance* (Dec 1980), pp 1073–103.

13 In other words, *the cost of capital results from the use you make of it and not really whence it comes*. This, however, requires that a bridge be built between real and financial variables: see for example: SC Myers and S Turnbull, 'Capital budgeting and the capital asset pricing model: good news and bad news,' *Journal of Finance* (May 1977), **32**: 321–36.

── CHAPTER 21 ──

The Cost of Debt and the Capital Structure Issue

21.1 DEBT LOOKS CHEAP BUT THIS MAY BE AN ILLUSION

Among the two most popular forms of external financing, debt and equity, one, debt, is obviously cheaper. As a consequence, one could be tempted to use it in preference to other forms of financing. An analysis of the impact of using debt shows, however, that this would not be a very good idea.

The case with no corporation tax

The fact that, when corporation tax is ignored, a company cannot achieve any advantage by using apparently cheap debt financing, was first demonstrated by Modigliani and Miller in 1958.[1] Their demonstration produced a very simple argument: shareholders who want to take risks can either buy the shares of companies which finance themselves with debt (levered companies), or can buy shares of all-equity financed companies (unlevered companies) and borrow by themselves. As a result, shareholders are perfectly indifferent whether firms borrow or not. *They merely require more return from levered firms, exactly the return they would achieve by borrowing themselves.*

How companies can increase their book return on equity by borrowing: the leverage effect

Let us consider the following example.

Based in Bahrain, a country with no corporation tax, Al Shirawi and Al Kantara are two identical companies, with the same activity, the same size (total assets = 10 000 BD) and the same operational profitability (15% of assets). The two companies differ in one respect only. Al Shirawi uses no debt, Al Kantara finances its assets with 50% of equity and 50% of debt at 10%. How much return on equity do the two companies give to their shareholders? (The book return on equity of Al Shirawi and Al Kantara is shown in Figure 21.1.)

AL SHIRAWI

| Assets 10 000 | Equity 10 000 |

AL KANTARA

| Assets 10 000 | Debt 5 000 |
| | Equity 5 000 |

Operational profit $\quad 0.15 * 10\,000 = 1\,500$

$\quad$ − interest $\hspace{5.5cm} 0$

$\quad$ = profit $\hspace{5cm} 1\,500$

Book return on equity $= \dfrac{1\,500}{10\,000} = 15\ \%$

Operational profit $\quad 0.15 * 10\,000 = 1\,500$

$\quad$ − interest $\qquad 0.10 * 5\,000 = \quad 500$

$\quad$ = profit $\hspace{4cm} 1\,000$

Book return on equity $= \dfrac{1\,000}{5\,000} = 20\ \%$

A **suggestion**: construct a small spreadsheet model for comparing the return on equity of Al Shirawi and Al Kantara in various situations. Design your model in such a way that return on assets, interest rate and debt to equity ratio can easily be changed. Use your model to test:

1. What happens to the return of equity of Al Kantara when the return on assets is lower than the interest cost.
2. The impact of higher debt ratios when:
   (a) Return on assets is higher than interest,
   (b) Return on assets is lower than interest.

You can then compare your model with the one in Figure 21.2 (rows 1 to 9).

Figure 21.1 The leverage effect.

Figure 21.1 shows the very popular effect of using the cheap source of finance, debt, that of *the leverage effect* (or *gearing*):

- When the return on assets is higher than the cost of debt, using debt increases the return on equity, and the more debt, the higher the return on equity.
- When the return on assets is lower than the cost of debt, then the effect is opposite, and using debt reduces the return on equity, and the more debt, the lower the return on equity.

How shareholders can achieve the same result by borrowing by themselves

Let us assume that Al Shirawi and Al Kantara have one single shareholder each.

- Bahrain Holdings, the shareholder of Al Shirawi, is not satisfied with the 15% return it gets from its 10 000 BD investment and wants to achieve the same 20% as the shareholder of Al Kantara. Let us further assume that Bahrain Holdings can borrow at the same rate as companies, 10%.
- Manama Holdings, the shareholder of Al Kantara, is not satisfied either, as it wants to achieve the 15% unlevered return offered by Al Shirawi. Let us assume that it can invest in a debt instrument that yields 10%.

In order to achieve their respective objectives, without switching companies, Bahrain Holdings and Manama Holdings can proceed as follows.

- Bahrain Holdings can borrow 10 000 BD by themselves, in the same proportion as the levered company does.
- Manama Holdings can invest in equity and debt in the same proportion as the levered company borrows.

The foreground of a spreadsheet model simulating the situations of Al Shirawi, Al Kantara, Bahrain Holdings and Manama Holdings is shown in Figure 21.2. The formulas are given in Figure 21.3. The model shows that shareholders can easily do or undo leverage by themselves, and do not need companies to do it for them.

The issue of risk

When borrowing, companies expose their shareholders to more risk. If you assume the occurrence of operational difficulties and set the return on assets to 0.06 in the model described in Figure 21.2, you realize that:

- The return on equity of the levered company falls to 0.02, while the return of the unlevered company only falls to 0.06. In case of operational difficulties, and because the cost of debt is fixed, the return on equity of levered companies falls more. This risk is called the *volatility risk*. This risk might be the reason why Manama Holdings was not happy with its levered return.
- The return of the shareholder who makes his own leverage falls to 0.02 (the

	A	B	C	D	E
1	Return on assets	0.15			
2	COMPANY AL SHIRAWI			COMPANY AL KANTARA	
3	Total assets	10 000		Total assets	10 000
4	Debt/equity ratio	0.0		Debt/equity ratio	1.0
5	Operational profit	1 500		Operational profit	1 500
6	Interest cost	0		Interest cost	500
7	Profit after interest	1 500		Profit after interest	1 000
8	Equity	10 000		Equity	5 000
9	**Return on equity**	0.15		**Return on equity**	0.20
10					
11	SHAREHOLDER BAHRAIN HLDs			SHAREHOLDER MANAMA HLDs	
12	Own equity investment	10 000		Own equity investment	5 000
13	Debt/own investment	1.0		Debt/own investment	0.0
14	Total equity investment	20 000		Total equity investment	5 000
15	Own debt investment	0		Own debt investment	5 000
16	Income from equity	3 000		Income from equity	1 000
17	Interest paid	1 000		Interest paid	0
18	Income from debt	0		Income from debt	500
19	Total income	2 000		Total income	1 500
20	**Return on own investment**	0.20		**Return on own investment**	0.15

Width of columns: A:24; B:8; C:8; D:24 and E:8.

Figure 21.2 Shareholders and leverage: a spreadsheet model.

same as the levered company) and the return of the shareholder who has undone the leverage, falls to 0.06 (the same as the unlevered company), in spite of the fact that he holds shares in a levered company.

B1:	0.15		
B3:	U 10 000	E3:	(F0) +B3
B4:	(F2) U 0	E4:	(F2) U 1
B5:	(F0) +B3*B1	E5:	(F0) +E3*B1
B6:	(F0) +B4/(B4+1)*0.1*B3	E6:	(F0) +E4/(E4+1)*0.1*E3
B7:	(F0) +B5−B6	E7:	(F0) +E5−E6
B8:	(F0) 1/(1+B4)*B3	E8:	(F0) 1/(1+E4)*E3
B9:	(F2) +B7/B8	E9:	(F2) +E7/E8
B12:	+B8	E12:	(F0) +E8
B13:	(F2) 1	E13:	(F2) 0.0
B14:	(F0) (1+B13)*B12	E14:	(F0) (1+E13)*E12
B15:	(F0) 0.0	E15:	(F0) 5 000
B16:	(F0) +B14*B9	E16:	(F0) +E14*E9
B17:	(F0) +B12*B13*0.1	E17:	(F0) +E12*E13*0.1
B18:	(F0) +B15*0.1	E18:	(F0) +E15*0.1
B19:	(F0) +B16−B17+B18	E19:	(F0) +E16−E17+E18
B20:	(F2) +B19/B12	E20:	(F2) +E19/(E12+E15)

Figure 21.3 Formulas of the spreadsheet model.

So, whatever companies do in terms of leverage, shareholders can achieve their own objectives. What is the consequence of this?

- Companies should not be able to create any additional value from the use of debt.[2]
- Shareholders should not be sensitive to the increase in book return caused by leverage. As they can achieve the same levered return at the price of additional risk, shareholders should adjust the return they require from companies in relation to the amount of debt they use. Shareholders should actually require from levered companies exactly the same return as they would get by borrowing by themselves.

The effect of borrowing on the cost of capital of companies can be shown on a graph. Figure 21.4 shows what happens to the cost of equity capital and to the combined cost of equity capital and debt of a company when it borrows.

As shown in Figure 21.4, the increase in the cost of equity that occurs when companies borrow, results in the fact that the combined cost of any mix of debt and equity capital remains constant and equal to the cost of equity when there is no borrowing (cost of unlevered equity).

The proportion of debt to the total capital of the company (debt and equity) is known as the *capital structure*.[3] Using financial language, we can say that Figure 21.4 shows that, when there is no corporation tax, the capital structure of a company does not seem to matter.

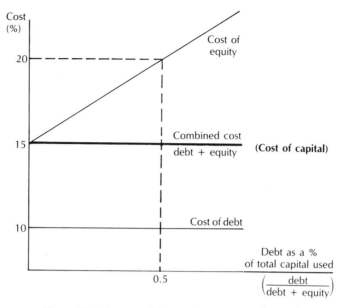

Figure 21.4 Impact of borrowing on cost of capital.

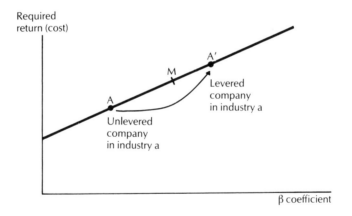

Figure 21.5 Impact of borrowing on cost of capital: CAPM approach.

The consequence of borrowing on the cost of capital of companies can also be shown on a graph representing the security market line. This is done in Figure 21.5.

Within the CAPM framework, companies which use debt increase their beta coefficient, and the relationship between the beta of an unlevered company and the beta of the same company with debt is as follows:

$$\beta_{A'} = \beta_A + \frac{D}{E} * (\beta_A - \beta_D)$$

where $\beta_{A'}$ = beta coefficient of the levered company
$\quad\quad\beta_A$ = beta coefficient of the same company without debt (the beta coefficient of the industry for the non-levered company)
$\quad\quad$D = amount of debt used
$\quad\quad$E = amount of equity used
$\quad\quad\beta_D$ = beta coefficient of the debt.

This relationship has important implications:

- As most companies are levered (use debt), companies' beta coefficients are the result of their business, or industry, risk *and* of their financial risk.
- As a consequence, the beta coefficients of individual companies cannot be used directly for calculating the return required from companies by the market. In order to calculate this, one must first remove the impact of the financial risk from the beta coefficient of individual companies.
- When the impact of the financial risk is removed, their beta becomes equal to the beta of the industry they operate in, provided they operate in one industry only.[4]
- *The required return to be used for evaluating strategic alternatives is far more related to the beta of the industry than to the beta of the company.* In other words, what counts when you consider committing funds is the cost of capital of the industry you are investing in, not the cost of capital of your own company. In many ways this is a reassuring statement. Success in a given industry depends on the intelligence of the strategies of the competitors, not on their financial muscle.

The case with corporation tax and some other factors ✳

Corporation tax exists in most countries and generally does not have a neutral effect on financing since it treats the various sources of capital differently. In most countries, interest related to debt financing is tax deductible, whereas dividends related to equity financing are not.[5]

When interest is tax deductible, debt financing suddenly becomes attractive to companies. *Using debt enables companies to create an additional value equal to the present value of the tax savings* created by the tax deductibility of interest charges. An example can help you understand how this additional value can be calculated. A company raises a loan of 120 000 FFR which will cause interest charges equal to 9 600 FFR in the three coming years. The corporation tax rate is 40%. What is the additional value created by the loan?

In the three coming years, and because interest payments are tax deductible, the loan will enable the company to reduce its tax by an amount equal to:

$$9\ 600 * (\text{tax rate}) = 9\ 600 * (0.4)\ 3\ 840\ \text{FFR}$$

The present value of this tax saving is equal to:[6]

$$\frac{3\ 840}{(1.1)} + \frac{3\ 840}{(1.1)^2} + \frac{3\ 840}{(1.1)^3} = 9\ 550\ \text{FFR}$$

This is the additional value created by the use of debt.

An alternative way to describe the advantage of debt is to say that debt-induced tax shields reduce the cost of debt and consequently reduce the aggregate cost of debt and equity or cost of capital. In order to illustrate this, let us come back to the graph in Figure 21.4. This graph shows that, in the absence of corporation tax, the proportion of debt in the capital structure has no impact on the aggregate cost of capital. With corporation tax, the result is quite different as is shown in Figure 21.6.

	No debt		Debt = 50% of total capital used	
No corporation tax	Cost of debt:	0.10	Cost of debt:	0.10
	Cost of equity:	0.15	Cost of equity:	0.20
	Aggregate cost:		Aggregate cost:	
	(equity cost)	0.15	(0.5*0.1)+(0.5*0.2) =	0.15
Corporation tax (50% rate)	Cost of debt:	0.10	Cost of debt:	0.10
	Cost of equity:	0.15	Cost of equity:	0.20
	Tax savings:	0.00	Tax savings: 0.5*(0.1*0.5) =	0.025
	Aggregate cost:	0.15	Aggregate cost: 0.15−0.025 =0.125[†]	

[†] This is equal to either:

Cost of unlevered equity − tax savings: 0.15−0.025 = 0.125

or to:

Weighted sum, of cost of equity and debt after tax: 0.5*0.20+0.5*0.05 = 0.125

Figure 21.6 Impact of debt on cost of capital with and without corporation tax.

Because of corporation tax, companies should therefore borrow as much as they can. The issue of debt financing is more complicated, however, since using debt increases the chances of the firm running into a financially difficult situation. As it commits the firm to compulsory cash outflows in the future, debt reduces the flexibility of the firm.[7] This may mean the loss of valuable opportunities, or, worse, cash difficulties. Ultimately, an excessive use of debt can result in bankruptcy. Consequently, the value of the firm which uses debt can be expressed as follows:

Present value of the levered firm	=	Present value if all equity financed	+	Present value of debt induced tax shields	−	Present value of cost of financial inadequacy

As both the value of the tax shields and the cost of financial inadequacy increase with the amount of debt used, this formula suggests the existence of an optimal capital structure which is reached when the difference between tax shields and cost of financial inadequacy is maximum, an intuitively appealing idea which is unfortunately not consistent with actual practices. Many large companies, for whom the risk of financial inadequacy is very remote, borrow very little which contradicts the above formula.

The capital structure issue[8] has been widely discussed in financial literature but, as stated by SC Myers,[9] 'when asked "How do firms choose their capital structures?" The answer is we don't know'. Even though a full treatment of this issue, a very specialized topic, goes beyond the scope of this book, refer to Further Model VI.5 for some guidelines and useful references.

Because of our limited understanding of the capital structure issue, we would like to recommend you to be very cautious each time you feel that you have to include capital structure considerations in your models. Are these considerations supported by theory? Are they fully consistent with actual practices?

21.2   WHAT SHOULD YOU DO IN PRACTICE? THE CONCEPT OF ADJUSTED PRESENT VALUE (APV)

In Chapter 20, we said that you should use the cost of the capital of the industry you invest in as the discount rate. We can now be more precise.

- You should discount the operational cash flows attached to a strategic alternative at the unlevered cost of equity capital that prevails in the industry in which you invest. This enables you to calculate the net present value of this alternative.
- You should then analyze the financing side effects of this strategic alternative, particularly the additional recourse to debt that it will cause. When doing so, make sure that the relationship that you assume between the alternative and the additional debt is valid. In particular, do not take for granted the existence of a standard debt to total financing ratio since the very concept of a target capital structure is not clear.
- You should then add to the net present value of the strategic alternative, the present value of its financing side effects. The resulting net present value is known as the Adjusted net Present Value (APV).[10]
- One last recommendation: in most cases, financing side effects are not that important. What matters most in general is the net present value at the unlevered cost of equity capital.

The example described in Figure 21.7 will help you understand how you can use the APV approach.

Gamma is contemplating an investment in its usual and unique line of business. The after tax cash flows attached to this opportunity are:

			(in 000 FFR)
1993	1994	1995	1996
−900	400	950	520

The unlevered cost of equity to Gamma is 15%. The corporate tax rate is 50%. Gamma believes that if implemented this opportunity will enable the company to borrow an amount equal to 569 000 FFR. This borrowing would correspond to the following cash flows:

1993	1994	1995	1996
569	−56.9	−56.9	−625.9

(which corresponds to an interest rate of 10%).

What is the NPV attached to the new investment?

Figure 21.7 Using the APV approach.

When you apply the APV approach to the situation at Gamma, you obtain the following results:

1. NPV of project (in 000 FFR):

$$- 900 + \frac{400}{1.15} + \frac{950}{(1.15)^2} + \frac{520}{(1.15)^3} = 508$$

2. NPV of financing side effects:

$$\frac{56.9 * 0.5}{1.1} + \frac{56.9 * 0.5}{(1.1)^2} + \frac{56.9 * 0.5}{(1.1)^3} = 71$$

where: 56.9 is the interest paid
56.9 * 0.5 is the tax shield from interest
0.1 is the discount rate which corresponds to the debt (assuming that the tax shield is certain)

3. APV: NPV of project   508
     + APV of financing side effects   71
     = APV   579

These results show that, when you consider the impact of the financing side effects, the project looks more attractive (14% higher NPV).

One very important thing to realize about APV calculations is that they are not easy to perform. Four difficulties stand out.

The first difficulty relates to the evaluation of the debt attached to the project. How did Gamma assess that the project would enable them to borrow 569 000 FFR? In practice, you may find yourself in two different types of situation.

- Either there is a specific debt tied to the project, which is the easier case but, unfortunately, not the most common.
- Or no specific debt tied to the project exists but you want to reflect that the project is going to increase the debt capacity of the company. In this case, the evaluation of the debt is a very complex matter.
  - · The idea that a new project can increase the debt capacity of the firm is related to the concept of the existence of a target capital structure. As we discussed earlier, this is not an obvious concept.
  - · Assuming that you have clear beliefs about the capital structure policy of your firm and that, in particular, you believe that your company pursues a target debt to equity ratio, then a further problem arises. Is this general debt to equity ratio valid for the project? You may actually think that some projects are more able than others to support debt.[11] Let us skip over this difficulty and assume that the target debt to equity ratio applies to the project and go back to the Gamma example to illustrate some further problems.

Does the 569 000 FFR loan correspond to the policy of having debt equal to 63% of total capital (the initial capital being 900 000 FFR)? Because the project corresponds to a present value of 1 408 000 FFR, it is more correct to say that the loan corresponds to a 569/1408, or 40%, debt to total capital ratio.[12] But then a further difficulty arises. Over the life of the project, its present value will change, whereas the value of the loan will remain constant. Consequently, the loan envisaged at Gamma does not correspond to a constant 40% debt to total capital ratio. You will find, in Further Model VI.6, a model for estimating a loan corresponding to a target capital structure maintained over the life of the project.

The second difficulty relates to the discount rate you should use for the debt related tax shields. We considered above that you should use the debt rate on the basis that tax shields are certain. How sure can we be about this?

The third difficulty relates to the estimation of the cost of financial inadequacy. In general, you can consider that these are small and can be neglected.[13]

The final difficulty is related to the estimation of the unlevered cost of capital. As discussed earlier (page 313), this cannot generally be derived directly from observed betas. As soon as debt is used, the impact of the financial risk has to be removed from betas before you can use them to estimate the unlevered cost of capital.

Fortunately, as we said above, *the most important thing is the estimation of the NPV component of the APV*, so do not be afraid of the complexities attached to the adjustment factor (tax shield and financial inadequacy).

21.3 THE ALTERNATIVE TO THE APV APPROACH: THE WEIGHTED AVERAGE COST OF CAPITAL (WACC)

A very popular alternative to the APV approach is the weighted average cost of capital (WACC).

Both WACC and APV deal with the impact of debt financing but they do not approach the problem in the same way. APV suggests that you add the present value of the debt induced tax shields to the NPV of the project, while WACC suggests that you discount the cash flows of the project at a lower rate, which embodies the tax shields (or that you compare the IRR of the project with this lower rate used as a hurdle).

The WACC approach has one great advantage in that it seems to be more simple than the APV approach. But this simplicity is only apparent and hides some serious difficulties. *It implies the existence of a target debt to equity ratio* maintained constantly over the life of the project, it poses calculation problems and it is not easy to reconcile with APV. In order to illustrate the use of the WACC, let us return to the Gamma example.

A popular way[14] to calculate WACC to Gamma would be as follows:

$$\text{WACC} = \text{cost of equity} * \frac{E}{E+D} + \text{cost of debt} * \frac{D}{E+D}$$

where D = value of debt
        E = value of equity

The equity cost to be used is the levered cost of equity, which is a further argument in favor of the WACC approach since, in practice, the levered cost of equity is easier to estimate than the unlevered cost. Gamma's levered cost of equity can be derived from Figure 21.6.

$$\frac{\text{cost of}}{\text{equity}} = \frac{\text{cost of}}{\text{unlevered}} + \frac{D}{E} * \left(\frac{\text{cost of}}{\text{unlevered}} - \frac{\text{cost of}}{\text{debt}} \right)$$
$$\qquad\qquad\quad \text{equity} \qquad\qquad\qquad \text{equity}$$

The problem is to decide which debt to total capital ratio should be used. Market values (1 408 for the project and 569 for the loan) suggest a 40% debt to total capital ratio.[15] You can then calculate the WACC and the NPV.

$$\text{cost of equity} = 0.15 + \frac{0.4}{1-0.4} * (0.15 - 0.10) = 0.183$$

$$\text{WACC} = 0.183 * 0.6 + 0.10 * 0.5 * 0.4 = 0.13^{16}$$

$$\text{NPV} = 558$$

This NPV is not equal to the APV, the main reason being that the WACC approach assumes that the debt ratio is kept constant over the life of the project, which is not true with the loan considered at Gamma. A reconciliation of WACC and APV approaches is shown in Further Model VI.6.

Final recommendations

In the absence of a consensus among finance specialists, we would like to take the risk of proposing our own views.

- The WACC approach is simple and popular but it makes a very strong assumption about the existence of a target capital structure, a notion which is intuitively appealing but challenged by a number of theoreticians and practitioners.
- As the capital structure assumption is implicit in the WACC approach, there is a danger of using WACC and forgetting to check the validity of this capital structure assumption.
- We would therefore recommend that you use the APV approach, which has the advantage of forcing you to make an explicit assumption about the financing side effects in each situation you analyze. When a problem is complex, it is always preferable to remain aware of the assumptions you make.
- However, the bad news is that it is difficult to estimate the cost of unlevered equity that you need in order to use the APV approach.

R.T.C. LIBRARY
LETTERKENNY

NOTES

1 F Modigliani and MN Miller, 'The cost of capital, corporation finance and the theory of investment', *American Economic Review* (June 1958), **48**: 261–97.

2 For the impact of debt financing on the Dhahran Roads contract, refer to Further Model VI.4.

3 Leverage may be measured according to two different ratios:
   - Debt to equity ratio (DR = Debt/Equity)
   - Debt to total capital ratio (dr = Debt/(Debt + Equity))

   The relationship between these two ratios is: $DR = dr/(1 - dr)$ and $dr = DR/(1 + DR)$.

4 If they operate in several industries their beta becomes equal to the weighted average of the betas of the industries they operate in.

5 This encouragement given to corporations to raise debt rather than equity is rather strange since one would expect tax authorities to be neutral, or, at least, not to encourage corporations to use the most risky source of capital. In some countries,

for example France in 1976, there have been some timid attempts at changing this situation by making dividends also tax deductible in special circumstances. For a description of attempts to create tax deductible equity in the USA, refer to: AN Chen and JW Kensinger, 'Innovations in corporate finance: tax deductible equity', *Financial Management* (Winter 1985), pp 44, 51.

6 As we consider that the tax savings are certain, we discount at the cost of debt.

7 See for example: G Donaldson, 'Corporate debt capacity', Division of Research, Graduate School of Business Administration, Harvard University (1962).

8 Here we restrict the capital issue structure to the debt v equity choice. The problem is more complex, however, since capital structure relates to the internal v external financing choice and to the choice among the various types of external financial instruments. In most countries, firms can choose among a very large variety of external financing instruments, equity, various types of debt, leasing, convertibles, etc, this choice being made greater by the availability of different maturities, borrowing short, medium or long term.

9 SC Myers, 'The capital structure puzzle', *Journal of Finance* (July 1984), **39**: 575–92.

10 For more about the APV, refer to: SC Myers, 'Interactions of corporate financing and investment decisions – implications for capital budgeting', *Journal of Finance* (March 1974), **29**: 1–25.

11 Refer to SC Myers, 'Determinants of corporate borrowing', *Journal of Financial Economics* (November 1977), **5**: 147–75.

12 1408 and 569 are also the market values of the project and of the loan, and are equal to the present value of the future cash flows discounted at the relevant rates, 15% for the project and 10% for the loan.

13 For an estimation of bankruptcy costs, refer to: J Warner, 'Bankruptcy costs: some evidence', *Journal of Finance* (May 1977), **32**: 337–48.

14 For other methods of calculating WACC: F Modigliani and M Miller, 'Corporate income taxes and the cost of capital: a correction', *American Economic Review* (June 1963), **53**: 433–43, and JA Miles and JR Ezzel, 'The weighted average cost of capital, perfect capital markets and project life: a clarification', *Journal of Financial and Quantitative Analysis* (September 1980), **15**: 719–30.

15 With a 63% ratio (debt ratio calculated in relation to initial capital), you get an NPV equal to 590. It is higher due to the fact that more debt is envisaged.

16 Could also be calculated as the result of: $0.15 - 0.10*0.5*0.4$.

CHAPTER 22

Cost of Capital: Some Rules for Action

22.1 EXTERNALLY AND INTERNALLY RAISED CAPITAL HAVE BASICALLY THE SAME COST

Our initial worry about the existence of many different costs attached to different types of capital was not really founded. We know that as far as externally raised capital is concerned what really counts is the cost of unlevered equity. We also know that this cost depends primarily on the risk of the strategic alternative under consideration. We know finally that this cost depends not on the total risk of that alternative but on part of that risk only, the market risk component.

Another worry we had was the fact that the cost of capital could differ according to whether capital was raised externally or internally. This is not a problem either. If we accept that the cost of capital comes from the return required by the shareholders, each time we envisage committing new capital, we should ask ourselves the question, is this investment better than the shareholders require or, in other words, is this investment better than the shareholders could achieve by themselves? If the answer to this question is negative, do not commit capital. In the extreme case where there are internal funds available and no attractive opportunities to invest them in, you should distribute these funds to the shareholders through dividend payments.[1]

As a result, whether it is internally generated or externally raised, capital has basically the same cost,[2] so there is no need to trace the source of capital you need.[3]

22.2 COST OF CAPITAL CORRESPONDS TO A VALUE MAXIMIZATION APPROACH

Value maximization

One key dimension of the use of cost of capital as a hurdle rate is that it corresponds to a value maximization approach.

When it invests in only the opportunities that have a positive net present value, a company creates the maximum possible additional value. If most opportunities undertaken have large net present values, undertaking some decisions with negative present values would probably not jeopardize the fact that the net result of all decisions would correspond to a positive value. This would, however, no longer be the maximum possible value.[4]

A common misuse of the cost of capital concept can help illustrate this point. Let us consider the following example.

A company operating in a one single line of business has a 20% cost of capital. As the specific competitive position of the company becomes very uncertain in 1993, it decides to keep a significant amount of cash available: 30 million FFR, 25% of its typical investment budget. For the sake of simplicity, let us assume that this amount of cash is kept uninvested and has, therefore, a zero return.

In such a situation, a number of people would be tempted to consider that, since the 1993 projects will have to contribute to the financing of the cash investment, more should be demanded from them, ie about 27% ((20 × 100)/75 = 26.66). This would actually be wrong, since doing so would make the company reject projects which have positive net present values at rates ranging between 20 and 27% which could contribute to creating the additional value that the company needs for financing its cash investment.

The cost of capital should never be adjusted to take into account unprofitable investments. It should be used as it is, whatever these unprofitable investments are. The only thing to do is to compare the total additional value the company is able to create from its profitable projects with the unprofitable investments. If the additional total value is higher, then things are all right; if on the other hand it is less, the company should think about leaving the business it is in since the maximum value it can create is not sufficient. This leads to a fundamental question: what makes net present values positive?

What makes net present values positive?

Theory tells that, when an industry settles into long-run competitive equilibrium, all its assets are expected to earn their opportunity cost of capital, and as a result generate zero net present values.

Finding a strategy that generates a positive net present value is finding a strategy that is able to out-perform the market and create what economists call a rent, and is not that easy. This has a number of practical implications.

- *You should never take for granted that the NPV attached to a decision is positive.* You should always make sure that this does not result from over-optimistic forecasts but rather from a well-thought-out strategy. Only strategies that can build up some kind of sustainable competitive advantage for the firm are the ones that have positive NPVs.[5]

- *NPV calculations should not be done by specialists but rather by the managers who make the strategic decisions.* As positive NPVs can only be created by superior strategies, who is in a better position for this than the managers themselves? They have good information about, and a good understanding of, the market forces and the competition. When used by the strategic decision maker the NPV helps probe the validity of the moves envisaged and make clear how they can become even more effective.

22.3 THE UNLEVERED COST OF EQUITY IS THE DISCOUNT RATE YOU SHOULD USE: THE DANGER OF DOUBLE COUNTING RISK

Use of the unlevered cost of equity as the discount rate

- The discount rate we recommend you to use for screening strategic alternatives is the *cost of unlevered equity*, the return expected by the financial markets when they provide equity to the industry in which you are investing.
- This unlevered cost of equity is equal to the cost of debt increased by a *risk premium*. This risk premium depends on the risk of the envisaged strategic alternative or of the industry with which it is concerned and not so much on your company. The important thing to realize is that this risk premium does not depend on the total risk of the strategic alternative but on its *market risk*, which is only *part of the total risk*. Estimating this price premium is difficult. It has been a headache for finance specialists for a very long time and will probably continue to be so in the future. One other important thing to be aware of is that, since most companies carry some debt, the unlevered cost of equity is not readily observable and requires adjustment to remove the effect of this existing debt.
- *Make a rule not to adjust the unlevered cost of equity.* The existence of unprofitable investments should not make you use an adjusted cost of equity. If you believe that your project is going to have financing side effects, try to evaluate their present value and add them to the NPV of your decision (APV approach).
- Finally, keep in mind that at present we only have *rules of thumb* for evaluating cost of equity.

Two final problems

Is it right to discount future cash flows at a constant rate?
The discount rate depends a great deal on the market risk of your decision (or

its beta). The problem is that the models we have to relate return and risk, and the CAPM in particular, *look at rates of return and risk over one period at a time.* There is considerable literature[6] available concerning the application of the CAPM to the valuation of cash flows in a multi-period context but they are not easy to use.[7]

The danger of double counting risk

Using unlevered cost of equity as the discount rate poses a further problem, however. As cost of equity incorporates a risk premium, should we just discount the expected cash flows attached to a decision at this cost and forget about any further risk analysis?

This problem is very difficult and it is fair to say that no definite answer has yet been found. Not wishing to leave the question completely unanswered, let us risk some arguments.

Since cost of equity incorporates a risk premium, discounting at the cost of equity is a way to adjust the cash flows of a decision for risk. When the decision is risky you use a high cost of equity to discount, and as a result you penalize the expected cash flows. If you assume that the risk premium is right, and there is no reason not to do so, this should be just enough for taking risk into account. Any attempt at building decision diagrams and risk profiles would merely result in double counting risk. Since the objective of analyzing strategic alternatives is to recognize what the risk involved is and definitely not to overestimate it, further risk analysis should not be carried out.

But we have seen that *the risk incorporated into the cost of equity is only the market risk.* The specific risk attached to the decision is completely absent from the risk premium embodied in the cost of equity. As mentioned by several authors, even though this risk might not be important to shareholders, it is probably crucial to managers who are sensitive to the total risk of the projects they undertake.

As a result we should perform risk analysis according to the approaches explored in Part V, but *it should be limited to the risk factors that correspond to the specific risk component attached to the decision.*

What does this mean in practice?

- You will probably use cost equity as the discount rate for calculating the NPVs of strategic alternatives.
- You will also analyze the various risk factors, build risk and decision diagrams and risk profiles of NPVs.
- But when performing risk analysis you will probably try to distinguish between:
  - Those risk factors which are directly related to the evolution of the economy as a whole, *market risk* factors.
  - And those which are *specific* to the strategic alternative you consider and

which result from its specific success and failure factors (specific environmental, market, competitive, internal factors).

As they are already incorporated in the cost of equity, the first risk factors should be ignored. *Risk analyses should envisage the risk factors belonging to the second category only*.

Is this easy to do in practice? Obviously not, since we have very few clues for classifying the various risk factors of a strategic alternative into one of the two categories identified above.[8] One thing to keep in mind is what Brealey and Myers state in *Principles of Corporate Finance*: risk and decision diagrams are mostly aimed at understanding the working of projects, *at opening up black boxes*. Consequently, we recommend you to perform such analyses and not to worry too much about the danger of double counting.

NOTES

1 One might actually envisage a very useful role of hygiene for companies. First distribute to shareholders all cash generated, then ask shareholders for any amount needed for new capital expenditures. However, dividend decisions are not so simplistic. A short bibliography on dividends: H Baker, G Farrelly and R Edelman, 'A survey of management views on dividend policy', *Financial Management* (Autumn 1985), pp. 78–84; J Lintner, 'Distribution of incomes of corporations among dividends, retained earnings, and taxes', *American Economic Review* (1956), **46**: 97–113; F Black, 'The dividend puzzle', *Journal of Portfolio Management* (Winter 1976), **2**: 5–8; MN Miller and MS Scholes, 'Dividend and taxes', *Journal of Financial Economics* (Dec 1978), **6**: 333–64; S Bar-Yosef and L Nuffman, 'The information content of dividends', *Journal of Financial and Quantitative Analysis* (March 1985), **21**: 47, 58.

2 Except, obviously, for the transaction costs associated with the raising of external capital.

3 Although this is true in general, cases exist where some alternatives are tied to specific sources of capital. Here, the cost of the specific source should be taken into consideration. But obviously in such cases tracing it is not a problem.

4 Such an investment rule would actually aim at maximizing the size of the firm rather than its value. Recent tests have confirmed that managers act as if they were maximizing value and not size. For an example, refer to: JJ McConnell and CJ Muscarella, 'Corporate capital expenditure decisions and the market value of the firm', *Journal of Financial Economics* (1985), **14**: 399–422.

5 About the problem of biases in evaluating strategic alternatives, refer to: L Bower, 'Managing the resource allocation process', Division of Research, Graduate School of Business Administration, Harvard University (1970); and M Statman and TT Tyebjee, 'Optimistic capital budgeting forecasts: an experiment', *Financial Management* (Autumn 1985) (this contains a list of useful references).

6 Refer for examples to: MC Bogue and R Roll, 'Capital budgeting of risky projects with "imperfect" markets for physical capital', *Journal of Finance* (May 1974), pp 601–13; EF Fama, 'Risk adjusted discount rates and capital budgeting under uncertainty', *Journal of Financial Economics* (August 1977), pp 3–24; GM Constantinides, 'Admissible uncertainty in the intertemporal asset pricing model', *Journal of Financial Economics* (Mar 1980), pp 71–86.

7 A further difficulty relates to the fact that most strategic decisions require companies to commit capital for a long period of time. This suggests that the discount rate to be used is a long term interest rate, a rate comparable to the one investors require from long term investments. The difficulty is that, in the real world, the relationship between short and long term interest rates, or the term structure of interest rates, is complex. For example, if today the two-year interest rate is 0.10 and the one-year interest rate is 0.08, intuition tells you that the one-year expected rate, one year from now, should be: $((1 + 0.10)^2/(1 + 0.08)) - 1$, ie 0.12. Unfortunately, things are not so simple, since investors seem to prefer short term investments (liquidity preference) and therefore require from long term investments a rate higher than the result of the compounded short term interests. Consequently, in the example above, the two-year 0.10 rate may well correspond to a sequence of two one-year interest rates equal to 0.08 and to a liquidity premium. For more on the term structure of interest rates, refer to: BG Malkiel, *The Term Structure of Interest Rates: Expectations and Behavior Patterns*, Princeton University Press (1966) and to: R Roll, *The Behavior of Interest Rates: An application of the efficient market model to US treasury bills*, Basic Books (1970).

8 One assumption you may often make is that specific risk is probably much bigger than market risk. Consequently, the risk of double counting might be relatively limited.

Further Models VI

FURTHER MODEL VI.1
ASSESSING A FINANCIAL LEASE

The literature of accounting and finance has devoted considerable attention to the issue of leasing. The objective of this appendix is limited to the definition of leasing, and the presentation of a spreadsheet model for assessing a financial lease. For more about leasing, refer to the references given at the end of this Further Model.

What is leasing?

A lease is a contract between the owner of an asset called the lessor and another party called the lessee who is given the right to use the asset against the promise to make a series of payments (the first payment being generally made as soon as the lease is initiated). Provisions of leasing contacts depend very much on the country in which you operate. In the USA, where leasing is well established since the mid 60s, it is common to make a distinction between financial leases and operating leases.[1]

Financial leases

Even though there exist many varieties of financial leases, we can consider that, in general, financial leases have most of the following characteristics:

- Long-term contract between the lessee and the lessor. Generally, financial leases are concluded for most of, or all, the useful life of the asset. Consequently, total lease payments are close to the value of the asset.
- Non-cancellable contract.
- The lessee is responsible for maintenance, insurance and the payment of property taxes, if any (net lease as opposed to full-service lease).
- The lessee may acquire the full ownership of the asset at the end of the lease (strict transfer of property or bargain purchase option).

Contracting a financial lease is therefore very close to buying an asset and borrowing money from a bank. In most cases, leased assets are new ones. But it sometimes happens that firms sell an asset which they already own to another party and then lease it back from the buyer. This arrangement is called sale and lease back, as opposed to direct leasing. In some cases, the lessor borrows part of the price of the leased asset, using the lease contract as security for the loan. Such arrangements are called leveraged leases.

Operating leases

Operating leases are short term leases (the contract term is only a small fraction of the useful life of the asset). In general, they provide for both financing and other services (maintenance, insurance, property tax, etc), and are cancellable during the contract at the option of the lessee. Vehicles, computers, copiers are among the assets commonly acquired through operating leases.

Accounting and tax issues

One dubious advantage of leasing is that it represents off balance sheet financing. Rentals are included in the income statement but neither the leased asset nor the lease obligation are shown in the balance sheet (though a footnote to the accounts indicates the existence of the lease). In many countries, and in particular in the USA (since 1976), this way to account for leases is only allowed for operating leases. For finance (or capital leases) the firm should explicitly show the lease in its assets and liabilities. In any case, it is somewhat naive to consider that external investors can be fooled by off balance sheet financing.

As far as tax is concerned, and even though this again very much depends on the country you operate in, it can be said in general that the lessor retains the tax benefit of ownership (depreciation, tax investment credit, etc) whereas the lessee is entitled to deduct the lease rentals from its taxable income.

Leasing is not a miracle form of financing and as stated by Miller and Upton[2] 'The decision to lease or buy is neither a matter of indifference for the typical firm nor one for which any general presumption can be established a priori. Each case must be examined on its merit'.

An example of a financial lease

The Constructor Company has decided to execute a project which requires the use of a piece of equipment worth $125 000. Constructor has the option of entering the following financial lease scheme, rental fee is $22 500 to be paid from 1993 to 1998, maturity six years with no cancellation clause. The leasing company does not provide Constructor with any maintenance, insurance or tax property service (a net lease). Should Constructor buy the equipment, it would have to pay the asset cost in 1993, and would benefit from a tax credit equal to 10% of the value of the asset. If it owned the equipment, Constructor would be able to depreciate it over five years for 15%, 22%, 21%, 21%, and 21% of its depreciable value each year (the depreciable value being equal to the asset cost minus half of the investment tax credit taken). The tax rate is 46%. How can we approach this problem?[3]

1. The actual choice for Constructor is between leasing, or buying and

borrowing. Prior to the financing decision Constructor has assessed that the project was worth being undertaken and the operational cash flows of the project did not depend on the financing solution. These operational cash flows can therefore be ignored in the lease v borrow analysis.

2. What are the differential cash flows of the solution lease v the solution buy and borrow?
   - Lease payment.
   - Equipment acquisition cost.
   - Loss of investment credit.
   - Loss of depreciation tax shield.

   These differential cash flows and the net differential cash flows are shown in the spreadsheet model presented in Figure VI.I (a).

3. If we believe that financial leasing is a form of debt, then we can consider that the net differential cash flows are equivalent to the interest and

	A	B	C	D	E	F	G
1	PARAMETERS:						
2	Capital outlay	125					
3	Tax credit rate	0.1					
4	Depreciation rates	0.15	0.22	0.21	0.21	0.21	
5	Tax rate	0.46					
6	Debt rate	0.1					
7	Annual lease fee	22.5					
8							
9	CALCULATIONS						
10	Years	1993	1994	1995	1996	1997	1998
11	Capital outlay	125.00					
12	Lease payment	22.50	22.50	22.50	22.50	22.50	22.50
13	Tax shield lease	10.35	10.35	10.35	10.35	10.35	10.35
14	Loss investment credit	12.50					
15	Loss tax shield depreciation	8.19	12.02	11.47	11.47	11.47	
16	DIFFERENTIAL CASH FLOWS	92.16	−24.17	−23.62	−23.62	−23.62	−12.15
17							
18	After tax interest rate	0.05					
19	PRESENT VALUE	92.85					
	EQUIVALENT LOAN						
20	PRESENT VALUE LEASE	−0.69					

Background:
   Width of columns: A 30, global 7
   Format: fixed two decimals
   Range B2.G10: data
   Formulas:
      B11: +B2;B12: +$B$7 (to be copied across)
      B13: +B12*$B$5, (to be copied across)
      B14: +B2*B3
      B15: ($B$2−0.5*$B$2*$B$3)*B4*$B$5 (to be copied in the range C15.F15)
      B16: +B11−B12+B13−B14−B15 (to be copied across)
      B18: +B6*(1−B5)
      B19: −@NPV(B18,C16.G16)
      B20: +B16−B19

Figure VI.I (a) Evaluation of a financial lease. A spreadsheet model.

repayment cash flows caused by a loan. Since the after tax interest rate to Constructor is 0.054, we can calculate the present value of a loan which would cause the same cash outflows as the net differential cash flows. Such a loan would be equivalent to the leasing proposal. As shown in Figure VI.1(a), this present value is equal to $92 850.

4. The advantage of leasing over the equivalent loan can be calculated as the difference between the present value of the leasing ($92 160) and the present value of the equivalent loan ($92 850). In the present case, leasing is not an attractive proposal.

What can make leasing a worthwhile solution? It is difficult to generalize but we may, however, say that: the potential advantage of leasing is not due to a miraculous financial or tax trick, but to the fact that in some cases companies are not in a position to take advantage of all tax subsidies available. In this case they may use the services of leasing companies which specialise in the maximum utilisation of these subsidies, a maximum utilisation which is in turn reflected in the rental rates. You can, for example, check that if Constructor plans not to pay tax (set the tax rate and the investment credit to zero), then the lease becomes a valuable proposal.

A final note

Until the recent development of option valuation theory,[4] most of the literature concentrated on the analysis of valuation of financial, non-cancellable, leases. More recently, attention has shifted towards the analysis of operating leases and of their cancellable features.[5]

NOTES

1 In the USA, the distinction between capital and operating leases has been defined by the Financial Accounting Standards Board (SFAS no. 13, Nov 1976). For more about accounting for leases in the USA, refer to B Jarnagin and J Booker, 'Financial accounting standards – explanation and analysis'. Commerce Clearing House. For a discussion of some problems encountered with the distinction between capital and operating leases in the USA, refer to: Richard Dieter, 'Is lessee accounting working?' *The CPA Journal* (Aug 1979), pp 13–15, 17–19.

2 MN Miller and CW Upton, 'Leasing, buying and the cost of capital services', *Journal of Finance* (June 1976), **31**: 761–86.

3 This lease valuation method is derived from: SC Myers, DA Dill and AJ Bautista, 'Valuation of financial lease contracts, *Journal of Finance* (June 1976), **31**: 799–819, and from: JR Franks and SD Hodges, 'Valuation of financial lease contracts: a note', *Journal of Finance* (May 1978), **33**: 657–69. There are many proposed approaches for

evaluating a financial lease contract. For a review, refer to: R Bower, 'Issues in lease financing', *Financial Management* (Winter 1973), pp 25–33.

4 Refer to Part IX.

5 For an example of such an analysis, refer to JJ McConnell and JS Schallheim, 'Valuation of asset leasing contracts', *Journal of Financial Economics* (1983) **12**: 237–61.

FURTHER MODEL VI.2
MEAN, VARIANCE, STANDARD DEVIATION, COVARIANCE AND COEFFICIENT OF CORRELATION

Let us go back to Mr Dubois' problem as described in Chapter 20 (see page 298). The results in Figure 20.3 can be presented as follows:

	State A	State B	State C	State D
Probability	0.36	0.24	0.24	0.16
Return from a portfolio of Alma and Opéra	0.40	0.15	0.15	−0.10
Return from Alma only	0.40	0.40	−0.10	−0.10
Return from Opéra only	0.40	−0.10	0.40	−0.10

Mean, variance and standard deviation

The mean is the sum of the various possible outcomes weighted by their probabilities of occurrence. The variance and the standard deviation measure the dispersion of the possible outcomes from their mean. Variance and standard deviation treat in the same way deviations resulting from outcomes both below and above the mean. The concept is that risk corresponds to the fact that actual results may differ from what is expected (the mean), and may be more, or less, than expected. In order to calculate the variance, you have first to compute the differences between each outcome and the mean, to square these differences (in order to treat in the same way deviations above and below the mean) and to weight these differences according to the probabilities. The standard deviation is the square root of the variance (calculating the standard deviation enables you to come back to the original units).

Some useful relationships

If X and Y are two random variables (for example, X corresponds to the returns from Alma and Y to the returns from Opéra) and if E(X) is the mean of X, V(X) its variance and $\sigma(X)$ its standard deviation, then:

$$E(X + a) = E(X) + a$$
$$E(aX) = aE(X)$$
$$V(aX) = a^2V(X)$$
$$\sigma(aX) = a\sigma(X)$$

where a is a constant

A spreadsheet model

Figure VI.2(a) shows the foreground and background of a spreadsheet model for calculating the mean, variance and standard deviation of the returns of the three investments contemplated by Mr Dubois, investment in Alma only, investment in Opéra only, and investment in hoth Alma and Opéra.

The impact of diversification

The model confirms the results shown in Figure 20.4: diversification reduces risk.

	variance of returns (unit = square returns)	standard deviation (unit = returns)
Investment in Alma only	0.06	0.24
Investment in Opéra only	0.06	0.24
Investment in both Alma and Opéra	0.03	0.17

Covariance and correlation coefficient

Covariance and correlation coefficient assess the extent to which two series of outcomes, such as the returns Mr Dubois may get from Alma or Opéra, vary together, or are correlated.

The covariance is equal to the weighted sum of the products of the deviations of each series of outcomes from its mean. The weights are the joint probabilities of the outcomes. When the covariance is equal to zero, then the two series of outcomes are said to be independent (which is our assumption regarding Alma and Opéra). When the covariance is big (close to the total risk of the two series of outcomes), then the two series of outcomes are highly correlated. As the covariance has a sign, a high correlation may be positive (the two series of outcomes vary together), or negative (the two series of outcomes have opposite variations).

The correlation coefficient aims to express the covariance as a proportion of the total risk of the two series of outcomes. It is equal to the covariance divided by the product of the standard deviation of the two series of outcomes. Consequently, correlation coefficients always lie between -1 and $+1$ inclusive:

	A	B	C	D	E	F	G
1	States	A	B	C	D		
2	Probabilities	0.36	0.24	0.24	0.16		
3	Return Alma	0.40	0.40	−0.10	−0.10		
4	Return Opéra	0.40	−0.10	0.40	−0.10		
5	Return Alma + Opéra	0.40	0.15	0.15	−0.10		
6							
7	ALMA:						
8	RETURN*PROBABILITY	0.144	0.096	−0.024	−0.016	MEAN	0.200
9	(RETURN−MEAN) ∧ 2*PROBABILITY	0.014	0.010	0.022	0.014	VARIANCE	0.060
10	OPERA:					STD DEV	0.245
11	RETURN*PROBABILITY	0.144	−0.024	0.096	−0.016	MEAN	0.200
12	(RETURN−MEAN) ∧ 2*PROBABILITY	0.014	0.022	0.010	0.014	VARIANCE	0.060
13	ALMA+OPERA:					STD DEV	0.245
14	RETURN*PROBABILITY	0.144	0.036	0.036	−0.016	MEAN	0.200
15	(RETURN−MEAN) ∧ 2*PROBABILITY	0.014	0.001	0.001	0.014	VARIANCE	0.030
16						STD DEV	0.173
17							

Width of columns: A:27, B,C,D,E:7, F:10, G:7. Format: fixed 3 decimals for the calculations.
Background:
Range B2.E5: data
In B8: +B3*B2; B9: +B2*(B3−$G$8) ∧ 2; B11: +B4*B2;
  B12: +B2*(B4−$G$11) ∧ 2; B14: +B5*B2; B15: +B2*(B5−$G$14) ∧ 2
Range B8.B15 is to be copied across (C.E)
In G8: @SUM(B8.E8); G9: @SUM(B9.E9); G10: +G9 ∧ 0.5
  Range G8.G10 is to be copied in ranges G11.G13 and G14.G16
Width of columns: A:27; B,C,D,E:7; F:10; G:7. Format: fixed 3 decimals for the calculations.

Figure VI.2(a)   Mean, variance and standard deviation: a spreadsheet model.

- A +1 correlation coefficient means that the two series of outcomes have a perfect correlation.
- A zero correlation coefficient means they are independent.
- A −1 correlation coefficient means they have a perfect negative correlation.

The process for introducing a covariance and correlation coefficient calculation in the model is shown in Figure VI.2(b).

The impact of diversification

The model enables you to check that the returns from Alma and Opéra are independent. In this case, the risk of investment in both Alma and Opéra, as measured by the variance, is half of the risk of an investment in either Alma or Opéra.[1]

What if the returns of Alma and Opéra were perfectly correlated? Perfect correlation means that in each of the states A to D, Alma and Opéra show the same results, good or bad. You can simulate this by changing the probabilities and returns of Opéra to:

	State A	State B	State C	State D
Probabilities	0.25	0.25	0.25	0.25
Return Opéra	0.40	0.40	−0.10	−0.10

	A	B	C	D	E	F	G
1	States	A	B	C	D		
2	Probabilities	0.36	0.24	0.24	0.16		
3	Return Alma	0.40	0.40	−0.10	−0.10		
4	Return Opéra	0.40	−0.10	0.40	−0.10		
5	Return Alma + Opéra	0.40	0.15	0.15	−0.10		
6							
7	ALMA:						
8	RETURN*PROBABILITY	0.144	0.096	−0.024	−0.016	MEAN	0.200
9	(RETURN−MEAN) ∧ 2*PROBABILITY	0.014	0.010	0.022	0.014	VARIANCE	0.060
10	OPERA:					STD DEV	0.245
11	RETURN*PROBABILITY	0.144	−0.024	0.096	−0.016	MEAN	0.200
12	(RETURN−MEAN) ∧ 2*PROBABILITY	0.014	0.022	0.010	0.014	VARIANCE	0.060
13	ALMA+OPERA:					STD DEV	0.245
14	RETURN*PROBABILITY	0.144	0.036	0.036	−0.016	MEAN	0.200
15	(RETURN−MEAN) ∧ 2*PROBABILITY	0.014	0.001	0.001	0.014	VARIANCE	0.030
16	DEVIATIONS FROM MEAN:					STD DEV	0.173
17	ALMA	0.200	0.200	−0.300	−0.300		
18	OPERA	0.200	−0.300	0.200	−0.300		
19	DEV. ALMA*DEV. OPERA*PROB.	0.014	−0.014	−0.014	0.014	COVARIANCE	0.000
20						CORR COEFF	0.000

Additional background:
In B17: +B3−$G$8; B18: +B4−$G$11; B19: +B17*B18*B2
(to be copied across)
In G19: @SUM(B19.E19); in G20: +G19/(G10*G13)

Figure VI.2(b)   Mean, variance, standard deviation, covariance and correlation coefficient.

You can check that the covariance is equal to the variance of either Alma or Opéra and that the correlation coefficient is equal to 1. In such a case, the variance of investing in both Alma and Opéra is the same as the variance of investing in either Alma or Opéra, and therefore diversification brings no benefit.

What if the returns of Alma and Opéra were perfectly negatively correlated? You can simulate this by changing the returns of Opéra to:

State A	State B	State C	State D
−0.10	−0.10	0.40	0.40

The covariance becomes equal to minus the variance of Alma or Opéra and the correlation coefficient to −1. In such a case, the variance of investing in both Alma and Opéra is equal to zero. The risk has been totally eradicated by diversification. We shall see, in Part IX, how options can enable investors to achieve such perfect hedges.

In real life, the impact of diversification of an investment across shares will lie somewhere in between the impact of diversification when the outcomes are independent and when the outcomes are positively correlated. This is due to the fact that all shares are exposed to economy-wide hazards.

NOTE

1 If X and Y are two random variables and if V(X) and V(Y) are their variance and cov(X, Y) their covariance, then:

$$V(aX + bY) = a^2V(X) + b^2V(Y) + 2abcov(X,Y)$$

In the present case a = b = 0.5, V(X) = V(Y) and cov(X, Y) = 0, then:

$$V(0.5X + 0.5Y) = 0.25V(X) + 0.25V(X) = 0.5V(X)$$

FURTHER MODEL VI.3
USING THE APT MODEL[1]

A problem

In 1993, the Eagle company is considering the launch of a new product which should have a two year life. Figure VI.3(a) shows the cash flows attached to this project in 1993, 1994 and 1995. In 1994, the uncertainty is limited to two possible situations only, that things go well (state A) or not so well (state B). In 1995, the uncertainty is limited to the possible occurrence of states C, D, E or F.

When preparing the analysis of the new product, Eagle has estimated the 1994 and 1995 values of a stock listed on the market in each possible state. Eagle has also estimated the interest rate that will prevail in each of these states. This information is shown in Figure VI.3(b)

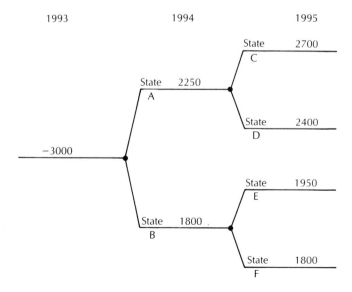

Figure VI.3(a)   Using the APT model. Expected cash flows.

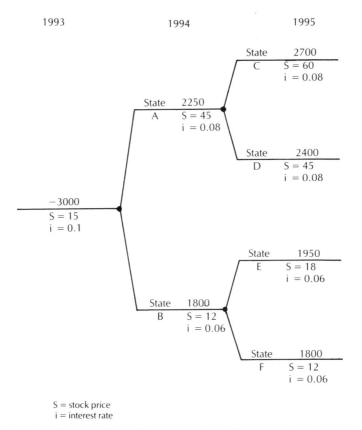

Figure VI.3(b)   Using the APT model: expected cash flows, stock values and interest rates.

An arbitrage approach to valuation

Let us assume that we are in 1994, that things have gone well (state A) and that we want to assess the 1994 value of the project.

One approach would be to do as we have done in many other situations and calculate this 1994 value directly from the 1995 value of the project (2 700 or 2 400). We would, however, face two obstacles. How much weight should be given to each of the two possible values, and which discount rate should we use? Another approach is to deduct the 1994 value of the project from the comparison of the project with an asset, of which we know the value in 1994 and 1995 and which has the same value as the project in 1995.

If such an asset exists, the problem is solved. The 1994 value of the asset is equal to the 1994 value of the project. If this was not true, investors would benefit from a riskless arbitrage opportunity between two assets which have the same 1994 value. The existence of such an arbitrage opportunity is inconsistent with the hypothesis that markets are in equilibrium.

	A	B	C	D E F		G	H I		J
1	PERIOD 1			PERIOD 2			PERIOD 3		
2						State A			State C
3	Cash flow		−3 000	Cash flow		2 250	Cash flow		2 700
4	Interest		0.10	Interest		0.08	Interest		0.08
5	Stock price		15	Stock price		45	Stock price		60
6									State D
7	EQUIVALENT PORTFOLIO			EQUIVALENT PORTFOLIO			Cash flow		2 400
8	Number stocks		31	Number stocks		20	Interest		0.08
9	Amount debt		2 857	Amount debt		1 389	Stock price		45
10	Value		3 322	Value		2 289			
11	Net present value		322						
12						State B			State E
13				Cash flow		1 800	Cash flow		1 950
14				Interest		0.06	Interest		0.06
15				Stock price		12	Stock price		18
16									State F
17				EQUIVALENT PORTFOLIO			Cash flow		1 800
18				Number stocks		25	Interest		0.06
19				Amount debt		1 415	Stock price		12
20				Value		1 715			

Width of columns: A:8; B:11; C:8; D:2; E:1; F:13; G:8; H:2; I:11; J:8.
Format: 0 decimals except for interest rates.
Background:
J3, J4, J5, J7, J8, J9, J13, J14, J15, J17, J18, J19: data
G3, G4, G5, G13, G14, G15: data
C3, C4, C5: data

G8: (J3−J7)/(J5−J9); G9: (J3−J5*G8)/(1+G4);
G10: +G5*G8+G9; G8, G9 and G10 can be copied into the range G18.G20

C8: (G3+G10−G20−G13)/(G5−G15); C9: (G3+G10−C8*G5)/(1+C4);
C10: +C5*C8+C9; C11: +C10+C3

Figure VI.3(c) Using the APT model: a spreadsheet model.

We know the 1994 and 1995 values of two assets:

- The stock = 45 in 1994, 60 or 45 in 1995.
- The loan = its value in 1995 is equal to its 1994 value multiplied by (1 + 0.08).

The problem is then the construction of a portfolio of the share and the loan which would have the same value as the project in 1995.

If n is the number of stocks in the portfolio and L the 1994 value of the loan, n and L should be such that:

$$\text{If state C occurs: } (n \times 60) + (L \times 1.08) = 2\ 700$$
$$\text{If state D occurs: } (n \times 45) + (L \times 1.08) = 2\ 400$$

which guarantees that the portfolio has the same value as the project in 1995, whatever happens (only states C and D are possible). From these two equations, you can deduce the values of n and L:

$$n = 20$$
$$L = 1\ 389 \text{ (1994 value of the loan)}$$

The 1994 value of the portfolio, and of the project, follows:

$$20 \times 45 + 1\ 389 = 2\ 289$$

This approach, which was originally used by Modigliani and Miller in 1958, bypasses a number of difficulties (discount rate, probability of the outcomes, investors' attitudes towards risk) but poses one major problem, how do you identify the reference stock? In many practical situations, it is impossible to answer this question.[2]

A spreadsheet model for solving the problem of the Eagle company is shown in Figure VI.3(c). It shows that the new product is worth being launched (positive NPV).

NOTES

1 This further model is based on the approach presented by A Gehr, 'Risk adjusted capital budgeting using arbitrage', *Financial Management*, (Winter 1981), pp 14–19.

2 This approach has been used in particular for the valuation of options (see Part IX). In that case, the problem of the reference stock has been removed since it is possible to compare portfolios of options with a riskless asset.

FURTHER MODEL VI.4
ASSESSING THE IMPACT OF FINANCING ON THE DHAHRAN ROADS CONTRACT

In order to illustrate the impact of debt financing let us go back to the Dhahran Roads case, where there is no corporation tax, and to the model we built in order to help us decide about the contract.

Let us also assume that SADE is contemplating using a 4 m SR, three-year loan in order to finance part of the capital required by the project. Such a loan would carry 15% interest and would have to be reimbursed in full in 1996. In order to assess the impact of this loan we can modify the model we developed in Part IV (Figure 11.2). This can be done by:

- Inserting eight rows above row 16.
- Entering the inputs described in Figure VI.4(a).

The way in which the model shown in Figure VI.4(a) is built calls for an explanation. *Why discount the contract and the debt cash flows at different rates?* The explanation for this is related to the risk–return relationship we identified in Part VI.

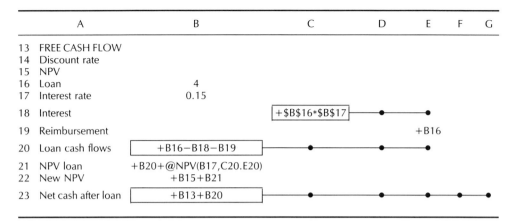

	A	B	C	D	E	F	G
13	FREE CASH FLOW						
14	Discount rate						
15	NPV						
16	Loan	4					
17	Interest rate	0.15					
18	Interest		+$B$16*$B$17 • •				
19	Reimbursement				+B16		
20	Loan cash flows	+B16−B18−B19	• • •				
21	NPV loan	+B20+@NPV(B17,C20.E20)					
22	New NPV	+B15+B21					
23	Net cash after loan	+B13+B20	• • • • •				

Note: Following these adjustments, you should then adjust the calculation of change in cash as well as the income statement and balance sheets.

Figure V1.4(a)   Inputs for modelling the impact of debt financing.

- The cash flows of the contract correspond to a construction activity in a specific country. SADE estimates that, given the risk of this activity investors require a minimum return of 25%. They should therefore be discounted at 25%.
- The cash flows related to the debt are certain and should therefore be discounted at the lower rate required by the lenders. As a result the NPV of the debt cash flows is zero.[1]

Whatever the debt used by SADE to finance the Dhahran Roads contract *the NPV of the contract will remain the same* (the extra value created will remain the same), and *the risk will also remain the same*. When performed with the model shown in Figure VI.4(a), the risk analysis we made in relation to the Dhahran Roads (C) case leads exactly to the same risk profile as the one shown in Figure 18.5.

This shows that using *debt financing has no impact on the result SADE will obtain from its contract*. Such a conclusion obviously goes against our immediate intuition. Using cheap debt financing should give SADE an advantage.

When looking again at the NPV of the combination of the contract and of the loan, one realizes that the same net present value is now generated by a smaller initial investment (7 m SR instead of 11). This means that the internal rate of return of the cash flows resulting from the contract and loan package should be more than the one we initially found for the Dhahran Roads contract. We can easily introduce two more rows into our model and enter:

- in A24: guess rate
- in B24: 0.6

- in A25: IRR
- in B25: @IRR (B24,B23.G23)

We can then estimate the internal rate of return corresponding to the cash flows of the contract and loan package as equal to 75%. It corresponds to the new *return on equity*. So we are now on more familiar grounds. Using a cheap source of finance does indeed increase the return on equity.

Realizing that the use of debt may increase the return on equity is only one aspect of the problem. It is true that if SADE uses debt it will increase the return on its equity, but what about the risk? As the risk of the contract is basically unchanged whatever the level of debt, this same risk will now apply to a smaller capital, and as a result the degree of risk in relation to each SR of capital will increase just as much as the internal rate of return has.

As a result of the simultaneous increases in return and risk, no advantage will be derived by SADE from using debt. We discovered this when calculating the net present values of the project before and after the loan.

NOTE

1 The breakdown of the package, contract + debt, into its two components contract and debt, is possible due to the additive property of the NPV.

FURTHER MODEL VI.5
CAPITAL STRUCTURE: MILLER'S 'DEBT AND TAXES' MODEL

The capital structure issue

If we restrict the capital structure issue to the debt equity choice, we can say that many competing views exist in financial literature to explain why a company decides to borrow or not to borrow.[1]

The main criticism which is made of the tax shields/financial inadequacy analysis of debt presented in Chapter 21, Figure 21.6, is that it is not consistent with the fact that many successful companies with very low risk of financial inadequacy do not borrow. As phrased by MH Miller, 'For big businesses, at least (and particularly for such low levered ones as IBM or Kodak), the supposed trade-off between tax gains and bankruptcy costs looks suspiciously like the recipe for the fabled horse-and-rabbit stew – one horse and one rabbit'.

In his famous *Debt and Taxes*,[2] Miller has offered a new approach to the capital structure issue. According to Miller, debt/equity equilibrium is not to be analyzed at the level of individual firms but rather at the aggregate level of all firms. At this aggregate level, there exists an equilibrium between equity and corporate debt which depends on the levels of the corporate tax rate and of the individual tax rates on income from stocks and from bonds. Depending on the relative position of these tax rates, corporate borrowing may present advantages or disadvantages for the investors.

Because the debt/equity equilibrium is an issue which matters for all firms taken together and not for the single firm, Miller concludes that borrowing is immaterial at the level of any individual firm. Use of debt should not change the value of any company but only the type of investors it appeals to. Firms with low leverage should appeal most to investors in the high tax brackets and highly levered firms to investors in low tax brackets but, since one clientele of shareholders is worth another, use of debt should not make any difference.[3] If you believe Miller, you should therefore not worry about the impact of debt financing in your models.

Starting from Miller's model, DeAngelo and Masulis[4] have reached a different conclusion, however. According to them, debt is only one among many other sources of tax shields, such as depreciation, investment tax credits, etc. When these are taken into account, it can be seen that different firms may have very different opportunities for reducing their taxes. Consequently, firms which have access to few tax shields other than debt will view debt as more desirable than firms which have access to many tax shields other than debt, so borrowing is no longer immaterial at the level of the individual company and different firms should aim at different capital structures. So financial models *should* take into account the impact of debt. The debate is far from over.[5]

A third view, or rather family of views, is that firms borrow or do not borrow for many other reasons than tax shields. This view, which is not new,[6] has gained popularity with the recent developments of the closely related theories of agency,[7] information asymmetry, signalling and screening.[8]

As shown by Jensen and Meckling,[9] the relationship between the management of a firm and its shareholders can be analyzed as an agent/principal relationship. Potential conflicts of interest between the two parties result in agency costs that management can try to avoid by using debt instead of equity financing. But issuance of debt also has agency costs caused by the conflict of interest between existing shareholders and would–be lenders. Consequently, when deciding if they should use debt, companies will compare two agency costs. Jensen and Meckling suggest that equity and debt agency costs differ depending on the industry and the size of the company, hence the motivation for different capital structures.[10]

A related view is the one characterized by Myers[11] as the pecking order approach to financing. According to this approach, managers do not pursue any optimal target debt equity structure but rather tap financing resources according to the following process:

1. They prefer internal finance. Thus, they adapt their dividend pay out to their investment opportunities.
2. When unexpected investment opportunities arise, and because dividends cannot be cut brutally, firms first tap their liquidity reserves.
3. When these are not enough, they have recourse to external funds, starting with debt. At times, and when its value is right, they issue equity.
4. The level of debt at a given moment in time depends on the stage in this process which the company has reached.

Myers and Majluf[12] have further demonstrated that, when financial markets are perfect and efficient with respect to publicly available information and when managers have superior information about new investment opportunities:

- It is in the shareholders' interest that firms issue debt rather than equity. As investors do not yet know the good news, new equity would be issued at an undervalued price. So, it is better to issue debt, the price of which does not depend on the information about new investment opportunities.
- It is in the shareholders' interest that firms have liquidities available. This can prevent them from passing up good investment opportunities which cannot be financed because debt is not available.

Along the same lines, several authors have argued that financing choices are used by firms to signal to the market their true value, without having to disclose confidential information.[13]

As you can easily realize, the capital structure issue has not finished challenging finance specialists. Consequently, *be very cautious each time you have to include capital structure considerations in your models.*

Miller's 'debt and taxes' model

The idea
The model presented below will enable you to understand more clearly that:

- When there are no taxes, companies have no incentive to borrow.
- When you consider only the impact of corporation tax, then companies have plenty of reasons to borrow.
- When you consider the impact of corporation and personal taxes combined, then companies' incentive to raise debt depends very much on the structure of the different tax rates.

The following model is based on the works of Miller and Fama and Miller.[14] Behind it lies an arbitrage concept.

Shareholders can buy shares of levered or unlevered companies.

If you assume that there exist two companies which are exactly similar on the operational side (same assets yielding the same return with the same risk) but which differ from the point of view of their financing (one is levered, the other is not), then you can imagine that some investors will buy the shares of the levered company while others will buy the shares of the unlevered one. Let us assume that there are two investors only. One buys all the shares of the levered company, the other one all the shares of the unlevered company.

If you believe that it is not possible to achieve arbitrage gains, then both shareholders should be able to achieve the same return. In order to do so the shareholder of the unlevered company will have to borrow. Let us assume that this can be done at the same rate as the company.

Starting from the income obtained by the shareholder of the levered company, you can estimate how much the shareholder of the unlevered company should borrow in order to achieve the same income.

When this level of personal borrowing is achieved, you can deduct the amount of the net investment of the shareholder of the unlevered company (shares purchased minus borrowing).

Since, by construction, this net investment produces the same income as all the shares of the levered company, then its value should be equal to the value of the shares of the levered company.

Having estimated the value of the shares of the levered company you can compare them to the value of the shares of the unlevered one and deduct the impact of leverage.

Let us make one further assumption. The operations of the two companies and the debt of the levered company can be considered as perpetuities. Investment and debt decisions are made in period 1, profit and interest costs are constant in all subsequent periods.

The model

The structure of the model is presented in Figure VI.5(a), its foreground is presented in Figure VI.5(b) and its background is presented in Figure VI.5(c).

The arrows in Figure VI.5(a) show the logic of the model:

- Five parameters are needed:
  - The return on the operations of the levered and of the unlevered companies (unlevered return).
  - The debt rate (for corporations and individuals).
  - The corporation tax rate.
  - The personal tax rates on income from shares and from debt.[15]
- You can then model the unlevered and the levered companies, except that for the unlevered company you cannot yet calculate the value of its shares. (NB) The use of two different columns for value and expected income relates to the concept of period 1 and period 2 and subsequent ones).

- You can then model the position of the shareholder of the levered company and calculate the target income you will aim to for the other shareholder.
- You can then model the position of the shareholder of the unlevered company and calculate the value of his/her net investment which is also the value of the stock of the levered company.
- You can then calculate the value of leverage for a shareholder.
- Finally as a test you can enter in the model Miller's formulas[16] for calculating:
  · The amount to be borrowed by the shareholder of the unlevered company.
  · The advantage of leverage.

Using the model

You can use the model to check that:

- When all tax rates are set to zero, then borrowing by companies does not bring any benefit to shareholders, and this is true whatever the unlevered return and the interest rate are.
- When the personal tax rates on incomes from stock and debt are the same

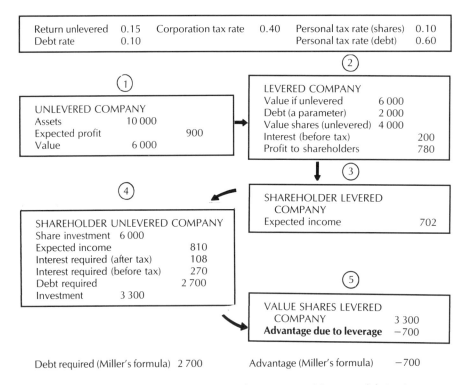

Figure VI.5(a) Impact of leverage: an arbitrage spreadsheet model. Logic.

	A	B	C	D	E	F	G	H
1	Unlevered return	0.15	Corp tax rate			0.40 Pers tax rate (shares)		0.10
2	Debt rate	0.10				Pers tax rate (debt)		1.60
3								
4	UNLEVERED COMPANY					LEVERED COMPANY		
5	Assets	10 000				Value if unlevered	6 000	
6	Expected profit		900			Debt (a parameter)	2 000	
7	Value	6 000				Value shares (unlevered)	4 000	
8						Interest (before tax)		200
9						Profit to shareholders		780
10								
11	SHAREHOLDER UNLEVERED COMPANY					SHAREHOLDER LEVERED COMPANY		
12						Expected income		702
13	Share investment	6 000						
14	Expected income			810				
15	Interest required (after tax)			108				
16	Interest required (before tax)			270				
17	Debt required			2 700				
18	Investment	3 300				VALUE SHARES LEVERED COMPANY		3 300
19						**Advantage due to leverage**		**−700**
20	Debt required (Miller's formula)			2 700		Advantage (Miller's formula)		−700

Width of columns: A:17; B:6; C:8; D:5; E:8; F:14; G:7; H:7.

Figure VI.5(b)   Impact of leverage: an arbitrage spreadsheet model. Foreground.

A1:	W17	'Unlevered return		E9:	W8	'Profit to shareholders
B1:	(F2)	W6 0.15		H9:	W7	+C6−H8*(1−E1)
C1:	W8	'Corp tax rate		A10:	W17	'
E1:	(F2)	W8 0.4		A11:	W17	'SHAREHOLDER UNLEVERED COMPANY
F1:	W14	'Pers tax rate (shares)		E11:	W8	'SHAREHOLDER LEVERED COMPANY
H1:	(F2)	W7 0.1		E12:	W8	'Expected income
A2:	W17	'Debt rate		H12:	(F0)	W7 +H9*(1−H1)
B2:	(F2)	W6 0.1		A13:	W17	'Share investment
F2:	W14	'Pers tax rate (debt)		B13:	W6	+B7
H2:	(F2)	W7 0.6		A14:	W17	'Expected income
A3:	W17	'		D14:	(F0)	W5 +C6*(1−H1)
A4:	W17	'UNLEVERED COMPANY		A15:	W17	'Interest required (after tax)
E4:	W8	'LEVERED COMPANY		D15:	(F0)	W5 +D14−H12
A5:	W17	'Assets		A16:	W17	'Interest required (before tax)
B5:	W6	10 000		D16:	(F0)	W5 +D15/(1−H2)
E5:	W8	'Value if unlevered		A17:	W17	'Debt required
G5:	W7	+B7		D17:	W5	+D16/B2
A6:	W17	'Expected profit		A18:	W17	'Investment
C6:	W8	+B5*B1*(1−E1)		B18:	(F0)	W6 +B13−D17
E6:	W8	'Debt (a parameter)		E18:	W8	'VALUE SHARES LEVERED COMPANY
G6:	W7	2 000		H18:	(F0)	W7 +B18
A7:	W17	'Value		E19:	(F0)	W8 'Advantage due to leverage
B7:	W6	+C6/B1		H19:	(F0)	W7 +H18−G7
E7:	W8	'Value shares (unlevered)		A20:	W17	'Debt required (Miller's formula)
G7:	(F0)	W7 +G5−G6		D20:	W5	+G6*(1−E1)*(1−H1)/(1−H2)
E8:	W8	'Interest (before tax)		E20:	W8	'Advantage (Miller's formula)
H8:	W7	+G6*B2		H20:	(F0)	W7 (1−(1−E1)*(1−H1)/(1−H2))*G6

Figure VI.5(c)   Impact of leverage: an arbitrage/spreadsheet model. Background.

then the advantage of leverage is the same as when there are no personal taxes at all. In this case it is equal to the present value of the tax shield on corporate debt,[17] and this is true whatever the return and interest rates are.

■ When there exist a corporation tax rate (0.4), a higher personal tax rate on debt income (0.6) and a low personal tax rate on share income, then borrowing by companies is harmful to shareholders, and this is true whatever the unlevered return and the interest rates are.

NOTES

1 Useful reviews of the issue are: M Harris and A Raviv, 'The Theory of Capital Structure', *The Journal of Finance*, March 1991, p 297–355; and 'Capital Structure Theory', by Pinegar and Wilbricht, *Financial Management*, Winter 1989, p 82–91. One of the conclusions of the Pinegar–Wilbricht survey is that 'the financing decision is the most flexible of all the sources and uses of funds constraints. That is, it is the least binding' p 89.

2 M Miller, 'Debt and taxes', *Journal of Finance* (May 1977), **32**: 261–76. You should know that since then, the 1986 Tax Reform Act has changed the US tax system and the effective tax rate on equity income is no longer substantially lower than on interest.

3 Even though there is empirical evidence to support the existence of such clienteles, it is difficult to be sure of their essential cause, whether leverage, dividends or other factors. Refer to: O Sarig and J Scott, 'The puzzle of financial leverage clienteles', *Journal of Finance* (December 1985), **60**: 1459–67.

4 H DeAngelo and RW Masulis, 'Optimal capital structure under corporate and personal taxation', *Journal of Financial Economics* (1980), **8**: 3–29.

5 See for example: SA Ross, 'Debt and taxes and uncertainty', *Journal of Finance* (July 1985), **60**: 637–56.

6 See for example: G Donaldson, *Strategy for financial mobility*, Division of Research, Graduate School of Business Administration, Harvard University (1969).

7 For a review, refer to: MC Jensen and CW Smith, 'Stockholder, manager and creditor interests: applications of agency theory' in *Recent Advances in Corporate Finance*, EI Altman and MG Subrahmanyam (eds), RD Irwin (1985), pp 93–131.

8 Refer to: M Spence, 'Job market signalling', *Quarterly Journal of Economics* (August 1973), pp 355–79, and JE Stiglitz, 'The theory of "screening", education and the distribution of income', *American Economic Review* (June 1975), pp 283–300.

9 MC Jensen and WH Meckling, 'Theory of the firm: managerial behavior, agency costs and ownership structure', *Journal of Financial Economics* (1976), **3**: 305–60.

10 One example they mention is the bar/restaurant industry. In this activity it is very difficult for shareholders to control management (because perk consumption is very easy). Consequently, equity agency cost should be very high and, as a result, this

industry should be characterized by a relatively low outside equity (owner managers being typical) and high leverage. Along the same lines, WS Kim and EM Soerensen have found that firms with high insider ownership (a sign of high equity agency costs) have greater debt ratios than firms with widely diffused ownership. Their results are reported in 'Evidence of the impact of agency cost of debt on corporate policy', *Journal of Financial and Quantitative Analysis* (June 1986), **21**.

11 SC Myers, 'The capital structure puzzle', *Journal of Finance* (July 1984), **39**: 575–92.

12 SC Myers and NS Majluf, 'Corporate financing and investment decisions when firms have information that investors do not have', *Journal of Financial Economics* (1984), **13**: 187–221.

13 See for example: WL Lee, AV Thakor and G Vora, 'Screening, market signalling and capital structure theory', *Journal of Finance* (December 1983), and MJ Flannery, 'Asymmetric information and risky debt maturity choice', *Journal of Finance* (March 1986), **61**: 19–37.

14 M Miller, 'Debt and taxes', *Journal of Finance* (May 1977), **32**: 261–76, and E Fama and M Miller, *The Theory of Finance*, Holt, Rinehart & Winston (1972).

15 In many countries capital tax gains are not taxed. It follows that, since the income from shares is made of dividends (often very small) and of capital gains (often the main income), the taxation of the income from shares is often very low.

16 Here are Miller's formulas:

Bs = borrowing by the shareholder of the unlevered company
L   = advantage of leverage
B   = borrowing by the levered company
tc   = corporation tax rate
tps = personal tax rate on share income
tpb = personal tax rate on borrowing

$$Bs = B * \frac{(1 - tc)(1 - tps)}{(1 - tpb)}$$

$$L = 1 - \frac{(1 - tc)(1 - tps)}{(1 - tpb)} * B$$

17 When personal tax rates are set to zero and the corporation tax rate to 0.4, then, the advantage of leverage is equal to 800. When the unlevered return is 0.15 and the debt rate 0.10, then the interest before tax is 200. The annual interest tax shields are therefore equal to 80 and their present value to 80/0.1 = 800, the same value as the leverage advantage. This result is valid whatever the unlevered return is.

FURTHER MODEL VI.6
WACC and APV[1]

In order to help you understand the difficulties of using the WACC and the APV, we would like to invite you to build a spreadsheet model for calculating the NPV attached to the new project opportunity available to Gamma in Chapter 21. Let us remind you of the cash flows attached to this project:

In 000 FFR	1994	1995	1996
Operational profit	500	1 600	740
Depreciation	300	300	300
Operational profit before tax	200	1 300	440
Profit after tax (50% rate)	100	650	220
CFE/CFO (no working capital needs)	400	950	520

Capital expenditures amount to 900 (to be made in 1993). There is no residual value. The risk adjusted cost of unlevered equity for such a project is 15%. Let us assume further that Gamma aims at a debt to total capital ratio of 39% (or debt to equity ratio of 64%), and thinks that the new project opportunity will sustain the same level of debt as the overall company. Consequently, it considers that the project will generate an additional debt constantly equal to 39% of its value. A spreadsheet model for comparing the WACC and APV approaches when a constant debt to equity ratio (market values) is assumed is shown in Figures VI.6(a) and VI.6(b).

Notes on the model
The upper part of the model shows the parameters:

- Discount rate for unlevered equity (0.15)
- Tax rate (0.5)
- Interest rate (0.10)
- Leverage rate (0.39).

The second part shows the cash flows and their present values. The loan is calculated each year as 39% of the present value of the project, this present value including the present value of the debt-related tax shields (hence the circular reference in the model).[2]

The third part shows the results of the APV and WACC approaches. The WACC is calculated according to the formula proposed by Miles and Ezzel (a close alternative to the popular formula shown in Chapter 21).

$$ WACC = \frac{unlevered}{equity\ rate} - \frac{debt\ to}{total\ funds} * \frac{interest}{rate} * \frac{tax}{rate} * \frac{1 + unlevered\ equity\ rate}{1 + interest\ rate} $$

As far as APV is concerned, you should note that the tax shields are discounted at the unlevered equity rate except for the first year they materialize.[3]

A fourth part shows the annual cash flow statements, income statements and balance sheets of the project.

	A	B	C	D	E	F	G	H
1	Discount rate (unlevered)			0.15	interest rate			0.10
2	Corporation tax rate			0.50	debt/total funds			0.39
3					implied D/E ratio			0.64
4								
5	OPERATING PROFIT BEFORE DEPRECIATION				500	1 600	740	
6	DEPRECIATION				300	300	300	
7	PROFIT AFTER TAX				100	650	220	
8	CASH FLOWS			−900	400	950	520	
9	PRESENT VALUE AT UNLEVERED RATE			1 408	1 219	452		
10	PRESENT VALUE INTEREST TAX SHIELDS			51	29	8		
11	ADJUSTED PRESENT VALUE (APV)			1 459	1 249	460		
12	DEBT			569	487	180		
13	INTEREST AFTER TAX				28	24	9	
14	INTEREST TAX SHIELDS				28	24	9	
15								
16	APV					WACC		
17								
18	NPV			508				
19	INTEREST TAX SHIELDS			51		RATE		0.130
20	**APV**			**559**		**NPV**		**559**
21	NET CASH			−900	372	926	511	
22	DEBT			569	487	180	0	
23	EQUITY			331				
24	LOAN REPAYMENT			0	569	487	180	
25	DIVIDEND			0	0	0	0	
26	CHANGE IN CASH (BALANCE SHEET)			0	289	618	331	
27								
28	PROFIT BEFORE TAX				500	1 600	740	
29	INTEREST				57	49	18	
30	DEPRECIATION				300	300	300	
31	PROFIT AFTER TAX				72	626	211	
32								
33	CASH			0	289	908	1 239	
34	NET FIXED ASSETS			900	600	300	0	
35	TOTAL ASSETS			900	889	1 208	1 239	
36								
37	DEBT			569	487	180	0	
38	NET WORTH			331	402	1 028	1 239	
39	TOTAL EQUITIES			900	889	1 208	1 239	
40								
41	Book debt/equity ratio			1.7	1.2	0.2	0.0	
42	Book debt/total funds ratio			0.6	0.5	0.1	0.0	

Width of columns: Global: 7; A:23.
Format: 0 decimal, except for rates and ratios.

Figure VI.6(a) WACC and APV. Foreground of the model.

Comments

So it is possible, with hard work, to get the same results through the WACC and APV approaches, provided that you assume in both cases that the debt to equity ratio (with market values) is kept constant over the life of the project.

You can use the model to check that this result is true whatever the timing of

1　D1, D2, H1, H2: data; H3: +H2/(1−H2).
　　Operating profit before depreciation: data.
2　Depreciation: in E6: −D8/3; in F6: +E6; in G6: +F6.
3　Profit after tax: in E7: (E5−E6)*(1−$D$2) (to be copied).
4　Cash flows: in D8: −900; in E8: +E6+E7; etc.
5　Unlevered present value is the present value of the future cash flows (not including tbe cash flow of the current year) in F9: +G8/(1+D1); in E9: (F9+F8)/(1+Dl)(you can copy into D9).
6　Present value interest tax shields: it is assumed that the company keeps an amount of borrowing equal to the target debt equity ratio times its present levered value (the latter being equal to the present unlevered value plus the value of the interest tax shields). In order to model this assumption you have to build a circular reference.* The formulas for interest tax shields are starting from F10:
　　　　in F10: +F11*$H$2*$H$1*$D$2/(1+$H$1)
　　　　in E10: +E11*$H$2*$H$1*$D$2/(1+$H$1)+F10/(1+$D$1)
　　　　in D10: copy the formula from E10.
7　Present levered value: +D9+D10 in D11 (to be copied).
8　Borrowing: +D11*$H$2 in D12; to be copied.
9　Interest after tax: +DI2*$H$1*(1−$D$2) in E13 (to be copied).
10　Interest tax shields: +D12*$H$1*$D$2 in E14 (to be copied).
11　NPV: +D9+D8 in D18; interest tax shield in DI9:
　　　　+G14/((1+H1)*(1+D1) ∧ 2)+F14/((1+H1)*(1+D1))+E14/(1+H1)
　　APV: +D18+D19 in D20.
12　Rate for WACC: +D1−D2*H1*H2*(1+D1)/(1+H1) in H19; NPV:
　　@NPV(H19,E8.G8)+D8 in H20.
13　Cash flow statements:
　　　　Net cash: +D8−D13 in D21 (to be copied).
　　　　Borrowing: +D12 in D22 (to be copied).
　　　　Equity: −D21−D22 in D23.
　　　　Loan repayment: 0 in D24; then +D22 (to be copied).
　　　　Dividend: a data
　　　　Change in casb: +D21+D22+D23−D24−D25 in D26 (to be copied).
14　Income statements:
　　　　Profit before tax: +E5 in E28 (to be copied).
　　　　Interest: +E13+E14 in E29 (to be copied).
　　　　Depreciation: +E6 in E30 (to be copied).
　　　　Profit after tax: (E28−E29−E30)*(1−$D$2) in E31 (to be copied).
15　Balance sheets:
　　　　Cash: +D26 in D33; then +D33+E26 in E33 (to be copied).
　　　　Net fixed assets: −D8 in D34; +D34−E30 in E34 (to be copied).
　　　　Total assets: + D33+D34 in D35 (to be copied).
　　　　Debt: +D12 in D37 (to be copied).
　　　　Net worth: +D23−D25 in D38; +D38+E31−E25 in E38 (to be copied).
　　　　Total equities: +D37+D38 in D39 (to copied).
16　Debt equity ratio: +D37/D38 in D41 (to be copied).
17　Debt total funds ratio: +D37/D39 in D42 (to be copied).

＊ Because of the circular reference you may obtain slightly different values for the APV and the NPV. In order to get the same value depress the F9 key as many times as necessary.

Figure VI.6(b)　Constructing the WACC/APV spreadsheet model.

the cash flows (you only have to change the operational profit before depreciation in the range EG.G4).

Two points are worth noting:

1. Borrowing 39%[4] of the market value of the project leads to borrowing much more than 39% of the 900 initially needed. Actually, the model shows that borrowing 39% of the market value of the project leads to financing the

initial 900 by more debt than equity.[5] This phenomenon is fairly general, since, as soon as a project has a positive net present value, the present value of its expected cash flows is necessarily higher than the initial investment.

2. Borrowing 39% of the market value does not imply that the book debt to equity ratio will be 64%. In the present case, this ratio is 170%, then 120%, then 20% then 0%, a similar problem to the one we faced when trying to reconcile accounting with financial measures in the Dhahran Roads case.

NOTES

1 This model uses the approach presented by J Miles and R Ezzell in 'The weighted average cost of capital perfect capital markets and project life: a clarification', *Journal of Financial and Quantitative Analysis* (Sept 1980), **15**: 719–30.

2 Because of this circular reference, you may get slightly different values for the APV and the NPV implied by the WACC. If this happens, press F9 and the two values will converge.

3 The rationale for this is that, since the rule is to borrow in relation to the present value of the project, the level of borrowing becomes uncertain.

4 The reason why a 569 000 FFR loan corresponds to a 39% debt ratio rather than the 40% ratio assumed in Chapter 21, is due to the fact that, in the model, the value of the project incorporates the present value of the tax shields.

5 The model also shows that, beyond a 0.60 debt to total funds ratio, you no longer need to invest any equity.

Part VI   Bibliography

Altman EI and Subrahmanyam MG (eds) (1985), *Recent Advances in Corporate Finance*, RD Irwin.

Bachelier L (1900), *Théorie de la Spéculation*, Gauthier Villars.

Baker H, Farrelly G and Edelman R (1985), 'A survey of management views on dividend policy', *Financial Management* (Autumn), pp 78–84.

Bar-Yosef S and Huffman L (1985), 'The informarion content of dividends', *Journal of Financial and Quantitative Analysis* (Mar), **21**: 47–58.

Black F (1976), 'The dividend puzzle', *Journal of Portfolio Management* (Winter), **2**: 5–8.

Bogue MC and Roll R (1974), 'Capital budgeting of risky projects with "imperfect" markets for physical capital', *Journal of Finance* (May), pp 601–13.

Bower L (1970), 'Managing the resource allocation process', Harvard University, Division of Research, Graduate School of Business Administration.

Bower R (1973), 'Issues in lease financing', *Financial Management* (Winter), pp 25–33.

Chen AH and Kensinger JW (1985), 'Innovations in corporare finance: tax deductible equity', *Financial Management* (Winter), pp 44–51.

Constantinides GN (1980), 'Admissible uncertainty in the intertemporal asset pricing model', *Journal of Financial Economics* (Mar), pp 71–86.

Copeland T and Weston F (1988), *Financial Theory and Corporate Policy*, Addison Wesley.

DeAngelo H and Masulis RW (1980), 'Optimal capital structure under corporate and personal taxation', *Journal of Financial Economics*, **8**: 3–29.

Dieter R (1979), 'Is lessee accounting working?', *CPA Journal* (Aug), pp 13–15, 17–19.

Donaldson G (1962), 'Corporate debt capacity', Harvard University, Division of Research, Graduate School of Business Administration.

Donaldson G (1969), 'Strategy for financial mobility', Harvard University, Division of Research, Graduate School of Business Administration.

Fama E and Miller M (1972), *The Theory of Finance*, Holt, Rinehart & Winston.

Fama EF (1977), 'Risk adjusted discount rates and capital budgeting under uncertainty', *Journal of Financial Economics* (Aug), pp 3–24.

Flannery MJ (1986), 'Asymmetric information and risky debt maturity choice', *Journal of Finance* (Mar), **61**: 19–37.

Franks JR and Hodges SD (1978), 'Valuation of financial lease contracts: a note', *Journal of Finance* (May), **33**: 657–9.

Friend I, Granito M and Westerfield R (1978), 'New evidence, on the capital asset pricing model', *Journal of Finance* (June).

Gehr A (1981), 'Risk adjusted capital budgeting using arbitrage', *Financial Management* (Winter), pp 14–19.

Harris M and Raviv A (1991), 'The Theory of Capital Structure', *The Journal of Finance* (March), pp 297–355.

Jarnagin B and Booker J (current edition), *Financial Accounting Standards: Explanation and Analysis*, Commerce Clearing House.

Jensen, M (1968), 'The performance of mutual funds in the period 1945–64', *Journal of Finance* (May), pp 389–416.

Jensen MC and Meckling WN (1976), 'Theory of the firm: managerial behavior, agency costs and ownership structure', *Journal of Financial Economics*, **3**: 305–60.

Jensen MC and Smith CW (1985), 'Stockholder, manager and creditor interests: applications of agency theory', in Altman EI and Subramanyam MG (eds), *Recent Advances in Corporate Finance*, RD Irwin.

Jensen MC and Smith CW (eds) (1986), *The Modern Theory of Corporate Finance*, McGraw-Hill.

Kim WS and Soerensen EM (1986), 'Evidence of the impact of agency cost of debt on corporate policy', *Journal of Financial and Quantitative Analysis* (June), **21**.

Lee WL, Thakor AV and Vora G (1983), 'Screening, market signalling and capital structure theory', *Journal of Finance* (Dec).

Lintner J (1956), 'Distribution of incomes of corporations among dividends retained earnings and taxes', *American Economic Review* (May), **46**: 97–113.

McConnell JJ and Muscarella CJ (1985), 'Corporate capital expenditure decisions and the market value of the firm', *Journal of Financial Economics*, **14**: 399–422.

McConnell JJ and Schallheim JS (1983), 'Valuation of asset leasing contracts', *Journal of Financial Economics*, **12**: 237–61.

Malkiel BG (1966), *The Term Structure of Interest Rates: Expectations and Behavior Patterns*, Princeton University Press.

Merton R (1990), *Continuous-Time Finance*, Basil Blackwell.

Miles J and Ezzell R (1980), 'The weighted average cost of capital perfect capital markets and project life: a clarification', *Journal of Financial and Quantitative Analysis*, **15**: 719–30.

Miller M (1977) 'Debt and taxes', *Journal of Finance* (May), **32**: 261–76.

Miller MH and Scholes MS (1978), 'Dividend and taxes', *Journal of Financial Economics* (Dec), **6**: 333–64.

Miller MH and Upton CW (1976), 'Leasing, buying and the cost of capital services', *Journal of Finance* (June), **31**: 761–86.

Modigliani F and Miller MH (1958), 'The cost of capital, corporation finance and the theory of investment', *American Economic Review* (June), **48**: 261–97.

Modigliani F and Miller MH (1963), 'Corporate income taxes and the cost of capital: a correction', *American Economic Review* (June), **53**: 433–43.

Myers SC (1974), 'Interactions of corporate financing and investment decisions – implications for capital budgeting', *Journal of Finance* (March), **29**: 1–25.

Myers SC (1977), 'Determinants of corporate borrowing', *Journal of Financial Economics* (Nov), **5**: 147–75.

Myers SC (1984), 'The capital structure puzzle', *Journal of Finance* (July), **39**: 575–92.

Myers SC, Dill DA and Bautista AJ (1976), 'Valuation of financial lease contracts', *Journal of Finance* (June), **31**: 799–819.

Myers SC and Majluf NS (1984), 'Corporate financing and investment decisions when firms have information that investors do not have', *Journal of Financial Economics*, **13**: 187–221.

Myers SC and Turnbull S (1977), 'Capital budgeting and the capital asset pricing model: good news and bad news', *Journal of Finance* (May), **32**: 321–36.

Pinegar and Wilbricht (1989), 'Capital Structure Theory', *Financial Management* (Winter), pp 82–91.

Roll R (1970), *The Behavior of Interest Rates: An Application of the Efficient Market Model to US Treasury Bills*, Basic Books.

Roll R (1977), 'A critique of the asset pricing theory's tests', *Journal of Financial Economics* (May), **4**: 129–76.

Roll R and Ross SA (1980), 'An empirical investigation of the arbitrage pricing theory', *Journal of Finance* (Dec), pp 1073–103.

Rosenberg B and Guy J (1976), 'Prediction from investment fundamentals', *Financial Analysts Journal* (May/June), **32** (3): 60–72.

Ross S (1976), 'The arbitrage theory of capital asset pricing', *Journal of Economic Theory* (Dec), **13**: 341–60.

Ross SA (1985), 'Debt and taxes and uncertainty', *Journal of Finance* (July), **60**: 637–56.

Sarig O and Scott J (1985), 'The puzzle of financial leverage clienteles', *Journal of Finance* (Dec), **60**: 1459–67.

Sharpe WF (1990, 1978), *Investments*, Prentice Hall.

Spence M (1973), 'Job market signalling', *Quarterly Journal of Economics* (Aug), pp 355–79.

Statman M and Tyebjee TT (1985), 'Optimistic capital budgeting forecasts: an experiment', *Financial Management* (Autumn).

Stiglitz JE (1975), 'The theory of "screening", education and the distribution of income', *American Economic Review* (June), pp 283–300.

Wagner W and Lau S (1971), 'The effects of diversification on risk', *Financial Analysts Journal* (Nov/Dec), **26**: 7–13.

Warner J (1977), 'Bankruptcy costs: some evidence', *Journal of Finance* (May), **32**: 337–48.

Capital Budgeting and Strategy
How to Launch a New Product

We would now like to invite you to help BA International, a German-based multinational company, to imagine a strategy for launching, if it should be launched, a new compressor called P12.

The BA International case is derived from a real business situation and it has been discussed several times with the executives who were involved in the actual decision, a decision which was not easy to make.

We would like to make our usual recommendations. Be prepared to invest sufficient time in analyzing the case and solving it by yourself. In order to help you in this process, we suggest that you:

- Read carefully the first BA International case only.
- Put yourself in the position of a consultant to BA International and try to answer the following questions:
  · How easy/difficult is it to launch a new product in an industry such as the one in which BA International operates?
  · What are the options open to BA International?
  · What kind of model can you build in order to select the best of these options?
- A further suggestion – why not start by following BA International's approach and then improving it, if need be?

When preparing the BA International case, it may be a good idea to go back to the tables which describe the key learning points in Parts III, IV and V.

The need for a new mentality

In most industries today, managers are confronted with increasing complexity and a quicker pace of change. Complexity and change exist in the environment, in the competitive game, in the technology and within the organizations themselves. Business situations evolve as the result of the complex interplay between a very large number of variables. Within the multi-variable and multi-relationship complexity with which they are confronted, managers should aim to identify the few basic variables and relationships which really matter. As once expressed in the Shell company, effective managers are the ones who are able to develop a helicopter mentality. Such a mentality

- Helps them take the necessary perspective and avoid being overwhelmed by unnecessary complexities.
- Helps them *simplify and structure* problems and situations.
- Helps them *not to give too much importance to short term events* and *turbulence* which may not recur in the long term.
- Helps them *transfer insight* from other business experiences, from the experience of other managers, from literature.
- Enables them to exercise their imagination and business sense on adequately simplified problems.

What some people do not always realize is that the new availablity of personal computers and spreadsheet software increases the need for such a mentality.

Personal computers and spreadsheets enable managers to complicate problems and situations all too easily. When used this way, the new technology is totally counter-productive and as a result people become disappointed with it. Personal computers and spreadsheet software should always be used to *structure and simplify problems and situations*. When progressively developing a spreadsheet model, you should aim to make it more and more effective but also more and more simple. Models which are really helpful for strategic decision-making are the ones in which you understand the interplay between the variables. This understanding may not be immediate, it may require some deep thinking and some learning but it should exist. How can you trust a model which generates results you cannot explain? As a consequence, helpful models necessarily have a limited number of relationships and variables.

Personal computers and spreadsheets enable managers to do calculations fairly easily and to prove arguments with numbers. The problem, however, is always to be sure that the proof is valid. This is again a matter of taking the right perspective, of making sure that the approach is suitable, that the data are adequate and that the calculations are appropriate.

There are also many stories in business about decisions which have been taken on purely intuitive grounds and which have been justified afterwards by carefully selected numbers. This is now much easier to do with personal computers. Number crunching is simple with a personal computer but crunching numbers does not necessarily correspond to good quantitative analysis. In order to perform a good quantitative analysis, you need to think about the kind of analysis you need to carry out and elaborate a game plan to organize this.

BA International: summary of the steps of the analysis

Step 1 Case (A), Chapters 23, and 24.1: **first definition of the problem**.

Step 2 A **global evaluation** of the different alternatives, Figure 24.7, page 385.

Step 3 Building an **initial model** which corresponds to the consensual view of the problem. NFV is equal to zero.

Step 4 Chapter 24: **Criticizing the model**. Identifying potential improvements. What would a good NPV be? 5 million at least.

Step 5 Case (B): New thoughts, additional references to experience and theory, new information. **Correcting the time horizon**: with a period of study equal to the expected life-cycle, at 10 years, the NFV becomes 3.3 million. A new base model, (Figure G.2, page 391).

Step 6 Chapter 25: **Correcting one mistake at a time** and assessing its impact as compared with the base model. Tax and depreciation, accounts payable, inventory delays, currency risk, inflation, CGS, cannibalization, cost of production, fixed and variable costs, impact of experience, differential experience, product life-cycle, timing of selling costs, competition. Results are shown in Figure 25.11, page 414.

Step 7 Chapter 26: Building an **improved model incorporating all the potential improvements** except for cgs (Figure 26.3, page 420). The NPV is 8.1 million (Figure 26.4, page 421). Testing that the model is robust (results of the **sensitivity analysis** are in Figure 26.5, page 422).

Step 8 Chapter 27: Improving the ease of use of the model. **Building a control panel** (Figures 27.5, 27.7, 27.9, and 27.10, pages 429, 431 and 433). Two first evaluations of alternative strategies:
- Without taking risk into account, the best niche strategy corresponds to an 8.1 million NPV, the best volume strategy to a 22.6 million NPV (Figure 27.6, page 430).
- **When risk is taken into account** (competitive and production risks*), we get a range of possible NFVs:
  - from 0.8 to 8.1 million for the best niche strategy (15% price premium)
  - from −16.8 to 22.6 million for the best volume strategy (0% price premium) (Figure 28.1, page 435)

Step 9 Chapter 28: **Making a decision.** Assigning probabilities and constructing a risk profile (Figure 28.4, page 438).

Step 10 Chapter 28: A **final critical review** of the decision. Have we given a fair chance to the two contending strategies?
- Have we evaluated capital expenditures properly? Structure costs?
- What about a more aggressive pricing strategy if we were to adopt a volume strategy?
- Is our cannibalization model correct in case of niche strategies?
- The niche strategy as a step by step approach. Its option value.

* Currency risk is analyzed in Further Model VII.2: see Figure VII.2(a).

KEY LEARNING POINTS

SPREADSHEETS

MODELS

FINANCE AND RELATED APPROACHES

A DISCIPLINED PROCESS FOR MODELLING STRATEGIC ALTERNATIVES

THE PROBLEM
It results from your own analysis; its specification evolves with your understanding; the need to identify the alternatives
A global evaluation helps you to understand the problem

THE INITIAL MODEL
It results from your initial understanding of the situation. It is the outcome of a process: paper and pencil analysis, one-year spreadsheet model verification and extension – *Figure 24.6, page 380*

CHASING MISTAKES/LOOKING FOR IMPROVEMENTS AND EVALUATING THEM
Testing the initial model against your experience, the experience of others and theory. Identifying the need for new information and obtaining it. Using the initial model as a base for testing the impact of potential improvements.

A GOOD ENOUGH MODEL
Building a model which embodies all meaningful improvements – *Figure 26.3, page 420*
Testing its robustness – *Figure 26.5, page 422*

AN EASY TO USE MODEL
Driving the model with the key parameters – *Chapter 27, page 424*
Building a control panel with key parameters and outcomes. Using the model to test competitive strategy – *Figure 27.10, page 433*

THE DECISION
The need to feel sufficiently confident about the economy of the decision before choosing – *Chapter 28, page 435*

CHAPTER 23

The Evaluation of New Products and New Markets

New product/market decisions are the result of a series of complex strategic choices, the decision to be in an industry, competitive strategy, marketing strategy, manufacturing strategy, etc. Consequently, new product/market decisions should be viewed as a general management problem which is part of the overall strategic planning process. New product/market decisions are also the result of complex organizational processes. When contemplating a move into a new market, managers cannot ignore the fact that such a move may change the structure of power within the organization, and their own position.

New product/market decisions cannot be reduced to financial approaches. Financial approaches are tools which help managers to act at the various stages of a long and complex process. Personal computers and spreadsheets provide managers with new opportunities:

- They can now use financial approaches by themselves, which presents two major advantages.
  - · Managers can learn more effectively about strategic moves by using simultaneously their intuition and a powerful methodology.
  - · Managers can put all the unique information they have in their financial models.
- They can use financial approaches at the various stages of this long process and, in particular, at its earlier stages when most alternatives are still open.

Financial approaches for evaluating new product/market alternatives

From a financial standpoint, good actions are those which generate positive net present values. From a theoretical viewpoint, there is no difficulty in assessing new product/market alternatives; it is just a matter of assessing their cash flows and discounting these at the relevant discount rate.

The evaluation of the cash flows attached to new product/market alternatives is not that easy in practice since:

- The cash flows should be assessed on an incremental basis. The only cash flows to be considered are those which will be created by the decision to launch the new product or to enter the new market. As a result, all costs previously incurred should be ignored. In accounting/finance literature, these costs are called sunk costs.

▪ Even though the concept of incremental cash flows is very simple, its application is very difficult in practice. Before considering any cash flow, you should check that this cash flow is the direct result of your decision to go ahead with the new product or market you are studying. In particular, pay attention to:

· The nature of cost data you use. Much cost data in real life comes from accounting and is the result of allocation processes. This cost data is true on the average in the long run, but not necessarily on an incremental basis.

· The eventual impact of your decision on the existing business portfolio of your company. Very few new decisions can be considered as totally independent from the firm's existing cash flows.

· The eventual impact of your decision on your company's future strategic opportunities. If the decision you contemplate is likely to change the future competitive position of your firm, you should recognize this advantage in your analysis.

▪ In addition, one difficult problem with new product or market decisions is to select the adequate horizon for study. The theory gives you a clear answer. New products and markets should be studied over their entire expected life. But, again, doing it is not easy in practice, as we shall see when we analyze the BA International case.

New product/market decisions: A long and complex process

The example in Figure 23.1 can help explain the new product/market decision process.

Financial studies should be prepared at the various stages of the new market/product decision process. In the example described in Figure 23.1, one could imagine that financial studies are prepared in at least four different stages.

A large multinational company produces industrial products which are sold through a network of selling subsidiaries all over the world. For many years, this company has been selling products to a segment of customers and, in order to keep and improve its competitive edge, it has had to introduce new products every 3–5 years. This product introduction is a rather long process since it is generally 2–3 years between the initial identification of the new product and the final decision to launch it.

These 2–3 years are used for market research and product development. (During these 2–3 years, a number of ideas are abandoned.) When the decision is finally made to start production, 1–2 more years are necessary to prepare the production facilities, organize the relationships with suppliers and develop the definitive marketing plan.

Figure 23.1 The situation.

- When the new product is made available to the selling subsidiaries (Stage 4).
- When the decision to put the new product into production is about to be made (Stage 3).
- When the new product idea is identified – or at least when it is identified with sufficient precision (Stage 2).
- When the management periodically reflects about the position of the company on its markets and tries to increase its competitive edge, new products being one of the possible strategic moves (Stage 1).

The fact that financial analyses can be performed at so many different stages raises two fundamental questions.

- Do analyses made at different stages lead to similar results? Will they lead to the same conclusions regarding the value of the envisaged new product (as measured by NPV)?
- If the analyses do not lead to similar results, which results should be believed?

The 'profitability of a new product' does not exist

Financial approaches aim to describe the *value of alternative decisions at a given moment in time.* The consequence of this is that, depending on the moment when the analysis is made, the results will differ quite significantly. In order to understand this better, let us assume that the company described in Figure 23.1 has the cost structure shown in Figure 23.2.

The cash inflows and outflows that would be taken into account in the analysis at different stages are shown in Figure 23.3.

Financial analyses when made at different stages will therefore, as expected, lead to very different results:

- At Stage 1, financial analysis will conclude that the company has to leave its

Sales	100
Cost of goods sold (cgs)	40
Research and development (R&D)	40
Administration at headquarters (HQ)	5
Administration at selling subsidiaries level	20
Profit	(5)

Further assumptions:
  All new product ideas lead to the same revenue and cost structure. (This structure is to be maintained in the future.)
  Revenues and costs can be assimilated to cash receipts and disbursements.
    There is no tax.
    In the short run, administrative costs at headquarters are fixed, administrative costs at selling subsidiaries level are divided into fixed (15) and variable (5).

Figure 23.2   The company's cost structure.

	Stage 1 Assessment of competitive position	Stage 2 A new idea is found	Stage 3 A new product is going to be launched in production	Stage 4 A new product is made available to selling subsidiaries
Cash inflows	100*	100*	100*	100*
Cash outflows	105[†]	85[‡]	45[§]	90'
Net	(5)	15	55	10

* Sales.

[†] *Assumption*: Since the company is operating on one market only, all revenues and costs are to be taken into account over the long run.

[‡] *Assumption*: Disbursements envisaged are cgs (40), R&D (40), variable administrative costs at subsidiaries level (5).

[§] *Assumption*: Disbursements envisaged are cgs (40), variable administrative and selling costs in subsidiaries (5). All other costs are not taken into account since they are considered as sunk (R&D) or as fixed structure at both HQ and subsidiary levels.

' *Assumption*: HQ charge to selling subsidiaries through the transfer price: cgs (40), R&D (40), Administration (5). Selling subsidiaries consider as outflows only the variable part of their selling costs (5).

Note: The cash inflows and outflows depend on the assumptions made and other assumptions are possible.

Figure 23.3 Four different stages of the analysis.

present market/products.

■ At Stages 2, 3 and 4, the conclusion will be the opposite.

One has to realize, however, that the analysis itself is technically correct at each stage. For example, it is true that, if one looks at Stage 3, when the product has been developed, it makes sense to launch it since not launching it would make the situation even worse. What has to be understood, however, is that the problem for this company is not really to decide whether or not products already developed should be launched but rather to examine why these products are not generating enough money to cover their costs of development and structure. If time has to be spent on financial analyses, it would be better in this case to spend time on decisions at Stage 1, and to examine then whether the company should stay in this line of business.

Using financial approaches for evaluating relevant strategic alternatives

Financial analyses always attempt to place a value on decisions, *to assess which value can be created by making a specific move rather than doing nothing more than usual.*

In order to ensure that only useful analyses are made, you have to:

■ Make sure they relate to the relevant decisions.
■ Develop them in a strategic fashion.
■ Understand the real meanings of the decision and of the related analysis.

The most useful analyses are those made in relation to the firm's critical strategic decisions. In the above example, it is probably useful to make analyses at Stages 3 and 4 (although the scope of decisions made at Stage 4 is fairly limited) but it is crucial to carry out analyses at Stage 1, and perhaps at Stage 2 also.

In another firm, the situation may be completely different and priority may have to be given to analyzing Stage 3. This would be the case, for example, in a highly profitable industry with high entry costs, low product development costs and many opportunities for new product introduction.

You also have to realize that, made at different stages, financial analyses have different natures.

- The time horizon changes with the stage at which the analysis is made, from very long-term at Stage 1, to relatively short-term at Stage 4.
- The degree of uncertainty is different at each stage. At Stage 4, much data is available (production cost, market price, etc). On the other hand, very little is known at Stage 2.
- The nature of the data itself is different at each stage. At Stage 4, it is possible to identify fixed and variable costs, whereas at Stage 1 most costs are probably variable since, when a long-term view is taken, most costs can be changed.

The concept of making analyses in a *strategic* fashion relates to three main ideas:

- Useful analyses should incorporate *adequate models of the various dimensions of the new market/product decisions*, marketing, production, etc. Making a sales forecast, for example, is not as useful as establishing a model that explains sales in relation to relevant variables (growth of a primary market, market share, etc). With such a model, you are able to test the impact of an increase in market share given the effort that would be required. Only analyses based on a model that describes simultaneously all the various aspects of a new market/product are useful since what is required is to test the impact of specific actions on the total financial result.
- Useful analyses focus on the evaluation of *alternative strategies*. In many respects, it is a waste of time to build a model of a new product to test just one strategy. This merely allows you to check that the strategy is acceptable, which is probably the case anyway, if this is the result of discussions among a large number of managers. *Testing one single strategy never allows you to check that this strategy is the best one available.*
- Recognize the *stage of development of the industry* and explicitly take into account this dimension when analyzing new market/product opportunities.

Competition is generally of a different nature at each stage of development of an industry, emergence, maturity and decline.[1] In emerging industries, uncertainty is very high and competitive rules are not established. New market/product analyses should therefore explore *a wide spectrum of possible product/technology, market and competitive alternatives*. This calls for the use of simple models focusing on a small number of key parameters. Such models should help you to explore a wide range of scenarios and imagine innovative strategies.

In mature industries, the situation is different. Growth slows down, marketing becomes more sophisticated and adequate pricing becomes of greater importance, new product introductions occur less often and great care has to be given not to cannibalize existing products, sophisticated control of costs becomes a major strategic weapon, etc. The new market/product analysis should explore in depth the factors which are critical at this stage of development, pricing, positioning of products (searching for niches), cannibalization, manufacturing costs, purchasing costs, etc. Evaluation of alternative strategies will require, at this stage, financial models which analyze, in detail, the marketing and production aspects, and you should not be surprised to find relatively low returns.

In declining industries, situations have a lot in common with maturity but an additional problem arises. When will it be time to pull out? When analyzing such industries, your models should address this issue.

NOTE

1 For more about this, refer to M Porter, *Competitive Strategy*, The Free Press (1980). Competition in emerging industries is described in Chapter 10, competition in mature industries in Chapter 11 and competition in declining industries in Chapter 12.

BA INTERNATIONAL (A)

In December 1991, the time had come at BA International to submit the final report on P12, a new product to be introduced on the market in 1993, to the Board of Directors for their approval. Mr Keller, the Head of the Product Planning Department, was responsible for preparing this final report from the numerous memoranda about P12 as well as from the minutes of the New Product Committee.

The company

BA International was a large, German-based multinational corporation which specialized in the production and sales of industrial compressors. Its production facilities were located in Dusseldorf. The company sold through a network of wholly owned international sales subsidiaries in forty countries, as well as through distributors.

In the past, BA International had been more successful in the more powerful end of the market (see Appendix F.1 to this case study) selling to large industrial firms and/or those using large equipment (100–1 000 kW range). It offered to these market segments products of high quality, in particular a very successful line of oil-free rotary screw compressors.

With P12, BA International was planning to offer the oil-free quality to a new market segment consisting of medium and small firms using medium size equipment (15–100 kW range).

Traditionally, BA International had a strong market position with a worldwide market share of about 15% in the 100–1 000 kW range. In most of these markets, BA International had played the role of a price leader which resulted in high profitability. In recent years, however, growth had been sluggish and short-term prospects were not very favorable. As a consequence, BA International's profitability had declined sharply recently, but to a lesser extent than its competitors. The worldwide stagnation of the compressor market, due to the economic recession, as well as the intense competition from dynamic compressors in the most powerful range, led management to believe that the basis for developing the group activities should lie in a downward extension rather than in a deeper penetration of the large or top power range markets.

P12

The introduction of P12 represented such a downward extension of its market position for BA International. It was not absent from the 15–100 kW segment. When the competition actively developed oil lubricated rotary screw compressors for that segment, BA launched a line of comparable products with a view to preventing the competition in this segment from becoming too strong. In 1991, BA International was

This case was developed by the author and Bernard Dubois, Professor at Centre HEC-ISA (France). The pedagogy of this case has been developed by the author, Bernard Dubois, Sherwood Frey, Professor at Colgate Darden (USA) and Foster Rogers, Professor at IFL (Sweden).

R.T.C. LIBRARY
LETTERKENNY

serving this segment through distributors rather than its own sales subsidiaries, except for the large firms served directly. But, although BA International had introduced a line of medium sized oil lubricated rotary screw compressors, its long term objective was to promote the oil-free solution in the entire 15–1 000 kW range.

The Concept for P12 was an old one at BA International. The first formal meeting about this product had taken place in the company as early as 1980. P12 was to be priced higher than the existing lubricated rotary screw compressors since it was providing a better service, oil free air and lower maintenance costs. (BA International also provided maintenance services to its customers.)

BA International had been particularly concerned with the marketing of P12. Some questions had not been easy to answer.

1. Were the prospective customers for P12 really sensitive to the oil-free argument? Apparently some were not, and that led BA International to conclude that P12 should be introduced only in those industries where specific characteristics required oil-free air (the electronics and food industries, for example). Another strategy, however, would be to promote P12 on a larger scale and invest in educating customers about the advantages of oil-free air. A spin-off effect of that effort would also help the sales of the more powerful equipment and reinforce BA International's image as a technological leader. However, the evaluation of such an effect was very difficult.
2. What premium over currently available products should P12 carry? The higher the premium, the more difficult P12 would be to sell in larger volume. In the end, a 15% premium over existing products was considered the most suitable.
3. Would P12 cannibalize the rotary screw compressors presently sold by BA International? As these were a profitable mature product this was a sensitive issue. The cannibalization issue depended very much on the strategy adopted for P12. If P12 were marketed only to those customers who were sensitive to the oil-free air argument, and if those customers were medium and small firms presently served by distributors, then it was felt that only limited cannibalization would take place. Obviously, if a higher price premium were charged, this would reinforce the argument for the absence of cannibalization. On the other hand, if BA International decided to aim at a larger market for P12, then it would be necessary to consider the impact of a cannibalization of the existing oil lubricated compressors. Generally, when existing products are cannibalized, it is assumed that they are cannibalized in the proportion of their market share.
4. Would competition move in on this market? At present, no competitor seemed to have a product with a similar design. Even though it was finally considered at BA International that no competitor would offer a product similar to P12 in the near future, some engineers claimed that the major world competitor of BA International could well introduce such a product on the market at any time.

The new products development process

In a mature industry of the type in which BA International was operating, products have a long life cycle, some 10 to 15 years. During their life cycle, a number of the products require additional investment (engineering expenditures, change in the organization of production, even revamping of the product). In the case of P12, a 10-year life with no additional capital expenditures could reasonably be expected.

New product development and introduction was the responsibility of Headquarters which was frequently secretive about new product development since it was felt that, if sales subsidiaries knew about new products too early, they would put less effort into selling existing products and wait until the new product was available. As a result, sales subsidiaries were generally informed about new products only when these were available for sale (the end of 1992 for P12).

The Product Planning Department headed by Mr Keller was a staff department. Its mission was to co-ordinate the three functions involved in new product development, the technical, production and marketing functions. This co-ordination was formally made through a New Product Committee, the secretariat of which was provided by the Product Planning Department.

New product development, described in Appendix F.2, was a long process, maybe too long, according to the new financial manager. As shown in Appendix F.2, this process involved mainly Headquarters staff who were, in any case, the only ones concerned with technical and production problems. Marketing issues related to the introduction of new products were dealt with by the Marketing Department at Headquarters. When needed, this department tested new product ideas and characteristics (especially price) with the management of sales subsidiaries but had to remain discreet in order to avoid disclosing too much about the new products envisaged (the summary of the marketing studies for P12 is given in Appendix F.3).

During the process, numerous alternatives were explored until a consensus was reached on the most reasonable assumptions and strategy. These were the basis for the comprehensive profitability study submitted to the Board (see Appendix F.4). This profitability study was obviously not the first to be carried out in the product development process but was the only really comprehensive one.

Generally, this study presented one single set of assumptions and strategy, the one that had been progressively built up through successive consensuses about the most realistic assumptions and the best strategic alternatives.

The final report on a project, including the profitability study, was not submitted to the Board so that they could decide whether or not the project should be launched, but was intended rather to provide the senior management of BA International with the opportunity to summarize the various dimensions of the decision in a comprehensive and structured way, and to double check the strength of the arguments in favor of the introduction of a new product on the market and the robustness of the consensual strategy that had progressively emerged. In fact, substantial changes were often made to the consensual strategy during the process of preparing the final report.

APPENDIX F.1

THE INDUSTRIAL COMPRESSOR MARKET

Air compressor technology, dating back to the industrial revolution of the last century, is based on a very simple idea. A given volume of air is confined in a cylinder, compressed by a piston usually driven by an electric motor) and the resulting energy, characterized by a volume of air at a given pressure, is used to drive a machine, move a piece of equipment or an air motor. Over the years, compressed air technology has evolved to the point where it is possible to distinguish three categories of product (in 1991 it appeared that technology had reached a stage of maturity).

1. Piston (reciprocating) compressors

Piston compressors are the oldest type but, even now, represent intrinsically the most energy-efficient solution (in terms of the number of kWs necessary to produce one cubic meter of air). Their main advantages (from the user's point of view) are their familiar technology and their lower purchasing cost. Their main disadvantages are:

- Substantial installation costs (foundation mountings).
- Vibration.
- Noise level when in use.
- High maintenance costs. It can be estimated that a 100 kW piston industrial compressor has a life expectancy of 80 to 100 000 hours but must be checked on average every 8 000 hours.

The piston compressor family covers a wide range, including oil-lubricated and oil-free (pure air), single or double-acting, one or two-stage compression, air- or water-cooled, etc.

2. Rotary screw compressors

Instead of being compressed in a cylinder, air is squeezed between two screws rotating in a housing. The main advantages of rotary screw compressors are their reduced installation cost (rotary screw compressors are packaged units which only need to be connected up to the electricity supply) and reduced maintenance costs (a major maintenance operation such as replacing a screw is necessary, on average, every 25 to 50 000 hours) as well as a reduced level of noise and vibration. the trade-off for this reduction in maintenance costs is that the initial capital cost is about 20% more than for a piston compressor.

Like piston compressors, rotary screw compressors include several types of machine, particularly oil-lubricated and oil-free machines. Oil-lubricated screw compressors have the advantage of being a packaged unit and are capable of delivering air at 7 to 10 bar pressure in a single stage of compression (such a performance would require a two-stage process for oil-free piston compressors), but the delivered air is not totally free from oil and must be purified through a series of filters, the effectiveness of which may vary considerably from one application to another. Since certain types of applications require very high quality air (the food and electronics industries) there also exist oil-free rotary screw compressors. Their main advantage is the purity of the compressed air delivered, but two compression stages are necessary as well as an intercooler in order to obtain a 7 to 10 bar final pressure. These compressors cost more than oil-lubricated ones (15% more than the sum of the costs of an oil-lubricated compressor and of the filters). The initial difference in capital cost between oil-lubricated and oil-free compressors is, however, compensated for by the savings obtained in energy consumption and maintenance. As the yearly maintenance costs are about 10% lower in the case of an oil-free screw compressor, the payback of selecting an oil-free solution lies somewhere between three and four years.

3. Dynamic compressors

The basic principle of dynamic compressors consists of an impeller accelerating air to a high velocity and converting the speed of the air into pressure in the diffuser. There are two main, categories of dynamic compressor, centrifugal and axial. Given the high cost and level of sophistication, the dynamic compressor technology is only justified at a power range greater than 1 000 kW. Dynamic compressors always deliver oil-free air. Their main advantage lies in their excellent input/output ratio and their compactness and limited number of components.

Industrial compressors may be driven by any type of motor, electrical or steam and gas turbine and are used in many applications in almost all industrial sectors. The different types of compressor correspond to different application areas.

(a) The market for very small compressors (smaller than 15 kW) is dominated by oil-lubricated piston technology. This market is highly competitive and a large number of manufacturers engage in price wars. Products which are technologically simple are sold in large quantities, most often through wholesalers at unit prices averaging a few thousand DM. The bottom end of this line consists of small workshop compressors as well as do-it-yourself products. BA International was neither interested nor active in this market.

(b) The middle range (15–100 kW) compressor market worldwide was estimated at about 24 000 units in 1993. Given the standard nature of their product, manufacturers compete very actively with each other. Given the current economic situation, price and delivery criteria tend to be more important than company image and technical features. Traditionally dominated by piston technology, this market has changed fundamentally in the last ten years, under pressure from big international manufacturers who introduced oil-lubricated screw compressors to try to gain market share from the local producers. It was this development which prompted BA International to launch, slightly later than its competitors, its own line of oil-lubricated screw compressors. Most manufacturers sell directly through sales subsidiaries as well as through distributors.

(c) The market for large compressors (100–1 000 kW) is more structured as far as demand and competition are concerned. Compressors in this range are often sold directly to customers by the manufacturer, to customer specifications. A potential customer interested in buying a compressor provides the specifications required for the particular application, a feasibility study is then made by each manufacturer interested in the contract and a proposal is made. If an agreement is reached, the contract is signed and the equipment is delivered and installed on site. The selection of a manufacturer is made on the basis of three criteria, technical (air quality, kW/m^3 output), commercial (price, delivery) and reputation and image factors. This market segment is dominated by international companies.

(d) The market for very large compressors (greater than 1 000 kW) is a market dominated by technical considerations and each sale is dealt with on an ad hoc basis. In 1991, BA International was not active in this segment.

APPENDIX F.2

NEW PRODUCT DEVELOPMENT PROCESS

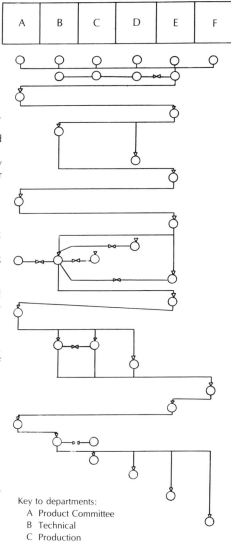

1.1 Introduction of ideas and proposals.
1.2 Technical screening, developing recommendations.
1.3 Decision regarding priority and research objective.

2.1 Distribution and co-ordination of investigation tasks.
2.2 Investigation of alternative technical solutions.
2.3 Preliminary appraisal of market requirements and potential fields of application.
2.4 Evaluating market and technical findings. Preliminary cost and profitability analysis. Recommendations for further action.
2.5 Decision.

3.1 Developing project specification.
3.2 Market research on field of application, market requirements etc. including five years' sales forecast.
3.3 Engineering functional analysis, service planning testing of functional prototype. Reporting progress. Investigating investments for production.
3.4 Coordinating and evaluating technical data and market information. Profitability analysis. Recommendations as to further action. Network plan.
3.5 Decision.

4.1 Engineering, value analysis, drawings and specifications, testing of production prototype. Review of investments in production.
4.2 Review of market research, five years sales forecast. Marketing planning.
4.3 Precalculation.
4.4 Profitability analysis.
4.5 Final decision.

5.1 Release of drawings.
5.2 Production.
5.3 Marketing.
5.4 Introduction into BA International product programme.
5.5 After calculation.

Key to departments:
  A Product Committee
  B Technical
  C Production
  D Marketing
  E Product Planning
  F Other
Key to symbols:
  □ = action ▽ = transportation ▷◁ = co-ordination

APPENDIX F.3

MARKETING STUDIES

The determination of the potential market for P12 has been studied by the Marketing Department at Dusseldorf. This has been accomplished by desk and field research (interviews of managers in sales companies, industrial analysis). The conclusions of the studies on the market for P12 are summarized as follows:

- The total annual world market for compressors in the range of 40–100 kW is estimated at 5 780 units in 1993. This market is estimated to grow at 3% per year (P12 was aimed at only part of the 15–100 kW market).
- Within this total market, the users who need oil-free air represent 11%, corresponding to 635 units, the sales being equaliy shared between small and large firms. BA International currently sells to small firms through distributors (world market share 10%) and to large firms through subsidiaries (world market share 13%).
- There is potential for some other customers to be converted to the use of oil-free air since this solution could reduce their maintenance costs. This would, however, require BA International to undertake a major educational effort. If these customers were convinced, the potential market for P12 could progressively rise to 19% of the total market. If BA International were ready to spend about 17 m DM (equally spread over 1992 and 1993), P12's market segment could rise to 14% of total market in 1993, 16.5% of total market in 1994 and 19% of total market in 1995 and afterwards. Additional customers would be 50% small firms, 50% large firms although, given the technical characteristics of P12, BA International was planning to sell P12 directly and not through wholesalers.
- All other customers can be considered as non-sensitive to the oil-free argument, as long as oil-free compressors are more expensive than oil-lubricated ones.
- It is recommended that there is no education campaign. In which case, BA International could potentially change the size of P12's segment through its pricing policy.

Premium over present products	Estimated size of P12 segment
10% (sales price 32 140 DM)	12%
15% (sales price 33 600 DM)	11%
25% (sales price 36 520 DM)	9%
35% (sales price 39 443 DM)	7%

If the education campaign is carried out, the relationship between price premium and P12's additional segment size is estimated as follows:

Premium over present products	Estimated size of additional P12 segment (% of total market) 1995[1]
10%	12%
15%	8%
25%	5%
35%	2%

- It is recommended that a premium of 15% is charged which should ensure an 11% segment share for P12. Two factors influence the selection of the 15% premium:
  - The estimate of the cost of providing an alternative solution to P12 by using a rotary screw compressor plus filters plus higher maintenance costs.

· BA International's experience with larger equipment which is selling at a similar premium.

■ It is recommended that no account is taken of the possible introduction of a similar product to P12 by any competitor. The only possible competitor who could launch a similar product has a smaller market share than BA International (4 to 6 ratio).

APPENDIX F.4

PROFITABILITY STUDIES

1. Sales assumptions

The volume of the market segment of P12 in 1993 is 635 units. This segment is assumed to grow at 3% a year after 1993. A 100% market share is assumed (no competitor present). A progressive market penetration is envisaged: 22.5% in 1993, 50% in 1994, 75% in 1995 and 100% in 1996 and afterwards.

2. Price assumptions

The average world price for P12 is estimated to be 33 600 DM (customers' price) in 1993. The entire profitability study is made at revenue and cost prices of 1993. Currency values considered are also 1993 values.

3. Costs

Production costs are determined on the basis of 17 013 DM per unit in 1993. No allowance has been made in future years for increases in prices. The calculation of costs is detailed in Appendix F.5. The cost of 17 013 DM represents the cost of P12 in 1993 for a volume of production of 100 units. This cost includes direct material, material overheads, direct labour, labour overheads, product costs (10% of the other costs) and packaging and transportation (9% of the total of the other costs). Since the volume of P12 is to remain small in comparison with other products, no attempt has been made to charge any cost relating to the structure of the production unit and Headquarters. The cost of goods sold is assumed to be equal to the cost of production.

Selling costs in the sales companies are estimated to be 20% of sales. No attempt has been made to charge any cost related to the general structure of the sales companies.

Other costs. No interest charges have been considered. Inflation and foreign exchange rate fluctuations have been considered as neutral, and their impact has been ignored. As a simplification, it has been assumed that corporation tax is paid at a rate of 50% on the profit before tax, and no reduction of tax due to depreciation has been considered.[2]

4. Working capital needs

The collection period is assumed to be three months. Inventories are estimated at three months of production costs (excluding packaging and transport costs) at the factory and three months of production costs (including packaging and transport costs) in the sales companies. The profitability study does not consider any accounts payable, even though materials are paid for with a three month delay.

5. Capital expenditures

The only capital expenditures envisaged are related to the preparation of the production facilities, and amount to 4.64 m DM, the disbursement of which takes place in 1993. The disbursements relating to the development of P12 were about 5 m DM, but by 1991 they are largely sunk costs. It has thus been decided to disregard them.

6. Profitability calculation

It is normal practice at BA International to calculate the internal rate of return over the first five years of the life of a new product. In 1991, even though there was no formal system of hurdle rate at BA International, it was felt that comparable projects to P12 should yield at least 14%. This yield could be considered as the risk adjusted cost of capital in 1991. Profitability is calculated for one set of assumptions and strategy. In case of doubt, the most cautious and conservative alternative is considered; this is why accounts payable are not considered. Cash flows beyond five years are also not considered.

APPENDIX F.5

PRODUCTION COSTS

When estimating unit costs of production, the engineering department envisaged these costs after the introduction phase was completed (after the production of 500 units). A new unit cost estimate was prepared at an earlier production stage (100 units). This led to a new unit cost estimate of 17 013 DM. In order to take a cautious view, this unit cost estimate was then used in the profitability study.

Unit cost in DM (1993 prices)	100 units	500 units
Direct material	12 151	11 168
Material overhead (2.7%)	328	302
Direct labour	786	786
Overhead labour	924	924
= Production cost	14 189	13 180
+ Product line cost (10% of production cost)	1 419	1 318
= Unit cost 1	15 608	14 498
+ Packaging, transport (9%)	1 405	1 305
= Unit cost 2	17 013	15 803

NOTES

1 For example if the educational campaign is undertaken, the total segment for P12 is equal to 24% (12 + 12) with a 10% price premium.

2 This is a cautious assumption, since the capital expenditures would be depreciated 50% in 1993, 25% in 1994 and 1995. The actual average tax rate for the group was about 45%.

CHAPTER 24

The Initial Model

24.1   THE ENVIRONMENT OF THE PROBLEM

The problem

In December 1991, the time had come at BA International to make the final decision about the introduction of P12 and the strategy to adopt for this introduction. Over the years,[1] a consensual strategy had progressively emerged for P12.

- P12 should be introduced.
- It should be targeted at those firms which need oil-free air, and as a result there would be no need to undertake an educational campaign.
- It should be priced at a 15% premium above comparable oil-lubricated compressors.
- It should be sold direct through BA International's selling subsidiaries.

The key issues in December 1991 seemed to be:

- Is it really worth introducing P12? Even though a strong organizational commitment seems to exist, it would be useful to check that such a move makes sense. In order to do so we should estimate the NPV attached to the decision of introducing P12.
- Have all the strategic alternatives been explored? Have these alternatives been described properly?
- Is the consensual strategy clearly superior to all the other alternatives available? If not, which alternative is the best?

Over the years BA International has developed a methodology for evaluating the alternative strategies related to the introduction of P12. This methodology is described in the case and is a series of assumptions, variables and relationships which has enabled them to estimate the volume to be sold, the revenues and costs, and the working capital needs, etc.

To make the decision, the first two steps are to make sure that we understand:

- The environment of the decision. What are the characteristics of the market? What are the alternatives for positioning P12 on the market? More generally, what are the key characteristics of the industry?
- Which financial model does the methodology developed at BA International for evaluating the decision to launch P12 correspond to?

P12

Figure 24.1 describes the market segments at which BA International aims. P12 would be the first rotary oil-free compressor in the 40–100 kW segment. Potentially P12 can be targeted at either a part of this segment, the customers who need oil-free air (niche strategy), or to the whole segment. P12's selling point would in this case be its lower maintenance costs (volume strategy).

The alternative strategies for the introduction of P12 are described in Figure 24.2.

Figure 24.2 calls for several comments.

- The diagram only shows decision nodes. This is because, if we believe the case, BA International does not seem to envisage any uncertainty, no competitive response, no manufacturing risk, etc.
- The diagram does not show any decision related to distribution. The characteristics of P12 and the need to make use of the capacity of the selling subsidiaries (downward extension) eliminate the alternative of indirect selling.
- Some of the branches shown in Figure 24.2 seem to be inconsistent. Why sell P12 at a low price when a niche strategy is adopted? Is it really reasonable to

Segment	Small < 15 kW	Medium 15–100 kW	Large 100–1 000 kW	Very large > 1 000 kW
Market size		24 000 units in 1993 5 780 units in the 40–100 kW range		
Technology	Piston Oil-lubricated	Piston and rotary (new) Oil-lubricated	Rotary Oil-lubricated and oil-free	Dynamic Oil-free
Distribution	Independent distributors	Independent distributors and direct sales	Direct sales	Direct sales
BA International's position and competition	BA is not present	BA is strong but has been late introducing rotary World-wide competition International and local firms	BA is very strong (15% market share) World-wide competition; market dominated by international firms	BA is hardly present

Figure 24.1 Market segments.

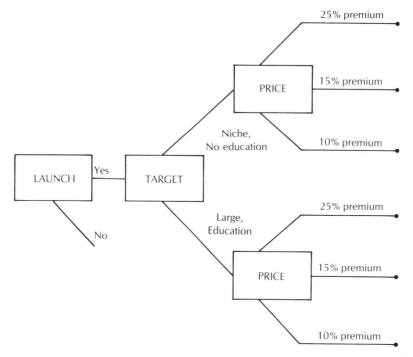

Figure 24.2 Alternative strategies.

think that P12 can be sold at a 25% premium when a volume strategy is adopted?

The industry

The industry in which BA International operates seems to present many characteristics specific to a mature industry. A saturated mass market with limited growth. Standard products with limited innovation. Well-segmented markets where service has become very important. Some production over-capacity with cyclicality. Falling profitability for manufacturers. Severe competition.

What are the implications of this for the launch of a new product like P12? In mature industries new products are not easy to find. Efforts are often more productive when concentrated on existing products. Competitors are not likely to surrender their market share. They may be ready to fight back and to engage in price wars. High quality, premium price strategies may be difficult to sustain. International competition increases and international companies try to eliminate local firms. Marketing changes and redistribution of power may occur between manufacturers and distributors. Profitability is at risk and manufacturers find it more and more difficult to create value.

We may therefore consider that the introduction of P12 is not going to be easy for BA International. Consequently, we should not expect easily to find launch strategies corresponding to big NPVs. But we should not be too pessimistic, however.[2] It might well be that P12 is the chance for BA International to overcome the problems of maturity and to reinforce its competitive position. In particular, P12 might be the chance for BA International to achieve a dominant position on the 15–100 kW segment at the expense of local competition and of independent distributors as has already happened in the 100–1 000 kW segment.

BA International

BA International is a successful firm in the industry. Its selling subsidiaries network is a definite strength when service becomes a key competitive weapon, and its price consciousness is also a strength in a mature industry. We might, however, have some worries when analyzing the available data. The company seems to perceive itself as the champion of oil-free air, but is that what the market really wants? The secrecy of the Headquarters when they introduce new products protects BA International against cannibalization but it may be unwise for the company not to take advantage of the knowledge subsidiaries have of their markets. The company also seems to perceive itself as a technology leader, but it was not the first one to introduce the rotary technology in the 15–100 kW segment, and the decision to launch P12 has taken a long time to come.

24.2 BUILDING AN INITIAL MODEL

In 1991, a consensual strategy and a methodology for evaluating it exist at BA International. Even though we may have reservations about them, let us start by building a model which corresponds to them. This will help us understand how the company approached the problem and subsequently build a systematic list of the improvements we would like to make to its approach.

When working with a spreadsheet, we shall probably build this initial model according to the following steps.

- The construction of a one-year pencil and paper model describing the 1993 cash flows attached to the consensual strategy. Such a model is shown in Figure 24.3.
- The construction of a one-year spreadsheet model of these same cash flows. The background of such a model is described in Figure 24.4.
- The extension of the one-year spreadsheet model to four more years and

	1993
Total market	5 780
P12 segment share	0.11
Market penetration	0.225
Sales volume	143.1
Unit price	33.6
SALES	4.8
Unit cost	17.0
CGS	2.4
Selling cost/sales	0.2
SELLING COST	1.0
Tax rate	0.5
PROFIT AFTER TAX	0.7
Collection period	3
RECEIVABLES END	1.2
RECEIVABLES OPEN	0.0
Inventory period production	3
Inventory period sales	3
INVENTORY END	1.2
INVENTORY OPEN	0.0
CFO	−1.7
CAPITAL EXPENDITURES	4.6
FREE CASH FLOW	−6.3

Format: the results of all calculations are shown with one decimal.

Figure 24.3 Pencil and paper model.

1		1993
2	Total market	5 780
3	P12 segment share	0.11
4	Market penetration	0.225
5	Sales volume	+B2*B3*B4
6	Unit price	33.6
7	SALES	+B5*B6/1 000
8	Unit cost	17.013
9	CGS	+B8*B5/1 000
10	Selling cost/sales	0.2
11	SELLING COST	+B10*B7
12	Tax rate	0.5
13	PROFIT AFTER TAX	(B7−B9−B11)*(1−B12)
14	Collection period	3
15	RECEIVABLES END	+B7/12*B14
16	RECEIVABLES OPEN	0
17	Inventory period production	3
18	Inventory period sales	3
19	INVENTORY END	((B9/1.09/12*B17)+(B9/12*B18)
20	INVENTORY OPEN	0
21	CFO	+B13−B15+B16−B19+B20
22	CAPITAL EXPENDITURES	4.64
23	FREE CASH FLOW	+B21−B22

Figure 24.4 Background of a spreadsheet model.

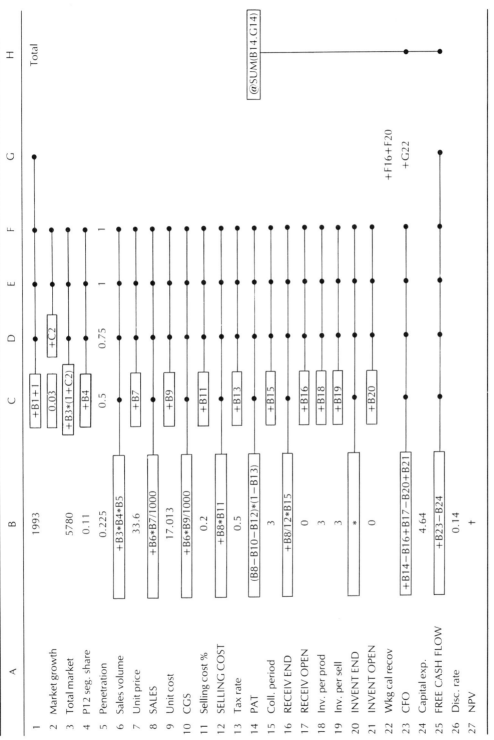

* ((B10/1.09)/12*B18)+(B10/12*B19)

† (B25+@NPV(B26, C25.G25))/(1+B26) ∧ 2

Format: total market and sales volume: zero decimals; NPV: two decimals; all the other calculations: one decimal; (tax rate and discount rate: two decimals).

Width of columns: because you will extend the model at a later stage, we advise you to fix the width of column A at 12 and to abbreviate the labels.

Figure 24.5 Building a five-year spreadsheet model.

	1993	1994	1995	1996	1997	1998	Total
Market growth		0.03	0.03	0.03	0.03		
Total market	5 780	5 953	6 132	6 316	6 505		
P12 segment share	0.11	0.11	0.11	0.11	0.11		
Market penetration	0.225	0.5	0.75	1	1		
Sales volume	143	327	506	695	716		
Unit price	33.6	33.6	33.6	33.6	33.6		
SALES	4.8	11.0	17.0	23.3	24.0		
Unit cost	17.0	17.0	17.0	17.0	17.0		
CGS	2.4	5.6	8.6	11.8	12.2		
Selling cost/sales	0.2	0.2	0.2	0.2	0.2		
SELLING COST	1.0	2.2	3.4	4.7	4.8		
Tax rate	0.50	0.50	0.50	0.50	0.50		
PROFIT AFTER TAX	0.7	1.6	2.5	3.4	3.5		11.8
Collection period	3	3	3	3	3		
RECEIVABLES END	1.2	2.8	4.2	5.8	6.0		
RECEIVABLES OPEN	0.0	1.2	2.8	4.2	5.8		
Inventory per production	3	3	3	3	3		
Inventory per sales	3	3	3	3	3		
INVENTORY END	1.2	2.7	4.1	5.7	5.8		
INVENTORY OPEN	0.0	1.2	2.7	4.1	5.7		
Working capital recovery						11.8	
CFO	−1.7	−1.4	−0.5	0.3	3.2	11.8	11.8
CAPITAL EXPENDITURES	4.6						
NET CASH	−6.3	−1.4	−0.5	0.3	3.2	11.8	7.1
Discount rate	0.14						
NPV	0.25						

Figure 24.6 Results of the initial model.

introduction of a NPV calculation. The process for doing so is described in Figure 24.5. The results are shown in Figure 24.6.

Figure 24.5 calls for two comments, one related to model building and one to the financial evaluation of strategic decisions.

- As shown in the Dhahran Roads case, profit and cash are the same in the end. This fundamental relationship is worth being tested in all financial models. It is the rationale behind the calculation of cumulated profit, CFO and net cash. *Working capital needs correspond to an adjustment of the timing of the cash flows, not to an adjustment of their cumulated value.* As a result you should always make sure that all amounts frozen into working capital needs are released in the end. This is the necessary condition for making cash equal to profit in the end.[3]
- NPV is calculated as at the end of 1991 (when the decision is made).

The results of the initial model do not portray the introduction of P12 as a very attractive move as this would apparently result in a net present value close to zero.

24.3 ANY OBVIOUS MISTAKES?

When forming a critical analysis of the initial model built according to the methodology described in the case, some questions immediately arise.

1. Is it correct to limit the period of study to five years?

At BA International they decided to limit the period of study to five years, based on the fact that cash flows beyond this are too uncertain to be considered. Even though future cash flows are uncertain, and probably more so as we go further into the future, what is the rationale behind so much discrimination between some cash flows (the first five) and the others? Why not analyze the decision to introduce P12 over the whole period during which this decision is expected to have an impact, the expected life of P12?

2. How sure are we about the timing of the cash flows?

The model assumes a 6.3 m DM cash deficit in 1993 and further assumes that this deficit is going to occur at the end of the year. What if BA International has to pay the capital expenditures at the beginning of 1993? This would obviously decrease the NPV.

3. Is it acceptable to ignore the tax impact of depreciation?

In order to exercise a certain amount of caution, BA International has ignored the tax impact of depreciation and envisaged a pessimistic tax rate of 50%. This creates a bias against the decision to launch P12 and this is not acceptable.

4. Is it correct to ignore the impact of accounts payable?

Ignoring the impact of accounts payable obviously creates a further bias against the decision to introduce P12, especially when we take into account, as in the initial model, the impact of the accounts receivable and of the inventories. This is especially true since, as indeed for P12, BA International mainly carries out assembly work. As a result of the significant value of external purchases, ignoring the impact of suppliers' credit can create a significant bias.

5. Is it correct to assume that inventory turnover will remain constant over years?

At the beginning of the life of P12, BA International probably needs large inventories (to cover the need to show the product to customers, uncertainty of demand, etc). But later it should be possible to reduce inventories to a lower level. Another problem related to inventories is the way in which we calculate them. It would be better to calculate them in relation to future sales rather than to current sales.

6. Is it correct to assimilate cgs and cost of production?

As P12 is a manufacturing project, the calculation of cgs cannot really be carried out in the same way as in the initial model. A much more accurate way to calculate cgs would be to:

- Evaluate first the total production cost. This could be done from an evaluation of the volume produced and of the unit production cost, volume produced being equal to the sum of volume sold and finished goods inventory build-up.
- Then calculate cgs as the difference between total production cost and increase in the value of inventory of finished goods.

7. Is it right to ignore inflation and currency variations?

Can we reasonably expect that prices and exchange rates will remain constant over the period of study? How does this assumption relate to the assumption relative to the discount rate? Is the discount rate used at BA International consistent with the assumption that prices will not change over the period of study?

8. Is it correct to ignore cannibalization?

A product like P12 is not going to be sold to many customers who would not have operated without a compressor had P12 not been launched. Almost all the sales of P12 will probably be made to customers who will buy P12 instead of buying another compressor. In other words, P12 will oust other compressors made by the industry, by both BA International's competitors and BA International itself. As a result and due to the introduction of P12, BA International will sell less of its existing compressors, as much less as its share of the total market multiplied by the volume of P12 sold. Consequently, we should deduct from the cash flows of P12 the cash flows corresponding to existing compressors that will not be sold due to the introduction of P12.

9. Is it right to assume that unit production costs will remain constant over the period of study?

When evaluating the decision to launch P12 at BA International, they assumed that the unit production cost will remain constant and equal to 17 013 DM. This is a cautious approach but is in strong contradiction to the data shown in Appendix F.5 of the case which indicates that, at a production level of 400 units per year, the unit production cost should fall to 15 803 DM. Since this level of production should be reached as early as 1995,[4] keeping the unit cost at 17 013 DM creates a bias against the decision to launch P12. *It also creates a bias against any volume strategy, which is not acceptable as we want to choose between niche and volume strategies.*

10. Is the sales profile during the period studied acceptable?

The sales profile of P12 which is assumed in the initial model is worth testing against the product life cycle concept. This is especially true if we consider that the period of study should be extended to ten years, the total expected life for P12. The shape of the sales profile of P12 during its life is generated in the initial model through the parameter market penetration. Are the values of this parameter correct, and in particular those relating to the last years of P12's life?

11. Is the relationship for calculating selling costs acceptable?

In the initial model, and following BA International, we assumed that selling costs were fully variable and equal to 20% of the sales in each of the years of P12's existence. If this were true, it would be nice since it would mean that when sales are low at the beginning of the life of P12 selling costs are also low. It may be quite different; BA International will probably need to make a special effort to promote P12 at the beginning of its life.

This is a mistake often made when evaluating strategic decisions. Data from past accounting records will no doubt indicate for example, as at BA International, that, *on average*, for products similar to P12, selling expenses represent 20% of the sales. Such information is not accurate enough to use to assess the decision to introduce P12 since we need to know the timing of these expenses.

12. Can risk be completely ignored?

There are at least two areas of uncertainty one should investigate when analysing the decision to launch P12. The reaction from competition and the manufacturing risk.

If BA International decides to introduce P12, its competitors may well not have an equivalent product in 1993. At BA International they consider that this is very likely and as a result do not even consider the risk that their competitors may have a similar product. This may be true in 1993 but one can seriously question the assumption that the competitors will *never* introduce a product similar to P12. In a mature industry where all firms have comparable technological capabilities, it seems far more reasonable to assume that the advantage BA International could achieve can only be temporary. If the competition does not have a similar product in 1993, it will probably develop and introduce one within a few years. The question asked should be when will it be introduced rather than if.

We should also consider manufacturing risk. P12 is a technological innovation, and whether the manufacturing of this new product will proceed smoothly or not is uncertain. This risk seems to be completely ignored by BA International.

13. Are the revenues and costs envisaged relevant?

In the analysis of the decision to launch P12 we have followed BA International in envisaging only the incremental revenues and costs. As a result we have ignored:

- All allocated costs of structure. This was made on the basis that P12 should remain a small part of the overall activity of BA International. Is it realistic to consider that introducing P12 will not change these costs? Is it realistic in the particular case of a volume strategy?

- All costs incurred on P12 before the decision is made in 1991. The development costs of P12 are clearly sunk costs but does that mean that they should be completely ignored?

- Is it correct to ignore two further effects of the launching of P12 on the company's present businesses, that with P12, BA International will reinforce its image as the oil-free air champion, which might increase the profitability of the existing products and P12 will decrease the need for BA's maintenance services, a negative impact.[5]

14. Finally (and most importantly) why not start with a global evaluation?

Even though they are not sufficient, global evaluations are a very useful starting point. The expected profit over the entire life of P12 can be estimated as follows:

Annual market volume	5 780
Number of years (5–1.5 due to progressive penetration)	3.5
Total market	20 230
P12 segment share	0.11
Volume sold over the entire life of P12	2 225
Total sales (million DM)	75
Total cgs	38
Total selling costs	15
Total depreciation	5
Total profit before tax	17
Total profit after tax	9
Profit after tax/investment ÷ 5	0.37

As it ignores working capital needs, this approach tends to make P12 look a better opportunity than it probably is. The value of this global approach is, however, to enable you to make a first and rough assessment of the various alternatives. In order to do so, you can build the simple spreadsheet model described in Figure 24.7. With the model in Figure 24.7, you can quickly generate results over the entire life of P12. If you set the year factor at 8.5 (3.5 + 5), you get quite different results:

	Niche strategy				Volume strategy			
Premium	0.35	0.25	0.15	0.10	0.35	0.25	0.15	0.10
Profit after tax	23	25	24	23	21	31	35	41

This shows that:

- In order to give a fair chance to the volume strategy, you have to study the alternatives over the entire life of P12.
- The impact of pricing seems to differ with the target you envisage. It does not seem to matter much in the niche strategy but seems to become a key variable in the volume strategy. Consequently, when evaluating volume strategies, we should be prepared to investigate the impact of aggressive pricing strategies.

	A	B	C	D	E	F	G	H	I	J
1		NICHE STRATEGY					VOLUME STRATEGY			
2										
3	Annual market	5 780								
4	Year factor	3.5								
5	Total market	20 230	20 230	20 230	20 230		20 230	20 230	20 230	20 230
6	Premium	0.35	0.25	0.15	0.10		0.35	0.25	0.15	0.10
7	P12 segment share	0.07	0.09	0.11	0.12		0.09	0.14	0.19	0.24
8	Total volume sold	1 416	1 821	2 225	2 428		1 821	2 832	3 844	4 855
9	Unit selling price	39.44	36.52	33.60	32.14		39.44	36.52	33.60	32.14
10	SALES	56	66	75	78		72	103	129	156
11	Unit cost	17	17	17	17		17	17	17	17
12	CGS	24	31	38	41		31	48	65	83
13	SELLING COST	11	13	15	16		14	21	26	31
14	EDUCATION CAMPAIGN	0	0	0	0		17	17	17	17
15	DEPRECIATION	5	5	5	5		5	5	5	5
16	PROFIT BEFORE TAX	16	18	17	16		5	13	16	21
17	PROFIT AFTER TAX	8	9	9	8		2	6	8	10

Formulas:
    B5: +$B$3*$B$4   B12: +B11*B8/1 000
    B8: +B5*B7   B13: +B10*0.20
    B9: 33.6/1.15*(1+B6)   B16: +B10−B12−B13−B14−B15
    B10: +B8*B9/1 000   B17: +B16*0.5

All these formulas should he copied across.
Width of columns: global:6, A:21, F:3.
Format: 0 decimal except for rows 4, 6, 7 and 9.
Capital expenditures are equal to 4.64.

Figure 24.7 Global evaluation of the alternatives.

24.4 WHAT WOULD A GOOD NPV BE?

As we are concerned with the decision to launch P12, any positive NPV should satisfy us, and since we know that launching P12 is not going to be an easy task we should not expect to find very big NPVs. If we find big NPVs we have to be very cautious and check out possible errors in our calculations.

We do need to know whether we should be happy with a launching strategy which results in a slightly positive NPV. We should not forget that we make the study at a very late stage, which means that a lot of money has already been spent in relation to P12 (about 5 m DM). If when evaluated in 1991, the best strategy for launching P12 corresponds to a very small positive NPV, *P12 should be launched as this will be better than forgetting about* P12, but it will not mean that the efforts devoted to P12 have been very successful. In order that these efforts should be successful in the end we need to find a strategy which generates a NPV significantly bigger than simply a positive one.

- If BA International wants to recover its development costs, the NPV should be at least bigger than 5 m DM.[6]
- If we take into consideration that in order to launch a new product a company like BA International will have explored many ideas and developed only a few, then the NPV attached to the launching of P12 should be much more than 5 m DM if BA International wants to justify its research and development activities. If one idea out of two results in the launching of a new product, P12 should generate at least a 10 m DM NPV; if it is one out of three, P12 should generate at least a 15 m NPV, etc.

NOTES

1 The process for developing P12 has been extremely long. For a more aggressive new product development process, refer to H Takeuchi and I Nokaka, 'The new product development game', *Harvard Business Review*, (Jan/Feb 1986).

2 A major problem with maturity is its unexciting nature. Firms need a lot of managerial talent to break out into a dematurity stage. Refer to D Quinn Mills, '*The New Competition*', John Wiley (1985, Ch 8, pp 145–59).

3 The modelling of working capital needs recovery as proposed in Figure 24.5 is not the only one possible. One could also model more precisely the end of the life of P12. As the company expects its life to end in 2002, production will probably stop early that year so as not to leave inventories.

4 Probably even earlier than 1995. In the initial model we assimilate cgs to cost of production and, as a result, we do not calculate the volume of production which is necessarily higher than the volume of sales, due to the need to build up inventories.

5 Which might, however, be compensated for by offering customers the option to pay for insurance against maintenance costs, a favorable deal for BA International, due to the very little maintenance expected.

6 If you consider that these 5 m DM have been spent over the past 10 years, then their present (1991) value is much higher than 5 m DM. If you assume that the 5 m has been equally spent over the past 10 years you find a NPV equal to 10 m DM.

R.T.C. LIBRARY
LETTERKENNY

BA INTERNATIONAL (B)

ADDITIONAL DATA, EXPERIENCE AND THEORETICAL BACKGROUND

1. Period of study

When reviewing the estimates of cash flows related to the decision to introduce P12, it was felt at BA International that limiting the period of study to five years was looking at the bad news only. Due to the working capital needs required by P12 at the beginning of its life, early cash flows were not very attractive. In order to make a better assessment of the decision it was necessary to analyze it over the whole expected life of P12. The memorandum sent by Mr Lefranc, the Financial Manager, is reproduced in Appendix G.1. The cash flows estimated over a period of ten years are also in Appendix G.I.

2. Inventories

After having carefully reviewed the logistics of P12, it had been felt that the inventory period estimates (in months) should be reconsidered as follows:

	1993	1994	1995 and subsequent years
Production	3	2	1
Sales companies	3	2	2

It was also felt that inventory estimates should be based on future rather than current sales.

3. Discount rate

One could consider that the 14% discount rate used at BA International in 1991 embodied a 3% expected yearly inflation.

4. Cannibalization

In order to clarify this issue, Mr Keller had further meetings with managers responsible for marketing at Headquarters. Even though the situation was different on each national market, it seemed possible to simplify the situation as follows when taking a worldwide view. The assumed segment for P12 was made up of 50% of the small firms that BA International was presently serving through distributors and 50% of the large firms BA International served through its sales subsidiaries. As far as the first segment was concerned, BA International had a 10% market share only. In this market, the contribution after tax of each compressor sold could be estimated at about 4 000 DM. In the second segment, BA International had a 13% market share and a much higher contribution per unit, about 8 000 DM. If an educational campaign was undertaken, it

This case was developed by the author and Bernard Dubois, Professor at Centre HEC-ISA (France). The pedagogy of this case has been developed by the author, Bernard Dubois, Sherwood Frey, Professor at Colgate Darden (USA) and Foster Rogers, Professor at IFL (Sweden).

would probably achieve results in both the first and second segments. Finally, no cannibalization was to be considered after 1997.[1]

5. Cost/volume relationships[2]

When analyzing the manufacturing characteristics of P12, it had been concluded at BA International that an 85% experience curve would apply to both the material and assembly costs of P12.[3]

Due to its very strong position with its suppliers, BA International would be able to reap most of their cost savings due to experience. P12 was, however, not a totally new product for the suppliers since a similar but bigger product had already been manufactured. As a result, increasing the accumulated production of P12 from 100 to 500 units corresponded to a 43% increase in experience only (it could also be considered that 830 units had been produced before 1993).

Assembly costs were also to decrease in relation to an 85% learning curve but the previous experience was larger. It could be estimated that increasing the accumulated production of P12 from 100 to 500 units corresponded to a 17% increase in experience only (or that about 2 200 units had been produced before 1993).

6. Product life cycle

After checking the initial sales estimate of P12 against the concept of product life cycle and the experience of comparable products launched by BA International in the past, it had been felt that the following penetration coefficients should be considered.[4]

Year	1993	94	95	96	97	98	99	00	01	02
Coefficient	0.3	0.5	0.7	1	1	1	1	1	0.7	0.5

7. Selling costs

On average, it could be estimated that selling costs were equal to 20% of the sales of P12. Selling costs could not, however, be considered as equal to 20% of the sales of P12 each year. Only half of total selling costs could be considered as variable, mainly salesmen's commissions. The other half of the selling costs corresponded to launching costs and were to be incurred in the first three years of the life of P12 (in equal amounts). As they corresponded to a specific intensity of selling efforts, fixed costs were largely independent of the pricing policy. One could thus assume that they would not change if the price premium were modified. Consequently, it was decided to consider only two levels of fixed selling costs; one for the situation where the educational campaign was not undertaken and the other for the situation where it was undertaken.

8. Competition

Even though it has been assumed in the initial study that no competitor was going to introduce a product similar to P12, discussions had shown that there was a chance that the main world competitor of BA International could introduce a product similar to P12. For some marketing people, that could happen as early as 1993. In this case, the market share of BA International would be equal to 0.6 throughout the period. To the others, it seemed likely that this would happen within five years (in 1998). In a mature industry, major competitors had all mastered the technology, and five years was to be the maximum time needed by the major world competitor to find its answer to P12. In this case, BA International's market share would be equal to 0.8 in 1998 and to 0.6 in the period 1999–2002.

If the major competitor was going to offer a product similar to P12, it could opt for two extreme types of pricing policy. It could decide to offer the competing product at the same price as P12, or, on the other hand, decide to price very aggressively. According to some marketing managers, this could mean a selling price never more than 175% of the cost per unit. It was also felt that the likelihood of a price war was much higher if BA International decided to make an aggressive bid for market share (educational campaign and low price premium).

9. Production risk

Production problems should never be ignored when putting a new product into manufacture. This was especially true in the case of P12 which introduced some innovative technological solutions which were not common in the industry. When this issue was discussed, one engineer reminded the committee about a previous manufacturing difficulty. SP4 had had a unit production cost 15% higher than expected and outputs significantly lower than expected. The company had expected to start with a 200/300 unit yearly output and rapidly reach 700/800 units per year, but had only achieved 25 units in the first year, 100 in the second, 200 in the third and 300 in the fourth year, and never managed to produce more than 400 units per year. However, the numerous meetings of the new product committee on P12 had convinced Mr Keller that it was likely that manufacturing would go smoothly, but he knew he must also remember the risk of the same difficulties as with SP4.

NOTES

1 For more about cannibalization, refer to R Kerin, M Harvey and J Rothe, 'Cannibalism and new product development', *Business Horizons* (Oct 1978), pp 25–31.

2 Refer to Appendix G.2.

3 Experience effects apply to existing products also. Given the large experience accumulated, the low growth and the severe competition, it was considered at BA International that the unit price of existing products would decrease by 1% per year in real terms in the coming years.

4 Refer to Appendix G.3.

APPENDIX G.1

MEMORANDUM

FROM: M Lefranc, Financial Manager
TO: M Keller,   Product Planning
SUBJECT: **PERIOD OF STUDY FOR THE DECISION TO INTRODUCE P12**

The length of the period of time to be studied has a significant impact on the net present value. This impact is shown in Figure G.I.

Duration	NPV (million DM)	Annual cash flows (the bold figure corresponds to working capital recovery)									
		1993	1994	1995	1996	1997	1998	1999	2000	2001	2002	2003
1	−3.8	−6.3	**2.4**									
2	−3.1	−6.3	−1.4	**5.4**								
3	−2.2	−6.3	−1.4	−0.5	**8.4**							
4	−1.1	−6.3	−1.4	−0.5	0.3	**11.5**						
5	−0.2	−6.3	−1.4	−0.5	0.3	3.2	**11.8**					
6	+0.6	−6.3	−1.4	−0.5	0.3	3.2	3.3	**12.2**				
7	1.4	−6.3	−1.4	−0.5	0.3	3.2	3.3	3.4	**12.5**			
8	2.1	−6.3	−1.4	−0.5	0.3	3.2	3.3	3.4	3.5	**12.9**		
9	2.7	−6.3	−1.4	−0.5	0.3	3.2	3.3	3.4	3.5	3.6	**13.3**	
10	3.3	−6.3	−1.4	−0.5	0.3	3.2	3.3	3.4	3.5	3.6	3.7	**13.7**

Notes on the calculation of NPVs:
1. It is assumed that the capital expenditures occur early in 1993 and that all annual cash flows occur at year end.
2. NPVs are calculated as of end-1991 NPVs.
   As an example, the formula for the NPV with a 5-year horizon is:

$$\left(\text{Capital expenditures} + \frac{CFO_{93}}{1.14} + \frac{CFO_{94}}{(1.14)^2} + \frac{CFO_{95}}{(1.14)^3} + \frac{CFO_{96}}{(1.14)^4} + \frac{CFO_{97}}{(1.14)^5} + \frac{WC\ recovery}{(1.14)^6} \right) \Big/ (1.14)$$

Figure G.1   Influence of the length of period to be studied.

These results call for the following comments. When the period studied is short, the net cash flows consist mainly of working capital recovery. With a horizon of five years, working capital recovery represents 166% of the total net cash flow. The value of the NPV depends a great deal on the period. With a six year period, the NPV criterion indicates that BA International should introduce P12, but with a five year period, the same criterion indicates that P12 should not be launched. As a consequence, we should not adopt any arbitrary time horizon but rather study P12 over its entire expected life of ten years. When we do so, we obtain the cash flows shown in Figure G.2. These cash flows correspond to an NPV at 14% of 3.3 m DM.

	1993	1994	1995	1996	1997	1998	1999	2000	2001	2002	2003	Total
Market growth		0.03	0.03	0.03	0.03	0.03	0.03	0.03	0.03	0.03		
Total market	5 780	5 953	6 132	6 316	6 505	6 701	6 902	7 109	7 322	7 542		
P12 share	0.11	0.11	0.11	0.11	0.11	0.11	0.11	0.11	0.11	0.11		
Penetration	0.225	0.5	0.75	1	1	1	1	1	1	1		
Sales volume	143	327	506	695	716	737	759	782	805	830		
Unit price	33.6	33.6	33.6	33.6	33.6	33.6	33.6	33.6	33.6	33.6		
SALES	4.8	11.0	17.0	23.3	24.0	24.8	25.5	26.3	27.1	27.9		211.7
Unit cost	17.0	17.0	17.0	17.0	17.0	17.0	17.0	17.0	17.0	17.0		
CGS	2.4	5.6	8.6	11.8	12.2	12.5	12.9	13.3	13.7	14.1		
Selling cost/sales	0.2	0.2	0.2	0.2	0.2	0.2	0.2	0.2	0.2	0.2		
SELLING COST	1.0	2.2	3.4	4.7	4.8	5.0	5.1	5.3	5.4	5.6		42.3
Tax rate	0.5	0.5	0.5	0.5	0.5	0.5	0.5	0.5	0.5	0.5		
PAT	0.7	1.6	2.5	3.4	3.5	3.6	3.7	3.9	4.0	4.1		31.1
Collection period	3	3	3	3	3	3	3	3	3	3		
RECEIVABLES END	1.2	2.8	4.2	5.8	6.0	6.2	6.4	6.6	6.8	7.0		
RECEIVABLES OPEN	0.0	1.2	2.8	4.2	5.8	6.0	6.2	6.4	6.6	6.8		
Inv period production	3	3	3	3	3	3	3	3	3	3		
Inv period sales	3	3	3	3	3	3	3	3	3	3		
INVENTORY END	1.2	2.7	4.1	5.7	5.8	6.0	6.2	6.4	6.6	6.8		
INVENTORY OPEN	0.0	1.2	2.7	4.1	5.7	5.8	6.0	6.2	6.4	6.6		
WC RECOVERY											13.7	
CFO	−1.7	−1.4	−0.5	0.3	3.2	3.3	3.4	3.5	3.6	3.7	13.7	31.1
CAPITAL EXPENDITURES	4.6											
FREE CASH FLOW	−6.3	−1.4	−0.5	0.3	3.2	3.3	3.4	3.5	3.6	3.7	13.7	26.4
Discount rate	0.14											
NPV	3.3											

Notes

1. These cash flows correspond to the methodology presented in the case BA International. They relate to the consenual strategy.
2. To show all the columns of such a model on one single screen, you need to set the global column width to 5 and the width of column A to 12.
3. The formula for the NPV is: (−B24+@NPV(B26, B23.L23))/(1+B26). With two decimals, the NPV is 3.27.

Figure G.2   Assessment of cash flows over the whole expected life of P12.

APPENDIX G.2

MEMORANDUM

FROM: J Muller, Production Engineer
TO: M Keller, Product Planning
SUBJECT: **RE-EXAMINATION OF THE COST/VOLUME RELATIONSHIP FOR P12**

Cost/volume relationships constitute a very important issue in management and a voluminous amount of literature exists about them in at least two areas of management, accounting and strategy.

The traditional accounting view: fixed and variable costs
In accounting, costs are traditionally analyzed into two basic categories, fixed and variable costs.

- Fixed costs are defined as those costs, the total of which does not depend on the volume of activity.

- Variable costs are defined as those costs, the total of which is a function of the level of activity.

The words fixed and variable are somewhat confusing and one should realize that they apply to total costs only. When looking at unit costs, fixed and variable costs are quite different.

- The unit cost of an item that accounting calls fixed is a function of the level of activity. Since the total cost is fixed, the unit cost is obviously low when the activity is high and high when the activity is low.
- The unit cost of an item that accounting calls variable is obviously fixed. It is because of this that the total cost is a function of the level of activity.

The concept of fixed and variable costs can be applied to P12. In the study of P12, we get the following information about the relationship between total production costs and volume:

Volume produced	Total production cost
100	1 701 300
400	6 321 200

(Data in the study actually refers to cumulative levels of production. Let us assume that these cumulative levels correspond to annual production levels of respectively 100 and 400 units.) These figures can be shown on a graph as in Figure G.3.

When you assume that the relationship between total production cost and volume is linear, total production cost may be expressed as:

$$y = ax + b$$

where y = total production cost and x = volume.
   You can calculate a and b:

$$a = \frac{6\,321\,200 - 1\,701\,300}{400 - 100} \simeq 15\,400$$

$$b = 6\,321\,200 - (15\,400 * 400) \simeq 161\,333$$

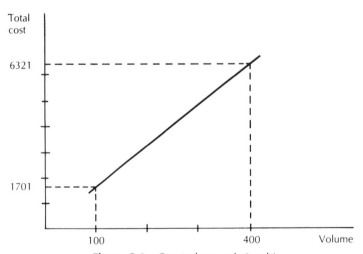

Figure G.3   Cost/volume relationship.

where a = the variable cost per unit and b = the part of the total cost which is fixed and independent of volume.

The relationship between total cost and volume enables us to derive the relationship between unit production cost and volume:

$$y = 15\,400 + \frac{161\,333}{x}$$

where y = unit production cost and x = volume.

The strategy approach: the concept of experience[1]

The distinction between fixed and variable costs fundamentally portrays the effect of economies of scale within a specific range of volumes. Within a specific range of volumes, among all the production costs some are fixed. When spread over more units, their impact is less and, as a result, the total unit cost decreases and ultimately tends towards the variable unit cost.

The effect of experience is a different concept that states that the unit production cost decreases, and tends towards no limit, when the cumulated volume of production increases. The relationship between unit production cost and cumulative production is known as the experience curve. The most popular way to describe the effect of experience is to say that: each time cumulated production doubles, unit production cost decreases by a constant percentage. If the learning rate is 80%, unit production cost decreases by 20% (100 − 80) each time cumulated production doubles.

The reasons why unit cost decreases with the accumulation of experience can be set out as follows:

- Greater labour efficiency.
- Better work organization.
- Innovative processes.
- Better use of resources.
- Better product standardization.
- Product re-designs.
  - Better performance obtained from equipment.

The concepts of experience and scale effects are not easy to distinguish since gains in experience occur at the same time as the size increases. The main difference between these two concepts is probably that the scale effect is more static and the experience effect more dynamic. The important things to realize about the experience effect are that:

- It is not automatic. Experience provides opportunities for decreasing the unit cost but these can be overlooked.
- The experience effect is difficult to measure.
  - As experience effects can generally only be observed over a long period, one should remove the impact of inflation, and also be careful with potential biases introduced by accounting measures.
  - Be careful with shared experience. A new product may benefit from the experience of products already manufactured and not correspond to a great deal of additional experience for the firm. As a result, its unit cost will not decline very quickly.
  - If it applies within an individual firm, the concept of shared experience may also apply within a whole industry.

The experience concept states that each time cumulated production doubles, the unit production cost decreases by a constant percentage. How can we express this relationship in mathematical terms? An example may help. A company has produced, as of today, 1 000 units of the A product. The current unit production cost is 10 DM. What will the unit production cost be when the company reaches production levels of 2 000 and 4 000 units, if the experience rate is 80%?

This question can be answered as follows:

	Current	Future	
Accumulated volumes	1 000	2 000	4 000
Unit cost	10	8	6.4
		(ie 10*0.8)	(ie 8*0.8)

You can define two variables:

$$X = \frac{\text{future accumulated volume}}{\text{current accumulated volume}}$$

$$Y = \frac{\text{future unit cost}}{\text{current unit cost}}$$

At present, X and Y are equal to 1. When cumulated volume doubles, X will be equal to 2 and Y to 0.8. When cumulated volume doubles again and becomes four times what it is today, X will be equal to 4 and Y equal to 0.64. When cumulated volume doubles again and becomes eight times what it is today X will = 8 and Y = 5.12. The values of X and Y can be plotted on a graph (Figure G.4).

The curve that fits the points corresponding to the points shown in Figure G.4 is not a straight line but a curve[2] corresponding to a function of the kind:

$$Y = \frac{1}{X^n} \text{ or } Y = X^{-n}$$

The steepness of such a curve depends on the value of the exponent of X. Let us try with an exponent with an absolute value equal to 1;

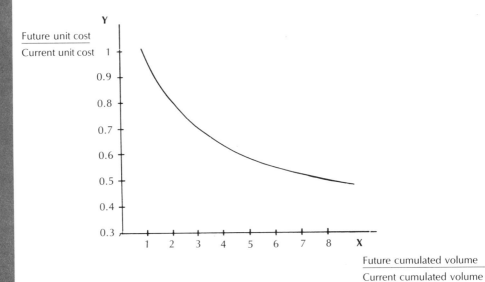

Figure G.4   Relationship of variables X and Y.

$$Y = X^{-1}$$

X	1	2	4	8
Y	1	0.5	0.25	0.125

This corresponds to a 50% learning curve, a curve much steeper than the 80% learning curve shown in Figure G.4. Let us now try with an exponent with an absolute value equal to 2:

X	1	2	4	8
Y	1	0.25	0.0625	0.0156

In order to fit the points shown in Figure G.1, and, as a result, to portray an 80% experience curve, we should assign to the exponent of X an absolute value inferior to 1. Mathematics show that in order to get an experience curve of 80%, the exponent of X should have an absolute value of 0.322.[3] In this case, the relation between X and Y is: $Y = X^{-0.322}$.

NOTES

1 For more about this concept, refer to: A Hax and N Majluf, 'Competitive cost dynamics: the experience curve', *Interfaces* (Oct 1982, pp 50–61; K Clark and P Adler (1991), 'Behind the Learning Curve: A Sketch of the Learning Process', *Management Science*, March, pp 267–81; W Abernathy and K Wayne, 'Limits of the learning curve' in *Survival Strategies for American Industries*, John Wiley (1983), pp 114–31, and PB McNamee, *Tools and Techniques for Strategic Management*, Pergamon Press (1985), pp 67–102.

2 The experience curve formula is usually presented as:

$$C_q = C_n \times \left(\frac{q}{n} \right)^{-b}$$

where C_q = cost of producing the qth unit
C_n = cost of producing the nth unit
b = experience parameter

3 The formula for calculating the exponent (n) is as follows: if ex is the experience rate (ex = 80 when learning rate is 80%)

$$n = \frac{\ln 100 - \ln ex}{\ln 2}$$

when ex = 80

$$n = \frac{\ln 100 - \ln 80}{\ln 2} = \frac{4.61 - 4.38}{0.69} = 0.322$$

Some values of n:

Experience rate	Exponent (n)
90	0.152
85	0.234
80	0.322
75	0.415
70	0.515
65	0.621
60	0.737
50	1.000

APPENDIX G.3

MEMORANDUM

FROM: L Lundquist, Marketing
TO: M Keller,   Product Planning
SUBJECT: **RE-EXAMINATION OF THE INITIAL SALES ESTIMATES FOR P12 IN THE LIGHT OF THE PRODUCT LIFE CYCLE CONCEPT**

The concept
In industrial marketing, as for consumer goods, it is widely accepted that products experience a life cycle although the exact shape and duration of this cycle is not easy to predict. The product life cycle (PLC) concept is an attempt to identify different stages in the sales history of a product to which correspond distinct opportunities and problems and therefore strategies and tactics. Although it is not possible to find in the marketing literature a universally accepted shape for the PLC,[1] one may consider that a reasonably well accepted description is in terms of the bell-shaped (annual sales) and S-shaped (cumulative sales) curves shown in Figure G.5. The curves are then divided into several stages known as introduction, growth, maturity and decline. These stages are generally related to different steps of the innovation/diffusion process.

In applying the PLC concept to a particular problem, it is very important first to specify the scope of the analysis, which may be the industry as a whole, a given segment or an individual product.

As far as quantitative models of the PLC are concerned it seems fair to say that there are very few models aimed at predicting the whole PLC. *Most models aim rather at predicting the first phases of the PLC.* Many different models exist corresponding to different assumptions regarding the process by which the diffusion of a new product takes place and the factors that influence that diffusion.

The experience of BA International
When considering the past experience of comparable products, it appears that the PLC concept applies to our products. Testing the validity of the PLC concept on past data raises a major issue, however. *Past data shows the sales history that has resulted from the management of the PLC.* When the company feels that a product is going to reach decline, measures are taken in order to sustain the sales. A company like BA International would never accept such a sharp decline in sales as that shown in Figure G.5(a). Production requirements always lead to declining products being killed off very quickly.

The approach used for estimating the penetration coefficients of P12 was that past data related to the introduction of the rotary oil-free compressors shows that cumulative sales have followed an S-shaped curve. The company decided then to try to fit the curve generated by a popular substitution model, the Fisher and Pry model, to these data. As a good fit was found, it was decided to use this model to estimate the penetration coefficients for P12.

The Fisher and Pry model aims to predict the rate at which the potential market is going to switch to a new substitute. It rests upon the assumption that the adoption process results from word-of-mouth activity initiated by the first adopters (the pioneers) and aimed at those who have not yet adopted (the followers).

In mathematical terms:

$$\frac{dF}{dt} = b * F * (I - F)$$

(a)

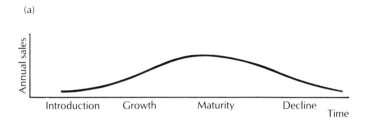

(b)

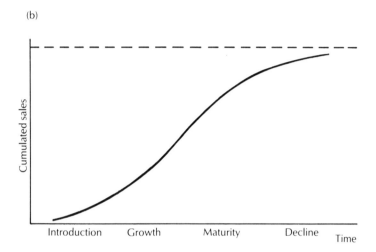

Figure G.5 Product life cycle curves. (a) Annual sales. (b) Cumulated sales.

where   F = the cumulative percentage of adopters of the new product at a given point in time
        dF/dt = the percentage of those who are going to adopt the new product at that time
         b = an industry related coefficient.

This mathematical formulation corresponds to the so-called bell-shaped curve as can be seen from the following numerical values.

F	0%	10%	20%	30%	40%	50%	60%	70%	80%	90%	100%
F*(l−F)	0%	9%	16%	21%	24%	25%	24%	21%	16%	9%	0%

This is shown graphically in Figure G.6.

When F is small (when the pioneers are few), little word-of-mouth activity can take place and the number of new adopters is limited. When F grows, so does dF/dt but beyond a certain threshold (50%), the number of new adopters decreases, not because word-of-mouth activity diminishes but because the market potential is now limited due to ceiling effects. In the end, only the laggards have yet to join the majority.

To understand more about the industry related coefficient b, let us consider again the numerical values below:

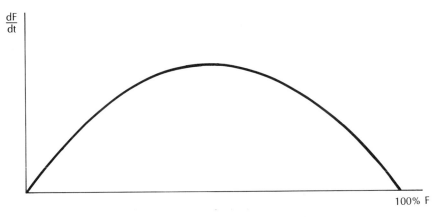

Figure G.6   The Fisher and Pry model.

F	0%	10%	20%	30%	40%	50%	60%	70%	80%	90%	100%
b=1 b*F*(l−F)	0%	9%	16%	21%	24%	25%	24%	21%	16%	9%	0%
b=2 b*F*(l−F)	0%	18%	32%	42%	48%	50%	48%	42%	32%	18%	0%
b=½ b*F*(l−F)	0%	4.5%	8%	10.5%	12%	12.5%	12%	10.5%	8%	4.5%	0%

This is shown graphically in Figure G.7.

Thus b plays the role of an amplifier or reducer of the impact of word-of-mouth activity. It is related to the tight, or loose, nature of contacts existing between companies in a given sector. In that respect it is an industry related coefficient. Mathematically, the Fisher and Pry equation can be rewritten as:

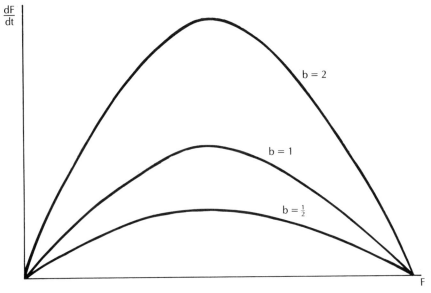

Figure G.7   Introducing b, an industry-related coefficient.

$$F = \int \frac{dF}{dt} = \frac{1}{1 + e^{-b(t-t_0)}}$$

where t = time since introduction

t_0 = time when half of the market has switched to the new product.

The graphical representation of F results in the logistic curve (S-shaped) where t_0, corresponds to the inflection point (see Figure G.8).

Generating the coefficients

The best fit of the rotary oil-free compressors data with the curve generated by the above model was found when the b parameter was set to 1.20 and t_0 was set to 2.67 (half of the potential market having switched to oil-free two years and eight months after the introduction). Using the same values for b and t_0, we were able to generate the following penetration coefficients for P12[2]:

Year	1	2	3
Penetration	0.29	0.47	0.71

It was thus decided to revise the coefficients of the initial model and to replace them with 0.30 in 1993, 0.50 in 1994 and 0.70 in 1995.[3]

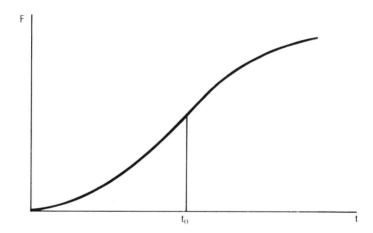

Figure G.8   Logistic curve.

The impact of the educational campaign

If the educational campaign were undertaken, the P12 segment by 1995 is supposed to become equal to 19% of the total market if a 15% price premium is adopted. In such a case the P12 segment would be equal to 14% of the total market in 1993 and to 16.5% in 1994. This progressive penetration can be considered as an adjustment of the penetration coefficients in the initial study. The implied penetration coefficients are calculated in Figure G.9.

	1993	1994	1995	1996	1997	1998	1999	2000
P12 Segment share	0.140	0.165	0.190	0.190	0.190	0.190	0.190	0.190
(a) P12 segment/0.19	0.740	0.870	1.000	1.000	1.000	1.000	1.000	1.000
(b) Penetration coefficient	0.300	0.500	0.700	1.000	1.000	1.000	1.000	1.000
Implicit penetration coefficient (a × b)	0.220	0.430	0.700	1.000	1.000	1.000	1.000	1.000

Figure G.9   The implied penetration coefficients.

NOTES

1 This is due to the fact that many authors approach the PLC issue from more a qualitative than a quantitative viewpoint. For more about the concept of substitution, refer to: M Porter, *Competitive Advantage*, The Free Press (1985), Ch 8. For more about the modelling of product life cycles, refer to V Mahajan, E Muller and F Bass (1990), 'New Product Diffusion Models in Marketing: A Review and Directions for Research', *Journal of Marketing*, January pp 1–26; R Dolan and A Jeuland (1981), 'Experience curves and Dynamic Demand Models: Implications for Optimal Pricing Strategies', *Journal of Marketing*, Winter, pp 52–62; G Lilien, P Kotler and K Sridhar Moorthy, *Marketing Models*, Prentice Hall (1992), and S Mullick, G Anderson, R Leach and W Smith, 'Life cycle forecasting', in *The Handbook of Forecasting*, S Makridakis and S Wheelwright (eds), John Wiley (1982).

2 When b=1.20 and t_0=2.67, F is equal to 0.12 in 1993, 0.31 in 1994 and 0.60 in 1995. When these coefficients are applied to the total volume sold over the period 1993–5 (1 574 units as estimated by the initial model when growth is set to zero), you get the following cumulative volumes: 187 in 1993, 487 in 1994 and 941 in 1995. The corresponding annual volumes represent respectively 0.29, 0.47 and 0.71 of the oil-free segment (no growth).

3 Following the same logic, it was decided to use the following symmetrical coefficients for 2001 and 2002:

2001	2002
0.70	0.50

Given the policy of BA International, to abandon declining products very early for production considerations, it was decided to assume that P12 would be phased out at the end of 2002.

CHAPTER 25

Putting the Model into Perspective
Correcting the Mistakes

The first imperfection we should remove from our initial model is the limitation of the period of study to five years. So let us extend the period of study to ten years and consider the model shown in Figure G.2 (see page 391) as our base model. This model corresponds to a 3.3 m 1991 NPV. We can then review each of the other imperfections we listed above and for each of them decide how the base model should be changed to remove it and see how this modification affects the value of the NPV. In this process we may discover that some imperfections do not have any significant impact on the NPV and can therefore be ignored thus keeping the model reasonably simple.

25.1 LOOKING AT ONE MISTAKE AT A TIME

1. Correcting the impact of corporation tax

In order to introduce depreciation, you can proceed as described in Figure 25.1.

---

1 Insert a row above row 13 and introduce depreciation:
   in B13: +B25/2; in C13: +B13/2; in D13: +C13.
2 Correct the calculation of profit after tax in row 15: in B15:
   (B8−B10−B12−B13)*(1−B14); then copy across.
3 Insert a row above row 16 and introduce CFE: in B16 type +B15+B13 and copy across.
4 Correct the calculation of CFO in row 25 in order to replace profit after tax by CFE in the formula.

Test You can check that you get the following key figures (with a 50% tax rate):

	1993	1994	1995	1996	1997	1998	1999	2000	2001	2002	2003
PAT	−0.5	1.0	1.9	3.4	3.5	3.6	3.7	3.9	4.0	4.1	
CFE	1.9	2.2	3.1	3.4	3.5	3.6	3.7	3.9	4.0	4.1	
CFO	−0.5	−0.9	0.1	0.3	3.2	3.3	3.4	3.5	3.6	3.7	13.7

Format: one decimal (one decimal for NPV also).

Figure 25.1 Introducing depreciation.

When the tax rate is 0.5, NPV is equal to 4.9 m DM (50% more than the base). When the tax rate is 0.45, NPV is equal to 6 m DM (83% more than base).

When depreciation is introduced, profit before tax becomes negative and as the model is built, tax becomes negative also. This is acceptable provided that the other activities of BA International are profitable, the loss due to P12 will provide the company with a tax credit which will decrease its overall corporation tax.

2. Introducing the impact of accounts payable

The procedure for introducing accounts payable in the base model is described in Figure 25.2.

---

1   Insert 3 rows above row 22; in row 22 introduce payment period (3 for 3 months).
2   In row 23 introduce accounts payable end. The formula to enter in B23 is:
     (B10+B20−B21)*12.151/17.013/12*B22. It can then be copied across.
3   In row 24 introduce accounts payable open: 0 in B24; +B23 in C24, then copy across.
4   Modify the formula for calculating CFO in B26:
     +B14−B16+B17−B20+B21+B23−B24+B25. Copy it across.
5   Finally, change the formula for calculating working capital recovery in L25: +K16+K20−K23.

Test   You can check that you get the following key figures.

	1993	1994	1995	1996	1997	1998	1999	2000	2001	2002	2003
PAYABLES END	0.6	1.3	1.8	2.4	2.2	2.3	2.3	2.4	2.5	2.6	11.2
Working capital recovery											
CFO	−1.0	−0.8	0.1	0.9	3.0	3.3	3.4	3.6	3.7	3.8	11.2

Format: one decimal

Figure 25.2   Introducing accounts payable.

The modified model described in Figure 25.2 generates a 4.3 m DM NPV, 31% more than the base.

3. Correcting the inventories

There are two corrections to make at this level.

- You should first introduce a calculation which estimates inventories end in relation to next year's sales. In order to do so you have to modify the formulas in row 20:
  · ((C10/1.09)/12*B18) + (C10/12*B19) in B20
  · then copy across
  When this is done you can check that inventory end in 2002 is zero and that NPV becomes 3 m DM or 7% less than the base, a small difference.
- You should then correct the value of inventory periods. When this is done (with the new inventory calculations), you get a NPV of 4.2 m DM, 29% more than the base.

4. Dealing with inflation[1] and foreign exchange rates

As it is now, the base model does not treat inflation in a consistent way. Prices of revenue and cost items are considered as constant but the discount rate embodies a 3% annual inflation. In order to be consistent we should either:

- Increase prices of revenue and cost items by 3% a year and keep the discount rate as it is.
- Or keep prices of revenue and cost items as they are and remove the 3% inflation from the discount rate.

Since the second alternative is easier to implement, let us change the discount rate and make it equal to: $(1.14/1.03) - 1 \simeq 0.107$. When you do so you get a NPV equal to 6.1 m DM, 86% more than the base.

The approach we used above to deal with inflation (constant prices and discount rate equal to the real interest rate) is used a great deal in practice. Among its major advantages are its consistency and its simplicity. You do need to check that it gives the same results as the alternative approach (current prices and discount rate equal to the current interest rate). In order to do so, you can modify the base model as follows.

- Insert a row above row 2 and enter inflation rate in A2 and the value of the inflation rate 0.03 in B2.
- Change, in row 8, the estimates of unit selling prices. In B8 enter: 33.6*(1+$B$2), in C8: +B8*(1+$B$2), copy across.
- Change, in row 10, the estimates of unit production cost. In B10 enter: 17.013*(1+$B$2), in C10: +B10*(1 +$B$2), copy across.
- Introduce a formula to calculate the discount rate in B27: (1.14/1.03*(1+B2))−1.
- Change the NPV calculation in order to get the NPV at the end of 1992: (−B25+@NPV(B27, B24.L24)).

When you run the model, you find the following results:

	NPV
Constant prices and real interest rate (B2 = zero)	6.7^2
Current prices and current interest rate (B2 = 0.03)	5.2

Contrary to what we were expecting, the two methods do not give the same results and the NPV estimated with current prices and current interest rate is about 22% lower. Why is this so? The two methods make the same assumption about inflation, and consider it as neutral, giving the same price evolution of revenue and cost items. But they differ in their treatment of the impact of inflation related to working capital needs. The constant prices method ignores this impact whereas the current prices method takes it into account. If this is not clear to you, you can make collection period and inventory periods equal to zero, then you will get a NPV equal to 12.2 m with both methods. You can check further that you always get a 12.2 m NPV with both methods whatever the inflation rate is (provided that the discount rate remains equal to

T.C. LIBRARY, LETTERKENNY

(1.14/1.03)*(1+i)−1; where i is the inflation rate).

The model we have just built shows that, provided there are no working capital needs, neutral inflation has no impact and consequently we can use either the real rate-constant prices or the current rate-current prices approach, as they both return the same NPV (12.2 m). *This is not totally true, however, due to the impact of depreciation* which is ignored in the model as it is. You can check what would happen when depreciation is introduced.

- Insert a blank row above row 15 and use it for depreciation.
- Correct the calculation of profit after tax.
- Insert a blank row above row 17 and use it for CFE.
- Correct the calculation of CFO to make it related to CFE instead of profit after tax.

When this is done you get the following results:

Inflation rate	NPV (with no working capital needs)
0.00	14.1
0.03	14.0
0.05	14.0
0.10	13.8

Why does NPV decrease with inflation? It decreases due to the tax impact of depreciation[3] which gives a tax shield, the value of which is fixed (since it is based on the value of the acquisition cost of the assets). As a result the more inflation the less the value of the tax shield as compared to the overall cash flows.

What, then, can we conclude? In spite of its consistency and simplicity the real-rate constant-price method somewhat over-estimates the NPV (due to working capital needs and depreciation). This over-estimation may be important when working capital needs are high. In the base model the over-estimation of the NPV seems to be sufficiently high to make us prefer the current prices current rate approach. We have to realize, however, that the base model significantly over-estimates working capital needs[4] (no impact of accounts payable, inventory turnovers too low). When you compare the two methods with a more realistic description of working capital needs you realize that the difference between them is in the range of 10%. *So let us keep the model simple and adopt the real-rate constant-price approach.*[5]

We must also consider *currency rate variations*. If BA International goes ahead with P12, it will sell this product in many different countries. The base model ignores this and assumes that all sales of P12 will be made in Germany, or, rather, that all sales made in any other country will be equivalent to sales made in Germany. This assumption is true provided that sales to foreign countries will be made in DM, which is not realistic, or that sales to foreign countries will be made in foreign currencies at prices such that they will offset any future changes in the exchange rate between these foreign currencies and the DM.

This second assumption is consistent with a well-known principle in international economics and finance, the *purchasing power parity law*. This states that *in the long run, on the average, changes in prices and in currency exchange rates offset each other.*[6]

Even though many deviations from purchasing power parity exist, this relationship is very important.

- It helps you to realize that currency exchange rate variations are not a problem in themselves. What really matters is the possible imbalance between changes in prices in the foreign currency and changes in exchange rates.
- It helps you to simplify problems such as the one we are dealing with. Because BA International is strong in its markets, we can assume that, on average, and in the long run, it will be able, through price increases, to pass on the impact of exchange rate variations to its customers.

Although when modelling a problem like the decision to launch P12 it is generally acceptable to start by ignoring the impact of currency risk and to plan as if the product were sold in the local currency, it is necessary in practice to return to the model afterwards and to reflect on:

- The impact of short-term discrepancies between changes in prices and changes in exchange rates. The purchasing power parity law is fundamentally a law that is valid over the long-term.
- The impact of medium-term discrepancies. Recent monetary history has shown that some currencies could be undervalued or overvalued over a relatively long period. Some companies have been able to build a competitive advantage from this whilst others have suffered losses.[7] The problem remains, however, to know whether or not it is possible to predict such competitive advantages. Most of the theories available today tell us that this is not really possible.

Returning to BA International and P12, let us assume as a first step that it is reasonable to consider that the purchasing power parity law is going to hold. We can thus ignore currency rate variations, an assumption which simplifies the calculations. At a later stage, we will analyze the currency risk resulting from possible deviations from purchasing power parity (this is done in Further Model VII.2).

5. Introducing a better calculation of cgs

Since P12 is a manufacturing project, the calculation of cgs cannot really be carried out directly as in the base model. First of all, manufacturing cost must be calculated. Cgs should then be estimated as the difference between manufacturing cost and increase in inventory of finished goods. The process for changing the model and getting a more correct evaluation of cgs is described in Figure 25.3.

When modified as indicated in Figure 25.3, the model returns a NPV equal to 3 m DM,[8] which is hardly worth the effort made when changing the model. It is interesting to note that total cumulated profit and cash have not changed and are still equal to 31.3 m DM as in the base model. *The cgs calculation we have introduced has not changed the total cash flows, but only modified their timing.*

---

1 Delete row 9 and 10 and introduce 14 blank rows above row 9.
2 In row 9 introduce inventory period production.
3 In row 10 introduce inventory period selling companies.
4 In row 11 introduce inventory end production.* The formula in B12 is +C6/12*B9. (Format: zero decimal.) Copy the formula across.
5 In row 12 introduce inventory end selling companies. The formula in B12 is +C6/12*B10. Copy the formula across.
6 Use row 13 for inventory volume open. Type in 0 in B13; +B11+B12 in C13 and copy across.
7 In row 14 introduce production volume. Type in B14: +B6+B11+B12−B13. Copy across.
8 Use row 15 for unit production cost 1. 15.608 in B15; +B15 in C15. Copy across.
9 Introduce production cost 1 in row 16. The formula in B16 is +B15*B14/1 000. Copy across.
10 Use row 17 for packaging and transport. The formula in B17 is:
    +B15*0.09*(B6+B12)/1 000. In C17: +C15*0.09*(C6+C12−B12)/1 000. Copy across.
11 Introduce production cost 2 in row 18. The formula is:
    +B16+B17. You can copy it across.

Test   You can check that you get the following key figures:

	1993	1994	1995	1996	1997	1998	1999	2000	2001	2002
Production volume	307	417	600	705	726	748	771	794	817	415
Production cost 2	5.1	7.0	10.1	12.0	12.3	12.7	13.1	13.5	13.9	7.3

Format: zero decimal for production volume and one decimal for cost

12 Use row 19 for inventory end, the formula in B19 is
    ((B11*B15)+(B12*B15*1.09))/1 000. Copy it across.
13 Put in row 20 inventory open; 0 in B20; +B19 in C20; copy across.
14 Introduce cgs in row 21: +B18−B19+B20 in B21. Copy across.

Test   You can check that you get the following figures for cgs:

	1993	1994	1995	1996	1997	1998	1999	2000	2001	2002
cgs	2.4	5.6	8.6	11.8	12.2	12.5	12.9	13.3	13.7	14.1

Format: one decimal

15 Use row 22 for unit cgs; type +B21/B6*1 000 in B22 and copy across.
16 Change the calculation of PAT. Type in B26: (B8−B21−B24)*(1−B25) and copy across.
17 Delete rows 30 and 31.
18 Change the formulas for inventory in rows 30 and 31: in B30 type +B19 and copy across. In B31 type +B20 and copy across.

---

* In this model we assume that inventory is related to sales planned in the subsequent year.

† This formula assumes that inventory end is evaluated at the average production cost during the year which might not be fully adequate when unit production costs change dramatically during the year. In such a case it would be better to evaluate inventory end in relation to production cost as it is towards the end of the year: ie, when the goods in inventory end are produced.

Figure 25.3   Introducing a better calculation of cgs.

6. Taking cannibalization into account

When you evaluate the impact of a new decision, you should evaluate the incremental cash flows caused by this new decision, and should account for the negative impact that this decision may have on the existing business. The process for introducing the impact of cannibalization is described below in Figure 25.4.

---

1   In row 28 introduce big firms as a fraction of total customers, 0.5 in B28; copy across (range C to F).
2   Use row 29 for the market share with big firms: 0.13 in B29; copy across (range C to F). (Format: two decimals.)
3   Put in row 30 the market share with small firms: 0.10 in B30, copy across (range C to F).
4   Put in row 31 the margin related to big firms: 8 in B31. Copy across.
5   Put in row 32 the margin related to small firms: 4 in B32. Copy across.
6   Introduce in row 33 the calculation of margin lost on existing products: type in B33:
      ((B6*B28*B29*B31)+(B6*(1−B28)*B30*B32))/1 000. Copy across.
7   Calculate new CFO in row 34: +B23−B33 in B34 and copy across (range C to L).
8   Calculate the new NPV in B35: (−B24+@NPV(B26,B34.L34))/(1+B26).

Figure 25.4   Introducing cannibalization.

When cannibalization is introduced, the NPV is 2.3, ie 29% less than in the base model.

Is our description of cannibalization correct? In order to evaluate it, we need to make an assumption about who is going to buy P12. At present, we assume that P12 will be bought by a wide range of customers among whom the present customers of BA International will not represent a percentage higher than the present market share of the company. Consequently, the impact of cannibalization is relatively small. Another assumption would be that P12 will be bought primarily by the existing customers of BA International. It might happen that any sale of P12 would replace the sale of an existing product, and then the impact of cannibalization would become much bigger, as shown in Figure 25.5.

As we do not have detailed data about who the customers of P12 might be, let us consider that our description of cannibalization is correct.

7. Introducing a more long term/strategic description of production costs

In the base model, unit production cost is considered as a constant. This is hardly acceptable since there should be some fixed costs. A better attempt at describing unit production costs can be made by changing unit production cost to 15 803 starting from 1995. This leads to a 4.8 m NPV, 45% more than the base. Since the NPV seems to be very sensitive to the value of the unit production cost, we should go further and introduce the impact of experience. The process for doing so is described in Figure 25.6.

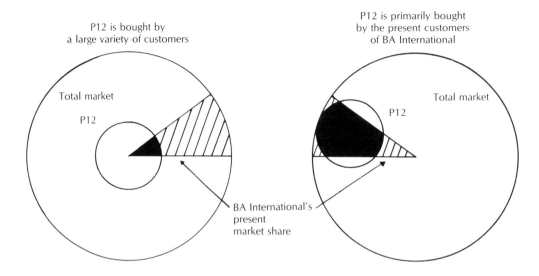

= volume cannibalized

Figure 25.5 Two models of cannibalization.

---

1 Insert 4 blank rows above row 9.
2 Introduce cumulative sales (volume) in row 9: +B6 in B9; +B9+C6 in C9; then copy across. Use a zero decimal format.
3 Use row 10 for cumulative sales at mid-year:* type +B9/2 in B10; (B9+C9)/2 in C10, copy across.
4 Introduce unit material cost in row 11. Formula in B11 is: 12.151*((B10+830)/930) $\wedge$ − 0.234. Copy across.

   Test You can check that you get the following unit material cost figures:

1993	1994	1995	1996	1997	1998	1999	2000	2001	2002
12.2	11.6	10.8	10.0	9.3	8.9	8.5	8.2	7.9	7.7

   Format: one decimal

5 Introduce unit assembly packaging and transport costs in row 12.
   Formula to be entered in B12 is:
   (17.013−12.151)*((B10+2 200)/2 300)/$\wedge$−0.234. Copy across.

   Test You can check that you obtain the following unit costs for assembly, packaging and transport:

1993	1994	1995	1996	1997	1998	1999	2000	2001	2002
4.9	4.8	4.6	4.4	4.2	4.1	3.9	3.8	3.7	3.6

   Format: one decimal

6 Change the calculation of unit production cost in B13. This should become: + B11+B12. Copy across.

---

* Manufacturing cost is an average figure for the year, consequently you should not evaluate it from the end unit cost but from the unit cost at mid-year instead.

Figure 25.6 How to introduce the impact of experience.

When the impact of experience is introduced in the model, the NPV becomes 8.1 m DM, a very sharp increase compared to the base (almost 150%).

When you have introduced formulas which describe the impact of experience, you can check that the results displayed behave as expected. You will see that unit material cost decreases quicker than unit assembly and other costs, because there is less accumulated experience for material, and that you have to wait until 1998 in order to double the experience related to assembly and other costs, and to gain 15% on unit costs. You can also draw a graph showing unit material cost, unit assembly and other costs and total unit production costs. This graph is shown below in Figure 25.7.

One interesting thing to note in the graph is the small bump in the curves in 1994. *In order to obtain smooth curves you should plot unit cost against cumulative experience and not against time.*[9]

The dramatic impact of experience calls for three questions.

- How sure can we be about the fact that experience will be 85%?
  · If it were 80%, NPV would be 9.6 m, 192% more than the base.
  · If it were 90%, NPV would still be 6.6 m, 101% more than the base.
- How sure can we be about the values assigned to previous experience?
  · If previous experience for material were 913 (10% more), NPV would be 8.0 m DM, 143% more than the base.

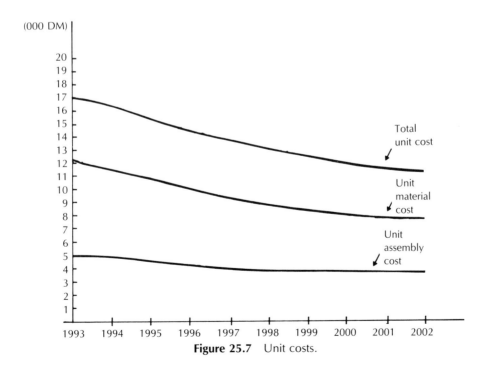

Figure 25.7 Unit costs.

· If previous experience for assembly were 2 420 (10% more), NPV would be equal to 8.1 in DM, 146% more than the base.

■ How can we be sure that BA International is going to reap all the effects of experience from its suppliers? Since BA International's operations consist mainly of assembly work, most of the experience effects are going to take place with the suppliers. In order to benefit from experience BA International will have to put a lot of pressure on its suppliers and get them to price their products along the experience curve. This is possible provided that BA International manages its relationships with suppliers effectively.

The need to take the experience on existing products into account, the concept of differential experience
The assumption in the model is that P12 is going to be sold at a premium of 15% above existing oil-lubricated products. This gives a price of 33 600DM for P12 in 1993, but if experience applies to existing oil-lubricated products, their cost (and because of competition, their price) is going to decline with the increase in cumulative volume. Therefore, in order to keep a 15% premium above these products the P12 price should follow the same evolution as the existing oil-lubricated compressors (dropping 1% per year as indicated on p 377). The company is not going to benefit from its experience with P12 but rather from the differential between its experience with P12 and that of the existing products.

In order to introduce this in the model you have to change the calculation of unit selling price. To do so, starting from the model we adjusted for experience, you can change the calculation of unit selling price; in B7: $33.6*(1-0.01) \wedge (B1-1993)$; and copy across. When you have done so, the model generates a NPV equal to 6.7 m DM; + 105% more than the base (instead of +148%).

8. Introducing a more realistic long-term profile for sales
Using the graph facilities of your spreadsheet again you can generate a curve showing the evolution of sales over the period studied. Such a sales profile is hardly consistent with the usual product life cycle concept. The case suggests that a more realistic sales profile can be obtained when making the penetration coefficients equal to the following values:

1993	1994	1995	1996	1997	1998	1999	2000	2001	2002
0.3	0.5	0.7	1	1	1	1	1	0.7	0.5

When you introduce such coefficients in the base model you get a more familiar sales profile over the long-term and an NPV equal to 2.8 m DM, 13% less than the base, so a more realistic sales profile does not have a lot of impact on the NPV.

9. Introducing a more realistic timing of selling costs over the period of study

In the base model, selling costs are assumed to be strictly proportional to sales.[10] The case suggests that this is not realistic and that selling costs are on average equal to 20% of sales but they tend to be higher than this percentage at the beginning of the life-cycle and less when maturity is reached. In order to depict this behaviour, you should modify the model as indicated in Figure 25.8.

With the new timing of selling costs, the model returns a NPV of 0.3 m DM, 90% less than the base. You can check that this huge impact is a pure timing effect; cumulative profit and cash are still equal to 31.1 m DM.

The formula we have used for calculating fixed selling costs is not completely satisfactory. With such a formula they are not really fixed, since they vary with both volume and price of sales. As suggested in the case, fixed selling costs should probably remain fixed in relation to the price premium BA International decides to adopt, but change in relation to volume. The case actually suggests that they may take two different values depending on volume, one corresponding to the smaller volume of the niche strategy, the other to the larger volume expected with the educational campaign. We will therefore have to come back to the formula for calculating fixed selling costs and change it before we start testing alternative strategies (see Chapter 27, Figure 27.5 p 429).

---

1 Introduce 2 blank rows above row 12.
2 Replace the heading in A11 by variable cost/sales, enter 0.1 in B11.
3 Introduce a calculation of total cumulative selling cost in M11: @SUM(B8.L8)*0.20.
4 Use row 12 for calculating variable selling cost: +B11*B8 in B12. Copy across.
5 Introduce fixed cost in row 13: +$M$11/6 in B13. Copy across to the range C13.D13. Erase the range E13.K13.
6 Correct the heading and formula in row 14. Total selling cost in A14. Formula to be entered in B14 and to be copied is +B13+B12.
7 Put a formula in M14 to check that total selling cost is not changed.

Figure 25.8   Introducing a more realistic timing of selling costs.

10. Introducing competition

The influence diagram in Figure 25.9 describes how BA International evaluates the sales of P12. This diagram calls for some comments.

- The size of the segment of P12 is not very dependent on the marketing strategy for P12. More precisely it ignores the alternatives available to BA International in terms of the selection of specific national and/or industrial segments. The approach at BA International deliberately ignores one key concept in marketing, the concept of *market segmentation*. Even though one may question the existence of an homogeneous market for all countries and industries, one can accept such an homogeneity as an assumption necessary to keep the problem manageable. What should be kept in mind, however, is that because of this simplification, we will only be able to derive *broad strategies* for P12 at the worldwide level. These will not be very operational as they will not tell us which specific segments should be attacked. Detailed operational strategies will be elaborated at a later stage in the sales subsidiaries. When formulating these strategies, subsidiaries will have to identify the market segments for P12 and its positioning on these segments. This two-step approach obviously presents risks since the decision to launch P12 will he taken using simplified data which may not completely reflect the complex data of the different national and industrial market segments. The role of the Headquarters is to try to limit this risk, whilst keeping the worldwide model simple enough so as not to be suhmerged in details. So let us assume that the model used by BA International Headquarters is a fairly good compromise between simplicity and accuracy.

- The penetration factor does not appear as a variable that can be influenced by BA International. Let us assume, as we have already done earlier, that this factor reflects a more general parameter related to the shape of the life cycle of P12.

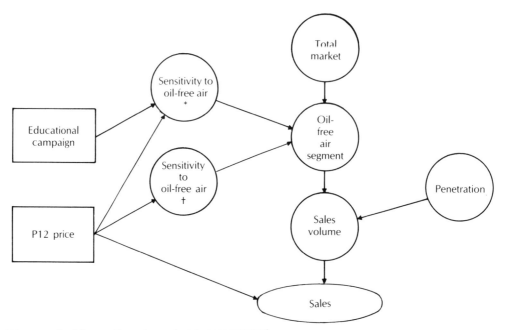

* Non-naturally oil-free sensitive customers (maintenance argument).
† Naturally oil-free sensitive customers.

Figure 25.9   Influence diagram describing the evaluation of P12 sales.

- Sales are driven by the market and not by production. This assumes that there will not be any major manufacturing problems, to which we shall come back later.
- Competition is absent from the diagram. This seems an unrealistic assumption since competition may exist as early as 1993 and in any case will start to exist in 1998. The impact of competition can be entered in the model through an additional variable, market share. The process for doing so is described in Figure 25.10.

---

1   Insert a blank row above row 6 and use it for market share: 1 in 1993; copy into range C6. F6; 0.8 in G6; 0.6 in H6. copy across.
2   Change the formula for calculating sales volume in B7: +B3*B4*B5*B6. Copy across.

Figure 25.10   Introducing competition.

The new model returns a 2.0 m NPV, 38% less than the base. This description of competition corresponds to the minimum reaction of other manufacturers, and it might well happen, as we have seen, that they offer a similar product as early as 1993. In this case the NPV falls to 0.3 m, 90% less than the base.

25.2   REVIEWING THE CORRECTIONS

Many of the corrections we have made have a significant impact on the NPV, and at this stage it is very difficult to get any feeling about what the NPV attached to the launching of P12 could actually be. The corrections made are reviewed in Figure 25.11, which calls for several comments.

- The mistakes we aimed to correct are not all of the same nature. Some of them are pure accounting or finance mistakes; one cannot ignore depreciation, consider a wrong tax rate, ignore accounts payable, take an inconsistent discount rate, calculate cgs inadequately, ignore cannibalization. Some mistakes are, however, more a result of the fact that the base model does not take a long-term/strategic/competitive view.

  Inventory turnover cannot be seen as constant over years, unit production cost should reflect experience, sales should behave according to a product life cycle, selling costs are higher at early stages, competition cannot be ignored. This suggests a method for checking for mistakes in any model you build. Check it against experience and theory; is there any violation of these? Check that the model takes a long-term/strategic/competitive view; in the long run, there are few constants and straight lines.
- The improvements we analyzed have impacts of a different nature.

	Total cumulated CFO	% Difference with base	NPV	% Difference with base
Base	**31.1**		**3.3**	
1 Depreciation	33.4	+7%	4.9	+50%
Depreciation + 45% tax rate	36.2	+16%	6.0	+83%
2 Accounts payable	31.1	—	4.3	+31%
3 Inventories				
In relation to future sales	31.1	—	3.0	−7%
Shorter delays	31.1	—	4.2	+29%
4 Real interest rate	31.1	—	6.1	+86%
5 CGS	31.1	—	3.0	−7%
6 Cannibalization	29.4	−6%	2.3	−29%
7 Unit production cost				
Fixed/variable cost	34.6	+11%	4.8	+45%
85% experience	43.5	+40%	8.1	+148%
Differential experience	39.1	+26%	6.7	+105%
8 Life cycle	27.9	−10%	2.8	−13%
9 Timing of selling costs	31.1	—	0.3	−90%
10 Competition	24.1	−23%	2.0	−38%

Figure 25.11 Comparison of model improvements.

· Some are pure timing effects, accounts payable, inventories, interest rate, cgs, selling costs.
· Some correspond to a change in the cumulative cash generated and in its timing.
■ Some improvements seem to have a very big impact (experience, interest rate, timing of selling costs) whereas some seem not to matter very much (cgs).

NOTES

1 By inflation we mean a global increase in prices which affects equally revenues and costs.

2 This corresponds to the 6.1 m DM NPV calculated previously as at the end of 1991.

3 For more about this, you can refer to: CR Nelson, 'Inflation and capital budgeting', *Journal of Finance* (June 1976), **31**: 923–31, and JR Ezzell and WA Kelly Jr, 'An APV analysis of capital budgeting under inflation', *Financial Management* (Autumn 1984), pp 49–54.

4 One comment about the dangers of modelling: the process we have followed for exploring the impact of each possible improvement (looking at one improvement at a time) could well have made us miss one of the impacts of inflation. *Looking at one improvement at a time is fully acceptable only when the improvements are independent* of one another.

5 And at a later stage you may analyze the risk resulting from possible changes in interest rate and inflation. See Further Model VII–3.

6 Key economic equilibrium/parity relationships are decribed in Further Model VII–1.

7 There are many examples of this. In the late 70s, European and US companies exporting to Latin American countries with overvalued currencies had a definite competitive advantage over local manufacturers. In Europe in the early 80s, Japanese exports were favoured by an undervalued yen. In 1984 European exports to the USA were favored by an overvalued US$, etc.

8 Which is the NPV we got when changing the calculation of ending inventories and estimating them in relation to next year's sales; more about this later.

9 You can obtain such a graph by using the X–Y type graph in Lotus 1-2-3. In order to do so, name your initial graph, cancel all graph settings, define the type of your new graph as X–Y, define the X range as cumulative sales (B9.K9), the A range as the unit material cost (B11.K11), the B range as the unit assembly cost (B12.K12) and the C range as the total unit cost (B13.K13). Then view.

10 One of the very difficult problems you often encounter when building models is the lack of information about what are the real causes or *drivers* of those costs. The accounting profession has started becoming aware of the need for changing cost allocation systems. Among the abundant literature on 'new' costing approaches and systems:

Berliner C and Brimson J (eds), (1988), *Cost Management for Today's Advanced Manufacturing*, Harvard Business School Press.

Borden J (1990), 'Review of Literature on Activity-Based Costing', *Cost Management* (Spring) pp 5–13.

Bromwich M and Hopwood A (eds), (1986), *Research and Current Issues in Management Accounting*, Pitman.

Cooper R (1989), 'You Need a New Cost System When . . .', *Harvard Business Review* (Jan–Feb), pp 77–82.

Johnson T and Kaplan R (1987), *Relevance lost*, Harvard Business School Press.

Kaplan R (ed), (1990), *Measures for Manufacturing Excellence*, Harvard Business School Press.

Monden Y and Hamada K (1991), 'Target Costing and Kaizen Costing in Japanese Automobile Companies', *Journal of Management Accounting Research* (Fall) pp 16–34.

Robinson M (ed), (1990), 'Contribution Margin Analysis: No Longer Relevant/ Strategic Cost Management: The New Paradigm', *Journal of Management Accounting Research* (Fall), **2**: pp 1–32.

CHAPTER 26

Building an Improved Model

26.1   THE CGS ISSUE

It is now time to come back to the base model and to incorporate in it the improvements we have analyzed so far. Are we going to incorporate all of them?

As discussed above, the introduction of a proper cgs calculation does not seem highly desirable since it would increase the complexity of the model but would not change the results very much. What, then, is the real impact of the introduction of a proper cgs calculation?

First, it changes the timing of operational disbursements since they become related to production instead of sales. With a proper cgs calculation, operational disbursements in early years are pushed up due to the building-up of inventories (which we also assume with our new calculation of inventory end), this being limited, however, by the increase in accounts payable.

Second, it changes the estimation of the cost of goods sold. This is not a problem when production prices are constant as in the initial model, but might be when production costs change dramatically under the pressure of experience. Before deciding whether or not to introduce a proper cgs calculation in the improved model, we should test the impact of such a calculation when experience effects are introduced.

Figure 26.1 describes how you can build two models for comparing alternative cgs calculations. The first is built from the model in which we introduced the impact of differential experience. The idea is to change this model and introduce a different inventory calculation and the impact of accounts payable. The second model is built from the model in which we introduced a proper cgs calculation. The idea here is to introduce the impact of differential experience. This results are shown in Figure 26.2.

When you compare the results of the two analyses shown in Figure 26.2, you realize that they are very close. Let us therefore decide *not to introduce a complex cgs calculation into the improved model*. Finally, you can use the first model in Figure 26.1 to test the impact of a more simple calculation of accounts payable end. To do so, you can:

I   Differential experience, inventory based on future sales, accounts payable

1   Start from the model with differential experience (the one which returns a 6.7 m NPV).
2   Change the inventory period in rows 22 and 23.
3   Change the inventory end calculation in row 24:
    ((C14/1.09)/12*B22) + (C14/12*B23). Copy across.
4   Insert 3 blank rows above row 26
    Use row 26 for payment period: 3
    Introduce accounts payable end in row 27: (B14+B24−B5)*(B11/B13)/12*B26 in B27.
    Copy across. Use row 28 for accounts payable open.
5   Correct the calculation of working capital recovery in row 29:
    +K24+K20−K27. Correct the calculation of CFO in row 30:
    +B18−B20+B21−B24+B25−B28+B27+B29.
    Copy across
    When you have done so, you get a NPV equal to 8.23 million DM.

II   Cgs and differential experience

1   Start from the base model in which you have introduced the cgs calculation (NPV = 3.0).
2   Correct the calculation of selling price: 33.6*(1−0.01)^(B1−1993) in B7. Copy across.
3   Change the inventory periods in rows 9 and 10.
4   Insert 4 blank rows above row 15.
5   Calculate accumulated production in row 15:
    +B14 in B15; +B15+C14 in C15. Copy across. (0 decimal format.)
6   Calculate mid-year accumulated production in row 16:
    +B15/2 in B16; (B15+C15)/2 in C16. Copy across.
7   Calculate unit material cost at mid-year in row 17:
    12.151*((B16+830)/930) ^ −0.234 in B17. Copy across.
8   Calculate unit assembly cost at mid-year in row 18:
    (15.608−12.151)*((B16+2 200)/2 300)^ −0.234. Copy across.
9   Change the calculation of unit production cost in B19:
    +B17+B18. Copy across.
10 Change the calculation of packaging and transport cost* in row 21; in B21 the formula to enter is:
    (B18*1.405/(15.608−12.151)*(B6+B12))/1 000
    in C21 the formula is:
    (C18*1.405/(15.608−12.151)*(C6+C12−B12))/1 000
    Copy across.
11 Insert 4 blank rows above row 23.
    Calculate end unit material cost in row 23
    12.151*((B15+830)/930)^ −0.234 in B23. Copy across.
    Calculate end unit assembly cost in row 24:
    3.457*((B15+2 200)/2 300)^ −0.234 in B24.
    Copy across.
    Calculate total end unit cost at year end production level in row 25:
    +B23+B24 in B25. Copy across.
    Calculate total end unit cost in sales companies in row 26:
    +B25+B24*1.405/(15.608−12.151) in B26. Copy across.
12 Change the inventory end calculation† in row 27:
    (B11*B25+B12*B26)/1 000 in B27. Copy across.
13 Introduce accounts payable: insert 3 blank rows above row 40.
    Introduce payment period in row 40. Use row 41 for accounts payable end. Type in B41:
    +B14*B17/12*B40/1 000. Copy across.
    Introduce accounts payable open in row 42. Change the calculation of working capital recovery and of CFO.
    When you have done so, you get a NPV equal to 8.22 m DM.

---

*   When introducing experience effects, we have considered two different effects, one for material and one for assembly costs including packaging. Because of this, packaging is no longer equal to 9% of total unit cost. To estimate packaging you can consider that the relationship between packaging and other assembly costs is kept.

†   This calculation is not fully correct as it would be better to evaluate inventory end at a somewhat lower cost, ie at the cost when goods in inventory end was produced; with the present formula, cgs is somewhat overvalued.

Figure 26.1   Building a model with cgs and changes in prices due to experience.

	1993	1994	1995	1996	1997	1998	1999	2000	2001	2002	2003	Total
Initial cgs calculation												
SALES	4.8	10.9	16.7	22.7	23.1	23.6	24.0	24.5	25.0	25.5		
CGS	2.4	5.4	7.8	10.0	9.7	9.5	9.4	9.4	9.3	9.4		82.3
Unit CGS	17.1	16.4	15.4	14.4	13.6	12.9	12.4	12.0	11.6	11.3		
PROFIT AFTER TAX	0.7	1.7	2.8	4.1	4.4	4.7	4.9	5.1	5.3	5.5		39.1
INVENTORY END	2.6	2.5	2.4	2.4	2.3	2.3	2.3	2.3	2.3	0.0		
INVENTORY OPEN	0	2.6	2.5	2.4	2.4	2.3	2.3	2.3	2.3	2.3		
PAYABLES END	0.9	0.9	1.4	1.7	1.7	1.6	1.6	1.6	1.6	1.2		
PAYABLES OPEN	0	0.9	0.9	1.4	1.7	1.7	1.6	1.6	1.6	1.6		
Work, capital recovery											5.2	
CFO	−2.2	0.3	1.8	3.0	4.3	4.5	4.8	5.0	5.2	7.3	5.2	39.1
CAPITAL EXPENDITURES	4.6											
FREE CASH FLOW	−6.8	0.3	1.8	3.0	4.3	4.5	4.8	5.0	5.2	7.3	5.2	
NPV	8.23											
Second cgs calculation												
SALES	4.8	10.9	16.7	22.7	23.1	23.6	24.0	24.5	25.0	25.5		
Production volume	307	332	511	700	721	743	765	788	811	622		
Production cost 1	4.7	4.8	7.0	9.0	8.8	8.6	8.5	8.5	8.5	6.3		
Packaging, transport	0.3	0.4	0.7	0.9	0.9	0.9	0.9	0.9	0.9	0.7		
PRODUCTION COST 2	5.0	5.3	7.7	9.9	9.6	9.5	9.4	9.4	9.3	7.1		82.3
Unit production cost	16.5	15.9	15.1	14.1	13.4	12.8	12.3	11.9	11.5	11.4		
CGS	2.5	5.3	7.8	10.0	9.7	9.5	9.4	9.4	9.3	9.3		82.3
Unit cgs	17.4	16.3	15.4	14.4	13.6	12.9	12.4	12.0	11.6	11.3		
PROFIT AFTER TAX	0.7	1.7	2.8	4.1	4.4	4.7	4.9	5.1	5.3	5.5		39.1
INVENTORY END	2.6	2.5	2.5	2.4	2.3	2.3	2.3	2.3	2.3	0.0		
INVENTORY OPEN	0.0	2.6	2.5	2.5	2.4	2.3	2.3	2.3	2.3	2.3		
PAYABLES END	0.9	0.9	1.3	1.7	1.7	1.7	1.6	1.6	1.6	1.2		
PAYABLES OPEN	0.0	0.9	0.9	1.3	1.7	1.7	1.6	1.6	1.6	1.6		
Work, capital recovery											5.2	
CFO	−2.2	0.2	1.8	3.0	4.3	4.5	4.8	5.0	5.2	7.3	5.2	39.1
CAPITAL EXPENDITURES	4.6											
FREE CASH FLOW	−6.8	0.2	1.8	3.0	4.3	4.5	4.8	5.0	5.2	7.3	5.2	
NPV	8.22											

Figure 26.2 The two cgs calculations.

- enter to B27: +B11*B6/1 000/12*B26 and copy this formula across.

When you do so, you get a 8.20 m DM NPV. As a result let us also decide to estimate accounts payable end as a direct function of cgs and not of purchases.[1]

26.2 HOW TO BUILD THE IMPROVED MODEL

You have to go back to the base model and introduce into it each of the improvements described in Chapter 25 except for cgs. Before doing so, you should think about the sequence for this.

- You start, not with the base model but rather with the model adjusted for cannibalization (NPV = 2.3).
- You can then successively carry out the following improvements:
  · Life cycle (the NPV becomes 1.9).

· Competition (the NPV becomes 0.8).
· Differential experience (the NPV becomes 3.2.).
· Inventories (the NPV becomes 3.8).
· Timing of selling costs (the NPV becomes 2.2).
· Depreciation and tax rate (the NPV becomes 4.7).
· Accounts payable (the NPV becomes 5.3).
· Discount rate (the NPV becomes 8.1).

You may prefer to adopt another approach. We will not, therefore, give you the detailed steps to take, but you will find instead, in Figure 26.3, a description of the structure of the completed model.

26.3 THE RESULTS: HOW ROBUST ARE THEY?

When you have incorporated all the improvements described in Chapter 25 (except for cgs) in the base model, you get an NPV equal to 8.1 m DM. The results of this improved model are shown in Figure 26.4.

Our previous analysis has shown how sensitive the NPV is; how confident can we be about this 8 m DM estimate? So, perform some sensitivity analysis. The results of such an analysis are shown in Figure 26.5.

What do the results indicate? NPV is most sensitive to unit price factors and especially to unit selling price. If we had the opportunity to check data and relationships further, we should give priority to these unit price data and relationships.

	A	B	C	D	E	F	G	H	I	J	K	L	M
1		1993	+B1+1										
2	Market growth		0.03	+C2									
3	Total market	5 780	+B3*(1+C2)										
4	P12 segment share	0.11	+B4										
5	Market penetration	0.3	0.5	0.7	1	1	1	1	1	0.7	0.5		
6	Market share	1	1	1	1	1	0.8	0.6	0.6	0.6	0.6		
7	Sales volume	+B3*B4*B5*B6											
8	Cumul vol end	+B7	+B8+C7										
9	Cumul vol mid year	+B8/2	(C8+B8)/2										
10	Unit price	33.6*(1−0.01)∧(B1−1993)											
11	SALES	+B10*B7/1000											
12	Unit mat cost mid year	(a)											
13	Unit ass cost mid year	(b)											
14	Unit prod cost mid year	+B12+B13											
15	CGS	+B7*B14/1000											

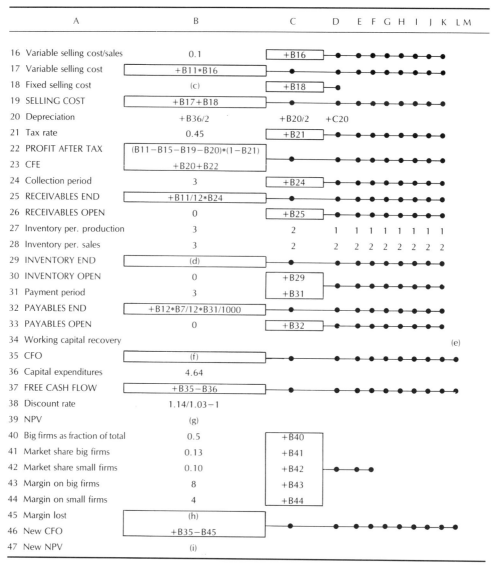

	A	B	C	D	E	F	G	H	I	J	K	L	M
16	Variable selling cost/sales	0.1	+B16										
17	Variable selling cost	+B11*B16											
18	Fixed selling cost	(c)	+B18										
19	SELLING COST	+B17+B18											
20	Depreciation	+B36/2	+B20/2	+C20									
21	Tax rate	0.45	+B21										
22	PROFIT AFTER TAX	(B11−B15−B19−B20)*(1−B21)											
23	CFE	+B20+B22											
24	Collection period	3	+B24										
25	RECEIVABLES END	+B11/12*B24											
26	RECEIVABLES OPEN	0	+B25										
27	Inventory per. production	3	2	1	1	1	1	1	1	1	1		
28	Inventory per. sales	3	2	2	2	2	2	2	2	2	2		
29	INVENTORY END	(d)											
30	INVENTORY OPEN	0	+B29										
31	Payment period	3	+B31										
32	PAYABLES END	+B12*B7/12*B31/1000											
33	PAYABLES OPEN	0	+B32										
34	Working capital recovery												(e)
35	CFO	(f)											
36	Capital expenditures	4.64											
37	FREE CASH FLOW	+B35−B36											
38	Discount rate	1.14/1.03−1											
39	NPV	(g)											
40	Big firms as fraction of total	0.5	+B40										
41	Market share big firms	0.13	+B41										
42	Market share small firms	0.10	+B42										
43	Margin on big firms	8	+B43										
44	Margin on small firms	4	+B44										
45	Margin lost	(h)											
46	New CFO	+B35−B45											
47	New NPV	(i)											

(a) 12.151*((B9+830)/930)/\ −0.234
(b) (17.013−12.151)*((B9+2 200)/2 300)/\ −0.234
(c) 4.822 ie 20% of total sales/6
(d) ((C15/1.09)/12*B27)+(C15/12*B28)
(e) +K25+K29−K32
(f) +B23−B25+B26−B29+B30+B32−B33+B34
(g) (−B36+@NPV(B38, B35..L35))/(1+B38)
(h) ((B7*B40*B41*B43)+(B7*(1−B40)*B42*B44))/1 000
(i) (−B36+@NPV(B38, B46..L46))/(1+B38)
Width of columns: global 5, A:12, M:7.

Figure 26.3 Structure of the improved model.

	1993	1994	1995	1996	1997	1998	1999	2000	2001	2002	2003	Total
Market growth		0.03	0.03	0.03	0.03	0.03	0.03	0.03	0.03	0.03		
Total market	5 780	5 953	6 132	6 316	6 505	6 701	6 902	7 109	7 322	7 542		
P12 segment share	0.11	0.11	0.11	0.11	0.11	0.11	0.11	0.11	0.11	0.11		
Market penetration	0.3	0.5	0.7	1	1	1	1	1	0.7	0.5		
Market share	1	1	1	1	1	0.8	0.6	0.6	0.6	0.6		
Sales volume	191	327	472	695	716	590	456	469	338	249		
Cumul vol end	191	518	990	1 685	2 401	2 990	3 446	3 915	4 253	4 502		
Cumul vol mid year	95	354	754	1 338	2 043	2 696	3 218	3 680	4 084	4 378		
Unit price	33.6	33.3	32.9	32.6	32.3	32.0	31.6	31.3	31.0	30.7		
SALES	6.4	10.9	15.5	22.7	23.1	18.8	14.4	14.7	10.5	7.6		145
Unit material cost mid year	12.2	11.5	10.7	10.0	9.3	8.9	8.6	8.4	8.2	8.1		
Unit assembly cost mid year	4.9	4.7	4.6	4.4	4.2	4.1	4.0	3.9	3.8	3.8		
Unit prod cost mid year	17.0	16.2	15.3	14.4	13.5	13.0	12.6	12.3	12.1	11.9		
CGS	3.2	5.3	7.2	10.0	9.7	7.6	5.7	5.8	4.1	3.0		62
Variable selling cost/sales	0.1	0.1	0.1	0.1	0.1	0.1	0.1	0.1	0.1	0.1		
Variable selling cost	0.6	1.1	1.6	2.3	2.3	1.9	1.4	1.5	1.0	0.8		
Fixed selling cost	4.8	4.8	4.8									
SELLING COST	5.5	5.9	6.4	2.3	2.3	1.9	1.4	1.5	1.0	0.8		29
Depreciation	2.3	1.2	1.2									
Tax rate	0.45	0.45	0.45	0.45	0.45	0.45	0.45	0.45	0.45	0.45		
PROFIT AFTER TAX	−2.5	−0.8	0.4	5.7	6.1	5.1	4.0	4.1	2.9	2.1		27
CFE	−0.2	0.3	1.6	5.7	6.1	5.1	4.0	4.1	2.9	2.1		32
Collection period	3	3	3	3	3	3	3	3	3	3		
RECEIVABLES END	1.6	2.7	3.9	5.7	5.8	4.7	3.6	3.7	2.6	1.9		
RECEIVABLES OPEN	0.0	1.6	2.7	3.9	5.7	5.8	4.7	3.6	3.7	2.6		
Inventory period prod	3	2	1	1	1	1	1	1	1	1		
Inventory period sales	3	2	2	2	2	2	2	2	2	2		
INVENTORY END	2.5	2.3	2.4	2.4	1.9	1.4	1.4	1.0	0.7	0.0		
INVENTORY OPEN	0.0	2.5	2.3	2.4	2.4	1.9	1.4	1.4	1.0	0.7		
Payment period	3	3	3	3	3	3	3	3	3	3		
PAYABLES END	0.6	0.9	1.3	1.7	1.7	1.3	1.0	1.0	0.7	0.5		
PAYABLES OPEN	0.0	0.6	0.9	1.3	1.7	1.7	1.3	1.0	1.0	0.7		
Working capital recovery											1.4	
CFO	−3.8	−0.2	0.6	4.5	6.4	6.3	4.7	4.4	4.0	3.4	1.4	32
CAPITAL EXPENDITURES	4.6											
FREE CASH FLOW	−8.4	−0.2	0.6	4.5	6.4	6.3	4.7	4.4	4.0	3.4	1.4	27
Discount rate	0.11											
NPV	9.1											
Big firms as fraction of total	0.5	0.5	0.5	0.5	0.5							
Market share big firms	0.13	0.13	0.13	0.13	0.13							
Market share small firms	0.10	0.10	0.10	0.10	0.10							
Margin on big firms	8.0	8.0	8.0	8.0	8.0							
Margin on small firms	4.0	4.0	4.0	4.0	4.0							
Margin lost	0.1	0.2	0.3	0.5	0.5							2
New CFO	−3.9	−0.4	0.3	4.0	5.9	6.3	4.7	4.4	4.0	3.4	1.4	30
New NPV	8.1											

Figure 26.4   Results of the improved model.

The 8 m DM result seems, however, fairly robust. P12 should be launched and this decision should allow BA International to do better than just recoup its development cost.

One thing to note is that the same sensitivity analysis would have given different results if performed earlier. If performed, for example, on the initial model, a sensitivity analysis would have shown that NPV was extremely sensitive to unit price estimates *and generally very sensitive to changes in any parameter.* We actually had a chance of seeing this when working on improving the initial model.

	% change	NPV at 10.6%	% change/ base NPV
Base		**8.1**	
Market size	+10%	10.0	+24%
	−10%	6.2	−23%
Growth	+10%	8.3	+3%
	−10%	7.8	−3%
P12 segment size	+10%	10.0	+24%
	−10%	6.2	−23%
Sales price	+10%*	11.7	+45%
	−10%	4.4	−45%
Unit production cost	+10%†	6.2	−24%
	+10%	9.9	+24%
Unit production cost	90% learning curve‡	6.8	−16%
	80% learning curve§	9.3	+16%
Unit production cost	10% more previous experience	7.9	−2%
	10% less previous experience	8.3	+3%
Variable selling cost	+10%	7.6	−5%
	−10%	8.5	+5%
Fixed selling cost	+10%	7.5	−7%
	−10%	8.6	+7%
Tax rate	+10%	7.1	−12%
	−10%	9.0	+12%
Collection period	+10%	7.9	−2%
	−10%	8.2	+2%
Capital expenditures	+10%	7.8	−3%
	−10%	8.3	+3%
Discount rate	+10%	7.1	−12%
	−10%	9.1	+13%
Margins cannibalized	+10%	7.9	−1%
	−10%	8.2	+1%
Life duration**	11 years	9.3	+16%
	9 years	7.1	−11%

* 37.0, ie 33.6*1.1 in 1993; then minus 1% each year.

† Unit costs at a cumulative production level of 100 are increased by 10%: (12.151 × 1.1) for material and (4.862 × 1.1) for other costs.

‡ With a 90% learning curve, total production cost is equal to 66.43 million DM, ie about 8% more than the base. (The exponent is −0.152, see p 395).

§ With an 80% learning curve, total production cost is equal to 57 million DM, ie about 8% less than the base. (The exponent is −0.322, see p 395).

** To extend the life by one year, you can insert a column on the left of column I and copy the range H1.H46 into I1.J1.

Figure 26.5 Sensitivity analysis.

NOTE

1 Even though accounts payable are directly related to purchases and not to cgs, it is often a good idea to model them in relation to cgs as:

· Estimating accounts payable in relation to purchases makes you assume that purchases are equally spread over the year which is not necessarily valid (see the analysis of Delta Metal pp 88 and 134).
· Estimating the exact value of purchases is difficult due to the fact that cgs and inventories may have different material components.

CHAPTER 27

Making the Model Work for Us

Having built a reasonably good model is nice, but not enough. We do not build models for the sake of having them, but to use them for analyzing alternatives. Let us go back to Figure 24.2 (page 376). As it is, the model can help us evaluate the end points of the diagram, but this would require a great deal of manipulation especially if we introduce competition and manufacturing risks. So why do we not think first about how we actually want to use the model and then try to make it easier to use.

27.1 IMPROVING THE ABILITY OF THE MODEL TO TEST TARGETING AND PRICING DECISIONS

The impact of targeting and pricing decisions can be shown with the influence diagram in Figure 27.1.

Pricing and segment size

Data in the case BA International (A) suggests the following relationship between the price premium and the size of the oil-free segment:

Price premium	10	15	25	35
Segment size	12	11	9	7

The data can be shown on a graph, as in Figure 27.2.

Figure 27.2 suggests that a linear relationship exists between price premium and segment size. This relationship corresponds to the following equation:

$$x = -0.2y + 14$$

where x = segment size and y = price premium.

Identifying such a relationship may prove very useful for testing different pricing strategies. We can now test the impact of more than four price premiums and in particular explore the impact of extreme pricing strategies.

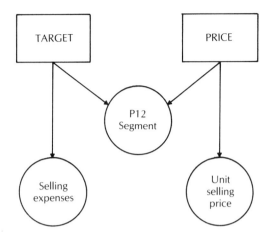

Figure 27.1 Impact of targeting and pricing decisions.

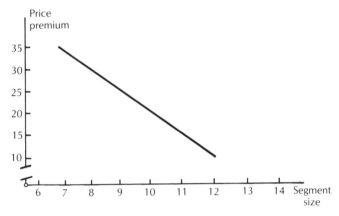

Figure 27.2 Price premium and segment size without education campaign.

Price, segment size and education

When the educational campaign is undertaken, the data suggests the following relationship between the price premium and the size of the *additional* segment (in 1995):

Price premium	10	15	25	3
Additional segment size	12	8	5	2

This data can also be shown on a graph as in Figure 27.3.

Figure 27.3 suggests the existence of a turning point which corresponds to a 15% price premium. If this is true and if there is no other turning point in the relationship between the price premium and the segment size, then BA

International cannot expect to capture more than 34% of the market with P12: 14% for the oil-sensitive customers and 20% for all the other customers.

This somewhat contradicts the intuitive idea one may have about P12. As P12 is a better product than the existing ones (lower maintenance costs), all customers should theoretically buy it if it is sold at no premium. The issue is more complex, however, since it might be unrealistic to envisage that BA International could achieve a monopolistic position on a worldwide segment in such a market. There are, however, many local competitors still in the segment, and maybe, with P12, or a P12-like product, BA International, or BA International and its worldwide competitor, could gain a substantial market share over local competition. If you consider this a real possibility, then the 34% maximum seems a bit pessimistic.[1] Let us, however, assume for the time being that this 34% maximum is acceptable and therefore that the relationship shown in Figure 27.3 is realistic.

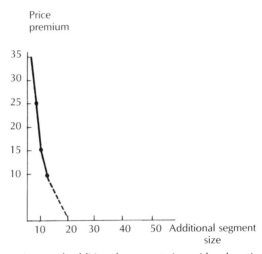

Figure 27.3   Price premium and additional segment size with educational campaign.

The problem of the first two years

We have now the following relationships between price premium and P12 segment size.

No educational campaign
$$x = -0.2y + 14$$

Educational campaign
If $y < 15$
$$x = -0.2y + 14 + (-0.8y + 20)$$
If $y > 15$
$$x = -0.2y + 14 + (-0.3y + 12.5)$$

where x = segment size and y = price premium.

These two relationships are valid for the period 1995–2002 but not for the first two years. As indicated in BA International (A), the impact of the educational campaign is not immediate, and, for example, when a 15% price premium is selected, the segment size is 14 in 93, 16.5 in 94 and only reaches 19 in 1995. This corresponds to the following sizes for the additional segment:

1993	1994	1995
3	5.5	8

Let us assume that whatever the price premium is, the relationship between the sizes of the additional segment in 1993, 1994 and 1995 is kept. Consequently, the sizes of the segments in 1993 and 1994 will be:

$$\text{Size of segment in 1993} = (\text{size of segment in 95}) * \frac{3}{8}$$

$$\text{Size of segment in 1994} = (\text{size of segment in 95}) * \frac{5.5}{8}$$

The relationships between price premium and P12 segment size therefore become those shown in Figure 27.4.

No educational campaign
  $x = -0.2y + 14$

Educational campaign

	1993	1994	1995 and afterwards
$y < 15$	$x = -0.2y + 14$	$x = -0.2y + 14$	$x = -0.2y + 14$
	$+ \frac{3}{8}(-0.8y + 20)$	$+ \frac{5.5}{8}(-0.8y + 20)$	$+(-0.8y + 20)$
$y > 15$	$x = -0.2y + 14$	$x = -0.2y + 14$	$x = -0.2y + 14$
	$+ \frac{3}{8}(-0.3y + 12.5)$	$+ \frac{5.5}{8}(-0.3y + 12.5)$	$+(-0.3y + 12.5)$

Figure 27.4 Relationships between price premium and P12 segment size.

Modifying the model

To make the test of the impact of alternative targeting and pricing decisions easy, you can add to the model two new parameters which will drive the model.

- The first parameter will be the educational campaign, to which we will assign only two values:
  · 1 for situations when the campaign is not undertaken.

· 2 for situations when the campaign is undertaken.
- The second parameter will be the price premium. This parameter will take any value and will drive both segment size and selling price.

To see the outcome variable, the NPV, which is presently at the bottom of the model, easily, you can display it near to the value of the key parameters which drive the model. You can not only show the NPV but also some other key intermediate variables, NPV before cannibalization and total cash.

Impact of the campaign on the selling costs

If BA International decides to target P12 at a wider market and consequently to undertake an educational campaign, then fixed selling costs will be higher. 8.5 m DM will have to spent in 1992 and 1993. This will come as an addition to fixed selling costs. Fixed selling costs as they are presently specified in the model will also increase due to a larger target requiring a higher level of commercial effort. At present, fixed selling costs are estimated at 4.822 m in 1993, 1994 and 1995 when there is no educational campaign (and this is true whatever the price premium). We shall calculate later the level of fixed selling costs which corresponds to the level of commercial effort needed for reaching a wider target.

Improving the model

To test the impact of alternative targeting and pricing strategies easily, you can modify the model as described below in Figure 27.5. The results are shown in Figure 27.6.

- When there is no educational campaign the final outcome is not very sensitive to the price premium but a price premium equal to 15% (or a bit less)[2] seems to be the best.
- When the educational campaign is undertaken, there is a strong argument in favor of a very low price premium.
- The strategy corresponding to the educational campaign and a very low price premium seems to dominate the others.[3]

27.2 IMPROVING THE ABILITY OF THE MODEL TO TEST THE IMPACT OF COMPETITION

The impact of competition is easier to test if we introduce two additional variables:

1 Insert 3 blank rows above row 1.
2 Type in A1: Educational campaign, no = 1, yes = 2.
3 Type in F1: 2.
4 Type in A2: premium.
5 Type in B2: 15; type in C2: + B2 and copy across.
6 Type in A3: NPV; type in B3: + B50; in D3: NPV before cannibalization; in H3: +B42; in I3: Total cash; in L3: +M49−B39.
7 Change the calculation of P12 segment share in row 7; in B7 type:
   (−0.2*B2+14+@IF(F=2,3/8*@IF(B2<15, −0.8*B2+20, −0.3*B2+12.5),0))/100
   in C7 type:
   (−0.2*C2+14+@IF($F$1=2,5.5/8*@IF(C2<15, −0.8*C2+20, −0.3*C2+12.5),0))/100
   or copy the content of B7 into C7 and change 3 to 5.5
   in D7 type:
   (−0.2*D2+14+@IF($F$1=2, @IF(D2<15, −0.8*D2+20, −0.3*D2+12.5),0))/100
   or copy the content of C7 into D7 and erase 5.5/8*
8 Copy the content of D7 into the range E7.K7.
   Tests: Now check that P12 segment share is equal to:

1993	1994	1995	1996	1997	1998	1999	2000	2001	2002
0.14	0.17	0.19	0.19	0.19	0.19	0.19	0.19	0.19	0.19

Also check that with educational campaign (F1=2) and a price premium equal to 0(B2=0), P12 segment share is equal to:

1993	1994	1995	1996	1997	1998	1999	2000	2001	2002
0.21	0.28	0.34	0.34	0.34	0.34	0.34	0.34	0.34	0.34

9 Change the price calculation in row 13: in B13 type:
   (33.6*(1−0.01)/\(B4−1993))/1.15*(1+B2/100)
   Copy the content of B13 across.
10 Calculate the amount of fixed selling cost with the educational campaign and a price premium of 15: when you set F1 to 2 and B2 to 15 you realize that annual fixed selling cost is equal to 8.149 m DM.
11 Change the calculation of fixed selling costs in row 21; type in B21: @IF(F1=1,4.822,8.149+8.5).
   Half of the educational campaign budget is spent in 1993. Type in C21:
   @IF($F$1=1,4.822,8.149)
   Copy the content of C21 into D21.
12 Change the calculation of the NPVs to introduce the educational campaign in 1992: you should have after that:
   In B42:
   ((−B39+@NPV(B41,B38.L38))/(1+B41))−@IF(F1=1,0,8.5*(1−B24)/(1+B41))
   Check the computer returns 11.1 m DM
   In B50:
   ((−B39+@NPV(B41,B49.L49))/(1+B41))−@IF(F1=1,0,8.5*(1−B24)/(1+B41))
   Check the computer returns 9.3 m DM
13 Change the calculation of total cash in L3:
   +M49−B39−@IF(F1=1,0,8.5*(1−B24))
   Check that the computer returns a total net cash of 39.7 m DM

Width of columns: B, H and L:6

Figure 27.5 Introducing two new parameters.

- A variable describing the date of entry of competition; we can assign two values to this:
  1 for a late entry (1998) of competition.
  2 for an early entry (1993) of competition.
- A variable describing the pricing policy of competition; we can also assign two values here:

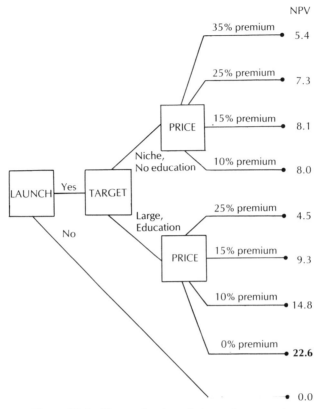

Figure 27.6   First evaluation of alternative strategies.

1 when competition adopts a conservative pricing policy.
2 when competition adopts an aggressive pricing policy. In this case BA
   International is obliged to follow competition, and selling price is never
   more than 1.75 times the unit cost. Let us assume that such a situation can
   only occur if BA International itself pursues an aggressive strategy (ie
   undertakes the educational campaign), and when competition enters early
   (ie in 1993). The process for introducing these two new variables is
   described below in Figure 27.7. The results are shown in Figure 27.8.

Returning to cannibalization

Should we always consider the NPV after cannibalization? This is acceptable
when competition enters late, but may be not when competition enters as early
as 1993: if competition enters in 1993 our existing products will probably be
attacked by competition and launching P12 would cause no further reduction
of their sales, so why not consider NPV before cannibalization for all situations
which correspond to early entry of competition.

1   Start from the model in Figure 27.5 and introduce two blank rows above row 3.
2   In A3 type: entry of competition 1 = 1998, 2 = 1993; in F3 type 2.
3   In A4 type: comp. pricing pol. 1 = cons, 2 = agg; in F4 type 2.
4   Change the calculation of market share in row 11:
      in B11 type: @IF($F$3=2,0.6,1)
      copy into range C11.F11
      in G11 type: @IF($F$3=2,0.6,0.8)

      Test   You can check that when there is no educational campaign and a 15% price premium
            NPV is equal to 2.9 m DM when competition enters in 1993.

5   Introduce a row above row 16. In A16 type: competitive price
      In B16 type:
      @IF($F$1=1,B15,@IF($F$3=1,B15,@IF($F$4=1,B15,@IF(B15<1.75*B20,B15,1.75*B20)))).
      Copy across.

      Test   You can check that where the educational campaign is undertaken, a premium of 15% is selected,
      competition enters in 1993 and follows an aggressive pricing policy, competitive prices are:

1993	1994	1995	1996	1997	1998	1999	2000	2001	2002
29.9	28.7	27.0	25.3	23.7	22.6	21.7	20.9	20.3	20.0

6   Change the calculation of sales in row 17: in B17 type:
      +B12*B16/100 and copy across.
      Test   You can check that when the educational campaign is undertaken, a premium of 15% is selected,
            competition enters in 1993 and follows an aggressive pricing policy, NPV is equal to −11.3 m DM.

Figure 27.7   Improving the ability of the model to test the impact of competition.

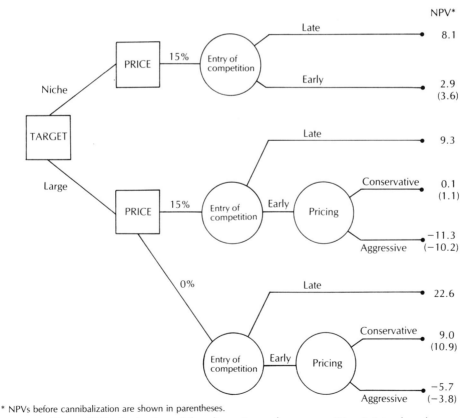

* NPVs before cannibalization are shown in parentheses.

Figure 27.8   Evaluation of the alternatives when competition is introduced.

27.3   INTRODUCING PRODUCTION RISK[4]

In our model, sales are always driven by the market which is acceptable provided that there are no production problems. If there are, sales would no longer be driven by the market, but by production capacity instead. We do not have any estimate of what the maximum production volumes could be in the case of production difficulties. The only thing we can do is extrapolate from the experience of SP4 as described in BA International (B) case. Let us therefore assume that in case of production problems, the maximum volumes produced would be as follows:

1993	1994	1995	1996	1997	1998	1999	2000	2001	2002
25	100	200	300	400	400	400	400	400	400

Another problem is to account for the increase in unit cost. Again we have little data for doing so. In our model, however, we calculate unit production cost as a function of cumulative production. Let us assume that this relationship would adequately reflect the increase in unit production cost when manufacturing problems occur.

The final problem with production difficulties is to know whether such difficulties can occur at BA International only, or at BA International and its competitor as well. In the latter case there is no risk of the competitor engaging in a price war while BA International is struggling with its production problems. In the former case the competitor may well take advantage of its ability to produce large volumes with no manufacturing difficulties to engage in a price war that would affect BA International when it is unable to produce P12 at a competitive price. The process for changing the model to evaluate situations with manufacturing problems is described below in Figure 27.9.

27.4   FINALIZING THE PRESENTATION OF THE MODEL

We now have a model which adequately describes the impact of the decision to launch P12 and enables us easily to test the various options related to this decision. We can at this stage carry out a last modification which will improve the presentation of the model. To do so:

− Insert four blank rows above row 1.
− Insert seven blank rows above row 10.
− Insert three blank rows above row 18.
− Type in titles:
  · Decision and environment variables
  · Outcomes

1 Start from the model in Figure 27.7 and introduce a blank row above row 5. In A5 type production problems, yes = 2, no = 1; in F5 type 2.
2 Insert two blank rows above row 13. In A13 type: theoretical sales volume. In B13 type: +B9*B10*B11*B12, and copy across.
3 In A14 type: volume if prod. problems. Enter the following values in row 14: 25 in B14, 100 in C14, 200 in D14, 300 in E14, 400 in the range F14.K14.
4 Change the calculation of sales volume in B15: @IF($F$5=1,B13,B14). Copy across.
5 Insert a row above row 18. Type in A18: price with aggressive competition. Enter the following values in row 18:

	B18	C18	D18	E18	F18	G18	H18	I18	J18	K18
	29.94	28.70	27.04	25.25	23.74	22.59	21.66	20.89	20.32	19.95

6 Change the calculation of competitive price in row 20.
Change the formula in B20:
@IF($F$5=2#AND#$F$3=2#AND#$F$4=2,B18,@IF($F$1=1−the rest unchanged except for an additional close the parenthesis at the end. Copy across.

Test Check the model returns a 0.8 NPV (with no educational campaign, 15% price premium and 1998 entry of competition).

Figure 27.9 Adapting the model to test production risk.

DECISION AND ENVIRONMENT VARIABLES

Educational campaign no = 1, yes 2				1						
Premium	15	15	15	15	15	15	15	15	15	15
Entry of competition 1 = 1998, 2 = 93				1						
Comp pricing policy 1 = Cons, 2 = Agg				1						
Production problems 2 = yes, 1 = no 1				1						

OUTCOMES

NPV 8.1   NPV before cannibalization 9.1   Total cash 25.4

Figure 27.10 Control panel with key parameters and outcomes.

You can have, as shown in Figure 27.10, a summary on top of your model and you can concentrate on this summary when testing alternative strategies. A further step would be to protect the model except for the decision and environment variables.

NOTES

1 From the data in the case, you can very well assume that the turning point is somewhere between a 10% and a 15% premium. As it seems unrealistic to imagine that BA International or even BA International and its world competitor could completely eradicate local competition, let us consider graph b as more realistic than graph a. Let us further assume that it is impossible for international companies to gain a market share higher than 70%, which means that the maximum additional segment size could be equal to 70 − 14 = 56%.

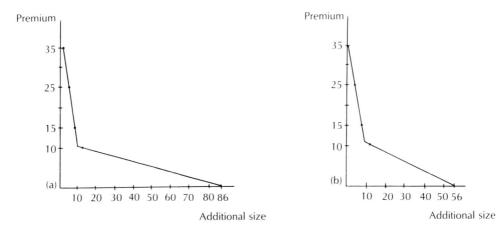

2 If you try different price premiums, you get the highest NPV for a 13% price premium. Let us not try to make the model say too much and let us accept the idea that a 15% price premium is adequate if we go for a niche strategy.

3 This would be even more true had we assumed a more optimistic relationship between price premium and market share (see note 1 above). When you assume that the educational campaign and a zero price premium would enable BA International to capture 70% of the segment, then the NPV is as high as 79 m DM.

4 Another risk is currency risk. For an analysis of this issue, refer to Further Model VII.2.

CHAPTER 28

Deciding about the New Product

28.1 MAKING A DECISION

You may feel that the time has come for us to make a decision about the launching of P12. This feeling is justified since it seems that we now know enough to make a well-argued decision. When you run the model we built, you get the results shown in Figure 28.1.

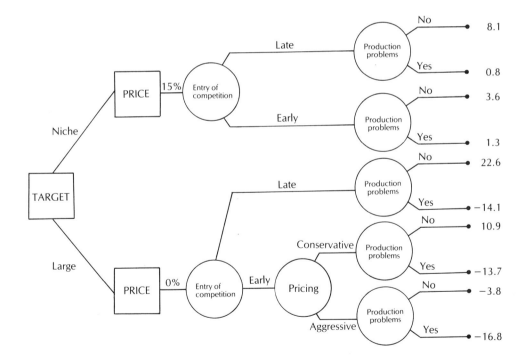

Figure 28.1 Evaluation of alternatives.

What shall we decide?

It seems that we have two basic options.

- Niche strategy with a standard price premium, the consensual strategy which emerged at BA International.
- Volume strategy with no price premium.

The first strategy appears to be less risky than the second one, but is it really

	A	B	C	D	E	F	G
1	Probability late entry					0.8	
2	Probability conservative pricing (large target)					0.5	
3	Probability no production problems.					0.9	
4							
5	EXPECTED NPV NICHE STRATEGY					7	
6	EXPECTED NPV LARGE TARGET					16	
7							
8							
9							
10	**NICHE STRATEGY**						EXPECTED
11	Probability late entry	0.8			NPV		NPV
12	Probability no production problems		0.9	0.72	8.1	5.832	
13	Probability production problems		0.1	0.08	0.8	0.064	
14	Probability early entry	0.2					
15	Probability no production problems		0.9	0.18	3.6	0.648	
16	Probability production problems		0.1	0.02	1.3	0.026	**6.57**
17	**LARGE TARGET**						
18	Probabillty late entry	0.8					
19	Probability no production problems		0.9	0.72	22.6	16.272	
20	Probability production problems		0.1	0.08	−14.1	−1.128	
21	Probability early entry	0.2					
22	Probability no production problems		0.9				
23	Probability conservative pricing		0.5	0.09	10.9	0.981	
24	Probability aggressive pricing		0.5	0.09	−3.8	−0.342	
25	Probability production problems		0.1	0.02	−13.7	−0.274	**15.5**

Formulas

F1:	U[W7]0.8	D15:	+C15*B14	F20:	[W7]+D20*E20
F2:	U[W7]0.5	E15:	[W6] 3.6	B21:	[W6]+B14
F3:	U[W7]0.9	F15:	[W7]+D15*E15	C22:	+C15
F5:	(F0)[W7]+G16	C16:	+$C$13	C23:	+F2
F6:	(F0)[W7]+G25	D16:	+C16*B14	D23:	+C23*C22*B21
B11:	[W6]+F1	E16:	[W6] 1.3	E23:	[W6]+10.9
C12:	+F3	F16:	[W7]+D16*E16	F23:	[W7]+D23*E23
D12:	+B11*C12	G16:	@SUM(F12..F16)	C24:	1−C23
E12:	[W6]8.1	B18:	[W6]+B11	D24:	+C24*C22*B21
F12:	[W7]+D12*E12	C19:	+$C$12	E24:	[W6]−3.8
C13:	1−C12	D19:	+C19*B18	F24:	]W7]+D24*E24
D13:	+C13*B11	E19:	[W6] 22.6	C25:	1−C22
E13:	[W6] 0.8	F19:	[W7]+D19*E19	D25:	+C25*B21
F13:	[W7]+D13*E13	C20:	1−C19	E25:	[W6]−13.7
B14:	[W6] 1−B11	D20:	+B18*C20	F25:	[W7]+D25*E25
C15:	+$C$12	E20:	[W6]−14.1	G25:	@SUM(F19..F27)

Width of columns: global 5; A:37; B and E:6; F:7.

Figure 28.2   Model for testing the impact of different probabilities.

superior? In order to explore this issue, we have to try to weigh the different situations. Since we have very little idea about the probabilities, we can build a model which helps us understand the impact of different probabilities. Such a model is described in Figure 28.2.

This model considers that, since the industry is mature, all competitors are faced with similar problems. As a result if there are production problems, they will be shared by BA International and its major competitor, and consequently there will be no price war in such a situation. *We should not overestimate the manufacturing risk . . . If at BA International they thought that production problems were likely to occur, they would not even have considered launching P12.* Let us assign a 0.9 probability to the absence of production difficulties.

As shown in Figure 28.3, the volume strategy is always superior unless you think that it is extremely likely that the competition will offer a similar product to P12 in 1993 and it is likely that the competition is going to adopt an aggressive pricing strategy. This contradicts the consensual strategy which emerged at BA International. Did they refuse the volume strategy because they were afraid of the possibility of adverse outcomes? Let us examine the risk profiles attached to the niche and volume strategies which are shown in Figure 28.4.

Once more, the analysis does not generate any definite answer. You have to make up your own mind. It is clear that the volume strategy may generate very adverse outcomes; but the probability of such outcomes is low and if successful the volume strategy would generate a great value.

Probabilities			Results	
Probability late entry	Probability conservative pricing	Probability no production problems	Expected NPV niche strategy	Expected NPV volume strategy
0.8	0.5	0.9	7	16
0.8	0.8	0.9	7	16
0.8	0.2	0.9	7	15
0.8	0.5	0.8	6	12
0.5	0.5	0.9	5	10
0.5	0.8	0.9	5	12
0.5	0.2	0.9	5	8
0.5	0.5	0.8	5	8
0.2	0.5	0.9	4	5
0.2	0.8	0.9	4	8
0.2	0.2	0.9	4	2
0.2	0.5	0.8	4	3

Figure 28.3 Expected NPVs.

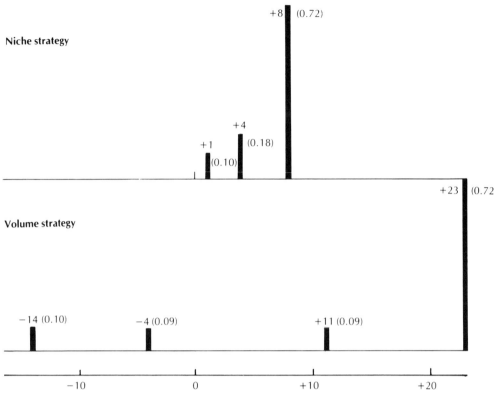

Probability late entry: 0.8; Probability conservative pricing: 0.5; Probability no production problems: 0.9.

Figure 28.4   Risk profiles.

28.2   HAVE WE MISSED SOMETHING?

When you review the analysis you may have three main worries.

- How sure can we be that capital expenditures are not going to change, whatever the strategy?
- Have we made a fair assessment of the volume strategies?
- Have we given a fair assessment to the niche strategies?

The capital expenditures issue

In our analysis, we have assumed that capital expenditures are not going to change when volume strategies are chosen. The problem is, however, that volume strategies imply a much higher capacity as shown in Figure 28.5.

If you believe the results in Figure 28.5 and consider that some additional capacity may be required by volume strategies, then those strategies look less attractive.

	Index		Required capital expenditures according to index
No educational campaign			
15% premium, late entry of competition	4 502	100	4.64
15% premium, early entry of competition	3 394		
Educational campaign			
0% premium, late entry of competition	13 513	300	13.92
0% premium, early entry of competition	10 250	228	10.58

Figure. 28.5 Cumulative volumes over ten years.

Have we made a fair assessment of the volume strategies?

One could argue that we might have underestimated the value of volume strategies. When assessing volume strategies, we have not considered the possibility of a negative price premium. When you do so (see Figure 28.6) you realize that selling P12 at a price 10% lower than substitute products would lead to a better result.

If you are attracted by volume strategies and think that P12 might be the chance for BA International successfully to attack local competition then you might consider that we have not given a fair chance to extremely low price strategies. If we retained the idea expressed in Chapter 27 (see page 426) and consider that P12 segment could reach a maximum of 70%, then, as shown in Figure 28.7, the results would look quite different. But this would correspond

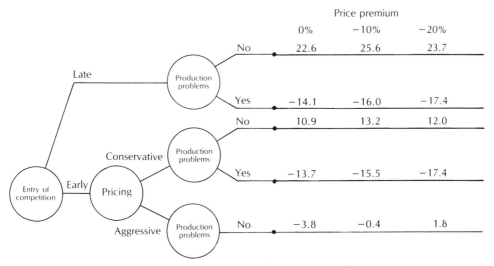

Figure 28.6 Impact of negative price premiums (volume strategy).

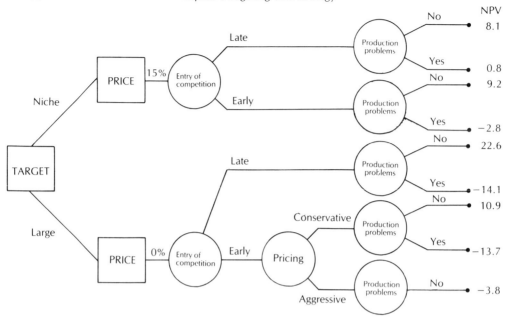

* Would correspond to a cumulative volume sold of 27 240. This might require (see Figure 28.5) about 23 m DM more
  capital expenditures.
† or much less if additional capital expenditures are made before the problem is encountered.
‡ Might require 17 m more in capital expenditures.

Figure 28.7   Possible impact of extremely low price volume strategy.

to a grand strategic move for BA International and would probably require
much more capital expenditures and costs of structure. As no mention of the
possibility of such a grand strategic move is made in the case, let us not dream
about it.

Have we given a fair assessment to the niche strategies?

In our analysis we have considered that an early entry of the competition would
only result in the sharing of an unchanged total market. But what if this also
changed the size of the segment of P12 as shown in the influence diagram of
Figure 28.8?

When you analyze the level of fixed selling costs, you realize that they are
quite significant when compared with the amount of the educational campaign.
If BA International's competitor introduces a product similar to P12 in 1993 it
will also incur fixed selling costs. The combined impact of its effort and that of
BA International may well be as effective as the impact of an educational
campaign undertaken by BA International alone, and fought by competition.

If you accept this idea, you have to carry out further modifications to the
model in order to give a fairer assessment to the niche strategies. The process
for this is described below in Figure 28.9. The results are given in Figure 28.10.

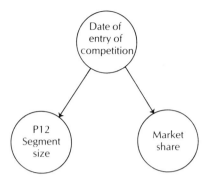

Figure 28.8 Impact of competition.

The three things you need to do* are to change the calculation of P12 segment share in row 9 and the calculation of fixed selling costs in row 25.

1   In order to change the calculation of P12 segment share,
    type in B24:
       (−0.2*B6+14+@IF($F$5=2#OR#($F$5=1#AND#$F$7=2),3/8 – the rest unchanged
    type in C24:
       (−0.2*B6+14+@IF($F$5=2#OR#($F$5=1#AND#$F$7=2),5.5/8 – the rest unchanged
    type in D24:
       (−0.2*B6+14+@IF($F$5=2#OR#($F$5=1#AND#$F$7=2),@IF – the rest unchanged
    Copy across.

2   In order to change the calculation of fixed selling costs,
    type in B42
       @IF(FS=1,@IF(F7=1,4.822,8.149),8.149+8.5)
    type in C42:
       @IF($F$5=2#OR#($F$5=1#AND#$F$7=2),8.149,4.822). Copy into D42.

3   Change the calculation of competitive price in order to introduce the possibility of a price war in the situation corresponding to: production difficulties, no educational campaign and early entry of competition. In order to do so, change the calculation of competitive price in row 34:
    @IF($F$9=2#AND#$F$8=2#AND#($F$5=2#OR#($F$5=1#AND#$F$7=2)),B32 – the rest unchanged. Copy across.

   Test   After these modifications, your model should return a −2.8 m DM NPV (before cannibalization) for the situation corresponding to:
       No educational campaign
       15% premium
       Early entry of competition, conservative pricing
       Production difficulties.

---

    * Starting from the summary model (Figure 27.10).

Figure 28.9   Introducing the idea of sharing a bigger market.

If you believe in the idea that an early entry of competition would result in the opportunity to share a bigger market then, as shown in Figure 28.10, the niche strategy looks much better than we thought. When analyzing carefully the results in Figure 28.10, you find something totally unexpected. In the case where there are no production problems, the outcome of the niche strategy looks better when competition enters the market early. If competition offers a

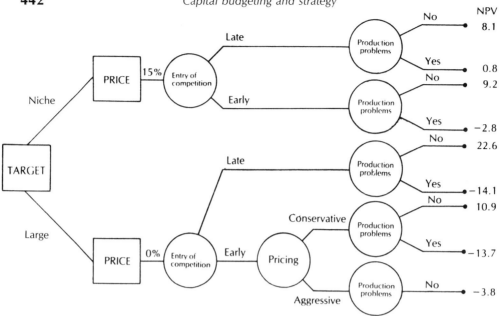

Figure 28.10   Results of sharing a bigger market.

product similar to P12 in 1998 the NPV is 8.1 m but if it offers the same product as early as 1993, the NPV is 9.2 m DM.

As a consequence, BA International should hope that competition is able to introduce a product similar to P12 in 1993, a very counter-intuitive idea. You must realize, however, that, within the framework of our new model, the situation with a niche strategy decided in 1991 and competition entering in 1993 does not result in P12 being sold to a niche market in 1993. *On the contrary, such a situation actually results in P12 being sold to a large market.* This is clear when you look at the values of P12 segment sizes. They are equivalent to what could be achieved by BA International if it undertakes the educational campaign. This has several implications.

- The diagram in Figure 28.10 should be modified in order to acknowledge that the market becomes a volume market in this situation.
- The diagram in Figure 28.10 has to be further modified in order to show the option which becomes available to BA International if this situation materializes in 1993. Why keep the premium at 15%? As the nature of the market has changed under the pressure of competition, why not cut the price premium to enlarge the P12 segment size further? But if BA International does so, the competition may react by cutting its prices further and a price war might start.
- Not only the diagram has to be changed but also the model, since you should introduce into it the possibility of a price war in the situation where there is

no production problem, no educational campaign and early entry of competition. In order to do so you simply come back to the previous model and change the calculation of competitive price in B34:

@IF($F$9=2#AND#$F$8=2#AND#($F$5=2#OR#($F$5=1#AND#
$F$7=2)),B32, @IF($F$5=1#AND#$F$7=1,B33,. . .

The rest is unchanged (what you have to change is underlined). Copy across. The results you can generate with this modified model are shown in Figure 28.11.

What do the results in Figure 28.11 indicate? You can first compare the NPVs attached to the following series of situations.

■ Niche strategy chosen in 1991, early entry of competition, cut in price premium, in 1993. NPVs are as follows:
  · Conservative competitive pricing:
No production problems	18.9
Production problems	−5.6
  · Aggressive competitive pricing:
No production problems	4.3
Production problems	−8.7
■ Volume strategy chosen in 1991 and early entry of competition. NPVs are as follows:
  · Conservative pricing strategy:
No production problems	10.9
  · Aggressive competitive strategy:
No production problems	−3.8

All the strategies belonging to the first group are higher by the same amount (about 8 m DM), the after-tax cost of the educational campaign. When a niche strategy is chosen and competition enters early the oil-free segment is as large as with volume strategies but there is no educational campaign to undertake.

The results in Figure 28.11 make the niche strategy look more attractive than it appeared in Figure 28.1. If you modify the model described in Figure 28.2 to calculate expected NPVs, you realize that, when you assume a 50% probability of early entry of competition, a 50% probability of conservative pricing and a 10% probability of no production problems, the niche strategy and the volume strategies return NPVs close to one another, provided BA International cuts the price premium in 1993.[1] Since the niche strategy is less risky, you can understand more clearly why the consensual recommendation in the end was for a niche strategy.

This analysis suggests that the niche strategy has a hidden additional value. If selected, *the option to change to a volume strategy if need be at a later stage* is retained. You may now think that we have dissected the problem sufficiently, and

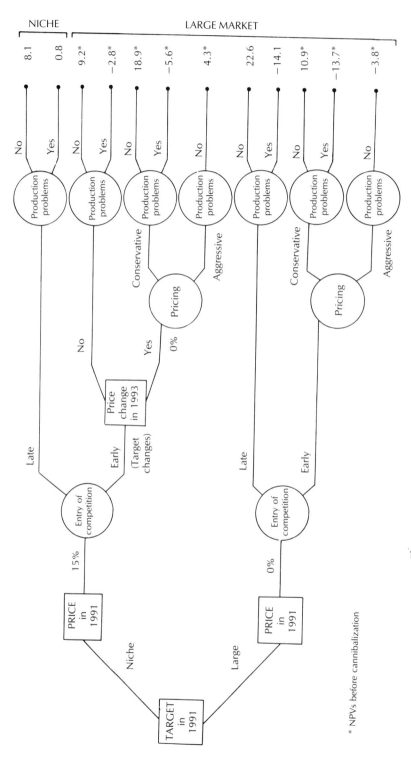

Figure 28.11 Results of sharing a bigger market: modified model.

* NPVs before cannibalization

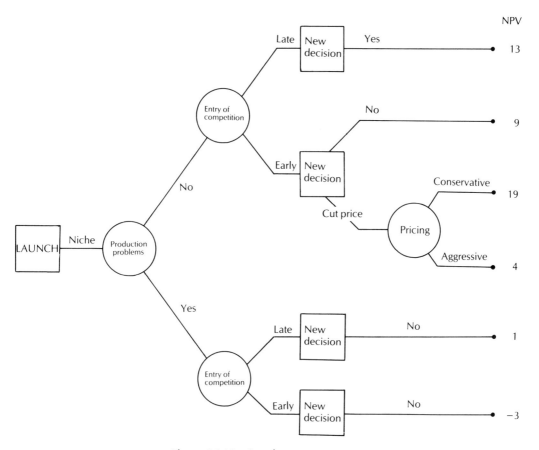

Figure 28.12 Step-by-step strategy.

perhaps the alternatives at BA International should be stated simply as either to decide as soon as 1991 to go for a volume strategy or to decide to start with a niche strategy and to keep the option open in the future either to continue to sell on a small market or to change and attack a larger market.

The niche strategy as a step-by-step approach

The advantages of starting with a niche strategy are obvious. This would enable BA International to know about the two main risk factors (early entry of competition and production risk) before embarking on a volume strategy. Consequently, risk would be very much reduced. Unfortunately, however, potential benefits would also be reduced.

In order to test the possible impact of such a step-by-step strategy, you can modify the model as follows:

- Using the last model we built set price premium to 15 in 1993 and 1994 and to zero afterwards
- Introduce the following values for P12 segment share

93	94	95	96	97	98	99	00	01	02
0.11	0.11	0.15	0.21	0.27	0.34	0.34	0.34	0.34	0.34

You obviously have to make an assumption regarding these values. In our model P12 segment size is equal to 21% with the educational campaign and a zero price premium. Will BA International be able to reach such a result as early as 1995 with the step-by-step strategy? We assume here that the repositioning of P12 will take some time and that therefore the 21% will be reached only in 1996. The 15% size in 1995 is a further assumption.
- Change the calculation of fixed selling costs. The decision you make about their level will very much affect the NPV. One difficulty here is that we do not know anything about the cost of changing the positioning of P12 after its introduction. Let us consider the following figures:

1993	4.822
1994	16.649
1995	16.649
1996	3.327

The 1996 figure is equal to 8.149 − 4.822. With this 1996 figure you get the same total fixed selling costs as in any volume strategy (no additional cost attached to the repositioning of P12).
- Remove from the NPV calculations the impact of the campaign.

When you do these modifications you get a 13.1 m NPV when competition enters late. The diagram corresponding to this strategy is shown in Figure 28.12.

When envisaged as a step-by-step approach, the niche strategy becomes very attractive. It might well be the reason why the consensual strategy that emerged at BA International recommended it.

NOTE

1 Provided that BA International cuts the price premium in 1993, the model shown in Figure 28.2 can be used to calculate the NPVs corresponding to keeping the same price premium in this situation. This would not be as good.

Further Models VII

FURTHER MODEL VII.1
INFLATION, INTEREST AND EXCHANGE RATES:
EQUILIBRIUM RELATIONSHIPS

One of the challenges of building models and risk scenarios is to construct sets of parameters which are internally consistent – or compatible. Economic theory is very useful for this as it suggests that key parameters such as *inflation, discount rate and exchange rates tend to be linked by equilibrium relationships*. When using these relationships, you should always keep in mind that they may be very useful and very dangerous:

- Equilibrium relationships are very powerful means to simplify situations like the one BA International is analyzing.
- But you should not forget that it is unusual to observe equilibrium situations in the real world. Consequently you should always assess the impact of likely deviations from equilibrium and remember that these relationships do not enable you to make predictions: experience shows, for example, that *predicting future exchange rates is impossible.*[1]

A spreadsheet model

The model in Figure VII.1 enables you to understand the nature and the implications of the equilibrium relationships between inflation, interest and exchange rates: when all these equilibrium relationships hold, then inflation, changes in exchange rates and changes in discount rate offset each other and as a result *values remain the same whatever inflation is*. In other words, you can start with models which ignore inflation and exchange rates: you can simplify the analysis of P12 and start with a model that assumes there is no inflation and all sales are made in DM.

Spot and forward exchange rates: implications for pricing

The model in Figure VII.1 shows two exchange rates, the current or spot exchange rate and the expected or future exchange rate. One of the important characteristics of foreign exchange markets[2] is that they provide you with the opportunity to buy and sell currencies:

- for immediate delivery (spot or cash rate) and,
- for future delivery (forward or future rate): this is one of the paradoxes[3] of

	A	B	C	D
1	Exchange rate as of end 1992	1		
2	Real 1-year real discount rate as of end 1992	8%		
3	Expected home inflation rate in 1993	5%		
4	Expected foreign inflation rate in 1993	20%		
5	EXPECTED RESULTS IN 1993:	Real	Current	Change
6	Exp. cash flow generated at home	500	525.0	1.05
7	Exp. interest gain generated at home	25	26.3	1.05
8	Exp. cash flow generated in foreign country	80	96.0	
9	Exp. exchange rate as of end 1993	1.000	0.875	
10	Exp. cash flow converted to home currency	80	84.0	1.05
11	Exp. interest gain generated to foreign currency	12	14.4	
12	Exp. cash flow converted to home currency	12	12.6	1.05
13	TOTAL EXPECTED CASH FLOW	617	647.9	1.05
14	Discount rate (home cash flow)	8%	13%	
15	Discount rate (foreign cash flow)	8%	30%	
16	VALUE	571.3	571.3	
17				
18	Future/current exchange rate	1	0.8750	
19	(1+ home inflation)/(1+ foreign inflation)	1	0.8750	
20	(1+ foreign interest)/(1+ domestic interest)	1	0.8750	

Formulas:

B2:	this rate includes a risk premium	C11:	+B11*(1+B4)
C6:	+B6*(1+B3)	C12:	+B9*B11 Copy in C11
D6:	+C6/B6 Copy in D7, D10, D12, D13	B13:	+B6+B7+B10+B12 Copy in C13
C7:	+B7*(1+B3)	B14:	+B2
C8:	+B8*(1+B4)	C14:	(1+B14)*(1+B3)−1
B9:	+B1	B15:	+B2
C9:	+B1*(1+B3)/(1+B4)	C15:	+(1+B15)*(1+B4)−1
B10:	+B9*B8 Copy in C10	B16:	+B13/(1+B14) Copy in C16
		C18:	+C9/B9
		C19:	(1+B3)/(1+B4)
		C20:	(1+C14)/(1+C15)

Figure VII.1 Parity relationships: a model.

the foreign exchange markets:
· today, you cannot predict the rate at which you will buy a foreign currency three months from now *and*
· today you can also decide to buy this currency three months forward and as a result fix, as of today, the rate that will apply to your transaction three months from now.[4]

Forward rates have a very important implication for pricing decisions in international business. When you need to use an exchange rate for pricing a transaction, you should use the exchange rate as of the date of payment[5]: for an immediate cash payment use the spot rate, for all deferred payments, use the *relevant forward rate*.

The relationships

Domestic and foreign inflation

The model shows that when equilibrium relationships hold, then foreign cashflows, when converted into domestic currency, behave according to domestic inflation (compare the outputs in cells D10 and D6 in the model of Figure VII.1(a)). This equilibrium relationship is called the Law of One Price or *Purchasing Power Parity (PPP)*.[6] It states that, in the long run, international trade irons out differences in the price trends of traded goods. As a result, similar goods should be priced – and should remain priced – roughly the same all over the world, or at least all over trading countries. This is obviously a simplification that ignores important realities such as the existence of restrictions to trade and of local monopolies, the fact that international companies differentiate their products which render international comparisons difficult, etc. Yet, over a long period of time, or over a short period of time during which wide price movements occur, one should expect similar price trends for similar traded goods in all trading countries. The validity of Purchasing Power Parity has been extensively tested and even though the evidence is mixed,[7] it is a very good starting point for building models.

Please also check in Figure VII.1 that the relationship between the future and the current exchange rate is the same as the relationship between the home and foreign inflation: when Purchasing Power Parity holds, then the inflation differentials among countries predict how the exchange rates will change.

Inflation and discount rate

Observed – or nominal or current – interest rates embody the expectations of inflation, or in other words, nominal interest rates can be decomposed into a 'real' interest rate and an expectation of inflation. This equilibrium relationship is due to Irvin Fisher.[8] Even though the evidence of its validity is also mixed,[9] this relationship constitutes again a very good starting point for building models. This relationship is used several times in Figure VII.1:

- The domestic and foreign interest gains increase with the domestic and foreign inflations. When Purchasing Power Parity also holds, then the interest gain generated abroad shows the same increase as the domestic gain (see cells D7 and D12).
- The discount rate increases with the domestic inflation: as cash flows similarly increase with inflation, value is not changed by inflation.
- The difference between the domestic and foreign inflations creates differences in interest rates which are offset by the change in exchange rate. This relationship which is called *Interest Rate Parity* – or International Fisher Effect – states that active international markets should iron out interest rates differences all over the world. If that was not the case, all investors would be

willing to invest in the currency/country with the highest interest and all borrowers to borrow in the currency/country with the lowest interest and no market equilibrium would be possible. When Interest Parity holds, the differential in interest rates predicts the changes in exchange rates.

Interest rate parity in the international money market

The international money market is a reasonably good example of a perfect market. This market provides continuous quotes for interest rates in different currencies as well as the exchange rates between these different currencies for immediate delivery (spot rates) as well as for deliveries at a series of future dates (forward rates). On this market, forward rates are used to allow for different interest rates for the different currencies to be quoted while giving all investors the same effective interest rate:

- An investor who is willing to capture the higher interest of a foreign currency may use the spot market and convert its holdings into that currency.
- When it uses the forward market and converts its holding back to its own currency at the end of the investment period, the forward rate is such that the interest advantage is destroyed.[10]

This relationship between interest rates, spot and forward exchange rates is called *Covered Interest Parity* and is much stronger than all the other equilibrium relationships presented above.[11] Interest covered parity is actually used by traders to quote forward rates: starting from the spot exchange rates and the interest rates in the different currencies, traders quote forward rates that exactly offset the interest rate differentials and allow the different currencies to keep different interest rates.

Using the equilibrium parity relationships for building and using models

These equilibrium relationships suggest the use of a three-step approach for building models and risk scenarios:

1. It is a very good idea to start with assuming that these relationships hold which enables you to build much simpler models.
2. Then you should check that the strategy that you contemplate does not prevent you from benefiting from those equilibrium relationships: if your strategy implies that you fix your selling price in a foreign currency, then you will no longer benefit from the price/exchange rate offsetting effect implied by Purchasing Power Parity.
3. Finally, you should get closer to reality and ask yourself how deviations from the equilibrium relationships may affect the outcome of your strategies.

NOTES

1 Refer for example to: R Levich (1982), 'Evaluating the Performance of the Forecasters', and J Frenkel (1983), 'Flexible Exchange Rates, Prices and the Role of "News": Lessons from the 1970s', both in D Lessard (ed), (1985), *International Financial Management*, John Wiley & Sons, and 'The Value of Forecasts' by G Dufey and R Mirus in *Management of Foreign Exchange Risk*, B Antl and R Ensor (eds), Euromoney Publications, 1982.

2 For a description of foreign exchange markets, refer to *A Guide to Foreign Exchange Markets*, K Chrystal, Federal Reserve Bank of St Louis, March 1984, pp 5–17.

3 This might actually not be a paradox: since it is impossible to forecast future exchange rates, companies have had to create instruments that enable them to escape this uncertainty. Forward rates are one of these instruments. An example may help you understand the value of forward rates.

In January 1993, a UK manufacturer of aero-engines is pricing the sale of three engines to a US airline (price is to be quoted in USD). These engines will be delivered and paid in 1995. The cost of building each engine is estimated at 4.5 million GBP. The spot UK/USD is 1.66 (1.66 USD for 1 GBP). A 3-year forward contract has recently been made at 1.50 USD per 1 GBP. The US Airline is willing to pay 7.2 million USD per engine. The USD/GBP rate has recently varied by more than 30% in a single year.

In January 1993, a US contractor is considering signing a contract in GBP with a British company. The proceeds of this contract are to be paid in 1996 for a total amount of 14.4 million GBP. The costs, all incurred in USD, are expected to amount to 20 million USD. A 3-year forward contract has recently been made at 1.50 USD per 1 GBP. The USD/GBP rate has recently varied by more than 30% in a single year.

Both companies are considering large, low-margin and risky businesses that are difficult to accept without a protection against exchange rate movements. If these companies are able to meet and decide to swap their foreign currency receipts in 1995, then they would both improve the value of their respective business. If the UK company sells forward its 21.6 million USD at a 1.50 rate, then it is sure to receive 14.4 million in 1996 which should enable it to generate a 0.9 million profit (provided the costs are as expected). If the US company sells forward its 14.4 million GBP at the same rate, then it is sure to receive 21.6 million USD in 1996 and generate a 1.6 million profit (provided the costs are as expected).

4 The forward rate may be considered as a forecast of the future spot exchange rate: E Fama, 'Forward and Spot Exchange Rates', *Journal of Monetary Economics*, 14, 1984, pp 319–38 and Wolff, 'Foreign Exchange Rates, Expected Spot Rates and Premia: A Signal Extraction Approach', *Journal of Finance*, June 1987, pp 395–406.

5 In international business, time is explicitly priced which makes cash much more relevant than profit.

6 The Purchasing Power Parity theory which originated in the 1920s is attributed to Gustav Cassel. Refer for example to AC Shapiro, 'What does purchasing power parity mean?' in *International Financial Management: Theory and Application*, DR Lessard (ed), John Wiley (1985), pp 235–59; RZ Aliber, *Exchange Risk and Corporate International Finance*, John Wiley (1978).

7 Refer to N Abuaf and P Jorion, Purchasing 'Power Parity in the Long Run', *Journal of Finance*, March 1990, pp 157–74 and M Adler and B Lehman 'Deviations from Purchasing Power Parity in the Long Run', *Journal of Finance*, December 1983, pp 1471–87.

8 *The Theory of Interest: As Determined by Impatience to Spend Income and Opportunity to Invest It*, 1930, republished in 1965 by Augustus M. Kelley Publishers.

9 Refer to E Fama 'Short-Term Interest Rates as Predictors of Inflation', *American Economic Review*, 65, June 1975, pp 269–82; P Hess and Bicksler, 'Capital Assets Prices Versus Time Series Models as Predictors of Inflation', *Journal of Financial Economics*, 2, December 1975, pp 341–60; and to C Nelson and G Schwert, 'Short-Term Interest Rates as Predictors of Inflation: On Testing the Hypothesis that The Real Rate of Interest is Constant', *American Economic Review*, 67, June 1977, pp 478–86.

10 The forward transaction is necessary for the investors to accept investing in a foreign currency. Without the forward transaction, the investment in foreign currency is more risky than the investment in domestic currency.

11 See 'Covered Interest Arbitrage: Unexploited Profits?', J Frenkel and R Levich, *Journal of Political Economy*, April 1975, pp 325–38; and K Clinton, 'Transaction costs and Covered Interest Advantage: Theory and Evidence', *Journal of Political Economy*, 96, April 1988, pp 358–70.

**FURTHER MODEL VII.2
CURRENCY RISK**

Currency risk, or currency exposure, is the risk that the value of a transaction in foreign currency be different from what is expected.[1] This risk results from the fact that the change in exchange rate and the change in price may not offset each other.

The environmental and competitive sources of currency risk

Currency risk may be due to external causes ie to the existence of deviations from the Purchasing Power Parity. Such deviations are common for economies as a whole and even more common for specific products and companies. An analysis of the impact of a possible deviation from Purchasing Power Parity on the outcome of P12 is shown in Figure VII.2(a).

Analyzing the full impact of possible – and unfortunately very likely – deviations from Purchasing Power Parity is very difficult as these deviations should be analyzed within the competitive context:

- A firm with a strong competitive position will probably be in a better position to adjust its prices with a view to offset changes in exchange rates.

Let us assume that BA International expects to make about 40% of its sales in US dollars. Since BA International manufactures P12 in Germany, it will be vulnerable to the fact that the US dollar and the German mark do not behave according to PPP. If the dollar is overvalued in relation to the mark, BA International will get more from its sales than we estimated. If the dollar is undervalued, it will get less.

As it is impossible to predict the evolution of exchange rates, the only thing we can do is to simulate potential deviations from PPP and assess their impact on the NPV we expect to derive from P12. This will give us an idea of the risk to which we are exposed. In order to do so, we can start from the model in Figure 26.3 and modify it as follows.

- Insert three rows above row 11 (sales).
- Introduce in row 11 a scenario of PPP discrepancies:

1993	1994	1995	1996	1997	1998	1999	2000	2001	2002	Average
0.0	–0.2	–0.6	–0.6	–0.2	0.2	0.6	0.6	0.2	0.0	0.0

- Introduce in B12 the percentage of sales made in USD: 0.4
- Introduce a new calculation of the selling price in row 13; in B13: +B10*(1–$B$12)+B10*$B$12* (1+B11), copy across.
- Change the formulas for sales in row 14: +B7*B13/1000 in B14. Copy across.

Your new model should generate an NPV equal to 6.4 m DM, 20% less than the model in Figure 26.3. Then you can change the scenario of PPP discrepancies.

For example:

1993	1994	1995	1996	1997	1998	1999	2000	2001	2002	Average
0.0	0.2	0.6	0.6	0.2	–0.2	–0.6	–0.6	–0.2	0.0	0.0

If you do so, you will find an NPV 20% higher than the one in Figure 26.3.

What can we conclude from this analysis? Provided that our models of PPP deviations are realistic, which is a matter of judgement, we can say that the outcome of P12 is not very much exposed to currency risk.

Figure VII.2(a)   Assessing the currency risk of P12.

The fact that P12 might be a unique product should help reduce its currency exposure.

- Deviations in Purchasing Power Parity may have complex consequences on the respective positions of competitors in an industry: if the main international competitor of BA International is an American firm, then a temporary overvaluation of the USD can jeopardize its short-term position and also encourage it to invest and improve which could reinforce its long-term competitive position.[2]
- The deviations in Purchasing Power Parity which matter are not easy to identify and may even affect those purely domestic competitors which operate in one currency only: if the USD becomes temporarily overvalued, then BA International will suddenly enjoy a stronger competitive position vis-à-vis its local competitors in the USA. Even though they do not deal in foreign currency, the local competitors of BA International have a significant currency exposure!

The operational sources of currency risk

Currency risk can also be created by the way in which a company decides to operate. As soon as it fixes prices in a foreign currency, a company renders its receipts or payments in foreign currency totally dependent on the changes in exchange rate which cannot be compensated any longer. Many operational events create currency exposure:

1. Accounts receivable, accounts payable, fixed interest investments and loans create currency exposure.
2. Orders received and placed at a fixed price, fixed price long term contracts also create currency exposure.
3. Finally currency exposure is also created by bids submitted at a fixed price and more generally by all contractual and quasi-contractual relationships which make a company commit itself to a fixed price in a foreign currency: published list prices, wage agreements, etc.

An example showing how to identify the exposed cash flows of a subsidiary is in Figure VII.2(b).

It is interesting to note that:

- Currency exposure is not a matter for finance specialists only. Rather than asking finance specialists to manage the currency exposure, it is much more effective to educate all those managers who deal with customers and suppliers in order that they avoid creating currency exposure. Operating with minimum currency exposure is a matter of *avoiding fixed price commitments and minimizing payment delays.*
- Currency exposure cannot all be captured by the accounting system: category 1 items are shown in the balance sheet, orders are captured also by accounting, but capturing category 3 items requires a specific information system.
- Assessing the category 3 items is a matter of judgement: for how long will it be difficult to change the prices published in a price list? What are the chances of having a fixed price bid accepted? Etc.
- Currency exposure only deals with risk and only captures one dimension of risk. The value of foreign sales is a function of the unit price and of their volume sold: what if international diversification reduces volume risk more than it increases price – or currency – risk? In any case what is important is not to know what the risk is but to know if this risk is worth being taken.

The opportunity to hedge

Figure VII.2(c) shows how a company can hedge exposed receipts and payments in foreign currency.

FIVE-YEAR PLAN:

The following data correspond to the 5-year plan of the UK subsidiary of a Swedish company as prepared on January 1st, 1993. All data, originally in pounds, have been expressed in Swedish kronor.

(in million SEK)	1993	1994	1995	1996	1997
Sales	12 000	12 400	13 000	14 000	14 000
Cost of sales	8 400	8 680	9 100	9 800	9 800
Operating expenses	750	800	900	990	1 000
Other expenses	450	450	500	500	550
Interest	396	252	144	0	0
Taxes	150	180	200	250	300
Cash Flow Earnings	1 854	2 038	2 156	2 460	2 350
Receivables open	950	1 000	1 033	1 083	1 167
Receivables end	1 000	1 033	1 083	1 167	1 167
Inventory open	1 000	1 050	1 085	1 138	1 225
Inventory end	1 050	1 085	1 138	1 225	1 225
Payables open	1 000	1 056	1 089	1 144	1 236
Payables end	1 056	1 089	1 144	1 236	1 125
Cash from Operations	1 810	2 003	2 108	2 381	2 239
New investments	600	1 100	800	600	
Loan repayments	1 200	900	1 200		
Change in Cash	10	3	108	1 781	2 239

Notes:

Prices on sales and cost of sales can be adjusted in case of a change in the exchange rate at the exception of one supply contract at fixed prices: 500 per year for the period 1993 to 1997. Supplies within this contract have been ordered for 1993, but not beyond that year.
Orders received or placed with a fixed price as of January 1st, 1993:
– Orders received from customers: 2 000
– Orders placed with suppliers: 1 100 (500 within the above mentioned contract).
– Equipment to be paid in 1988 (600) and in 1989 (1 000)
Salary costs for 1988 (5 000) can be considered as fixed.
Loans carry a fixed interest rate.

ESTIMATION OF CURRENCY EXPOSURE AS OF JANUARY 1, 1993:

When you take into account all fixed-price transactions recorded in the balance sheet and the income statements only:

Receivables open	950	Net exposed position: –4 142
Payables open	1 000	
Loan repayments	3 300	
Interest	792	

When you consider all fixed price orders also:

Receivables open	950	Net exposed position: –4 842
Customers' orders	2 000	
Payables open	1 000	
Loan repayments	3 300	
Interest	792	
Suppliers' orders	1 000	
Equipment	1 700	

When you consider all other factors that may result in fixed-price transactions also:

Receivables open	950	Net exposed position: –11 842
Customers' orders	2 000	
Payables open	1 000	
Loan repayments	3 300	
Interest	792	
Suppliers' orders	1 000	
Equipment	1 700	
Suppliers' contract	2 000	
Salaries	5 000	

Figure VII.2(b)   Estimating the currency exposure of a foreign subsidiary.

On January 10, 1993:

Exchange rates:

USD/FRR   spot: 5.3975   3-month: 5.4743
USD/SFR   spot: 1.4100   3-month: 1.4233

3-month interest rates:

USD: 4%   FFR: 9.75%   SFR: 7 13/16 (7.8125%)

A US company wants to hedge 4 million FFR to be received on April 11, 1993 and 2 million SFR to be paid on April 11, 1993.

1 Hedging the receipt:

Solution 1:

Sell the FFR forward and be sure to get 4 000 000/5.4743 ie 730 684.24 USD on April 11

Solution 2:

1 Borrow 3 904 820.01 FFR in order to have to repay 4 000 000 FFR on April 11: 3 904 820.01*(1+1.0975/400)= 4 000 000

2 change the proceeds to USD on January 10 and get: 3 904 820.01/ 5.3975 = 723 449.75 USD

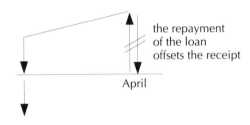

the repayment of the loan offsets the receipt

April

With solution 1, the company gets 730 684.20 USD for sure in April,
With solution 2, the company gets 723 449.75 USD for sure in January,
The difference is equal to the time value of money (1% for 3 months)

2 Hedging the payment:

Solution 1:

Buy the SFR forward and be sure to pay 2 000 000/1.4233 ie 1 405 179.21 USD on April 11

Solution 2:

1 Change today 1 391 266.54 USD in order to get 1 961 685.82 SFR: 1 391 266.54*1.41

2 Invest this amount at 7 15/15 in order to grow it to 2 000 000 SFR on April 11: 1 961 685.82*(1+7.8125/400)

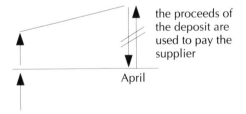

the proceeds of the deposit are used to pay the supplier

April

With solution 1, the company pays 1 405 179.21 USD for sure in April,
With solution 2, the company pays 1 391 266.54 USD for sure in January,
The difference is equal to the time value of money (1% for 3 months)

Figure VII.2(c)   Hedging a receipt and a payment in foreign currency.

Deciding whether it is valuable to hedge is a difficult decision and both literature and actual practice do not provide us with clear-cut answers. When analyzing such a decision you should consider the following issues:

- Hedging is an insurance: instead of accepting currency risk, you decide to insure against it. When thinking about hedging, you should probably think as you think about other types of insurances.
- Hedging works fully provided that your foreign currency cash flows come on time: if you have hedged a customer's payment in foreign currency and if the customer does not pay because you deliver late or because the customer has financial difficulties, then your hedge does not work any longer.
- As they correspond to uncertain cash flows (amount and/or timing uncertainty) categories 2 and 3 items are very difficult to hedge. Even though instruments like options and hybrids are sometimes used to hedge such items, this remain somewhat exceptional.[3]

Assessing foreign currency risk with @RISK

Currency risk corresponds to the price risk dimension of international activities which are undertaken by companies for a variety of reasons and in particular for securing an access to a bigger market and for reducing the volume risk of their operations.

The model in Figure VII.2(d) compares two portfolios of activities in the same industry, the two portfolios have the same size but the first one is purely domestic while the second one is diversified equally among 10 different countries. You can use this model to assess the value and limitations of hedging.

Translation risk

In addition to the currency risk related to their future cash flows, international firms also face an accounting or translation exposure. This exposure is caused by the fact that balance sheets are cumulative statements valued at historical rates. Because of these characteristics of balance sheets, changes in exchange rates – even when equilibrium relationships hold – create disturbances in the balance sheets in international companies. Translation risk is the risk that such disturbances happen.[4]

The model enables you to test the value of international diversification (you can vary the number of foreign countries from one to ten). It also enables you to test the value of three different strategies for dealing with currency risk:

1 Keep your prices in foreign currencies as flexible as possible and do not hedge (the outcome of this strategy is in J20).
2 Fix your prices in foreign currency and do not hedge (K20).
3 Fix your prices in foreign currency and hedge (L20).

The outcome of the purely domestic strategy is in L4.

	A	B	C	D	E	F	G	H	I	J	K	L	M	N	O
1	HOME:			Real				dev.							
2		Volume	ch.v	ExRt	Unit P	ch. u	ExRte	PPP		RECEIPTS					
3		1 400	0%		12.0	0%	1			16 800					
4	Deviation Interest parity					0%				VALUE......16 404					
5	Discount rate:			0.1	4	2%									
6															
7	INTERNATIONAL:														
8	Number of foreign countries (1–10):						10			**VPNH**	**FPNH**	**FPHED**			
9	1	140	0%	6.0	2.0	0%	6.0	0%		1 680	1 680	1 680	1 680	0	0
10	2	140	0%	4.0	3.0	0%	4.0	0%		1 680	1 680	1 680	1 680	0	0
11	3	140	0%	3.0	4.0	0%	3.0	0%		1 680	1 680	1 680	1 680	0	0
12	4	140	0%	2.0	6.0	0%	2.0	0%		1 680	1 680	1 680	1 680	0	0
13	5	140	0%	6.0	2.0	0%	6.0	0%		1 680	1 680	1 680	1 680	0	0
14	6	140	0%	4.0	3.0	0%	4.0	0%		1 680	1 680	1 680	1 680	0	0
15	7	140	0%	3.0	4.0	0%	3.0	0%		1 680	1 680	1 680	1 680	0	0
16	8	140	0%	2.0	6.0	0%	2.0	0%		1 680	1 680	1 680	1 680	0	0
17	9	140	0%	6.0	2.0	0%	6.0	0%		1 680	1 680	1 680	1 680	0	0
18	10	140	0%	4.0	3.0	0%	4.0	0%		1 680	1 680	1 680	1 680	0	0
19										16 800	16 800	16 800			
20							VALUE			16 404	16 404	16 404			

B3: 1400*(1+C3)
E3: 12*(1+F3)
J3: +B3*E3
L4: +J3/(1+F5)
F5: (((1+D5)^(1/E5))*(1+F3)*(1+F4))−1
B9: @IF(A9>0,($B$3/(1+$C$3))/$G$8,0)*(1+C9)
E9: (+$E$3/(1+$F$3))/D9*(1+F9)
G9: (+D9*(1+$F$3)/(1+F9))*(1+H9)
J9: +B9*E9*G9
K9: +B9*E9/(1+F9)*G9
L9: +M9+N9+O9

M9: @IF(C9>0,(+B9/(1+C9))*(E9/(1+F9))*D9,B9*(E9/(1+F9))*D9)
N9: @IF(C9<0,(B9/(1+C9)*E9/(1+F9)−B9*E9/(F9+1))*(D9−G9),0)
O9: @IF(C9>0,C9*B9/(1+C9)*(E9/(1+F9))*G9,0)
Copy B9,E9,G9,J9,K9,L9 and O9 into rows 10 to 18
A10: @IF(A9=0,0,@IF(A9+1>$G$8,0,A9+1)) Copy into A11.A18
J19: @SUM(J9..J18). Copy into K19.L19
J20: +J19/(1+$F$5). Copy into K20.L20

Column width: A: 3; F I, and H: 5; C, J, K and L: 6; B, D, E, and G: 7.

Figure VII.2(d) Doing business internationally: the value of hedging.

@ RISK (pronounce 'at Risk') is a software system that complements Lotus 1–2–3 and enables you to generate a risk analysis model from a 'best estimate' spreadsheet. In order to generate a risk analysis model from the model shown in Figure VII.2(d):

1 Install @ RISK and access 1–2–3 through RISK,
2 Define uncertainty cells:
   @ RISK enables you to replace your best estimates with probability functions. In order to check the value of hedging, you can simulate the situation where it works best: no uncertainty except on prices in foreign markets and on purchasing power parity. Among the many probability functions of @ RISK, you can select triangular distributions:
   · In F9: @TRIANG(–0.05,0,0.20), Copy to F10.F18.
     which means that you believe that the increase in the foreign prices can be anywhere between –5% and + 20% but you believe that no change is the most likely.
   · In H9: @TRIANG(–0.20,0,0.20), Copy to H10.H18.
3 Select output variables:
   · Depress ALT F7 to access the command menu of @ RISK
   · 'Outputs' 'Select' to define the name and the position of the output variables: home (L4), variable price-no hedge (J20), fixed price-no hedge (K20) and fixed price-hedge (L20).
4 Simulate this scenario:
   · 'Iterations' 'Iterations' 100, to select 100 samples.
   · 123-Recalc' 'Monte Carlo' Enter, to select random Monte Carlo sampling.
   · 'Execute' 'Start' to get the simulations performed by @ RISK.
5 View the results
   · 'Results' 'Current' to view the results: you can view the histogram, statistical data as well as a cumulative curve for each output variable.
Check that you get results like:

	Expected value	Standard deviation	Minimum value	Maximum value
HOME	16 404			
VPNH	16 404	360	15 332	17 239
FPNH	15 667	432	14 460	16 784
FPHED	16 404			

(one single value, ie no uncertainty for Home and Hedge)

Hedging does not work as well in all situations and you can check it with changing the uncertainties. You can for example introduce the following probability distributions:

In C3:	@TRIANG(–0.10,0,0.10)
In C9:	@TRIANG(–0.20,0,0.20). Copy into C10.C18
In F3:	@TRIANG(–0.05,0,0.20)
In F4:	@TRIANG(–0.01,0,0.01)
In F9:	@TRIANG(–0.05,0,0.15). Copy into F10.F18
In H9:	@TRIANG(–0.20,0,0.20). Copy into H10.H18

	Expected value	Standard deviation	Minimum value	Maximum value
HOME	16 405	666	14 869	17 890
VPNH	16 403	611	15 275	17 854
FPNH	15 897	651	14 670	17 530
FPHED	15 660	905	13 601	17 856

Figure VII.2(e)   Using @ RISK.

NOTES

1 See in *New Developments in International Finance*, J Stern and D Chew, Basil Blackwell, 1988:
Managing Foreign Exchange Risks by B Cornell and A Shapiro, pp 44–59.
The Nature and Management of Foreign Exchange Risk by N Abuaf, pp 29–43.
See also 'Exposure to Currency risk: Definition and Measurements', M Adler and B Dumas, *Financial Management*, Summer 1984, pp 41–50; 'On the measurement of Operating Exposure to Exchange Rates: A conceptual Approach', E Flood and D Lessard, *Financial Management*, Spring 1986, pp 25–36; and DR Lessard and JB Lightstone, 'Volatile exchange rates can put operations at risk', *Harvard Business Review* (July/Aug 1986), pp 107–14.

2 See 'Finance and Global Competition: Exploiting Financial Scope and Coping with Volatile Exchange rates', D Lessard, in *New Developments in International Finance*, J Stern and D Chew, Basil Blackwell, 1988, pp 3–26; 'Are We Feeling More Competitive Yet? The Exchange Rate Gambit', W Kester and T Luehrman, *Sloan Management Review*, Winter 1989, pp 19–28.

3 See 'The Foreign Exchange Option as a Hedging Tool', I Giddy, in *New Developments in International Finance*, J Stern and D Chew, Basil Blackwell, 1988.

4 For a review of the issues involved, refer to 'Foreign Currency Translation Research: Review and Synthesis', C Houston, *Journal of Accounting Literature*, Vol 8, 1989, pp 25–48.

FURTHER MODEL VII.3: INTEREST RATE RISK

Definition

Interest rate risk is the risk that the value of a project, of a strategy or of a whole company changes as a result of a change in interest rates. While it is widely used in financial institutions, the concept of interest rate risk is much less used in industrial organizations.

Interest rate risk in financial institutions

Interest rate risk is the most important risk for all those financial institutions which hold portfolios of fixed income securities.

The model in Figure VII.3(a) shows the sensitivity of the value of a particular fixed income security, a zero-coupon bond (a bond with a single cash flow at maturity) to small changes in interest rates: for small changes in interest rates, the value of a zero-coupon bond changes at a rate of −m per cent per unit increase in the interest rate, with m being equal to the maturity of this zero-coupon bond. Fixed income securities with interim coupon payments can be analyzed as a combination of several zero-coupon bonds (using the principle of

	A	B
1	Maturity	5
2	Initial yield to maturity	10%
3	Initial value	100
4	Payment at maturity	161
5		
6	Change in interest rate	0.5%
7	New interest rate	10.6%
8	New value	98
9	Percentage change	−2.5%
10	− Maturity * change in interest rate	−2.5%

Formulas:

B4:	(F0) +B3*(1+B2)^B1
B7:	(P1) (1+B2)*(1+B6)−1
B8:	(F0) +B4/(1+B7)^B1
B9:	(P1) +B8/B3−1
B10:	(P1) −B1*B6

R.T.C. LIBRARY LETTERKENNY

Figure VII.3(a)   Interest rate risk of a zero.

A bond:

	1993	1994	1995
Cash Flows	−100	10	110
Yield to maturity	10%		

This bond can be decomposed into two zero-coupon bonds:

	1993	1994	1995
Cash Flows	−9.09	10	
Yield to maturity	10%		
Cash Flows	−90.91		110
Yield to maturity	10%		

The duration of this bond can be estimated as the weighted average of the duration of the two zero-coupon bonds:

$$((9.09 * 1) + (90.91 * 2))/100 = 1.91$$

This duration is called the Macaulay duration. For small changes in interest rates, the value of the bond changes at a rate of $-d/(1+y/n)$ per cent per unit increase in interest rate (with d = the Macaulay duration, y = the new yield to maturity and n = the number of coupons per year). $d/(1+y/n)$ is called the modified duration.

Value change with a 2% change in interest:

Cash Flows	−100	10	110
Yield to maturity	10%		
Change in interest	2.0%		
New interest	12.2%		
New value	96.29		
Change in value	−3.7%		
− Modified duration * change in interest	−3.7%		

Figure VII.3(b)   Duration and interest rate risk of a bond.

value additivity) which allows for the calculation of their duration. Figure VII.3(b) shows an example of calculation of the duration of a bond with interim coupons. It shows that the interest rate risk of a fixed income security increases with its duration.[1]

Interest rate risk in non financial organizations

In a non financial firm, interest rate risk can be defined as the risk that the value of the operations of this firm and the value of its debts change as a result of a change in interest rates.

Interest rate risk of operations

As changes in interest rates and changes in prices are related to each other (see parity relationships in Further Models VII.1), the interest risk of operations cannot be analyzed independently from a more general 'inflation risk'. An example of the analysis of such a risk has been done in the discussion of BA International (p 402). It shows that the interest-inflation risk of a business increases with its working capital needs and depreciation as well as with the existence of any fixed price transactions. Reducing the interest rate risk is therefore a matter of shortening working capital delays, accelerating depreciation and avoiding fixed price transactions.

Interest rate risk of debts

Debts have an interest rate risk as soon as a firm uses fixed interest rate debt. The magnitude of this risk is a function of the duration of these debts. Using floating rate debt is the strategy for avoiding interest rate risk.

NOTE

1 Even though it is a key concept for removing the interest rate risk of a portfolio of fixed income securities, or 'immunizing' this portfolio, matching durations is generally not sufficient and other characteristics of the portfolio – such as its convexity – have to be considered also. For more about interest rate risk and interest immunization of a portfolio of fixed income securities, refer to F Fabozzi and D Fabozzi (1989), *Bond Markets Analysis and Strategies*, Prentice Hall, and to D Duffie (1989), *Future Markets*, Prentice Hall, p 251–78.

Part VII   Bibliography

Abernathy W and Wayne K (1983), 'Limits of the learning curve', in *Survival Strategies for American Industries*, John Wiley (pp 114–31).

Abuaf N and Jorion P, 'Purchasing Power Parity in the Long Run', *Journal of Finance* (March), pp 157–74.

Adler M and Dumas B (1984), 'Exposure to Currency Risk: Definition and Measurements', *Financial Management* (Summer), pp 41–50.

Adler M and Lehman B (1983), 'Deviations from Purchasing Power Parity in the Long Run', *Journal of Finance* (December), pp 1471–87.

Alliber RZ (1978), *Exchange Risk and Corporate International Finance*, John Wiley.

Antl B and Ensor R (eds) (1982), *Management of Foreign Exchange Risk* Euromoney.

Berliner C and Brimson J (eds) (1988), *Cost Management for Today's Advanced Manufacturing*, Harvard Business School Press.

Borden J (1990), 'Review of Literature on Activity Based Costing', *Cost Management* (Spring), pp 5–13.

Bromwich M and Hopwood A (eds) (1986), *Research and Current Issues in Management Accounting*, Pitman.

Chrystal K (1984), 'A Guide to Foreign Exchange Markets', *Federal Reserve Bank of Saint Louis* (March), pp 5–17.

Clark K and Adler P (1991), 'Behind the Learning Curve: A Sketch of the Learning Process', *Management Science* (March), pp 267–81.

Clinton K (1988), 'Transaction Costs and Covered Interest Advantage: Theory and Evidence', *Journal of Political Economy* (April), **96**: pp 358–70.

Cooper R (1989), 'You Need a New Cost System When . . .', *Harvard Business Review* (January–February), pp 77–82.

Dolan R and Jeuland A (1981), 'Experience Curves and Dynamic Demand Mode Models: Implications for Optimal Pricing Strategies', *Journal of Marketing* (Winter), pp 52–62.

Duffie D (1989), *Future Markets*, Prentice Hall.

Fabozzi F and Fabozzi D (1989), *Bond Markets Analysis and Strategies* Prentice Hall.

Fama E (1975), 'Short Term Interest rates as Predictors of Inflation', *American Economic Review* (June), **65**: pp 269–82.

Fama E (1984), 'Forward and Spot Exchange Rates', *Journal of Monetary Economics*, **14**: pp 319–38.

Fisher I (1935 and 1965), *The Theory of Interest: As Determined by Impatience to Spend Income and Opportunity to Invest*, Augustus M. Kelley.

Ezzell JR and Kelly WA Jr (1984), 'An APV analysis of capital budgeting under inflation', *Financial Management* (Autumn), pp 49–54.

Flood E and Lessard D (1986), 'On the Measurement of Operating Exposure to Exchange Rates: A Conceptual Approach', *Financial Management* (Spring), pp 25–36.

Frenkel J and Levich R (1975) 'Covered Interest Arbitrage: Unexploited Profits?', *Journal of Political Economy* (April), pp 325–38.

Hax A and Majluf N (1982), 'Competitive cost dynamics: the experience curve', *Interfaces* (October), pp 50–61.

Hess P and Bicksler (1975), 'Capital Assets Prices Versus Time Series Models as Predictors of Inflation', *Journal of Financial Economics* (December), **2**: pp 341–60.

Houston C (1989), 'Foreign Currency Translation Research: Review and Synthesis', *Journal of Accounting Literature*, **8**: pp 25–48.

Johnson T and Kaplan R (1987), *Relevance Lost, The Rise and Fall of Management Accounting*, Harvard Business School Press.

Kaplan R (ed.) (1990), *Measures for Manufacturing Excellence*, Harvard Business School Press.

Kerin R, Harvey M and Rothe J (1978), 'Cannibalism and new product development', *Business Horizons* (October), pp 25–31.

Kester W and Luehrman T (1989), 'Are We Feeling More Competitive Yet? The Exchange Rate Gambit', *Sloan Management Review* (Winter), pp 19–28.

Lessard D (ed.) (1985), *International Financial Management*, John Wiley & Sons.

Lessard DR and Lightstone JB (1986), 'Volatile exchange rates can put operations at risk', *Harvard Business Review* (July/Aug), pp 107–14.

Lilien G, Kotler P and Sridhar Moorthy K (1992), *Marketing Models*, Prentice Hall.

Mahajan V, Muller E and Bass F (1990), 'New Product Diffusion Models in Marketing', *Journal of Marketing* (January), pp 1–26.

McNamee PB (1985), *Tools and Techniques for Strategic Management*, Pergamon Press.

Monden Y and Hamada K (1991), 'Target Costing and Kaizen Costing in Japanese Automobile Companies', *Journal of Management Accounting Research* (Fall), pp 16–34.

Mullick S, Anderson G, Leach R and Smith W (1982), 'Life cycle forecasting', in Makridakis S and Wheelwright S (eds) *The Handbook of Forecasting*, John Wiley.

Nelson CR (1976), 'Inflation and capital budgeting', *Journal of Finance* (June) **31**: 923–31.

Nelson C and Schwert G (1977), 'Short-term Interest Rates as Predictors of Inflation: On Testing the Hypothesis that the Real Rate of Interest is Constant', *American Economic Review* (June), **67**: pp 478–86.

Porter M (1989), *Competitive Strategy*, The Free Press.

Porter M (1985), *Competitive Advantage*, The Free Press.

Quinn Mills D (1985), *The New Competition*, John Wiley.

Shapiro AC (1985), 'What does purchasing parity mean?', in Lessard DR (ed), *Financial Management: Theory and Application*, John Wiley.

Shapiro AC (1992), *Multinational Financial Management*, Allyn and Bacon.

Robinson MA (ed.) (1990), 'Contribution Margin Analysis: No Longer Relevant/ Strategic Cost Management: The New Paradigm', *Journal of Management Accounting Research*, (Fall), **2**: pp 1–32.

Stern J and Chew D (1988), *New Developments in International Finance*, Basil Blackwell.

Takeuchi H and Nokaka I (1986), 'The new product development game', *Harvard Business Review* (Jan/Feb).

Wolff (1987), 'Foreign Exchange Rates, Expected Spot Rates and Premia: A Signal Extraction Approach', *Journal of Finance* (June), pp 395–406.

Acquisitions, Mergers, Joint Ventures and Strategic Alliances

Models for Creating and Implementing Cooperative Strategies

We would now like you to practise one of the most powerful uses of models: *models as a tool for creating and implementing cooperative strategies.*

Part VIII is devoted to a case that was developed from the negotiation that took place between two major automotive groups in the mid 1980s.[1] F, the leader of the truck industry in the United Kingdom has offered I to acquire its operations. For I, the second-largest European manufacturer of trucks, this is a unique opportunity to build a very strong position in a key market and to close the overall market share gap it has with the industry leader in Europe.

Even though they both have a lot to gain from an agreement, I and F have to solve a series of difficult problems: how to structure an agreement that minimizes the risk of the acquisition, how to fix a price that satisfies both parties, etc. Our task is to help I capture this strategic opportunity.

Part VIII starts with a framework for evaluating companies. Then, the case I in the United Kingdom introduces the situation as it is viewed by I. Please do as we recommend you to do with the previous cases:

- Read the case very carefully.
- Prepare the negotiation with F as if you were going to run it.

Part VIII will provide you with a unique advantage over most real-life situations.

- A second case, F Trucks, will enable you to discover the actual position of F.
- A third case, the negotiation between I and F, will tell you how the actual negotiation developed and reached a critical stage. This will enable you to reassess the conditions of a successful deal between the two companies.

Cooperation

Part VIII deals with a critical process for creating and sharing value in business: the process by which two or more parties work side by side against problems, ie the negotiation process, or more generally, the cooperation process.[2]

As shown by Axelrod,[3] cooperation is primarily a very pragmatic and effective rule for action. Cooperation does not require altruism, friendship or the existence of a central authority. Cooperation only requires that 'egoists', or self-interested and opportunistic people, driven by their own interests recognize that:

- They are not alone, there are many other egoists around.
- Life is not a zero-sum game, ie there are other ways to create value than to grab it from somebody else.
- Their interactions with other egoists will be durable, or as expressed by Axelrod, that the 'shadow of the future' is large. When interaction with others is sufficiently durable, cooperation is the most effective strategy to advance your own interests.

Cooperation is a process that does not necessarily require the existence of negotiated agreements[4] between the parties, it may simply grow out of the interactive behaviour of the parties.[5]

In the business world of today cooperation has become a very important strategic and operational issue:

- When adopting innovative manufacturing technologies, numerous companies have discovered that a critical success factor is the creation and the effective management of more cooperative, long term – or repeat – relationships with their suppliers.[6]
- Companies operating in complex, rapidly changing industries have realized that effective competition should not necessarily aim at simply destroying other companies and sometimes requires the establishment and successful implementation of strategic alliances with some key competitors.[7]
- In complex, decentralized and global organizations, accountability is increasingly concentrated while authority and resources are more and more shared or diffused. In such organizations, managers can only succeed through cooperation and influence.[8]

Successful cooperation requires a series of attitudes that can be greatly enhanced by effective modelling and simulation. According to Raiffa,[9] successful cooperation requires careful preparation, the main elements of which are: know yourself, know the other parties, give thought to the negotiating conventions, consider the logistics of the situation, use simulated role playing, iterate and set your aspiration levels.

Spreadsheet modelling is the powerful and flexible tool you need to perform the many simulations that can help you imagine how to design and implement valuable cooperation. It is also the tool that can help you enhance your cooperating or negotiating skills and in particular your ability to simulate the point of view of the other parties and your capacity to reformulate business situations into win–win solutions.[10]

KEY LEARNING POINTS

■ **MODELS AS A TOOL FOR CREATING AND IMPLEMENTING COOPERATION**

Mapping the alternatives available to the parties involved in a cooperative situation, page 505.
Modelling the integrative or win-win dynamics of a situation, page 507.
Using models to try to understand what the other parties think their interests are, pages 509 and 528. Reversing roles, page 536.
Assessing the value of alternative agreements, page 555. Evaluation of a joint venture agreement, page 552.
Anticipating the termination of a joint venture agreement, page 557.

■ **OTHER MODELLING ISSUES**

Using models to further our understanding of the competitive dynamics of an industry, page 522.
A model to assess the value of a new product, page 514.
Using simple models and 'rules of thumb' to frame results, pages 484 and 525.
Dealing with inflation pages 473, 477 and 510.

■ **VALUING AN ACQUISITION TARGET**

Deriving value from an assessment of future cash flows, page 470.
Breaking future cash flows into future cash flows from past activities (page 483), future cash flows during a planning period (page 471) and future cash flows beyond that period, or terminal or continuing value (page 474).
Cash flow and perpetuity formulas, page 476; Finite period of superior performance (page 479).
Using Price-to-earnings ratios (PER), page 479. Which PER to use, Figure 29.3 page 481.
Other approaches to valuation (page 482). Formulas and 'rules of thumb' pages 482 and 485.

■ **CREATING VALUE OUT OF RISK**

Reducing risk through cooperative behaviours, pages 549 and 552.
Using Time as a way to destroy risk, page 551.
Agreeing to disagree as a powerful way to create value out of differences in risk perceptions, page 550.

■ Cumulative cash equals cumulated profit, page 476.
■ Conditions for creating value out of growth, pages 476 and 523.

■ **COOPERATION AND NEGOTIATION**

Cooperation as the most effective way to maximize your own interests in the long run, page 466.
The integrative and claiming dimensions of a cooperative situation, page 505.
BATNAs and zone of agreement, page 507.
How to create value through cooperation page 505, differences as a source of value, pages 506 and 550.
The danger of negotiating over positions, page 537.

■ **JOINT VENTURES AS AN ALTERNATIVE TO STRAIGHT BUY OUTS**, pages 539 and 552.

■ Niche vs volume strategies in the European truck industry, page 523.
■ Accounting treatment of business combinations (page 561), the notion of goodwill (page 562).

NOTES

1 Part VIII has been developed from the negotiation that took place between Iveco, the truck company of the Fiat group, and Ford in the mid 1980s. The situation and the data have been modified in order to preserve business confidentiality.

2 The essence of negotiation and cooperation situations is to entwine two dimensions: creation of value and sharing of value. The problem with the word 'negotiation' is that for many people it is associated with sharing of value, conflict of wills, compromise, etc. Consequently we prefer using the word cooperation.

3 *The Evolution of Cooperation*, R Axelrod, Basic Books, New York, 1984.

4 Actually, as stated by P Rubin in *Managing Business Transactions*, The Free Press, New York, 1990, 'it is impossible to write complete contracts which take account of any and all possible events and which eliminate all forms of opportunism or cheating'. Processes other than negotiated agreements are needed to control opportunism. Among those processes, Rubin mentions the 'creation of a reputation', a concept which is very close to the 'shadow of the future'.

5 In *The Selfish Gene*, Oxford University Press, Oxford, 1989, R Dawkins shows that cooperative strategies apply in the world of nature also: consciousness is irrelevant to the development of cooperative strategies.

6 Refer for example to 'Mixed Motive Marriages: What's next for Buyer-Supplier Relations?', J Henke, R Krachenberg and T Lyons, *Sloan Management Review*, Spring 1990, pp 29–36; Managing Suppliers: Incentive Systems in Japanese and US Industry', J McMillian, *California Management Review*, Summer 1990, pp 38–55; 'How Much Has Really Changed Between U.S. Automakers and their Suppliers', S Helper, *Sloan Management Review*, Summer 1991, pp 15–28.

7 Refer for example to 'Beyond Vertical Integration – The Rise of the Value-Adding Partnership', *Harvard Business Review*, July–August 1988, pp 94–101; 'Cooperate with Your Competitors and Win', Y Doz and CK Prahalad, *Harvard Business Review*, Jan–Feb 1989.

8 Refer for example to *Power and Influence – Beyond Formal Authority*, J Kotter, The Free Press, New York 1985; *The Manager as a Negotiator – Bargaining for Cooperation and Competitive Gain*, DA Lax, and JK Sebenius, The Free Press, New York 1986; *Influence Without Authority*, A Cohen and D Bradford, John Wiley & Sons, New York, 1990.

9 *The Art and Science of Negotiation*, The Belknap Press of Harvard University Press, 1982, Chapter 9.

10 Research shows that most negotiators tend to make similar mistakes, or have similar biases:

> Assumption of a 'fixed pie'.
> Framing of the situation in term of potential losses rather than in term of potential gains.
> Belief that too much has been invested to quit.
> Belief that their positions will prevail in the end, provided they do not give in.
> Underestimation of the importance of accurate information.
> Assumption that the other party is fairly inactive.

These biases are analyzed in *Judgement in Managerial Decisions*, MH Bazerman, John Wiley & Sons, New York, 1986.

CHAPTER 29

A Framework for Evaluating Companies[1]

29.1 EVALUATING COMPANIES: MODELLING OPPORTUNITIES AND CHALLENGES

The value of a company that you are considering acquiring is equal to the difference between two present values:

- the present value of the additional free cash flows that *you* expect to generate as a result of this acquisition.
- the price that you need to pay for acquiring this company.

Assessing a company creates unique modelling opportunities and challenges.

When considering acquiring a company, you need to build models that help you understand how this company works and what its risks are. If, as is often the case, you envisage changing the strategy of the acquired company, you need to assess the possible outcomes of the new strategy as well as the results of the transition to the desired new situation.

Structuring and implementing acquisition or merger agreements mean that several parties decide to cooperate. Establishing effective cooperation requires that each party understands its own interests as well as the interests of all the other parties involved. Models can help you role-play the situation of the other parties and further your understanding of their specific points of view.

Acquisitions and mergers present specific modelling challenges; unique situations, need for innovative solutions, high uncertainty, incomplete or unreliable information, etc. A further problem is that companies generally have very long lives – infinite, or at least long and indefinite lives. When assessing the value of an acquisition opportunity, you need to build and use genuine long-term, strategic models.

When, as is usually the case, the seller is paid in cash at the date of acquisition,[2] the immediate payment creates an asymmetry in the risk exposures of the two parties. When you are in the position of the buyer and are asked for an immediate cash payment, you need to assess your risk in a systematic fashion.

Finally, a warning; acquiring companies sounds like a very exciting activity, but it is a difficult business. Even though it does not give any definite answers, the literature[3] suggests that it is not easy to create value through mergers and acquisitions and that buyers tend to pay a premium over market prices. As a consequence, be very careful with your acquisition models.

- Do not use models so as to become overconfident about the value that you can achieve. As shown in Part VI, positive net present values only result from superior competitive strategies. Believing that you can derive a positive value from an acquisition should mean that you are confident that this acquisition will lead to a superior performance; either superior future performance and/or exceptionally low acquisition price.[4]
- Specify very clearly the key assumptions which drive your value estimates and make explicit decisions regarding the complexity of your models. When evaluating a very uncertain situation it is generally not a good idea to use very detailed models. Detailed models require a lot of data and when these data are not reliable the final result might be misleading.
- Do not rely on one single valuation method. When you are confronted with a new and unique situation the methods you are comfortable with might be challenged. A useful precaution is to use a variety of methods and check that they lead to similar results.
- Finally, make sure that your models envisage all the tax implications.[5]

29.2 BREAKING THE VALUE OF AN ACQUISITION INTO THREE COMPONENTS

The future free cash flows[6] that you expect to derive from an acquisition belong to two main categories.

- The cash flows that will be generated by the future activity; it is common practice to break these cash flows into two successive periods:
  - · an initial – or explicit planning period corresponding, for example, to the first five years after the acquisition and
  - · a second period corresponding to all subsequent years beyond the initial planning period. The value of these cash flows is often called the *continuing* or *terminal value*.
- The future cash flows that will result from the pre-acquisition activity; when acquiring a company, you generally inherit from debts raised in the past, from accounts receivable, from accounts payable, etc.

When estimating the value of an acquisition prospect, it is a good idea to:

- Evaluate successively each of the three value components: *(1) present value of the cash flows during the initial planning period, (2) continuing value and (3) value of the inheritance from the pre-acquisition activity.*

■ Estimate the value as the sum of these three components and frame your estimate through a comparison with similar transactions or any other relevant benchmark. This enables you to put your valuation in perspective and to check that it is not excessive – or that there are good reasons for it being very high.

29.3   ASSESSING THE PRESENT VALUE OF THE CASH FLOWS DURING THE INITIAL OR EXPLICIT PLANNING PERIOD

Three common reasons for using an initial or explicit planning period

A first, and not necessarily valid, reason for singling out an initial planning period, relates to the belief that the initial cash flows are the ones which matter most. One thing to remember is that even though each of the early cash flows has a much greater weight than any more distant one, it is not necessarily true that discounting makes the sum of all the distant cash flows negligible. Figure 29.1 shows the proportion of the total value of a potential acquisition that is captured by the initial planning period depending on the profile of the future cash flows, the length of the initial planning period, and the discount rate.[7]

Figure 29.1 shows that there are many situations where the value of the cash flows beyond the planning period matters and should get all your attention.

■ When you evaluate an acquisition with high growth prospects, the long-term cash flows are the ones which matter most. When acquiring a business in an emerging industry, the value of the cash flows during the first years might even be negative.
■ Even when the future cash flows decline by 5% a year, the value of the cash flows beyond five years represents as much as 38% of the total value when you use a 15% discount rate!

A second, and very good reason for singling out an initial planning period relates to the fact that you, as the new owner, plan to change the strategy or the operations of the acquired company or to integrate this company into another company. This will cause the years immediately following the acquisition to be transition years that should be modelled in great detail. When the rationale for the initial planning period is the modelling of a transition:

■ the length of the initial planning period should correspond to the time needed for the transition;
■ the cash flows should probably be modelled according to the traditional accounting approach (like the one we used for the analysis of Delta Metal)

MODEL

	A	B
1	Length of the planning period	5
2	Constant annual growth	3%
3	Discount rate	10%
4	Total value of the future cash flows	14
5	Value captured by the planning period	4
6	Percentage of value captured by the planning period	28%

Formulas:
B4: 1/(B3–B2) . For the formula see page 295.
B5: (1–((1+B2)/(1+B3))^B1)/(B3–B2) . For the formula see page 231.
B6: +B5/B4

RESULTS

Percentage of value captured by the planning period

1   When future cash flows grow 3% each year

Discount rate	Length of the planning period (in years)		
	5	10	15
10%	28%	48%	63%
15%	42%	67%	81%
20%	53%	78%	90%

2   When future cash flows are constant

Discount rate	Length of the planning period (in years)		
	5	10	15
10%	38%	61%	76%
15%	50%	75%	88%
20%	60%	84%	94%

3   When future cash flows decline 5% each year

Discount rate	Length of the planning period (in years)		
	5	10	15
10%	52%	77%	89%
15%	62%	85%	94%
20%	69%	90%	97%

Figure 29.1   Proportion of the total value captured by the planning period.

which is well adapted to a detailed, short-term assessment of a business. Long-term strategic modelling approaches based on concepts like product life cycle profiles and learning cost dynamics (like the approach that we used for the analysis of BA International) are probably more adapted to the longer term when a more stable situation has been reached.

A third very good reason for using an initial planning period relates to the belief that superior strategies cannot be sustained forever. It is not easy for a company to maintain a superior competitive position that enables it to generate above market returns and economic theory tells us that, in the long run, companies' returns tend towards their cost-of-capital or industry-required return. As a consequence you may decide to break the future cash flows into two successive periods:

- the period during which you believe that the acquired company will sustain a superior competitive performance;
- the subsequent years in which performance will just equal the cost of capital.

In this case you should probably use a relatively long planning period – as long as the superior competitive position will last – and you should probably adopt a long-term modelling approach similar to the one we used in the BA International case.

A three-step approach for assessing the value of the free cash flows in the initial planning period

The first step is to ask yourself why you want to use an initial planning period and how long you want this initial planning period to be. You can then simulate the strategy of the acquired company during the planning period. Which are the underlying competitive ideas? How can these ideas be implemented and sustained? What are the expected revenues and costs – including the potential synergies? What are the capital expenditures needed? What are the resulting free cash flows? You should also choose a modelling approach suited to the problem: traditional accounting approach, long-term strategic approach or a mixture of both.

Finally, if you plan to change the strategy of the acquired company, you should carefully simulate the transition from the old to the new strategy: how much of the existing inventories can be used? (Any inventory used will decrease the expected future disbursements.) Are the existing fixed assets suited to the new strategy? Do some of these assets need to be modified? Are some fixed assets not needed any longer? How much cash can be derived from their disposal? More generally, what are the costs involved in adapting the existing structure and resources to the new strategy; people-related costs (training, recruitment, dismissals), administrative systems costs, etc. The simulation of the transition process and of its financial implications is generally very difficult and requires a lot of 'what-if' analyses.

The inflation issue

As in any financial model you have the choice between the constant prices–real rate and the current prices–current rate approaches (see Chapter 25). When the initial planning period is short and when the cash flows are modelled according to an accounting approach, it is common practice to use the current prices–current rate approach. When you use a long initial planning period and a long-term strategic modelling approach, it is probably better to use the constant prices–real rate approach and eventually adjust the value in order to remove the bias introduced by this approach.

29.4   A SERIES OF APPROACHES FOR ASSESSING THE CONTINUING OR TERMINAL VALUE

A variety of approaches are used in practice to assess the value of the cash flows beyond the initial planning period. The price-to-earnings (PE)[8] ratio and the cash flow or profit perpetuity formula approaches are probably the most widely used but various approaches based on an explicit assessment of the free cash flows or profits beyond the initial planning period are gaining acceptance. Other approaches are used also.

The explicit cash flow or profit forecast approaches

These approaches are the ones that we recommend you to use whenever possible; they can be more or less detailed. A detailed approach would be similar to the one we have used to assess the value of P12 at BA International. A non-detailed approach is the one shown in Figure 29.2. Rather than building a full cash flow model, you make a direct estimate of the annual free cash flows after the initial planning period.

- You start with the estimate of three interrelated parameters: return, cash flow before new investments (or profit), and capital needed to generate such a cash flow – or capital or assets in place – at the end of the initial planning period.
- Then, you estimate the annual free cash flows as the difference between the cash flow before investments generated by the capital in place at the beginning of the year and the additional investments required by growth.
- Finally, you estimate the continuing value as the net present value of the free cash flows. The difference between this value and the value of the capital in place at the end of the planning period corresponds to the additional value created by growth.

It is worth noting that the annual free cash flow increases as long as the return is higher than the cost of capital. But as soon as the return becomes equal to the cost of capital, the annual free cash flow does not increase any longer.[9] This is

	A	B	C	D	E	F	G	H	I	...	CU	CV	CW
1	Return of acquired company during planning period					0.2							
2	Length of the period of above market return (years)					5							
3	Annual growth					0.04							
4	Cost of capital					0.12							
5	Base profit in year 1 after planning period					10							
6													
7	**FREE CASH FLOW APPROACH**												
8	Year (after planning period)	1	2	3	4	5	6	7	8		98	99	100
9	Return	0.2	0.2	0.2	0.2	0.2	0.12	0.12	0.12		0.12	0.12	0.12
10	Capital invested open	50	52	54	56	58	61	63	66		2 245	2 335	2 428
11	Additional capital needed	2	2	2	2	2	2	3	3		90	93	97
12	Cash flow before investments	10	10	11	11	12	12	13	13		449	467	486
13	Cash flow above market return	8	8	9	9	9	10	10	11		359	374	388
14	Actual free cash flow	8	8	9	9	9	7	7	7		7	7	7
15	NPV (last year planning period)	65											
16	NPV Capital in place	50											
17	NPV Growth	15		Growth as a %			24%						
18													
19													
20													
21													
22	**PROFIT APPROACH**												
23	Year (after planning period)	1	2	3	4	5	6	7	8		98	99	100
24	Return	0.2	0.2	0.2	0.2	0.2	0.12	0.12	0.12		0.12	0.12	0.12
25	Profit	10	10	11	11	12	7	8	8		269	280	291
26	Capital invested open	50	52	54	56	58	61	63	66		2 245	2 335	2 428
27	Additional capital needed	2	2	2	2	2	2	3	3		90	93	97
28	Cost of capital	6	6	6	7	7	7	8	8		269	280	291
29	Above market profit	4	4	4	4	5	0	0	0		0	0	0
30	NPV (above market profit)	15											
31	NPV Capital in place	50											
32	NPV (last year planning period)	65											

Formulas

B9: @IF(B8‹=$F$2,$F$1,$F$4); Copy to C9..CW9.
B10: +F5/F1; C10: +B10+B11; Copy to D10..CW10
B11: +B10*$F$3; Copy to C11..CW11
B12: +F5; C12: +C10*$F$1; Copy to D12..CW12
B13: +B10*$F$1– B11; Copy to D13..CW13
B14: @IF(B8‹=$F$2,B13, ($B$10*(1+$F$3)^(F2))*$F$4)
B15: @NPV(F4,B14.CW14)
B16: +B10
B17: +B15–B16   in G17: +B17/B15

B24: @IF(B23‹=$F$2,$F$1,$F$4); Copy to C24..CW24.
B25: +F5   C25: +C24*(B26+B27); Copy.
B26: +B25/B24; C26: +B26+B27; Copy.
B27: +B26*$F$3; Copy.
B28: +B26*F4. C28: +$F$4*(B26+B27); Copy.
B29: +B25–B28; Copy.
B30: @NPV(F4,B29..CW29)
B31: +B26
B32: +B30+B31

Figure 29.2 A model for assessing the continuing value.

due to the fact that the additional investments become exactly equal to the increase in cash flow.

An alternative model based on annual profits is also shown in Figure 29.2. The value is estimated as the sum of the value of the capital in place at the end of the planning period and the value of growth. The value of growth is equal to the present value of the additional annual profits caused by growth. As long as the return is higher than the cost of capital, the additional investments required by growth generate an additional profit equal to the difference between the above-market return and the cost of capital. As soon as the return becomes equal to the cost of capital, the additional investments break even and no additional profit is created any longer. Since working capital needs are ignored, the cash flow and profit approaches give similar results.

The model in Figure 29.2 assumes:

- a very long modelling period. This enables you to assess the impact of the length of the period of above-market returns and growth;
- constant above-market returns and growth. If you want to test the impact of variable returns and growth, we advise you to use the profit model and (1) insert a blank row above row 27 and use it to introduce annual growth, (2) correct the formula for additional capital, and (3) introduce the annual return and growth rates.

Growth is not always a source of value

The model in Figure 29.2 can help you check once more that growth has a positive impact on value only when the company generates a return higher than the industry-required return of cost of capital. If the company has no superior competitive advantage and just generates the industry-required return, its value is not increased by growth. If the company generates a return lower than its cost of capital, then growth reduces its value.

The cash flow and profit perpetuity formula approaches

These approaches also estimate continuing value as the present value of a stream of annual free cash flows or profits. But these approaches further assume that cash flows or profits behave steadily after the end of the planning period: ie constant or growing at a constant rate up to infinity which enables you to use simple perpetuity formulas (see note 4 on page 294). Even though they look very simple, these approaches pose a series of problems.

Which variable should you discount, profit or cash?

Cash is obviously the variable to be discounted but since the only difference between cash and profit is time, you may assume that beyond the planning period cash will lag behind (or lead) profit by a constant period of time.

Consequently, you can discount either annual profits or annual free cash flows, keeping in mind that the profit-based NPV will differ from the cash-based NPV by a factor corresponding to the cash–profit timing difference. When assessing long-term outcomes, you might find it easier to focus on profit and assess the continuing value as the present value of the stream of future annual profits. You may eventually decide to adjust this present value through discounting: for example, if you believe that cash will lag by one year behind profit, you may discount the profit-based present value by one additional year in order to get the cash-based NPV.

The inflation issue

Here again you have to decide which approach you want to use: constant prices–real rate or current prices–current rate. When doing so, be careful and check the internal consistency of your assumptions beyond the planning period (profit or cash flow level, superior return, growth, cost of capital) as well as their consistency with the assumptions made for the initial planning period.

The case when performance is equal to the industry-required return

When you assume that the company will not have a superior competitive position beyond the planning period and as a result will generate a return just equal to the industry-required return or cost of capital, you actually mean that future growth will not matter. If sales grow after the planning period, the company will have to invest in order to sustain this growth and:

- the additional investments will return exactly as much as they cost (i.e. their net present value will be nil) and the annual profit will remain constant for ever;
- the additional investments will be exactly equal to the additional cash flows and as a result the annual cash flow will remain constant for ever.

When profit is constant forever, the calculation of the continuing value is very simple:

$$\text{Continuing value} = \frac{\text{PAT 1}}{\text{rr}}$$

Where PAT1 = Profit after tax in the first year after the planning period.
  rr = industry required return (cost of capital).

Even though it looks simplistic, this assessment of the continuing value is, and should be, of a wide use. It corresponds to the reasonable assumption that, in the long run, the return of a company is equal to the industry-required return or cost of capital. It is the formula you should always use when you believe that the superior performance of the acquired company will not extend beyond the initial planning period.

A problem however is that the perpetuity formula assumes that the company will generate the industry required return up to infinity. If the company generates the industry-required return for a limited period of time only, then the perpetuity formula overestimates the true value:

Actual period of industry-required returns	Overestimation of the true value (with a 10% discount rate)
40 years	2%
30	6%
25	10%
20	17%
15	31%

Since there are few companies and industries which have been around for a very long period of time, these results should encourage you to be careful when using a perpetuity formula!

The case where you believe that the company can sustain a superior performance forever

As the company generates a return higher than its cost of capital, then growth is valuable and should be taken into account. The perpetuity formula to be used is the following:

$$\text{Continuing value} = \frac{PAT1}{r} + \frac{PAT1 * (r-rr)}{r} * \frac{1}{(rr - g)}$$

Where PAT1 = Profit after tax in the first year after the explicit planning period.

g   = growth rate
r   = above market return
rr = required return (cost of capital)

To derive this formula, you should consider that the continuing value is equal to the sum of the values of:

- the capital in place at the end of the planning period, ie

PAT1/r, and

- the additional profits that will result from valuable growth. In the first year, the additional profit is equal to the value of the capital in place multiplied by the difference between the above market return of the additional investments required to sustain the growth and the cost of capital

PAT1/r * (r−rr)

As annual additional profits grow at a constant rate g, and provided that g is small[11] and lower than rr (the cost of capital) their present value can be approximated by

PAT1/r * (r−rr) * 1/(rr−g)

The perpetuity formula can be rewritten as:

$$\text{Continuing value} = \text{PAT1} * \frac{(1 - g/r)}{(rr - g)}$$

Introducing the perpetuity formula into the model

To introduce the perpetuity formula in the model shown in Figure 29.2, the inputs are the following:

In A18: NPV perpetuity formula
In B18: +B12*(1−F3/F1)/(F4−F3)
In C18: Difference with exact formula
In G18: +B18/B15−1

The finite period of superior performance approach

As you might find it difficult to believe that superior performance can be maintained forever, you might feel more comfortable with using a formula[12] that assumes that the superior performance is limited to a period of P years.

$$\text{Continuing value} = \text{PAT1}*(1/r + \frac{(r-rr)}{r*(rr-g)} * (1-((1+g)/(1+rr))\char`\^P)$$

where P = length of the period of superior performance.

This formula assumes that return and growth rates are constant but, contrary to the perpetuity formula, is not an approximation.

Introducing the finite period formula into the model

To introduce the finite period formula in the model shown in Figure 29.2, the inputs are:

In A19: NPV finite period formula
In B19: +F5*(1/F1+(F1−F4)/(F1*(F4−F3))*(1−((1+F3)/(1+F4))^ F2))

The price-to-earnings (PE) ratio approach

This approach assumes that the value of the company at the end of the initial period is equal to its profit after tax multiplied by the relevant PE ratio. Profit after tax might correspond to a single estimate (profit after tax in the first year after the explicit planning period), or to an average of several – usually three to five – estimates. The PE ratio might be the PE ratio observed in the industry, the PE ratio of 'comparable' companies, or a purely judgemental PE ratio. Multiplying the profit after tax in the first year following the planning period by a PE ratio is the same as using a perpetuity or finite period formula.

- When you believe that the company has no superior competitive position after the planning period, then the PE ratio is equal to: 1/rr (rr = cost of capital). Some PE ratios and their corresponding implied cost of capital are:

PE ratio	Implied cost of capital
12.5	8%
10	10%
8.3	12%
6.7	15%
5	20%

  Even though it looks simplistic, this approach is of wide use and is the one you should use when you assume that the superior competitive position of the company will not be maintained beyond the initial planning period.
- When you believe that the company will be able to sustain a superior competitive position and benefit from growth for a very long period of time, then the PE ratio is equal to: (rr − g)/(1 − g/r). With g = growth rate, r = above market return.
- When you believe that the company will be able to sustain a superior return during a finite period of time P only, then the PE ratio is equal to:

  1/(1/r + (r−rr)/r*(rr−g)*(1 − ((1+g)/(1 + rr))^P)

  With P = length of the period of superior performance.

Introducing PE calculations into the model

To introduce PE calculations in the model shown in Figure 29.2, the inputs are the following:

In A20: PE ratio (based on exact formula)
In B20: +B15/F5
In D20: PE ratio (based on perpetuity formula)
In I20: +B18/F5

You can also calculate the PE to be applied to the normalized profit, ie the profit that would be generated by the capital in place if the return were equal to the cost of capital:

In C20: +B15/(F5*F4/F1).

The problem with the PE approach is that it fails to specify its assumptions

Period	5 years				10 years				15 years				Ever		
Cost of capital **Growth Return**	10%	15%	20%	25%	10%	15%	20%	25%	5%	10%	15%	20%	2.5%	5%	10%
12% 15%									8.4	9.0	9.9	11.2	8.8	9.5	13.9
									10.5	11.3	12.4	14.0	11.0	11.9	17.4
20%	6.7	6.9	7.1	7.3	8.3	9.0	10.0	11.1	8.5	9.7	11.5	14.1	9.2	10.7	20.9
	11.2	11.5	11.8	12.1	13.8	15.1	16.6	18.6	14.2	16.2	19.1	23.5	15.3	17.8	34.8
25%	6.2	6.4	6.7	6.9	8.3	9.2	10.5	12.0	8.6	10.2	12.4	15.8	9.5	11.4	25.1
	13.0	13.4	13.9	14.4	17.3	19.3	21.8	25.0	17.9	21.2	25.9	32.9	19.7	23.8	52.2
30%	5.9	6.2	6.4	6.7	8.3	9.4	10.8	12.6	8.6	10.4	13.1	16.9	9.6	11.9	27.8
	14.8	15.4	16.1	16.8	20.7	23.5	27.0	31.4	21.6	26.1	32.7	42.4	24.1	29.7	69.6
40%	5.5	5.8	6.1	6.4	8.3	9.6	11.2	13.3	8.7	10.8	13.9	18.4			
	18.4	19.3	20.3	21.5	27.6	31.9	37.3	44.2	29.0	36.0	46.2	61.3			
Return	10%	15%	20%	25%	10%	15%	20%	25%	5%	10%	15%	20%	2.5%	5%	10%
15% 20%	6.0	6.1	6.2	6.3	6.8	7.2	7.7	8.3	6.9	7.4	8.3	9.5	7.0	7.5	9.9
	8.0	8.1	8.2	8.4	9.1	9.6	10.2	11.0	9.1	9.9	11.0	12.6	9.3	10.0	13.2
25%	5.6	5.7	5.9	6.1	6.9	7.5	8.2	9.2	7.0	7.9	9.2	11.1	7.2	8.0	11.9
	9.3	9.6	9.8	10.1	11.5	12.5	13.7	15.3	11.6	13.2	15.4	18.6	12.0	13.3	19.8
30%	5.3	5.5	5.7	5.9	6.9	7.7	8.6	9.8	7.1	8.2	9.9	12.3	7.3	8.3	13.2
	10.7	11.0	11.4	11.8	13.8	15.4	17.3	19.7	14.1	16.4	19.7	24.5	14.7	16.7	26.4
40%	5.0	5.2	5.5	5.7	7.0	7.9	9.1	10.6	7.2	8.6	10.7	13.7	7.5	8.7	14.8
	13.3	13.9	14.6	15.3	18.6	21.2	24.4	28.4	19.1	22.9	28.4	36.4	20.0	23.3	39.5

Note
The first PE is the PE to apply to the actual profit, the second PE is the PE to apply to the normalized profit.

Figure 29.3 Growth, above-market returns, cost of capital and PE ratios.

which might be misleading. In Figure 29.3 you will find the correspondence between some PE ratios and the values of their key drivers: above market returns, length of the period of superior performance, growth and cost of capital.

The results in Figure 29.3 show that you should be careful and not use unrealistically high PE ratios.

- A high (let us say higher than 10) PE ratio is justified only if you are very confident that the superior performance of an acquisition target is sustainable.
- A high PE ratio is not justified for a company with a short-lived superior performance. Expecting that the company will soon return to a normal performance means that its profits will soon fall from their exceptionally high current level. When you set the above-market return to 30%, the length of period of superior return to 5, the growth to 15%, and the cost of capital to 12%, you get a PE of 6.2. This is less than the PE of 8.3 that you would use if the same profit were the profit of a company generating a 12% return for a very long period of time. Using a PE higher than 8.3 would be valid only if this PE were applied to a normalized profit.

A paradox to finish with PEs: even though the results in Figure 29.3 show that high PE ratios are not easy to justify, some companies do enjoy very high PEs. For example, the 1991 survey of the 1000 most valuable companies in the world[13] showed:

- PEs higher than 20 for many pharmaceutical companies; 25 for Merck, 104 for Astra. These companies were generating superior current returns and the market seemed to expect this to last for a long period of time.
- A few PEs higher than 100 for companies generating very low current returns (Rhone–Poulenc 127, Citicorp 230, Kubota 235, etc.). The rationale for such high PEs was probably more related to the expectation that these companies would quickly return to a normal level of profit rather than benefit from a long period of exceptional returns. In the case of the latter companies, it was extremely difficult to use formulas assuming constant returns and growth rates!

Some other approaches[14]

The *value-to-book value* approach estimates the value as the result of the multiplication of the book value at the end of the planning period by an adequate multiple. This approach poses several problems. A first difficulty is that the book value primarily reflects what has been achieved so far and not the future prospects which drive the continuing value. A second problem is how to find an adequate multiple. There is however one – but not unusual – situation where the book value might be relevant: this is the case when you assume that the acquired company will generate a return equal to its cost of capital after the initial planning period. In this case, the continuing value is equal to the capital in place which should be close to the book value. The multiple you should use in this situation is 1.

The *value-to-sales* approach assesses the continuing value as the result of the multiplication of the estimated sales by an adequate multiple. This approach requires the estimate of sales only, which might be an advantage when the cost structure is very uncertain. The problem though is to find an adequate sales multiple.

The *liquidation-value* approach assumes that the continuing value is equal to the proceeds that could be obtained from the liquidation of the assets. This approach poses a series of problems. A first problem is that the liquidation value remains a mere estimate for as long as the company is actually not liquidated. Another difficulty is that the liquidation value is nothing more than an estimate of the lower limit of the continuing value; if the operations are considered as worth being pursued, it is because the continuing value is higher than the liquidation value.

Formula-based approaches. All over the world, investment bankers, tax authorities and courts often use formulas which derive value as a weighted average of the capitalized value of earnings, dividends, book value, etc. A formula used by the US courts to value privately held stock is the one reported by K Hickman and G Perry:[15]

$$\text{VALUE} = (A * EPS * PE + B * \frac{DIV}{DIVY} + C * BV * BVM) * DISC$$

Where A, B and C are weighting coefficients (A+B+C=1). Typically, A has the highest share value (often 0.5).

EPS = earnings per share or average of the most recent earnings per share (last 5 years for example)

PE = industry related price earning ratio.

DIV = dividend per share

DIVY = dividend yield

BV = book value per share

BVM = industry related book value multiple

DISC = discount factor reflecting the lack of liquidity.

Formula-based approaches are sometimes also called 'rules of thumb': their main value is to reflect expert knowledge.

29.5 ASSESSING THE VALUE OF THE INHERITANCE FROM THE PRE-ACQUISITION ACTIVITY

When you buy a company, you generally inherit the consequences of some of its pre-acquisition operations. The inheritance that matters is the one which will result in future cash flows.

Starting with an analysis of the opening balance sheet

In order to assess the future cash flows that will result from past activities, you should probably start from the balance sheet at the date of acquisition. Some balance sheet items are easy to deal with.

- Cash and marketable securities. Except for the cash balance that might be required by the operations, this is a potential cash inflow (book value of cash and market value of marketable securities), the present value of which increases the value of the acquired company.
- Accounts and notes receivable. Their collection will result in cash inflows, the present value of which also increases the value of the company.
- Accounts payable and other debts. Their payment will cause cash outflows, the present value of which decreases the value of the company.

Some balance sheet items are more difficult to deal with.

- Inventories. The inventories which are going to be used in the new operations enable you to save on future operating costs (as this might already have been taken into account when assessing future operations, be careful to avoid double counting). The inventories which are not going to be used should be liquidated, their liquidation value increases the value of the acquisition.
- Fixed assets. As for inventories, you should make a distinction between those assets which are going to be used for future operations and those which are going to be liquidated. As the value of the assets to be kept has already been implicitly taken into account in the assessment of the future operations, the only additional thing to take into consideration is the present value of the tax savings caused by their depreciation. The value of the assets which are not going to be kept is equal to their liquidation value.

The need to go beyond the analysis of the opening balance sheet

All future cash flows resulting from pre-acquisition activities are not necessarily reflected in the balance sheet. In its past relationships with its customers, banks, competitors, local authorities, personnel, etc, the acquisition candidate might have concluded contracts, created a reputation or conflictual situations that can result in future cash flows – or which might affect future cash flows.

29.6   A FINAL PRECAUTION: FRAMING THE VALUE ESTIMATE

Because the value of an acquisition prospect depends on your unique perspective and ideas, it is very difficult to check that your assessment is correct. Even when you plan to acquire a company listed on the stock market, you might come up with a value that differs from the market value and be very confident – and rightly so – in your estimate. A reason for that might be that you are the only one in the position to merge this company with other operations and capture significant synergies.

When trying to frame an estimate of the value, you should probably:

- actively look for other estimates keeping in mind they are probably going to be different from yours;
- check that you are able to explain why your own estimate differs from these other estimates. If you are not able to explain the differences, check your estimate and revise it if needed.

Among the benchmarks you should use are: value of other transactions, market value, value-to-current earnings, value-to-sales of comparable companies, or even value-to-real parameters.

When the uncertainty is very high it might be very useful to estimate a few value-to-real parameters relationships. In the late 1980s, the industry of cellular operators was emerging in the USA and some companies were actively buying smaller operators in order to build a national coverage. Estimating the value of these small operators was very difficult (starting operations in emerging markets) and as a result it was common practice to frame the value of the small cellular-telephone operators by the number of inhabitants in the geographical area they were licensed to serve (or 'pops'). Industry experts[16] had developed an industry-based model reflecting their educated guess of the future of the industry and had assessed that in 1990, a typical 'pop' was worth something like 200 USD. As the number of 'pops' controlled by a system operator was often the only reliable data available, the total 'pop' value was considered as a very useful framing approach.

29.7 ACCOUNTING FOR MERGERS

This issue is dealt with in Further Models VIII.1.

NOTES

1 For an analysis of acquisitions from a strategic perspective, refer to: P Haspeslagh and D Jemison (1991), *Managing Acquisitions: Creating Value Through Corporate Renewal*, The Free Press and to M Forsgren (1989), *Managing the Internationalization Process: The Swedish Case*, Routledge (Chapters 4 and 5).

2 Cash is a very popular way of paying for mergers. According to *Mergers & Acquisitions*, almost 60% of the acquisition deals in the USA were all cash financed in 1989. May/June 1990, p 63.

3 In 'From Competitive Advantage to Corporate Strategy', *Harvard Business Review*, May–June 1987, pp 43–59, M Porter states that 'the track record of corporate strategy has been dismal' and that his records of 33 large, prestigious US companies over the 1950–86 period show that most of them have divested many more acquisitions than they have kept. Several studies of the post-merger performance of acquiring firms are not very encouraging either. In 'The Market for Corporate Control: The Scientific Evidence', *Journal of Financial Economics*, 11, 1983, pp 5–50, M Jensen and R Ruback report an average abnormal return of −5.5% during the twelve months after takeover. However, in 'The Postmerger Share–Price Performance of Acquiring Firms', *Journal of Financial Economics*, 29, 1991, pp 83–96,

J Franks, R Harris and S Titman argue that poor performance after takeover is likely due to benchmark errors.

4 The idea that overconfidence may lead managers to overpay acquisitions is documented in several studies. See for example: 'The Hubris Hypothesis of Corporate Takeovers', R Roll, *Journal of Business*, 59, 1986, pp 197–216 and 'Do Managerial Objectives Drive Bad Acquisitions?', R Morck, A Shleifer, and R Vishny, *The Journal of Finance*, March 1990, pp 31–48. In 'Do Bidder Managers Knowingly Pay Too Much for Target Firms?', *Journal of Business* Vol 63, 1990, H Nejat Seyun argues that it does not seem that bidder managers pay too much knowingly.

In 'Merger Bids, Uncertainty, and Stockholder Returns', *Journal of Financial Economics*, 11, pp 51–83, P Asquith shows that while selling firms receive substantial premiums, stockholders of buying firms roughly break even. The literature suggests that the value which corresponds to the target gains is created either by synergies or by the shifting of the control of the business to more effective managers (see for example: 'Synergy, Agency, and the Determinants of Premia Paid in Mergers', A Slusky and R Caves, *The Journal of Industrial Economics*, XXXIX, March 1991, pp 277–95).

5 In spite of its critical importance, this issue cannot be dealt with in a general text like this one. When dealing with an acquisition, make sure that you understand all the tax implications of the transaction.

6 The need to value acquisitions from their future cash flows is now well accepted. See for example: *Valuation: Measuring and Managing the Value of Companies*, T Copeland, T Koller, and J Murrin, 1990, John Wiley & Sons, New York.

7 It is worth noting that the approach shown in Figure 29.1 is not easy to use and can result in over-optimistic estimates. The difficulty stems from growth: when assessing the growth of the future free cash flows, you need to recognize the impact of the additional investments required by growth. Due to these investments, the annual free cash flow increases only when the additional investments generate a return higher than the cost of capital. This is shown in the model in Figure 29.2.

8 See definition on page 295.

9 'Capital' or 'Assets in Place' are the same as Capital Employed and 'Return' is the same as Return on Capital Employed. Estimating return and capital in place is not easy and as shown in Further Model IV.4, estimates derived from income statements and balance sheets can be misleading.

10 This means that the NPV of the free cash flows could be calculated as the sum of:

- the NPV of the free cash flows during the period of above market returns;
- the NPV of the capital in place at the end of that period. The value of the capital in place is the present value of a perpetuity; the stream of constant cash flows after the period of above market returns.

You can modify the model in Figure 29.2 and check that you get the same results.

11 Lower than 5–6%, which is not a major problem since it is difficult to imagine high growth rates lasting for ever and always corresponding to above market return situations.

12 The formula is derived as follows:

Value = Value of capital in place + Value of growth

$$= \quad PAT1/r \quad + \quad VG$$

$$VG = \frac{PAT1 - C1}{(1+rr)} + \frac{PAT2 - C2}{(1+rr)^2} + \ldots + \frac{PATp - Cp}{(1+rr)^p}$$

with C1, C2, Cp = cost of financing the capital in place.

$$PAT1 - C1 = PAT1 * (1 - rr/r)$$
$$PAT2 - C2 = PAT1 * (1 - rr/r) * (1 + g)$$
$$PATp - Cp = PAT1 * (1 - rr/r) * (1 + g)^{p-1}$$

$$VG = PAT1 * (1 - rr/r) * \left(\frac{1}{(1+rr)} + \frac{(1+g)}{(1+rr)^2} + \ldots + \frac{(1+g)^{p-1}}{(1+rr)^p} \right)$$

$$VG = PAT1 * \frac{(1-rr/r)}{(1+g)} * \left(\frac{(1+g)}{(1+rr)} + \frac{(1+g)^2}{(1+rr)^2} + \ldots + \frac{(1+g)^p}{(1+rr)^p} \right)$$

$$VG = PAT1 * \frac{(1-rr/r)}{(1+g)} * \left(\frac{1 - (1+g)/(1+rr)^p}{1 - (1+g)/(1+rr)} \right)$$

$$VG = PAT1 * \frac{(r-rr)}{r*(rr-g)} * (1 - (1+g)/(1+rr)^p)$$

13 *Business Week*, 15 July, 1991.

14 Approaches to business valuations are extremely numerous. For an overview of the many approaches used in practice, refer to: T and J Jones (eds) (1992), *Handbook of Business Valuation*, Wiley & Sons. Chapter 12 lists more than 200 rules of thumb for evaluating businesses in different trades!

15 K Hickman and G Petry (1990), 'A Comparison of Stock Price Predictions Using Court Accepted Formulas, Dividend Discount, and P/E Models', *Financial Management* (Summer), pp 76–87.

16 One of the expert models was the one developed by Donaldson, Lufkin & Jenrette Securities Corporation, 140 Broadway, New York, NY 10005.

R.T.C. LIBRARY
LETTER

I, IN THE UNITED KINGDOM

On 16 June 1985, Mr Corsi, the Managing Director of I, the second-largest truck manufacturer in Europe, was replacing the phone after a conversation with Mr Jones, the president of F. He had just agreed to a meeting in Torino on 29 June 1985, to discuss the conditions of an eventual takeover of F by I. The two companies had been discussing this question since the end of 1984, when F approached I. From the very beginning, I had shown interest, but the value of an acquisition of F's truck operations was not easy to assess, and now Mr Corsi was a bit puzzled by F's pressure to strike a deal. Mr Corsi asked his secretary to organize quickly a meeting with the two senior managers who had represented I at the last meeting at F's UK headquarters in May, 1985.

I's strategy in Europe

In 1985, I was one of the leading manufacturers of trucks in Europe with a 16% share of the market:

Market shares of the main manufacturers of trucks in Europe
(according to the numbers of units sold. 3.5 tons and above)

Daimler Benz	23.5%	Scania	4.6%
I	16.2%	Daf	4.0%
Renault	10.7%	Leyland	3.7%
Man-VW	7.1%	GM-Bedford	1.8%
Volvo	6.5%	Japanese	4.7%
F	4.6%	Others*	12.6%

* (including car manufacturers for light vehicles)

I's policy was to offer a full range of trucks to all national markets in Europe as well as to a number of markets outside Europe. In 1985, I was present on all European markets and, except for the UK, had achieved strong positions in the main markets: 16% in France, 12% in Germany, 69% in Italy, 6% – but rapidly growing – in Spain. Increase in market share was seen at I as one of the key conditions for improving profitability and recouping the high cost of new product development.

I had been formed in 1975 from the integration of Italian, French and German truck companies. Since its creation, I's strategy had been to increase its size and to rationalize its operations, which involved closures of plants in France and Germany. Rationalization had enabled I to cut the number of product lines from 21 to 6, the number of

This case has been prepared by Damir Borsic, Professor of Business Administration at Isvor Fiat (Italy) and the author from a real business situation which has been modified in order to serve as a basis for class discussion. The pedagogy of this case has been developed by the author, Damir Borsic and Sherwood Frey, Professor at Darden (USA). This document is not intended to reflect the real business situation of the truck industry.

engine groups from 12 to 6 and the variety of cabs from 21 to 4. In 1985, I had manufacturing and R&D facilities in Italy, France and Germany, which was both a disadvantage (complexity of operations) and an advantage (image of a national manufacturer able, for example, to sell to armed forces in three key European markets). I's policy was to manufacture, or at least to control the manufacturing of the main components, engines and drivelines.

I was spending 3% of its sales on R&D – and was planning an increase to 4% to keep ahead of the technology and to introduce new products. The cost of new product introduction was very high; I estimated that they would need to spend about 900 million GBP to introduce the new generation of trucks they were planning to launch in the early 1990s.

The very high cost of new product introduction was making the long-term survival of smaller truck manufacturers very unlikely, with the exception of those which had been able to focus on the most profitable segments and to achieve a wide geographic coverage. The early 1980s had been very difficult for most European truck manufacturers. Even for a market leader like I, profitability had been unsatisfactory (see Figure H-1). Fortunately, the late 1980s were expected to be more favourable.

- For the first time since 1979, demand in Europe was increasing again in 1985. A further increase of about 5% was expected in 1986, but I remained very cautious about the future. Though confident in the long-term prospects of the commercial vehicle industry, I's management believed that it was a low-growth industry: the long-term growth trend of the overall European market was slightly below 1% a year.
- The industry was likely to go through a difficult restructuring phase during the next few years, as a number of competitors unable to renew their product lines would have to leave the industry. It was expected at I that this restructuring would improve the overall profitability of the industry.

A brief description of the industry is in Appendix H1.

	1979	1980	1981	1982	1983	1984	1985
Sales (million GBP)*	2203	2459	3097	2725	2362	2373	2543
Annual growth		12%	26%	−12%	−13%	0%	7%
Profit before tax	−121	−98	16	5	−67	−113	43
As a % of sales	−5%	−4%	1%	0%	−3%	−5%	2%
Number of vehicles sold (000)†	110	110	113	102	96	90	99
Annual growth		0%	3%	−10%	−6%	−6%	10%
Personnel (000)	50	47	46	42	39	36	35

* I was selling products other than trucks: buses, military vehicles, engines, spare parts, fire-fighting equipment, fork lifts, etc. In 1985, I had sold about 56 000 trucks on the European market and had exported some 20 000 more units outside Europe. As an estimate, one could consider the average unit selling price of I trucks to be equal to about 17 000 GBP in 1985.
† Trucks, buses, military vehicles, etc.

Figure H.1 Key financial data of I.

I on the UK market

The UK market was one of the largest in Europe and the share and status of the different competitors was as follows:

	Share	Status
F	20%	Foreign owned, local production
Leyland	16%	UK, State owned, local production
Daimler Benz	13%	Foreign, importer
GM-Bedford	8%	Foreign owned, local production
Renault-Dodge	8%	Foreign, local production
Volvo	6%	Foreign, importer
Daf	4%	Foreign, importer
I	3%	Foreign, importer
Scania	3%	Foreign, importer
Seddon Atkinson	2%	UK, local production
Man	2%	Foreign, importer
Erf	2%	UK, local production
Foden-Paccar	1%	Foreign owned, importer

The UK market was characterized by its large number of competitors, the largest in Europe, and the growing importance of large fleet operators. The UK market was not very profitable (more so than France but significantly less than Finland or Italy). During the early 1980s continental European manufacturers increased their pressure on the UK market: Daimler Benz managed to get ahead of GM–Bedford, while Renault acquired Dodge, and became aggressive on prices. In 1985, F, Leyland and GM–Bedford were making losses.

There were several reasons why I was weak on the UK market.

- Late entry and relatively low priority given to this market so far. However, in the early 1980s, I had merger talks with Leyland and tried to acquire Seddon Atkinson.
- Strength of competitors such as F, Bedford or Leyland. Leyland had been the largest truck company in the world immediately after World War II.
- The relative weakness of I's dealer network in the UK. In 1985, I had 40 dealers in the UK who were not always located in prime sites and were often lacking in financial strength.

I was not satisfied with its position in the UK and was planning to become more aggressive in this market over the next five years. Its objective was to capture share and to be in a stronger position when the new generation of products was introduced. I was aware of the obstacles it would have to face.

- In spite of their good reputation, I's products were not well known in the UK.
- As the margins in the UK market were not very high, there was not much room for implementing an aggressive strategy.
- The UK market presented some specific characteristics which differed from the ones I was used to in continental Europe.

However, as it expected several competitors to leave the market, the management of I believed that it was the right time to focus its attention on the UK market and do better than the initial plan shown in Figure H2.

The initial and conservative plan

To compare this plan with other alternatives and in particular with the acquisition of F, the management of I had estimated the value that would result from this strategy. The value as of the end of 1985 had been estimated as the net sum of:

- The value of the working capital needs as of 31 December 1985.
- The present value of the cash flows that the company was expecting to generate in the period 1986–90.
- The present value of the cash flows to be achieved beyond 1990. This value had been estimated on the basis of 10 million GBP per point of market share.

In million GBP, except for unit prices in 000 GBP:

	1986	1987	1988	1989	1990	1991	Cum.
Growth	5.0%	5.0%	5.0%	3.0%	3.0%		
Total market	84 000	88 200	92 610	95 388	98 250		
Market share	3.00%	3.25%	3.50%	3.75%	4.00%		
Unit selling price	18 000	18 000	18 000	18 000	18 000		
SALES	45	52	58	64	71		
Unit cost	12 780	12 780	12 780	12 780	12 780		
CGS	32	37	41	46	50		
CGS/sales	71%	71%	71%	71%	71%		
OPERATING EXPENSES	14	14	14	15	16		
Operating expenses/sales	31%	27%	24%	23%	23%		
PROFIT BEFORE TAX	−1	1	3	4	5		
PROFIT AFTER TAX	−1	1	2	2	3		7
Working capital open	0	5	5	6	6	7	
Working capital/sales	10%	10%	10%	10%	10%		
Working capital end	5	5	6	6	7		
CFO 1986–90	−5	0	1	2	2	7	7
Discount rate	0.10						
NPV 1986–90 cash flows	3						
WORKING CAPITAL OPEN	4						
Market share in 1990	0.04						
VALUE CASH FLOWS BEYOND 1990	40						
TOTAL VALUE (million GBP)	47						

An alternative and aggressive plan

The management of I had prepared an aggressive plan for bringing its share of the UK market from 3 to 8% in 1990. Though difficult to achieve, this goal did not seem unrealistic: I had a share higher than 8% in most European markets and had been able to progress quickly in those markets where local competitors were losing ground. As an example, I had been able to increase its share of the Spanish market from less than 2% in 1982 to more than 6% in 1985 even though it operated as an importer. The plan envisaged:

- An increase in marketing and selling expenses; 15 million in 1986 and 1987, 16 million in 1988, 17 million in 1989 and 18 million in 1990.
- A reduction in prices; average selling price would be reduced from 18 000 GBP in 1985 to 14 400 in 1986 (a 20% reduction), kept at this level for three years, then brought back to 15 000 in 1989 and 18 000 in 1990.

Figure H.2   I's plans for the UK market.

One alternative was to implement an aggressive pricing strategy (see Figure H2) but this was risky and was falling short of reaching the long-term goal of the company, to capture at least 20% of the market. Under current conditions such a goal could only be reached by external acquisitions. However, acquiring market share was not easy, and past experience had shown that it was generally impossible to maintain the market share of the acquired company: losing 25% to 50% of this share was not unusual.

The negotiations with F

At the end of 1984, F offered I to acquire its truck operations. The management of I responded that such an acquisition might fit their strategy but that there was debate within the senior management of the company as to the real value of such a deal for I.

F Trucks was part of the international automotive group F. Within the F group, the commercial vehicle business had traditionally been centred on the UK market, where it enjoyed a very strong position. However, its market share had declined under the pressure of competition (see in Figure H3 the evolution of the UK market and of F sales). In the UK, F was operating as an integrated manufacturer focusing on the medium range since the discontinuation of the heavy trucks in 1983.

The financial data of F Trucks, as they were given to I, at the May meeting are in Figure H4. As F Trucks was integrated into the other activities of F, these data had to be considered with some caution and during the meeting, the representatives of I had the feeling that the management of F did not have full knowledge of their costs and were over-optimistic about their ability to reach a break-even situation.

UK market
(number of units)

	1979	1980	1981	1982	1983	1984	1985
Heavy (16 tons)	37 300	27 200	19 300	20 800	24 200	26 900	27 900
Annual growth		−27%	−29%	8%	16%	11%	4%
In % of total UK market	40%	36%	34%	34%	35%	36%	35%
Medium (5–15.9 tons)	37 700	29 800	22 900	21 800	23 200	23 600	24 600
Annual growth		−21%	−23%	−5%	6%	2%	4%
In % of total UK market	40%	40%	40%	35%	34%	32%	31%
Light (3.5–4.9 tons)	18 100	18 400	14 800	19 400	21 300	24 200	27 500
Annual growth		2%	−20%	31%	10%	14%	14%
In % of total UK market	19%	24%	26%	31%	31%	32%	34%
Total	93 100	75 400	57 000	62 000	68 700	74 700	80 000
Annual growth		−19%	−24%	9%	11%	9%	7%

F Trucks:

F Sales (number of units sold)	24 000	19 000	14 000	15 000	16 400	15 400	16 000
Annual growth		−21%	−26%	7%	9%	−6%	4%
Market share	26%	25%	25%	24%	24%	21%	20%

Figure H.3   Evolution of the UK market and of the position of F Trucks.

(million GBP)		
Income statements	1984	1985
Sales	187	192
Cost of goods sold	167	169
Other expenses	30	27
Profit before tax	−11	−4
Balance sheets		End 1985
Inventory and receivables		44
Accounts payable		24

It was not F's intention to sell their plant to I. In the case of an acquisition, the plant would be leased, and the annual lease payments had been included in the financial forecasts.

Figure H.4   Key financial data of F.

As far as F's products were concerned, they were very good and very well accepted by the market. F's problem was that:

- The products were produced in insufficient quantities to allow adequate economies of scale. When it had introduced these products, F had planned for much higher volumes, but it had to face disappointing export markets as well as some erosion of its domestic position.
- Introduced four years earlier, these products could not be expected to be sold beyond an horizon of five to six years without major capital investments which F was not ready to make.

The main strength of F was actually its dealer network which was among the best in the UK: F had 120 dealers, most of whom were car and truck dealers.

I was considering the following strategy in the case of an acquisition:

- Continue to produce the current F products for as long as they sold. The continuation of these products which were well accepted by the market would obviously help maintain the relationships with the dealers. I believed that the profitability of F's operations could not be improved during the next five years.
- When these products reached the end of their lives, I would invest in F's manufacturing facilities which would then assemble the new generation of products developed by I.

I's position vis-à-vis F

As the value of acquiring F's truck operations was obviously very dependent on the price to be paid, I wanted to avoid falling into the trap of paying too much.

Acquiring F was a unique opportunity for I to build a strong position in the UK market without having to exert pressure on prices and threatening the profitability of the market. Among all the UK companies, F was probably the best company to acquire. But acquiring the operations of F was a very risky move.

- Experience in other countries had taught I's management that up to half of the market share might be lost. Even though F's products were enjoying a good market response, it was not easy to predict how they would sell when manufactured by a not very well known foreign company. How would fleet operators and large customers like the Post Office react? Would they trust the new company to maintain the level of service presently provided by F?

- How would the dealers react to the prospect of working with I instead of F, a company with a strong and long-established reputation? Would the wealthy individuals owning F dealerships be willing to invest in the risky business of developing a new brand on the UK market? Would it be possible to integrate the F and the I networks?

- How would the management and personnel of F react to a takeover by I? F had a reputation as a very good company to work for, and some people could find the change in ownership difficult to accept. People might actually believe that I was only interested in the dealer network and was going to close the manufacturing facilities as soon as the first recession occurred.

- Finally, what growth could be expected in the UK market? Growth had been better than in other European countries recently, but this could mean bad news for the future as the UK market could not grow forever.

On the other hand, there were also arguments that the risks of this specific acquisition were limited.

- Because of its car business, F did not want its dealers to be frustrated and leave for competition. I could probably expect F to arrange for a smooth transition process, but it was clear also that F could do nothing as far as its customers were concerned.

- F's narrow product range made it difficult for the F dealers to compete; the full range of I would put them in a much better competitive position against Daimler Benz.

- As the truck business had never been a core activity for F, that company's employees in this sector might actually welcome the idea of being part of a company totally committed to the commercial vehicle industry.

The management of I had estimated the value of an eventual acquisition. This estimate, which is reproduced in Figure H5, shows that given the risks involved, I could not reasonably agree to pay very much for this acquisition. However, this was not necessarily a problem, since F was generating losses: an estimate of the value of F's operations if not acquired by I is in Figure H6.

Obviously, the situation would have been completely different had the acquisition of the truck operations of F really meant acquiring 20% of the UK market. In such a case, I would obviously have been prepared to pay much more!

Finally, Mr Corsi was wondering why Mr Jones and the management of F in general were so optimistic about the future and apparently so confident that I would succeed with the acquisition. The attitude of F's management could well be just negotiation tactics, but since the beginning of his discussions with F, Mr Corsi had had two somewhat conflicting feelings. One was telling him he had to find ways to help F adopt more realistic views, the other one was that he should not waste his time trying to change their views. After all, they were perfectly entitled to their own opinions about the future. Perhaps Mr Corsi should fully accept the optimism of the other party and find ways to take advantage of it for the benefit of both parties. This was obviously possible only if F's optimism was genuine.

The value of the combined operations of I and F, as of the end of 1985, had been estimated as the net sum of:

- The value of the working capital as of 31 December 1985.
- The present value of the cash flows that the operations were expected to generate in the period 1986–90.
- The present value of the cost of reorganization (30 million GBP), to be incurred in 1990.
- The present value of the cash flows to be achieved beyond 1990. This value had been estimated on the basis of 10 million GBP per point of market share.

The most likely scenario
In million GBP, except for unit prices in 000 GBP:

	1986	1987	1988	1989	1990	1991	Cum.
Growth	5.0%	5.0%	5.0%	3.0%	3.0%		
Total market	84 000	88 200	92 610	95 388	98 250		
Share I	3.5%	4.0%	4.5%	5.0%	5.5%		
Share F	18.0%	16.0%	14.0%	12.0%	10.0%		
Unit price I	18 000	18 000	18 000	18 000	18 000		
Unit price F	12 000	12 000	12 000	12 000	12 000		
SALES	234	233	231	223	215		
Unit cost I	12 780	12 780	12 780	12 780	12 780		
Unit cost F	10 407	10 643	10 956	11 468	12 189		
CGS	195	195	195	192	189		
CGS/sales	83%	84%	85%	86%	88%		
OPERATING EXPENSES	54	46	46	44	40		
Operating expenses/sales	23%	20%	20%	20%	19%		
PROFIT BEFORE TAX	−15	−8	−11	−13	−14		
PROFIT AFTER TAX	−15	−8	−11	−13	−14		−60
Working capital open	0	23	23	23	22	22	
Working capital/sales	10%	10%	10%	10%	10%		
Working capital end	23	23	23	22	22		
CFO 1986–90	−38	−8	−10	−12	−13	22	−60
Discount rate	0.10						
NPV 1986–90 cash flows	−53						
WORKING CAPITAL OPEN	24						
REORGANIZATION COST					30		
NPV REORGANIZATION	19						
TAX SHIELD	11						
NPV TAX SHIELD					21		
Market share in 1990	0.155						
VALUE CASH FLOWS BEYOND 1990	155						
TOTAL VALUE (million GBP)	118						

Note
The unit cost of F's products had been estimated with the following formula: 7 100 + 50 000 000/volume.

Other scenarios
A pessimistic scenario with the following assumptions had also been prepared:

	1986	1987	1988	1989	1990
Share I	0.03	0.03	0.03	0.03	0.03
Share F	0.16	0.12	0.10	0.08	0.07
Operating expenses	54	46	46	44	40
Market share beyond 1990	0.10				
Cost of reorganization	40 (in 1990)				

This scenario – which was not the most pessimistic – would lead to catastrophic results. Finally, the management of I had prepared an optimistic scenario:

	1986	1987	1988	1989	1990
Share I	0.04	0.05	0.06	0.07	0.12
Share F	0.19	0.18	0.17	0.16	0.11
Operating expenses	54	46	46	46	46
Market share beyond 1990	0.23				
Cost of reorganization	30 (in 1990)				

Figure H.5 The value of the combined operations of I and F.

The value of the operations of F had been estimated as the net sum of:

- The value of the working capital as of 31 December 1985.
- The present value of the cash flows that the company was expecting to generate in the period 1986–90. It has been assumed that the present products could not be sold beyond 1990.
- The present value of the cost of closure: 30 million, to be incurred in 1990.

In million GBP, except for unit prices in 000 GBP:

	1986	1987	1988	1989	1990	1991	Cum.
Growth	5.0%	5.0%	5.0%	3.0%	3.0%		
Total market	84 000	88 200	92 610	95 388	98 250		
Market share	18.0%	16.0%	14.0%	12.0%	10.0%		
Unit selling price	12 000	12 000	12 000	12 000	10 000		
SALES	181	169	156	137	98		
Unit cost	10 407	10 643	10 956	11 468	12 189		
CGS	157	150	142	131	120		
CGS/sales	87%	89%	91%	96%	122%		
OPERATING EXPENSES	30	25	23	20	15		
Operating expenses/sales	17%	15%	15%	15%	15%		
PROFIT BEFORE TAX	−6	−6	−9	−14	−37		
PROFIT AFTER TAX	−4	−4	−6	−9	−24		−47
Working capital open	0	18	17	16	14	10	
Working capital/sales	10%	10%	10%	10%	10%		
Working capital end	18	17	16	14	10		
CFO 1986–90	−22	−3	−5	−7	−20	10	−47
Discount rate	0.10						
NPV 1986–90	−37						
WORKING CAPITAL OPEN	20						
COST OF CLOSURE					30		
NPV CLOSURE	19						
TOTAL VALUE (million GBP)	−36						

Notes
The unit cost of F's products had been estimated with the following formula: 7 100 + 50 000 000/volume.
As F's other operations in the UK were profitable, any loss on the truck operations would generate a tax credit.

Figure H.6   Value of the operations of F if not acquired by I

APPENDIX H.1

THE EUROPEAN TRUCK INDUSTRY

Since the 1950s when they were as many as 55, competitors in the European truck industry had not found it easy to create value, as the overall industry had been characterized by its

- low margins,
- large and increasing capital expenditures,
- low growth and volatile demand.

In this difficult market, competitors had traditionally adopted a variety of strategies ranging between two extremes.

- Strategies for overall market dominance. In the mid-1980s two companies were emerging as overall market leaders with respective shares of 20 and 16% of the number of new vehicles delivered.

■ Focused strategies. Focus on specific segments and/or specific national markets. Among the competitors, one had been very successful at pursuing a strategy focusing on the heavy-vehicle segment.

In the mid-1980s several competitors were facing an even more difficult challenge as they had to invest in the renewal of their product lines at a time when profitability had been depressed by the price wars of the early 1980s. This was expected to force several competitors out of the industry.

Salient features of the commercial vehicle industry

A low growth and cyclical market
The annual number of new commercial vehicles registered in Western Europe had evolved as shown in Figure AH.1 during the period 1970–85. For the European manufacturers, the situation had been made worse by the collapse of the export markets, which fell from 175 000 units in 1981 to less than 75 000 units in 1985. It was expected that these exports would further decrease in 1986.

(Registrations in units – 3.5 tons and above)

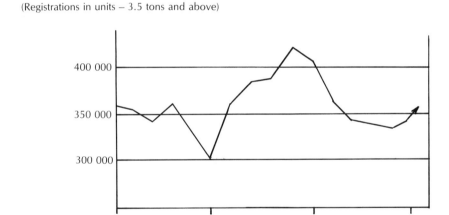

Figure AH.1   Evolution of the Western European truck market.

In spite of the rapid development of road transportation and the growing importance of this form of transport in the infrastructure of modern economies, the commercial vehicle industry was a very low-growth industry: slightly less than 1% a year on the average over a 20-year period. As a basis for comparison, the GNP of OECD countries grew by 3.8% a year in the period of 1950–73 and 1.9% in the period 1973–87. The different segments of the market were not behaving in the same way and, as shown in Figure AH.2, the trend seemed to be towards a polarization of the market: heavy trucks for long-distance haulage and light trucks for city transportation.

New registrations	1979	1980	1981	1982	1983	1984	1985
TOTAL MARKET							
Number of units (000)	425	405	362	340	339	333	343
Annual growth		−5%	−11%	−6%	0%	−2%	3%
HEAVY (>16 tons)							
As a % of total	31%	31%	30%	30%	32%	34%	34%
Annual growth		−7%	−13%	−5%	7%	3%	1%
MEDIUM (5–15.9 tons)							
As a % of total	38%	38%	35%	33%	33%	32%	31%
Annual growth		−6%	−16%	−12%	0%	−6%	1%
LIGHT (3.5–4.9 tons)							
As a % of total	30%	32%	35%	37%	34%	34%	36%
Annual growth		0%	−3%	0%	−6%	−2%	7%

Figure AH.2   Segments of the European truck market.

In 1984, the size of the respective national markets (in 000 units) was:

UK	75	Italy	40
France	75	Spain	19
Germany	56	Others	68

Because of the registration procedures, volume data were easily available in the industry. While more difficult to obtain and probably much less reliable, value data were very interesting, since they showed a different picture:

Average unit selling price for the manufacturer (000 GBP):

Heavy (>16 tons)	34
Medium (5 to 15.9 tons)	17
Light (3.5 to 4.9 tons)	10

Relative size of segments (sales as a % of total sales):

Heavy (>16 tons)	57%
Medium (5 to 15.9 tons)	26%
Light (3.5 to 4.9 tons)	18%
Total	100%

Numerous laws and regulations
The truck industry was affected by numerous national laws related to:

- Standards for commercial vehicles in each country: maximum weight (from 28 tons in Switzerland to 52 tons in Sweden), maximum width and length, number of axles, speed, noise levels, exhaust emissions, etc. Pollution-control factors had become very important; according to industry sources, more than one-third of the cost of designing new truck engines was spent on pollution control.
- The organization of the road transport industry. In several European countries, like Germany, regulations were keeping numerous inefficient companies in existence, while in countries like the Netherlands and the UK, the transport industry had been largely deregulated.

The impact of the creation of a unified market in Europe was difficult to assess:

- On the one hand, there were forecasts suggesting that cross-border transportation could grow by more than one-third in Europe before the end of the century and that the share of freight moved by trucks could increase to 55% from its current 40% level.
- On the other hand, improvement in logistics and the removal of regulations would keep trucks from operating empty. Disappearance of borders would also mean that the speed of operations would increase dramatically. Therefore, some industry experts believed that the volume of road transport in year 2000 could be handled by the same number of vehicles as today. Another unfortunate consequence for European manufacturers would be that a unified European market might become more attractive to Japanese manufacturers.

Demanding customers
Commercial vehicles were industrial products sold to:

- Well-informed customers. Large fleet operators and leasing companies had built up extensive statistics of the ownership costs of the different makes and models. A typical breakdown of the ownership costs of a truck over its full life is in Figure AH.3.
- Customers requiring ever-increasing productivity. The industry of road transportation, or large sectors of it, had become very efficient.

There were numerous specification requirements and very few trucks were identical.

Driver	30
Fuel	21
Tax	12
Maintenance	10
Tyres	7
Insurance	7
Depreciation	7
Interest	6
TOTAL	100

Figure AH.3   Typical breakdown of ownership cost over full life.

Higher technology products requiring very high investments
The 1985 Frankfurt Motor Show witnessed attempts by European truck manufacturers to outdo each other in their claims to superiority in advanced engineering.

After the car industry, the truck industry was now being penetrated by electronics, and the hot issues in Frankfurt were vehicle management systems – aimed at improving performance and fuel efficiency – and computer-aided gearchange systems. Electronics were also present in the anti-skid systems. Diesel engines had progressed also; they were becoming cleaner, quieter and more efficient. Use of exhaust-gas driven turbochargers allowed engines to burn fuel more completely and efficiently. Intercoolers, which reduce the temperature of the air delivered by the turbocharger before it goes into the engine, had also improved efficiency.

European manufacturers had invested a lot in manufacturing technology, in order to deal with erratic demand and to benefit from vertical integration. Competitors like Scania and Volvo were producing all their driveline components (engines, gearboxes and rear axles) and had dramatically reduced the number of basic components, thus achieving scale effects comparable to those of higher volume manufacturers often plagued by manufacturing diversity. Advances in product and manufacturing technology had made the development of new products very expensive: Scania and Volvo had announced that they each had invested 900 million GBP for the development and introduction of their new generation of trucks launched in 1984–85.

A variety of competitive strategies . . . and very few successes so far
According to many industry observers, the economics of the market (limited growth, volatility of demand, low margins and large investment requirements) were going to lead to a further reduction of the number of competitors. Competitors could be classified according to their positioning on the market:

- Full product and geographic coverage   (I)
- Full product range but limited geographic coverage   (II)
- Focused product range and full geographic coverage   (III)
- Focused product range and limited geographic coverage   (IV)

According to most observers in the industry, only those companies which had positioned themselves in I or III had strong chances to survive in the long run. These two groups of competitors had very different strategies:

- Strategies aimed at succeeding through maximizing volume and achieving economies of scale, on the one hand.
- Focused strategies aimed at creating high customer value (superior product design, high quality, service, etc.), premium pricing and innovative manufacturing, on the other.

Figure AH.4 shows the positioning of the European manufacturers in 1985.

Product coverage	Market coverage	
	All countries	Selected countries
Full range	Mercedes Benz Iveco	RVI British Leyland
Selected segment	Scania Volvo	Man Ebro Pegaso/Seddon Sizu ERF Foden Ford Astra Daf Steyr Bedford

Figure AH.4   Positioning of the European truck manufacturers in 1985.

Another characteristic of the industry was the strong presence of state-owned and state-supported companies:

France:	Renault
Spain:	Enasa, Pegaso
UK:	Leyland
Austria:	Steyr
Finland:	Sizu
Netherlands:	Daf

Fights for market shares, attempts at maintaining workloads in volatile markets, priority given to volume over profitability, etc. had triggered numerous price wars which had eroded the margins of all competitors. In 1985, very few competitors were profitable.

■ Scania and Volvo were showing operating profits equal, respectively, to 13% and 7% of their sales.
■ Daimler Benz was not publishing profitability data on its truck operations. I was expecting to report a small profit.
■ Renault was expecting to sustain losses of 270 million GBP in 1985. The company had lost 640 million in the period 1983–85.
■ Man had to sell assets to Daimler Benz in order to resist an acquisition by GM.
■ Daf was expecting to make a marginal profit after heavy losses in 1984.

Key financial data of the main competitors are shown in Figure AH.5.

Europe and the world market

In the mid-1980s, the world truck industry was fragmented into regional markets, each having its specific regulations and demand characteristics but, as shown in Figure AH.6, all equally volatile.

The US market
The US was quite a different market from Europe.

■ The products were very different (for example, the traditional cab behind the engine was still popular in the USA).
■ US competitors were much less integrated than their European counterparts. Paccar, the most profitable competitor, was one of the less vertically integrated companies.
■ The US market was more heavily dominated than Europe by large fleet operators (Ryder, for example, had a fleet of more than 100 000 trucks).

In the late 1970s, most US competitors were suffering from the collapse of the market, and this allowed several European competitors – Volvo, Renault, Daimler Benz – to strengthen their position through acquisitions. However, the substantial differences between the US and European markets prevented these companies from achieving much industrial integration of their European and US operations.

	Strategy	Output	Estimate average selling price (authors' estimates)	Operating profit/sales
Daimler Benz	Strategy for world market dominance. Numerous production sites. Wide range of products.	110–150 000	19 000 GBP	Not published, did not seem very high.
I	Strategy for European market dominance plus exports outside of Europe.	76 000 in 1985 56 000 in Europe	17 000 GBP	5% in 1985.
F	Activity limited to the UK market (plus some exports) and to medium trucks. Suffered from over-capacity.	16 000 in 1985	12 000 GBP	Loss
Volvo	Leadership in heavy/medium segment. Strong vertical integration.	28 700 European trucks and 13 200 American trucks, e.g. 41 900 in 1985 42 200 in 1984	32 000 GBP (European trucks)	6% in 1985 7% in 1984
Scania	Leadership in the heavy segment in Europe and Latin America. High-quality products, high level of service, premium prices Strong vertical integration with the lowest number of components in the industry. Distribution through independent dealers.	22 970 in 1985 21 800 in 1984 17 500 in 1983	35 000 GBP	13% in 1985 13% in 1984

Figure AH.5 Key financial data of the main European truck manufacturers.

Annual number of new registrations (3.5 tons and above)							
	1979	1980	1981	1982	1983	1984	1985
TOTAL WORLD MARKET (000 vehicles)	1315	1205	1162	1000	995	1083	1138
Annual growth		−8%	−4%	−14%	−1%	9%	5%
WESTERN EUROPE As a % of world market	32%	34%	31%	34%	34%	31%	30%
Annual growth		−5%	−11%	−6%	0%	−2%	3%
USA As a % of world market	42%	30%	26%	28%	31%	38%	39%
Annual growth		−35%	−17%	−7%	11%	32%	7%
REST OF THE WORLD As a % of world market	26%	37%	43%	38%	35%	31%	31%
Annual growth		29%	14%	−24%	−9%	−1%	4%

* Slightly less than half of the 'rest of the world' was accounted for by Japan, the second-largest market in the world.

Figure AH.6 World truck markets.

The Japanese market
This was another market with its own specific features. There were four competitors: three with a share slightly higher than 25%; Hino (part of the capital of Hino was held by Toyota), Isuzu, and Mitsubishi; the fourth with a share somewhat lower than 20%, Nissan.

Japanese truck competitors were less aggressive than the Japanese car competitors on the world market. However, they were very active in South Eastern Asia, and they had started actively looking for niches in the European and US markets. Hino entered the US market in 1984. Other Japanese companies had established joint ventures with US companies. Nissan had signed an agreement to supply a new generation of medium-weight trucks to International Harvester, and GM, which had a 40% interest in Isuzu, was distributing Isuzu's light- and medium-weight trucks.

The European market in the mid-1980s
At the end of the 1970s, the truck market had been very buoyant all over the world, and manufacturers installed new capacity in expectation of a continually expanding market. According to some industry sources, the total capacity of the industry had risen to as much as 600 000 vehicles per year. Starting in 1980, the market collapsed as, one after another, key export markets in Africa and the Middle East ran out of foreign currency to pay for imports. To make things worse, demand also fell on most European markets. This led the European truck manufacturers to

- cut part of their production capacity; about one-fourth was eliminated between 1980 and 1985;
- compete more intensely among themselves;
- rely more on the European market.

1985 was the first year to show some improvement, with demand expected to grow by 3% above its level in 1984. Another improvement in 1985 was related to the fact that capacity reductions were beginning to have an impact, and it was expected that several manufacturers who had been incurring heavy losses would break even. However, the feeling was that the restructuring of the industry would continue and even accelerate with a recovery, which could encourage potential buyers to invest. Another reason for further industry restructuring to occur was the fact that several competitors were no longer able to renew their product range and would therefore be in a critical position in the late 1980s or early 1990s. The industry was expecting further recovery in 1986, but in spite of the feeling that demand should come back to a 'normal' level, many people in the industry were taking a very cautious view of the future.

In the mid-1980s, one US truck manufacturer, GM, was attempting to implement the same acquisition strategy that had allowed some European competitors to establish themselves on the US market five years earlier. GM was aiming at building a world-wide truck business and had been engaged in acquisition and collaboration talks with several companies in Europe, particularly those finding it more difficult to compete: Enasa, Leyland and Man.

CHAPTER 30

A Step-by-Step Analysis of the Dynamics of an Opportunity for Cooperation

30.1 RECOGNIZING THE MOTIVATIONS TO COOPERATE

The case suggests that a deal would be beneficial to both companies.

- I is the second-largest competitor, it holds a 16% share of the European market but is weak in the UK, one of the biggest European markets. To be consistent with its strategy, I has to reinforce its position in the UK. When considering an acquisition, F is probably the best candidate: leading market share, superior dealer network, strong local reputation, quality products, private ownership, etc. A more debatable advantage is the local manufacturing capacities brought by F: producing in the UK would increase the complexity of the operations of I for a benefit that Daimler Benz does not seem to need to succeed in the UK.

  By acquiring F and retaining its market share, not only would I build up a strong local position but it would also close its overall European market share gap with Daimler Benz. If it misses the acquisition of F, I will probably not have such an opportunity in the near future ie before the introduction of the new product generation.

- F has decided to withdraw but still commands a leading share of the UK market. This is a short-lived but precious asset provided that an adequate buyer is found. I is obviously the ideal buyer and it is no surprise that it is I that F decided to approach.

The case also suggests that the two companies have further motives to cooperate.

- For both companies the issue at stake is of strategic importance. Because it will continue working with most of its current truck dealers through its car business, F cannot only be interested in getting a high price from I. F most probably also wants the acquisition to succeed.
- The positions of the two companies are equally strong and their respective strengths depend on the other party. The value of the market share of F is created by the interest of I and the acquisition of F is a unique opportunity

for I. Neither I nor F can use the threat of time. If an agreement is not reached, the customers of F may quickly lose interest for a brand that is going to disappear. But if the market share of F collapses, a great opportunity will be lost for I as the customers leaving F will turn more to the market leaders – and to Mercedes Benz in particular – than to marginal competitors like I. Both F and I are working under the pressure of time.

■ Both companies are key players in the world automotive industry, both have a long-term view about the industry, both have a reputation to keep and both probably consider the present deal as part of a long-term competitive and cooperative relationship. At the same time I and F compete with each other and each want to gain as much as possible from the potential agreement.

30.2 MAPPING THE ALTERNATIVES AVAILABLE TO EACH PARTY

Figure 30.1 shows a tentative mapping of the alternatives available to I and F.

■ I does not seem to be in a position to buy any other company than F. If it does not acquire F, I will have to rely on internal growth. When considering internal growth, I might decide to pursue its current conservative strategy or adopt a more aggressive approach. When analyzing alternatives, and in particular the acquisition of F, I has to realize that these alternatives may result in a variety of outcomes.

■ F does not seem to be able to sell its operations to any other company than I. If F fails to reach an agreement with I, its only option will be to decide when to close its operations.

30.3 UNDERSTANDING THE INTEGRATIVE AND DISTRIBUTIVE DYNAMICS OF THE SITUATION

In order to understand a cooperative situation you should analyze its two critical dimensions.

■ What is the value, or 'the pie', to be shared? What are the critical factors that drive the value to be shared? How can this value be increased? This is the *integrative dimension* of cooperative and negotiation situations.
■ How can this value be shared? This is the *distributive or claiming dimension.*

Even though it is too often reduced to its claiming dimension, negotiation is

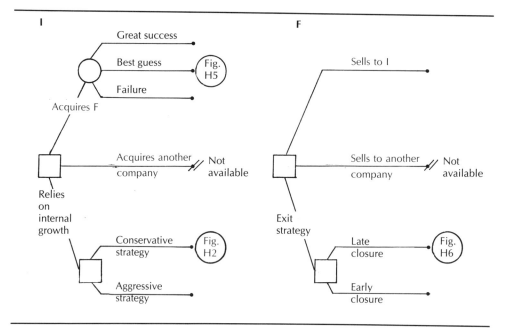

Figure 30.1 The alternatives of I and F.

primarily a powerful approach for creating value. Value can be created by various means[1]:

- Identification of *common interests*. I and F have several common interests: reaching an agreement quickly, retaining the current customers of F, satisfying the current dealers of F, etc. I and F should not find it difficult to discover that they want the same resolution of several issues and are in a position to work at creating common value. One interesting property of common – or 'public' – value is that it can be shared by all parties simultaneously; no one can be excluded unless all are.
- Recognition of *valuable differences*. A classic image is the one suggested by MP Follett[2]: two sisters quarrel over an orange until they realize that one wants only the fruit to eat and the other only the peel for baking.
- *Redefining* the situation. The negotiating parties might reformulate their apparent conflict and invent new options that can fulfil their underlying interests.

Means to create value – or to enlarge the pie – are like alternatives to decisions. They do not appear spontaneously but are created out of the analysis and imagination of managers. Experience and research actually show that most negotiators find it difficult to see all the opportunities for creating value and the literature prescribes a series of rules of hygiene.

- *Start with the analysis of the integrative dimension.*
- Define the goal as 'designing an outcome that fits the needs of the parties involved'.[3]
- Invent first, decide later, focus on interests, not on positions, separate the problem from the people.[4]
- Listen and question.[5]

The integrative dynamics: value, BATNAs, and zone of agreement

The mapping of the alternatives of I and F shown in Figure 30.1 enables us to understand the integrative dimension of the situation. The value of an agreement between I and F is equal to the difference between:

- the value of the combined operations of I and F and
- the sum of the maximum values that I and F could achieve by themselves in the absence of an agreement or using the term coined by Fisher and Ury,[4] the sum of their *BATNAs – Best Alternatives To a Negotiated Agreement.*

For I, the value of an agreement with F is equal to the difference between the value of the combined operations of I and F, the value of the best internal growth strategy I can choose (I's BATNA), and the price paid to F. The maximum price that I can pay is equal to the difference between the value of the combined operations and the value of its best internal growth strategy. Any price above this maximum, or *walk-away*, or *reservation* price should be rejected by I as it would render an agreement with F less valuable than the best internal growth option.

For F, the value of an agreement with I is equal to the difference between the price paid by I and the best exit strategy F can adopt. The minimum price that F can accept is equal to the value of the best exit strategy it can select. This is the walk-away price of F.

The integrative dimension of the situation is driven by three critical values:

- The value of the combined operations of I and F.
- The value of the BATNA of I (best internal growth strategy).
- The value of the BATNA of F (best exit strategy).

As shown in Figure 30.2, the first two critical values drive the walk-away price of I, the third value drives the walk-away price of F and the two walk-away prices drive the existence and size of a *zone of agreement*.

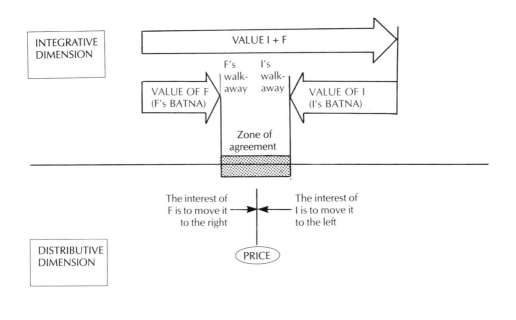

Figure 30.2   The integrative and distributive dynamics of the situation.

What does this tell about the dynamics of the situation?

A zone of agreement should exist in order that a deal be possible. This zone is bounded by three critical values: combined operations, BATNA of I and BATNA of F. The zone of agreement shows the value of the deal, or the size of the potential pie to be shared. It is increased by any increase in the value of the integrated operations and by any decrease in the value of each stand-alone company.

The concept of zone of agreement is actually more complicated than shown in Figure 30.2 as you should realize that:

- both I and F probably have their own *perceived zones of agreement*. These perceived zones depend on the opinions that I and F have on the three critical values. As a result, the two parties may see quite different zones of agreement which may overlap or not. A further complication is that neither I nor F know what is the perceived zone of agreement of the other party. Trying to unveil the expected zone of agreement of the other party is one of the very important parts of the negotiation process.[6]
- The perceived zones of agreement of each party are not necessarily stable as

their perception of each of the three critical values may change over time and in particular may change with new information unveiled during the negotiation process.

The distributive dimension and the 'fair' price issue

Figure 30.2 also shows the distributive dimension of the situation. An interesting question is what I and F would consider as a fair sharing. In particular would I be happy with a 50–50 sharing? A fundamental problem with sharing is that the true value of the pie to be shared is not known for sure today. This value will only be known a few years from now when the major uncertainties will be resolved. Sharing such an expected value can be done in two ways.

- Either you decide today about a rule for sharing (50–50 for example) and wait until the uncertainties are resolved in order to determine the amount to be shared and to proceed with the actual payments.
- Or you make the actual payments today. When doing so, you create an asymmetry between the two parties since the buyer acquires a share of an expected value in exchange for a certain payment. In such a situation I might not consider that a 50–50 sharing is fair, or might require that the expected value be adjusted downwards before a 50–50 sharing becomes acceptable.

30.4 A MODEL FOR EVALUATING THE THREE CRITICAL ALTERNATIVES

We can use the model described in Figures 30.3 and 30.4 to assess the value of the three critical alternatives: the BATNA of I, the BATNA of F and the combined operations of I and F. The model breaks the value of each alternative into three components.

- The value of the inheritance from the pre-acquisition activity. Here the inheritance is limited to the working capital needs at the date of acquisition. Neither of the companies carries debt obligations, owns fixed assets, holds significant cash balances, or faces potential costs of litigation.
- The value of the cash flows during the transition period up to the introduction of the new product generation. If it does not acquire F, I will try to take advantage of the expected restructuring of the UK market in order to increase its share. If I acquires F there will be additional costs related to the integration of the two dealer networks and to the reinforcement of the brand image of I in the UK. Costs of reorganizing the production facilities of F will have to be faced also. If it does not reach an agreement with I, F will have to design and implement an exit strategy.
- The continuing value. This value is based on the expected gains from the

	1986	1987	1988	1989	1990	1991	Cum.
Growth	5.0%	5.0%	5.0%	3.0%	3.0%		
Total market	84 000	88 200	92 610	95 388	98 250		
Share I	3.5%	4.0%	4.5%	5.0%	5.5%		
Share F	18.0%	16.0%	14.0%	12.0%	10.0%		
Competitive price change	0						
Unit price I	18 000	18 000	18 000	18 000	18 000		
Unit price F	12 000	12 000	12 000	12 000	12 000		
SALES	234	233	231	223	215		
Unit cost I	12 780	12 780	12 780	12 780	12 780		
Unit Cost F	10 407	10 643	10 956	11 468	12 189		
CGS	195	195	195	192	189		
CGS/sales	83%	84%	85%	86%	88%		
OPERATING EXPENSES	54	46	46	44	40		
Operating expenses/sales	23%	20%	20%	20%	19%		
PROFIT BEFORE TAX	−15	−8	−11	−13	−14		
PROFIT AFTER TAX	−15	−8	−11	−13	−14		−60
Working capital open	0	23	23	23	22	22	
Working capital/sales	10%	10%	10%	10%	10%		
Working capital end	23	23	23	22	22		
CFO 1986–90	−38	−8	−10	−12	−13	22	−60
Discount rate	0.10						
NPV 1986–90	−53						
WORKING CAPITAL OPEN	24						
REORGANIZATION COST					30		
NPV REORGANIZATION	19						
TAX SHIELD					21		
NPV TAX SHIELD	11						
Market share in 1990	0.155						
Market share in 1991	0.155						
Adjustment continuing value	0.0%						
VALUE CASH FLOWS BEYOND 1990	155						
TOTAL VALUE (million GBP)	118						

Figure 30.3   The foreground of a model to evaluate the alternatives of I and F.

new generation of products. There is obviously no continuing value for F in case it does not reach an agreement with I.

The model uses a constant prices–real rate approach for assessing both the initial planning period and the continuing value. It also includes parameters aimed at simulating different industry scenarios and in particular the impact of a possible price war.

NOTES

1 In *The Manager as Negotiator*, Lax and Sebenius claim that all joint gains derive from transactions involving various combinations of 4 basic factors:

values and attitudes toward risk and time;

beliefs and forecasts;
original endowments of the parties and
the capabilities of the parties to produce.

2 'Constructive Conflict', MP Follett, in *Dynamic Administration: the Collected Papers of Mary Parker Follett*, HC Metcalf and L Urwick, eds, New York Harper, 1940.

3 Refer to *Conflicts, A Better Way to Resolve Them*, Edward De Bono, Penguin Books, London, 1985.

4 *Getting to Yes, Negotiating Agreement without Giving In*, R Fisher and W Ury, Houghton Mifflin Company, Boston, 1981.

5 The art of questioning is critical to the unveiling of creative solutions; for the use of questioning in negotiation, refer to Chapter 8, *Fundamentals of Negotiating*, G Nierenberg, Hawthorn Books, Inc, New York, 1968.

6 For a treatment of this issue, refer to Chapter 4, *The Art and Science of Negotiation*, H Raiffa, The Bellknap Press of Harvard University Press, Cambridge, 1982.

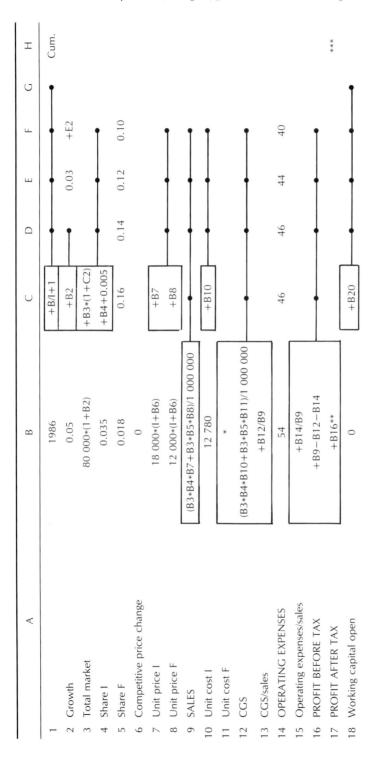

Row	A	B	C	D	E	F	G	H (Cum.)
1		1986	+B1+1					
2	Growth	0.05	+B2	0.03	0.03	+E2		
3	Total market	80 000*(1+B2)	+B3*(1+C2)					
4	Share I	0.035	+B4+0.005	0.14	0.12	0.10		
5	Share F	0.018	0.16					
6	Competitive price change	0						
7	Unit price I	18 000*(1+B6)	+B7					
8	Unit price F	12 000*(1+B6)	+B8					
9	SALES	(B3*B4*B7+B3*B5*B8)/1 000 000						
10	Unit cost I	12 780	+B10					
11	Unit cost F	*						
12	CGS	(B3*B4*B10+B3*B5*B11)/1 000 000						
13	CGS/sales	+B12/B9						
14	OPERATING EXPENSES	54	46	46	44	40		
15	Operating expenses/sales	+B14/B9						
16	PROFIT BEFORE TAX	+B9−B12−B14						***
17	PROFIT AFTER TAX	+B16**						
18	Working capital open	0	+B20					

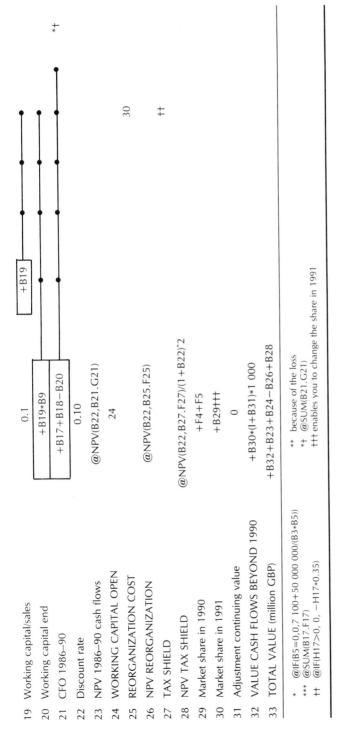

19	Working capital/sales	0.1
20	Working capital end	+B19*B9
21	CFO 1986–90	+B17+B18−B20
22	Discount rate	0.10
23	NPV 1986–90 cash flows	@NPV(B22,B21.G21)
24	WORKING CAPITAL OPEN	24
25	REORGANIZATION COST	30
26	NPV REORGANIZATION	@NPV(B22,B25.F25)
27	TAX SHIELD	††
28	NPV TAX SHIELD	@NPV(B22,B27.F27)/(1+B22)^2
29	Market share in 1990	+F4+F5
30	Market share in 1991	+B29†††
31	Adjustment continuing value	0
32	VALUE CASH FLOWS BEYOND 1990	+B30*(1+B31)*1 000
33	TOTAL VALUE (million GBP)	+B32+B23+B24−B26+B28

+B19

*   @IF(B5=0,0,7 100+50 000 000/(B3*B5))
***   @SUM(B17.F17)
††   @IF(H17>0, 0, −H17*0.35)

**   because of the loss
*†   @SUM(B21.G21)
†††   enables you to change the share in 1991

Figure 30.4   The background of a model to evaluate the alternatives of I and F.

CHAPTER 31

Using a Model to Further our Understanding of the Competitive Structure of the Industry and to Check the Assessment of the Continuing Value

The model in Figure 30.3 shows that the cash flows beyond 1990, or the continuing value, represent 131% of the total value of the combined operations of I and F. This is hardly a surprise since the period 1986–90 is a transition period that allows I to build its new competitive position in the UK. The benefits come at a later date, ie after 1990, when I will introduce the new generation of products.

How can we check that the continuing value can be estimated on the basis of 10 million GBP per point of market share?

- A first approach is to start from the new generation of products that I is planning to introduce in 1991. What is the value of this new generation of products? How would the additional sales resulting from the acquisition of F increase this value?
- A second approach is to start from the UK operations and estimate their profit or cash flows in the long run.

31.1 A MODEL TO ASSESS THE VALUE OF THE NEW GENERATION OF PRODUCTS

The model described in Figures 31.1 and 31.2 is built according to the approach followed in the analysis of BA International. It proceeds in two steps:

- assessment of the value of the new products without the acquisition of F;
- assessment of the impact of the additional sales resulting from the acquisition of F.

The value of the new products without the acquisition of F

The value of the new products is estimated as follows:

- the model starts with the appraisal of the total volume of sales over the whole life of the products;
- then, the total volume of sales is allocated over the years to estimate the annual sales.
- Annual unit costs, including all costs except for depreciation, are calculated using a 85% learning formula.
- Annual unit selling prices are derived from unit costs: the model assumes that, as was the case in the past, all learning gains are passed on to the customers. Consequently, annual selling prices decrease with unit costs. As an option, the model also envisages an umbrella pricing situation with the decrease in the selling price lagging behind the decrease in unit cost.
- Working capital needs are assumed to be equal to 15% of sales.
- Capital expenditures take place during the period 1986–90. The model assumes that the other activities of the company are profitable. This enables the company to benefit from a tax shield in the period 1986–90. An option of the model envisages the situation when the company is not able to benefit from this tax shield. The model also allows for the simulation of a shorter time to market (three instead of five years).

The impact of the acquisition of F

In order to assess the impact of the additional volume resulting from the acquisition, the model assumes that:

- The annual selling prices are kept the same. This is consistent with the fact that one of the key advantages of the acquisition is to enable I to improve its competitive position without having to exert any pressure on the market price. This is also consistent with the fact that the UK market has an 'average' profitability.
- The basic cost structure is also kept the same and the acquisition helps reduce the unit cost: in the model, the additional volume increases the gains derived from experience. This assumption is consistent with the fact that most of the transition costs have been incurred during the 1986–90 period.

31.2   THE VALUE OF THE NEW GENERATION OF PRODUCTS

The value of the new products without the acquisition of F

With the assumptions of the model, the new generation of products would generate a 15 million NPV. This is small which is not surprising. Except for a higher unit price (22 000 instead of 17 000) and a higher operating profit, the

PARAMETERS

Level of sales in unit in 1991 (000)	80
Annual growth	2%
Unit selling price	22
Capital expenditures	900
DEPRECIATION/SALES an output	**0.04**
Profit before depreciation/sales	0.11
OPERATING PROFIT/SALES an output	**0.07**
Working capital/sales	15%
Life cycle length	12
Time for development (5 or 3 years)	5
Ability to depreciate early, yes=1, no=2	1
Learning gains kept, no=1, yes=2	1
Additional units from acquisition	0

OUTPUTS

NPV OPERATIONAL CASH FLOWS	450
NPV INVESTMENTS	−435
NPV (million GBP)	15

	86	87	88	89	90	91	92	93	94	95	96	97	98	99	100	101	102	103	104	105	106	Cum.
Total volume sold over period						1073																
Years						1	2	3	4	5	6	7	8	9	10	11	12	13	13	13	13	13
Scaling factor						0.08	0.15	0.23	0.31	0.38	0.46	0.54	0.62	0.69	0.77	0.85	0.92	1.00	1.00	1.00	1.00	1.00
Product life cycle coefficient						0.45																
Annual sales coefficient						0.30	0.40	0.46	0.50	0.52	0.53	0.53	0.52	0.50	0.46	0.40	0.30	0.00	0.00	0.00	0.00	0.00
Cumulated sales coefficient						0.30	0.70	1.16	1.66	2.18	2.72	3.25	3.78	4.27	4.73	5.13	5.44	5.44	5.44	5.44	5.44	5.44
CUMULATED VOLUME						60	139	229	328	431	536	642	745	843	934	1013	1073	1073	1073	1073	1073	1073
ANNUAL VOLUME						60	79	91	98	103	105	105	103	98	91	79	60	0	0	0	0	0
Cumulated volume as of the start of the new product						1600																
Learning rate						85																
Exponential learning coefficient						0.234																
Unit selling price						21.8	21.6	21.3	21.1	20.8	20.6	20.3	20.1	19.9	19.8	19.6	19.5	19.5	19.5	19.5	19.5	19.5
SALES (in million GBP)						1309	1701	1932	2072	2146	2168	2144	2075	1960	1790	1546	1171	0	0	0	0	0
Unit cost						19.4	19.2	19.0	18.7	18.5	18.3	18.1	17.9	17.7	17.6	17.5	17.4	17.4	17.4	17.4	17.4	17.4
COSTS (in million GBP)						1165	1514	1720	1844	1910	1929	1908	1847	1744	1593	1376	1042	0	0	0	0	0

Total volume sold over period with additional sales	1073															
CUMULATED VOLUME WITH ADDITIONAL SALES	60	139	229	328	431	536	642	745	843	934	1013	1073	1073	1073	1073	1073
ANNUAL VOLUME WITH ADDITIONAL SALES	60	79	91	98	103	105	105	103	98	91	79	60	0	0	0	0
SALES WITH ADDITIONAL VOLUME (in million GBP)	1309	1701	1932	2072	2146	2168	2144	2075	1960	1790	1546	1171	0	0	0	0
Unit cost with additional sales	19.4	19.2	19.0	18.7	18.5	18.3	18.1	17.9	17.7	17.6	17.5	17.4	17.4	17.4	17.4	17.4
COSTS WITH ADDITIONAL VOLUME (in million GBP)	1165	1514	1720	1844	1910	1929	1908	1847	1744	1593	1376	1042	0	0	0	0
PROFIT BEFORE TAX WITH ADDITIONAL VOLUME	144	187	213	228	236	238	236	228	216	197	170	129	0	0	0	0
PROFIT BEFORE TAX	144	187	213	228	236	238	236	228	216	197	170	129	0	0	0	0
Cumulated profit before tax	−756	−569	−356	−128	108	346	582	810	1026	1223	1393	1521	1521	1521	1521	1521
TAX	50	65	74	80	83	83	80	75	69	60	45	0	0	0	0	
PROFIT AFTER TAX	94	122	138	148	153	155	153	148	140	128	111	84	0	0	0	0
WORKING CAPITAL OPEN	0	196	255	290	311	322	325	322	311	294	269	232	176	0	0	0
WORKING CAPITAL END	196	255	290	311	322	325	322	311	294	269	232	176	0	0	0	0
CFO	−103	63	103	127	142	152	157	159	157	153	147	140	176	0	0	0
Discount rate	0.1															
NPV OPERATIONAL CASH FLOWS	450															
R&D AND CAPITAL EXPENDITURES	100	100	200	200	300											
TAX SAVINGS	35	35	23	47	82	58	35									
INVESTMENTS AFTER TAX SAVINGS	−65	−65	−177	−153	−218	58	58	35	0	0	0	0	0	0	0	0
NPV INVESTMENTS	−435															
FREE CASH FLOW	−65	−65	−177	−153	−218	−44	98	103	127	142	152	157	159	157	153	147	140	176	0	0	0
NPV OPERATIONAL CASH FLOWS	450															
NPV	15															

Figure 31.1   Foreground of the model.

	A	B	C	D	E	F	G	H	I
21		86	87	88	89	90	91	92	93 06
22	Total volume sold over period								
23	Years						(1)		
24	Scaling factor						+G23/$V$23 (2)		
25	Product life cycle coefficient						0.45		
26	Annual sales coefficient						(G24*$G$25)*(1−G24)*$G$25		
27	Cumulated sales coefficient						+G26	+H26+G27	
28	CUMULATED VOLUME						+$G$22*G27/$V$27	+H28−G28	
29	ANNUAL VOLUME						+G28		
30	Cumulated volume as of the start of the new product						20*D2		
31	Learning rate						85		
32	Exponential learning coefficient						(@LN(100)−@LN(G31))/@LN(2)		
33	Unit selling price						(3)		
34	SALES (in million GBP)						+G33*G29		
35	Unit cost						(4)		
36	COSTS (in million GBP)						+G35*G29		
37									
38	Total volume sold over period with additional sales						(5)		
39	CUMULATED VOLUME WITH ADDITIONAL SALES						+$G$38*G27/$V$27	+H39−G39	
40	ANNUAL VOLUME WITH ADDITIONAL SALES						+G39		
41	SALES WITH ADDITIONAL VOLUME (in million GBP)						+G40*G33		
42	Unit cost with additional sales						(6) +G42*G40		
43	COSTS WITH ADDITIONAL VOLUME (in million GBP)						+G41−G43		
44	PROFIT BEFORE TAX WITH ADDITIONAL VOLUME								
45									
46	PROFIT BEFORE TAX						@IF($D$14=0,G34−G36,G44)		

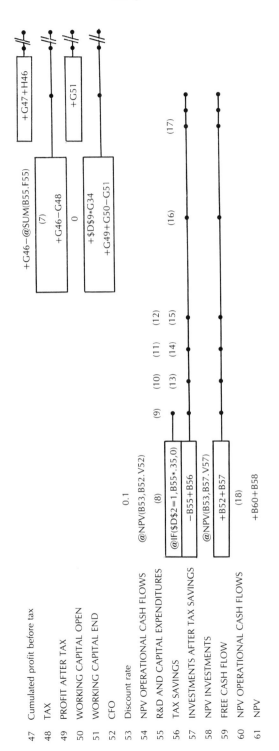

Control panel

	A	B	C	D	E	F	H
1	PARAMETERS						
2	Level of sales in unit in 1991 (000)			80			
3	Annual growth			0.02			
4	Unit selling price			22			
5	Capital expenditures			900			
6	DEPRECIATION/SALES an output			(19)			
7	Profit before depreciation/sales			0.11			
8	OPERATING PROFIT/SALES an output			(20)			
9	Working capital/sales			0.15			
10	Life cycle length			12			
11	Time for development (5 or 3 years)			5			
12	Ability to depreciate early, yes=1, no=2			1			
13	Learning gains kept, no=1, yes=2			1			
14	Additional units from acquisition			0			
15							
16							
17	OUTPUTS						
18	NPV OPERATIONAL CASH FLOWS	+B54					
19	NPV INVESTMENTS	+B58					
20			NPV (million GBP)				+B61

Notes

1 +D2*((((1+D3)^D10)-1)/D3)

2 @IF(C21-90<$D$10+1,G21-90,$D$10+1)

3 in G33: @IF($D$13=2,$D$4,$D$4*((G28+$G$30)/$G$30)^-$G$32) Copy to H33. In I33:@IF($D$13=2,$D$4*((G28+$G$30)/$G$30)^-$G$32,$D$4*((I28+$G$30)/$G$30)^-$G$32)-$G$30)^-$G$32). Copy

4 +$D$4*(1-$D$7)*((G28+$G$30)/$G$30)^-$G$32

5 +G22+D14*((((1+D3)^D10)-1)/D3)

6 +$D$4*(1-$D$7)*((G39+$G$30)/$G$30)^-$G$32

7 @IF($D$12=1,C46*0.35,@IF(G47<0,0,@IF(G47<C46,0.35*G47,0.35*G46)))

8 @IF($D$11=5,$D$5/9,$D$5/3)

9 @IF($D$11=5,$D$5/9,$D$5/3)

10 @IF($D$11=5,$D$5*2/9,$D$5*4/9)

11 @IF($D$11=5,$D$5*2/9,0)

12 @IF($D$11=5,$D$5*3/9,0)

13 @IF($D$12=1,$D$55/3*.35,0)

14 @IF($D$12=1,($E$55/3+$D$55/3)*.35,0)

15 @IF($D$12=1,($E$55/3+$D$55/3+$F$55/3)*.35,0)

16 @IF($D$12=1,($E$55/3+$F$55/3)*.35,0)

17 @IF($D$12=1,$F$55/3*.35,0)

18 @NPV(B53,C52..V52)*(1/(1+B53)^(@IF(D11=5,5,3)))

19 +D5/@SUM(G34..V34)

20 @SUM(G46..V46)-@SUM(B55..F55)/@SUM(G34..V34)

Column width: Global: 6, A: 29, H: 7

Figure 31.2 Background of the model.

model assumes that the conditions that will prevail in the future are fundamentally the same as those which prevailed in the past (eg the model assumes that the gains of learning are passed on to the customers) and which did not allow I to do better than breaking even. When you perform a sensitivity analysis (see results in Figure 31.3) you realize that:

- A small variation in any parameter can result in a very significant – positive or negative – change in the NPV. This is due to the fact that the initial assumptions describe a break-even situation.
- An increase in learning gains would not help I generate more value. As the learning gains are passed on to the customers, more learning only results in annual cash flows with smaller absolute values.
- A different pricing policy aimed at keeping part of the learning gains would dramatically change the picture. An umbrella pricing strategy enabling I to keep the learning gains for two years would create an additional value of 102 million GBP.
- The inability to benefit from the tax deductibility of the capital expenditures results in a significant loss of value. The many competitors who are not profitable should find it very difficult to launch a new generation of products.
- Finally, the proximity to the break-even point makes the company very vulnerable to a recession especially if the recession results, as in the past, in losses. Even though the model does not enable you to simulate their impact, such losses would probably have a dramatic impact on the total value.

The impact of the acquisition of F

With the assumptions of the model, the acquisition of F could have a significant impact on the value of the new products.

- One thousand additional units create an additional value of 10 million GBP, 5 000 additional units create 50 million, 10 000 additional units create 101 million and 20 000 additional units create 207 million. This result is consistent with the strategy of I which aims at increasing its size. However, it is worth noting that 20 000 more units increase the total volume by 25%, but create a value which is only twice as big as the value created by a two-year umbrella pricing strategy.
- The sensitivity analysis shows that the additional value created by 20 000 additional units remains in the range of 200 million GBP, even though this value is obviously sensitive to the overall market and operating conditions. The additional value is increased most by a shorter time to market and an umbrella pricing policy.
- The value created by 20 000 additional units is easily destroyed. When you set operating profit to 10% of sales, the additional value falls to 160 million

	Value	Difference with base	Value 20 000 additional units
Base	15		207
Level of sales			
+10%	60	45	206
−10%	−30	−45	208
Annual growth			
+10%	40	25	221
−10%	−8	−23	194
Unit selling price			
+10%	60	45	228
−10%	−30	−45	186
Capital expenditures			
+10%	−29	−43	208
−10%	58	43	207
Operating expenses			
10%	−36	−51	196
12%	66	51	218
Working capital needs			
10%	50	35	207
20%	−20	−35	207
Life cycle length			
13	37	22	220
11	−8	−23	193
3-year development	60	45	251
Late depreciation	−49	−64	214
Umbrella pricing	117	102	234
80 Learning rate	5	−10	227
90 Learning rate	24	9	188
Previous experience=1 200	8	−7	218
Previous experience=2 000	20	5	199

Figure 31.3   Sensitivity analysis.

GBP. You can actually check that each additional percentage point of operating profit results in a 62 million GBP loss of value.

31.3   USING THE MODEL TO FURTHER OUR UNDERSTANDING OF THE COMPETITIVE STRUCTURE OF THE INDUSTRY

With some precautions, the model can be used to further our understanding of the competitive situation in the European truck industry. Among the limitations of the model to be kept in mind are:

- The fact that the model ignores many of the complexities of the industry as well as key differences among competitors (distribution strategies, management of variety, degree of integration, etc). Another limitation of the model is the assumption that all competitors need to invest the same amount and that this amount is independent of the segment aimed at, and of the number of segments aimed at.

- The fact that the model extrapolates the conditions of the past. As expressed by M Leontiades,[1] it is a deadly management myth to assume stable industry structures with strong competition as this necessarily biases the conclusion towards the inevitability of pressure on prices and the need for competitors to become the lowest-cost champion.

Figure 31.4 shows the sets of parameters that you can use in order to explore some key competitive issues in the truck industry.

It seems clear that F made the right move when deciding to withdraw from the market. Even if it were able to reduce the size of the investment needed, F would not be in a position to generate a positive value from the introduction of a new product. As the leaders have decided to innovate, F had better sell its market share before it disappears.

Since several competitors are in the same position as F, it seems that the introduction of the new generation of products should correspond to a further step in the restructuring of the industry. The total value, before capital expenditures, of the new generation of products for the whole industry is between four to six times the value of the capital expenditures (their NPV is equal to 435 million, provided that tax allowances are used). You can try to guess who the four to six survivors might be!

An interesting result is that the value does not seem equally distributed among the heavy, medium and light segments. Competitors who specialize in the heavy segment have a stronger position. For a competitor that is strong in this segment, there is probably not much value to be gained through a downward extension of its range. The existence of competitors who specialize in the heavy segment probably reduces the number of competitors who can survive. If conditions do not change, there might be three or four survivors only. You may want to reconsider your guess about the survivors and eliminate one or two more names! Another interesting result is that a pricing strategy that would enable manufacturers to retain part of their learning gains would allow one additional competitor to find room in the industry.

The tentative simulation of the position of a competitor like Scania shows that a high value–high price competitor can prosper provided it has positioned itself on the right segment and also sells outside Europe in order to achieve a sufficient volume.[2] The model also shows the very high value of growth for a competitor like Scania; for such a competitor and provided its economics are kept the same, 20 000 more units would create some 800 million additional value ie four times more than for I. The tentative simulation of the position of a

	Sales	Growth	Price	Investment	Operating profit	Working capital	Life	Development	Tax deduction	Pricing	Additional units	Value
BASE	80	2%	22	900	11%	15%	12	5	1	1	0	15
SITUATION OF F												
Base . . .	20	2%	12	900	11%	15%	12	5	2	1	0	−374
With 30% higher price	20	2%	16	900	11%	15%	12	5	2	1	0	−353
With half investment	20	2%	12	450	11%	15%	12	5	2	1	0	−156
WHOLE INDUSTRY												
Base . . .	400	1%	20	0	11%	15%	12	5	1	1	0	1939
With 30% higher price	400	1%	26	0	11%	15%	12	5	1	1	0	2521
With 50% higher price	400	1%	30	0	11%	15%	12	5	1	1	0	2909
10% operating profit	400	1%	20	0	10%	15%	12	5	1	1	0	1721
With 30% higher price	400	1%	26	0	10%	15%	12	5	1	1	0	2238
12% operating profit	400	1%	20	0	12%	15%	12	5	1	1	0	2157
With 30% higher price	400	1%	26	0	11%	15%	12	5	1	1	0	2804
Market is 350 000 units	350	1%	20	0	11%	15%	12	5	1	1	0	1697
With 30% higher price	350	1%	26	0	11%	15%	12	5	1	1	0	2206
With 50% higher price	350	1%	30	0	11%	15%	12	5	1	1	0	2545
Umbrella pricing	400	1%	20	0	11%	15%	12	5	1	2	0	2361
With 30% higher price	400	1%	26	0	11%	15%	12	5	1	2	0	3069
With 50% higher price	400	1%	30	0	11%	15%	12	5	1	2	0	3541
HEAVY SEGMENT	136	2%	34	0	11%	15%	12	5	1	1	0	1182
MEDIUM SEGMENT	124	0%	17	0	11%	15%	12	5	1	1	0	485
LIGHT SEGMENT	144	2%	10	0	11%	15%	12	5	1	1	0	368
A COMPETITOR LIKE SCANIA												
At 1985 price level	23	3%	35	900	21%	15%	12	5	1	2	0	26
Umbrella pricing	23	3%	35	900	21%	15%	12	5	1	2	0	78
With 30% higher price	23	3%	46	900	21%	15%	12	5	1	2	0	171
A COMPETITOR LIKE VOLVO												
At 1985 price level	42	3%	32	900	12%	15%	12	5	1	2	0	−32
Prices 30% higher	42	3%	42	900	12%	15%	12	5	1	2	0	94

Notes
1 Average industry price in 1985: 34*0.34+17*0.31+10*0.36.
2 Average price 20% higher than the 1985 price (the price assumed by 1 for the new products is 30% higher than its average 1985 price).
3 Average price 30% higher than the 1985 price.
4 34% of a 400 000 units market, prices of 1985 (to be compared with the base scenario for the global market).
5 31% of a 400 000 units market, prices of 1985.
6 36% of a 400 000 units market, prices of 1985.
7 An operating profit before depreciation of 21% is needed to generate the 13% operating profit after depreciation shown in Figure AH.5.
8 An operating profit before depreciation of 12% is needed to generate the 7% operating profit after depreciation shown in Figure AH.5.

competitor like Volvo tends to show that a strategy of downward extension does not necessarily create value.

31.4 USING THE MODEL TO CHECK THE ASSESSMENT OF THE CONTINUING VALUE

The results of the model are apparently consistent with the statement made in the case that each point of market share in the United Kingdom (ie 1 000 trucks) is worth 10 million GBP. You have however to consider that:

- The model assumes that the UK market has the same characteristics as the 'average' European market which is probably not fully true.
- The model ignores the cost of the additional complexity caused by the acquisition of F; I plans to continue using the manufacturing facilities of F in the UK. If this reduced the total operating profit by only 1 percentage point of sales, then about 30% of the 200 million would be lost!
- The model ignores the value that additional volume will create with the future generations of products. If I believes in the future of the industry, this means that I is confident that, in the long run, the economics of the industry will change and enable the survivors to create value. The economics of a competitor like Scania suggest that the industry could create a lot of value, but assessing how much this value could be is extremely difficult. A further problem with this long-term perspective is the impact of time: 200 million 15 years from now are equivalent to 50 million today ie less than the impact of one point of operating profit to sales.

In conclusion, it seems that the value of 10 million per percentage point of market share is a reasonable estimate provided however that some industry restructuring happens before 1990 and allows for an improvement of the economics of the industry.

31.5 FRAMING THE ESTIMATE WITH A SIMPLER MODEL

The large size of the continuing value should encourage you to attempt to frame your estimate. In the absence of comparable transactions, you might try a much simpler approach: what is the present value of 12 years' contribution of 20 000 trucks? The very simple model in Figure 31.5 helps you answer this question. It shows that:

- With an 11% marginal contribution (before depreciation and tax), you get a value of 146 million GBP.

	A	B	C	D	E	F	G	H	I	J	K	L	M
1		91	92	93	94	95	96	97	98	99	100	101	102
2	Growth	0.02											
3	Market	100	102	104	106	108	110	113	115	117	120	122	124
4	Share	0.2											
5	Volume	20	20	21	21	22	22	23	23	23	24	24	25
6	Price	22											
7	SALES	440	449	458	467	476	486	496	505	516	526	536	547
8	Contribution	0.11											
9	PAT	31	32	33	33	34	35	35	36	37	38	38	39
10	Rate	0.1											
11	NPV 1990	234											
12	NPV 1985	146											
13	Capital in place												391
14	NPV 1990	125											
15	NPV 1985	77											
16	Total value	223											

Formulas

```
C3:   +B3*(1+$B$2)
B5:   +B3*$B$4
B7:   +$B$6*B5
B9:   +B7*$B$8*0.65
B11:  @NPV(B10,B9..M9)
B12:  +B11/(1+B10)^5
M13:  +M9/B10
B14:  @NPV(B10,B13..M13)
B15:  +B14/(1+B10)^5
B16:  +B12+B15
```

Figure 31.5 A simpler model.

- If you assume that, beyond the new generation of products, the activity in the UK will generate a normal return, ie a return equal to the cost of capital, then the value of the capital in place in 2002 is equal to 391 million which corresponds to a 1985 value of 77 million GBP.
- This leads to a total value of 223 million.

This model, which again seems to confirm the assessment of 10 million per percentage points, has a number of limitations:

- It ignores the impact of the additional volume on the operations of I as a whole.
- It ignores the fact that the activities beyond 2002 might generate more than a normal return. I actually believes that the industry will be more profitable in the long run.
- It does not take into account the erosion of the selling price caused by the passing of experience gains on to the customers.

NOTES

1 *Myth Management, An Examination of Corporate Diversification as Fact and Theory*, M Leontiades, Basil Blackwell, 1989. The example of the industry of equipment for telecommunications is a case in point: in the mid-1980s, most of the analysts – and some of the competitors – were convinced that competition was leading to the survival of a limited number of low-cost producers. Competitors – AT&T, Siemens, Ericsson, Northern Telecom, etc were fighting against each other, the overall climate in the industry was gloomy and very few competitors were creating value. The only thing very few had realized was that the cellular technology and the radio-based technologies in general were about to change the rules of the game and introduce a new competitor that very few had identified: Motorola. In the early 1990s, competition in the industry was still strong but the climate was very different as everybody was focusing on innovation and often (Ericsson for example) creating much more value than earlier.

The truck industry may also experience radical changes in the future.

2 In 'Survival Strategies in a Hostile Environment', *Harvard Business Review*, 1980, Sept–Oct, W Hall shows that, in hostile environments, success seems to come to those firms that achieve either the lowest cost or the most differentiated position.

Designing a Cooperative Strategy and Preparing for its Implementation

When preparing for the negotiation, I should understand both its interests and the interests of F. The problem is that understanding the interests of another party is extremely difficult.

- Taking the other parties' perspective is not easy.
- What you need to understand is not what the interests of the other parties should be, but *what the other parties think their interests are.*

In order to try to understand how F views its interests, we would like to propose a three-step approach.

- Let us start with an 'objective' analysis of the situation and let us design a deal that should satisfy their interests and ours.
- Then, let us put ourselves in their shoes and imagine how they might react to our 'objective' deal. This should help us go one step further in the process of understanding their perceived interests and perhaps make us revise our strategy.
- Finally, let us make sure that we devise a negotiation strategy, that will enable us to ask them, directly or indirectly, what they think their interests are. Even though it is essential, a careful preparation should never make you believe that you can guess what is in other people's minds.

32.1 STARTING WITH AN 'OBJECTIVE' ANALYSIS OF THE INTERESTS OF THE TWO PARTIES

Specifying the industry risk

The data suggested in the case for making 'best guess' assessments are reproduced in Figure 32.1.

Both the history of the market and its current situation (a competitor seems to be willing to start a price war) encourage us to explore more than one industry scenario. Even though it is very difficult to anticipate the evolution of

I Grows internally and pursues a conservative strategy

	1986	1987	1988	1989	1990
Growth	5.0%	5.0%	5.0%	3.0%	3.0%
Share I	3.00%	3.25%	3.50%	3.75%	4.00%
Share F					
Unit price I	18 000	18 000	18 000	18 000	18 000
Unit price F					
Unit cost I	12 780	12 780	12 780	12 780	12 780
Operating expenses	14	14	14	15	16
Working capital/sales	10%	10%	10%	10%	10%
Working capital open	4				
Cost of reorganization					

TAX: loss in 1986, carry forward in 1987, normal tax in 1988–90

I Grows internally and adopts an aggressive strategy

	1986	1987	1988	1989	1990
Growth	5.0%	5.0%	5.0%	3.0%	3.0%
Share I	4.0%	5.0%	6.0%	7.0%	8.0%
Share F					
Unit price I	14 400	14 400	14 400	15 000	18 000
Unit price F					
Unit cost I	12 780	12 780	12 780	12 780	12 780
Operating expenses	15	15	16	17	18
Working capital/sales	10%	10%	10%	10%	10%
Working capital open	4				
Cost of reorganization					

TAX: no tax losses during the whole period 1986–89

F closes its operations as late as possible

	1986	1987	1988	1989	1990
Growth	5.0%	5.0%	5.0%	3.0%	3.0%
Share I					
Share F	18.0%	16.0%	14.0%	12.0%	10.0%
Unit price I					
Unit price F	12 000	12 000	12 000	12 000	10 000
Unit cost I					
Operating expenses	30	25	23	20	15
Working capital/sales	10%	10%	10%	10%	10%
Working capital open	20				
Cost of reorganization					30

TAX: losses create tax credits for the other operations of the group

F closes its operations as early as possible

	1986	1987	1988	1989	1990
Growth	5.0%	5.0%			
Share I					
Share F	16.0%	10.0%			
Unit price I					
Unit price F	12 000	10 000			
Unit cost I					
Operating expenses	30	28			
Working capital/sales	10%	10%			
Working capital open	20				
Cost of reorganization		30			

TAX: losses create tax credits for the other operations of the group

I acquires F: the best guess case

	1986	1987	1988	1989	1990
Growth	5.0%	5.0%	5.0%	3.0%	3.0%
Share I	3.5%	4.0%	4.5%	5.0%	5.5%
Share F	18.0%	16.0%	14.0%	12.0%	10.0%
Unit price I	18 000	18 000	18 000	18 000	18 000
Unit price F	12 000	12 000	12 000	12 000	12 000
Unit cost I	12 780	12 780	12 780	12 780	12 780
Operating expenses	54	46	46	44	40
Working capital/sales	10%	10%	10%	10%	10%
Working capital open	24				
Cost of reorganization					30
Market share in 1991	15.5%				

TAX: no tax, losses during the whole period

I acquires F and the acquisition is a great success

	1986	1987	1988	1989	1990
Growth	5.0%	5.0%	5.0%	3.0%	3.0%
Share I	4.0%	5.0%	6.0%	7.0%	12.0%
Share F	19.0%	18.0%	17.0%	16.0%	11.0%
Unit price I	18 000	18 000	18 000	18 000	18 000
Unit price F	12 000	12 000	12 000	12 000	12 000
Unit cost I	12 780	12 780	12 780	12 780	12 780
Operating expenses	54	46	46	46	46
Working capital/sales	10%	10%	10%	10%	10%
Working capital open	24				
Cost of reorganization					30

TAX: loss in 1986, carry forwards in 1987–88, normal tax afterwards

I acquires F and the acquisition is a failure

	1986	1987	1988	1989	1990
Growth	5.0%	5.0%	5.0%	3.0%	3.0%
Share I	3.0%	3.0%	3.0%	3.0%	3.0%
Share F	16.0%	12.0%	10.0%	8.0%	7.0%
Unit price I	18 000	18 000	18 000	18 000	18 000
Unit price F	12 000	12 000	12 000	12 000	12 000
Unit cost I	12 780	12 780	12 780	12 780	12 780
Operating expenses	54	46	46	44	40
Working capital/sales	10%	10%	10%	10%	10%
Working capital open	24				
Cost of reorganization					40

TAX: no tax, losses during the whole period

Figure 32.1   Sets of data for 'best guess' assessments.

such a volatile market, let us specify a very optimistic and a very pessimistic scenario.

- 'Profitable boom'. A temporary market upswing will result in the following growth rates: 15% in 1986 and 1987, 10% in 1988, −5% in 1989, and −10% in 1990. This temporary boom will not lift the total market in 1991 which will remain equal to 100 000 units. Taking advantage of the boom, the

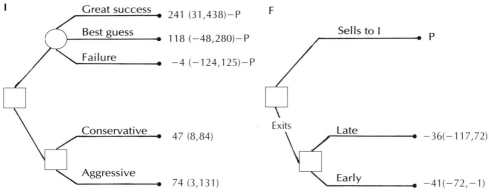

Notes
1 The first number corresponds to the 'best guess' scenario, the second to the 'cutthroat recession', the third to the 'profitable boom'.
2 To generate the results of the very difficult integration:
    For 'cutthroat recession', assume a 14 400 unit selling price for I and a 9 600 unit selling price for F (whole period). For 'profitable boom', take the 1990 loss into account for the tax shield.
3 To generate the results of aggressive internal growth with 'cutthroat recession', assume that in spite of a unit selling price of 14 400, I keeps the same market share as with the conservative strategy.
4 To generate the results of late closure, make the tax shields and the value beyond 1990 equal to zero. For 'cutthroat recession', make all unit prices 20% less than with the best guess scenario, for 'profitable boom', make them 20% higher.
5 To generate the results of early closure, erase the range C1.F16.

Figure 32.2 Outcomes of the alternatives available to I and F.

industry will be able to increase its average selling price by 20% in 1986.
■ 'Cutthroat recession'. There will be no market growth at all in the period 1986–90. A price war will cause a 20% price reduction in the period 1986–90 and the overall market value in 1991 will be 15% less than expected.

Figure 32.2 shows the results of the simulations of the situations of I, F, and of the combined operations of I and F within the three industry scenarios.

Assessing the BATNA of I
A 3–4% share of the UK market does not fit the ambition of I. It is why some managers are in favor of a more aggressive strategy. Is such a strategy a valuable alternative for I? Figure 32.2 suggests that the outcomes of the aggressive strategy are attractive but you should consider risk also and recognize that the aggressive strategy may start an industry-wide price war. In order to compare the conservative and the aggressive strategies, you should assign a much higher probability to the pessimistic industry scenario[1] in case I adopts the aggressive strategy. As risk easily destroys the advantage of the aggressive strategy, let us assume that the BATNA of I corresponds to the conservative internal growth strategy with a 47 million GBP best guess value and an 8 to 84 million GBP range.

Assessing the 'objective' BATNA of F

Figure 32.2 compares two exit strategies: closing as late as possible and closing as early as possible, ie within the next two years. The late closing strategy exposes F to a risk of very large losses, which might even be higher than shown by the model as the market may brutally lose confidence in products which are about to be discontinued. If, as seems reasonable, F adopts an early closing strategy, then its BATNA corresponds to a negative value: −36 million GBP for the best guess industry scenario.

The interesting thing, though, is that only a late closing strategy would give F a chance to leave the market without a loss (in the case of a market boom). As a result, it is difficult to guess what F perceives as its BATNA.

- Our analysis suggests that F had better close as early as possible. As this BATNA corresponds to a negative value, F should be willing to pay a price for getting rid of its operations.
- However, one may also imagine that if it believes that there is a good chance of a market upswing, F might be tempted to continue for as long as it can. If that were the case, F might consider that its BATNA is a positive number (if F assigns a 60% probability to the 72 million outcome, a 35% probability to the −36 million outcome and a 5% probability to the −117 million outcome, then its BATNA is as high as 25 million GBP).

Assessing the 'objective' value of the combined operations of I and F

Figure 32.2 shows nine possible outcomes for the combined operations: three acquisition scenarios (best guess, very successful integration and very difficult integration) and three values for each acquisition scenario (one for each industry scenario). These nine values are also shown in Figure 32.3 together with the three estimated outcomes of the BATNA of I.

Figure 32.3 confirms that, even though it might create a significant value, the acquisition is a risky option for I. If the industry becomes difficult, only a very successful integration process can avoid a disaster. Even though they are difficult to assess, the probabilities attached to the different integration and industry scenarios are critical. As shown in Figure 32.4, when you assign the same probability to each of the nine scenarios, you get an expected value of some 116 million which is about the same as the 118 million of the best guess scenario (best guess industry and best guess integration scenario). However when you take a more pessimistic view, the expected value of the combined operations becomes equal to 57 million only. At the opposite, when you take a more optimistic view, the expected value of the combined operations almost doubles.

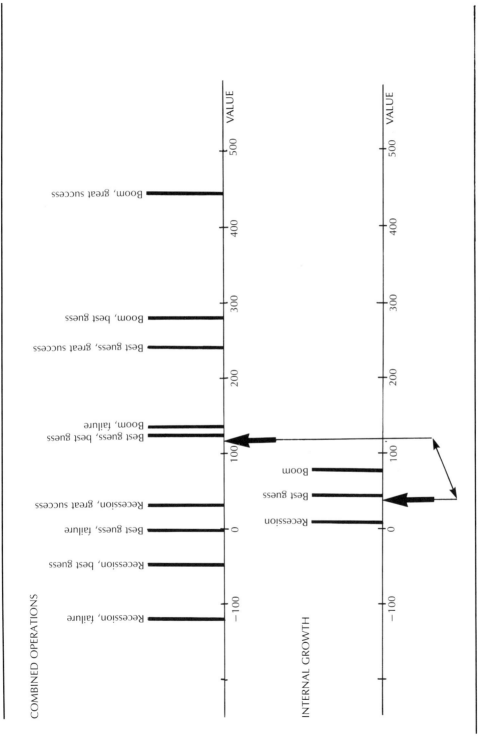

Figure 32.3 Outcomes of the integrated operations and of internal growth.

	Equal weights	Pessimistic view	Optimistic view
Industry scenario			
Cutthroat recession	33%	40%	20%
Best guess	33%	40%	30%
Profitable boom	33%	20%	50%
Integration scenario			
Failure	33%	40%	20%
Best guess	33%	40%	30%
Great success	33%	20%	50%
VALUE (in million GBP)	117	57	225

Figure 32.4   Value of the combined operations of I and F.

A model for assessing the zone of agreement: initial assessments of the situation

The model in Figure 32.5 can help us assess the value of an agreement, the walk aways of I and F and a 'fair' price (corresponding to an equal sharing of the value created) depending on:

- the values and probabilities of the outcomes of the three critical alternatives: integrated operations, BATNA of I and BATNA of F;
- the values and probabilities of the three industry scenarios. (The industry and integration outcomes are assumed to be independent.)

When the probabilities of each integration and industry scenarios are set to 1/3, the model in Figure 32.5 suggests that:

- A deal between I and F would create a substantial expected value: 110 million GBP. The value is especially high when the market becomes better. A large portion of the value is created by the suppression of the losses of F.
- F should accept any price above −38 million GBP (ie F should be prepared to pay up to 38 million to I in order to get rid of its truck operations) and I should be willing to pay as much as 72 million: this creates a large zone of agreement and suggests a fair price of 17 million GBP.

The model in Figure 32.5 enables you to test the robustness of this initial assessment. Let us assume that a pessimistic view of the industry or of the integration would make I assign a 50% probability to the worst outcome, a 40% probability to the middle outcome and a 10% probability to the best outcome. Let us further assume that an optimistic view of the same scenarios would make I assign a 10% probability to the worst outcome, a 40% probability to the middle outcome and a 50% probability to the best outcome. When you run the model with these assumptions you get the results shown in Figure 32.6. The sensitivity of the value created by a deal has a series of implications.

	A	B	C	D	E	F	G	H
1		Recession			Best guess			Boom
2	INTEGRATED OPERATIONS							
3	Very difficult	−124			−4			129
4	Probability	0.33						
5	Best guess	−48			118			280
6	Probability	0.33						
7	Great success	31			241			438
8	Probability	0.33						
9	EXPECTED VALUE	−47			118			282
10								
11	BEST INTERNAL GROWTH (I's BATNA)	8			47			84
12								
13	BEST EXIT STRATEGY (F's BATNA)	−72			−41			−1
14								
15	VALUE CREATED	17			112			199
16	Probability industry scenarios	0.33			0.33			0.33
17								
18	**VALUE CREATED (expected)**	**110**			**WALK-AWAYS**	F	**−38**	I **72**
19	**FAIR PRICE (equal sharing of value)**	**17**			**VALUE FOR**	F	**17**	I **101**
20					**ADDITIONAL VALUE FOR**	F	**55**	I **55**

Formulas
B9 +B3*$B$4+B5*$B$6+B7*$B$8; copy into E9 and H9.
B15 +B9−B11−B13; copy into E15 and H15.
B18 +B15*B16+E15*E16+H15*H16
F18 +B13*B16+E13*E16+H13*H16
B19 +B18/2+F18
F19 +B19
H18 (B9−B11)+B16+(E9−E11)*E16+(H9−H11)*H16
H19 +B9*B16+E9*E16+H9*H16−B19
F20 +F19−F18
H20 (B9−B11−B19)*B16+(E9−E11−B19)*E16+(H9−H11−B19)*H16

Figure 32.5   A model to assess the integrative dynamics.

In million GBP

	Value created	Zone of agreement	Fair price
I is pessimistic about the integration and pessimistic about the industry	32	−53 to −21	−37
optimistic about the industry	93	−24 to 68	22
I is optimistic about the integration and pessimistic about the the industry	115	−53 to 62	5
optimistic about the industry	200	−24 to 176	76

Figure 32.6   Sensitivity analysis.

- I has to assess the risks involved very carefully. What are these risks? How can they be reduced? Is it possible to design a deal that can accommodate the remaining risks?
- If they happen to have different views about the risks of the integration or of the industry, I and F will find it very difficult to make a deal.

Let us assume, for the time being, that I assigns a 1/3 probability to the different integration and industry scenarios and therefore aims at a 'fair' price of 17 million GBP (see Figure 32.5).

32.2   TRYING TO INTRODUCE THE SUBJECTIVITY OF THE OTHER PARTY

Reversing roles

If you were F, would you easily agree that 17 million GBP is a fair price for your business?

When you realize that your working capital has a value of 20 million and that each point of market share is worth 10 million GBP, ie that a 20% share is worth 200 million, you might consider that 17 million is a very low price! It seems obvious that F will find it difficult to understand that I believes that the costs and risks of transferring their operations are so high that they wipe out almost all the intrinsic value of these operations.

If you were F, how would you evaluate the combination of your operations with those of I?

- F's assessment should present many similarities to I's. The valuation model of F should have the same general structure, similar key relationships and numbers (value of initial working capital, value of each percentage point of market share, size of the market in 1986, market shares of F and I in 1986, selling prices of F and I trucks in 1986, unit costs of F and I trucks in 1986, operating costs of F and I in 1985 and possibly in 1986, etc). When you consider it, it is not unreasonable to assume not only that I and F have similar valuation models but also that the numbers shown in the first year of their models are very close.
- However, it is likely that the models of F present some fundamental differences also as there is no reason for F to share the views of I regarding the future of the UK market and the potential of integrating the operations.
  · F has built a leading position in the UK; I has always been marginal in this market.
  · F has access to the best network of dealers in the UK; the dealers of I are of a relatively low quality.
  · F has a very strong brand in the UK; the brand of I is hardly known on this market.

· F has strong management capabilities in the UK; I has never devoted much management attention to this market.
· F has no experience of integrating the operations of another truck company; I has been built through a series of acquisitions and some of these acquisitions have not been easy to integrate.
· If it sells its operations to I, and gets paid in cash, F will be able to forget about the truck business; I will have to implement the merger.

What if F were more optimistic than we are?

Let us formulate an extreme, but not necessarily unrealistic, scenario. Let us assume that F, who never had a difficult integration experience and who has an intimate knowledge of the market, believes that:

■ The integrated operations of I and F could result in a market share bigger than the sum of the individual shares of I and F. In order to simulate the impact of this synergy, you can run again the very successful integration scenario and set the market share of I in 1990 at 14% (using the model in Figure 30.4).
■ This new very successful scenario is the most likely: 60% chances against 35% for the middle scenario and 5% for the difficult scenario.
■ The most likely industry scenario is the 'profitable boom': 60% chances against 35% for the middle scenario and 5% for the pessimistic one.
■ Running their operations until 1990 is their best alternative to an agreement with I.

The model in Figure 32.5 can help you simulate the consequences of this optimistic view of F. As shown in Figure 32.7, F now requests a price higher than 25 million and aims at a 'fair' price of 129 million GBP. If I sticks to the view corresponding to our initial assessment (see Figure 32.5) and if F adopts the optimistic view, an agreement becomes much more difficult.

■ F wants to get a price between 25 and 233 million, while I is willing to pay a price between −38 and 72 million.
■ As a result there is a narrow zone of agreement: between 25 and 72 million. However, it might be difficult to find a price within that zone that would satisfy both I and F as any price in the zone might look a bit low for F and a bit high for I.

The danger of negotiating over positions

A typical negotiation process is to have each party state its position, argue for it and engage in a 'dance' of concessions aimed at reaching a compromise somewhere in the middle of the initial positions.

	Recession	Best guess	Boom
INTEGRATED OPERATIONS			
Very difficult	−124	−4	129
Probability	0.05		
Best guess	−48	118	280
Probability	0.35		
Great success	49	265	465
Probability	0.60		
EXPECTED VALUE	6	200	383
BEST INTERNAL GROWTH (I's BATNA)	8	47	84
BEST EXIT STRATEGY (F's BATNA)	−117	−36	72
VALUE CREATED	115	189	227
Probability industry scenarios	0.05	0.35	0.6
VALUE CREATED (expected)	**208**	**WALK-AWAYS F 25**	**I 233**
FAIR PRICE (equal sharing of value)	**129**	**VALUE FOR F 129**	**I 171**
		ADDITIONAL VALUE FOR F 104	**I 104**

	I's VIEW	F's VIEW
Integrated operations	118	300
Best internal growth	46	67
Best exit strategy	−38	25
VALUE CREATED	110	208
I's WALK-AWAY	72	233
F's WALK-AWAY	−38	25
FAIR PRICE	17	129
ZONE OF AGREEMENT		
F's walk-away	25	
I's walk-away		72

Figure 32.7   What if F were to be more optimistic?

Where could such a process lead I and F? Let us now assume that while F considers that the results of Figure 32.7 give a fair assessment of the situation, I wants to be cautious and ends up espousing the most pessimistic view described in Figure 32.6 (pessimistic view about the integration and the market). Let us further assume that I and F are so confident in their analyses that they decide to state their respective positions regarding a 'fair' price at the very beginning of the negotiation:

> F: 'We estimate that you should pay 129 million to us'
> I: 'We estimate that you should pay   37 million to us'

This could obviously upset both parties and jeopardize the whole negotiation even though both I and F are perfectly able to understand the rationale behind such distant positions.

In the present situation, *it is better for I and F to decide to defer the statement of any position regarding a 'fair' price.* The priority for I and F is to design a process that will enable them to work together at establishing the integrative dimension of the situation they are dealing with.

32.3   DESIGNING A COOPERATIVE STRATEGY FOR NEGOTIATION

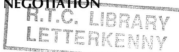
R.T.C. LIBRARY
LETTERKENNY

The analysis suggests the following negotiating agenda:

- I should acquire a better understanding of the perspective of F: how does F see the future of the market, its own future and the potential of a merger?
- I should try to close part of the potential gaps between its point of view and the point of view of F. If, as is likely, I is more concerned with risk than F, the two companies should define joint actions that they could undertake for helping reduce the risks for I.
- The two companies should design a solution to create value out of their remaining differences.
- Finally, I and F should find a solution for claiming a fair share of the value created by the negotiation.

As the priority is to create the value of a potential deal and not to share this value, I should adopt a cooperative approach. This requires the implementation of a specific strategy and of specific behavioral characteristics.

- Axelrod[1] has established that the negotiating strategy that works best in most cases is a very simple cooperative strategy: adopt a cooperative attitude from the very beginning and continue cooperating for as long as the other party reciprocates. In case the other party stops cooperating and 'attacks', retaliate immediately but be forgiving and turn again to cooperation straightaway after retaliation.
- Cooperation also requires specific behavioral attitudes aimed at building mutual trust: clear distinction between facts that can be agreed on and beliefs that can be accepted as being different, honesty in the presentation of facts and beliefs, openness to new information and differences in beliefs, joint problem solving, establishment of jointly accepted criteria and . . . patience. One thing I has to decide is how much information it is prepared to share with F; for example, is I willing to show its business plans (BATNA and integrated operations) to F?

When trying to simulate the discussions with F, I should realize that not all critical issues are to be dealt with in the same way.

- If they show mutual respect, the two parties should probably recognize that the other party knows best about its own situation. F should probably easily accept the value stated by I regarding its best internal growth scenario and I should probably do the same for the value of the best exit strategy stated by F. I should also probably realize that the discussion of the eventual liquidation of the operations of F is difficult as such a discussion can easily turn into an investigation of the weaknesses of F and destroy the cooperative climate.

- At the opposite, the evaluation of the combined operations is the real opportunity for I and F to recognize their shared interests, to go for a two-way exchange of information and to engage in joint problem-solving activities. One very important thing that the two companies should quickly realize is that they have a common interest: the success of the merger of the operations of I and F. This means that F should be willing to help I reduce the risks of the merger. Consequently, I should identify how F could help reduce the risk and think about what it could reasonably request from F in the negotiation: authorization to use the F brand name for a period of time, guarantee that the key managers will not leave, assistance in the negotiation with the dealers, etc.

Finally, I should think about how to deal with the differences that will probably remain in the end. Because the uncertainties are very big, I should probably remain flexible and wait until more is known to decide about the best structure for a deal. The problem however for I is to be aware that the great uncertainty will probably make it look for either:

- A straight buy-out solution with a relatively low payment made to F at the date of signature (less than 50% of the value created paid to F and/or conservative assessment of the value created).
- Or a merger of the operations of F and I that would keep F involved for a period of time and would defer the payment to F to a future date when the major uncertainities are resolved. F might actually be interested in such a solution. If they are very confident about the success of the merger, F could see such a deal as an opportunity to get a higher payment. F could also realize that such a solution could help it contribute to the success of the merger and make sure that no damaging conflicts surface with its dealers.

These two extreme solutions are consistent with different negotiation climates (distributive vs cooperative). If, as seems reasonable, I decides that the second type of solution is preferable, then the need for establishing a cooperative climate is even greater.

A final problem that I should consider is the chance that F is not willing to adopt a cooperative approach. Analysis says that F should adopt an integrative approach, but there is at least one indication in the case which suggests that F might have decided to adopt a claiming approach: F is putting pressure on for a quick deal. This might mean that F believes that the value is easy to assess and that the only thing to do is to agree on how to share it, a pure distributive issue. If it has this view, F will probably show impatience with the efforts of I to establish a cooperative climate and will push for a price. F might even come very quickly with a price proposal. Such a proposal would help I understand the perspective of F but could also create difficulties associated to position bargaining. Dealing with a difficult other party[2] might make the task of I much more complicated but should not make I abandon its cooperative strategy.

NOTES

1 The *Evolution of Cooperation*, Basic Books, New York, 1984.

2 For how to negotiate with difficult people, refer to *Getting Past No, Negotiating with difficult people*, W Ury, Business Books, London, 1991.

F TRUCKS

(Abridged version)

On 28 June 1985, Reginald Jones, the president of F in the United Kingdom was busy reviewing his files before leaving for Torino where he was going to meet the senior management of I on the following day. Reginald Jones was optimistic about the issue of the meeting which he had pressed I's management to organize before the summer break. Since a deal was very clearly beneficial to both parties, Reginald Jones was confident that it should be easy to agree quickly about a fair price.

F Trucks was part of the international automotive group F. Within the F group, the truck business had traditionally been centered on the UK market where it enjoyed a strong position. However, the market share of F Trucks had progressively declined under the pressure of competition. Since it discontinued its heavy truck product line in 1984, F was selling medium trucks only. One of the major strengths of F was its network of dealers which was probably the strongest car and truck dealers network in the UK. In 1985, F had 120 truck dealers, most of whom were car dealers also. Like most companies in the automotive sector, F had to face difficult labor relations in the 1970s, but these improved a lot in the early 1980s and the company launched a major change programme aimed at reaching world-class quality. The programme was successful and in 1985, F Trucks had been able to suppress quality inspectors, to reduce the number of its suppliers from 15 000 to 400 and to operate with 3 unions instead of 9 in the early 1980s. F had also taken measures for reducing its capacity and lowering its break-even point. In particular, F had decided to abandon the manufacturing of its own axles.

The divestment plan

In November 1984, the Board of F made the decision not to develop a new generation of trucks as the investment required would not be profitable due to the insufficient size of F's operations. Following this decision, F started preparing a divestment plan. The obvious option for F was to try to sell their operations to one of their competitors. Among those, I appeared to be the one which would benefit most from the acquisition of F Trucks. F approached I at the end of 1984 and as expected by F, I expressed interest in exploring the issue further. During the first meeting that took place between the representatives of the two companies in January 1985, I tried to show that:

- F was in a weak position;
- the benefits that I would derive from the acquisition were not that great.

It was not the first time that Reginald Jones had been involved in such negotiations and he was convinced that the young I team who took part in the first meeting had been

This case is an abridged version of the F Trucks case which was developed by the author and Damir Borsic, Professor at ISVOR-FIAT (Italy). The F Trucks case can be obtained from the author.

	1986	1987	1988	1989	1990	1991	Cum.
Growth	5.0%	5.0%	5.0%	3.0%	3.0%		
Total market	84 000	88 200	92 610	95 388	98 250		
Share F	19.0%	19.0%	18.0%	17.0%	15.0%		
Unit price F	12 000	12 000	12 000	12 000	10 000		
SALES	192	201	200	195	147		
Unit Cost F	10 233	10 084	10 099	10 183	10 493		
CGS	163	169	168	165	155		
CGS/sales	85%	84%	84%	85%	105%		
OPERATING EXPENSES	25	20	15	15	10		
Operating expenses/sales	13%	10%	7%	8%	7%		
PROFIT BEFORE TAX	3	12	17	14	−17		
PROFIT AFTER TAX	2	8	11	9	−11		19
Working capital open	0	19	20	20	19	15	
Working capital/sales	10%	10%	10%	10%	10%		
Working capital end	19	20	20	19	15		
CFO 1986–90	−17	7	11	10	−6	15	19
Discount rate	0.10						
NPV 1986–90 cash flow	9						
WORKING CAPITAL OPEN	20						
REORGANIZATION COST					20		
NPV REORGANIZATION	12						
TOTAL VALUE (million GBP)	17						

Note
This scenario corresponds to the best guess industry scenario.
With the 'profitable boom' scenario, the value is 151 million GBP.
With the 'cutthroat recession' scenario, the value is −84 million GBP.
The expected value is (−84+17+151)/3=28 million.

Figure I.1   Evaluation of an exit strategy at F.

playing tough to prepare for a quick agreement in their favor. As far as the position of F was concerned, Reginald Jones did not believe it was that weak. Even though I was the only possible buyer, F could very well implement a plan for closure, and as shown in Figure I.1, achieve reasonable results. As it did not include some opportunities to export to South Africa and Turkey (about 1 500 vehicles), this plan could be considered as conservative.

The potential benefits for I

Reginald Jones was convinced that the acquisition of F was a great opportunity for I: the estimate of the value of the combined operations of F and I that had been prepared by F is in Figure I.2.

Through acquiring F, I would be able to get access to a 20% market share without having to put any pressure on the prices. Obviously, a critical success factor was that I would be able to retain the dealers and customers of F, but according to Reginald Jones, this should not present any major difficulty.

The continuation of F's current products until 1990–91 should allow for a smooth transition and Reginald Jones was convinced that the dealers would welcome the business of I which, contrary to F, was offering a full range of products. As they were

	1986	1987	1988	1989	1990	1991	Cum.
Growth	5.0%	5.0%	5.0%	3.0%	3.0%		
Total market	84 000	88 200	92 610	95 388	98 250		
Share I	4.0%	4.0%	5.0%	6.0%	12.0%		
Share F	19.0%	19.0%	19.0%	18.0%	11.0%		
Unit price I	18 000	18 000	18 000	18 000	18 000		
Unit price F	12 000	12 000	12 000	12 000	12 000		
SALES	252	265	294	309	342		
Unit cost I	12 780	12 780	12 780	12 780	12 780		
Unit Cost F	10 233	10 084	9 942	10 012	11 726		
CGS	206	214	234	245	277		
CGS/sales	82%	81%	79%	79%	81%		
OPERATING EXPENSES	45	43	43	43	43		
Operating expenses/sales	18%	16%	15%	14%	13%		
PROFIT BEFORE TAX	1	8	17	21	22		
PROFIT AFTER TAX	0	5	11	14	14		44
Working capital open	0	25	26	29	31	34	
Working capital/sales	10%	10%	10%	10%	10%		
Working capital end	25	26	29	31	34		
CFO 1986–90	−25	4	8	12	11	34	44
Discount rate	0.10						
NPV 1986–90 cash flow	21						
WORKING CAPITAL OPEN	24						
REORGANIZATION COST					30		
NPV REORGANIZATION	19						
Market share in 1991	0.23						
Adjustment continuing value	0.0%						
VALUE CASH FLOWS BEYOND 1990	230						
TOTAL VALUE (million GBP)	256						

Figure I.2 Estimate of the value of a merger between F and I.

	1986	1987	1988	1989	1990	1991	Cum.
Growth	5.0%	5.0%	5.0%	3.0%	3.0%		
Total market	84 000	88 200	92 610	95 388	98 250		
Market share	3.0%	5.0%	7.0%	9.0%	10.0%		
Unit selling price	14 400	13 680	13 680	13 680	14 000		
SALES	36	60	89	117	138		
Unit cost	12 780	12 780	12 780	12 780	12 780		
CGS	32	56	83	110	126		
CGS/sales	89%	93%	93%	93%	91%		
OPERATING EXPENSES	10	15	20	22	22		
Operating expenses/sales	28%	25%	23%	19%	16%		
PROFIT BEFORE TAX	−6	−11	−14	−14	−10		
PROFIT AFTER TAX	−6	−11	−14	−14	−10		−55
Working capital open	0	4	6	9	12	14	
Working capital/sales	10%	10%	10%	10%	10%		
Working capital end	4	6	9	12	14		
CFO 1986–90	−10	−13	−17	−17	−12	14	−55
Discount rate	0.10						
NPV 1986–90 cash flow	−44						
WORKING CAPITAL OPEN	4						
Market share in 1991	0.1						
VALUE CASH FLOWS BEYOND 1990	100						
TOTAL VALUE (million GBP)	60						

Figure I.3 Estimate of the value that can be achieved through internal growth by I.

generally selling both trucks and cars, dealers were very important to F and Reginald Jones was prepared to make all the efforts needed to ensure a smooth transition and to avoid any of the dealers going to the competition. There was obviously a risk related to the integration of the two operations but since I, contrary to F, was strongly committed to the truck business, management and employees should welcome their new owner. Finally, the manufacturing facilities of F were among the most modern in Europe and could easily be converted to assemble the new products of I in the 1990s. In any case, acquiring F trucks was a much better solution for I than relying on internal growth (an assessment of what I could achieve without acquiring F is in Figure I.3).

Reginald Jones's intuition was that in such a situation, where a deal was clearly beneficial to both parties, the best approach was to try to strike the deal quickly. This is why he pressed for a meeting to take place before the summer break.

THE NEGOTIATION BETWEEN I AND F

On 15 October 1985, Mr Corsi was very happy. I and F had agreed to form a 50–50 joint venture to run the merged operations of F Trucks and of I in the UK and were going to meet at the end of the month to finalize the agreement. It had been already agreed that the joint venture would be managed by I.

The joint venture proposal was made by Mr Corsi when opening the meeting held on 29 June. The discussions that took place during the meeting and several subsequent meetings during the autumn, allowed the two parties to:

- agree to form a 50–50 joint venture;
- exchange a lot of information. I and F exchanged their strategic plans and agreed about their respective positions in case they failed to reach an agreement.
  - · The value of the best internal growth strategy for I was estimated at 47 million GBP according to the strategic plan of I.
  - · The value of the best exit strategy for F was estimated at 28 million GBP according to the strategic plan of F.
- Recognize their common interest in reducing the risk of the future merged operations. F agreed that the joint venture would be allowed to use the F brand name for a period of three to five years, F agreed to play an active role in the negotiation of the new contracts with the dealers and confirmed that the key managers of its truck operations were enthusiastic about the opportunity to work for I.
- Agree on the sharing of the results of the joint venture: at the end of each year, any profit would be distributed to the two partners, any loss would be covered by a new equity issue subscribed equally by the two partners.

However, the two parties had not been able to agree on the value of the expected outcome of the operations of the joint venture. The solutions found with F to limit the risks of the merger had made Mr Corsi disregard the failure scenario that he had envisaged initially but as shown in Figures J.1 and J.2, I was still more pessimistic than F about the future of the joint venture. As the two parties were not willing to change their views, it was decided to keep two scenarios for planning the future of the joint venture. Rather than 'I' and 'F', these two scenarios were called 'pessimistic' and 'optimistic'.

This case has been prepared from a real business situation by Damir Borsic, ISVOR FIAT (Italy) and the author.

	1986	1987	1988	1989	1990	1991	Cum.
Growth	5.0%	5.0%	5.0%	3.0%	3.0%		
Total market	84 000	88 200	92 610	95 388	98 250		
Share I	4.0%	4.0%	5.0%	6.0%	12.0%		
Share F	19.0%	19.0%	19.0%	18.0%	11.0%		
Competitive price change	0						
Unit price I	18 000	18 000	18 000	18 000	18 000		
Unit price F	12 000	12 000	12 000	12 000	12 000		
SALES	252	265	294	309	342		
Unit cost I	12 780	12 780	12 780	12 780	12 780		
Unit Cost F	10 233	10 084	9 942	10 012	11 726		
CGS	206	214	234	245	277		
CGS/sales	82%	81%	79%	79%	81%		
OPERATING EXPENSES	45	43	43	43	43		
Operating expenses/sales	18%	16%	15%	14%	13%		
PROFIT BEFORE TAX	1	8	17	21	22		
PROFIT AFTER TAX	0	5	11	14	14		44
Working capital open	0	25	26	29	31	34	
Working capital/sales	10%	10%	10%	10%	10%		
Working capital end	25	26	29	31	34		
CFO 1986–90	−25	4	8	12	11	34	44
Discount rate	0.10						
NPV 1986–90 cash flows	21						
WORKING CAPITAL OPEN	24						
REORGANIZATION COST					30		
NPV REORGANIZATION	19						
TAX SHIELD					0		
NPV TAX SHIELD	0						
Market share in 1990	0.23						
Market share in 1991	0.23						
Adjustment continuing value	0.0%						
VALUE CASH FLOWS BEYOND 1990	230						
TOTAL VALUE (million GBP)	256						

The above assessment of the optimistic integration scenario corresponded to the 'best guess' market scenario. When run within different market scenarios, the optimistic integration scenario was giving the following values:
- 'profitable boom' 454 million GBP
- 'cutthroat recession' 47 million GBP

The average value of this optimistic integration scenario was equal to (47+256+454)/3 ie 252 million GBP. This scenario is the same as the integration scenario prepared by F (see Figure I.2).

Figure J.1   The 'optimistic' scenario for the joint venture.

	1986	1987	1988	1989	1990	1991	Cum.
Growth	5.0%	5.0%	5.0%	3.0%	3.0%		
Total market	84 000	88 200	92 610	95 388	98 250		
Share I	3.5%	4.0%	4.5%	5.0%	5.5%		
Share F	18.0%	16.0%	14.0%	12.0%	10.0%		
Competitive price change	0						
Unit price I	18 000	18 000	18 000	18 000	18 000		
Unit price F	12 000	12 000	12 000	12 000	12 000		
SALES	234	233	231	223	215		
Unit cost I	12 780	12 780	12 780	12 780	12 780		
Unit Cost F	10 407	10 643	10 956	11 468	12 189		
CGS	195	195	195	192	189		
CGS/sales	83%	84%	85%	86%	88%		
OPERATING EXPENSES	54	46	46	44	40		
Operating expenses/sales	23%	20%	20%	20%	19%		
PROFIT BEFORE TAX	−15	−8	−11	−13	−14		
PROFIT AFTER TAX	−15	−8	−11	−13	−14		−60
Working capital open	0	23	23	23	22	22	
Working capital/sales	10%	10%	10%	10%	10%		
Working capital end	23	23	23	22	22		
CFO 1986–90	−38	−8	−10	−12	−13	22	−60
Discount rate	0.10						
NPV 1986–90 cash flows	−53						
WORKING CAPITAL OPEN	24						
REORGANIZATION COST					30		
NPV REORGANIZATION	19						
TAX SHIELD					21		
NPV TAX SHIELD	11						
Market share in 1990	0.155						
Market share in 1991	0.155						
Adjustment continuing value	0.0%						
VALUE CASH FLOWS BEYOND 1990	155						
TOTAL VALUE (million GBP)	118						

The above assessment of the pessimistic integration scenario corresponded to the 'best guess' market scenario.

When run within different market scenarios, the pessimistic integration scenario was giving the following values:

- 'profitable boom' 280 million GBP
- 'cutthroat recession' −48 million GBP

The average value of this pessimistic integration scenario was equal to (−48+118+280)/3 ie 117 million GBP.

Figure J.2 The 'pessimistic' scenario (same as I's best-guess integration).

CHAPTER 33

Creating Value Out of Shared Interests and Differences: the Rationale for a Joint Venture[1]

The essence of a joint venture is to entwine agreement and disagreement. A joint venture has the same fabric as the negotiation that led to its establishment. With the joint venture, the cooperative relationship between I and F will continue and develop within a new frame.

33.1   THE POSITIONS ON 29 JUNE 1985

With the I and F cases, we are in the unusual situation of knowing what the two parties to a negotiation were thinking when they started to discuss. Figure 33.1 shows the initial positions of I and F as they can be assessed with the help of the model in Figure 32.5. I and F had a narrow zone of agreement and the design of a distributive agreement was very difficult.

33.2   THE JOINT VENTURE ENABLES I AND F TO IMPLEMENT A SERIES OF AGREEMENTS FOR CREATING COMMON VALUE

Even though they had reached different positions regarding a 'fair' price, I and F were agreeing on many critical factors when they met on 29 June 1985. The negotiation process enabled them to discover that:

- They had the same basic understanding of the situation. This shows in the scenarios developed by the two companies. I and F were sharing similar views about the market, they were considering the same alternatives, and they were making almost the same assumptions for future revenues and costs.
- Both companies were recognizing the risks involved in an acquisition as well as the common interest they had in limiting these risks. This led them to organize a process for an effective transfer of know-how from F to I. As they

	I's VIEW	F's VIEW
Integrated operations	118	252
Best integral growth	46	59
Best exit strategy	−38	28
VALUE CREATED	110	166
I's walk away	72	194
F's walk away	−38	28
FAIR PRICE	17	111
ZONE OF AGREEMENT		
F's walk away	**28**	
I's walk away		**72**

Note
It is assumed that F considers the same three industry scenarios as I (equal probabilities). For F, there is only one integration scenario.

Figure 33.1   Positions before the June negotiation.

have decided to stay, the key managers of F will make I benefit from their unique knowledge of the market, the use of the F brand name will help I build its position in the UK, F will make I benefit from its successful experience in managing a network of dealers in the UK.

The joint venture institutionalizes the agreement reached by I and F for limiting the risks of the merger, it provides them with the time they need to implement a successful transfer of know-how. Finally it creates for both of them, and for F in particular, a strong incentive to succeed.

33.3   THE JOINT VENTURE ALSO ENABLES I AND F TO DISAGREE AND TO CREATE VALUE OUT OF THIS DISAGREEMENT

In spite of the agreements that they managed to establish during the negotiation, I and F were still in disagreement regarding the risks involved.

Figure 33.2 shows the impact of the joint actions decided by I and F to reduce the risks of a merger: as a result of these actions I values the integrated operations at 172 million GBP (ie 44% more than its initial estimate). These joint actions have reduced the gap between the points of views of I and F. The paradox however is that the value of an agreement, as seen by I, has decreased; this is due to the fact that I has revised its assessment of the BATNA of F which contributes now much less to the value of an agreement.

At this stage of the negotiation, I and F were in a much better position to agree on a fair price. A first approach for reaching an agreement would have been to continue discussing the risks involved with the hope that the two

	I's VIEW	F's VIEW
Integrated operations	171	238
Best internal growth	46	46
Best exit strategy	28	28
VALUE CREATED	97	164
I's walk away	125	192
F's walk away	28	28
FAIR PRICE	76	110
ZONE OF AGREEMENT		
F's walk away	**28**	
I's walk away		**125**

Figure 33.2 Positions after the June negotiation.

companies would manage to resolve their remaining differences, ie that at least one of the parties would change its mind. A possible solution could have been that F finally agrees with I that a merger is always a risky venture and accepts a price of 76 million GBP, a price significantly higher than its walk away.

A second and more creative approach was to design the deal in such a way that neither F nor I had to change its mind. As nobody can claim to know what the future will be, *why not agree to disagree about the future* and find a way to create a deal that can leave each party free to believe what it wants regarding the future? The key to the creation of such a deal was to take advantage of time. A few years after I and F decide to merge their operations, ie in 1990–91, there will no longer be any uncertainty about the success of the deal. Both I and F will know perfectly the situation of the integrated company: market share, dealers network, internal climate, selling prices, costs, profits, etc. Consequently, there will no longer be any major difficulty for I and F to agree on a fair price.

- If the acquisition has enabled I to capture 23% of the UK market and to derive a large profit from this position, I will have no objection to paying a high price to F.
- If at the opposite, the UK market has collapsed, a severe price war has occurred and if these adverse events have made the combined operations of F and I, and the rest of the industry, generate losses, F will easily agree that its operations have a very low value.

I and F decided to take advantage of time and of their disagreement regarding risk. They agreed to form a joint venture and to get through its future dividends whatever these future dividends may be. This is a very effective approach for creating value and belongs to the option framework which is presented in Part IX.

33.4   THE VALUE OF THE JOINT VENTURE AGREEMENT[2]

A model to assess the value of the joint venture

You can compare the value of the joint venture with the value of the following two alternative situations: no deal, and a 76 million fixed price deal (the case in which F would finally accept the view of I regarding the risk of the merger). A model for establishing this comparison is shown in Figure 33.3.

- In the no agreement situation, the values for I and F are equal to their BATNAs and the total value for I and F is equal to the sum of their BATNAs.
- In the fixed price deal situation, I gets the difference between the outcome of the integrated operations and the price paid to F. To estimate the additional value created by the deal for I you have to further deduct the outcome of the best internal growth strategy of I.

  F gets the fixed price whatever the final outcome of the merger is. The additional value of the deal for F is equal to the difference between the price and what F would have obtained with its best exit strategy.
- In the joint venture situation, I gets the difference between the outcome of the integrated operations and the dividend paid to F (or the new equity contributed by F). To estimate the additional value created by the deal for I, you have to further deduct the outcome of its best internal growth strategy. In this situation, F receives a dividend or contributes new equity depending on the outcome of the integrated operations. The additional value created by the deal for F is obtained by further deducting the outcome of the best exit strategy.

The joint venture reduces risk

With a 76 million GBP price paid in 1985, the merger creates an additional expected value of 48 million for I, but this is a very risky solution as the additional value may range between a loss of 132 million and a profit of 294 million GBP.

Figure 33.3 shows that the expected value of the joint venture agreement is equal to 39 million. This value is 17% lower than the value of the fixed price deal but is less risky as it only varies between −32 and 143 million. If the joint venture agreement creates value through a reduction of the risk for I, it is worth noting that this reduction of risk is not achieved at the expense of a reduction of the expected value. The 17% difference with the fixed price solution is only due to the fact that the dividend paid to F is based on the value of the joint venture and not, as it should be, on this value adjusted for the difference between the two BATNAs of I and F. To avoid the bias introduced

	A	B	C	D	E	F	G	H	I	J
1	Industry scenarios	R	BG	B						
2	Probabilities	0.33	0.33	0.33						
3	POINT OF VIEW OF I						POINT OF VIEW OF F			
4	INTEGRATED OPERATIONS									
5	Success	47	256	454			47	256	454	
6	Probability of success	0.4					0.9			
7	Difficulties	−48	118	280			−48	118	280	
8		−10	173	350	171		38	242	437	239
9	BATNA I	8	47	84	46		8	47	84	46
10	BATNA F	−84	17	151	28		−84	17	151	28
11	Value created	66	109	115			114	178	202	
12	EXPECTED VALUE	97					164			
13	FAIR PRICE	76					110			
14	**NO DEAL** VALUE FOR I	**46**			VALUE FOR F		28	TOTAL		74
15	FIXED PRICE DEAL	PRICE	76.3							
16	Value, success	−29	180	378			76	76	76	
17	Value, difficulties	−86	97	273			76	76	76	
18										
19	Additional value, success	−37	133	294			160	59	−75	
20	Additional value, difficulties	−132	−5	120			160	59	−75	
21	**FIXED PRICE** VALUE FOR I	**48**			VALUE FOR F		48	TOTAL		97
22	% of I in the joint venture	0.5								
23	Value, success	24	128	227			24	128	227	
24	Value, difficulties	−24	59	140			−24	59	140	
25	Expected net dividends	Paid by I			85		Received by F			119
26	Additional value, success	16	81	143			108	111	76	
27	Additional value, difficulties	−32	12	56			60	42	−11	
28	**JOINT VENTURE** VALUE FOR I	**39**			VALUE FOR F		91	TOTAL		122

B8: +B5*$B$6+B7*(1−$B$6). Copy to C8.D8.
G8: +G5*$G$6+G7*(1−$G$6). Copy to H8.I8.
E8: +B8*$B$2+C8*$C$2+D8*$D$2. Copy to E9,E10,J8,J9 and J10.
B11: +B8−B9−B10. Copy to C11,D11,G11,H11 and I11.
B12: +B11*$B$2+C11*$C$2+D11*$D$2. Copy to G12.
B13: +E10+B12/2. Copy to G13.
B14: +E9
G14: +E10
J14: +G14+B14
B16: +B5−$C$15. Copy to C16.D16.
G16: +$C$15. Copy to H16,I16 and G17.I17.
B17: +B8−$C$15. Copy to C17.D17.
B19: +B5−B9−$C$15. Copy to C19.G19.
G19: +$C$15−G10. Copy to H19.I19.
B20: +B7−B9−$C$15. Copy to C20.D20.
G20: +G19. Copy to H20.I20.
B21: +B6*(B19*$B$2+C19*$C$2+D19*$D$2)+(1−B6)*(B20*$B$2+C20*$C$2+D20*$D$2). Copy to G21
J21: +B21+G21
B23: +B5−B5*(1−$B$22). Copy.
G23: +G5*(1−$B$22). Copy.
B24: +B7−(1−$B$22)*B7. Copy.
G24: +G7*(1−$B$22). Copy.
E25: +B6*((B5−B23)*$B$2+(C5−C23)*$C$2+(D5−D23)*$D$2)+(1−B6)*((B7−B24)*$B$2+(C7−C24)*$C$2+(D7−D24)*$D$2)−H22
J25: +G6*(G23*$B$2+H23*$C$2+I23*$D$2)+(1−G6)*(G24*$B$2+H24*$C$2+I24*$D$2)−H22
B26: +B5−B9−(1−$B$22)*B5. Copy.
G26: +G23−G10. Copy.
B27: +B7−B9−(1−$B$22)*B7. Copy.
G27: +G24−G10. Copy.
B28: +B6*(B26*$B$2+C26*$C$2+D26*$D$2)+(1−B6)*(B27*$B$2+C27*$C$2+D27*$D$2)+H22
G28: +G6*(G26*$B$2+H26*$C$2+I26*$D$2)+(1−G6)*(G27*$B$2+H27*$C$2+I27*$D$2)−H22
J28: +B28+G28

Figure 33.3 A model to evaluate the joint venture.

by the basis for calculating the dividend, I and F could either agree on slightly different shares in the joint venture (you can check that 55–45 would do), or on a compensating payment made by F to I at the date of signature. In order to introduce such a payment in the model, you can:

- enter in H22 the amount of this payment: set it to half of the differences between the two BATNAs (9 million);
- correct the joint venture values: + H22 for I and − H22 for F (already done in Figure 33.3).

When you do so, you will check that the value for I of a 50–50 joint venture is equal to 48 million GBP: the 50–50 joint venture creates the same value as the fixed price deal but is much less risky. With the compensating payment, the additional value for F is equal to 82 million GBP.

As with most conditional agreements, the joint venture is valued differently by I and F

Another interesting result of Figure 33.3 is that:

- I believes that it will pay a net amount of 76 million GBP to F (85 million dividend minus the 9 million initial payment) and values the agreement at 48 million. I has obtained exactly what it wanted and has obtained it at a lower risk than it was willing to take.
- F believes that it will get a net amount of 110 million GBP from the joint venture with I (119 million dividend minus the 9 million initial payment). F has obtained exactly what it wanted, ie 82 million more than its 28 million BATNA.

This is a great advantage of the joint venture solution. It enables I and F to keep believing that they will get the amounts they wanted to reach. As the amounts they will ultimately obtain will not be known until a much later date, why quarrel about them? I and F know that they are going to get half of the future results but they have been wise enough not to try to force an agreement on what each of them mean by 'half of the future results'. They have agreed on a process for sharing the results and since nobody can predict the future, they fully accept that the other party may genuinely have its own opinion about the future – a very personal matter which should not prevent serious people from doing business together. This recognition of and respect for individual differences is materialized by the decision to have two business plans for the joint venture: an optimistic plan (F's preferred scenario) and a pessimistic one (I's preferred scenario).

A potential problem with contingent agreements is their sustainability: how will I and F react when the final outcomes are known? The real issue is to make sure that both I and F have exchanged all the information which was available to them and will continue doing so. If this is the case neither I or F should have any problem accepting that the future might be full of surprises!

The joint venture is a genuine 'win-win' agreement

A final result of Figure 33.3 is the sum of the values for I and F or total value of the different situations:

- The no-deal situation corresponds to a total value of 74 million GBP.
- The 76 million fixed price deal corresponds to a 97 million total value, 31% more than the no-deal situation.
- The joint venture solution corresponds to a 131 million total value, 35% more than the fixed price deal and 77% more than the no-deal situation. With the joint venture solution, both I and F get a better deal than with the fixed price solution.

33.5   THE SUPERIORITY OF JOINT VENTURE AGREEMENTS OVER PROFIT SHARING AND OTHER TYPES OF CONDITIONAL AGREEMENTS

As an alternative to their joint venture agreement, I and F could have crafted a profit sharing agreement: F could have brought its operations to I which would have then paid a share of the profit of the merged operations to F. Even though it is very close to a joint venture agreement, such a profit sharing agreement is not as effective for I if the losses are not shared also. This is shown in the model in Figure 33.4 which is an extension of the model in Figure 33.3.

Other types of conditional agreements could also have been designed by I and F:

- in 1985, F brings its operations to I;
- at a later date, 1990 for example, I pays to F a price linked to some critical performance indicator (for example, the market share of the combined operations in 1990).

How does such a conditional sale agreement compare with a joint venture solution? If it aims at the same risk sharing goal as a joint venture, a conditional sale agreement has a number of drawbacks.

- A first difficulty is to specify the critical performance indicator(s). In addition to being 'objective' and easily measurable, critical performance indicator(s) should be relevant also. In the I–F negotiation, the 1990 market share is definitely critical to the overall performance of the integrated operations but other parameters can greatly influence the overall performance, for example, levels of selling price and cost of goods sold, operating expenses, and other factors that we are not even able to imagine now! At the

	A	B	C	D	E	F	G	H	I	J
1	Industry scenarios	R	BG	B						
2	Probabilities	0.33	0.33	0.33						
3	POINT OF VIEW OF I						POINT OF VIEW OF F			
4	INTEGRATED OPERATIONS									
5	Success	47	256	454			47	256	454	
6	Probability of success	0.4					0.9			
7	Difficulties	−48	118	280			−48	118	280	
8		−10	173	350	171		38	242	437	239
9	BATNA I	8	47	84	46		8	47	84	46
10	BATNA F	−84	17	151	28		−84	17	151	28
11	Value created	66	109	115			114	178	202	
12	EXPECTED VALUE	97					164			
13	FAIR PRICE	76					110			
14	**NO DEAL** **VALUE FOR I**	**46**			**VALUE FOR F**		**28**		**TOTAL**	**74**
15	FIXED PRICE DEAL	PRICE	76.3							
16	Value, success	−29	180	378			76	76	76	
17	Value, difficulties	−86	97	273			76	76	76	
18										
19	Additional value, success	−37	133	294			160	59	−75	
20	Additional value, difficulties	−132	−5	120			160	59	−75	
21	**FIXED PRICE** **VALUE FOR I**	**48**			**VALUE FOR F**		**48**		**TOTAL**	**97**
22	% of I in the joint venture	0.5		Initial payment			9			
23	Value, success	24	128	227			24	128	227	
24	Value, difficulties	−24	59	140			−24	59	140	
25	Expected net dividends	Paid by I			85		Received by F			119
26	Additional value, success	16	81	143			108	111	76	
27	Additional value, difficulties	−32	12	56			60	42	−11	
28	**JOINT VENTURE** **VALUE FOR I**	**48**			**VALUE FOR F**		**82**		**TOTAL**	**122**
29	% Profit for I	0.5								
30	Value, success	24	128	227			24	128	227	
31	Value, difficulties	−48	59	140			0	59	140	
32										
33	Additional value, success	16	81	143			108	111	76	
34	Additional value, difficulties	−56	12	56			84	42	−11	
35	**PROFIT SHARING VALUE FOR I**	**34**			**VALUE FOR F**		**92**		**TOTAL**	**127**

B30: +B5−@IF(B5>0,(1−$B$29)∗B5,0). Copy.
G30: @IF(G5>0,(1−$B$29)∗G5,0). Copy.
B31: +B7−@IF(B7>0,(1−$B$29)∗B7,0). Copy.
G31: @IF(G7>0,(1−$B$29)∗G7,0). Copy.
B33: +B30−B9. Copy.
G33: +G30−G10. Copy.
B34: +B31−B9. Copy.
G34: +G31−G10. Copy.
B35: +$B$6∗(B33∗$B$2+C33∗$C$2+D33∗$D$2)+(1−$B$6)∗(B34∗$B$2+C34∗$C$2+D34∗$D$2)+H29
G35: +$G$6∗(G33∗$B$2+H33∗$C$2+I33∗$D$2)+(1−$G$6)∗(G34∗$B$2+H34∗$C$2+I34∗$D$2)−H29
J35: +G35+B35

Figure 33.4   A model to evaluate alternative deals.

opposite the joint venture solution naturally organizes the sharing of the overall results without requiring that the two parties specify how these results will be generated.

- A further difficulty is to find and agree on a performance indicator that enables the two parties to share both profits and losses. A major advantage of joint venture solutions is that their very nature implies the sharing of both profits and losses.

- A final difficulty with conditional sales is that the seller is generally no longer part of the operations which are under the sole control of the buyer. This asymmetry is not consistent with the idea of risk sharing and in case things turn sour, there is a great danger that the seller believes that the bad results were caused by the poor management of the buyer (even though the latter has no real motivation to mismanage the operations). Again this danger is probably less in the case of a joint venture.

33.6 SOME IMPLEMENTATION PROBLEMS

The need to enable F to withdraw from the joint venture

Even though it looks like a very good solution, the joint venture does not enable F to achieve one of its key objectives ie to divest its truck operations. A solution for this is to decide, in 1985, when and how F could withdraw from the joint venture.

The very rationale of the joint venture implies that F stays for a sufficiently long period of time, that is, until the major risks are resolved. In both scenarios the major risks should be resolved fairly early, in 1987 or 1988, even though one might argue that a very important risk will only be resolved when the market adopts or not I's new generation of products. This will not be known until 1992 or 1993. However, F might not be willing to share this latter risk as the success of the new products of I is very much out of the control of F.

If F leaves the joint venture, there will be a need to value its equity in the joint venture. An approach for assessing the equity price is to estimate the present value of the future dividends that F would have received had it stayed in the joint venture. The problem is that F and I might disagree on the forecast of these future dividends which might bring them back to the problem they managed to avoid with the joint venture solution! As this could be a difficult problem, you cannot believe that F will enter a joint venture if the rules for evaluating its equity are not fixed in the joint venture agreement. Figure 33.5 shows the nature of the problem.

- If the optimistic scenario materializes, F will get 15 million (1985 value) of dividends during the period 1986–90 and will therefore still have 111 million to claim if it leaves in 1990.

F – or optimistic – scenario (Figure J.1)

		1986	1987	1988	1989	1990
Value claimed by F	128					
Profit after tax		0	5	11	14	14
Dividends/new equity		0	3	6	7	7
Value achieved during 86–90	15					
Value still to be claimed	113					
in 1990 value	181					
Price to 1990 earnings ratio	26					
Price to 1990 sales ratio	1.06					

I – or pessimistic – scenario (Figure J.2)

		1986	1987	1988	1989	1990
Value claimed by F	59					
Profit after tax		−15	−8	−11	−13	−14
Dividends/new equity		−8	−4	−6	−7	−7
Value achieved during 86–90	−23					
Value still to be claimed	82					
in 1990 value	132					
Price to 1990 earnings ratio	Negative					
Price to 1990 sales ratio	1.23					

Figure 33.5   Optimistic vs pessimistic scenarios.

- If the pessimistic scenario materializes, then F will have invested 23 million (1985 value) and will therefore still have 82 million to claim if it leaves in 1990.

It is worth noting that the values to be claimed in 1990 have a lower dispersion (82–113) than the values claimed in 1985 (59–128). As the dispersion reflects the difference between the points of view of I and F, this means that I and F differ more on the short than on the long term. Both consider that in the long run the joint venture will succeed, they differ on the assessment of the costs and risks of the transition.

Among the possible solutions that can be specified in the joint venture agreement to value the equity of F are:

- A price based on the results achieved. Even though this seems to be the most adequate solution, this is not easy to implement; a multiple of profit will not work in case the pessimistic scenario materializes. A multiple of sales could eventually be used but the relationship between value and sales is not a very good one.
- A fixed price; even though I and F have different opinions about the future, Figure 33.5 shows that I and F differ more on the short than on the long term. Consequently, an agreement on a fixed price might not be impossible to reach, especially if F is not allowed to leave the joint venture too soon. (Extending the model in Figure 33.5 to a few more years would probably reduce the dispersion of the values to be claimed by F.)

The joint venture agreement has to specify also the conditions in which F will be able to get out of the joint venture. Many solutions are possible. The agreement may specify that F will leave at a given date, it may give F an option to leave at that date (or starting from that date), it may give F an option to leave and I an option to force F to leave, etc.

The need to protect the interests of I and F

Even though I and F will have an equal share in the joint venture, their interests are fundamentally different. I has a long-term commitment to the truck market while F has decided to leave this market. This asymmetry in interests explains why the management of the joint venture has been entrusted to I. Even though it might give F the option to reconsider its decision to leave the market, the joint venture solution also exposes F to the consequences of decisions made by I in its own interest. In 1989–91, I will focus on the launch of its new generation of products and might be willing to engage in heavy investments. As these investments will pay only in the long run F might find that 1989–91 is not a good time for leaving the joint venture. F might therefore either:

- impose a right to veto the decisions made by I, and in particular the investment decisions of I. Such a veto would not necessarily be a useful protection for F as it could just cause conflict;
- or choose an earlier or later date for leaving the venture (mandatory or optional exit).

33.7 HOW TO ASSESS THE QUALITY OF THE DEAL

Even though it has enabled I and F to reach a deal, the joint venture solution is not exempt from problems as conflicts between the two partners may easily surface in the future. Assessing the value of the deal from I's point of view is a difficult matter: is I getting a good deal? Is I getting a better deal than F? Is I getting the best deal it could get? etc. In *The Evolution of Co-operation*, R Axelrod suggests that the relevant standard for evaluating a deal is to ask yourself 'how you are doing relative to how well someone else could be doing in your shoes'.[2] As there were plenty of opportunities for I and F to fail to agree and as I and F have managed to create a significant value out of their agreement, you should probably conclude that both I and F have done very well.

NOTES

1 There exists a considerable literature on the creation and management of strategic alliances and joint ventures and especially in the area of international management. Among many useful references: K Harrigan (1986), *Managing for Joint Venture Success*, Lexington Books, J Carter, R Cushman and CS Hartz (eds) (1988), *The Handbook of Joint Venturing*, Dow Jones Irwin. J Lewis (1990), *Partnerships for Profit*, The Free Press (this book contains useful information on the Iveco–Ford deal) and F Contractor and P Lorange (1988), *Cooperative Strategies in International Business*, Lexington Books.

2 On the choice between a full takeover and the creation of a joint venture: J-F Hennart (1991), 'The Transaction Costs Theory of Joint Ventures: An Empirical Study of Japanese Subsidiaries in the United States', *Management Science* (April), pp 483–97. On joint ventures and strategic alliances as a learning process, refer to: J Badaracco Jr (1991), *The Knowledge Link: How Firms Compete through Strategic Alliances*, Harvard Business School Press.

Further Model VIII

BUSINESS COMBINATIONS: POOLING VS PURCHASE

There exist two main methods for acquiring companies.

- The buyer can *buy the shares* of the acquired company from its shareholders and keep the acquired company operating as a separate business entity. This corresponds to the *'pooling'* accounting method.
- The buyer can *buy the assets* of the acquired company. The acquired company is dissolved and its assets are integrated into the assets of the buyer. According to the historical concept, assets are posted in the books of the buyer at their fair value at the date of the acquisition. When the fair value is higher than the book value, additional depreciation opportunities are created

	A	B	C	D	E	F	G
1	All data in million FFR						
2	**Projected cash flows and value of Electra**						
3			1993	1994	1995	1996	1997
4	SALES		500	500	500	500	500
5	Expenses (65% of sales)		325	325	325	325	325
6	Depreciation		0	50	50	50	50
7	Income		175	125	125	125	125
8	Taxes		79	56	56	56	56
9	NET INCOME		96	69	69	69	69
10	CASH FLOW EARNINGS		96	119	119	119	119
11	Investment		0	50	50	50	50
12	FREE CASH FLOW		96	69	69	69	69
13	Dividend		96	69	69	69	69
14	Discount rate				0.12		
15	NP(92)V 93–97 Free cash flows				272		
16	CASH as of end of 1992				200		
17	TERMINAL VALUE (97 Free cash flow/disc. rate)				290		573
18	VALUE				763		
19							
20	**Agreed price**	500					
21							
22	**Balance sheet of Electra as of 31 Dec. 1992**						
23	Cash	200		Equity	200		
24	Net fixed assets	0					
25	Total	200		Total	200		
26							
27	**Balance sheet of ABC as of 31 Dec. 1992**						
28	Cash	1000		Equity	1000		
29	Total	1000		Total	1000		

Figure VIII.1 The acquisition of Electra

and, in most countries, result in additional tax savings. This corresponds to the '*purchase*' accounting method.

The example of the acquisition of Electra by ABC is shown in Figure VIII.1. The situation corresponding to the purchasing of the shares of Electra by ABC is shown in Figure VIII.2. The situation of ABC can be assessed at two different levels:

- the ABC company, or parent company level;
- the ABC group, or consolidated level. At the consolidated level you assess the situation as if ABC and its new subsidiary were one single business entity.

The results in Figure VIII.2 show that:

- The cash flows and consequently the value of the acquisition are the same when assessed at the parent company and at the consolidated levels.[1]
- The income statements and the balance sheets of ABC as a parent company reflect adequately the impact of the acquisition:
  · additional annual incomes in the income statement;
  · change in the structure of the assets; 500 million of financial assets replace 500 million of cash.
- However, the consolidated income is abnormally low. This is due to the amortization of a 'goodwill' of 300 million which corresponds to the difference between the price paid for Electra and the book value of its assets. Goodwill does not mean anything special and is only an adjustment account needed because the acquisition has established that the value of the assets of Electra was 500 million and not the 200 million shown in the books. This adjustment account called 'goodwill' generally has no impact on cash flows because most tax authorities do not accept that companies depreciate it. The problem however is that according to accounting practice goodwill is generally amortized: in the USA, accounting standards state that goodwill should be amortized over the period benefited, not to exceed 40 years. In Figure VIII.1, the period for amortizing goodwill is excessively short. Using a 40-year period would increase annual income by 52.5 million and make it much more realistic.

Figure VIII.3 shows the situation when ABC buys the assets of Electra. In this situation:

- The value is higher due to the assumption that the assets of Electra allow for an additional depreciation of 50 million in 1993. If you set the additional depreciation to zero in C43, then the value is the same as in Figures VIII.1 and VIII.2.
  When this depreciation opportunity exists, then acquiring assets gives an

	A	B	C	D	E	F	G
30	**Balance sheet of ABC after acquisition**						
31	Cash	700		Loan*			200
32	Financial assets	500		Equity			1000
33	Total	1200		Total			1200
34	**Consolidated balance sheet of the ABC group after acquisition**						
35	Cash	700		Equity			1000
36	Goodwill†	300					
37	Total	1000		Total			1000
38							
39	CASH FLOWS						
40	**Parent**	1992	1993	1994	1995	1996	1997
41	Price paid – loan	−300					
42	Net income (dividends‡)		96	69	69	69	69
43	**VALUE**	**263**					
44	**Consolidated**						
45	Price paid – loan	−300					
46	SALES		500	500	500	500	500
47	Expenses		325	325	325	325	325
48	Depreciation fixed assets		0	50	50	50	50
49	Amortization goodwill		60	60	60	60	60
50	Income before tax		115	65	65	65	65
51	Taxes		79	56	56	56	56
52	Income after tax		36	9	9	9	9
53	Investment		0	50	50	50	50
54	Free cash flow	−300	96	69	69	69	69
55	**VALUE**	**263**					
56							
57	**Balance sheets ABC**						
58	Parent	1992	1993	1994	1995	1996	1997
59	Cash	700	796	865	934	1003	1071
60	Financial assets	500	500	500	500	500	500
61	Total	1200	1296	1365	1434	1503	1571
62	Loan	200	200	200	200	200	200
63	Equity	1000	1096	1165	1234	1303	1371
64	Total	1200	1296	1365	1434	1503	1571
65	**Consolidated balance sheets**						
66	Cash	700	796	865	934	1003	1071
67	Goodwill	300	240	180	120	60	0
68	Total	1000	1036	1045	1054	1063	1071
69	Equity	1000	1036	1045	1054	1063	1071
70	Total	1000	1036	1045	1054	1063	1071

*   It is assumed that in order to transfer its cash to the parent, the new subsidiary makes a loan to the parent. This loan is
    supposed to carry no interest.
†   In the accounts of the subsidary, equity is worth 200 million while the same equity is worth 500 (the acquisition price) in
    the books of the parent: goodwill is used to reconcile these two amounts.
    Please note that in the consolidated accounts, the loan of the subsidiary to the parent has disappeared as it is a pure
    internal transaction. Actually, if the parent and the subsidiary have the same investment opportunities and the same
    corporate tax there is no need to assume such a loan.
‡   It is assumed that dividends are not taxed which is true in many countries. In some countries, dividends are taxed and
    generate a tax credit: this obviously impacts the value of the acquisition.

Figure VIII.2   Pooling method

	A	B	C	D	E	F	G
30	**Balance sheet of ABC after acquisition**						
31	(in this case there is only one company after the acquisition.						
32	There is therefore no need to build consolidated accounts)						
33	Cash	700		Equity			1000
34	Net fixed assets*	50					
35	Goodwill†	250					
36	Total	1000		Total			1000
37							
38	CASH FLOWS						
39		1992	1993	1994	1995	1996	1997
40	Price paid – cash	−300					
41	Sales		500	500	500	500	500
42	Expenses		325	325	325	325	325
43	Depreciation fixed assets		0	50	50	50	50
44	Depreciation revalued assets		50				
45	Amortization goodwill		50	50	50	50	50
46	Income before tax		75	75	75	75	75
47	Taxes		56	56	56	56	56
48	Net income		19	19	19	19	19
49	Cash flow earnings		119	119	119	119	119
50	Investment		0	50	50	50	50
51	Free cash flow		119	69	69	69	69
52	NPV free cash flows	292					
53	**VALUE**	**283**					
54							
55	**Balance sheets ABC**						
56		1992	1993	1994	1995	1996	1997
57	Cash	700	819	888	956	1025	1094
58	Net fixed assets	50	0	0	0	0	0
59	Goodwill	250	200	150	100	50	0
60	Total	1000	1019	1038	1056	1075	1094
61	Equity	1000	1019	1038	1056	1075	1094
62	Total	1000	1019	1038	1056	1075	1094

* When acquiring the fixed assets of Electra, ABC is allowed to revalue them, the new value ie 50, can be depreciated ie can be deducted from next year's taxable income.

† Goodwill is equal to the difference between the book value of the assets after revaluation: 200 cash plus 50 net fixed assets and the price paid: 250 million.
Goodwill is amortized over 5 years (no impact on taxes)

Figure VIII.3   Purchase method

advantage over acquiring shares.

advantage over acquiring shares.

- The net income is abnormally low. This is due again to the amortization of 'goodwill'. It is worth noting that goodwill is not calculated in the same way as in Figure VIII.2. Here, goodwill is equal to the difference between the acquisition price and the fair value of the assets of Electra (instead of their book value). Since the fair value of the assets is 50 million higher than their book value, goodwill is lower than in Figure VIII.2 and as a result has a smaller impact on the net income. If goodwill were amortized over 40 years annual net income would be 43.75 million higher.

NOTE

1 This explains why stock prices do not seem to be affected by the adoption of one of these two methods. For evidence of the ability of shareholders to see through the particular method adopted, refer to: H Hong, R Kaplan and G Mandelker (1978), 'Accounting for Mergers on Stock Prices', *The Accounting Review* (January), pp 31–47.

Part VIII   Bibliography

Asquith P (1984), 'Merger bids, uncertainty and stockholder returns, *Journal of Financial Economics*: 51–83.

Axelrod R (1984), *The Evolution of Co-operation*, Basic Books and Penguin Books.

Badarasco J (1991), *The Knowledge Link, How Firms Compete Through Strategic Alliances*, Harvard Business School Press.

Bazerman M (1986), *Judgment in Managerial Decision Making*, John Wiley & Sons.

Bazerman M and Lewicki R (1983), *Negotiating in Organizations*, Sage.

De Bono E (1985), *Conflicts, A Better Way to Resolve Them*, Penguin Books.

Carter J (ed) (1988), *The Handbook of Joint Venturing*, Dow Jones Irwin.

Cohen A and Bradford D (1990), *Influencing without Authority*, John Wiley & Sons.

Contractor F and Lorange P (eds) (1988), *Cooperative Strategies in International Business*, Lexington Books.

Copeland T, Koller T and Murrin J (1990), *Measuring and Managing the Value of Companies*, John Wiley & Sons.

Dawkins R (1976), *The Selfish Gene*, Oxford University Press.

Doz Y and Prahalad CK (1989), 'Cooperate with your competitors and win', *Harvard Business Review*, January–February 1989, pp 133–9.

Fisher R and Ury W (1981), *Getting to Yes, Negotiating Agreements without Giving In*, Houghton Mifflin Company.

Forsgren M (1989), *Managing the Internationalization Process: The Swedish Case*, Routledge.

Franks J, Harris R and Titman S (1991), 'The postmerger share-price performance of acquiring firms', *Journal of Financial Economics* **29**: 83–96.

Ghemawat P (1991), *Commitment, The Dynamic of Strategy*, The Free Press.

Hall W (1980), 'Survival strategies in a hostile environment', *Harvard Business Review* (September–October), pp 75–85.

Harrigan K (1986), *Managing for Joint Venture Success*, Lexington Books.

Haspelag P and Jemison D (1991), *Managing Acquisitions, Creating Value through Corporate Renewal*, The Free Press.

Helper S (1991), 'How much has really changed between US automakers and their suppliers', *Sloan Management Review*, Summer 1991, pp 15–28.

Henke J, Krachenberg R and Lyons T (1990), 'Mixed motive marriages: What's next for buyer-supplier relations?' *Sloan Management Review*, Spring 1990, pp 29–36.

Hennart J-F (1991), 'The Transaction Costs Theory of Joint Ventures: An Empirical Study of Japanese Subsidiaries in The United States', *Management Science* (April), pp 483–97.

Hickman K and Petry G (1990), 'A Comparison of Stock Price Predictions Using Court Accepted Formulas, Dividend Discount, and P/E Models, *Financial Management* (Summer), pp 76–90.

Hong H, Kaplan R and Mandelker G (1978), 'Pooling vs Purchase: the Effects of Accounting for Mergers on Stock Prices', *Accounting Review* (January), pp 31–47.

Jensen M and Ruback R (1983), 'The market for corporate control: the scientific evidence', *Journal of Financial Economics* **11**: 5–50.

Johnston R and Lawrence P (1988), 'Beyond Vertical Integration – The Rise of the Value-Adding Partnership', *Harvard Business Review* (July–August), pp 94–101.

Kotter J (1985), *Power and Influence – Beyond Formal Authority*, The Free Press.

Lax DA and Sebenius JK (1986), *The Manager as a Negotiator – Bargaining for Cooperation and Competitive Gain*, The Free Press.

Leontiades M (1989), *Myth Management, An Examination of Corporate Diversification as Fact and Theory*, Basil Blackwell.

Lewis J (1990), *Partnerships for Profit*, The Free Press.

McMillian J (1990), 'Managing suppliers: incentive systems in Japanese and US industry', *California Management Review*, Summer 1990, pp 38–55.

Metcalf HC and Urwick L (1940), *Dynamic Administration: The collected papers of Mary Parker Follett*, New York Harper.

Morck R, Shleifer A and Vishny R (1990), 'Do managerial objectives drive bad acquisitions?', *The Journal of Finance*, March, pp 31–47.

Nierenberg G (1968), *Fundamentals of Negotiating*, Hawthorn Books.

Porter M (1987), 'From competitive advantage to corporate strategy', *Harvard Business Review*, May–June 1987, pp 43–57.

Raiffa H (1982), *The Art and Science of Negotiation*, The Bellknap Press of Harvard University Press.

Roll R (1986), 'The Hubris hypothesis of corporate takeovers, *Journal of Business* **59**: 197–216.

Rubin P (1990), *Managing Business Transactions*, The Free Press.

Seyhun NH (1990), 'Do bidders knowingly pay too much for target firms?', *Journal of Business* **63**: 439–65.

Slusky A and Caves R (1991), Synergy, agency, and the determinants of premia paid in mergers, *The Journal of Industrial Economics*, **XXXIX** (March): 277–95.

Ury W (1991), *Getting Past No*, Business Books Limited.

West T and Jones J (1991), *The Handbook of Business Valuation*, John Wiley & Sons.

The Need to be Prepared to use Novel Approaches

Option Analysis as a Potential Future Tool

Throughout this book we have helped you develop the attitudes and skills you need for using the powerful toolkit offered by finance (and related disciplines) today. When you start using this toolkit, you will realize that it helps you understand strategic situations more clearly and become a more effective manager. We believe that the more you use this toolkit, the more you will enjoy using it and the more you will realize how powerful it is. However, we would like to advise you not to fall into the trap of believing that this toolkit is perfect and definitive. When using financial approaches, never forget:

- However powerful finance is for solving the problems of today, there may be completely different problems tomorrow. Will finance be as good at helping you to understand them?
- Finance is not the only possible approach for analyzing problems. Avoid reducing problems solely to financial problems and try to use other approaches as well, as we did in Part VII and Part VIII.
- There is usually more than one way to use finance in approaching a specific situation. Avoid using excessively standardized procedures. A good rule of hygiene is to scrap systematically the models which have achieved their purpose and to start analyzing new situations from a blank piece of paper and a blank screen.
- Finance is a changing field. It has changed a great deal over the last decades[1] and there is no reason for this process of change to come to an end. This is fortunate because finance, as it is now, does not satisfactorily answer all the questions you may have when building models.[2] Among those partially unanswered questions we would like to single out three:

  1. *How do you carry out risk analysis?*
     The approach presented in Part V (decision tree analysis) is very powerful for understanding the risk attached to a strategic situation but this approach is not easy to reconcile with the concept of the existence of two types of risk, market and specific risk.
  2. *Which discount rate should you use?*

As explained in Part VI, there is no definite answer to this question, only a series of clues which suggest that you should use a risk-adjusted discount rate but remain vague about how to do the adjustment in practice.

3. *How do you deal with the side effects of decisions?*

   When using the incremental approach recommended by finance, you very often face the difficult problem of evaluating the side effects of your decision on both the existing business of the organization[3] and its future competitive position.[4]

Consequently, while using the toolkit proposed in this book, be alert to innovation and be prepared to adopt novel approaches if they look more powerful. Among the potential innovations which finance may bring to model building for strategic decision making, there is an area particularly worth attention, that of options or, more generally, the area of contingent claim analysis (CCA). Of this very rapidly growing area of finance,[5] it is fair to say that it is not really new since its recent development originates from the break through made in 1973 by Black and Scholes with their article 'The pricing of options and corporate liabilities',[6] and its application to the analysis of strategic decisions is still in its infancy and hindered by a number of practical and theoretical difficulties.

The framework of options seems very promising, however, as among other potential advantages it seems able to bring more satisfactory answers to the three difficult questions expressed above. What we would like to invite you to do in Part IX is to use the power of spreadsheet modelling for understanding some of the major dimensions of option valuation and for making yourself aware of some of the potential of this exciting area.

KEY LEARNING POINTS

MODELS FOR UNDERSTANDING CONCEPTUAL APPROACHES AND TECHNICAL ISSUES
- Constructing a riskless hedge – *Further Model IX.2, page 590*
- A model of the Black and Scholes formula. Using it – *Further Model IX.3 page 595*
- Alternative strategies with options. A model for calculating gross values at expiration date – *Further Model IX.1, page 582*
- A model for calculating the profit of naked strategies, hedges, spreads and combinations – *Futher Model IX.4, page 602*
- Calculating continuously compounded return, evaluating its volatility – *Further Model IX.3, page 601*

BASIC OPTION THEORY
- What is an option? – *Figures 34.1 and 34.2, pages 573 and 574*
- How to evaluate options:
  - At expiration date – *Chapter 34, page 574 and Further Model IX.1, page 582*
  - At any other date: the Black and Scholes formula – *Further Model IX.3, page 595*
- The five parameters which determine the value of an option: stock price, striking price, total risk, time to expiration and interest rate – *Figures 34.3 and IX.3(e), pages 575 and 599*

THE POTENTIAL OF OPTION THEORY FOR THE ANALYSIS OF STRATEGIC ALTERNATIVES
- Strategic decisions as the process of creating, exercising and abandoning options – *Section 35.1, page 576*
- Options and strategic flexibility – *Section 35.2, page 578*
- What increases the value of flexibility? – *Section 35.3, page 579*
- Reconciliation of options and decision diagrams – *Section 35.3, page 579*

ARBITRAGE APPROACH TO VALUATION
- Constructing a riskless hedge and using it for valuation purposes. Relationship between the value of calls and puts – *Further Model IX.2, page 590*

- Using the power of graphics to understand difficult problems – *Further Models IX.1, IX.2, IX.3 and IX.4, pages 582, 590, 595, and 602*

NOTES

1 For a review of the recent development of finance, refer to JF Weston, 'Developments in finance theory, *Financial Management*, (10th Anniversary issue, 1981), to *The Modern Theory of Corporate Finance*, MC Jensen and CW Smith (eds), McGraw-Hill, (1986), to M Miller, *Financial Innovations and Market Volatility*, Basil Blackwell (1991) and to J Marshall and V Bansal, *Financial Engineering*, New York Institute of Finance (1992).

2 For a review of these unanswered questions, refer to R Brealey and SC Myers, *Principles of Corporate Finance. Conclusion: What we do and do not know about finance*, McGraw-Hill (1991), pp 915–24. For a review of the current state of finance theory, refer to DE Allen, *Finance – A theoretical introduction*, Martin Robertson (1983), Ch 9, pp 297–311.

3 When analyzing the launch of P12 at BA International, we accounted for the side effects of P12 on existing business by introducing the concept of cannibalization.

4 When analyzing BA International, we did not recognize this latter effect. One reason for this was that it was extremely difficult to envisage what benefits BA International could derive from being the oil-free air champion.

5 The area of options is a success story in finance as it has simultaneously developed very rapidly in the real world (option markets have developed tremendously in the USA and in Europe since the creation of the Chicago Board Options Exchange in 1973 which is now the second largest security in the world market after the New York Stock Exchange) and in the academic world.

6 *Journal of Political Economy* (May/June 1973), pp 637–59. For a review of other option pricing models, you can also refer to: Smith, 'Option pricing: a review', *Journal of Financial Economics* (Jan/Mar 1976), pp 3–51.

CHAPTER 34

The Value of Options

34.1   WHAT IS AN OPTION?

An option is a contract between two parties in which one party (the *holder* or *buyer*) is given the *right* (and not the obligation) to buy or sell an asset. This right has a price, the option price, and the other party (the *writer* or *seller*) assumes the *obligation* to sell or buy that same *underlying asset* or *underlying security*.

Option contracts exist and are traded for a wide variety of underlying securities. In order to simplify the exposition, let us focus on traded options on common stocks.

Option contracts are of two types, *call options* and *put options*. A call option (or a call) gives the holder the right to buy (or to call away) the underlying security from the writer at a fixed price on or before a given future date. The fixed price is termed the *exercise* or *striking price*. The future date at which or before which the option can be exercised is known as the expiration date. A *European call* option can only be exercised at the expiration date. An *American call* option can be exercised at any time up to the expiration date. Figure 34.1

EUROPEAN CALL CREATED ON 1ST JANUARY 1993
Underlying security: 1 RTB share
Price of the option: 10 FFR
Exercise date: 31st March 1993
Striking price: 100 FFR

On 1 January 1993	**On 31 March 1993 (expiration date)**
The holder receives the call option contract from the writer and pays 10 FFR (call price) to the writer.	The holder either: Does nothing Or exercises the option. In this case, the holder: Receives 1 RTB share from the writer against the call option contract and the payment of 100 FFR (striking price) to the writer.

Figure 34.1   Transaction between the writer and the holder of a European call.

describes the complete transaction between the writer and the holder of a European call.

A put option (or a put) gives the holder the right to sell (or to put to) the underlying security to the writer at a fixed price on or before a given future date. As with a call, the fixed price is known as the exercise or striking price and the future date as the expiration date. A put can be a European put (exercisable only on the expiration date) or an American put (exercisable at any time up to or on the expiration date). The transaction between the writer and the holder of a European put is described in Figure 34.2.

EUROPEAN PUT CREATED ON 1ST JANUARY 1993
Underlying security: 1 RTB share
Price of the option: 9 FFR
Exercise date: 31st March 1993
Striking price: 100 FFR

On 1 January 1993	**On 31 March 1993 (expiration date)**
The holder receives the put option from the writer and pays 9 FFR (put price) to the writer.	The holder either: Does nothing Or exercises the option. In this case, the holder: Gives 1 RTB share to the writer against the put option contract and the payment of 100 FFR (striking price) from the writer.

Figure 34.2   Transaction between the writer and the holder of a European put.

Options contracts raise a number of interesting questions. What makes the holder decide, whether or not to exercise the option? In the case of European options, this question depends on the value of the option at the expiration date. If the option is worthless at expiration date then the holder just forgets about it. If the option has a value then the holder takes advantage of that value through exercising the option. A further question: what are the determinants of the price of the option when it is created and between creation and expiration date?

34.2   CALCULATING THE VALUE OF OPTIONS

Calculating the value of an option is either very easy or very difficult, depending on when you want to do it.

- At expiration, the value of a call is either zero if the stock price is lower than the striking price or equal to the difference between the stock price and the striking price if the former is higher. Similarly, the value of a put at expiration is either zero (if the value of the stock is higher than the striking price) or equal to the difference between the striking price and the stock price. Please refer to Further Model IX.1 for a more detailed presentation of the value of options at expiration date.

WHEN	THE CURRENT VALUE OF A CALL	THE CURRENT VALUE OF A PUT
Striking price increases in relation to stock price	Decreases	Increases
Stock volatility increases	Increases	Increases
Time to maturity increases	Increases	Increases
Interest rate increases	Increases	Decreases

Figure 34.3 Effects of the five explanatory parameters on the values of calls and puts.

■ At any time before the expiration date, assessing the value of an option is much more difficult. Fortunately, in 1973, Black and Scholes[1] found a model for evaluating options and have demonstrated that their value depends on only five parameters:
· Current stock price.
· Striking price.
· Total risk of the stock (or volatility of its future price).
· Time to expiration.
· Interest rate (debt rate).
The impact of these parameters on the value of a call and a put option is shown in Figure 34.3.

For evaluating options, Black and Scholes use an arbitrage concept which does not require the use of a risk adjusted discount rate, a complex matter as we realized in Part VI. Their approach is based on the construction and evaluation of a riskless hedge: please refer to Further Model IX.2 to see how it is possible to achieve a riskless investment with options.

The Black and Scholes formula, and the process for constructing a spreadsheet model which will enable you to experiment with it, is shown in Further Model IX.3. This model will be particularly helpful for checking the results shown in Figure 34.3.

Finally, you will find, in Further Model IX.4, a model for evaluating some of the investment strategies which can be pursued when options are available.

NOTE

1 'The pricing of options and corporate liabilities', *Journal of Political Economy* (May/June 1973), pp 637–59.

CHAPTER 35

What the Option Framework Can Bring to the Modelling of Strategic Decisions

The application of the option framework to strategic decisions is still in its infancy; applications do exist[1] but it is fair to say that, at present their scope is still limited and they require mathematical treatment, the sophistication of which is accessible to specialists only.

Will that change in the future, and will option valuation tools become part of the standard toolkit for analyzing strategic decisions? Nobody really knows,[2] so our recommendation is watch out for new developments. Another question is what can this framework bring you today? We do not believe that the option framework is going to make you change radically the modelling approaches you have learned throughout this book. We believe rather that it is going to give you a new perspective on strategic situations and in particular on their flexibility dimensions and a better understanding of the determinants of the value of this flexibility. This should enable you to understand strategic decisions better and to build more effective models.

35.1 STRATEGIC DECISIONS AS THE PROCESS OF CREATING, EXERCISING AND ABANDONING OPTIONS

Let us consider two examples of strategic situations.

1. *You are considering the launch of a new product.* This can be analyzed as a call option where:
    · The required capital is the striking price.
    · The underlying security corresponds to the cash flows expected from the new product (and also the value of any growth opportunity that the new investment may create, a further option).
    · The expiration date is the deadline by which the go/no go decision should be made. If the decision is to be made immediately, the option is about to expire. If the decision can be deferred, then you are in the presence of a true option.

2. *You are organizing a project in such a way that it could be abandoned more easily.*
   This can be analyzed as the creation of a put option where:
   · The disposal value you can get from this specific project is the striking
     price.
   · The underlying security corresponds to the cash flows you expect to get if
     you continue the project.
   · The expiration date is the deadline for realizing the disposal value.
3. You are considering alternatives for expanding your activities in a very
   uncertain market. Establishing a joint venture with a company which
   controls complementary resources can also be analyzed as the creation of
   one or several options. This is the solution that I designed to expand its
   business in the UK market – see Part VIII.[3]

When you start thinking about it, you soon realize that a number of strategic
decisions can be analyzed using the framework of options. This is particularly
true for all decisions which require solutions which keep a number of future
alternatives open which you might decide to pursue or not depending on the
environment and the competition, and which are expected to create future
growth opportunities which you might or might not decide to seize.

Some examples might help you understand why some authors have
suggested that the essence of strategic management corresponds to the process
of creating, exercising and abandoning options.

- Adopting manufacturing solutions which provide flexibility in terms of
  sourcing of supplies, alternative uses, future expansion, etc, correspond to
  the creation of options.
- In projects and contracts, introducing minimum price clauses, change in
  invoicing currency clauses and various types of guarantee also corresponds
  to the creation of options.
- Starting an R&D project also corresponds to the creation of an option.
  Contemplating the launch of a new product derived from this R&D is
  deciding whether or not the option should be exercised. Stopping an R&D
  project is abandoning the option.
- When you have a new technology, deciding on the timing of its introduction
  is deciding on when an option should be exercised.
- Deciding to enter a new market, in spite of the fact that it is currently too
  competitive to generate positive values, might be a good decision if this
  move creates valuable options for future growth.
- When acquiring a company, agreeing to pay more than the present value of
  its existing activities might be justified by the acquisition of options that the
  company has managed to create.

This list of examples demonstrates two important facts.

- A wide number of strategic decisions can indeed be analyzed as the creation, the exercise or the abandonment of options.
- Most importantly, the option framework invites you to reflect on one essential dimension of strategic solutions, *their flexibility*:[4]
  · Dominating the timing vs acting under timing pressure.
  · Keeping alternatives open vs being locked into one solution.
  · Creating growth opportunities you may choose from vs doing all you can.

Because it seems to capture flexibility better than any other approach, the option framework could help put more strategic thinking into models and consequently could help make those models more useful for decision making.[5]

35.2   THE OPTION FRAMEWORK AS AN INCENTIVE TO LOOK FOR FLEXIBILITY IN STRATEGIC DECISIONS

Returning to the example of a new product launch decision as a call option, when analyzing such decisions, one usually assumes that the decision has to be made immediately (as we assumed for P12 in the BA International case). When you do so, the call option has a value equal to its expiration value, the difference between the security price and the striking price. In such a situation the option framework does not add much to your understanding of the problem.

Considering a new product launch as a call option should, however, also make you think about further issues which could have a significant impact on the value of this new product opportunity.

- Is it possible to defer the launch decision (or to increase the time to expiration)? How? In the BA International case, the niche alternative can be seen as a market test which could enable the company to delay the go/no go decision on the volume market until some major uncertainties are resolved. Projects which show such a flexibility have a higher value than projects which require an immediate decision, and this should show in the results of the calculations.
- Is the problem a simple option problem or is it a compounded option problem? The introduction of P12 on a large market might make BA International the leader of the oil-free air technology and create new competitive opportunities for the company. If you believe this, the problem is a compounded option problem and your calculations should show an extra value for this future flexibility.
- Would it not have been better to evaluate P12 earlier? If BA International had done so, they could have been able to evaluate P12 as an option, to explore more risky strategies and to identify the risk factors they should resolve before having to make the go/no go decision; This might have helped them to be more creative and to manage more effectively their search for

information about competition, potential manufacturing problems, etc.

Using the option valuation framework to investigate the flexibility of strategic decisions may prove very useful as it should help you imagine solutions which will provide you with more flexibility, a very important factor, and *help you assign a value to this flexibility* and therefore prevent you from undervaluing strategic alternatives.[6] The bad news is that option valuation as it is now does not provide you with clear answers about how to evaluate this flexibility. The good news is that it gives you some very useful clues about the determinants of the value of this flexibility.[7]

35.3   WHAT DETERMINES THE VALUE OF THE FLEXIBILITY OF A STRATEGIC DECISION?

If a strategic decision presents no flexibility, then its value is equal to the NPV of its attached cash flows as you have to face them without any possibility of reacting.[8] However, as soon as a decision presents some kind of flexibility, its value exceeds the NPV of its attached cash flows[9] and this extra value, or flexibility value, depends on:

- *The length of time the decision can be delayed.* The existence of an option to delay part or all of the decision is the *necessary condition for having flexibility.* What option valuation tells you is that *the value of this flexibility increases with the length of time the decision can be deferred.* The possibility of deferring choice gives you a chance to obtain more relevant information and to avoid costly mistakes. In a competitive context this length of time very much depends on the question whether you are the only one in the industry to own the option, or whether, conversely, the ownership of this option is shared between you and your competitors.[10] This key factor is very difficult to analyze as we realized in the BA International case.
- *The risk of the optional solution.* Provided you can defer the actual choice, you should not be worried about its risk; quite the opposite. Option valuation tells you that *the value of an option increases with the risk of the underlying security*; risk has a positive value provided that you can opt out.[11]

  Back to BA International, we realized that launching P12 on a grand scale was very risky. If the decision is to be taken now, we have to worry about this risk but if we can defer the decision then this risk becomes an advantage attached to P12. If adverse events materialize then we will not go ahead. If adverse events do not materialize then we will go ahead and that will make us benefit from a superior NPV since we know that due to the high risk there is a possibility to get large cash flows from the project.

  We have already met this very important concept in Chapter 18 when we analyzed decision diagrams and realized that they tell you not to be afraid of risk when you have the possibility of reacting. Option theory tells you basically the same thing but in a more powerful way. When exploring strategic alternatives, you should spend time exploring risky solutions and consider their risk as a good thing for as long as you keep the flexibility to opt out.

- *The level of interest rates.* When a solution has to be implemented immediately then the higher the interest rate the lower the NPV. When the decision can be deferred, and if it corresponds to a call option, then the situation is the opposite since the value of a call increases with the interest rate. Consequently, *the higher the interest rate, the higher is the value of flexibility* (when it corresponds to a call option).

NOTES

1 For examples refer to R Banz and M Miller, 'Prices for state-contingent claims: some estimates and applications', *Journal of Business* (1978), **51**: 653–72; MJ Brennan and ES Schwartz, 'Evaluating natural resource investments', Report prepared for the Division of Corporate Finance, Dept. of Finance, Ottawa (1983); S Mason and R Merton, 'The role of contingent claim analysis in corporate finance' in *Recent Advances in Corporate Finance*, E Altman and M Subrahmanyam (eds), RD Irwin (1985), Part 1, pp 7–54.

2 Some authors predict that it will become 'as important and commonplace a tool for capital budgeting decisions as it is for financial market decisions at present'. S Mason and R Merton in *Recent advances in Corporate Finance*, op. cit.

3 Refer also to B Kogut (1991), 'Joint Ventures and the Option to Expand and Acquire', *Management Science* (January), **37**(1): 19–33.

4 For more about this concept of flexibility, refer to S Mason and R Merton in *Recent Advances in Corporate Finance*, op. cit. Refer also to A Triantis and J Hodder (1990) 'Valuing Flexibility as a Complex Option', *The Journal of Finance* (June), pp 549–65 and to P Ghemawat (1991), *Commitment: The Dynamics of Strategy*, The Free Press.

5 As expressed by S Myers in 'Finance theory and financial strategy', *Interfaces* (1984) **14**(1): 'The Option Framework might be a chance to reconcile two different cultural approaches: finance theory and corporate or strategic planning'.

6 A number of papers exist in financial literature which stress the danger of NPV calculations; they are said to lead to wrong decisions because they under-estimate the value of strategic alternatives. For a recent example of this, refer to 'Managing as if tomorrow mattered', R Hayes and D Garvin, *Harvard Business Review* (May/June 1982), **3**: 71–9. We agree with the fact that NPV calculations can be wrong but it is our belief that they can both under- and over-value, and that in any case this does not cast a doubt on the NPV calculations themselves, but rather on the way in which they are performed.

7 The other good news is that it can make you approach old problems with a fresh view. As an example of this we can refer to the debt/equity issue. In an option framework, debt-holders become the owners of the firm and shareholders the

owners of call options on the assets. For more about this you can refer to RC Merton, 'On the pricing of contingent claims and the Modigliani–Miller theorem', *Journal of Financial Economics* (1977), **15**: 24–50.

8 Using the option framework this corresponds to the situation when the option is close to expiration. In such a case the value of the option is simply equal to its parity value. This situation is very much the same as the one described in the Dhahran Roads (B) case in Part V. Various scenarios are envisaged but no possibility of reacting to adverse outcomes is envisaged.

9 A simplistic example can help you to understand this. You consider undertaking an action which can either produce an outcome of 200 (50% chance) or an outcome of −100 (50% chance). With no possibility of reacting, the value of this action is 50 [0.5 * 200 + 0.5 * −100]. With the possibility of opting out if the −100 outcome materializes and if opting out leads to a zero outcome, then the value of the action becomes 100 [0.5 * 200 + 0.5 * 0]. This value of 100 can be analyzed as 50 created by the two possible outcomes without considering the option (200 and −100) plus 50 created by the option to react.

10 For the distinction between proprietary and shared options and its application to decision making, refer to WC Kester, 'Today's options for tomorrow's growth', *Harvard Business Review* (Mar/Apr 1984), pp 153–66.

11 Let us consider two potential actions:

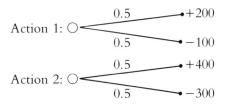

Without any possibility of reacting, both actions have a value of 50 but the risk of action 2 is higher. Let us now introduce an option to react:

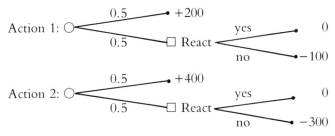

If we analyze the value of each action as the sum of its value without any option to react plus the value of the option to react, then actions 1 and 2 become very different.

	Value without option	Value of option	Total value
Action 1	50	50	100
Action 2	50	150	200

The total values of actions 1 and 2 are the same as those you obtain with the decision diagram approach. The advantage of the option framework is to invite you to break down this total value and to single out the value of the option.

Further Models IX

FURTHER MODEL IX.1
GROSS VALUE OF OPTIONS AT EXPIRATION DATE

Alternative investment strategies with options

Let us consider the situation described in Figure IX.1(a).

---

1   The stock of RTB is quoted 100 FFR today. (Let us call the current value of the stock S).
2   You contemplate the following alternative investment strategies:
    To buy 1 RTB stock and to hold it for 1 year – or to take a 'long position' in RTB stock.
    To take a short position* for 1 year in the same stock.
    To buy a European call written on 1 RTB stock.
    To write a European call on 1 RTB stock.
    To buy a European put written on 1 RTB stock.
    To write a European put on 1 RTB stock.
3   All calls and puts have the same time to expiration: 1 year, and the same striking price: 100 FFR. (Let us call the striking price K.)
4   You plan to calculate the value of each alternative investment one year from now (forgetting about the price you have to pay now in order to implement each alternative).
5   The stock is not paying any dividend. There are no taxes and no transaction costs.

---

* You can achieve this by borrowing one share for a year from an investor who owns RTB stock. At the end of the loan you will have to buy one share on the market in order to reimburse the lender. You will benefit from any decline (and lose from any increase) in the share price.

Figure IX.1(a)   Alternative investment strategies.

The gross values one year from now[1] attached to each of the alternative investment strategies described in Figure VIII.1(a) are the following.

- Long stock position (buy stock):
  Value = stock price one year from now. If we call the value of this stock price S* then
  Value = S*
- Short stock position (sell stock):
  Value = −S* (the value to be paid in order to buy the stock to be given back to the lender).
- Buy call:
  The value of this alternative depends on the value of the stock price at expiration.
  · If the stock price one year from now is equal to, or less than, the striking price, then it makes no sense for the holder to exercise the option and to pay more for the stock than he could if buying on the market.

R.T.C. LIBRARY
LETTERKENNY

Consequently, the option is worthless.

If $S* < K$, then value = zero

· If the stock price one year from now is more than the striking price, then the option gives an advantage to the holder who can buy from the writer at a cheaper price than the market price. In this case the option is worth the difference between the stock price and the striking price.

If $S* > K$, then value = $S* - K$

- Write call:

The value of this alternative is symmetric to the value of the buy call:

· If $S* < K$, then value = zero. The option is worthless for both the holder and the writer.

· If $S* > K$, then value = $K - S*$. The contractual relationship between the writer and the holder of an option is a zero-sum game, if one wins the other loses, and vice versa.

- Buy put:

The value also depends on the value of the stock price at expiration.

· If the stock price one year from now is equal to, or more than, the striking price, then the option is worthless.

If $S* > K$, then value = zero.

· If the stock price one year from now is less than the striking price, then the option is worth the difference between the striking price and the stock price.

If $S* < K$, then value = $K - S*$.

The gross values attached to each of the different investment alternatives described in Figure IX.1(a) all depend on the value of one uncertain variable, $S*$, the future stock price or, more precisely, the stock price at expiration date. In order better to understand the relationship between the value of each alternative and the possible values of $S*$, you can draw the pay-off diagram attached to each alternative. This can be done with a spreadsheet model.

A spreadsheet model for generating pay-off diagrams

The format of a spreadsheet model for generating pay-off diagrams is shown in Figure IX.1(b). The process for building it is described in Figure IX.1(c). The pay-off diagrams are shown in Figure IX.1(d).

- With options, you can make money whatever you expect from the market.
  · Buy call or write put are strategies which have a positive value if you expect the stock to go up (and if you find somebody who believes the contrary).
  · Buy put or write call are strategies which have a positive value if you expect the stock to go down. Put options are sometimes refered to as an insurance contract on the stock.

- The value of a call at expiration is either equal to zero or to S* − K (difference between stock price and striking price) whichever is higher. This relationship can be generalized to any date. The current value of a call should be at least equal to the greater of zero and S − K (S being the stock price at a given date and K the striking price). The greater of zero and S − K is known as the *exercise value* or *parity value of the call*. If the current price of a call is higher than its exercise or parity value, then the call is said to show a *premium over parity*. Finally when S − K is positive then the call is said to be *in-the-money*, if S − K is equal to zero, the call is *at-the-money*, while if S − K is negative, the call is *out-the-money*.[2] A similar terminology applies to put options. This is illustrated in Figure IX.1(e).

	A	B	C	D	E	F	G	H	I	J	K	L	M
1	Current stock price				100								
2	Striking price call				100								
3	Striking price put				100								
4													
5	Exp. stock price		0	20	40	60	80	100	120	140	160	180	200
6													
7	ELEMENTARY PAY-OFF DIAGRAMS												
8	Buy stock												
9		value	0	20	40	60	80	100	120	140	160	180	200
10	Sell stock												
11		value	0	−20	−40	−60	−80	−100	−120	−140	−160	−180	−200
12	Buy call												
13		value	0	0	0	0	0	0	20	40	60	80	100
14	Write call												
15		value	0	0	0	0	0	0	−20	−40	−60	−80	−100
16	Buy put												
17		value	100	80	60	40	20	0	0	0	0	0	0
18	Write put												
19		value	−100	−80	−60	−40	−20	0	0	0	0	0	0
20													

Figure IX.1(b) Format of a model for generating pay-off diagrams.

Using the model to assess the gross value of combined investment strategies

One of the great advantages of options is the flexibility they offer to investors. Investors can achieve this flexibility through various combinations of the elementary strategies (or naked strategies) described in Figure IX.1(a).

- Combinations of an option with its underlying stock are called *hedges*. Examples of hedges are buy one share and buy one put, buy one share and write two calls, take a short position on one share and buy two calls, etc.
  - *Combinations* correspond to combinations of options of different types[3] on the same underlying stock so that they are both bought or both written.

1   Set global column width at 5. Set the width of column A to 12.

2   Type in A1: current stock price; 100 in E1.
    Type in A2: striking price call; 100 in E2.
    Type in A3: striking price put; 100 in E3.

3   Type in A5: Expiration stock price;
    Then generate stock price values with the Data Fill command:
    in C5:/D (data) F (fill) C5.M5 [R][R] 20 [R] [R]

4   Type in A7: ELEMENTARY PAY-OFF DIAGRAMS
    A8: buy stock; in B9: value;
    in C9: +C5 and copy across.

5   Type in A10: sell stock; in B11: value;
    in C11: −C5 and
    copy across.

6   Type in A12: buy call; in B13: value;
    in C13: @IF(C5<$E$2,0,C5−$E$2) and copy across.

7   Type in A14: write call; in B15: value;
    in C15: @IF(C5<$E$2,0,$E$2−C5) and copy across.

8   Type in A16: buy put; in B17: value;
    in C17: @IF(C5>$E$3,0,$E$3−C5) and copy across.

9   Type in A18: write put; in B19: value;
    in C19: @IF(C5>$E$3,0,C5−$E$3) and copy across.
    Test check that you get the result shown in Figure IX. 1(b).

10 Generate the pay-off diagrams:
    ■ In order to generate the pay-off diagram for the long stock (buy stock) situation:
    · Position cursor in C5: then /G (graph) T (type) X (XY) X C5.M5 [R] A C9.M9 [R] you can then view the graph (V)*
    · Then you can name your graph /G (graph) N (name) C (create) buystock [R].†
    ■ In order to generate the second pay-off diagram (sellstock), you can:
    · use the Graph, Reset, A command to cancel the A range of the first graph (which has been previously saved).
    · Enter a new range: C11.M11 [R].
    · Give a name to your second graph: N C sellstock [R]. Etc.

---

* You can improve the presentation of the graph with titles and legends:
    The main title of the graph can be written through Option. Title, First (Lotus 1-2-3).
    The legend for the Y axis through Option, Title, Y axis (value).
    The legend for the X axis through Option, Title, X axis (price).

† In Lotus 1-2-3 graphs are saved through the Name sub-command. The Save sub-command is for saving graphs for printing purposes.

Figure IX.I(c)   Process for building a spreadsheet model for generating pay-off diagrams.

A *straddle* is the combination of a put and a call on the same underlying stock with the same striking price and the same expiration date.
· *Spreads* correspond to combinations of options of different series but of the same class[4] where some are bought and others are written.

The spreadsheet model you have just built enables you easily to generate the payoff diagrams of various hedges and combinations. The process for doing so is to:

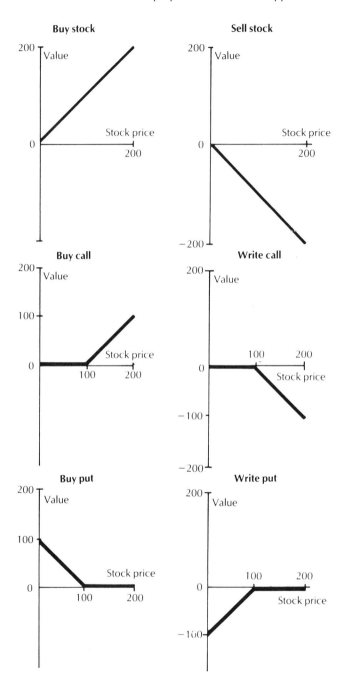

Figure IX.1(d)   Pay-off diagrams (values at expiration).

Type	Striking price K	Stock price S	Parity value S − K (call) K − S (put)	
Call	100	200	100	Deep in the money
Call	100	120	20	In the money
Call	100	100	0	At the money
Call	100	80	−20	Out the money
Call	100	20	−80	Deep out of the money
Put	100	120	−20	Out the money
Put	100	100	0	At the money
Put	100	80	20	In the money

Figure IX.1(e)   Parity values of options.

- Use a row to calculate the value of the combined strategy you consider. This value can be obtained from the values of the elementary investment strategies. For example, the value of the strategy corresponding to buying one stock and one call is equal to + C9 + C13 (to be then copied across), the value of the strategy buying one stock and two calls is equal to + C9 + 2*C13 (to be then copied across), etc.
- Generate the corresponding pay-off diagram with the graph facility.

Since our purpose is not to explore all the various possible combinations of investment strategies, we would like to invite you to consider only those envisaged in Figure IX.1(f). The values of these hedges are shown in Figure IX.1(g) and their pay-off diagrams in Figure IX.1(h).

The pay-off diagram of the hedge, buy one share, buy two puts (called *reverse hedge*) which is reproduced in Figure IX.1(g), is worth analyzing as it demonstrates the unique flexibility of options. Suppose you believe that a new technology about to be developed is going to affect the future of RTB drastically, but you do not know whether the impact will be good or bad. The investment strategy, buy one share, buy two puts, will give you a high value if

	A	B	C	D	E	... M
21	COMBINED PAY-OFF DIAGRAMS (HEDGES)					
22	Buy 1 stock buy 1 put					
23		value	+C9+C17	●——●		●
24	Buy 1 stock buy 2 puts					
25		value	+C9+2*C17	●——●		●
26	Buy 1 stock write 1 call					
27		value	+C9+C15	●——●		●
28	Buy 1 stock write 2 calls					
29		value	+C9+2*C15	●——●		●

* You could introduce the number of stock(s) and option(s) as parameters. This is done in Further Model IX.4.

Figure IX.1(f)   Values attached to four combined strategies.

Current stock price	100
Striking price call	100
Striking price put	100

Exp. stock price		0	20	40	60	80	100	120	140	160	180	200
ELEMENTARY PAY-OFF DIAGRAMS												
Buy stock												
	Value	0	20	40	60	80	100	120	140	160	180	200
Sell stock												
	Value	0	−20	−40	−60	−80	−100	−120	−140	−160	−180	−200
Buy call												
	Value	0	0	0	0	0	0	20	40	60	80	100
Write call												
	Value	0	0	0	0	0	0	−20	−40	−60	−80	−100
Buy put												
	Value	100	80	60	40	20	0	0	0	0	0	0
Write put												
	Value	−100	−80	−60	−40	−20	0	0	0	0	0	0

	0	20	40	60	80	100	120	140	160	180	200
COMBINED PAY-OFF DIAGRAMS (HEDGES)											
Buy 1 stock buy 1 put											
	100	100	100	100	100	100	120	140	160	180	200
Buy 1 stock buy 2 puts											
	200	180	160	140	120	100	120	140	160	180	200
Buy 1 stock write call											
	0	20	40	60	80	100	100	100	100	100	100
Buy 1 stock write 2 calls											
	0	20	40	60	80	100	80	60	40	20	0

Figure IX.1(g) Value of selected hedges at expiration.

the stock of RTB moves strongly, and this is true whatever the direction of the move. Without options it would be very difficult for you to find a strategy that would correspond so well to your belief about the future of RTB.

NOTES

1 Again, forgetting about the price you should pay in order to implement each alternative. The net value or profit attached to each alternative is obviously equal to the difference between the value one year from now and the price to be paid today. For investments in options you need to know the price of the call (or of the put), a variable we are not able to calculate yet. A spreadsheet model for calculating the profit attached to various investment strategies is described in Further Model IX.4.

2 When S is very superior to K the call is said to be deep-in-the-money, and when S is very inferior to K, the call is said to be deep-out-of-the-money.

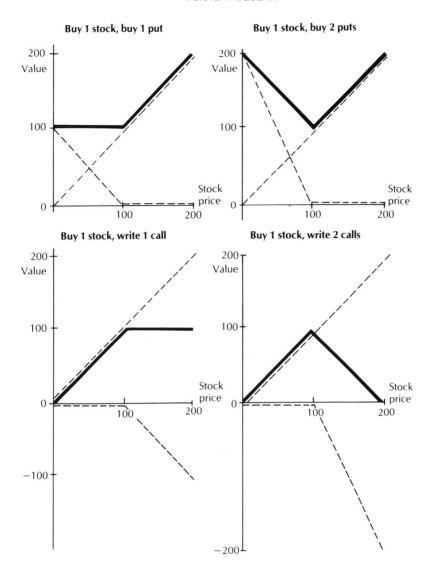

Figure IX.1(h) Pay-off diagrams for selected hedges: values at expiration.

3 Puts and calls are the two types of option.

4 Options belong to the same class if they are written on the same stock and they are of the same type (a put or a call). Within a given class, options may belong to the same series or not. In order to belong to the same series they should have the same expiration date and the same striking price.

FURTHER MODEL IX.2
USING OPTIONS TO ACHIEVE A RISKLESS INVESTMENT:
IMPLICATIONS FOR THE VALUATION OF OPTIONS

Riskless investment, arbitrage and valuation of a call

Options are a risky investment (they are usually riskier than the underlying stock) but they can contribute to achieving a riskless investment.

Let us go back to the results shown in Figure IX.1(g) and look at the value of the hedge, buy one stock, write two calls, to find that this value is the same for different values of the stock price at expiration. For example, the value of this hedge is equal to 60 FFR when the stock price is either 60 or 140 FFR.

Let us assume for a moment that the stock price at expiration cannot take a continuum of values but two values only, 60 or 140 FFR. If this is the case an investor who buys one stock and writes two calls is sure to achieve a value of 60 FFR in one year from now whatever the stock price is. The investment strategy, buy one stock and write two calls, is a *riskless investment* (or a riskless hedge) and consequently if there exist no arbitrage opportunities it should return exactly the same as an investment in a risk-free bond.

This simple idea is far-reaching as it enables you to calculate the value of a call option. In order to do so, you have to compare the positions of an investor who invests in the riskless hedge now and one year from now. This is done in Figure IX.2(a).

Today	At expiration date (1 year from now)	
	S* = 60	S* = 140
Value: 100 −2C†	Value: 60	Value: 60

† C = current value of the call

Figure IX.2(a)   Arbitrage table for a call.

As 60 and 140 FFR are the two only possible values for S at expiration date, the value of the investment is the same whatever the value of S. If the investment is risk-free, it should necessarily give the same return as an investment in a risk free bond. Let us further assume that the interest-free rate is 25% a year. It follows that the relationship between the value of the investment today and in one year from now is

$$100 - 2C = \frac{60}{1 + 0.25}$$

from which you can deduce:

$$2C = 100 - 48$$

$$C = 26 \text{ FFR}$$

This calculation of the current value of a call option is obviously made simplistic by the assumption of only two possible stock price values at expiration. It shows, however, the basic principle discovered by Black and Scholes which has been a breakthrough in option valuation. This principle is to construct a riskless hedge and to make it equal to a risk-free investment as we did above.

What influences the value of a call option?

1. *The risk of the stock.* We considered that the value of the stock price at expiration could be 60 or 140 FFR, but we could equally have considered it to be 20 or 180 FFR, only two possible values again but more distant from the current value of the stock (100). If we use the same approach to calculate the value of the call, we find:

$$100 - 2C = \frac{20^1}{1 + 0.25}$$

$$C = 42 \text{ FFR}$$

This shows a very important result. *When the risk of the stock increases, the value of the call increases.* The thing to note is that the risk of the stock which matters is the total risk and not, as in the CAPM framework, the sole systematic or undiversifiable risk.

2. *The interest rate.* Another factor which influences the value of a call option is the value of the interest rate. Let us go back to the first calculation of the call value:

$$100 - 2C = \frac{60}{1 + 0.25}$$

$$C = 26 \text{ FFR}$$

Let us now assume that the interest rate is 50% instead of 25%. If this is the case the value of the call becomes:

$$100 - 2C = \frac{60}{1 + 0.5}$$

$$C = 30 \text{ FFR}$$

This is another very important result. *The value of the call increases with the interest rate.*[2]

3. *The striking price.* In the model, you can change the value of the striking price and set it to 80 FFR. When you do so you realize that, if the stock price at expiration can be 60 or 140 FFR, the hedge, buy one stock and write two calls, is no longer a riskless hedge. By trial and error you can find that, buy three stocks and write four calls, is a riskless hedge (if the stock value at expiration is either 60 or 140 FFR).

$$S* = 60 \quad S* = 140$$

Buy three stocks and write four calls	180	180

You can then calculate the value of the call option:

$$300 - 4C = \frac{180}{1 + 0.25}$$

$$C = 39 \text{ FFR (instead of 26 with a 100 striking price)}$$

The lower the striking price is in relation to the stock price, the higher the call value is.

Riskless investment and valuation of a put

We can use a similar approach to value a put option. Let us assume again that the stock price at expiration can take two values only, 60 or 140 FFR. The model (see Figure IX.1(g)) shows that the hedge, buy one stock, buy two puts, is a riskless hedge. We can then construct the arbitrage table shown in Figure IX.2(b).

Today	At expiration date (1 year from now)	
	S* = 60	S* = 140
Value: 100 +2P[†]	Value: 140	Value: 140

[†] P = current value of the put option

Figure IX.2(b)   Arbitrage table for a put.

If we assume that the risk free interest rate is 25% a year, we can deduce the value of the put.

$$100 + 2P = \frac{140}{1 + 0.25}$$

$$2P = 112 - 100$$

$$P = 6 \text{ FFR}$$

You can also use the model as we did for testing the impact of the influence of the risk of the stock, of the interest and of the striking price on the value of the put. If you do so you will realize:

- The value of the put increases when the risk of the stock increases.
- The value of the put decreases when the interest rate increases.
- The value of the put decreases when the striking price decreases.

Establishing the relationship between the values of calls and puts

Let us go back to the value of the hedge, buy one stock, buy one put, shown in Figure IX.1(g), and to its pay-off diagram in Figure IX.1(h). The value of this hedge has something in common with the value of buying one call; it is actually always 100 FFR more than buying one call.[3] If we combine the hedge, buy one stock, buy one put, with write one call we get a riskless hedge, the value of which is 100 FFR, the value of the striking price. We can construct an arbitrage table (Figure IX.2(c)) and deduce from there the relationship between puts and calls.

If r is the risk-free interest rate we can write

$$S + P - C = \frac{K}{1 + r_f}$$

which can be generalized to more than one period. If T is the time to expiration, then

$$S + P - C = \frac{K}{(1 + r_f)^T}$$

from which we get

$$C = P + S - \frac{K}{(1 + r_f)^T}$$

or

$$P = C - S + \frac{K}{(1 + r_f)^T}$$

where C= value of a call

P = value of a put

S = stock price

K= striking price of the put and the call

T= time to expiration

r_f= risk free rate.

Today	At expiration date
Value: S+P−C	Value: K
(buy 1 stock, buy 1 put, write 1 call)	(whatever the value of S*)

Where S = current value of the stock.
P = current value of put.
C = current value of call.
K = striking price.

Figure IX.2(c)   Arbitrage table for buy 1 stock, write 1 call and buy 1 put.

Comment

The approach we have used to value options is at the same time similar to, and different from, the one we have used up to now. We have continued using the concept of discounting and of present value but for evaluating options we have used the risk free rate as the discount rate (because of the concept of the riskless hedge) and, finally, we have been concerned with total risk and no longer with market risk.

NOTES

1 The value 20 is obtained from the spreadsheet model (see Figure IX.1(g)).

2 One can also deduce intuitively from this result the influence of the time to expiration. *The value of the call should also increase with the length of the time to expiration.*

3 You can check it with the model. In order to do so you just have to calculate the value of the new combination as + C23 + C15 (and to copy across).

FURTHER MODEL IX.3
THE BLACK AND SCHOLES FORMULA

As shown in Further Model IX.2, it is possible to evaluate options using an arbitrage approach. You build a riskless portfolio of options and stocks (something options enable you to achieve). Then, as you know the return of this portfolio (the risk free rate), you can deduct the value of the option.

Black and Scholes have used this basic idea to derive their formula. They have demonstrated that it is possible continuously to adjust the quantities of stock and options as the stock price changes over time in order to maintain a riskless hedge. Their formula is as follows.[1]

$$C = SN(d_1) - Ke^{-r_fT}N(d_2)$$

where $d_1 = \dfrac{\ln(S/K) + r_fT}{\sigma\sqrt{T}} + \dfrac{1}{2}\sqrt{T}$

$d_2 = d_1 - \sigma\sqrt{T}$
C = Current value of a European call option
S = Current price of the underlying stock
N(d) = Probability that a normally distributed variable z will be less than or equal to d^2
K = Striking price or exercise price
r_f = Annual risk free rate of interest (continuously compounded)
T = Time to expiration
σ = Annual standard deviation of the continuously compounded return of the underlying stock or volatility of the stock.

This formula calls for several comments.

1. It shows that the current value of a European call option depends on five parameters only:
   - Current underlying stock price
   - Striking or exercise price
   - Time to expiration
   - Risk free interest rate
   - Volatility of the stock
   It is worth noting that some variables are absent from the formula, the return of the stock, the growth rate of the stock price, the investors' attitudes towards risk, etc. The risk which matters is the volatility of the stock price, its total risk, and not the systematic risk of the CAPM model.
2. The notion of annual standard deviation of the continuously compounded rate of return of the stock is worth some clarification. If we ignore dividends, the rates of return of a stock can be estimated from its past prices

at the end of short periods such as months, fortnights, weeks, etc.

If S_{-1}, S_{-2}, . . . S_t, S_{t-1}, are the prices of the stock at the end of consecutive past months, and if r is the monthly return then we have:

$$S_t = S_{t-1}(1 + r)$$

If we break the month into shorter periods, days for example, then the equation becomes:

$$S_t = S_{t-1}\left(1 + \frac{r}{30} \right)^{30}$$

which, if we compound continuously, tends towards:

$$S_t = S_{t-1}e^r$$

which is equivalent to:[3]

$$r = \ln\left(\frac{S_t}{S_{t-1}} \right)$$

Once a number of values of r have been obtained,[4] you can then estimate their mean and standard deviation.[5] You have further to multiply this standard deviation by $\sqrt{12}$,[6] in order to convert it into an annual standard deviation. Black and Scholes assume that continuously compounded returns $\ln(S_t/S_{t-1})$ are normally distributed and therefore that S_t/S_{t-1} and S_t are log-normally distributed. This may be shown graphically as in Figure IX.3(a).

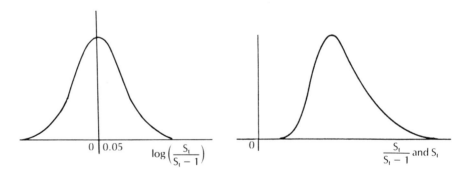

Figure IX.3(a)

The assumption that stock prices follow a log-normal distribution has some important practical implications.

- The stock price can never become negative, which is sensible.
- As the distribution is skewed to the right, there is no limit on how far the stock might rise but very large values are fairly unlikely.

	A	B	C	D	E	F	G
1							
2				Option Valuation Model			
3				(According to the Black-Scholes formula)			
4							
5							
6	PARAMETERS:						
7							
8							
9	CURRENT STOCK PRICE			100			
10	TIME TO EXPIRATION			0.4 (expressed in year)			
11	STRIKING PRICE			100			
12	VOLATILITY (standard deviation)			0.5			
13	RISK FREE RATE			0.05 (per year)			
14							
15							
16	RESULTS:						
17							
18	CURRENT VALUE OF CALL			13.45			
19	CURRENT VALUE OF PUT			11.52			
20							
21	CALCULATION OF D1 AND D2:						
22							
23	CALCULATION OF D1:						
24	D1=D11/D12+D13						
25	D11=LN(STOCK PRICE/STRIKING PRICE) RISK FREE RATE*TIME TO EXPIRATION						
26	D11=						0.02
27	D12=VOLATILITY (standard deviation)*(TIME TO EXPIRATION) $\wedge$ 0.5						
28	D12=						0.316227
29	D13=1/2*VOLATILITY (standard deviation)*(TIME TO EXPIRATION) $\wedge$ 0.5						
30	D13=						0.158113
31	D1=D11/D12+D13						0.221359
32							
33	CALCULATION OF D2:						
34	D2=D1−VOLATILITY (standard deviation)*(TIME TO EXPIRATION) $\wedge$ 0.5						
35	D2=						−0.09486
36							
37	POLYNOMIAL APPROXIMATION OF THE STANDARD NORMAL DISTRIBUTION FUNCTION:						
38							
39	CONSTANTS:						
40	B1	0.31938153	B4		−1.821255978		
41	B2	−0.356563782	B5		1.330274429		
42	B3	1.781477937	A		0.2316419		
43							
44			D1	D2			
45	z(D1 or D2)		0.221359	−0.09486			
46	Absolute value of z		0.221359	0.094868			
47	K=1/(1+A*z)		0.951224	0.978497			
48	N(absolute value of z)		0.587593	0.537790			
49	N(z)		0.587593	0.462209			
50							
51	Value of call		13.45363				
52	Value of put		11.52095				

Width of columns: global, 9; B and E, 13.

Figure IX.3(b) A spreadsheet model for using the Black and Scholes formula.

```
 D9:   100
D10:   0.4
D11:   100
D12:   0.5
D13:   0.05
C18:   +C51
C19:   +C52
G26:   @LN(D9/D11)+D13*D10
G28:   +D12*(D10 ∧ 0.5)
G30:   0.5*G28
G31:   (G26/G28)+G30
G35:   +G31−G28
B40:   0.31938153
E40:   −1.821255978
B41:   −0.356563782
E41:   1.330274429
B42:   1.781477937
E42:   0.2316419
C45:   +G31
D45:   +G35
C46:   @ABS(C45)
D46:   @ABS(D45)
C47:   1/(1+C46*$E$42)
D47:   1/(1+D46*$E$42)
C48:   1−(1/((2*@pi) ∧ 0.5)*@EXP(−(C46 ∧ 2)/2)*($B$40*C47+($B$41*C47 ∧ 2)+($B$42*C47 ∧ 3)
         +($E$40*C47 ∧ 4)+($E$41*C47 ∧ 5)))
D48:   1−(1/((2*@pi) ∧ 0.5)*@EXP(−(D46 ∧ 2)/2)*($B$40*D47+($B$41*D47 ∧ 2)+($B$42*D47 ∧ 3)
         +($E$40*D47 ∧ 4)+($E$41*D47 ∧ 5)))
C49:   @IF(C45>0,C48, 1−C48)
D49:   @IF(D45>0,D48,1−D48)
C51:   +D9*C49−@EXP(−D13*D10)*D11*D49
C52:   +C51−D9+(D11/(1+D13) ∧ D10)
```

Figure IX.3(c)   Formulas for the Black and Scholes spreadsheet model.

1 Start from the model described in Figure IX.3(b).
2 Create tables for sensitivity analysis; create a series of values for the stock price in the range A61.A71. For example from 20 to 170 FFR with a 15 FRR step. To do so, position the cursor in A61, then / D(data) F(fill) A61.A71 [R] 20 [R] 15 [R] [R].
3 Initialize the model by setting the stock value at 20.
4 Create a table of the call and put values. To do so, type +C51 in B61 and +C52 in C61. Then position the cursor in A61 and type / D(data) T(table) 1(1 input) A61.C71 [R] D9(the input cell) [R].
5 To keep the values in the table, use the range command / R(range) V(value) A61.C71 [R] A73 [R].
6 Graph the table using a XY graph with X corresponding to the A73.A83 range, A to the B73.B83 range and B to the C73.C83 range.
7 Reset the model and repeat the same process for creating tables for time to expiration, volatility, interest rate and striking price. We suggest you use the following ranges of values:

Time to expiration : 0.00001* to 2   (step: 0.2)
Volatility   : 0.00001* to 1   (step: 0.1)
Interest rate   : 0† to 0.25   (step: .025)
Striking price   : 20 to 170   (step: 15)

* If you make time to maturity or volatility equal to 0 then the model returns an error statement. In order to avoid this, take a very small value (.00001 for example).

† When interest rate is equal to 0 and when the stock price is equal to the striking price then the values of the call and of the put are equal (you can check it from the put-call parity relationship).

Figure IX.3(d)   Process for generating graphs showing the influence of the 5 explanatory factors.

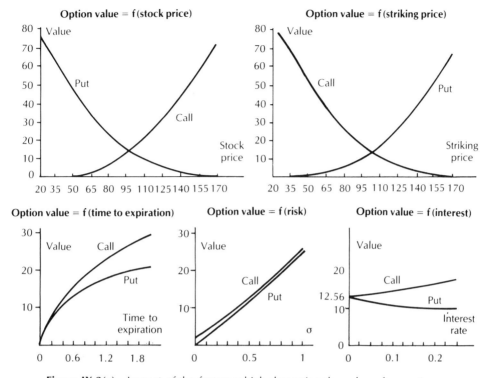

Figure IX.3(e) Impact of the factors which determine the value of an option.

3. What are the assumptions needed to derive the Black and Scholes formula?
   - No transaction costs or taxes.
   - Fixed risk-free rate at which it is possible to borrow.
   - The option can only be exercised at maturity (European option).
   - The stock does not pay dividends.
   - There are no market imperfections or restrictions to selling short options or stocks.
   - The distribution of stock prices is log-normal. The standard deviation of the rate of return is constant.

   A number of these assumptions may, however, be relaxed. For more about this, refer to Cox and Rubinstein.[7]
4. The value of European put options can be derived from the Black and Scholes formula using the call-put parity relationship established in Further Models IX.2. Also, since it does not pay for the holder of an American call to exercise the option early, the formula can also be used for American calls. Conversely, since it might pay off to exercise a put early, the value of an American put is higher than the value of its European counterpart.[8]

A spreadsheet model of the Black and Scholes formula

The design of a spreadsheet model for evaluating calls and puts following the Black and Scholes formula is straightforward. The format of such a model is shown in Figure IX.3(b), its formulas in Figure IX.3(c). This model calculates $N(d_1)$ and $N(d_2)$ from the polynomial approximation described in Note 2 on page 600.

You can use this model to analyze the impact of changes in the five parameters on the current value of calls and puts. The process for doing so is described in Figure IX.3(d). The results are shown in Figure IX.3(e).

NOTES

1 For the derivation of this formula, refer to: JC Cox and M Rubinstein, *Options Markets*, Prentice Hall (1985), Ch 5, pp 165–252.

2 The meaning of $N(d)$ can be illustrated with the density function of a normal distribution.

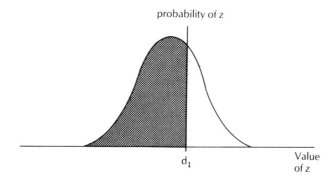

probability of z

d_1

Value
of z

$N(d_1)$ or the probability that z be equal to d_1 or less than d_1 is equal to the shaded surface below the curve. $N(d)$ can be either estimated from tables or from the following polynomial approximation:

$$N(d) \approx 1 - (1/\sqrt{2\pi})e^{-d^2/2}(b_1k + b_2k^2 + b_3k^3 + b_4k^4 + b_5k^5)$$

where $b_1 = 0.31938153$ $b_4 = -1.821255978$ $k = 1/(1+ad)$
$b_2 = -0.356563782$ $b_5 = 1.330274429$
$b_3 = 1.781477937$ $a = 0.2316419$

This calculation is valid for $d_1 > 0$. For $d_1 < 0$, the result is equal to 1 − the result of the above calculation for the absolute value of d_1.

3 As the continuously compounded return is a function of the change in the stock price from one period to another, you can understand why the term volatility of stock price is also used.

4 Here r is the monthly continuously compounded return. The annual compounded return is equal to 12r.

5 A spreadsheet model for estimating the mean and the standard deviation from past stock prices is shown in the appendix to this further model (see Figure IX.3(f)).

6 Or, more generally, by the square root of the number of periods of observation in a year. Here, since we have monthly observations, the number of periods is 12.

7 F Black and M Scholes, *Option Markets*, Prentice Hall (1985), Chs 5 and 7.

8 See for example: M Brennan and E Schwartz, 'The valuation of American put options', *Journal of Finance* (May 1977), pp 449–62.

Appendix

A spreadsheet model for calculating σ

In the Black and Scholes formula, σ corresponds to the standard deviation of the continuously compounded annual rate of return of the stock price, which is also called the volatility of the stock price. The process for calculating σ can be illustrated with an example. Let us assume that the stock of RTB has shown the following values over the last 12 months:

Current month −12	100
Current month −11	120
Current month −10	160
Current month − 9	140
Current month − 8	160
Current month − 7	150
Current month − 6	130
Current month − 5	160
Current month − 4	120
Current month − 3	130
Current month − 2	110
Current month − 1	120
Current month	100

The process for calculating is as follows:

· Calculate the continuously compounded return. Since the data is monthly, we will get a monthly return. If we call S_{-1} and S the values of the stock price in two consecutive months and r the continuously compounded return, we have:

$$S = S_{-1}e^r$$

$$e^r = \frac{S}{S_{-1}}$$

$$r = \ln\left(\frac{S}{S_{-1}}\right)$$

· Estimate the mean of the compounded monthly returns.
· Estimate the variance of the monthly returns. In order to remove the bias of our estimate of the variance, we have to multiply the previously found variance by a correction factor which depends on the sample size: $n/(n-1)$ where n is the number of observations.
· Estimate the variance of the annual returns. This is equal to 12 times the variance of the monthly returns.
· Estimate the standard deviation of the annual returns.

A spreadsheet model for performing the above calculations is described in Figure IX.3(f).

	A	B	C	D	E	F	G
1			Stock		Continuously compounded		
2		Month	price		return		(Return-mean)^2
3		n−12	100				
4		n−11	120		0.182		0.033
5		n−10	160		0.288		0.083
6		n−9	140		−0.134		0.018
7		n−8	160		0.134		0.018
8		n−7	150		−0.065		0.004
9		n−6	130		−0.143		0.02
10		n−5	160		0.208		0.043
11		n−4	120		−0.288		0.083
12		n−3	130			0.08	0.006
13		n−2	110		−0.167		0.028
14		n−1	120		0.087		0.008
15		Current	100		−0.182		0.033
16			Mean return:		0.0	Monthly variance	0.031
17						Adjusted monthly variance	0.034
18						using 1-2-3 built-in-function	0.034
19						Adjusted annual variance	0.412
20						ANNUAL STANDARD DEVIATION	0.642

Formulas:
  E4: @LN(C4/C3). Copied into E5.E15
  E16: @SUM(E4.E15)/12
   G4: (E4−$E$16) $\wedge$ 2. Copied into G5.G15
  G16: @SUM(G4.G15)/12
  G17: +G16/11*12
  G18: @VAR(E4.E15)*@COUNT(E4.E15)/(@COUNT(E4.E15)−1)
  G19: G17*12
  G20: G19 $\wedge$ 0.5

Width of columns: global, 7; A, 3; D, 12; F, 29.
Format: 3 decimals in columns E and G.

Figure IX.3(f)   Calculating σ with Lotus 1-2-3.

Please note that the measurement of volatility raises a series of complex issues which are not presented here. For more about the concept and the measurement of volatility, you may refer to S Figlewski *et al.* (1990), *Financial Options: From Theory to Practice*, Business One Irwin, p. 516.

	A	B	C	D	E	F	G	H	I	J	K	L	M	N
1							Striking price							
2						high	med	low						
3	Current stock price					100	100	100						
4	Current value of call					12.32	24.15	41.09						
5	Current value of put					11.10	3.18	0.39						
6	Striking price call					100	80	60						
7	Striking price put					100	80	60						
8	Time to expiration				0.25									
9	Interest rate				0.05									
10														
11	Stock			0	20	40	60	80	100	120	140	160	180	200
12														
13	ELEMENTARY PAY-OFF DIAGRAMS (high striking price)													
14	Buy stock													
15			Profit	−100	−80	−60	−41	−21	−1	19	38	58	78	98
16	Sell stock													
17			Profit	100	80	60	41	21	1	−19	−38	−58	−78	−98
18	Buy call													
19			Profit	−12	−12	−12	−12	−12	−12	7	27	47	67	86
20	Write call													
21			Profit	12	12	12	12	12	12	−7	−27	−47	−67	−86
22	Buy put													
23			Profit	88	68	48	28	9	−11	−11	−11	−11	−11	−11
24	Write put													
25			Profit	−88	−68	−48	−28	−9	11	11	11	11	11	11
26														
27	ELEMENTARY PAY-OFF DIAGRAMS (medium striking price)													
28	Write call													
29			Profit	24	24	24	24	24	4	−15	−35	−55	−75	−94
30														
31	ELEMENTARY PAY-OFF DIAGRAMS (low striking price)													
32	Buy call													
33			Profit	−41	−41	−41	−41	−21	−2	18	38	58	77	97
34	Write call													
35			Profit	41	41	41	41	21	2	−18	−38	−58	−77	−97
36														
37	HEDGES													
38	NER stock 1 sell stock(s) buy call(s) ie, reverse hedge													
39	NER calls 2 prof.			75	56	36	16	−4	−23	−4	16	36	56	75
40	NER stock 2 buy stock(s) write call(s)													
41	NER calls 3 prof.			−163	−124	−84	−44	−5	35	15	−5	−25	−44	−64
42														
43	SPREADS													
44		Bullish vertical												
45			Profit	−29	−29	−29	−29	−9	11	11	11	11	11	11
46		Bearish vertical												
47			Profit	29	29	29	29	9	−11	−11	−11	−11	−11	−11
48		Butterfly												
49			Profit	−5	−5	−5	−5	15	−5	−5	−5	−5	−5	−5
50														
51	COMBINATIONS													
52		Straddle												
53			Profit	75	56	36	16	−4	−23	−4	16	36	56	75
54		Bottom vertical												
55			Profit	47	27	7	−13	−13	−13	7	27	47	66	86
56		Top vertical												
57			Profit	−47	−27	−7	13	13	13	−7	−27	−47	−66	−86

Continued

	O	P	Q	R	S	T	U	V	W	X	Y
15	−200	−160	−121	−81	−42	−2	37	77	116	156	195
16											
17	100	80	60	41	21	1	−19	−38	−58	−78	−98
18											
19	−25	−25	−25	−25	−25	−25	15	54	94	133	173
20											
21	37	37	37	37	37	37	−22	−82	−141	−200	−259
22											
23											
24											
25											
26											
27											
28											
29	48	48	48	48	48	9	−31	−70	−110	−149	−189
30											
31											
32											
33											
34											

Width of columns; global: 5, A:9; B:3.
Note: The purpose of showing the strategies displayed in the range O15.Y29 is to enable you to graph the aggregate result of combined strategies as well as their components.
O15.Y15 shows; buy n(B40)stocks
O17.Y17 shows; sell n(B38)stocks
O19.Y19 shows; buy n(B39)calls
O21.Y21 shows; write n(B41)calls
O29.Y29 shows; write 2 calls with medium striking price

Figure IX.4(a)   Profit from selected investment strategies: foreground of the model.

FURTHER MODEL IX.4
A SPREADSHEET MODEL FOR CALCULATING THE VALUE OF NAKED STRATEGIES, HEDGES, SPREADS AND COMBINATIONS

In Further Model IX.1, we calculated the gross value of different investment strategies, ignoring the investment they require. We can now build a model to assess the net value or profit attached to naked strategies, hedges, spreads and combinations. The net value or profit of any strategy is equal to the difference between the present value of the value at expiration and the investment to be made today.

In order to calculate the profit attached to spreads and combinations, you need to consider more naked strategies than in Figure IX.1(a). For building spreads, you need puts and calls written on the same security but of different series ie of different striking prices and/or expiration date. Let us limit ourselves to options with three different striking prices, one high, one low and one medium. For building combinations you also need options with different striking prices.

If you want to build a wide range of spreads and combinations,[1] you have to enter a large variety of naked strategies. However, in order to keep the size of the model reasonable, we recommend that you limit yourself to the naked strategies shown in Figure IX.4(a). The foreground of the model is described in Figure IX.4(a). Its background is shown in Figure IX.4(b). The pay-off diagrams are shown in Figure IX.4(c).

---

1 Range F3.H7 and range E8.E9: data.

2 Range D11.N11: data.

3 D15:+D11/((1+$E$9) ∧ $E$8)−$F$3
   D17:+$F$3−D11/((1+$E$9) ∧ $E$8)
   D19:@IF(D11<$F$6,−$F$4,(D11−$F$6)/((1+$E$9) ∧ $E$8)−$F$4)
   D21:@IF(D11<$F$6,$F$4,((−D11+$F$6)/(1+$E$9) ∧ $E$8)+$F$4)
   D23:@IF(D11>$F$7,−$F$5,((−D11+$F$7)/(1+$E$9) ∧ $E$8)−$F$5)
   D25:@IF(D11>$F$7,$F$5,((D11−$F$7)/(1+$E$9) ∧ $E$8)+$F$5)
   D29:@IF(D11<$G$6,$G$4,(($G$6−D11)/(1+$E$9) ∧ $E$8)+$G$4)
   D33:@IF(D11<$H$6,−$H$4,((−$H$6+D11)/(1+$E$9) ∧ $E$8)−$H$4)
   D35:@IF(D11<$H$6,$H$4,(($H$6−D11)/(1+$E$9) ∧ $E$8)+$H$4)
   Copy all these formulas in the range E.N.

4 in B38, B39, B40 and B41; data.

5 D39:+D17*$B$38+D19*$B$39
   D41:+D15*$B$40+D21*$B$41
   D45:+D33+D21
   D47:+D19+D35
   D49:+D33+D19+2*D29
   D53:+D19+D23
   D55:+D33+D23
   D57:+D35+D25
   Copy all these formulas in the range E.N

6 O15:+D15*$B$40
   O17:+D17*$B$38
   O19:+D19*$B$39
   O21:+D21*$B$41
   O29:+D29*2
   Copy all these formulas in the range P.Y

7 GRAPHING:
   You can then graph each strategy (name each graph in order to be able to call it back). For hedges, spreads and combinations you can either graph the sole aggregate result or graph the aggregate result and its components – which is a bit difficult to read on the screen in some cases.

Figure IX.4(b) Profit from selected investment strategies: background of the model.

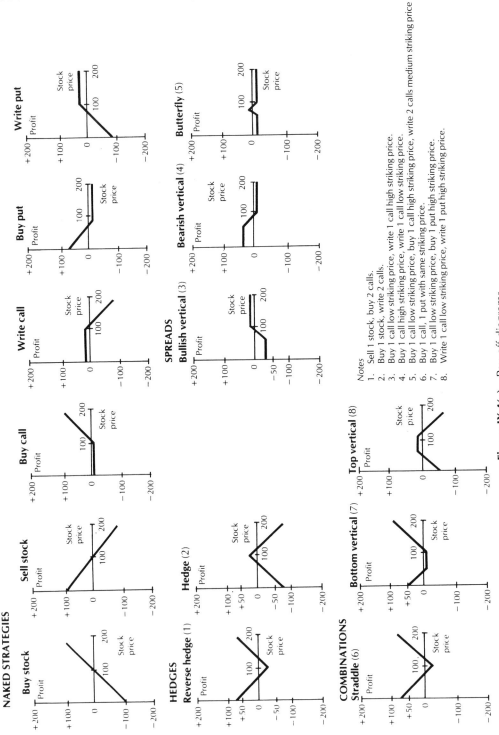

Figure IX.4(c) Pay-off diagrams.

Notes
1. Sell 1 stock, buy 2 calls.
2. Buy 1 stock, write 2 calls.
3. Buy 1 call low striking price, write 1 call high striking price.
4. Buy 1 call high striking price, write 1 call low striking price.
5. Buy 1 call low striking price, buy 1 call high striking price, write 2 calls medium striking price.
6. Buy 1 call, 1 put with same striking price.
7. Buy 1 call low striking price, buy 1 put high striking price.
8. Write 1 call low striking price, write 1 put high striking price.

NOTE

1 For a comprehensive description of those, refer to JC Cox and M Rubinstein, *Options Markets*, Prentice Hall (1985).

Part IX Bibliography

Allen DE (1983), *Finance: A theoretical introduction*, Martin Robertson.

Altman E and Subrahmanyam M (eds) (1985), *Recent Advances in Corporate Finance*, RD Irwin.

Banz R and Miller M (1978), 'Prices for state-contingent claims: some estimates and applications', *Journal of Business*, **51**: 653–72.

Black F and Scholes M (1973), 'The pricing of options and corporate liabilities', *Journal of Political Fconomy* (May/June) pp 637–53.

Brealey R and Myers SC (1986), *Principles of Corporate Finance*, McGraw-Hill.

Brennan M and Schwartz E (1977), 'The valuation of American put options', *Journal of Finance* (May) pp 449–62.

Brennan M and Schwartz E (1983), 'Evaluating natural resource investments', Division of Corporate Finance, Department of Finance, Ottawa.

Cox JC and Rubinstein M (1985), *Options Markets*, Prentice Hall.

Duffie D (1989), *Future Markets*, Prentice Hall.

Figlewski S, Silber W and Subrahmanyam M (1990), *Financial Options: From Theory to Practice*, Business One Irwin.

Ghemawat P (1991), *Commitment: The Dynamic of Strategy*, The Free Press.

Hayes R and Garvin D (1982), 'Managing as if tomorrow mattered', *Harvard Business Review* (May/June) **3**: 71–9.

Hull J (1989), *Futures and Other Derivative Securities*, Prentice Hall.

Jacob D, Lord G and Tilley J (1987), 'A Generalized Framework for Pricing Contingent Cash Flows', *Financial Management* (Autumn), pp 5–14.

Jenson MC and Smith CW (eds) (1986), *The Modern Theory of Corporate Finance*, McGraw-Hill.

Kester WC (1984), 'Today's options for tomorrow's growth', *Harvard Business Review* (Mar/Apr) pp 153–66.

Kogut B (1991), 'Joint Ventures and the Option to Expand and Acquire' *Management Science* (January), **37**: pp 19–33.

Mason S and Merton R (1985), 'The role of contingent claim analysis in corporate finance', in Altman E and Subrahmanyam M (eds) *Recent Advances in Corporate Finance*, RD Irwin.

Merton RC (1977), 'On the pricing of contingent claims and the Modigliani/Miller theorem', *Journal of Financial Economics*, **15**: 241–50.

Miller M (1991), *Financial Innovations and Market Volatility*, Basil Blackwell.

Myers SC (1984), 'Finance theory and financial strategy', *Interfaces* (Jan/Feb) **14** (1).

Smith C (1976), 'Option pricing: a review', *Journal of Financial Economics* (Jan/Mar) pp 3–51.

Smith A (1986) *Trading Financial Options*, Butterworths.

Triantis A and Hodder J (1990), 'Valuing Flexibility as a Complex Option', *Journal of Finance* (June), pp 549–65.

Walmsley J (1988), *The New Financial Instruments: an Investor's Guide*, John Wiley & Sons.

Weston JF (1981), 'Developments in finance theory', *Financial Management* (10th Anniversary Issue).

608

Conclusions

We hope that the analyses carried out in this book have helped you to understand how you can use modern corporate finance effectively for management decisions in the age of new information technology. It is now time, if you have not already started, for you to use this approach for your own benefit. In order to help you do so with maximum success, we would like to leave you with four guidelines.

X.1 DO NOT DELEGATE BUSINESS ANALYSES

Financial model building for management decisions is above all a learning process. As a manager, you start off with some understanding of what the problem is, what the alternatives are, what the relevant variables and relationships are but it is not until you have spent time progressively building and using a model and then testing its results against your business sense that you finally become aware of the real nature of your problem and of the alternatives.[1]

The opportunity to go through such a learning process is the unique advantage offered by information technology and in particular by PCs and spreadsheets. With this technology, organizing and processing calculations is no longer a problem. Consequently, managers now have the novel opportunity of using simultaneously, and interactively, their intuition and powerful tools for creating new strategies.

In the past, business analyses implied calculations requiring specialist knowledge and skills and, as a result, the majority of managers were not encouraged to perform business analyses themselves. Today, however, business analyses have changed in nature and become opportunities for self learning about strategies. Who would be prepared to delegate such an experience?

Figures X.1 and X.2 may help you to visualize the simplification brought into the business modelling process by PCs and spreadsheets. Figure X.1

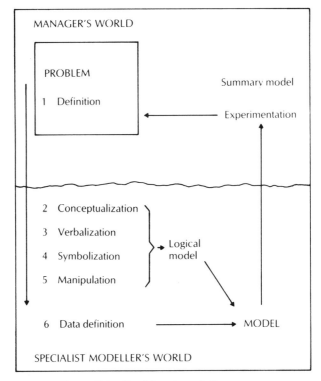

Figure X.1 Traditional modelling process.

shows a picture of the traditional business modelling process as described by Finlay.[2] Figure X.2 shows the business modelling process in the age of the PC and spreadsheet software.

The main differences between Figures X.1 and X.2 are:

- The modelling activity described in this book and summarized in Figure X.2 does not automatically call for specialists. It is carried out by the manager. That is why we described it as a personal modelling activity in the introduction.
- PCs and spreadsheets remove many of the cumbersome tasks of traditional model building.
  - *Symbolization* or expression of the variables and their relationships in mathematical terms is done automatically by spreadsheets.
  - *Manipulation* or rearrangement of variables and relationships in order to render their mathematical treatment more effective is not done by spreadsheets in a very inelegant way but, as they are supported by the power of a computer, inelegant relationships are not of any consequence (provided, however, that the model is not too big).

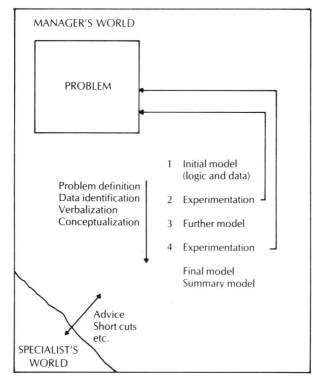

Figure X.2 Modelling with PCs and spreadsheets.

· *Logical v data model* In traditional modelling, it is a fairly common rule to separate the logic from the data. First, you build the structure and check that it works, then you introduce the data. With spreadsheets, the approach is completely different since you mix the logic and the data in the construction phase. This has the great advantage that you can check the logic at each step. A disadvantage which may be encountered is that, in the end, the logic of your model might be less elegant than if built independently from data.

■ Finally, PCs and spreadsheets allow for *more and quicker feedback between the problem and the model* than the traditional approach.

If you are a practising manager, used to the traditional organizational boundaries which still prevail in many businesses, the idea of building your own models might not look readily acceptable to you. If this is the case, please think once more about the following issues.

■ When you contemplate a new strategic move, how much do you really know about its true economics? Do you really know enough to specify to a specialist how to analyze the problem for you? Can you define all the information to analyze, all the variables to take into consideration, all the alternatives to evaluate?

- How much time are you prepared to invest in:
  - Specifying the problem to the specialist? (If the specification is not very good, the specialist cannot perform a useful analysis.)
  - Waiting for the first feedback and then remembering your initial ideas?
  - Understanding the rationale of the analysis made by the specialist? Explaining the new understanding of the situation you have achieved from the first results?
  - And so on.
- Are the analyses we made together in this book so difficult that you could not really do them by yourself more quickly and more effectively than through the necessarily difficult interaction with specialists?
- Finally, how do you value the unique advantages of doing business analyses by yourself which enable you:
  - To play freely with *confidential information* and *very innovative ideas* yourself. Never forget that business analyses become an organizational and political process as soon as another person than yourself is involved.
  - To build *your own confidence* about the decision you are contemplating and to interact better with the other managers involved, be they generalists or specialists. If you start building your own models, you are probably not going to stop working with specialists but your relationship with them will change; you will only need to call on them for their real specialisation.

X.2 ALWAYS KEEP IN MIND SOME FUNDAMENTAL CONCEPTS

In this book, we presented a number of fundamental concepts in corporate finance and some other related areas. Always remember that management is a discipline that cannot be reduced to one single approach, not even to finance. Let us review these concepts.

- Cash and profit are the same in the end. In any financial model you build, make sure that this key relationship is maintained. We particularly recommend that you test it each time you build overall financial plans; these plans should always show some sort of working capital recovery at the end.
- Even though cash and profit are the same in the end, we advise you to pay special attention to cash generation as it is a better reflection of timing. As soon as you accept the idea that cash deficits have to be financed and cash excesses can be invested, then cash generation is a better yardstick than profit.
- In order to operate at a profit, a firm should generate more CFO than the

capital expenditures it makes to generate this CFO. This is obviously a relationship which is true in the long term and not on a year-to-year basis, and which should take into account the timing effects. The longer it takes to generate CFOs, the higher they should be in relation to the capital expenditures.

- Assess the impact of your potential decisions on the basis of their operational characteristics. As debt financing can only be envisaged for strategic moves which correspond to successful operations, it is a good idea to ignore financing effects first.

- NPVs are an excellent tool for summarizing, with one single number, the value of a strategy that will affect your business over a long period of time. NPVs reflect how much value a strategy can create as of today above financing costs.

- When calculating NPVs, you should use a discount rate equal to the unlevered cost of shareholders' equity for the economic activity you are investing in. When you believe that your decision will have side financing effects, evaluate their net present value and add this to the NPV of your project in order to obtain its adjusted present value (APV).

- The unlevered cost of equity capital is necessarily higher than the cost of debt as it should reflect a risk premium. This risk premium is related to the amount of undiversifiable risk contained in the economic activity with which your decision is concerned. This undiversifiable risk is related to the relationship which exists between the volatility of the performance in this activity and in the economy as a whole. It is therefore largely independent of the specific risk of your own decision. Unfortunately, at present, there is nothing available for evaluating cost of equity other than rules of thumb.

- Be careful with your assumptions regarding inflation: if your cash flow forecasts do not incorporate inflation, then you should use a real interest rate. If, on the other hand, your cash flow forecasts reflect inflation, then a current rate is more appropriate. We recommend that you use the real rate–constant prices approach.

- More generally, start assuming parity conditions (see Further model VII.1, p 447): this will enable you to build a much simpler and more effective model. As real life does not behave as parity conditions, ask yourself at a later stage: what if parity conditions are not satisfied?

- The fact that the discount rate you use when calculating NPVs incorporates some risk should not prevent you from attempting to understand the risk of your decision. When doing so, you aim to understand the specific risk of this decision as opposed to its systematic risk as reflected in the discount rate. Understanding the specific risk is a matter of identifying possible scenarios and of weighing them up. Expected values are a way of reducing a range of possible scenarios with a single number. Risk profiles are a way of showing the same information by keeping the dispersion visible.

- When analyzing decisions, it is generally more effective to use an incremental approach. This approach, however, poses two problems:
  - · How to take into account the interaction between your decisions and existing business. The introduction of cannibalization in the analysis of BA International was an attempt to solve this problem.
  - · How to take into account the interaction between your decision and future decisions. You may well decide today to make a strategic move which results in a negative NPV in the hope that it will enable you to improve your future competitive position, and not be able to evaluate this improved future competitive position. Option valuation theory provides you with a framework for addressing this issue but no easy operational procedures as yet.
- Be careful when trying to describe evolutions over a long period as there are few variables which evolve according to straight lines. The concept of experience, introduced in Chapter 25, page 407 is a good example of replacing straight lines with curves.
- Finally, and most importantly, always remember that big NPVs can only correspond to great strategic ideas that make you benefit from what the economists call an economic rent. If a trivial decision seems to generate a lot of value, we suggest that you double-check your calculations.

X.3   ADOPT SOME BASIC RULES OF HYGIENE

Building financial models with a PC is an excellent learning activity but, unless you adopt some basic rules of hygiene, you might fall into some traps. After completing the models proposed in this book, we recommend that you adopt the following rules.

- Do not rush building a spreadsheet model. Always take time to understand the situation and its causes, design a game plan for the analysis. Perform some quick global calculations.
- *Think simple*. The purpose of a financial model is to help you to simplify a problem, not to complicate it.
- Proceed *step-by-step*. Start from your understanding of the situation, build a first model, review it, recognize the learning achieved, build a second model, etc.[3]
- *Make sure that you understand the results* generated by your models. This may take some time but, in the end, you must understand the results. If not, disregard them.

- *Make sure that your results make sense.* When building models, it is essential never to take results at their face value. Always check them against your experience and the experience of others – and here do not just think about your colleagues but also about the theory.[4]

- Use *what if analysis as a creative process.* If a strategy looks good, what about its opposite?

- Be ready to leave your problem for a while and to sleep on it. When you come back to it, you may see 'the' solution.

- *Always translate the results into words.* Quantification is a tool for helping you to understand a situation. When you have understood, you should be able to explain your results to anybody and in particular to people who are not at ease with numbers. Check that your explanations can be understood by such people.

- *Place value on your time.* Building models is not a game you play just to have fun. Model building is a process which enables you to reach more quickly a solid understanding of the possible consequences of your decisions. Understanding quickly is not automatic, however, since there are many potential traps, many of which may be avoided by a careful organization of your time.

- *Never aim at perfection.* Perfection does not exist and almost perfect approaches often require a lot of time. The great thing about spreadsheet software is that you can start with rough models and improve them progressively. Never forget to use this facility.

- *Try using different approaches/thinking languages.* One problem with modelling is that the approach you adopt may preclude the results you get. It is therefore often a very good idea to stop, restart from scratch and try a completely different approach. In some cases, it will enable you to check your results, in others it will show you quicker ways to get them, and in yet others it will tell you how contingent they are.

- *Be prepared to scrap your models.* Financial models are excellent learning aids but there is no point in preserving them when you have understood. Learning and experience accumulate but learning aids lose their value as soon as they have served their purpose. A further reason for scrapping your models and starting from scratch each time you approach a new situation is that it will help keep your creativity alive.

- *Be prepared to switch to new technology.* At present, the technology represented by the PC and a spreadsheet is enormously powerful. It probably has far more potential than we realize today. But don't believe that technological development will stop there. On the contrary, we recommend that you remain ready and willing to experiment with new technology as it arrives. This is not, however, a recommendation to wait for the next stage in technology before doing anything, since those who have developed their skills and attitudes with the present stage will be best prepared to take advantage of future developments.

■ Finally, *be eager to learn*. Building financial models for management decision making is a learning process. Your first models will probably be a bit clumsy but you will quickly learn more elegant solutions, and also learn what effective decisions are. Also when you have learned something, do not keep it to yourself, discuss it with other managers, which process will usually make you learn even more.

X.4   LEARN HOW TO ORGANIZE YOUR OWN LEARNING

As indicated in the introduction, this book has dealt with personal modelling, a creative activity which helps managers understand business situations and develop new strategies. As we envisage them, models are learning systems and not answer-generating machines. The classification of models developed by Earl[5] (see Figure X.3) may help you position personal models among other types.

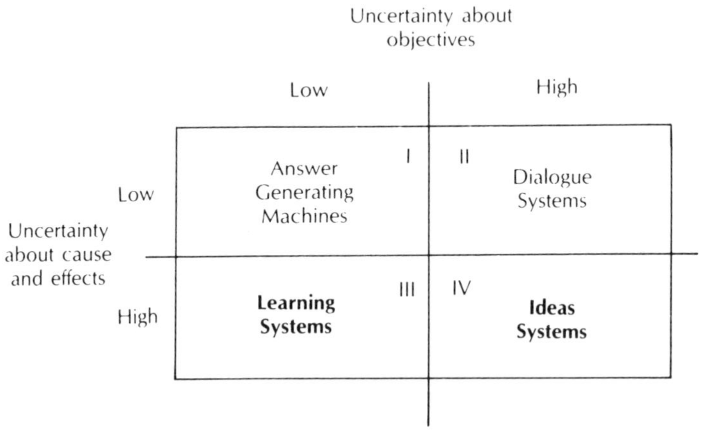

After MJ Earl in *Management Accounting Research and Practice*, Cooper and Scapens (eds), ICMA, London.
Figure X.3   A typology of models.

The modelling activity, or personal modelling, envisaged in this book, generally belongs to quadrant III and, in some cases, to quadrant IV. In most of the situations we envisaged, those with which managers are confronted, the problem is unstructured at the beginning but the objective is fairly clear, to create additional value (provided that managers understand the finance approach). In some case, however, the objective may also be unclear, for example, where a decision aims at an objective which cannot easily be

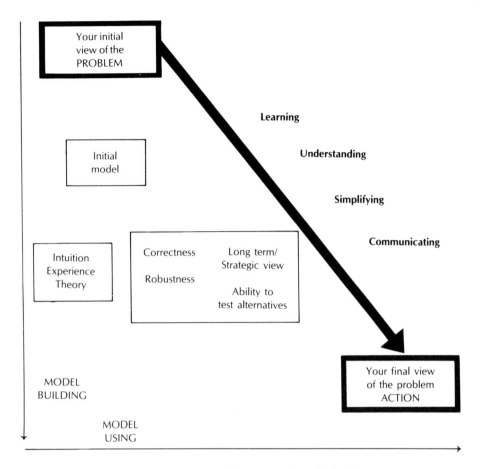

Figure X.4   Description of the personal model building process.

described in terms of additional value (such as improving the future competitive position of the firm).

This is obviously very different from the heavy duty corporate modelling activity (budgetary systems, planning systems, reporting systems, etc) which clearly belong to quadrant I. Within this activity, creativity has no more room as the purpose of the exercise is only aimed at generating results according to a well accepted framework.

Starting to build your own models for management decision making is to begin a process which aims to make you learn about new situations by using your intuition and powerful tools in an interactive fashion. The problem is to organize this process and make it effective. Although this is largely an individual matter very much related to your own mental process and experience, we would like to suggest some guide lines.

As shown in Figure X.4, you can divide the personal modelling activity into model building and model using. Contrary to what often takes place with traditional modelling processes (see Figure X.1), the model building phase does not really precede the model using phase. With PCs and spreadsheets, the two phases are closely integrated since you will usually start building a partial model, then test and use it, further develop it, then test and use the newly obtained model, etc.

This interplay between model building and model using should invite you to test the validity of the model at each step.

- Is it correct? Test your results against your intuition and experience, the intuition and experience of others and against a more general form of others' experience, theory.
- Does it take a long term/strategic perspective?
- Would a different approach give the same result (generality)?
- Is it robust? Sensitivity analysis is essential but it is probably most effective when made on a correct model, as shown in Section 26.3, page 419.

When you feel that your model is valid, think about its adequacy, its ability to evaluate strategic alternatives and their risk.

The difficulty with this step-by-step approach is that it tends to encourage you to make your model progressively more complex. So always try to simplify your model and build a summary model at the end. This will help you to analyze the various alternatives and communicate with the other managers involved in the decision.

NOTES

1 One of the problems with traditional strategic approaches is the process they recommend. First, definition of objectives, then formulation of strategy, finally identification of the necessary resources. As shown in RH Hayes, 'Strategic planning – forward in reverse?', *Harvard Business Review* (Nov/Dec 1985), this is an excessively mechanical process and a more interactive process is generally more effective.

2 PN Finlay, *Mathematical Modelling in Business Decision-making*, Croom Helm (1985), p 49.

3 The literature devoted to 'quality' has shown the value of step-by-step, continuous improvements. For an introduction to the quality literature refer to: D Hunt (1992), *Quality in America: How to Implement a Comparative Quality Program*, Business One Irwin.

4 Theoretical literature related to management seems to be mostly read by academics.

If you are a manager, you should invest some time in understanding the results of management research.

5 MJ Earl, *Management Accounting Research and Practice*, in Cooper and Scapens (eds), ICMA, London.

Part X   Bibliography

Earl MJ (1984), *Management Accounting Research and Practice*, Cooper and Scapens (eds), ICMA, London.

Finlay PN (1985), *Mathematical Modelling in Business Decision Making*, Croom Helm.

Hayes RH (1985), 'Strategic planning – forward in reverse?', *Harvard Business Review* (Nov/Dec).

Hunt D (1992), *Quality in America: How to Implement a Competitive Quality Program*, Business One Irwin.

Index